REASON AND REALITY

Front Cover Image © Keith Lehrer
<http://www.u.arizona.edu/~lehrer/ga.htm>
Reprinted By Permission

REASON AND REALITY
An Essay in Metaphysics

J. R. LUCAS

Charles Tandy, Ph.D., Editor

In this masterful and wide-ranging work by a prominent Oxford University philosopher, J. R. Lucas asks what reality is and how to reason about it. In 15 chapters he brings together his insights and arguments over many decades to offer a coherent view of a single reality which has to be understood in terms of many essential different types of explanation. The view of time and reality that emerges is one that takes full account of modern physics but has room for human beings and responsibility.

REASON AND REALITY
An Essay in Metaphysics

by

J. R. LUCAS
Fellow of Merton College, University of Oxford

Ria University Press

www.ria.edu/rup

2009

Printed in the United States of America

Ria University Press   **Palo Alto, California**

REASON AND REALITY
An Essay in Metaphysics

J. R. Lucas

Edited by Charles Tandy, Ph.D.

FIRST PUBLISHED IN HARDBACK AND PAPERBACK 2009

PUBLISHED BY
Ria University Press
PO Box 20170 at Stanford
Palo Alto, California 94309 USA

www.ria.edu/rup

Distributed by Ingram
Available from most bookstores and all Espresso Book Machines

---

Copyright © 2009 by J. R. Lucas

Hardback/Hardcover ISBN-13: 978-1-934297-04-9

Paperback/Softcover ISBN-13: 978-1-934297-06-3

TO

Bernard Williams
and
all who argued with me

REASON AND REALITY
An Essay in Metaphysics

J. R. Lucas

Distributed by Ingram
Available from most bookstores and all Espresso Book Machines

Hardback/Hardcover ISBN-13: 978-1-934297-04-9

Paperback/Softcover ISBN-13: 978-1-934297-06-3

Contents

Chapter 1 Fallibility and Reality 1
§1.1 Wrong
§1.2 Is Metaphysics Possible?
§1.3 Is Metaphysics Necessary?
§1.4 The Natural History of Reason
§1.5 Pro and Con
§1.6 Argument and Agreement
§1.7 Authority and Autonomy

Chapter 2 The Development of Normative Reason 25
§2.1 Non-contradiction
§2.2 'Not' and 'And'
§2.3 Gödelian Arguments
§2.4 Analyticity
§2.5 Mathematical Dialogues
§2.6 All, Any, Every and Each
§2.7 Induction
§2.8 Practical Reasoning
§2.9 Empathy and Other Minds
§2.10 Reason

Chapter 3 A Critique of Critical Reasoning 73
§3.1 Scepticism
§3.2 Knowledge and Doubt
§3.3 Autonomy
§3.4 Inductive Scepticism
§3.5 Predictions Vindicated
§3.6 A Gruesome Universe?
§3.7 Degrees of Similarity
§3.8 Natural Kinds
§3.9 Limits of Critical Reasoning

Chapter 4 Explanation and Cause 100
§4.1 Explanation
§4.2 Why?
§4.3 BeCauses
§4.4 Hume on the Meaning of Cause
§4.5 The Concept of Causal Cause
§4.6 Causal Necessity
§4.7 The Epistemology of Causal Laws
§4.8 Discovering Causal Connexions
§4.9 Causal Reductionism

Chapter 5 Projectivism and Probability 130
§5.1 Projectivism
§5.2 Degrees of Belief
§5.3 The Marriage of Arithmetic with Boole
§5.4 Assigning Probabilities
§5.5 . . . and Statistics
§5.6 The Limits of Ignorance
§5.7 Unprojected Reality

Chapter 6 The Tree in the Lonely Quad 147
§6.1 Phenomenalism
§6.2 How Do You Know?
§6.3 The Argument from Illusion
§6.4 The Argument from the Senses
§6.5 The Argument from Facts
§6.6 Rebuttals
§6.7 Arguments against Phenomenalism
§6.8 Reality Recovered
§6.9 The Analogy of Feeling
§6.10 Criteria
§6.11 The Argument from Deception
§6.12 Myself and Others
§6.13 Understanding People
§6.14 Conclusion

Chapter 7 **Existence and Reality**   178
    §7.1 Universals
    §7.2 Existence
    §7.3 Platonism
    §7.4 Mathematical Platonism
    §7.5 Nominalism
    §7.6 Conceptualism
    §7.7 Natural Kinds
    §7.8 Modifying Logic
    §7.9 Umbrian Universals
    §7.10 Aristotelian Actuality

Chapter 8 **Appearance and Unreality**   219
    §8.1 'Real'
    §8.2 Antirealisms
    §8.3 Appearances
    §8.4 Plato against Appearance
    §8.5 Empiricism
    §8.6 The Cave
    §8.7 Beyond

Chapter 9 **The Search for the Ultimate**   246
    §9.1 The Ontological Argument
    §9.2 "Existence Is Not a Predicate"
    §9.3 The Search for the Superlative
    §9.4 The Logic of the Mostest
    §9.5 Togetherness and *Res Extensa*
    §9.6 Corpuscularianism
    §9.7 The Plenum and the Void: Arena and Explanation
    §9.8 Penultimate Imperfections

Chapter 10 **Points of View**   279
    §10.1 Locality
    §10.2 Causal Cones
    §10.3 Minkowski Spacetime
    §10.4 Windowed Monads
    §10.5 Covariance
    §10.6 Perspectives
    §10.7 McTaggart and Mellor
    §10.8 Tense and Temporality

Chapter 11 **Quantum Mechanics**   307
    §11.1 Unhistory
    §11.2 The Inner Cave
    §11.3 Discreteness and Continuity
    §11.4 From von Neumann to Kochen-Specker
    §11.5 From EPR via JSB to GHZ
    §11.6 Non-locality
    §11.7 The "Measurement Problem"
    §11.8 Knowing and Being
    §11.9 The Uncertainty Principle
    §11.10 Nullary Qualities
    §11.11 Indiscernability and *Haecceitas*
    §11.12 Quantum Realism
    §11.13 Quantum Philosophy

Chapter 12 **Time**   347
    §12.1 Time and Change
    §12.2 Leibniz and Relationism
    §12.3 Spacetime
    §12.4 Time and Electromagnetism
    §12.5 Tense and Modality
    §12.6 Augustine, Instants and Intervals
    §12.7 The Topology of Time
    §12.8 The Metric of Time
    §12.9 Tense and Reality

Chapter 13 Reductionism 381
- §13.1 Pervasive Pressure
- §13.2 Laplace
- §13.3 Isolation and Chaos
- §13.4 Indeterminism
- §13.5 Supervenience
- §13.6 Haecceity
- §13.7 Levels of Explanation
- §13.8 The Virtues of Irrelevance
- §13.9 Pluralist Monism

Chapter 14 Persons 414
- §14.1 Minds and Bodies
- §14.2 Consciousness
- §14.3 A Mind of One's Own
- §14.4 Fusion and Fission
- §14.5 In Praise of Bodies
- §14.6 The Subjective View
- §14.7 Secondary Qualities
- §14.8 Conjugating Viewpoints

Chapter 15 Inconclusions 455
- §15.1 The Restoration of Reason
- §15.2 The Pressure of Reason on Reality
- §15.3 Personal Reason and Reality
- §15.4 Recalcitrance and Actuality
- §15.5 Metaphysical Argument
- §15.6 Questioning Quest

Index 477

J. R. Lucas

Fellow of the British Academy. Fellow of Merton College, University of Oxford. Author: *The Principles of Politics*, 1966, 1985; *The Concept of Probability*, 1970; *The Freedom of the Will*, 1970; (jointly) *The Nature of Mind*, 1972; (jointly) *The Development of Mind*, 1973; *A Treatise on Time and Space*, 1973; *Essays on Freedom and Grace*, 1976; *Democracy and Participation*, 1976 (Portuguese, 1985); *On Justice*, 1980; *Space, Time and Causality*, 1985; *The Future*, 1989; (jointly) *Spacetime and Electromagnetism*, 1990; *Responsibility*, 1993; (jointly) *Ethical Economics*, 1997; *The Conceptual Roots of Mathematics*, 2000; (jointly) *An Engagement with Plato's Republic*, 2003; *Reason and Reality*, 2009. More: <http://users.ox.ac.uk/~jrlucas>.

Chapter 1
Fallibility and Reality

§1.1 Wrong
§1.2 Is Metaphysics Possible?
§1.3 Is Metaphysics Necessary?
§1.4 The Natural History of Reason
§1.5 Pro and Con
§1.6 Argument and Agreement
§1.7 Authority and Autonomy

§1.1 Wrong

I can be wrong. But contrary to the arguments of the sceptics, my fallibility shows not only that I may be wrong, but that I can be right. Indeed, it shows more. Not only does my being wrong carry with it the possibility of my being right, but it implies that I often am. I would not jump to false conclusions, and suppose that the stick was bent where it went into the water, or that the distant tower was round, when really it was square, or that the moon was the size of a sixpence, unless jumping to conclusions was generally a sensible strategy to adopt, yielding for the most part reliable results. It is only because I am often led aright that I can occasionally be led astray.

Fallibility is a mark of objectivity. It shows that there is a standard other than myself which determines what is correct and what is not. It is not simply a matter of my say-so. Nor of your say-so. You too can be wrong. Indeed, IF I am right, and you disagree, then you are wrong. And equally for others: if we are right, then they, if they disagree with us, are wrong. It is not just for you and me that our claims hold good, but for everyone. Something cannot be true just for me, or just for you, or just for him. Truth is omnipersonal. We are all answerable to truth, and we all can be wrong.

But, again, though we all can be wrong, we cannot all be always wrong. How things seem to us, though not a conclusive guide to how they really are, is a good guide none the less. We cannot, with Plato,[1] dismiss out of hand how things seem. Appearances

---
[1] *Republic* VII, 529. See further, §4.7 and §15.5.

can deceive, but only if they also can be veridical, and usually are. We are led to a modified empiricism, and should follow Aristotle rather than Plato, and in giving an account of the world, try to save appearances, and reject them only for good reason.

But appearances are not our only guide to reality. Reason also can be a source of knowledge. The Logical Positivists were wrong in holding pure reason to be purely tautological, incapable of yielding any non-analytical truth. Our mathematical understanding is not just a simple matter of following specified rules of inference, but can go beyond them and recognise truths not validated by the rules hitherto accepted as canonical. That has important implications for our understanding of mathematics in particular and for any adequate account of the nature of argument in general. I claim that we acquire mathematical knowledge through pure deductive reason without thereby conceding that it is merely analytic, or that mathematics is simply a set of tautologies. Mathematics cannot be reduced to logic: the theorems of mathematics are not just theorems of first-order logic (the logic that computers can be programmed to do). We need to avail ourselves of second-order logic in order to characterize the natural numbers completely, as well as to formulate other definitions and arguments; that is, we are having to quantify over properties and relations, which therefore, according to Quine, must be supposed to exist. We are thus led to a version of Platonism as an account of what there is. There is a pervasive sense of hard rationality about mathematical truth which is deeply persuasive: it is objective, and not just a matter of the way we set up definitions or play pencil-and-paper games, nor just the mental experience mathematicians want to share with one another.

Gödel's theorem supports this view of mathematical truth. It shows that in any formal mathematical system with formal rules of inference there are truths that cannot be formally proved according to the formal rules of inference, but can be informally proved and seen to be true nonetheless. Gödel's theorem is a conclusive refutation of any Formalist view of mathematics. It refutes the widely-held belief that to be reasonable is to be in accordance with a rule. Reason is more than observance of rules: truth outruns provability. Gödel's theorem also shows beyond doubt that mathematical truths are not all empty tautologies, and suggests some sort of realism as regards mathematical truth.[2] The combination of

---

[2] See further below, §2.3.

epistemological Logicism and ontological Platonism I have already argued for[3] is thus further supported by the account of reasoning that Gödel's theorem establishes.

It is not only in mathematics that rationalist considerations can guide us into truth. Some commitment to the uniformity of nature is implicit in any use of inductive inference, and uniformity can be refined in various fundamental principles of sameness. Many thinkers have had intimations about the nature of reason and of reality. The hard part is not to have such intimations, but to articulate them in a way that takes account of difficulties, and to meet the counter-arguments of those who believe that the function of metaphysics is to cut our view of the world and of ourselves down to minimum size. To this I now turn.

§1.2 Is Metaphysics Possible?

Metaphysics has a bad reputation. It is widely supposed to be meaningless, senseless, pointless, incapable of being true or false; so much so that before I embark on any account of metaphysics, I need to deal with these charges, and attempt to show that, although, admittedly, much nonsense has been talked under the guise of metaphysics, metaphysical statements are not necessarily meaningless, and metaphysical arguments do not have to be fallacious.

Many thinkers claim that metaphysics is impossible:

1. A.J. Ayer said that metaphysical statements are meaningless because they do not satisfy the Verification Principle.[4]
2. G.E. Moore, maintained that metaphysical statements cannot be true because they conflict with ordinary language; we know that stones are solid, and that the will is free and there's an end on't.
3. Wittgenstein, held metaphysical statements are mistaken, because they seek to revise ordinary language, and ordinary language is quite all right as it is.[5]

---

[3] *The Conceptual Roots of Mathematics* London, 1999.

[4] A.J.Ayer, *Language, Truth and Logic*, London, 1936, ch.1. See also W.H. Walsh, *Metaphysics*, London, 1963, reprinted Aldershot, 1991, pp.14-16, 43-47.

[5] W.H.Walsh, *Metaphysics*, p. 16: N.A.Malcolm, "Moore and Ordinary Language", in P.A.Schilpp, ed. *The Philosophy of G.E.Moore*, Evanston, 1942, pp.343-368; L.Wittgenstein, *Philosophical Investigations*, Oxford, 1953.

4. Kant argued that metaphysical statements cannot be established as true, because they rest on bad arguments and go beyond the bounds of possible experience.[6]

None of these contentions succeed in showing that metaphysics is impossible. Ayer's Verification Principle refutes itself. He says

> The criterion which we use to test the genuineness of apparent statements of fact is the criterion of verifiability. *We say that a sentence is factually significant to any given person, if and only if, he knows how to verify the proposition which it purports to express—that is, if he knows what observations would lead him, under certain conditions, to accept the proposition as true, or reject it as being false.* If, on the other hand, the putative proposition is of such a character that the assumption of its truth, or falsehood, is consistent with any assumption whatsoever concerning the nature of his future experience, then, as far as he is concerned, it is, if not a tautology, a mere pseudo-proposition. The sentence expressing it may be emotionally significant to him: but it is not literally significant.[7]

But is the italicised sentence factually significant? What sense-experiences are, or could be, adduced in support of the claim made by this sentence? Is it then a tautology? If so, it must be true in virtue of the meaning of the words involved. It would be, if we were to define 'factually significant' to mean that the person concerned knows what observations would lead him, under certain conditions, to accept the proposition as true, or reject it as being false. But having thus defined 'factually significant', what right have we to stigmatize every other sort of sentence as expressing merely a pseudo-proposition? If the Verification Principle is a tautology, it can tell us only how Ayer is going to use words: if it claims to be factually significant, it lacks any empirical support: the only way it can be taken is as making a philosophical claim, and then it is hoist by its own petard, and is, unverifiable, and so, according to Ayer, meaningless.

This argument is of a type that turns up again and again in metaphysics—metaphysical claims are often to be rejected because if they were true, they would themselves be invalidated—Freud, Marx, Relativism, Protagoras' subjectivism.[8] It is decisive against

---

[6] W.H.Walsh, *Metaphysics*, London, 1963, pp.38-42.

[7] A.J. Ayer, *Language, Truth and Logic*, London, 1936, ch.1, p.48.

[8] See Roger Trigg, *Reason and Commitment*, Cambridge, 1979, pp.2-5; Bernard Williams, *Morality*, Penguin, 1972, pp.41-43; *Theaetetus*, 152 a.

§1.2   *Fallibility and Reality*   5

Ayer, but it does not stop the question 'How would you verify your statement?' being a perfectly pertinent one; nor does it invalidate some distinction being drawn between 'factually significant' and other types of proposition.

Moore's Argument from Common Sense likewise lacks cogency. Common sense once told us that the earth was flat and that the sun rose in the East. The bare fact that metaphysics makes out that reality is very different from how we had thought it was is not conclusive, although it is important to save the phenomena: we have to explain why we think that the sun rises; if Bradley holds that time is unreal, he must explain why it is none the less possible for him to catch trains. Similarly the Argument from Ordinary Language fails. Not all ordinary language is quite all right as it is. Some language games undercut others: astrology occupies many columns in the popular press, but its truth-claims are refuted by astronomy. Walsh compares Wittgenstein to Burke.[9] Both make good conservative points: ordinary language and existing societies are going concerns; they need to be understood sensitively before being criticized, and doctrinaire criticisms are likely to be crass. But not all criticisms of existing social arrangements are out of court; even radical criticisms may be cogent; and so, too, radical criticisms of existing linguistic practices or conceptual structures cannot be ruled out of court. More generally, if language games can be played, they can be evaluated. We can ask on occasion which language game we should play. Shall I do astrology or astronomy? And sometimes unequivocal answers will be forthcoming—astronomy, if you interested in discovering the truth.

Hume and Kant give a large number of arguments criticizing various metaphysical contentions. Some are quite good, many very difficult to understand. Quite often Kant demolishes only one version of a particular metaphysical argument—e.g. the Ontological Argument—leaving open the possibility that other versions might be valid. Some of the more wide-sweeping arguments rest on a limited view of logic, or idiosyncratic epistemological doctrines. Hume in his *Dialogues on Natural Religion* claims that all arguments from natural phenomena to the existence of God are flawed. But so then would be arguments to the existence of atoms. I have never experienced a quark, and cannot imagine what it would be like, but I

[9] W.H.Walsh, *Metaphysics*, pp.16, 122-124.

believe in quarks none the less. Similarly, in spite of Kant's critique, we have continued to reason about science and religion in ways he had pronounced impossible.[10] It is quite possible that the theologians are wrong; it is quite possible that the scientists are wrong; but it requires great reserves of faithlessness to believe that they both must be wrong. Though they deserve to be taken seriously, the criticisms of Hume and Kant are not conclusive; they do not rule out the possibility of metaphysics straight away, and when they make telling points against particular metaphysical arguments or metaphysical doctrines, they leave open the possibility that other arguments or other doctrines may be exempt from the criticisms thus far advanced.[11]

Underlying many assertions about the impossibility of metaphysics is an unduly narrow view of the range of meaning and the bounds of reason. Metaphysicians make statements of great generality about the universe, but the words they use get their meaning from necessarily limited uses. The Ionian philosophers were wont to say that Everything is Fire, or that Everything is Earth, or that Everything is Water, but we only understand the words 'fire', 'earth', and 'water', by virtue of the facts not everything is fire, that not everything is earth, and not everything is water. We know what the word 'fire' means because we can get away from the fire into a cold out-house, and use the word 'fire' to distinguish the one from the other. Similarly with 'earth' and 'water': the former cannot be applied to the sea, the latter cannot be applied to dry land. Hence, it is argued, we cannot meaningfully assert that Everything is Fire, or that Everything is Earth, or that Everything is Water, because in each case the claim is belied by the conditions for the meaningful use of the words concerned.

The argument is plausible, but must be wrong. At the beginning of the twentieth century materialists were claiming that Everything is Matter—some earth-like passive substance—and were understood. After Einstein, Matter was seen as a form of Energy—that which fires characteristically emit—and people were again able to have some idea of what was being said. Then cosmologists began

---

[10] M.C.Banner, *The Justification of Science and the Rationality of Religious Belief*, Oxford, 1990.

[11] For a modern example of Kant's "programmatic scepticism", see Stuart Hampshire, *Spinoza*, Penguin, 1951, ch.6, "The Nature of Metaphysics", pp.210-226.

§1.2 *Fallibility and Reality* 7

to speculate about the origin of the universe, either as continuous creationists or as advocates of the Big Bang, and maintained that hydrogen—that is, etymologically speaking, the water-generating element—was the stuff of creation; and again they were understood.

The error lies in a too simple theory of meaning. It is true only up to a point that words obtain their meaning from the paradigm case of its correct application. Although I may learn the meaning of the word 'elephant' by being shown an elephant, and told that the word 'elephant' is the correct name for it, the meanings of words are connected in many ways, and may well be used meaningfully in the absence of any paradigm example. Most obviously, we may learn the meaning of some comparative term, such as 'better', and then extrapolate to a superlative, and talk about the supreme good, without ever having come across an example of supreme goodness. So too we can attach enough meaning to the words 'matter', 'energy' and 'hydrogen', on the basis of our ordinary experience, to be able to use them coherently in talking about issues that transcend ordinary experience. The critic may fairly point out that the Ionian philosophers were using the words 'Earth', 'Fire' and 'Water' in an unusual sense—hence the capital letters—and he may properly warn us of the danger of being misled by metaphors not carefully scrutinised. But metaphors *are*, sometimes, understood, and a theory of meaning which denies this, and denies that much of the thought of the twentieth century was capable of being understood, is a theory of meaning that deserves scant respect.

Sceptics often also circumscribe the bounds of reaon unduly. They assume that nobody can responsibly claim knowledge, or even meaningfully make a statement, which goes beyond the evidence at his disposal. But that is what we habitually do, and must do if communication is to be possible. I predict rain tomorrow, but all my evidence for this future statement is information about the weather now and in the recent past. I tell you that there is a fox in yonder hedge, but all I have to go on is my sense-experience, which is necessarily different from yours. In each case I have good evidence. But what I say goes beyond the actual evidence. The evidence is evidence for what I say, but what I say is not just the evidence on which it is based. If I am to be believed, and more generally if we are to understand one another, I must not make, and we must not make, assertions which are not warranted. But the warrant for our assertions is less than what our assertions actually assert. In making them we are sticking our necks out, and on occasion we may find that what we said, though reasonable and responsibly uttered at the time, turns out to be mistaken in the event. The clouds cleared and there was no rain; there was a brown dog in the hedge, but no fox. And similarly, I shall argue, we may be able to make reasonable metaphysical assertions about the nature of reality which go beyond the appearances accessible to all of us.[12]

A final argument for the possibility of metaphysics is provided by contemporary disputes about materialism. Many people today have a world-view of scientific materialism: many other people feel that such a world-view must be wrong because it does not account adequately for consciousness, rationality or moral responsibility. Rather good arguments would be required before we could conclude that they were all mistaken, that there was no point of contention between them, and that all the arguments they adduced were necessarily invalid.

It seems reasonable, then, to conclude that metaphysics is possible. I have not proved that it is. Kant's arguments might turn out to be better than I have made out. Further arguments may emerge which bolster an unremitting scepticism about our ever being able to get genuine knowledge of reality. But they have not emerged yet, and the sweeping arguments which claimed to rule out the possibility of metaphysics altogether have turned out to be invalid. I have not proved the possibility of metaphysics, but I have disproved the current disproofs. In Alvin Plantinga's useful phrase, I have defeated the defeaters.

§1.3 Is Metaphysics Necessary?

Plato was led into metaphysical claims by his moral concerns. At the end of the first book of the *Republic*, Plato has Socrates say οὐ γὰρ περὶ τοῦ ἐπιτυχόντος ὁ λόγος, ἀλλὰ περὶ τοῦ ὅντινα τρόπον χρὴ ζῆν, *ou gar peri tou epituchontos ho logos, alla peri tou hontina tropon chre zen*, the argument is not about some trivial matter, but about what way one ought to live.[13] Plato was preaching a

---

[12] See further below, §3.5. §6.11, §8.6, §8.7 and §14.2. S.E.Toulmin, *The Uses of Argument*, Cambridge, 1958, first made me aware of the distinction between the grounds for an assertion and its content.

[13] *Republic* I, 352d5.

§1.3   *Fallibility and Reality*

gospel of moral seriousness, and postulated the Forms as a metaphysical underwrite to moral objectivity.[14] Democritus, Epicurus and Lucretius thought that the ultimate reality was constituted by material atoms, and had a different view of how one's life ought to be lived. It makes a difference to our view of ourselves and our obligations if we think that all our doings are known to a benevolent God, or that our whole life is a tale told by an idiot signifying nothing.

    The moral impetus towards metaphysical speculation is of great importance. In the first place it should make us cautious. Metaphysicians often are moralists, and form a view of the world that supports their moral prescriptions. It is always possible that the view offered to us has been adopted not on account of the reasons adduced for it, but for the sake of the philosophy of life it would support if adopted. Wishful thinking may engender an optimistic view of the world, malevolence a gloomy one. Bradley once said that metaphysics was the search for bad reasons for doctrines adopted on instinct, and the instincts may be deceitful. We need to be wary, ready to spot the operation of ulterior motives, leading to conclusions not justified by reason or resulting from the disinterested concern for truth. But although it is always possible that the arguments adduced are mere rationalisations, we should not assume that that could be the case always. The man who in his metaphysical thinking is pursuing a hidden agenda could not pass it off as cogent reasoning if no reasoning were ever cogent. We need to be wary, not cynical. Though for some thinkers the conclusions determine the arguments, the whole rationale of argument is for the arguments to determine the conclusion, and at least sometimes with some people that is what actually happens.

    Secondly, the moral concern of the metaphysician imports into his thinking the logic of practical choice. Practical reasoning is subject to the principle *Tertium Non Datur*. When I, as a rational agent, am making up my mind what to do, I cannot suspend judgement for long. I must, as I see the enemy advancing, decide whether to fight or flee. During the early years of our life we can try out various ideas and think of different life-choices and various possible careers, but then we will have to decide. We have to choose. Many people would like not to, and would rather take over current attitudes and opinions without thought. But that too is a choice, only

---

[14] *Republic* V, 475e-480.

one based on ignorance rather than the best assessment that can be made of one's real situation. We need a world-view to inform the fundamental choices we each have to make. Although we may also be fired by a strong desire to know the nature of reality for its own sake, yet one abiding theme will always be that expressed in the title of Iris Murdoch's book, *Metaphysics as a Guide to Morality*.

The *Tertium Non Datur* of practical decision-making shapes our metaphysical reasoning. We see things in terms of a stark Either-Or, between which we have to choose. Often we embrace one alternative as much because it is not the other as for any positive virtues of its own. Plato, and many philosophers since him, have felt threatened by materialism, the thesis that Things are the only things to exist, and feeling convinced that materialism cannot be true, have embraced the only other available alternative. And, *per contra*, other thinkers, sensing that Platonism cannot be correct, have embraced some other philosophy, less on account of its positive merits than for its not being Platonism.

Metaphysical argument, like practical reasoning, is, as will be argued in the next two sections, messy. It does not have stringent canons of relevance, it is often inarticulate, it lacks a decision-procedure, its arguments are holistic, cumulative and two-sided; altogether it is not academically respectable. Academically respectable disciplines, like mathematics, history, or natural science, can rule out of court various types of argument, and simply suspend judgment if adequate arguments and evidence are not available; but metaphysics cannot be equally brusque, since it cannot indefinitely suspend judgement, but must examine each consideration to see if it has a bearing on how the world should best be viewed. The final judgement is a cumulative, holistic one. Having taken everything into account, the metaphysician has to decide, often unable to articulate an adequate world-view by himself, just choosing to the best of his ability between the ones made available by other men's thought. There is no decision-procedure, no way of being sure that the decision arrived at is the right one. It is a personal decision, though not subjective. Different considerations will point in different directions. The argument will be "dialectical", with a *prima facie* case being rebutted by further arguments, themselves liable to being countered by counter-arguments, leading to a tentative conclusion which will hold, other things being equal, but which may be over-ridden by yet further considerations.

The fact that we cannot indefinitely suspend judgement forces us to relax our standards of stringency. Traditionally, philosophers have sought certainty, and have been prepared greatly to restrict the realm of what can be known in order to secure that what is known is indubitably so. But there is a trade-off between range and certainty: the more stringent the requirements of indubitability, the narrower the range of what can be known. If I want to be absolutely sure, beyond all conceivable doubt, that what I think I know I really do know, then, like Descartes, I shall conclude that I know very little. And if, on the other hand, I realise that I do not have time for unlimited cogitation, but must decide now in the time of my mortal life how best to use the time that remains, I must be prepared to decide under conditions of imperfect information, doing the best I can to decide aright, but aware that I have no copper-bottomed guarantee of not being wrong. We are faced with a choice: we can either despair of ever having any reason at all for preferring one world-view to another, and adopt a stance of resolute agnosticism; or we can try our best, knowing that we may be wrong, but being ready to correct our opinion if some other seems better founded. If we adopt the former, we guarantee ignorance; if the latter, we may be wrong, but are not necessarily so. The latter is therefore a rational strategy to adopt in the absence of convincing arguments that knowledge is in principle unattainable.

§1.4 The Natural History of Reason

Metaphysical reasoning is a form of reasoning. To understand it we need an account of reason generally. Two different approaches may be adopted. We may characterize reason as a phenomenon, or we may lay down principles to which it ought to conform if it is to be worthy of our intellectual allegiance. On the former approach we observe reasoning as a human activity, and pick out its characteristic features. Men reason about what to do, what is likely to happen, what is really the case, what arguments are worthy of acceptance, what is worthy of admiration. We are able to distinguish rational from non-rational activities, and rational from irrational decisions, beliefs, attitudes, procedures, and the like, and reasonable from unreasonable men. A careful examination of cases should enable us to distil the essential features of the rational and the reasonable, and make explicit the grounds of the judgements we already implicitly understand. In so doing, we may come not only to describe but to clarify and amend our practice, in much the same way as Socratic dialogue and discussion leads to our formulating a definition which in turn may lead to a reformed usage.

Most philosophers, however, have spurned the descriptive approach: it may show how men actually think, but men's thoughts are mostly wrong, and are largely prejudices engendered by upbringing and interest. Rather than observe the bad habits of present-day practitioners, they seek to make a fresh start in which we take great care to reason aright, uncontaminated by the errors of previous generations. But if we make a clean sweep of existing practices, we may fail to acknowledge some important types of reasoning; however pure our consequent understanding is, it may well be not *reason* that we are talking about, but only some part of it, or perhaps, even, something quite different. Any serious examination of reason, therefore, must start with a descriptive approach, in order to anchor the subsequent discussion. Neither approach is adequate by itself: each needs the other to complement it. In this and the following sections we shall survey how we actually reason, and give, as it were, a natural history of reasoning, and then in the next chapter adopt a normative approach.

§1.5 Pro and Con

Our powers of reasoning are characterized primarily by reference to the way we reason about what to do: for this is the basic and most typical case. Many thinkers have failed to recognise this, and, starting with some other paradigm of reasoning, have found themselves unable to accommodate practical reasoning, and have often been led to discountenance it, as not being a proper mode of reasoning at all. But that is a mistake. We all have to decide what we are going to do, and use our wits to figure out what would be the best course of action in difficult cases. We argue and debate far more about what to do than about mathematics or other academic disputes. Instead of trying to view practical reasoning as a strange type of academic reasoning, we do better to view theorizing as a special activity we undertake, and theoretical reasoning as a special case of reasoning generally; and then we shall find that much the same applies, *mutatis mutandis*, when the question at issue is not what is to be done, but what is to be believed, what is to be admired, what is to be accepted. Arguments about the truth of statements or the cogency of arguments, are, along with aesthetic arguments, fundamentally evaluative, and not all that different from purely practical ones. Indeed, if to assess a

§1.5   *Fallibility and Reality*   13

statement as true, or an argument as cogent, were not to evaluate it, and to recommend that something should be done, namely that the statement be believed or the argument accepted, truth and cogency would be uninteresting concepts. Academic arguments are remoter from the press of urgent business than practical arguments, but are not totally disconnected from practical concerns and the world of action: and if reason is inherently incapable of guiding us on what to do, then it is incapable of guiding us on anything at all; and *per contra*, if reason is any good at all, then we shall be able to assess its merits when we are wondering what to do, before going on to consider its more specialised applications in aesthetics or the academic disciplines.

We start, then, by examining what people do, both when they act rationally, and in particular when they argue about actions. We note first the similarities between human actions and the reactions of other organisms, and then what it is that differentiates rational action from mere animal behaviour. First, then, we consider all behaviour as a response to a situation. A response is an answer, in this case the organism's answer to the question what to do, if such a question could have been formulated. The future behaviour of the organism—amoeba, earthworm, honeybee, or ape—is at the outset unsettled, and then is settled: the amoeba swims away from a region of greater salinity, the earthworm turns left rather than right at a junction in a tube, the honeybee flies a particular distance in a particular direction, the ape snarls aggressively. In each case we are inclined to say that a choice has been made what to do, although such anthropomorphic language can be misleading: what we can more safely do is to apply the Law of the Excluded Middle and say that one pattern of behaviour rather than another has been manifested; and where the behaviour is homoeostatic and complicated, rather than continuously variable, the Law of the Excluded Middle is peculiarly apt, and we can say either that some sort of behaviour has been manifested or that it has not. Often, although not always, this behaviour can be seen as a response to some stimulus. There is some feature in the environment which has caused it: and very often the behaviour is not only the result of, but a very appropriate response to, an environment characterized by that feature. If an amoeba did not move away from regions of increasing salinity, it would be desiccated by osmosis and die. A worm has often taken the right-hand turn and suffered an electric shock in consequence; by turning to the left it avoids it. A honeybee, by responding to the dance of another bee in a particular fashion, arrives in the neighbourhood of honey-bearing flowers. An aggressive snarl may trigger off an escape-mechanism in a rival. Different species have evolved, each with a propensity to produce an appropriate response to many of the situations that are likely to arise. And in determining what response shall be given, the organism is likely to be affected by any factor that could be relevant to the range of possible responses. If the choice is between standing one's ground or fleeing, the robin redbreast needs to respond not only to a provocatively red breast of another robin close by but to the feline form stealthily approaching in the distance.

An organism needs to respond to the whole environment, and so do we. Our most basic classifications are in terms of appropriate responses: creepy, sinister, open, welcoming. Babies can recognise the smile on their mothers' faces long before they have ever experienced a sense-datum; and grown-ups are better at recognizing people than either the colours or the shapes of which their faces are said to be composed. Not that similarity of colour or shape are unimportant; we rapidly learn to notice such similarities on account of their use in identifying material objects, and they have a pre-eminent position in our philosophy of nature: but we are agents before we are observers, and our observations are undertaken more as a guide to action than out of idle curiosity. We therefore size up situations in terms of the actions to be performed. We are very quick to notice anything that may be a clue, but overlook irrelevant details. We are asking 'Is this man honest?', 'Is this the man I met last year?', 'Is the road slippery?', 'Can I get round the corner at this speed?', and in such matters our judgement becomes remarkably reliable.

That our assessment of situations is holistic has long been recognised. Plato, in the *Protagoras*, distinguishes our assessment of a face from that of a lump of metal.[15] When we weigh metals, our measure is simply additive, but when dealing with people we are on the look out for anything that may invalidate initial impressions; a child can often sense untrustworthiness that the social upbringing of adults has trained them not to notice. A flicker of the eyelids, an involuntary tightening of the mouth, may give the game away. When postage stamps were invented, the reason for having

---

[15] *Protagoras*, 329de. See further below, §2.7, fn.13.

§1.5   *Fallibility and Reality*   15

the Queen's head on them was that forgeries would be easier to detect, since everyone would notice the slightest difference of facial expression.

The fact that our assessments are holistic means that they are two-sided. If, when we size up a situation a further factor may entirely alter the appropriate responses, it will constitute a consideration against the original course of action. While on the one hand the succulence of the worm is an argument for staying put, the increasing propinquity of a predator is an argument against. Practical reasoning is two-sided. There are considerations in favour and considerations against, and we have to balance the *pros* and the *cons*. Since there is a possibility of a further *con*, which could prove decisive, we may have to reconsider and change our mind. This distinguishes holistic from deductive reasoning. Deductive reasoning is "monotonic". In deductive logic, adding a further premise may enable some further conclusion to be proved, but cannot invalidate the proof of one already proved; or, more formally,

If A and B are axiom systems, with $A \subset B$,
then $Th(A) \subset Th(B)$,

where $Th(S)$ = the set of sentences that can be proved from S.[16]

In contrast, the logic of practical reasoning, is not one of incontrovertible proof-sequences but of *prima facie* arguments and counter-arguments, of objections and rebuttals, of exceptional circumstances and special cases; with the conclusion following not conclusively but only in the absence of further considerations, only provided that other things are equal. and the fundamental connective is not 'therefore' but 'but'. We do not use the logic of the propositional calculus with its necessary and sufficient conditions, where propositions once proved remain so always, but a quite different "*dialectical* logic" of claim and counter-claim, presumption

---

[16] From L-E.Janlert, "Modeling Change—the Frame Problem", in Z.W.Pylyshyn, ed., *The Robot's Dilemma*, Norwood, N.J., 1987, p.25. For non-monotonic logic generally, see E.Sandewall, "An Approach to the Frame Problem and its Implementation", in B.Meltzer and D.Michie, eds., *Machine Intelligence 7*, Edinburgh, 1972, pp.195-204; and J.McCarthy, "Circumscription: A Non-monotonic Inference Rule", *Artificial Intelligence*, 13, 1980, pp.27-40. I owe these references to Professor D.A.Gillies, of King's College, London.

and *ceteris paribus* clauses, in which truths are seldom established beyond all possibility of further question.[17]

The fact that our assessments of situations is often non-monotonic has been a considerable embarrassment to advocates of Artificial Intelligence, who reckon that it should be possible, at least in principle, to program a machine to operate according to the rules of formal logic, but do not see how to program a machine to spot and take into account relevant factors that tell against the putative course of action the machine might otherwise undertake. In real life it is essential to be able to take cognizance of any detail: not every detail will be relevant, but any may. The same holds good in practical affairs, in political argument, and most notably in the law courts. Justice should take all relevant factors into consideration, in contrast to legality, which takes into account only those laid down by law. Guided by legality, we subsume the case under the relevant law, and see what follows, period. But often that seems harsh and we appeal to some idea of equity, which allows for a further 'but'.[18]

Two-sided logic is inherently fallible. We always may have overlooked some consideration which should have been decisive, had we known of it. Hence it is built into the logic of two-sided reasoning that we might be mistaken. It is hardly surprising. Organisms can behave inappropriately too, and if they do they may pay for it with their lives. To decide is to decide between alternatives, and however generous we are in accepting the decisions of others, we cannot, in regard to our own decisions and at least sometimes in regard to those of others, endorse them all equally: else, there would be no point in agonizing over what we ought to do, and no difference between saying that some decision of another was right and saying that it was wrong. To choose is to exclude, and if it is possible to choose right, then some of the excluded alternatives

---

[17] See H.L.A.Hart, "The Ascription of Rights and Responsibilities", *Proceedings of the Aristotelian Society*, 1948, pp.171-194; reprinted in A.G.N.Flew, ed., *Logic and Language*, I, Oxford, 1951, pp.145-165. W.D.Ross, *The Right and the Good*, Oxford, 1930, pp.19-20, and *The Foundations of Ethics*, Oxford, 1939, pp.85-86; S.E.Toulmin, *The Uses of Argument*, Cambridge, 1958, ch.3, pp.97-102; J.Raz, *Practical Reasons and Norms*, London, 1975, and Princeton, 1990, ch.1, §1.1, pp.25-35.

[18] See, more fully, J.R.Lucas, *The Principles of Politics*, Oxford, 1966 and 1985, §28; and *On Justice*, Oxford, 1980, pp.43-44, 78-79.

must have been wrong, and if actually chosen, would have been wrong decisions. To be an agent is to choose, and to be a rational agent is to try to choose right, and to be open to the possibility of choosing wrong. We are fallible: fallibility is a fact of life—the fundamental fact of life—for agents aspiring to rationality.

With men wrong decisions not only may prove to be mistakes in the event, but are always liable to be criticized. For we can communicate. We not only can act, but can tell others what we are doing, have done, or are going to do. This is what differentiates human actions from animal responses: the agent can, typically, say what he is doing and why he is doing it. In particular he can say what he is doing, and what he is going to do, and another agent can disagree and express his disagreement in words. If two animals assess a situation differently and respond to it in different ways, there is no conflict between them: they go their separate ways, and one may survive and the other not. But we can talk: so we can disagree.

§1.6 Argument and Agreement

"Argument never gets you anywhere", we say, after fruitless wordy debates have degenerated into mere verbal wrangling. We exaggerate. Arguments do sometimes—indeed, quite often—end in agreement. Were it not so, we should have abandoned arguing long ago, and resorted to fisticuffs. People sometimes reach agreement—else they would not waste breath arguing—but not always.

Arguments arise when we do not share a common view. It would be pointless to argue if we did not disagree about something. But it is fruitless, too, to argue if we disagree about everything. We must start with some points of agreement if our discussion is to get us anywhere, and only by taking them as agreed and in the present context unquestionably true can we hope to reach agreement over the point at issue. These points of agreement we often call *the facts*. On the basis of these we argue and may succeed in reaching a conclusion. If we do reach a conclusion, then this point now agreed between us will be *a fact* in any further dispute the pair of us may have. It is a point, largely unrecognised, but of great importance, that a fact is a fact *relative to a given dispute*, or relative to two or more persons at a given time arguing about something. Items both sides accept as true, each side will describe by the word 'fact': items whose truth one side would challenge should not be called facts, unless their truth can be established on the basis of other facts, premises that is, which are conceded as unquestionably true. The word 'fact' is an incomplete symbol; the complete locution being 'facts in respect of such and such a dispute'. Before we can answer the question "What are the facts?" we need to know, either from the context or by being told explicitly, with respect to what dispute the question is being asked. This runs counter to the widespread assumption that facts are the simple solid elements out of which the whole fabric of our knowledge is constructed. That the word 'fact' does not refer to some definite entity is best brought out by Aristotle's Method of Opposites. We ask "What is it being contrasted with? Is it a fact as opposed to a fiction? Or as opposed to a theory? Or as opposed to an interpretation? Or a question of fact as opposed to a question of law?" The argument can be elaborated, with instances to show the word being used in different, and incompatible, senses, showing that we cannot talk of Facts with a big F. Facts are not fundamental building blocks, but are systematically ambiguous counters in the dialectic of argument, with the consequence that as the issue in dispute varies, so also will the facts. The worship of facts is responsible for many of the obsessions which afflict academics.[19]

When arguing, we cast round for points on which we can agree, and proceed from them, each adducing facts or considerations or principles which the other recognises as cogent, but not conclusive. I may think I ought to stay and fight, you may counsel against it: we are talking about the same proposed action, and we are contradicting each other about it. And so we argue. I am claiming that my action would be appropriate in the situation, and if you fail to see this I must try and share with you the way I see it. But it may not be easy. There are many difficulties. One is a failure of language. I may not be able either to characterize the situation totally, or to formulate the correlation between the situation as I have characterized it and what I am proposing to do, in such a way as to enable you to see why I regard it as appropriate. We are often at a loss for words even when we are confident we are right: I reckon I am right—$\lambda\acute{o}\gamma o\nu$ $\check{\epsilon}\chi\epsilon\iota\nu$ (logon echein)—but cannot give an account in words—$\lambda\acute{o}\gamma o\nu$ $\delta\iota\delta\acute{o}\nu\alpha\iota$ (logon didonai).

Our inability to express in words what we inarticulately know is a pervasive feature of thought, which has attracted much attention.

---

[19] See more fully, J.R.Lucas, "On Not Worshipping Facts", *The Philosophical Quarterly*, **8**, 1958, pp.144-156. See further below §2.7 and §6.3.

§1.6   *Fallibility and Reality*   19

But I am not completely inarticulate: I can begin to formulate my reasons, but cannot do so completely. If I am minded to stick it out where I am, I may be able to cite some factor in favour of staying put, even though I recognise it falls far short of a complete justification. The very fact that we use language gives us some hope that we may sometimes reach agreement.[20] There is no particular level at which we must be able to agree any more than there is one at which we cannot but disagree; but we must be able to agree at some level or other; else, we could not speak the same language. Many arguments—many of the most important arguments—take place against a background of many shared assumptions, or agreed criteria of relevance, or canons of cogency. Historians do not reckon that if a thesis is well written it must be true, and lawyers look coldly on pleas of passion. Often we secure agreement by limiting the matter under dispute, or construing it as belonging to a particular discipline, whose premises and procedures we agree to abide by.[21]

But argument cannot be relied on to produce agreement. There is in most disciplines no algorithm, no decision-procedure which will in every case reach a definite conclusion in a finite number of steps, and tell us what the right answer is. The lack of a decision-procedure in practical reasoning was noticed by Plato, and has often been seen as a disqualification for being regarded as a proper sort of reasoning.[22] Much more weight has to be put upon the person who is making the decision than would be the case if every decision could be arrived at by anyone using the relevant procedure. So, although we can argue, and may by argument reach agreement, we cannot count on doing so; and where the argument is inconclusive, we have to exercise judgement, and must be prepared in the end to take a decision on our own authority, and carry the can should the consequences turn out ill.

---

[20] See below, §2.1.

[21] See further below, §15.1.

[22] Plato, *Phaedrus* 263ab.

§1.7 Authority and Autonomy

We disagree, because we are fallible, and do not all always reach a right conclusion about everything. Many philosophers have concluded that since we always may be wrong, we may be always wrong, and cannot really know anything.[23] The argument is invalid, and the conclusion false. We can know things. But I by myself cannot know them all. Contrary to much modern opinion, knowledge is communal. There are many things that other people know and I do not. If I am to know what they know, I must be ready to accept their considered word for the reliability of what they tell me.[24] I would not have been born if my ancestors had not accepted without question warnings that a predator was approaching, and though I am sometimes tempted by scepticism, the price—almost universal nescience—is too high. I need to adopt what Professor Swinburne calls a principle of credulity.[25] Better sometimes wrong than never mistaken: the ostrich's safety from false belief is perilous.

It follows that it is often reasonable to accept someone else's say-so about a matter of fact or about what ought to be done. We believe, approve, or act, on his authority. But authority is not absolute. Not only I, but other people, can be wrong. Unwilling though I should be to disbelieve them entirely, I cannot afford to be unreservedly credulous, nor should I expect them always unquestioningly to accept what I say. I need to be prepared to distance myself from their beliefs, as also from those I myself have been holding hitherto, and make a fresh assessment. Professor Waddington sees man's having "authority-bearing systems" within his mind and some form of "self-objectification" as the springs of conscience and moral action.[26] Certainly, I am often torn between

---

[23] See below §3.2.

[24] See again, §3.2.

[25] R.G. Swinburne, *The Existence of God*, Oxford, 1977, p.254; and *Epistemic Justification*, Oxford, 2001, p.125, and pp.141-149. he refers to Thomas Reid, *Essays on the Intellectual Powers of Man*, Essay 6 on Judgement, ch.5, and *Inquiry into the Human Mind*, ch.6, §24, who had earlier used the term in a similar sense; see R.E.Beanblossom and K.Lehrer, eds, *Thomas Reid's Intellectual Powers of Man*, Hackett, 1983, p.281, and K.Lehrer, ed.*Inquiry into the Human Mind*, pp.75 and 211.

[26] C.H.Waddington, *The Ethical Animal*, pbk. ed., Chicago, 1967, chs.12, 13.

§1.7   *Fallibility and Reality*   21

a presumption in favour of accepting knowledge-claims of other people and a lingering sense that I am somehow being marginalised, and that in the end it is up to me to make up my own mind about what is right and true.

For I, too, am an authority. It is for me, as an autonomous agent, to decide what to do, and hence I am the relevant authority on my future actions. I know what I am going to do. I also know, as Gilbert Ryle is reported as having said to an art critic, what I dislike. I am the authority on whether I have a headache or not. Similarly in the optician's chair, I and I alone, am to be believed about how the left-hand letter on the bottom row appears to me. My knowledge claims are not based on my having been through a certified procedure to ensure accuracy or eliminate error; the question 'How do you know' is out of place because it is not a question of 'how' but of 'who'. I, because I am me, am the relevant authority on my intentions, my preferences, my pains, my sense-experience.

The difference between my first-personal authority and the third-personal authority of others creates tension. I know that I can think wrong. But so can you, so can they. I am rationally reluctant to work on the assumption that I am wrong, but others are not. But they too are rationally reluctant to work on the assumption that they are wrong. Each side feels its authority impugned, and seeks to defend it, adducing incontrovertible arguments in favour of the contention put forward, and probing the arguments of the other side, in order to be able to convict them of error. Instead of the two sides having the common purpose of sharing understanding, they have the opposed purposes of convicting the other side of error. Plato's διαλεκτική (*dialektike*) gives way to ἐριστική (*eristike*), and in the conflict some fragile flowers of insight are trampled under foot. Maybe they have their reasons, but I have my reasons, of which their reasons know nothing. It could be that they, for all their arguments, are missing something, perhaps because they have altered or distorted the topic under discussion, so that they are no longer addressing the question that is really in issue; or perhaps because they are failing to recognise the understanding I bring to the problem, or give any credence to the insights it generates. Thinkers have noticed this finer sensitivity which on occasion informs our judgements, and talk of empathy, *verstehen* and humane insight. In popular, unprofessional philosophy, it is called intuition, and reckoned to be a predominantly feminine ability. Tolstoy devotes a chapter to it in *Anna Karenina*.[27] Levin was far more intelligent than his wife, had read many more books, had pondered great matters far longer, could articulate his thoughts much more clearly: but his wife understood the situation, whereas he did not: she did not have to think, because she knew, whereas try as he might, his thinking could never resolve the problems, never even come to grips with it, let alone come to a conclusion. The feminine sensibility shown by Kitty Levin and Agafya Mkhoylovna was nearly, but not quite, instinctive. It was like the reactions of animals in its immediacy and sureness, but unlike them in not being restricted to earthbound matters and in being refined by reflection and religion.

The difficulty Kitty Levin had in articulating her thought is due in part to inadequacies of language, but more fundamentally to the shift in viewpoints required. She needed to articulate reasons which seem cogent to her husband for a conclusion she had reached by some over-all assessment that seems cogent to her, though not to him. It is inherently difficult to oscillate between her first-personal viewpoint and his third-personal one, and achieve well-focused binocular vision from widely separated eyes. Intuition is in consequence often seen as giving support to some irrationalist position; but what is really being shown is that reason itself is not all of a piece, but has different varieties. The polemical reasoning that shows others to be wrong, and myself to be indisputably right is inevitably crude, and misses the finer subtleties as I explain every nuance in my agonizing over what to do. Rather than posit irrational powers of the mind, as many post-Kantian philosophers did, we should conclude that the power of reason had been unreasonably circumscribed, and that we could by reason attain an understanding that was sometimes right, though not indisputably so. It is a conclusion reached by many philosophers, but in the nature of the case not one easy to establish by coercive arguments as indisputably true. Tough-minded thinkers have therefore found it easy to ridicule talk of finer flights of reason that go beyond the range of coercive argument, and say dismissively that reasons of which the reason know nothing are not reasons at all. It is difficult to confute *l' esprit de géométrie* when it is defiantly ignorant of

---

[27] Pt V, ch. 19.

§1.7   *Fallibility and Reality*   23

other sorts of reasoning, but I shall in due course produce a proof *more geometrico* of the truth-fruitfulness of *l' esprit de finesse*.[28]

Even if we can vindicate the credentials of understanding, insight and judgement, tension remains. Polemical strategy imposes constraints on the free exercise of reason. There is pervasive pressure to formulate, even at the cost of distortion. There is also a preference for derivations—chains of argument, in which each step can be scrutinised separately, and for finitude, so that we can pursue an opponent until we have cornered him, and he must concede defeat, or, contrariwise, make our contention proof against all manner of objection. Coercive arguments can be framed, but at a price. Often the range of topics is limited: mathematicians cannot prove empirical truths, scientists cannot address moral issues. Often the argument is distorted and relevant factors excluded from consideration. And sometimes, especially with moral arguments, resentment is aroused, and we object to being made to do things by some moral law, instead of being able to decide for ourselves what we should choose to do. Coercive reason is all very well when I am telling you where you are wrong, where you get off, or what you have got to do, but inhibits my flights of fancy, my tentative insights, my explorations of the good life. It has its place in our thinking about thinking, because I may be wrong, you may be wrong, we may be wrong, they may be wrong. But it is also possible to think right, and we should be ready to recognise its non-coercive role, in explaining why I did what I did, and in inviting your understanding and support.

Although illuminating, a description of how human beings reason does not give foolproof guidance on how to reason. Human reasoning is fallible. In the face of that fact, it is not enough to maintain, as Strawson and others have done,[29] that "ordinary usage is quite all right as it is", and that since we do, as a matter of fact, reason in certain ways, these ways constitute the standards of what should count as good reasons. That would be to make reason immune to rational scrutiny. And while the presumption that any form of reasoning widely practised must be cogent is strong, it is not incontrovertible. As we have noted, astrology is much practised. Reason is concerned with what we ought to infer, believe, do: it cannot be conclusively decided by actual linguistic practice,

---

[28] In §2.3.

[29] See below, §3.4 n.14.

however weighty that may be in guiding our judgement as to what considerations are likely to be cogent. While, as we shall see later,[30] there is nothing wrong with grounding a value judgement on a factual premise, and in that sense deriving an 'ought' from an 'is', there is something wrong in making the derivation hold by virtue of the way the terms are defined. If we define 'cogent inference' as an inference that conforms to the currently accepted standards, then we are committing an intellectual version of the naturalistic fallacy. It is not enough simply to characterize reason as a phenomenon: we need also to consider why we should be guided by reason, and in what way cogent arguments are to be identified, in the absence of any overall decision-procedure. If we address the former question first, and ask, in the words of J.S. Mill, what are the sanctions of reason—that is, what goes wrong if we go against it—we can distinguish different types of argument, and then we can formulate criteria which will enable us, within limits, to distinguish cogent arguments from those that carry no weight.

[30] In §2.8.

Chapter 2
The Development of Normative Reason

§2.1   Non-contradiction
§2.2   'Not' and 'And'
§2.3   Gödelian Arguments
§2.4   Analyticity
§2.5   Mathematical Dialogues
§2.6   All, Any, Every and Each
§2.7   Induction
§2.8   Practical Reasoning
§2.9   Empathy and Other Minds
§2.10 Reason

§2.1 Non-contradiction

One can think wrong. The fact that after much thought one has reached a conclusion is no guarantee that the conclusion reached is right. Only a very opinionated man would refuse to concede the possibility of error, and once the admission of fallibility is made, the problem of justifying one's beliefs becomes acute. So we formulate our reasons as best we can. But even when formulated, they may fail to convince. Only if people are willing to be reasonable can they be reasoned with. None so obdurate as those who will not listen to reason, and with them at least it is better to save one's breath than to attempt to convince them. You just cannot argue with people who will not be argued with. With them we can only let them go their way, as did Socrates; ἔα χαίρειν (ea chairein).

And yet. Sometimes even the most unreasonable sophist can be caught out, and made to admit the force of an argument. Socrates was able to make Thrasymachus blush, and Aristotle gave some general rules for arguments which are absolutely incontrovertible. If I admit that All men are mortal and that Socrates is a man, I must then concede that Socrates is mortal. Why? What happens if I do not? If I do not concede that Socrates is mortal but say instead that he is not mortal, having already said that All men are mortal and that Socrates is a man, then I am contradicting myself.

The traditional syllogism

> All men are mortal
> <u>Socrates is a man</u>
> *therefore* Socrates is mortal

25

is valid[1] because the conjunction of the three propositions
> All men are mortal
> Socrates is a man
> Socrates is not mortal

is inconsistent. A man who utters this inconsistent triad of propositions is guilty of a self-contradiction. Having affirmed any two, he must not go on to affirm the third on pain of inconsistency, but must contrariwise concede the negation of that third proposition. If he affirms the first two he must concede the negation of the third, as in the familiar syllogism. If he had affirmed the second and the third, he would have to deny the first, as in the syllogism

> Socrates is a man
> <u>Socrates is not mortal</u>
> *therefore* Not all men are mortal,

while if he had affirmed the first and the third, he would have to deny the second, as in the syllogism

> All men are mortal
> <u>Socrates is not mortal</u>
> *therefore* Socrates is not a man.

Simple informal deductive arguments can be defined in terms of inconsistency in much the same way as analytic propositions can. A proposition is analytic if its negation is inconsistent, and similarly an argument is deductive if it would be inconsistent to affirm the conjunction of the premises and the negation of the conclusion; or, more colloquially, if a man would be contradicting himself if he affirmed the premises and denied the conclusion. We are bound to admit the force of deductive arguments because we should be contradicting ourselves if we did not. Having said that All men are mortal and that Socrates is a man, we cannot refuse to allow

---

[1] The use of the word 'valid' has caused difficulties. It is sometimes used as a general term of appraisal, at other times as applying only to deductive arguments. See J.O.Urmson, "Some Questions Concerning Validity", *Revue Internationale de Philosophie*, **25**, 1953, pp.217-229; reprinted in R.G.Swinburne, *The Justification of Induction*, Oxford, 1974, pp.74-84. In this book it will be used only of deductive arguments, which are either valid, or invalid, with no further value in between. Inductive and other arguments will be assessed as being of greater or less cogency. It follows that an "invalid" (i.e. not *deductively* valid) argument may nevertheless be extremely cogent. See further below §3.4.

§2.1   *The Development of Normative Reason*   27

that Socrates is mortal, any more than we can resist the claim that All red things are coloured, that All uncles are brothers, that All bachelors are unmarried, or that Either it is raining or it is not. Deductive arguments, like analytic propositions, flow from the Law of Non-contradiction, and thence obtain their incontrovertible validity.

But why should I not contradict myself? It is a free country, and it would be uncivilised to make me bridle my tongue out of deference to Plato or Aristotle. And indeed there are no legal penalties for inconsistency. The sanction is quite another one, namely that if I contradict myself I make myself unintelligible. A speaker must be consistent, or communication breaks down. In most systems of formal logic[2] it is easily shown that if both p and not-p are given, we can prove any other proposition we like; and one definition of the consistency—the "absolute consistency" of a system—is that not every proposition can be proved in it. The same thought is expressed in the colloquial rejoinder "If you would say that, you would say anything". And this is a rebuke, because if a person is prepared to say anything, then anything he says is no better than anything else. Only if there are some things he is not prepared to say does the fact of his saying some other thing signify. Where everything is free, nothing is of value. Propositions acquire meaning in as much as they have scarcity value. Only if Thrasymachus is not prepared to say absolutely anything, will people attend to what he actually does say. Else his words cease to have scarcity value or significance, and cease to be words at all, and become just babble.

Simple informal deductive arguments, therefore, are valid. Anybody who refuses to accept a deductive argument, puts himself out of court by making himself unintelligible. If he wishes to communicate, he must use a language, and abide by the rules of that language, which alone constitute it as a language and not a sequence of meaningless noises. They are therefore utterly incontrovertible,

---

[2] The word 'logic', like the word 'valid' is the cause of much confusion. Often it is taken to mean 'deductive logic', but philosophers used to talk of 'inductive logic', without its being a contradiction in terms. Scientists sometimes speak of the logic of an experiment, and historians of the logic of a situation, while feminists are furious when men say that women are emotional rather than logical. Confusion is best avoided by always asking what the words 'logic' and 'logical' are being contrasted with.

since only if he accepts them can he make himself understood. Even a sophist, even Thrasymachus, could not resist deductive arguments. They are absolutely cogent, and make no demands on a person's being reasonable, but only on his being able to use language. In that sense, man is a λογιστικόν ζῷον (*logistikon zoon*), a talking animal, even more ineluctably than that he is rational. Not all men are reasonable, but all who argue with us are of necessity language-users.

Although informal deductive arguments are valid, there may be in some cases a problem of recognising them for what they are. The informal deductive arguments which Plato has Socrates use against his opponents obtain their force from the rules of correct English (or Greek) usage. Sometimes it is the rules for certain key words, 'not', 'are', 'is', 'all', 'some', 'more': at other times it is the rules for some specialised word; for example, instead of the analytic proposition All red things are coloured, we may have the deductive argument

  This is red
therefore This is coloured

where the validity of the argument, like the truth of the analytic proposition, turns on the meaning of the words 'red' and 'coloured'. Similarly the arguments

  He is an uncle
therefore He is not an only child

and

  He is a bachelor
therefore He is not married

turn on the meanings of the words 'uncle', 'only', 'child', 'bachelor', 'not' and 'married'. But the meanings of words are not always clear. Although we often know how to use words we seldom know how they are used, in the sense of being able to give explicit definitions of them; indeed, we find it very hard to formulate adequate definitions, and normally we just rely on our unformulated "know-how". We are none the worse for that, so long as usage is clear and we agree about it. But often usage is not clear, and we are not agreed about how to use a crucial word. In the United States at one time to say 'He is red' meant that he had left-wing sympathies and to say 'He is coloured' meant that he numbered Negroes among his ancestors. But the inference from the former proposition to the latter is not deductively valid. Again the word 'uncle' is used in England not only of a parent's brother but of any middle-aged friend of the family, and also of pawnbrokers. It is not clear whether these peripheral uses of the word 'uncle' are standard ones or not. Certainly, we could not convict a man who used the word 'uncle' in either of these senses of not knowing English, although if he refused to distinguish the different senses of the word, communication would break down. But the criterion for distinguishing senses is simply the validity or invalidity of various patterns of deductive argument, and so our appeal is no longer to a common language but simply to a willingness to accept certain types of argument as valid. If the only cogent arguments were deductive ones, it might not matter making a willingness to accept them a precondition of communication: but since there are other arguments, many of which are felt by many people to be cogent, we shall be arguing in a circle if we explain deductive arguments in terms of linguistic usage, and linguistic usage in terms of deductive argument.

Language cannot be separated from the rest of life and thought. The meaning of the word 'gentleman' depends on an understanding of the considerations a gentleman is guided by. We speak the same language only because we share to some extent a common life and a common standard of rationality. We often say of a person who completely rejects our assumptions or refuses to acknowledge the cogency of any of the arguments commonly regarded as cogent that "he does not speak the same language as we do". Our language is not a formal logistic calculus but something much more flexible, often vague, sometimes shifting, impregnated with implicit assumptions, something almost alive. Sometimes its shifts reflect merely a social change. At one time the argument

> This person is a bachelor
> *therefore* This person is a male

was a valid deductive argument, because unmarried females were called spinsters. But now we have the term 'bachelor girl' and the validity of the argument is in doubt. The meaning of the word 'bachelor' is shifting, and now has connotations of bed-sits, doing for oneself and cooking for one, rather than of being as yet uncommitted and fancy-free. There may even come a day when the word 'bachelor' is so completely anchored in, say, a residential context, that from someone's being a bachelor it will no longer follow as an inference of deductive logic that he or she is unmarried. More serious, from our point of view, than social changes are intellectual ones. Our thoughts change, and our theories have to accommodate new insights or new facts. At one time

> This is gold
>
> *therefore* This is soluble in *aqua regia* but not in *aqua fortis*

would have been a reasonable argument, but not a deductive one, at another it might have been deductive, and at yet another it might have no longer been deductively valid. As our knowledge of chemistry has deepened, and the concepts of alleomorph and isotope have been introduced, the meaning of other concepts has been changed too. The change is sometimes gradual, and we cannot say whether some inference is or is not valid in consequence of the way we use words or in consequence of the way, we believe, the laws of nature operate. Similarly in moral arguments the distinction between moral and purely deductive arguments is sometimes difficult to draw. A man who says that it is always wrong to kill people but that capital punishment is quite all right is clearly failing to use the word 'always' correctly. But is a person who says 'I promise to marry you' and later denies that he ought to marry her failing on a point of linguistic usage or only of morality? If he gave some reason for not carrying out his promise, we should acquit him on the linguistic charge, even if we regarded his reasons as inadequate for going back on his obligations. But if he failed to see that saying the words 'I promise' put him under any obligation whatever, we might also say that he did not know what the word 'promise' meant. There are many other words—*justice, mercy, duty, love*—whose meaning is not constituted by any particular patterns of inference but rather to the recognition of the force of some lines of argument. We cannot separate considerations of language from those of reasonableness. A man who never sees reason to do justice or love mercy, altogether lacks these concepts and does not really understand the meaning of the words.

These difficulties tell not against our drawing the distinction between deductive and other agreements but against the claim that the distinction is always a clear one. Often we can draw the distinction, and it is useful to pick out those arguments which are basically verbal since they turn on the meaning of words, from other more substantial arguments. But we cannot always draw the distinction, and therefore in practice cannot wield simple informal deductive arguments as effectively as we should like, to force recalcitrant reasoners to concede conclusions.

§2.2 'Not' and 'And'

One natural response is to formalise. We pick out certain basic patterns of inference, and spell out explicitly what the essential pattern is. We choose basic patterns which are, beyond doubt, purely deductive. And if anyone denies their validity, he can be convicted by appeal to the explicit rules of formal logic. We might lay down that the following forms of argument are valid

> All Bs are C
> X is a B
> ─────────
> *therefore* X is a C

and if ever our opponent refuses to accept an argument of this form, we no longer need appeal to his unformulated sense of the meaning of the words 'all', 'are', 'is' *etc.*, but can simply point out that the argument in question is of this form, and therefore must be valid.

Forms of valid inference have not only been specified explicitly, but have been systematized, so that granted only a few, simple, patterns of inference, others can be validated by a succession of simple steps. Deductive logic is thus very like geometry. At first, in Aristotle's day, there were a number of separate patterns of inference, each recognised as valid, but only a few having been "reduced" to simpler forms. Now, however, there are many axiomatizations of formal logic with only three axioms, some with only one, and correspondingly few rules of inference. The difficulty is that a recalcitrant listener cannot be forced to accept cogent deductive inferences in these formal logics on pain of self-contradiction: If I fail to concede that once you have established the two premises p and $p \rightarrow q$, I cannot deny you the conclusion q, I do not thereby show myself ignorant of English. Rather, I am failing to play the game. The analogy is with cricket: it is as though I refused to leave the wicket after having been bowled. A person who refuses to leave the wicket when out is just not playing cricket; there is no law against it—the pitch may be in his own garden—but nobody will play with him. The sanction is the same: being ignored by others if we ignore the rules of the game. Formal deductive arguments thus appear as a species of rule-observance: we don't have to observe rules, but if we do not, we are not observing them. But cricket is optional, whereas logic is not. We could change the rules of cricket, and have bowlers bowl eight times in an over, instead of only six, but we should be chary of recognising "Australian logic" as an equally good way of arguing, simply because the Australians chose to adopt it. Although there is some room for dispute at the margins, the main body of logic is what it is for good reason. Its rationale arises from the need to avoid self-contradiction.

If I have *not both (p and not q)*, or *not p without q*, then if I am given p, I can infer q, because else I should have *p and not q* as well as *not both (p and not q)*, which would be an evident contradiction. We can express this in symbols. The older logicians wrote *not both (p and not q)*, as $-(p\& - q)$, but it is better to have a distinct sign for negation, $\neg$. which will not be mistaken for a dash. For reasons that will emerge later, instead of the simple ampersand, &, logicians now prefer to use a wedge-shaped symbol, $\wedge$. Then granted a very minimal sense of the word 'and', namely that if we have p and $\neg q$, we have $(p \wedge \neg q)$, it follows that if we have $(p \wedge \neg q)$ and $\neg(p \wedge \neg q)$ we have $(p \wedge \neg q) \wedge \neg(p \wedge \neg q)$ which is evidently a self contradiction. That is, if I have $\neg(p \wedge \neg q)$, then I can infer q from p, or granted $\neg(p \wedge \neg q)$, I have 'if p then q'. This suggests that we write $\neg(p \wedge \neg q)$ as $p \rightarrow q$: $p \rightarrow q$ is called material implication, and is often read as 'p implies q'. But it is important to note that in most ordinary uses of 'p implies q' there is a suggestion of some connexion between p and q justifying the inference.

Material implication does not carry this connotation. We can see this if we note that $\neg(p \wedge \neg q)$ is true automatically if p is false, so that if we know that p is false, we can assert $p \rightarrow q$ whatever q is, and without there being any connexion between p and q. Similarly if q is true, $\neg(p \wedge \neg q)$ must be true too, so that $p \rightarrow q$ holds vacuously. Material implication does not give the full sense of *if ... , then ...* , but only the minimal truth conditions it must satisfy. But these are important. They are *the* minimal conditions, and if an implication does not satisfy them, it cannot be an implication as we know it. We can express the force of material implication by the inference it legitimises. If I have p and $p \rightarrow q$, then I can conclude q, or, representing inference by $\vdash$, p, $p \rightarrow q \vdash q$.

In reaching this formulation, we have implicitly appealed to inference patterns expressing the force of 'and', $\wedge$, namely that p, $q \vdash p \wedge q$. The complete specification of the logical force of $\wedge$ has in addition to introduction rules, the elimination rules: $p \wedge q \vdash p$ and $p \wedge q \vdash q$. It follows that $p \wedge q \vdash q \wedge p$. Here, as with material implication, the logical symbol carries only part of the sense of ordinary language. $p \wedge q$ means the same as $q \wedge p$, whereas "They got married and had a baby" means something different from "They had a baby and got married".

§2.2   The Development of Normative Reason   33

Negation, $\neg$, is similarly defined by inference patterns. In addition to the ban on self-contradiction, it is commonly held that $p \vdash \neg\neg p$ and $\neg\neg p \vdash p$, though the latter inference is controversial. Some logicians work with an "intuitionistic logic" in which only $\neg\neg\neg p \vdash \neg p$ holds. Such a logical system can be developed without inconsistency, but fails to capture the two-sided nature of contradiction. If I say p, you can contradict me by saying not-p, $\neg p$, but I can then contradict you by saying $\neg\neg p$, thereby re-asserting my original claim. Although logical systems can be devised with only a truncated form of negation, or, indeed, without any form of negation whatsoever, they fail to capture the full force of dialogue, in which assertions on the one hand can be confronted by denials on the other, followed by a ding-dong of argument in which claim and counter-claim are made and defended.

Just as we can define $\rightarrow$ in terms of $\neg$ and $\wedge$, so can we similarly define $\wedge$ in terms of $\rightarrow$ and $\neg$. We can also define in terms of $\neg$ together with $\wedge$, or $\vee$, or $\rightarrow$, other connectives—'if and only if', the inclusive 'or', often now written 'and/or' (in Latin *vel*), and the exclusive 'or', that is 'either or , but not both' (in Latin *aut*).[3]

---

[3] Indeed, we can generate all the truth functions from a single binary 'neither . . nor . . ', $\downarrow$, joint denial, where $p \downarrow q$ is true just in case both p and q are false, or from $|$, alternative denial, which is false just in case both p and q are true. Whitehead and Russell took $p \vee q$ as basic, defining $p \rightarrow q$ as $\neg p \vee q$, and $p \wedge q$ $\neg(\neg p \vee \neg q)$.

§2.3 Gödelian Arguments

Formal logic saves us from being swamped by the fluidity of ordinary usage. We may disagree about whether 'or' should be construed in an inclusive or exclusive sense, but the rules for $\wedge$ and for $\not\leftrightarrow$ (which captures the sense of the exclusive 'or', *aut* in Latin) are unambiguous. It would seem natural, therefore, in carrying out the programme of formalisation, to seek total explicitness, with all the agreements expressed in propositions, so that everyone could know that they had been agreed, with nothing depending on an implicit know-how. But that cannot be achieved. As Lewis Carroll pointed out,[4] we cannot replace all rules of inference by propositions, but need at least one rule, telling us how to operate with the propositions we are given. It is not enough to have the explicit statement

$$((p \to q) \wedge p) \to q$$

which expresses the truth enshrined in the rule of inference

$$\frac{p \to q \quad p}{q}$$

We need also to be able to *apply* it, which involves being able to recognise symbols, and to see *when* we have premises of the form $p \to q$ and p, and then *allow* in *that* case that q also holds. There was implicit appeal to a rule of inference in the previous section, in recognising $(p \wedge \neg q) \wedge \neg(p \wedge \neg q)$ as a contradiction of the *same form* as $p \wedge \neg p$. Formally, the recognition is justified by a rule of substitution, which is taken for granted in all formal systems. Formal logic is concerned with formal patterns of inference, and has to be able to classify different particular inferences as being of the same general type. Know-how cannot be entirely reduced to know-that: there remains an ineliminable element of know-how: logic is ultimately about how to reason, not a set of formulas in a calculus.

---

[4] Lewis Carroll, "What the Tortoise Said to Achilles", *Mind*, 10, 1895, pp.278-290; reprinted in *The Works of Lewis Caroll*, ed. R.L.Green, London, 1965, pp.1049-51. See also, Gilbert Ryle, *The Concept of Mind*, London, 1949, ch.2, pp.25-61; or "Knowing How and Knowing That", *Proceedings of the Aristotelian Society*, 48, 1945-1946, pp.1-16; and Kant, *Critique of Pure Reason*, tr. Kemp Smith, A132-3/b171-2.

§2.3   The Development of Normative Reason   35

None the less, by formalising we hope to reduce the element of know-how to a minimal ability to recognise shapes, and we can go a very long way in formalising logic in terms of a finite number of axioms and rules of inference. Rules can be applied over and over again. There is a potential infinity of applications. We begin to go from simple deductive logic to mathematics.

Mathematics has long been regarded the paradigm of rigorous deductive reasoning. Many philosophers have sought to cast all reasoning into an incontrovertible chain of rule-validated inference *more geometrico*, supposing that only so could they establish thought on sure foundations. But much to everyone's surprise, mathematics itself has shown that such an ideal is impossible. This highly unexpected result was proved by Gödel in 1929.[5] Granted that we can represent both addition and multiplication in our formal system—it would be a very defective one, if we could not—we can prove in the system that, provided it is a consistent system, it will contain some formula which can be neither proved nor disproved in the system. When we examine the proof we come to the even more surprising conclusion that the proposition expressed by that formula must in fact be true. The Gödelian formula is considered both as an abstract formula in an abstract system, and as an arithmetical proposition with its ordinary meaning. Looking at it in the former way, we prove that, granted the consistency of elementary number theory, it is unprovable: and looking at it the latter way we see that it is true. Thus we have found a new way of establishing the truth of certain propositions of elementary number theory which could not be proved within the standard axiomatization of the theory.

Gödel's theorem is a variant on the Epimenides—or "liar"— paradox, "this statement is untrue", in which the wide-ranging

---

[5] K. Gödel, *"Über Formal Unentscheidbare Sätze der Principia Mathematica und verwandter Systeme"*, Part I, *Monatschefte für Mathematik und Physik*, Vol. XXXVIII (1931), 173-198. Reprinted with English translation in *Kurt Gödel: Collected Works*, vol.1, Oxford Univeristy Press, 1986, pp.144-195. There is also an English translation in Kurt Gödel, *Lectures at Institute of Advanced Study*, Princeton, N.J., 1934; and one by B.Meltzer, Edinburgh, 1962 (but see review in *Journal of Symbolic Logic*, 30, 1965, pp.357-359). In this paper Gödel proved two theorems. It is his first theorem that is here discussed.

'untrue' is replaced by a tightly defined 'unprovable-in-the-given-system'. Provided the system is a formal system, and contains enough simple arithmetic to define addition and multiplication, we can code the concept of being 'unprovable-in-the-given-system' into an arithmetical formula, and assign numbers ("Gödel numbers") to each formula of the system. It is then possible to find a number (in practice enormously large, but here pretended to be 1024) which is the Gödel number of the formula 'the formula with the number 1024 is "unprovable-in-the-given-system" ', where the property of being 'unprovable-in-the-given-system' has been given its appropriate code. It follows that the formula no.1024, which we shall call G, must be true, but unprovable-in-the-given-system, since if it were false, it would be provable-in-the-given-system, which would mean that elementary number theory was false.

The actual argument is enormously long, and needs to be stated with great care. But the upshot is that if we formalise any system rich enough to contain ordinary arithmetic, there will be some formula (in fact an infinite number of them) which cannot be proved in it but is obviously true. An obvious retort is that if the proof is valid, it can be formalised, so that a heuristic, informal proof at one stage can be replaced by a proper, formally valid one in due course. It can. But Gödel's theorem applies to any formal system strong enough for elementary number theory: and if we try to complete such a system by adding the Gödelian formula as an additional axiom, we can apply Gödel's theorem to this new system to find a new Gödelian formula which is unprovable in the new system. Even if we add a new rule of inference, which would be equivalent to adding an infinite sequence of axioms, we still should not have secured a system that was complete, because Gödel's theorem would again apply to the new system, with its new rule of inference and all, and would again enable us to find a formula which could not be proved or disproved in the new system, although we would be quite clear that in fact it was true.

Gödel's theorem is difficult to understand, easy to misunderstand. The formal proof shows only that if the system is consistent, then the Gödelian formula is unprovable in the system. Some philosophers have suggested that the system itself is inconsistent. But that is a counsel of despair; and if elementary number theory were inconsistent, deduction would cease to be a paradigm of valid argument. Other philosophers stick their feet in and refuse to recognise the Gödelian proposition as true. And of course if a man

§2.3   *The Development of Normative Reason*   37

refuses to concede as true anything except what can be proved in a formal system, he can avoid any further embarrassment, beyond that of having to be remarkably obdurate to cogent mathematical reasoning. Essentially what he is doing is to deny any application of the word 'true'. He can understand what the word 'provable' means, and can be forced to acknowledge that in a consistent formalisation of elementary number theory there must be formulas which can be neither proved nor disproved in the formalised system. But he refuses to understand what the word 'true' means, and see that the proposition expressed by the Gödelian formula must in fact be true.

But we do understand what 'true' means, and we learn from Gödel's theorem that truth outruns provability. That has always been believed by some thinkers, though denied by others, who have shied away from any concept of truth that could not be established against the sceptic by some copper-bottomed proof. But once the concept of proof has been made explicit, and the criteria for being provable clearly laid down, Gödel's theorem shows that there are truths which go beyond that concept of provable.

We are led, therefore, to reject certain minimalising views of truth and reason. It is possible for propositions to be true, even though we cannot verify them. It makes sense to claim truth, to wonder about truth, to seek truth, beyond the limits of assured knowledge. Equally with reason, to be reasonable is not just to be in accordance with a rule. Aristotle sometimes talks of κατὰ τὸν ὀρθὸν λόγον *kata ton orthon logon*, in accordance with correct reason, sometimes of μετὰ λόγου *meta logou*, with reason; Gödel's theorem underlines the difference, and extends the point made by the tortoise to Achilles in the previous section: however carefully or fully we specify rules of inference, not only is inference something different, but it is not always just rule-observance and can go beyond mere conformity to rules.

Many philosophers have sought to formalise inference. Rather than have inchoate appeals to reason, they seek a few rules of inference which can be precisely formulated, or better still, articulate them as axioms, which can act as premises for simple applications of the *Modus Ponens* rule. Formalisation along these lines can be useful. If the inference itself is in dispute, it helps to try and formulate it precisely, so that each party can spot hidden assumptions, or unjustified claims, made by the other. And treating a system purely formally enables important questions of consistency, completeness, or independence to be asked and sometimes answered. But the programme—we may call it "deductivism"—of always formalising every inference cannot be carried through. Deductivists in moral philosophy want to replace every moral inference by a moral major premise, which will apply syllogistically to a proposition describing a particular case. In the philosophy of history, they construe particular inferences about particular situations as covertly universal propositions saying that whenever a situation of the one sort arises, it will be followed by a situation of the other sort. These rational reconstructions always were implausible. Now that we see that the programme cannot in any case be carried through, we need feel no compunction in not formalising in cases where there is no special reason for doing so.

If reason transcends rules, we need to alter many of our views of rational activity. Rules will still be important, but not all important. They provide a useful check on the fallibility of individual reasoners, and a means of agreeing among ourselves about what may be commonly taken for granted. But they need validation by reasonable men recognising that the rules are in fact reasonable, and they are open to criticism. If to be reasonable was simply to follow a rule, then it would be self-contradictory to hold that a rule was unreasonable; but it is always intelligible to say that, and sometimes correct.

Rules should be evaluated at the bar of reason: reason need not necessarily be called to account in terms of rule-following. Often, of course, we are concerned with a rule-governed activity, but not of necessity in all cases. Judgement may be called for, and we may have to decide whose judgement is most to be respected in cases where the rules conflict, or have run out, or do not exist. Although there are disciplines, such as mathematics or mathematical logic, where the traditional aim has been to prove everything *more geometrico*, we do not need, nor should attempt, to reconstruct other disciplines on that model. In history or literary criticism it may be right to recognise the authority of great historians or sensitive critics without being able to reduce their reasoning to explicit syllogistic form. We often talk of originality and creativity in artistic work, and hold that the great artist breaks out from the canons of correct taste and achieves something that, although not conforming to them, is nevertheless absolutely right: Gödel's theorem underwrites this possibility, as one obtaining not only in artistic creation, but throughout the whole realm of rationality, even in the austere field of mathematical logic.

§2.4 Analyticity

Gödel proved another theorem, a completeness theorem. He proved that first-order logic is complete, that is that every well-formed formula in first-order logic is a theorem. This is most easily understood if we consider propositional calculus. Propositional calculus can be treated axiomatically, as it was by Russell and Whitehead, who postulated five axioms, and certain rules of inference, and proved well-formed formulas by deriving them from the axioms by means of the rules of inference. But we can also use truth-tables to work out the truth-value of a well-formed formula from the truth-values of its components; and if a well-formed formula comes out true whatever the truth-values of its components, we call it a tautology. It is a fairly easy exercise to check that the axioms are tautologies, and that the rules of inference are such that if the premise or premises are tautologies, then the conclusion must be one too. It is much harder to prove the converse of this, but it can be done: every tautology can be proved from the axioms. We say that propositional calculus is *complete* (or sometimes "semantically complete"). Gödel proved that the same holds good for first-order logic, the logic in which we have quantifiers, All, Some, None and Not All, with the quantifiers ranging over individuals, so that we can talk of All men being mortal, and the like. We can construe this as showing that the quantifiers, *when they range over individuals*, are subject to the same discipline as we have worked out for And and Not. If you deny the conclusion of some syllogism that holds whatever individual cases it is about, you are not only guilty of contradicting yourself, but can be brought step by step to a self-evident self-contradiction. This supports the claim by Kant and many modern philosophers that deductive logic is purely analytic, based on the principle of non-contradiction, and yielding only empty tautologies.

But Gödel's completeness theorem holds only for *first*-order logic, in which quantification is allowed only over individual variables, and not over predicate variables. In first-order logic we can talk about all Peter's children, and say that they have blue eyes, but not about all Peter's features, which none of his children possess in their entirety. Dedekind needed the latter sort of locution in order to define the natural numbers, and it is similarly needed to define the concept of being finite, and to formulate various different axioms of infinity. Second-order logic allows quantification over predicate variables, so that we can talk about all features, all properties, all qualities, and the like, but second-order logic is *not* complete in Gödel's sense, but only Henkin-complete, which secures completeness only by misinterpreting key logical terms. In second-order logic not all well-formed formulas that are true under all (reasonable) interpretations are theorems. Logical truths are not always provable by a step-by-step ("algorithmic") derivation. A sceptic can deny them without being led into patent self-contradiction. Deductive logic is not necessarily analytic: synthetic *a priori* propositions are possible.

And we need to have them.

§2.5 Mathematical Dialogues

The argument of the previous section is cogent, but not incontrovertible. All that has been formally proved in any system which contains simple arithmetic is that there is no formal proof in the system of the Gödelian formula or its negation. A determined sceptic could maintain the negation of the Gödelian formula without contradicting himself—just. We could argue with him—there are cogent arguments for not accepting the negation of the Gödelian formula—but his position, though weird, is tenable: we can understand what is being claimed; it is not a contradiction in terms, and if put forward, would need to be argued against, not simply dismissed as unintelligible. It follows that even this austerely mathematical reasoning is two-sided. And, contrary to orthodox opinion, much else in mathematics is best understood in terms of a two-sided dialogue between seekers after truth.[6]

Mathematics, with its unexpected incompleteness and unprovable consistency, is different from simple, first-order logic, which is provably consistent and complete. Poincaré[7] regarded the Rule of Recursion, often misleadingly called the Principle of Mathematical Induction,[8] as the key difference. In Peano's first-order axiomatization of arithmetic, it is expressed by the axiom schema

---

[6] See above, §1.5.

[7] H.Poincaré, *Science and Hypothesis*, pbk ed., New York, 1952, §§IV-VII, pp.8-13.

[8] Although it may be advantageous, for the purposes of logistic analysis, to articulate an axiom, which can be added or not added to an axiomatic system, we gain a deeper understanding of the principle involved, if we view it as a rule of inference. If we do regard it as an an axiom, it is evidently a synthetic *a priori* one, stating some fact about a strange universe of enormous size: we wonder not only whether it is true or false, but also how we could ever come to know its truth or falsity. A rule arising from a dialogue between two truth-seekers is much easier to understand and to justify.

§2.5   The Development of Normative Reason   41

$$(F(0) \land (\forall n)(F(n) \to F(n+1))) \to (\forall x)F(x),$$

which lays down that if the property F holds for 0, and is such that if it holds for any one natural number it holds for its successor, then it holds for all natural numbers. It seems a very reasonable rule to adopt. It does not seem to add anything that could be questioned to what we already have. If we had Peano's other four postulates without this axiom schema, we should have a system that could be called "*Sorites* Arithmetic", in which, granted the antecedents of the axiom schema, namely $F(0)$ and $(\forall n)(F(n) \to F(n+1))$, we could establish for each natural number n that $F(n)$. There could not be a counter-example within what we normally regard as the natural numbers. If anyone were to maintain that there was, and that for some number, say 257, it was not the case that $F(257)$, we could construct a *Sorites* argument

$F(0)$
$F(0) \to F(1)$ (particular case of $(\forall n)(F(n) \to F(n+1))$)
$F(1)$ by *Modus Ponens*
$F(1) \to F(2)$ (particular case of $(\forall n)(F(n) \to F(n+1))$)
$F(2)$ by *Modus Ponens*
$F(2) \to F(3)$ (particular case of $(\forall n)(F(n) \to F(n+1))$)
$F(3)$ by *Modus Ponens*
$F(3) \to F(4)$ (particular case of $(\forall n)(F(n) \to F(n+1))$)
$F(4)$ by *Modus Ponens*
. . .
. . .
$F(256)$ by *Modus Ponens*
$F(256) \to F(257)$ (partic. case of $(\forall n)(F(n) \to F(n+1))$)
$F(257)$ by *Modus Ponens*

Thus in the end he would be forced to withdraw his putative counter-example, on pain of self-contradiction. In fact, he could see that this would be the outcome long before we had finished the proof, and would concede rather than waiting to be checkmated. And he would see that the same would happen if he were to suggest any other putative counter-example. It would be reasonable, therefore, for him to concede the claim that $F(n)$ holds for all n.

But we have not actually proved that. We have shown how, for *each* n, we can prove $F(n)$; but without the Rule of Recursion, or some equivalent, we cannot actually produce a formal proof, the last line of which is $(\forall x)(F(x))$, expressing the proposition that *all* natural numbers x have the property F. There is a subtle difference between being able to prove, given any particular natural number n, that $F(n)$ holds, and actually proving that all numbers possess the property in question. Nevertheless, we are confident of the validity of the Rule of Recursion, and generally regard arguments invoking it, along with the rest of mathematics, as deductive.

But there is a difference. The difference shows up in a difference of sanction. The sanction against those who refuse to recognise the cogency of arguments by recursion is no longer that they are contradicting themselves or failing to abide by the rules of the calculus they are operating. The Rule of Recursion is independent of the other axioms and rules of inference of first-order Peano arithmetic (because our concept of natural number is not sufficiently tightly formulated to exclude the possibility of there being some "inaccessible" numbers, which could not ever be reached by a chain of argument, no matter how long it was). Someone who refuses to concede that every number has the property F, granted that 0 does, and that if any number does, so too does its successor, cannot be convicted of a straight contradiction, however unreasonable his stance seems, provided he sticks to his position without making any further move. Although it is very natural to give reasons for denying a claim made by a friend, it is not absolutely obligatory, and an antagonist who plays with his cards very close to his chest can avoid being brought up short in a self-contradiction. But once he starts considering the possibility of counter-examples, he is lost.

Why should he be reasonable? Or better, Why should I be reasonable? If my sole aim is the polemical one of not losing the contest, there is no reason why I should expose myself to being worsted in the argument. But the case is altered if I want to know the truth. In that case I value discovering what actually is true more than winning the argument, and indeed would rather be shown wrong in what I had previously believed, if by that means I come to exchange wrong opinions for better ones. If I have any idea of truth, it is something that my beliefs should conform to, rather than something that should be conformed to what I think. Truth is independent of me, or it is nothing. And however good an opinion I have of my opinions, once I am possessed of the idea of truth, I know that the opinions which are worthy to be believed are the true ones, not those that happen to be believed by me.

A reasonable man, therefore, will make the moves necessary for ascertaining the truth, even if he thereby exposes himself to being refuted. He will, "for the sake of argument", suppose that some particular natural number was a counter-example to the thesis being put forward, and, then seeing that any such supposition would involve him in inconsistency, allow that no counter-example could exist, and hence that the thesis must be true. The love of truth makes one vulnerable to pressures to which the purely contentious man is immune. Although the sanction against rejecting the Rule of Recursion is different from the sanction for rejecting *Modus Ponens*, arguments invoking recursion are properly regarded as deductive.

§2.6 All, Any, Every and Each

The terms 'all', 'any', 'every' and 'each', normally interchangeable when we are talking about the finite cases of ordinary converse, reveal logical differences when we are deploying formal proofs over infinite domains.

'All' is the strongest claim. Once admitted, it applies universally without more ado; I defy you to produce a counter-example; and—if my claim is admitted—you know you cannot. But before it has to be admitted, it needs to be justified to the hilt. In order to justify the claim 'all . . . ', I must produce a straightforward derivation, the last line of which is $(\forall x)(F(x)$. 'Any . . . ' is not so forthright. Instead of saying that I have got a proof, I invite you to choose some particular instance, x, and then show $F(x)$ by an incontrovertible derivation of a standard form. Since it is a standard-form derivation, I can myself apply it mechanically, and hence instruct you to apply it mechanically, and thus lead from an assured ability to prove any particular case you happen to choose, to a straight proof that my claim does, indeed, hold for *all* cases. *Any* entails *all* when the proof of *any* is always of the same form.

With recursive reasoning, the inference from *every* to *all*, the proof in each case is indeed valid, but not *quite* the same. The number of *Sorites* steps needed depends on the particular example chosen. The proof of $F(257)$ outlined in the previous section was similar to that of $F(4)$, but not *precisely* the same, inasmuch as it had 515 steps, whereas only 9 were needed to prove it for $F(4)$. Similarly the contra-positive disproof of the denial of $F(257)$ is much longer than that for $F(4)$. *Any* entails *all* because

$$(\forall x)(\exists\, Disproof_{standard-issue} \neg F(x)),$$

whereas *every* entails *all* because

$$(\forall x)(\exists \, Disproof_x \neg F(x)).$$

Since the disproof is an incontrovertible derivation, it is reasonable to expect any reasonable person to recognise that fact, and to concede without more ado, but if it is to be carried through to the bitter end, the respondent has to make the necessary adjustments to the length of the derivation, before he sees the inevitable outcome. The cooperation required of the respondent is minimal, but enough to mark the distinction between the inference from *any* to *all* and the inference from *every* to *all*.

Recursion is implicit in our ideal of a formal proof. A formal proof consists in a finite number of steps, each of which is a valid inference, in virtue of some stated rule of inference, of the proposition (or formula or sentence) in question from some proposition(s) which either is an axioms or is already established at some earlier stage in the proof. It must consist of only a finite number of steps, but can consist of any finite number of steps. That is, it can be as long as we please, but not infinitely long. It follows that as soon as a number, any number (but some definite one), is picked, we can prove our formula for that number; but that as long as the number has not been fixed, there is no guarantee that any particular proof we have produced will have reached that number.

The derivations adduced to make good a claim that 'every . . ', although not precisely the same in each case, are very similar, differing only in the length of the derivation, according to some specifiable formula. The respondent is required to exercise only minimal cooperative intelligence to see how the *Sorites* derivation should be adjusted in length to fit the case in under discussion. But it could be that in each case there was a derivation, but not so similar that the respondent could be given simple-to-follow instructions how to tailor the basic model so as to fit the particular case. The Gödelian argument sketched in §2.2 of this chapter can be deployed with regard to any first-order system strong enough to include elementary number theory, but there is no set formula giving instructions how to do it in each case. Some non-minimal cooperative intelligence is required on the part of the respondent to see how the general Gödelian argument should be tailored to fit the particular case under discussion. Just as the argument from *every* requires more

> Positive Universal Arguments
> 1. All. I have a proof of $(\forall x)F(x)$ and here it is.
> 2. Any. You choose x, and I will prove $F(x)$ by a standard procedure which will work for any other x you might choose.
> 3. Every. You choose n, and I will prove $F(n)$ by a *Sorites* derivation which will work, with suitable adjustments, for any other n you might choose.
> 4. Each. You choose x, and I will prove $F(x)$. You should be able to get the hang of my proof, and see how it could be altered to fit any other x you might have chosen.
>
> —oOo—
>
> Once dialogues (2), (3), or (4), have been concluded, you, if you are rational, will reckon that you cannot fault an All claim. So next time we meet, I claim All.
>
> Whereas in these latter dialogues, I give you the first move, and then persuade you to concede, I now make the first move myself, defying anyone to controvert me. All is a challenge I make to all comers, whereas with Any, Every and Each, I let you have the first move, so that you can see that try as you will, you cannot evade defeat.

cooperative intelligence than the argument from *any*, so the argument from *each* requires more cooperative intelligence than the argument from *every*.

The problem becomes tractable if we use the dialectical approach to cast these arguments in negative form. In the case of 'all . . . ', the negativity arises only from the nature of deductive proof. A formal derivation is a sequence of steps, each one of which must be allowed on pain of self-contradiction. In claiming 'all . . . ', I need to be able to produce a derivation which must be conceded on pain of self-contradiction. That is, if I say 'all . . . ', and you were to say 'not all . . . ', I could lead you step by step to inconsistency. 'All . . . ' is demonstrably ungainsayable.

With *any*, *every* and *each* the negative approach is much more significant. Instead of my saying that I have got a proof, whereupon you may challenge me to produce it, I challenge you to produce a counter-example, whereupon I show that it is not a counter-example in such a way that you realise that whatever purported counter-example you might propose, I should be able to refute your claim that it really was a counter-example. Provided you take up the challenge, and name some particular purported counter-example, I shall be able to prove you wrong.

If I claim 'any . . .', I challenge you to find a case that is not ungainsayable. If you deny $F(x)$ thereby claiming $\neg F(x)$, I shall show that $\neg F(x)$ leads to a self-contradiction, so that $F(x)$ is, as I claimed, ungainsayable. And, as argued before, since my proof is in a standard form, applicable without more ado to any case, you can see (and if you cannot see, I can tell you) how to assure yourself of the incontrovertibility of $F(x)$, whatever x you choose.

The difficulty with the positive approach to the inference from *every* to *all* was that the respondent had to make the adjustments necessary for the proof to fit his particular case. There was no upper bound to the length of proof that might be required, and since proofs have to be finite, we feel queasy at the prospect of their being indefinitely, even though not infinitely, long. Qualms are avoided in the negative approach, since although we have an infinite progression of numbers, for every individual number our argument can be put in the form of a regress which is necessarily only finite: I can prove my refutation of a purported counter-example for n, provided I can prove it for $n-1$; and I can prove it for $n-1$ provided I can prove it for $n-2$; and so on, until I come down to 0, where I have already established it. The dialectical challenge reverses the direction of the burden of proof. The burden of proof is still on my shoulders, but instead of my taking on the impossible task of scaling an infinite ascent and proving my claim for all of infinitely many cases, I get you to propose to me the manageable task of descending from any given stage and showing how well-grounded my argument is there. And this I always can do, in a finite number of steps. For although the natural numbers go on without ever coming to an end, they do have a definite beginning. And the Rule of Recursion secures its credit by trading on this fact.

The method of argument can be extended to transfinite numbers, since every transfinite ordinal can generate only a finite chain of descending ordinals. Transfinite set theory often appeals to the Axiom of Choice, which can again be illuminatingly viewed in terms of a dialogue, or alternatively, to the Axiom of Determinacy, which is explicitly dialectical in form.

In the straightforward positive justification of the Gödelian argument some significantly non-minimal cooperative intelligence was required on the part of the respondent, and if this is not forthcoming, it cannot be forced on an unwilling respondent. Hence again the polemical value of casting the argument in the negative form, where the respondent chooses some particular system, and I point out its Achilles' heel.

> Negative Universal Arguments
> 1. All. If you deny $(\forall x)F(x)$ I shall show that $\neg(\forall x)F(x)$ leads to an inconsistency, so that $(\forall x)F(x)$ is ungainsayable.
> 2. Any. You choose x, and if you deny $F(x)$, I shall show that $\neg F(x)$ leads to an inconsistency. I shall show it in a standard way, which clearly would apply to any x you might have chosen.
> 3. Every. You choose n, and if you deny $F(x)$, I shall show that $\neg F(n)$ leads to an inconsistency, by a step-by-step contrapositive *Sorites* argument, ending with a denial of $F(0)$, which was one of the premises originally given. You should be able to twig what is going on, and realise that whatever $F(n)$ you propose, I shall refute you, but if you do not, I can spell it out for you. If you cannot hoist it in, you can go on trying to produce a counter-example, and failing every time.
> 4. Each. You choose x, and if you deny $F(x)$, I shall show that $\neg F(x)$ leads to an inconsistency. You should be able to get the hang of my proof, and see how it could be altered to fit any other x you might have chosen; but if you cannot, you can go on trying to produce a counter-example, and failing each time.

§2.7 Induction

Induction perplexes philosophers. Inductive arguments are not valid deductive arguments, yet clearly possess some cogency. It is difficult to maintain a position of complete scepticism about them, but impossible to justify them by purely deductive means.

Many different characterizations of induction are given: the inference from the known to the unknown; from the past to the future; from the particular to the general; or from a certain number of particular instances that we have observed to another particular instance that we have not observed. These characterizations are not equivalent, nor does any constitute a definition. Not only do they pick on different aspects of inductive argument, but inductive arguments are of different types; sometimes posing different difficulties to the sceptic and requiring different sorts of justification. Nor is any one type adequately defined. Indeed, it is difficult to define induction. It is easy to begin, and lay it down as a necessary condition that inductive arguments are not deductive.

An older generation of philosophers used to divide all argument into deductive and inductive, and define inductive arguments as those that were not deductive. Hence the characterization of the Rule of Recursion, which was recognised as not being a simple deductive argument, as Mathematical Induction. Some philosophers would still stop there, though with a more adequate characterization of deduction, and offer, as a complete definition, that an inductive argument was a non-deductive one. But evaluative arguments, moral arguments, political arguments, legal arguments, historical arguments, literary arguments, philosophical arguments and theological arguments, are nearly all non-deductive, but very far from being all inductive. Some of these would be excluded if we defined inductive arguments as empirical arguments, or as arguments about matters of fact, but our idea of the empirical is hazy, and the concept of a fact is systematically ambiguous, varying very much with context.[9] Even if philosophy, theology, and literary criticism are deemed non-empirical and non-factual, history seems to be concerned with facts, and depends on empirical evidence, though few of its arguments conform to the canonical pattern of induction. As a rough criterion, we could say that inductive arguments are concerned with things rather than persons, and that anything evaluative or interpretative should be excluded. Some philosophers have attempted to exclude unwanted cases by stipulating that the conclusion of an inductive argument should be of the same logical type as the premises: if the premises are propositions about individual swans being white, so should the conclusion; from 'is's other 'is's may be derived inductively, but not 'ought's. Although types of inductive argument can be adequately defined in this way, others cannot: for example, the argument from particular instances to general laws, which was historically the first type of inductive argument to be distinguished. None of these definitions is satisfactory: like deduction, induction is fuzzy-edged. It is best to start with widely accepted standard cases, and recognise that the decision as to which other cases should be included is somewhat arbitrary, to be settled on grounds of convenience as much as anything else.

---

[9] See J.R.Lucas, "On Not Worshipping Facts", *The Philosophical Quarterly*, **8**, April, 1958, pp.143-156.

§2.7   The Development of Normative Reason   49

> **Induction**
> 1. Inference to the next case
> 2. Inference to the general case
> 3. Inference to natural law
> 4. ?Inference to best explanation?
>   (also called abduction, to distinguish it from the first three)

Let us start, then, with the simplest case, where we argue from particular to particular, and then extend it, in a natural but highly revealing way, to the argument from particular to general. In a simple induction we argue from a number of particular instances of a specified sort and having some further characteristic to some other particular instance's having the same further characteristic. The argument can be displayed crudely and inadequately by the following schema:

>   This swan is white
>   That swan is white
>   A third swan is white
>   . . .
>   . . .
>   A 256th swan is white
> *therefore*   The 257th swan is white.

We may call this type of inductive argument Inference to the Next Case. Other examples are the argument that the sun will rise tomorrow,[10] and Russell's chicken which on the basis of observation concluded that the farmer was coming to feed her on the day he was coming to wring her neck.[11] Inference to the Next Case is the type of inference that Hume had in mind, when he sought to explain it in terms of a conditioned reflex. Admittedly, reflexes can be conditioned; but Hume's contention that it is just a matter of habit is not plausible. For one thing, we sometimes cite reasons

---

[10] Some care is needed in expressing this inference, in order not to make it a tautology—days are often defined in terms of the sun's rising, so that tomorrow would not be tomorrow unless the sun rose.

[11] Bertrand Russell, *The Problems of Philosophy*, 2nd ed., Oxford, 1946, p. 63; reprinted in R.W.Swinburne, ed., *The Justification of Induction*, Oxford, 1974, p.21.

why a conclusion is to be believed, not just causes explaining how we have come to hold it; for another, we often jump to conclusions far more quickly than any habituation process could take place; often we bring to bear a whole lot of background information which justifies our taking a particular observation as indicative of the way things are, without needing to repeat it again and again.

Inference to the Next Case
Sun will rise tomorrow (note danger of tautology)
The Next Swan will be White
Russell's chicken—*The Problems of Philosophy*, Oxford, 1912, p.63.
Is it just a matter of habit, as Hume holds? No
(a) we give reasons, saying not only why we do, but why one should, accept the conclusion
(b) we jump to conclusions without waiting to be habituated to them.

Inference to the Next Case leads naturally to Inference to a Generalisation, or Inductive Generalisation, as it may be called. The schema of argument given above will yield conclusions not only about the 257th swan, but about the 258th, 259th, and indeed about any particular swan. Hence it is natural, much as in the case of the Rule of Recursion, to state the form of argument not as a schema that could be applied to yield a conclusion about any particular instance, but as a single argument yielding a conclusion about all instances, *i.e.* a conclusion in universal terms. This is the traditional form

     This swan is white
     That swan is white
     A third swan is white
      . . .
      . . .
     A 256th swan is white
therefore All swans are white.

The conclusion is of a different logical type from the premises. Its universality derived from the universality of reason. In simple induction we had a pattern of valid reasoning, which therefore applies in any particular case, and so is on universal application. And this is made explicit in the universal form.

§2.7   *The Development of Normative Reason*   51

As far as particular cases go, Inference to the Next Case and Inference to a Generalisation come to much the same thing. Granted the former, we can establish that something holds for each and every case, and granted the latter, we can obtain the particular case by one further step of deduction

                    All swans are white
therefore   The 257th swan is white.

Nevertheless, the difference in logical type of the conclusion is of considerable philosophical importance, and brings to light covert assumptions in drawing the inference, as well as possible justifications of the whole pattern of argument.

The pattern of argument thus far displayed is defective. It is not good enough to argue

                    This swan is white
                    That swan is white
                    A third swan is white
                    ...
                    ...
                    A 256th swan is white
therefore   All swans are white.

The premises, as it happens, are all true, but I do not draw the conclusion because I have heard tell of black swans, some growing naturally in Australia, others more accessibly visible in Chartwell. In order to reach the conclusion I need a further premise

    I have never seen, or heard of, a swan which was not white

This is expressed more traditionally

                    All the swans I have ever seen were white
therefore   All swans are white
therefore   The next swan will be white

in which the special force of the additional premise is played down. But this is a mistake. It plays down the two-sidedness of inductive inference, the importance for looking for arguments against the conclusion, and only accepting the conclusion after a reasonably sustained search has thrown up nothing substantial.[12] The importance of the additional premise is brought out in Popper's approach to inductive inference. Popper does not ask how the conclusion may be verified, but how it may be falsified, and since a

---

[12] See previous section and §1.5.

single counter-instance, unless it could be explained away, would be enough to falsify it, Popper's main concern is to look for counter-instances, and to regard any universal proposition that has not been refuted as a candidate for truth.[13] As soon as a black swan turns up, I abandon the claim that all swans are white: but until the existence of such a swan is brought to my notice, the law that all swans are white is a reasonable one; and therefore the critical issue is whether I have ever come across an un-white swan or not. Although Popper's account explains the importance of the additional premise, it does so at the cost of making all the others seem unnecessary. I do not need to have seen any white swans at all in order *not* to have *refuted* the universal proposition All swans are white. Exclusive emphasis on falsification does not accommodate our everyday belief that positive instances are as important as negative ones, and that a large number of positive instances does, in the absence of any negative ones, increase the evidence in favour of the conclusion. Nevertheless, even though it errs in neglecting the need for arguments in favour of any putative conclusion, Popper's account is valuable in stressing the importance of considering arguments against.

Although Inference to a Generalisation is inter-arguable with Inference to the Next Case, its conclusion is of a different logical type. 'The next swan is white' is not only a particular proposition, but a tensed one. 'Every swan is white', or, equivalently, 'All swans are white', is not only general, but tenseless; we can infer from 'Every swan is white' and 'Leda was a swan' the conclusion 'Leda was white'. Such an inference would not be valid if the 'is' of the first premise were a present-tense 'is'. It is, rather, an omnitemporal use of the verb 'to be' which is put into the present for lack of a better tense to put it into. Such a use of the present tense is sometimes indicated, following a suggestion of J.J.C. Smart, by italics.[14] So we write 'Every swan *is* white' or 'All swans *are* white', to indicate that the grammatically present tense is being used in

---

[13] K.R. Popper, *Logik der Forschung*, Vienna, 1934/5, tr. as *The Logic of Scientific Discovery*, London, 1959.

[14] J.J.C. Smart, *Philosophy and Scientific Realism*, London, 1963, p.133. Smart uses italicised but otherwise grammatically correct present tenses; for reading aloud the grammatically incorrect use of the infinitive is clearer. See, more fully, Nicholas Rescher, "On the Logic of Chronological Propositions", *Mind*, **75**, 1966, pp.75-76.

§2.7   *The Development of Normative Reason*   53

a logically tenseless way, or, better, use the grammatically incorrect 'Every swan *be* white' or 'All swans *be* white'. Such a use is entirely unobjectionable. But it heightens the profile of induction. Induction does not merely argue from particular to particular in the ordinary tensed indicative mood, but from particular in the ordinary tensed indicative mood to general in a different, tenseless mood. The mood is clearly different, not only because it does not conjugate like the ordinary indicative mood, but because it yields counterfactual propositions, such as 'If Zoe were a swan, she would be white', which the ordinary indicative mood does not.

Inference to a General Case

The sun rises every day. All swans are white.

(a) Importance of absence of negative instances: inductive arguments of this type are essentially dialectical, two-sided: only if I have looked for negative evidence and failed to find it, am I entitled to draw a general conclusion.

(b) Inference to Next Case and Inference to a General Case are interderivable, but differ in logical status of the conclusion: conclusion of former same logical type as premises (tensed indicative): conclusion of latter in tenseless present (*be*).

Often we go further still, and argue from particular premises not only to an omnitemporal generalisation in the tenseless present, but to a law of nature stating what must, under appropriate conditions, occur. It then becomes difficult to disallow, as also a species of inductive inference, arguments from actual instances to natural laws and from observed phenomena to unobserved entities. We argue from the regular whiteness of swans to a rule that they must be white, and from white appearances to a genetic make-up that accounts for them. Such inferences, although rejected by Hume, have commended themselves to scientists ever since. We seek generality, integration, unification and explanation in our account of the world, and it seems reasonable so to seek. Although quarks, psi-functions and wavicles all transcend the bounds of possible experience, we form some sort of concept of them, and succeed in saying things about them which can be significantly affirmed or denied. Nobody makes out that the Special Theory, the General Theory and Quantum Mechanics are plain sailing. They are difficult, and it is easy

> **Inference to a Natural Law**
> In any isolated system mass and energy must be conserved.
> The halogens can only have one valency bond.
>
> (a) Importance of a wide variety of efforts to falsify the law: only if I have tried hard to find negative instances and failed to find them, am I entitled to infer that I have come up against a law of nature.
> (b) Importance of consilience: natural laws should mesh together.
> Inference to a Natural Law yields a conclusion very obviously of a different logical type from premises. It shows us that reason can go from one mood to another: although we cannot *deduce* an 'ought' from an 'is', it may be possible to *derive*, or *infer*, it. This has consequences for metaphysics as well as for morals.
> It shows that we can go, with reason's aid, beyond the bounds of possible experience.

to be confused and talk nonsense about them. But it does not follow that rational argument about science is impossible, or that reason must acknowledge that such knowledge is too high for it, and it cannot attain unto it. The arguments Hume put forward for ruling out altogether knowledge of unobserved entities or explanations of the universe as a whole, would, if they were cogent, rule out all sub-atomic physics and cosmology. But, while many thinkers fear—or hope—they are cogent when deployed against metaphysics or natural theology, few seriously suppose they cast any aspersions on the reputability of modern science.

It is a moot point whether inferences leading to the acceptance of scientific theories should be called inductive. In recent years they have often been termed "inferences to the best explanation'. The term 'abduction' is sometimes used. The name indicates a difference of sanction. If having noticed a number of cases of people drinking hemlock and subsequently dying, I refuse to infer that if I drink hemlock I shall die, I shall pay for my scepticism with my life.

§2.7   *The Development of Normative Reason*   55

> **Inference to Best Explanation**
> An example of inference to entity of very different *ontological* type: Leibniz' argument from *La Liaison des Phénomènes* for the existence of material objects. See Chapter 6, §6.7.

The disutility of not reaching right conclusions about matters of fact, especially matters of future fact, is so great that even the most obdurate sceptic finds ways of not living down to his professions of ignorance. Omnitemporal generalisations are also useful, and the sceptic who disallows Inference to a Generalisation is depriving himself of much useful knowledge in a convenient and memorable form. Laws of nature and scientific theories can also be defended on grounds of utility, but the argument is more tenuous: many effective people lead happy and successful lives without having mastered Einstein's General Theory, or Quantum Electrodynamics. Although some knowledge of science is in some circumstances useful, the real sanction against the sceptic who will not admit inferences to scientific theories is that he will suffer from avoidable ignorance. I want to know the nature of the universe and to understand the causes of things. Natural laws and scientific theories claim truth and offer understanding. They integrate and explain. Diverse phenomena are unified by being brought under a single principle, and a welter of confusing events are explained by means of a theory. It is because they unify and explain that we believe that the laws and theories are true. But if they are true, we want to know them. The same motive applies also, though to a lesser extent, to accepting Inference to a Generalisation, and even to Inference to the Next Case. We like to know the way things happen, quite apart from any utility. Few bird-watchers eat birds, or obtain any material benefit from knowing which species the birds in the garden belong to, but want to know all the same. Although our motives may be mixed, our methods are the same: we apply various principles, often unconsciously, to distinguish good inductive inferences from bad ones.

By contrast to the systematic way in which we can test different combinations of possible causal factors, there is no systematic test for explanatoriness. We have a number of general ideas of what possible explanations there can be, and are much readier to accept a putative causal generalisation or law of nature if we can see how it might be explained—if it fits in with what we already know about the way things happen. Medical scientists are very reluctant to accept evidence in favour of homoeopathic remedies, and try hard to ascribe any indubitable cases to chance, because they do not see how homoeopathy could work. Consilience—the extent to which a new generalisation will fit in with what is already known—is a major factor in inductive inference, and one that cannot be reduced to a set of systematic rules. Nevertheless, all in all inductive inference is a rational activity, largely systematic, rule-governed, and we can properly speak of "inductive logic", as it used to be called.[15]

We are not obliged to accept inductive arguments as we are deductive ones. Communication will not break down if I, having seen many white swans, refuse to infer that the next one will be white too. It is perfectly intelligible to maintain that the next sample of hydrogen cyanide will not be poisonous—but highly unwise. Without the aid of inductive inferences I shall not be able to anticipate the situations I shall have to face; nor ward off untoward outcomes of conditions about to obtain. I shall know less, if I do not allow myself to infer universal propositions, under suitable safeguards, from particular observations, and I shall understand less, if I do not go beyond the phenomena to the best explanation available.

§2.8 Practical Reasoning

Once it is recognised that inductive inferences can lead from a tensed 'was' to a tenseless '*is*' or '*be*', it becomes hard to maintain as a matter of logical principle that we cannot derive an 'ought' from an 'is'. Even deduction can lead us to conclusions not contained in the original premises. And in Inference to the Best Explanation we argue from premises of one sort to conclusions of a very different logical type. The conclusions of practical reasoning are of a different type again. They are action-guiding. And the premises are factual, characterizing the situation to which the action commended is a response. But if we reason at all about what to do, our conclusions must point towards some action as appropriate, and if our reasoning is to be relevant and effective it must be based on the facts of the case.

The particularism of practical reasoning seems to run counter to its rationality. Rationality is universal, and enjoins us to act only on that maxim through which we can at the same time will that it

---

[15] See further above, §2.1, n.2.

should become a universal law.[16] This would require that we had a stock of universal laws under which we could subsume any action indicated by practical reason. But any such set of universal precepts would be too coarse-grained to accommodate the unbounded subtlety of human affairs. To accommodate that, we need a more flexible canon of universalisability. Instead of requiring that there be some universal precept which covers the proposed action, and that all similar ones should be treated similarly, we should require only that *if* we propose to treat some apparently similar case differently, there should be some difference between them to justify the difference of treatment.[17] Granted this different requirement of universalisability, we can have practical arguments being both rational and relevant to the particular case under consideration.

It is the particularity of the situations in which we have to act that requires our assessments to be holistic and gives rise to the two-sidedness of practical reasoning.[18] However fully we have specified a situation, there always may be a further feature that entirely alters the complexion of the case; and since circumstances, too, alter cases, there always may be some extraneous circumstance that requires a re-assessment of our response with a further 'but'. The fact that there is nearly always room for another 'but' has often been taken to show that there are no valid arguments in practical reasoning. But what it actually shows is that there are few *conclusive* arguments. Many arguments are cogent in the absence of counter-considerations, and we often state them explicitly with this proviso, "other things being equal", *ceteris paribus*, "in the absence of special circumstances", "as a general rule", ὡς ἐπί τὸ πολύ (*hos epi to polu*).

But other things may not be equal. That a certain action will cause you pain is a good reason for not doing it, yet I could well go on to say 'I am afraid this will hurt, but it is what I have to do': I might be a dentist, or a head-master, or an examiner, or a candid friend. But if I do conjoin 'this will cause pain' and 'this is what I ought to do', I need to explain why I ought to do it, in spite of its causing pain; perhaps because it will promote good

---

[16] Kant, *Groundwork of the Metaphysic of Morals*, 421/52, tr. H.J.Paton, as *The Moral Law*, London, 1947, p.88.

[17] See, more fully, J.R.Lucas, "The Lesbian Rule", *Philosophy*, **30**, 1956, pp.195-213.

[18] See above, §1.5.

health, or teach you a lesson, or uphold the integrity of some public system of evaluation, or enable you to make rational decisions in the face of unpalatable facts. It is something that calls for further explanation. The explanation need not be a moral or benign one: it would not be unintelligible, though it would show me in a bad light, if I explained that I was a sadist, and liked causing pain, or a Nietzschean, and wanted to make my mark on the universe.

Often a consideration is not so much countered as over-ridden. My having promised to return a borrowed weapon is a good reason for doing so, but if the person I had borrowed it from has in the meantime gone mad, the obligation to return is over-ridden by concern for his, and other people's, safety. But that does not abrogate the original obligation. If for good reason I have had to break a promise, it is not as though the promise had never been made: on the contrary, I am subject to further obligations to make good to the person I let down the damage my broken promise caused. We need to distinguish cases where a putative obligation does not hold at all—as if I made the promise having been deceived by the person to whom it was made—and cases where it is simply over-ridden.[19]

Our decision will depend not only on the strength of the arguments on one side, but on the weakness of those on the other. For only when there are alternative courses under consideration can I decide between them. If you counsel flight, I shall re-examine the situation to see whether it would be better after all to flee than to give battle, and with these alternatives in view I can try and tell whether this is a sticking-it-out situation or a cutting-one's-losses one. If, alternatively, you counselled me to advance, making propitiatory gestures, I should need to re-examine the situation in a different way, to attempt to make a different discrimination. So, again, if you had urged me to go on the offensive myself and launch a pre-emptive attack. The alternatives offered determine the factors that are relevant. I do not have to—very often cannot—justify my own judgement absolutely, but only relatively: I am not bound to show that I ought to do this, full stop, but only that I ought to do this rather than that. Different factors are relevant for deciding between different pairs of alternatives. If you counsel flight, it is pertinent to point out that I cannot run very fast: but my

---

[19] See further, J.Raz, *Practical Reasons and Norms*, London, 1975, and Princeton, 1990, ch.1, §1.1, pp.25-35; see also S.E.Toulmin, *The Uses of Argument*, Cambridge, 1958, ch.3, pp.97-102.

§2.8   The Development of Normative Reason   59

inability to run would be no argument against making propitiatory gestures, though the fact that my adversary was a cowardly bully would. Once the alternatives are fixed, we shall each look for features of the situation which will enable us to discriminate between its being a staying-and-sticking-it-out situation and its being a cutting-one's-losses one. We may be able to: language, used by both of us on many occasions before our present argument, enables us to pick out many sorts of features which might be relevant. We can compare this situation, which we each read differently, with others where we have no disagreement. 'But he looks very threatening', you may say of the adversary, 'Yes, but he is also anxious to secure his retreat', I counter; but because we are using some other, and usually more general, classificatory scheme than our primary one, we can work round to an agreed description of the situation we are considering. We may still be unable to reach agreement about what to do: we may argue that he is looking round nervously; or you may suggest that he is looking round not in order to see how he may beat a hasty retreat, but because he is expecting his accomplices to be on their way to join him. In that case we could agree only that he was looking round rather a lot. Even that description is not immune to objection. You may say that these few casual glances are no more than anyone might cast behind him, to note the terrain covered or to admire the view. In some situations you might question whether the man came with any hostile intent at all, in others whether it even was a man that I saw.

There is no uniform agreed level of facts from which our arguments can start. Rather, what counts as a fact depends on the question in issue. Almost anything may be disputed: but invariably there are some facts not in dispute, and it could not be the case that almost everything was disputed, for then there would be no common language in which to carry on the dispute.

Although we often disagree how the balance should be struck in some particular case, we very largely agree about the relevant considerations. When it comes to making decisions in particular situations, it always may be the case that peculiar circumstances may make it impossible to do all the things that normally ought to be done: but that does not affect the general reckoning that in all ordinary circumstances they should indeed be done. In general the reason is a good reason for acting in a particular way, even though in the exceptional case the reasons on the other side are weightier. Apart from a few disputed issues—abortion, capital punishment, sex—we all allow that in general promises should be kept, pain avoided, life preserved. If I have promised to do something, although in unusual circumstances I may meet your claim that I ought, therefore, to do it with a 'but'—'but I have got bronchitis and the doctor has told me to keep indoors'—I cannot brush off your claim with a 'so what?'. Not to recognise that a promise creates a *prima facie* obligation, or that a course of action might imperil life, is to put oneself outside the pale of moral discourse. Although no claim is incontrovertible, many are not to be overlooked. I can without inconsistency commend an action which will endanger life, cause pain, contravene a previous commitment, but if I do so, I need to explain myself, either in view of wholly exceptional circumstances or else by articulating some special moral view. Practical reasoning is not closed against the possibility of new situations or new insights, but the opinions of the many and the wise do to a large extent converge about what are the relevant considerations in the ordinary run of cases.[20]

There are many strands of argument within practical reasoning. The most primitive is the immediate decsion what to do, to fight or flee, to eat or to court a mate. Much human reasoning is on this level, but we criticize the man who pursues only τὸ παρὸν ἡδύ (*to paron hedu*), immediate pleasure, and responds only to immediate threats, and we think it more reasonable to be prudent, taking account of long-term future interests, and not only those close at hand. Reason, we hold, is not confined to present concerns, but to future ones too. But prudence alone is not enough. It is incoherent to have regard only to the future and not to the past, and it may be counter-productive to consider only myself, and not other people. Each of these points may be made with the aid of the Theory of Games, the Battle of the Sexes showing how I lay myself open to manipulation unless I take account of the past as well as the future, and the Prisoners' Dilemma showing how we fare worse if we are selfish than if we consider others' interests as well as our own.[21]

Practical reasoning is messy. It is easy to get it wrong. If we do, we may get away with it. Although wrong decisions can lead to disaster, there is no immediate, irresistible sanction against being unreasonable. The sanction is not the breakdown of communication, but, in the absence of dire consequences, just simply a failure to be sensible, accompanied by a loss of respect in the eyes of others, especially when some moral obligation has been disregarded.

---

[20] See further below §3.3.
[21] See further below, §14.8

§2.9 Empathy and Other Minds

The two-sidedness of practical reasoning gives a key to our knowledge of other minds and our understanding of the humanities. Besides making up my mind about what I shall do, I can consider what I should do if circumstances were different; and although in the present circumstances I must over-ride and reject some considerations in accepting and acting on others, I can fully appreciate how I might in other circumstances act on them, and so I can appreciate also how you in your circumstances might act on them. Because I know what I shall do in the actual situation, I can know what I should do in hypothetical situations, and so understand what I might do if I were you. Empathy is possible because I experience in my own deliberation the conflict of argument and feel the force of factors inclining me to act in various ways. I never have murdered any one, but I have been tempted, and so can understand the minds of those who have found the temptation irresistible. Equally I can enter into the minds of historical agents or those portrayed in literature, and although sometimes their reasoning and reactions will be entirely opaque to me, often there will be enough resemblance between their situation and my actual or possible ones for their response to be one I can see the rationality of. I do not have to suppose, counterfactually and sometimes implausibly, that I *would* in the event respond in the same way, but only that I *might*—only that there would be some reasons for so acting, in the absence of weightier considerations against. And that supposition is one it is much easier to make. I can understand what makes other people tick because of the many-sidedness of what goes on in making up my own mind. The messiness of practical reasoning, and the many decisions it partially leads me to take, gives me a width of understanding I could never otherwise obtain, and a partial *entrée* into the minds of all sorts and conditions of men far beyond my actual ken.

Anger, fear, resentment, spite, greed, jealousy, gratitude, pity, love, awe, exaltation and joy commonly issue in actions and activities. Feelings are not, as too many philosophers have supposed, bare physical sensations, but are for the most part to be described in terms of what we want to do or would like to do. They are, largely, incipient actions, frustrated actions, or failed actions, and the concomitants of these. And therefore our common rationality as agents gives further and detailed support for our belief that other men are of like passions with ourselves. I think that you feel angry because I know that I would be inclined to act angrily in like circumstances; and your subsequent actions constitute a further check on whether I am right or wrong. Thus, although it is neither logically impossible nor even emotionally impossible for you to overlook the slight, or alternatively to suppress the anger which you feel, nevertheless there are always cross-connections among different states of mind and between them and actions to make it unreasonable to deny that we have some sort of fellow feeling or empathy with others, or to suppose we might be always wrong in all our ascriptions of feeling to others. *Willst du die andem verstehen,* said Schiller, *blick in dein eigenes Herz.* If you want to understand others look into your own heart. Γνῶθι σεαυτόν (*gnothi seauton*), Know yourself; and then you will have insight into the minds of others too.

Insight, in popular, unprofessional philosophy, is important. Historians will say of a colleague that he has his facts right and his arguments are impervious to objection and his conclusions not demonstrably wrong, yet somehow he has not got the "feel" of his period, he has not worked his way "into" it. Thus, a reviewer can write that the author

> has the rare quality of entering into the minds of those he is studying and seeing things from their point of view; the result in this case is that perhaps for the first time it is possible to understand the Aztecs and sympathize with them in their painful predicament ... The book is one of the best ever written about the Aztecs: his portrait of their society is a triumph of scholarship, understanding and literary skill.[22]

On which Alan Richardson comments, "Each of these three words surely represents an essential feature of the historian's craft."[23] In the same way, literary critics will allow that a student knows all his texts, is well acquainted with the historical background, is able to manipulate parallel passages, can explain all the allusions, can comment on linguistic points, and has intelligent views on the cruces, and yet has not "got inside" his author. Scientists, it is alleged, are often insensitive: nobody denies that they are very clever men, but

---

[22] *Times Literary Supplement*, Nov. 10, 1961 (No.3, 115), p. 800; the work under review is Jaques Soustelle, *The Daily Life of the Aztecs*, Eng. trans. by P.O'Brian, London, 1961.

[23] A.R.Richardson, *History Sacred and Profane*, London, 1964, pp. 158-159.

they lack sympathy; they are well able to conduct difficult calculations and reach right conclusions about means to given ends, but they are unable to put themselves in other men's shoes, or sense what the human reaction will be. It is claimed for the humanities that they educate men's perceptiveness, and make them more sensitive in their dealings with other men. Education apart, different men are differently endowed with this faculty: some of our friends are, and always have been, very able; they will go far; but not all of them will notice much as they go: others are more *simpatico*; they may be less clear-headed, unable to put out arguments clearly, and having a less good memory for facts and a less adequate command of argument, but nonetheless more percipient in what they say.[24]

The untutored view is clear. Men have, besides the ability to draw conclusions from premises and to learn from experience, another, finer faculty, which enables them to "get inside". It is different from inductive reasoning both subjectively and in its operations. Subjectively, it feels different: the persons in question appear transparent, not opaque; one is unable to give as good reasons as one feels—one just knows; it is knowledge by acquaintance, not knowledge by description or by argumentation. It operates differently from induction: it does not generalise; we are quite clear that to the particular problem in mind a certain solution is the right one, but are not very ready to extend the solution to other cases; the role of evidence is unclear; we do not apply any canons of inductive inference; there seem to be no criteria of irrelevance; and often, very often, it operates when we should be unable to make any inductive inferences at all. It is as though each one of us had within him a well of singular hypotheticals, on which he was at times able to draw, and provide himself with immediate and complete solutions to certain of his problems. In ourselves we can recognize its happening: among others we can pick out those who are particularly gifted with it, those who have noses for human affairs. Sometimes it is insight into human character—Humane Insight, we might call it. Sometimes it is the ability to discard irrelevant, and fasten on important premises for an argument: this makes the good civil servant, the good historian. We value it so highly that we are constantly coining new names for it: sense, sensibility, sensitivity, being percipient, being perceptive, intuition, insight, sympathy, empathy, understanding, *verstehen*, being *en*

---

[24] Like Kitty Levin in §1.7 above.

rapport, being *simpatico*, and being able to put oneself inside other people's skins, all have been used at times to refer to it. Nor do we require it only of those engaged in practical affairs. Novelists, obviously, need to have it, and even philosophers are assessed according to, among other things, their understanding of human nature. We fault Hobbes' political doctrines because his view of man is not true to human nature. And we say this not after having examined all men and found them different from what Hobbes portrays, but merely from knowing a few men and knowing from within ourselves what it is to be a man, and what are the loyalties which can win men and move human beings to action. The attraction of Freud's doctrines lies not in the empirical evidence for them, which is often slender, but in their innate plausibility, which once Freud has expounded it, carries conviction because it corresponds to something in our own minds. We can see that this is how a man might respond, because it is how we might respond, even though we may have never responded in the fashion described, nor ever been in a situation comparable to that described. Freud's views have been accepted because he has been able to strike chords in the hearts of his readers, not because he has been able to furnish adequate statistics to establish his case. Where he is recounting some particular case or describing some typical situation, his reconstructions of the workings of the unconscious mind ring true: but where he or his disciples start trying to establish his conclusions in the way in which a medical scientist would establish his, our incredulity sets in. His conclusions are not inductive conclusions, they are not based on the evidence of our senses, nor built up from repeated, but opaque, conjunctions of observed fact. Rather, they are new ways of seeing human motives and construing human behaviour, new insights brought up from the depths of Freud's own mind. Little purpose is served by trying to assimilate this to ordinary inductive generalizations or by construing the actual experience Freud lived through himself and the hypothetical experience he could imagine for others, as a basis for an inductive generalisation in the way that our sense-experience is.

For the present we note that there seem to be inferential skills manifested by the historian and the literary critic, which do not fit into the account of inductive and scientific argument, but can be seen as stemming naturally from the two-sidedness of practical argument.[25]

[25] J.H.Newman, *The Grammar of Assent*, London, 1870, ch. VIII, §2, pp. 296-7; W.H.Walsh, *Introduction to the Philosophy of History*, London, 1951; and W.H.Dray, *Laws and Explanation in History*, Oxford, 1957. For further consideration of the role of empathy in history see C.Portal, ed. *The History Curriculum for Teachers*, Falmer Press, 1987.

§2.10   The Development of Normative Reason   65

§2.10 Reason

Reason is very different from what many philosophers have taken it to be. Even if we start with them, taking reason to be analytic deductive inference, we are led to a less restricted view of reason, as being typically two-sided, a dialogue between different people, conversing because they have some common objectives. Even deductive reason is not entirely analytic: and inductive arguments, and those of practical reasoning and its progeny, evidently lead to conclusions which were not implicit in the premises.

Looking back, we can now see the philosophers' ideal of valid inference as a special case, in which dialogue has been collapsed into a monologue, where the only common objective they need have—and must share—is to be understood. Whereas ordinarily, as I ratiocinate, my friend (or my *alter ego*), butts in with objections and counter-considerations, in an analytic deductive argument there is no room for interposing any 'but's. Any attempt to gainsay anything established by an analytic deductive argument ends in self-contradiction. As I argue, I do not need to pause, to hear objections raised, because no objection can be consistently— and therefore intelligibly—raised. Anyone who attempts to controvert what I say is contradicting himself, and can be ruled out of court as not saying anything meaningful. Monologous arguments are sometimes appropriate; in writing a book, for example, where the reader is, of necessity, in no position to interrupt. And monologous arguments are often attractive, since human nature is naturally inclined to brook no opposition. An "anti-deductivist" theme follows. Although deductive reason is the paradigm for coerciveness, it is not paradigmatic in other respects. We cannot adequately represent non-deductive inferences as deductions from additional major premises. Admittedly, sometimes, when a particular inference is in dispute, it may be helpful to articulate the rule of inference as a universal proposition, and if it proves acceptable, then the conclusion will follow deductively from it. But even in deductive logic, not all inferences can be so represented, as Lewis Caroll showed.[26] Often also, it is unhelpful to pose the question in terms of the truth or falsity of a proposition—it makes less sense to ask whether Peano's Fifth Postulate is true than to ask whether the Principle of Recursive Reasoning is cogent. Moreover, there are many inferences in the humanities which are too particular

---

[26] See above, §2.3.

to lend themselves to being formulated as a major premise, even though they are universalisable in a more flexible way. Reasoning is typically an open-textured dialogue in which the respondent can contribute, and the sort of contribution expected determines the structure of the dialogue. Therefore it cannot be adequately reconstructed into a deductive argument, which, since it is monologous, leaves no place for the respondent to join in. The solitary self-sufficiency of the deductivist thinker is purchased at the price of solipsistic vacuity. Reasoning is risky, and we do well to have candid friends who dare tell us that we are mistaken.

Most argument, though open-textured, is structured. As we have noted in §1.6, argument is fruitless, if we disagree about everything. Not only do we have to start from somewhere, but we have to have some aims and assumptions in common. Whereas simple deduction is subject to the one condition of being intelligible, usually we share a desire to know the truth, and often an aspiration to understand. Different aims and assumptions indicate different sorts of dialogue. Often in the course of one argument, we need for a time to confine the discussion to a particular type of dialogue for the sake of clarity, or in order to reach a resolution of a particular argument. It is good to be agreed about the facts of the case before embarking on interpreting them. We may need to work out the consequences of a particular hypothesis in order to test whether it is consistent with observations or falsified by them. We limit our shared commitment for the time being, in the hope of achieving some measure of agreement, before going on to more contentious matters. A serious argument is often composed of several sub-dialogues, each with its own standards of relevance and cogency. Unless we distinguish the way the different limbs are articulated into a coherent whole, we blunder, applying to one part canons only appropriate to another.

The sceptically minded may still be unwilling to go along with this account of reason. Thrasymachus may be forced to concede the cogency of simple deductive arguments, but can still refuse the invitation to enter into other men's minds. What are the sanctions against unreasonableness? They differ. I can resist the full force of Gödel's theorem by distinguishing the unprovability-within-the-system of the Gödelian formula of which there is a formally valid proof, from its being true, of which there is no formally valid proof, since there is no formal definition of the term 'true'. This, which can be seen as a consequence of Gödel's theorem, was established independently by Tarski.[27] He proved that the concept of truth cannot be defined in any adequate formal system, because if we add to such a system a term representing what we mean by our ordinary word 'true', we shall be led—again by an Epimenides argument—to a contradiction.[28] So, when you point out the implication of denying that the Gödelian formula is true, I fail to follow your reasoning, professing not to know what 'true' means. And that is the sanction. I have divested myself of knowing what 'true' means: I have deprived myself of the concept of truth. Although syntactically I am in the clear—I have not broken any of the rules of the communication exercise—semantically I am self-mutilated—I am no longer a man of truth. The same sanction was invoked against a refusal to move from *Sorites* Arithmetic to the Rule of Recursion. In these two cases there are further, arcane sanctions. I can, without self-contradiction, deny the truth of the Gödelian formula: there is no inconsistency between it and the axioms of Elementary Number Theory. It follows that there is a model of the negation of the Gödelian formula and the axioms of Elementary Number Theory. It is a weird model, but it cannot be faulted on formal grounds. If I refuse to acknowledge the truth of the Gödelian formula, I cannot exclude weird models, and so cannot specify that the numbers I am talking about are the same as the numbers that you, and everybody else, are talking about. Somewhat similarly, if I refuse to accept the Rule of Recursion, although I can specify each individual number separately, I cannot talk about them all collectively. I could be guilty of "ω-inconsistency", alleging that although each natural number possessed some property, some did not. The sceptic, who will not accept the truth of the Gödelian formula, or the validity of the Rule of Recursion, is not guilty of any straightforward inconsistency, but will be talking at cross purposes when he argues with those who have a firm grasp on the nature of the natural numbers.

Inductive sceptics have difficulty in living down to their unbeliefs. If I refuse to anticipate future events, I am in for nasty surprises. Even if my animal instincts enable me to avoid disaster in the particular situations I find myself in, I am handicapped, if I cannot generalise the better to communicate to others and to

---

[27] A.Tarski, "The Concept of Truth Formalized Languages" tr. J.H.Woodger in *Logic, Semantics, Metamathematics*, Oxford, 1956, Ch.VIII.

[28] See above, this chapter, §2.3.

remember myself what experience has taught me. And the price of not inferring to the best explanation is not to have the best explanation. I can live without understanding why things happen as they do. It is my choice. But if I choose to do so, I am the sufferer.

In practical affairs, again, I shall be the chief sufferer if I do not use reason, though others may suffer too as a result of my imprudence, lack of consideration, lack of public spirit, or lack of commitment to anything outside myself. Traditionally, philosophers have drawn a sharp distinction between counsels of prudence and precepts of morality, and have thought the former unproblematic, while seeing great difficulties in showing why we ought to be moral. There is indeed a distinction, but it is not as clear-cut as has been made out, and the sanctions are not as sharply separated as commonly supposed. Others, as well as I, may suffer if I am imprudent, and I, as well as others, if I am selfish. In part it is a question of identity and identification: if I have no consideration for others, I debar myself from meaningful use of the first person plural, and isolate myself into the logical loneliness of Plato's autistic autocrat; and if I am entirely insensitive to any obligation to any objective value, I cannot ground my agency, my actions, or my achievements in anything of greater worth than my own fleeting preferences. I do not have to enter into your concerns. Indeed, I economize on emotional drain, if I do not waste sympathy on you in your misfortunes, although in some cases the balance of advantage may go the other way—I shall gain more from your co-operation than I shall lose in bearing your troubles, but, whatever the balance of crude advantage, I lose out in knowledge and understanding if I make myself ignorant of the working of other men's minds, reducing my range of sensibility and diminishing myself.

Sanctions not only underwrite cogency, but impose a strategy. If you are obdurate, and do not feel the force of my argument, I must manoeuvre you into a tight corner, where you will pay the penalty for your obduracy. Hence the pressure to formulate; hence also the importance of chains of derivations. If I give a derivation, I can challenge you to say where I am wrong, and you have to specify, and I can then concentrate on that point. Often, in mathematical argument especially, I can show you to be inconsistent. In physics, I may show that you would be having to deny some important symmetry, or other rational requirement. Often in physics and in other sciences too the cost of resisting reason is a loss of understanding. If you persist in not accepting evolution, you will

§2.10   The Development of Normative Reason   69

not attain the wide-ranging perspective on how living creatures are related to one another, which the theory of evolution offers, and will not understand how different species came to be: I shall therefore seek, perhaps from the geological record, telling examples of intermediate species, or structural similarities not easily explained by any other theory. At a more mundane level unpleasant consequences flow from not believing scientific laws and maxims of common sense; and in a different way from not cooperating with others, and treating them well. The experience of living, unshielded by parental care, in a small community is often the means of instilling common sense and common decency by exposing the foolish and fickle to inescapable peer-group pressure.

Normative reason has an edge. It arises from our being able to think wrong. I can think wrong, you can think wrong, and we want to convict others' wrong thinking of error. Equally, in view of similar desires on the part of others, we seek to make our own arguments invincible. In either case the strategy is polemical. Each side seeks to pin down its opponents' arguments, and search for weak spots, where a decisive victory can be gained; and, anticipating similar moves on the part of the other side, tries to formulate defences against hostile probing. But some reasonings have no sanctions and no strategy for securing agreement. I give my reasons for having acted as I did, and you may be able to share them, and accept them as telling, but if you do not feel their force, and do not accept them, your only loss is not to be able to understand why I acted as I did.

Sanctions
1. Analytic statements and First-order Logic: Failure to communicate.
2. Gödel's theorem: No grasp of the concept of truth; inadequate grasp of the concept of number.
3. Rule of Recursion: No grasp of the concept of truth; ω-inconsistency; inadequate grasp of the concept of number.
4. Inference to the Next Case: Nasty surprises.
5. Inference to a Generalisation: No General Grasp.
6. Inference to Best Explanation: Inexplicability.
7. Practical Reason: No common sense.
8. Humane Insight: No understanding of fellow men.

The development of the idea of normative reason, starting from the minimal requirement for our communications to be intelligible, and moving through successive stages to a wide-ranging ability to enter into the minds of others, and to argue about what we, individually or collectively, ought to do, reveals a characteristic universality. If an argument is cogent on one occasion, it will be cogent on others too. Hence the move from *Sorites* arguments to the Principle of Recursive Reasoning, and from Induction to the Next Case to Inductive Generalisation. In practical reasoning, especially in moral, political and judicial argument, a similar move is made, giving rise to the principle of universalisability, cited in §2.8. But although often it is legitimate to argue that what is sauce for the goose is sauce for the gander, we had to recognise, at least where human beings are concerned, that one man's meat is another man's poison. Some principle of universalisability is still needed, but it needs to be a more flexible one, not only in moral discourse, but in explaining historical causes, and evaluating arguments in the humanities generally. Instead of positing some principle such that all cases falling under it are taken to be the same, we should require only that if some apparently similar case is taken to be different, a reason for the difference should be forthcoming.

If reason is universal, it can reason about reason itself, and from self-referential reasoning, it emerges that it is not possible to set bounds to reason, and in particular that metaphysical argument is not beyond the bounds of reason. Deductive argument gives rise not only to recursive arguments, but to Gödel's self-referential theorems; and inductive arguments merge into Inference to the Best Explanation, sometimes invoking entities beyond the bounds of possible experience. Practical reasoning leads on to empathy and moral argument, and they in turn lead to the humane insight of the humanities, and varieties of political, legal and judicial argument. Gödel's theorem shows that even with deductive argument, we cannot formalise completely; however far we formalise our rules of inference, there will still be some inference which is clearly valid but does not fall under any of the rules thus far formulated. Even deductive argument is fuzzy-edged, and the transition from one type of inductive inference to another shows that the same holds good for inductive arguments about matters of fact and their explanation—and counts against the contention that reason cannot lead on to the various styles of practical argument.

§2.10   The Development of Normative Reason   71

We can go further. The simple argument of the Logical Positivists against metaphysics does not work. If metaphysics could be ruled out by the Verification Principle, so too would the Verification Principle itself. Similarly, any claim to set a boundary to reason can be challenged. Clearly, if the bounds of reason are so tightly drawn as to exclude philosophical argument, the claim will exclude any possible justification of itself. But more generally, in order to determine the boundary exactly, it will need to specify what lies beyond it and is to be excluded, as well as what lies within it and is to be included. And if the boundary is really a boundary reason cannot overstep, reason will be precluded from stepping over it, to specify precisely what is to be excluded. Reason itself, then, is unbounded. We have a negative, self-referential argument, analogous to the negative, self-referential mathematical argument underlying Gödel's theorem, against any claim that reason can be corralled within any antecedently set limit, and are led to a crucial conclusion. Reason is not "thin".

Theses about Reason

1. Not all *a priori* arguments are analytic. For example, in mathematics, arguments by recursion: (point made by Poincaré): it is not straight inconsistent (though it is ω-inconsistent) to hold for *each* natural number, n, that $F(n)$, but to deny that $(\forall n)F(n)$, that is, for *all* natural numbers $F(n)$.
2. Not all deductive arguments are rule-bound, that is governed by some antecedently specified rule of inference. For example, Gödel's theorem shows that the Gödelian sentence of a formal system is true, though this cannot be proved in the system. We need to know how to argue, not just know that certain rules of inference are allowed. [Achilles and the Tortoise]
3. Not all sound arguments are deductive. For example, inductive arguments.
4. Not all inductive arguments are of the same type. For example, some inductive arguments argue from particular propositions as premises to another particular proposition as conclusion (the sun has risen every day hitherto, so it will rise again tomorrow), others argue from particular propositions as premises to a general proposition as conclusion (the sun has risen every day hitherto, so it rises every day).
5. Not all arguments about the way the world is are simple inductive arguments. For example, many scientific arguments go

from observational premises to theories about entities that cannot themselves be observed.
6. Not all arguments go from premises to conclusions of the same logical type. For example those instanced in (4) and (5).
7. Some arguments go from factual premises to evaluative conclusions. For example, moral arguments; also intellectual arguments about the acceptability of conclusions of arguments.
8. Most arguments, apart from deductive arguments, are two-sided. The addition of further information may weaken, not strengthen, a conclusion; they are not monotonic, but are a matter of argument and counter-argument, objection and rebuttal. For example, induction (even though I have seen 256 swans, and they are all white, and it was reasonable on that evidence to infer that all swans are white, if I now come across a black swan, I can no longer assert that all swans are white). The point has long been known in practical reasoning, where the very word 'deliberation' suggests weighing considerations pro against considerations con.
9. *Tertium non datur* (the principle of the excluded middle).
10. Reason is creative.
11. Cumulative arguments.
12. Nothing Venture, Nothing win.
13. Fallibility.
14. Self-reflective: metaphysical arguments often make use of this; as when we refute a metaphysical argument (e.g. the Verification Principle), on the grounds that it is sawing off the branch it is sitting on.

Chapter 3
A Critique of Critical Reasoning

§3.1   Scepticism
§3.2   Knowledge and Doubt
§3.3   Autonomy
§3.4   Inductive Scepticism
§3.5   Predictions Vindicated
§3.6   A Gruesome Universe?
§3.7   Degrees of Similarity
§3.8   Natural Kinds
§3.9   Limits of Critical Reasoning

§3.1 Scepticism

The word 'sceptic' comes from the Greek, σκεπτικός (*skeptikos*), itself from σκέπτομαι (*skeptomai*), with a root sense of examining, scrutinising, reflecting. Philosophers in this sense should be sceptics—indeed, we all should, if we agree with Socrates that ὁ δε ἀνεξέστατος βίος οὐ βιωτός ἀνθρώπῳ (*ho de anexestatos bios ou biotos anthropo$_i$*) the unexamined life is not worth living.[1] But to examine is not to reject. It is one thing not to take over beliefs and assumptions uncritically, another thing not to accept them at all. To question is to hold oneself in readiness to accept an answer. If I just ask questions, without being willing to wait for an answer, I am like a small boy, who keeps asking 'Why?', whatever his father says to him. At first the tactic works, and keeps father in play, but fathers soon tire of endless repetition, and cut off all requests for explanation with a curt 'Because I tell you' or 'That is the way it is'.

Philosophers too readily alternate between being small boys and impatient fathers. Obsessive questioning leads them into persistent doubt. Then common sense breaks in, and questions are given short shrift, with doubts being dismissed as absurd. Both positions are comprehensible, neither is commendable. Although the sceptic's doubts often seem silly, they are not to be dismissed out of hand. However unreasonable they seem to us in sober daylight, they are doubts experienced by many in moods of metaphysical madness. I

---

[1] *Apology* 38a5.

may suddenly find myself no longer believing the established verities of ordinary life: the people walking in the street cease to be people, and are only automatons, robotically behaving in some preset pattern; the trees in the park no longer exist if I turn my back on them; the stairs will not support me if I walk on them; water will not quench my thirst, but burn out my insides, if I drink it; I have a clear idea of what I ought to do, but still I don't see why I should. Doubts such as these sometimes afflict me, perhaps you, certainly others. I cannot always pass by the sceptic on the other side, for he is sometimes my own *alter ego*, needing to be taken seriously, and not just ignored.

We ought to take the sceptic seriously. He is asking a perfectly intelligible question, and we are not taking him seriously if we do not deign to offer any answer. But if we are to take him seriously, he must himself be serious too. He may ask questions, but we are entitled to question his questions, sometimes faulting them for being idle or wrongly formulated. And when his questions are answered, he should listen to the answers, and not shift immediately to some other question. If he demands a justification, he should be ready to indicate, at least in outline, what sort of justification he would be prepared to accept. He may find fault with what we say, but should be prepared to indicate, at least in outline, what he would say in our stead.

Scepticism
The sceptic is entitled to ask questions
BUT
In asking a question he commits himself to being willing in principle to accept some answer as satisfactory

---

Under questioning the sceptic's questions change: some may be reformulated; some may reveal themselves as idle; some as not seriously believed; some as not constituting a coherent critique. Often the sceptic fails to distinguish questions, and demands a justification that cannot in the nature of the case be given. The fiery radical rails against the monarch, and cannot see why Elizabeth Windsor is so marvellous that she should reign over us. Indeed, we cannot plausibly make out that she is as beautiful as Cleopatra, as warlike as Boadicea, as wise as the Queen of Sheba, or as wily as

§3.1   A Critique of Critical Reasoning   75

Queen Elizabeth the First. What we can do is to give reasons why there should be rulers, why monarchies are less likely to go wrong than republics, why Britain has evolved as a monarchy, and why the monarch is Elizabeth the Second. More generally in politics, we are often affronted by a bad decision of a bad person, and fail to see how it could possibly be justified. But "it" cannot be justified. And in other less emotive areas of philosophy too we need to articulate our discontent carefully and precisely.

Questions may reveal themselves as idle, or not seriously believed. The enthusiast who after going to W.E.A. classes on philosophy told the instructor "You know, I am entirely convinced by your arguments for solipsism: the only thing I find puzzling is why there are not more of us" was perhaps particularly *naive*, but many other sceptics, although too slippery to be as easily caught, are putting on a similar act. They do not really believe that other people are automata; and their complaint—that the assumption that other people really do have minds is unjustified—rings hollow. "Whom do you think you are complaining to?" we retort. Unless other people have minds, it is pointless to argue with them. Locke uses this argument to dismiss the sceptic who doubts the existence of the external world. "At least, he that can doubt so far . . . will never have any controversy with me; since he can never be sure I say anything contrary to his own opinion."[2]

Besides those who do not doubt seriously, there are many who doubt selectively. They press some questions, and are extremely difficult to convince of the soundness of the answers that are on offer, but are quite happy to allow other inferences, which could equally well be called in question. The behaviourist finds it very difficult to argue from people's behaviour to their conscious experience and their own point of view, but is quite happy to accept the existence of material objects on the basis of his sense-experience. Conversely, Berkeley doubted the existence of material objects, but had no difficulty with notions of God and of other conscious beings. Not that it is always wrong to be sceptical about some things, and not about others. We are, most of us, sceptical about ghost stories, but ready to accept astronomers' accounts of remote events in the universe. For this we can give reasons, and if sceptics who are selective in their unbelief can give good reasons for their selectivity, they

---

[2] *Essay Concerning the Human Understanding*, Bk IV, ch.11, §3.

deserve a respectful hearing. There are differences between material objects and other human beings, and these differences may justify doubts in the one case which would be unreasonable in the other. Sometimes, however, differences that are visible to us ought not to be visible to the sceptic. The concepts required in order to specify the difference are concepts the sceptic does not believe in. Mathematical Intuitionists baulk at actual infinities, and demand that all procedures should be "effective", but accept as effective operations involving such large numbers, that they could not be carried out in this universe before the Big Crunch.[3] In order to draw the distinction between effective and ineffective procedures, we need to be able to say when a procedure is ineffective; and we can say that a procedure is ineffective only if no result emerges even after an infinite number of operations. Even if the difference can be specified without using terms unavailable to the sceptic, its justification may be beyond his self-reduced abilities. Sextus Empiricus speaks of climbing a ladder, and then kicking it away—a practice not to be recommended in real life, as well as being incoherent philosophically. If I need to climb the ladder in order to kick it away, its having been kicked away shows that it is climbable, and the sensible thing to do is to climb it more carefully, and having climbed it, to argue more circumspectly, so as not to be misled to destructively absurd conclusions.

The final counter to the sceptical questioner is to ask what alternative he has in mind. Since reasoning is typically two-sided, it often involves an assessment of alternatives. If alternatives are offered, we can compare them with what we ourselves have put forward, possibly finding them preferable, but more probably finding them less well supported than the position under attack. But if, as often, no alternative is offered, we are not engaged in a serious exercise. It is the converse of an argument of Hume's, who concluded that "a total suspense of judgement is . . . our only

---

[3] Alexander George, "The Conveyability of Intuitionism", *Journal of Philosophical Logic*, **17**, 1988, pp.133-156. Crispin Wright, "Strict Finitism", *Synthese*, **51**, 1982, pp. 204, 208-210; and R.Gandy, "Limitations to Mathematical Knowledge", in D. van Dalen, D.Lascar, T.J.Smiley, eds., *Logic Colloquium '80*, North Holland, Amsterdam, 1982, pp.129-146. J.R.Lucas, *The Conceptual Roots of Mathematics*, London, 1999, ch.7, §7.7, pp.187-189.

§3.2   A Critique of Critical Reasoning   77

reasonable resource", arguing that, since "every attack and no defence . . . is successful, victory must go to the man who remains always on the offensive and has himself no fixed station or abiding city which he is ever, on any occasion, obliged to defend".[4] But guerilla warfare wins no territory. The metaphysician is looking for a position in which he *can* abide, and which he would be willing to defend. His thoughts and communications may sometimes be troubled by a Humean sceptic, but he will have no incentive to abandon his position for another, if no other is on offer. For he is *serieux*; metaphysics is not a *dilettante* occupation, but a guide to life, and life is short and will not allow an indefinite suspense of judgement.

§3.2 Knowledge and Doubt

Although arguments for scepticism are often based on very general themes, particular sceptical positions often rely on some particular understanding or misunderstanding of some particular concept. Knowledge is one such. Our understanding of knowledge has been distorted by misconceptions about the logical grammar of the word 'know'. The phrases 'I know', 'you know' 'he knows' 'we know' 'they know' do not merely introduce biographical statements about me, you, him, us, or them, but are "performative" locutions, committing the speaker to a certain position. The speaker is, as it were, issuing a cheque, signed either by himself or by the others mentioned, which guarantees the truth of what is said to be known.[5] If the cheque bounces, the speaker will be held to account; sometimes he may be under some obligation to put things right for those he misinformed; at the very least, he will be obliged to eat his words: "I thought we knew that beef was safe to eat, but I was wrong."

Plato, followed by most philosophers down to the present time, thought that knowledge must, therefore, be infallible.[6] The argument can be put in modern terms. To say that I (or you, or he, or we, or they) know that p, but p may not be true is self-contradictory.

$$(\text{know} p) \wedge (\Diamond \neg p) \vdash$$

---

[4] David Hume, *Two Dialogues on Natural Religion*, end of §viii.

[5] See above, §1.7.

[6] *Republic*, V, 476; and for example, Peter Ungar, *Ignorance*, Oxford, 1975, pp.103-105.

So
$$(\text{know}\,p) \vdash \neg(\Diamond \neg p)$$
that is
$$(\text{know}\,p) \vdash \Box p.$$
or, again in words,

From p is known, it follows that p is necessary

Plato concluded that only the necessary truths of mathematics and natural science could constitute genuine knowledge,[7] and in subsequent ages it has been widely held that where contingent things—things that could be otherwise—are involved, real knowledge is impossible, and we can do no more than have probable beliefs about them.

Descartes was similarly misled. He made the problem of what can be known a central question in philosophy, and introduced his method of doubt in order to ensure that what he thought he knew he really did know. Rather than rely on his unconsidered opinions, or take over anything from his predecessors, he wanted to think out everything for himself by incontrovertible argument from a starting point that was indubitably true. Only so could he be sure that his thoughts were free from error.

Plato and Descartes were not sceptics, but they provided the sceptic with a powerful weapon. It is easy to doubt. Almost every tenet can be called in question, and most attempts at justification can either be rejected out of hand or parried with a further demand for their premises to be justified. The realm of knowledge is cut down to very small size. Most of the things we think we know are things that could have been otherwise. I thought I knew that there was a train to London at 10.22, but it *could* be the case that there was not a train to London at 10.22; certainly I can imagine a world with no 10.22 to London. So it is not absolutely necessary that there should be such a train, and my belief that there is one, however well based, can never amount to knowledge, and should

---

[7] It is easy to confuse this argument with a comparable one, that if I (or you, or he, or we, or they) know that p, then *necessarily p* is true. The mediaeval schoolmen distinguished these, calling the latter *necessitas consequentiae* and the former *necessitas consequentis*. Some arguments for divine foreknowledge of human actions depend on a shift between these two necessities, but Plato's argument for the necessity of what is known does not.

> ### Plato and Descartes
> Plato:
> $$(\text{know} p) \vdash \Box p.$$
> From p is known, it follows that p is necessary
>
> Descartes:
> $$(\text{doubt} p) \vdash (\Diamond \neg p)$$
> From I can doubt p, it follows that $\neg p$ is logically possible So, it seems, p is not known if $\neg p$ is logically possible But (with possibly one or two exceptions) if p is not an empty tautology, $\neg p$ is logically possible So, it would follow, only empty tautologies can be known

not be represented as more than a probable belief. But trains are not the only things that may fail to run. Biology and geology are under a similar condemnation: they could have been different. The dinosaurs might not have become extinct, we humans might have evolved keeping our tails, a particular virus might mutate. Biology does not really count as genuine knowledge, because it does not have the hard necessity of chemistry and physics. But nor do chemistry and physics. The laws of nature are not analytically true. They can be denied without self-contradiction. We could live in a universe in which the velocity of light was only 186,000 furlongs a fortnight, instead of 186,000 miles a second, and Planck's constant a hundred thousand times larger than it is. Only the truths of deductive logic and mathematics have the logical necessity that cannot be gainsaid. And often they depend on axioms that are postulated rather than premises that are proved.

It can be a pleasing experience to show people that they do not know the things they thought they knew, and many philosophers have experienced that pleasure. But one may be sceptical of that sceptical success. There may be some special, philosophical, knowledge, defined as infallible, which is beyond the ken of most mortal thinkers, but that is not the knowledge we refer to when we talk about knowledge in our ordinary life. We commonly accept locutions in which contingent matters are said to be known: it follows that it cannot be against the meaning of words to use the word 'know' of things that could have been otherwise. Plato got it wrong. He failed to distinguish different degrees of necessity and possibility. It is indeed the case that I cannot consistently affirm that I know that p but p may not be true, but I can allow that p *might* not be true, even while claiming to know that p. "I know that the post goes at 4pm," I say. Admittedly, the postman might decide to go fishing instead of collecting the post, might go on strike, might even die; a wandering comet might blow us all to smithereens. All these are possible, but only *barely* possible. And bare possibilities do not detract from knowledge.

We know more than most philosophers will allow, but with less certitude than they demand. And that gives entry to sceptical arguments. We are easily led to make some claim to know, and then are asked quizzically: "Are you sure?", "Are you *really* sure?", and, knowing our own fallibility, are forced to confess that we might be wrong, whereupon our claim to knowledge is disallowed, and we are propelled step by step towards a state of sceptical agnosticism. We feel that something has gone wrong, but cannot say precisely what. We may be tempted, like Hume, to think it is just the effect of philosophy, and putting off philosophical speculation, resume the cheerfulness of ordinary life. But the fault lies not with philosophy, but with the arguments employed. And the remedy is not to stop thinking, but to think harder and more accurately, and work out what is wrong with the arguments the sceptic employs.

The method of doubt is flawed. People may doubt. That is their privilege. But before they can expect us to share their doubts, they should themselves share with us their reasons for doubting. Maybe there are reasons: what looks like water in the distance could well be a mirage, since the day is hot, and the map shows no lake in that direction. Maybe there will not be a train to London at 10.22: heavy storms have flooded the line; the engine-drivers are on strike; the Health and Safety Executive has imposed a 20 mph speed limit throughout the network. If the doubter can substantiate his doubts, then they should be taken seriously: but if they are just idle doubts, little time should be wasted on resolving them. To put it in forensic terms: before we even try to mount a defence in the face of the critic's questions, we ask him to say if there is a case to answer. We question whether there is a serious question to answer, and do not attempt to answer questions that need no reply.

But the method of doubt was a method. It was not just a succession of doubts raised one after another, but, rather, a programme designed to secure its conclusions against all possibility of

§3.2   A Critique of Critical Reasoning   81

error. It seems a sensible idea. If I am to be confident that my conclusions really are mine, and not taken over second-hand from the received opinion of my day, I must take care to believe *nothing* that could not be established by the most rigorous methods; since if any premise is false, the conclusion could be false too. Anything that was not absolutely certain was to be thrown out. Just as one bad apple can corrupt all the others in the barrel, so, Descartes feared, one dubious premise, or one shaky argument, would contaminate the whole corpus of belief with dubiety. The analogy is apt if the only cogent arguments are those of deductive logic. But once we realise that arguments can be two-sided, the infection of a false belief can be contained. Our beliefs do not depend upon a *chain* of argument, which can be no stronger than its weakest link, but on a network of interlocking and mutually supporting arguments, where if one strand fails, there are others to take the strain. I might, quite wrongly, believe that Mendeléef was a Bohemian monk, who did chemical experiments in the monastic garden, and arranged his specimens on a table. That false belief would be countered by other true beliefs I happened to have; and my actual belief in the Periodic Table would be supported by facts I knew about the chemistry of the halogens, the alkali metals, of carbon and silicon, and of oxygen and sulphur, quite independently of any historical misinformation I might happen to have.

The method of doubt is not the one and only means of avoiding error. It is like carbolic acid. It is a good antiseptic, but, incautiously used, it can damage living tissue. It led Descartes to ever greater feats of disbelief. Appearances might be illusions, contingent truths could be supposed to be false. A malicious demon might have been systematically misleading him. The only propositions which could not be doubted even if a malicious demon were at work were those that were logically necessary, where there was not even a bare logical possibility of their being false. The sceptic's victory is complete, but at the price of vacuity. If the only propositions to be admitted are those that follow deductively from premises that are logically necessary, the demand is that only tautologies and what follows tautologically from tautologies shall be allowed—propositions, that is, which are true solely in virtue of the meaning of the terms involved, propositions which it would be inconsistent to deny. But such propositions tell us nothing about the world. Nothing is excluded by them. If we try to ask ourselves what such propositions are ruling out, we find ourselves mired in self-contradiction as we seek to say what it is that, according to them, is not the case.

The method of doubt is not a sensible method to adopt if we seek knowledge. It will secure us against believing anything false, but at the price of ensuring that we do not believe anything at all, except for empty tautologies. If we want to acquire any substantial knowledge, then what we come to know must be something that it is meaningful to deny. We incur the logical possibility of being wrong in achieving content. One article in the mid-twentieth-century ended with the words: "If we have not said anything much, at least we have not said anything wrong." It is a sentence which could well be reversed: "If we have not said anything that might be wrong, we have not said anything much."

§3.3 Autonomy

The method of doubt commends itself to us as a means of securing intellectual autonomy. Rather than take over, unexamined, received opinions from other men, I should test each item before believing it myself. Only so can I be sure that my position really is one that I can really accept. Much as Luther had protested the importance of the individual's relationship with God, so Descartes emphasizes the importance of what *I* experience, and what *I* can know. There is a strain of egocentricity in the sceptics' arguments that sometimes led theologians to convict them of pride. They had a point. Often the inference being questioned is an inference across some border defined in egocentric terms.[8] The problem of Other Minds is the problem of how *I* can know minds other than *my own*;[9] if I am a phenomenalist, I am unable to argue from *my* experience to the existence of an objective, external world—a world independent of, and external to, *my* sense-experience;[10] the problem of induction is the problem of predicting the future—that is, the time

---

[8] Bertrand Russell introduced the term 'egocentric particulars' in *Human Knowledge*, London, 1948, ch.4, pp.100-108; H.Reichenbach, *Elements of Symbolic Logic*, New York, 1947, §50, pp.284-287, uses the term 'token-reflexive' of words such as 'I', 'this', 'here', 'now'; the term most commonly used is 'indexical', which is due to C.S.Peirce, and was popularised by Y.Bar-Hillel, "Indexical Expressions", *Mind*, **63**, 1954, p.365.

[9] See below, §6.12.

[10] See below, §6.2.

§3.3   A Critique of Critical Reasoning   83

after that at which *I* am speaking—on the basis of the past—that is, the time before that at which *I* am speaking. If I were not so self-important, I would not attach such significance to the distinction between *my*self and others, between *my* sense-experience and the things it is experience of, and between what has happened before, and what will happen after, the time of *my* speaking. To that extent the theologians were right to regard scepticism as an epistemological form of original sin.

But we need to be cautious in condemning. Original sin was a concomitant with knowing good and evil, or in modern terms, moral autonomy. Intellectual autonomy is also a good. I need to be on my guard against received opinion and other men's prejudices. But the method of doubt goes too far. The assumption that other men's views should carry no weight with me at all is unwarranted. While it is good to be aware that other men may make mistakes, it is stupid to assume that they always do. They are fallible, as I am: but as I can sometimes get it right, so they should be allowed to be often in the right. If I spurn the aid of other men's endeavours, I constrict my achievements to the small compass of what can be accomplished by a one-man band. I may not get very far on my own, refusing to avail myself of the benefits of other men's experience, and other men's thought. Newton could see far because he sat on the shoulders of giants.[11] If I spurn all help from others, I may spend my life re-inventing the wheel, and discovering that two and two make four. Rather than the method of doubt, we should adopt Swinburne's principle of credulity.[12] I should be willing to accept beliefs that have commended themselves to men of discernment, though always holding myself ready to revise my opinion if need be.

---

[11] In a letter to Robert Hook in 1675; it was said earlier by Bernard of Chartres.

[12] See above, ch.1, §1.7.

§3.4 Inductive Scepticism

Hume realised, quite rightly, that inductive inferences are not deductive, and concluded, quite wrongly, that they were therefore unjustified. Many philosophers since then have asked why inductive inferences should be accepted as cogent, and have been dissatisfied with the answers on offer. Often they have been confused, and have thought that the only justification of induction would be to make it into deduction. Some extra premise has been sought—a principle of natural uniformity, or of limited variability—which would, in conjunction with the other premises already available, yield the desired conclusion with deductive certainty. But though it may well be worth articulating a principle of natural uniformity, or of limited variability, neither will serve as an extra premise for a deductive argument, because there is always room for doubt how the principle is to be applied in the particular case. To search for some premise that will turn inductive arguments into deductive ones is to pursue a will o' the wisp. Inductive arguments are different from deductive ones—they would not be any use unless they were different, capable of being intelligibly denied, and hence informative, telling us, among the different things that could (logically could) be the case, what actually is going to be the case.

Some philosophers would leave it there. Inductive arguments are different from deductive arguments, and the fact that inductive arguments are not valid deductive arguments is neither here nor there. Inductive arguments are not valid deductive arguments but are cogent *inductive* arguments.[13] If asked what reason we have for accepting the conclusion of an inductive argument, we can cite the evidence, and leave it at that—that just *is* what constitutes having good reason for believing that conclusion.[14]

---

[13] See above, §2.1 n.1.

[14] Paul Edwards, "Russell's Doubts about Induction", *Mind*, **58**, 1949, pp.141-163; reprinted in A.G.N.Flew, ed., *Logic and Language*, vol.I, Oxford, 1951, pp.55-79; reprinted in R.W.Swinburne, ed., *The Justification of Induction*, Oxford, 1974, pp.26-47. A.J.Ayer, *British Empirical Philosophers*, London, 1952, pp.25-27; P.F.Strawson, *Introduction to Logical Theory*, London, 1952, ch.9, Pt II, §10, esp.pp.256-260. Nelson Goodman, *Fact, Fiction and Forecast*, Cambridge, Mass., 1979, pp.64-65. See above, §1.7.

§3.4   A Critique of Critical Reasoning   85

This response is an adequate answer to some enquirers, but not to those who want to call in question the whole practice under discussion. Their question is an intelligible one, and deserves serious consideration. But if their question is to be taken seriously, they must be serious too, and think through their question to determine what it really is asking for, and what alternative answers might be available. Too often sceptics oscillate between the general and the particular, complaining, when a general defence of a practice has been given, that it does not offer a justification of a particular instance, and when a particular difficulty is dealt with, that it does not justify the practice in general.

If a radical sceptic demands a reason why we should engage in inferring inductively at all, he needs to acknowledge at the outset that he is not looking for a *deductive* reason. Inductive inferences are by definition not deductive, and would be useless if they were. Their conclusions have substantial content, ruling out logically possible concatenations of events. If the sceptic is really yearning for a deductive justification of induction, he is crying for the moon. We cannot give him what he wants. It is useless to try. All we can do is help him to see that he has himself ruled out there being any possibility of getting what he wants. If he can bring himself to see that, we may be able to help him, but until then we can only feel sorry for him in his self-imposed incomprehension.

Can there be reasons which are not deductive? There is no reason why not.[15] Some philosophers define reason to be deductive reason, but that definition does not fit ordinary usage, according to which we often give reasons why events happen, or why people should undertake actions. They need, therefore, to give reasons for stipulating that only deductive reasons should be reckoned genuine ones. But since those reasons themselves could not be deductive ones, the project would never get off the ground. Even a sceptic, then, should allow that there could be a justification of inductive inference which was not itself deductive.

We need to know. If we are to survive, we must read the signs of coming events, and must try to predict the consequences of our actions. Of course, we may be wrong. But better the risk of being wrong than the certainty of not being right.[16] But why inductive

---

[15] See above §2.4.

[16] This account owes much to G.H. von Wright, *The Logical Problem of Induction*, Acta Philosophica Fennica, Helsinki, 1941 & 1957, Fasc. III, chs.IV, VIII & IX.

inferences? Why not adopt a "counter-inductive" principle of inference? Instead of assuming that the future will be like the past, the unknown like the known, assume that they will be "*unlike*". But unlike in which way? There are many ways of being unlike: the next swan could be blue, or green, or red. Which is it to be? The like has the advantage over the unlike in being relatively specific. The strategy of assuming that the next case will be like its predecessors, the future like the past, gives definite guidance, whereas the strategy of assuming that the next case will be unlike its predecessors, the future unlike the past, gives none. There is no feasible alternative to arguing inductively. Contrary to the way it is represented by sceptics, inductive inference is many-faceted,[17] and refines its methods to achieve more reliable results. It is not so much the application of some principle we know to be true, as a know-how, which we learn to use with increasing sophistication and skill. It may let us down sometimes—but then we can learn from our mistakes: in any case, better be sometimes wrong than never right.

We can fault counter-inductive principles on other grounds: they do not generalise, whereas those for induction do: if it had been right yesterday to infer counter-inductively that the next swan would be not-white, then there would be no basis today for inferring that tomorrow's swan would not be white. It would have to be neither white nor not-white. Indeed, it is evident today that if I had inferred yesterday counter-inductively that the next swan would be not-white, I should have turned out to be wrong. Sceptics are quick to disallow the fact that induction has hitherto proved successful in making predictions subsequently vindicated by events as an argument for its validity. That, they protest, would be to beg the question. But no objection can be raised against citing previous occasions as refuting rival rules. If it is rational to make inferences, albeit risky ones, from the known to the unknown, from the present and past to the future, and if it would have been evidently wrong to have used a counter-inductive principle of inference, then inductive inference is left as the sole rational resource.

The sceptic is not done yet. The man who justifies induction on these grounds, he says, is still guilty of a *petitio principii* at the meta level. The argument that counter-inductive inferences

---

[17] See above, ch.2, §2.7.

have reached the wrong results hitherto whereas inductive inferences have reached the right results is being appealed to as evidence that inductive inference works, and counter-inductive inference does not. But that is to assume that what worked in the past will continue to work in the future, which is just what is in question. Indeed, according to the counter-inductive principle, the fact that it has not worked hitherto is good reason for supposing that it will work now.

The Irish logic of this counter is beguiling, but not persuasive. Once we iterate inferences, we land ourselves in inconsistency. Thus far we have seen only white swans. Should we infer that the next swan will be not-white? If so, what about the next one after that? Perhaps we are to escape contradiction by refusing then to draw any inference. But it is a curious rule of inference which if successful, can only be used once—some genetically modified seeds are made sterile on purpose, but an un-reusable rule of inference scarcely qualifies as a rule at all.[18]

The pragmatic justification of induction answers the question posed by an enquirer who realises that it would be incoherent to look for a deductive justification, and is himself willing to survey possible alternatives. It will not convince the sceptic who is permitted only to ask questions, without being obliged to think them through, or to specify exactly what his alternative rule of inference actually is. He can make out that he does not accept the cogency of inductive arguments, and nothing we can say will shake him. But if we can consort with him for a time, we may find that his actions belie his words. A man who refuses to drink hemlock when proffered it, takes out a raincoat when he sees clouds, and puts the

[18] Hans Reichenbach, *Experience and Prediction*, Chicago, 1938, and *The Theory of Probability*, Berkeley, 1944, one of the original proponents of the "pragmatic justification of induction" expounds his argument in terms of probabilities. But probabilities are treacherous, and are by Reichenbach explicated in terms of von Mises *Kollectiv*s whose limiting frequencies tend towards a definite limit as the number of instances tends towards infinity. It seems better to concentrate upon the simple case, and avoid needless complexity, however elegant the mathematical treatment. A simple pragmatic justification is given by W.C.Salmon, "Inductive Inference", and criticized by J.W.Lenz, "Problems for the Practicalist's Justification of Induction", *Philosophical Studies*, **9**, 1958, pp.4-7; both reprinted in R.G.Swinburne, *The Justification of Induction*, Oxford, 1974, pp.74-101.

kettle on the stove before making a cup of tea, may profess not to accept the cogency of inductive arguments, but we shall remain sceptical of his sceptical protestations. He may be using the words 'reason' and 'cogency' in an idiosyncratic way. But in the ordinary sense of the words, the reason for what he does or refuses to do is that on the basis of facts already known to him he predicts the likely outcome of actions he may undertake, or the situation he finds himself in.

§3.5 Predictions Vindicated

Practically, we may have no alternative to arguing inductively, but theoretically we may still question whether inductive arguments lead to *truth*. Some philosophers have maintained that the history of science shows that they hardly ever do. The accepted truths of one generation are shown to be false in the next. Newton was refuted by Einstein, and quantum mechanics gives the lie to classical corpuscularianism. But that is to over-dramatize the development of scientific understanding. We still use Newtonian mechanics for building bridges and calculating trajectories and orbits. Einstein's Special Theory refined rather than refuted Newtonian mechanics, having Newtonian mechanics as a limiting case for low velocities. Similarly, the General Theory approximates to the Special Theory on the small scale, and quantum mechanics supports the kinetic theory of gases just as much as genuinely atomic theories did. It is rare for any generally accepted scientific theory to turn out to be completely wrong, though common for it to be subsumed under a new theory and seen in a new light. Even the phlogiston theory, currently condemned as bad chemistry, can be viewed more favourably as a first attempt at thermodynamics: when things burn, they do give off something—heat, or more generally, energy. Energy is not a chemical substance, but it is something—indeed, now we allow that it does have mass, though far less than a chemical substance. The history of science gives us no reason to be pessimistic, but only to be humble: our predecessors were not badly wrong, but our own beliefs are still open to improvement. If we change the question from "Why believe inductive inferences?" to "Do they reveal truths?", the track record suggests that the answer should be "Substantially yes".

The claim, although vague, is a large one. Whereas the pragmatic justification was concerned only with the next case, the truths inferred by induction are natural laws and explanatory

§3.5   *A Critique of Critical Reasoning*   89

schemata going far beyond the limits of our own experience. Can we justify sticking out our necks so far? Most thinkers reckon that the track record is justification enough. Admittedly, the claims are large. But for that very reason they are vulnerable. If they were incorrect, they would have been falsified. It is one thing to be cautious about accepting a newly constructed theory which does indeed explain the available evidence, but has not been further tested. It is quite a different thing when the theory has made numerous predictions which have in due course been found to be true. Although, of course, it is still the case that even with the added evidence of the confirmed predictions, it remains possible that the theory is false, it becomes increasingly implausible that, if the theory were false, the predictions made on the strength of it should none the less come out true.

The sceptic may seek leave to disagree. That is his privilege. We hear what he says, and cannot convict him of inconsistency. But if he is serious, he owes us an alternative explanation of the phenomena. He may offer one: it is always possible to construct a theory that will agree with all the evidence obtained hitherto, but yielding different predictions. Confident as we are of our own theory, we are ready to put the matter to the test: he could be proved right—in which case we shall have to eat our words and amend our views.[19] If, however, the sceptic ducks the test, or having taken it, refuses to accept it as decisive, we begin to question his seriousness. Is he really concerned to know the truth? or is he merely saying yet again that inductive inferences are not deductive? But perhaps this is an unfair dilemma. Perhaps he cannot offer an alternative explanation, because there is not one. Perhaps the correctness of the predictions was just a coincidence. After all, coincidences can and do happen, and arguments against accepting them are often fallacious. Colin Howson, the most trenchant exponent of Hume's inductive scepticism,[20] maintains that "The No-Miracles Argument" as he calls it, is fallacious, and can be seen to be so if it is cast into Bayesian form. He cites as a parallel the fallacious conclusion drawn in a test done in the Harvard Medical School for a rare condition, affecting only 0.1% of the population, where the probability of a false negative—that is of a

---

[19] There are a few famous cases where this has happened.

[20] Colin Howson, *Hume's Problem: Induction and the justification of belief*, Oxford, 2000.

patient with the condition being diagnosed as healthy—was zero, but the probability of a false positive—that is of a healthy patient being diagnosed as having the condition—was 5%. It was widely supposed that if someone had a positive result, then he had a one in twenty, 5%, chance of actually having the condition, whereas in fact he had only one in fifty chance. The fallacy is to argue from the true premise, that a healthy person has a 5% probability of being diagnosed positive, to the false conclusion that a person diagnosed positive has a 5% probability of being affected.[21] We can get a more intuitive sense of what is going wrong if we consider another example, highly relevant in modern legal cases, of a DNA match.[22] If the suspect's DNA matches that of blood at the scene of a crime, it seems highly like that the suspect did commit the crime, for the chance against the actual criminal just happening to have the same DNA profile as the suspect is several millions to one. But if the suspect turned out to have a water-tight alibi, we should have to allow that the match was due to a remarkable coincidence, and not to the suspect's having been at the scene of the crime. Howson discusses both examples in terms of Bayes' theorem, which is appropriate in the case of medical statistics, but can be misleading in other cases, where the attribution of prior probabilities is subjective and arbitrary. We need rather to see such cases as two-sided arguments, in which the improbability of a coincidence has to be weighed against the implausibility of the suggested explanation. That the suspect committed the crime is extremely implausible if he was at the time under constant observation locked up in a police cell several hundred miles away. Granted that, the DNA match has to be dismissed as no more that a remarkable coincidence. Similarly, claims to telepathic powers are considered by many scientists to be so implausible, that they are prepared to attribute to coincidence data discovered by researchers into psi phenomena. So what is the real rationale of the No-Miracles Argument? Can the determined sceptic's scepticism be convincingly countered? The answer is that there is no *single* counter to the sceptic. At any one stage, he can without evident irrationality, plead coincidence. Coincidences do happen. But they do not go on happening. If the sceptic is going to go on pleading coincidence, however many predictions turn out to be correct, then he is not taking account

---

[21] See further below, §5.4.

[22] Howson, p.58.

of empirical evidence at all, but is merely announcing his unshakeable determination not to allow a logical possibility to be abridged by any other rational consideration. On no single interchange can the sceptic be confuted, but in the course of a dialogue we can pin him down to outlining the circumstances in which he would be persuaded, or showing that he is not open to rational persuasion at all.

§3.6 A Gruesome Universe?

A determined sceptic can avoid the appeal to coincidence by putting forward a tailor-made theory which accommodates the available evidence, but yields different predictions. In a similar way he can avoid the inconsistencies of his simple counter-inductive rule of inference by offering a more sophisticated version. "Why not have the rule of arguing inductively hitherto, but counter-inductively from now on? Such a principle would not have been compromised by any past experience, and could, if put in some specific form, give definite guidance for the future."

Why not? The principle is formulated in essentially egocentric terms: 'the past' is the time before I am speaking, 'the future' the time after I am speaking; and egocentric distinctions are ones I must play down if I am to communicate with you and others. Although I do not make myself unintelligible if I make particular predictions contrary to the canons of induction, I need to curb my egocentricity, if I am to communicate effectively; if I am not to be confined in my conversation to myself alone, I need to recognise the continuing relevance of what does not depend on me, the time at which I speak, or the place from which I speak. Not that I can never report on my private experience, or on the current situation at the place where I am located. But to incorporate the time of utterance into a principle of inference would run counter to our canon of rationality, introducing a needless arbitrariness into what should be universal.

Discountenancing arbitrariness rules out other counter-inductive inferences which incorporate temporal dates or spatial positions. Although many general laws apply differently at different times or in different places, it would be irrational to propose a principle of inferring inductively up to 2035 AD, and thereafter in some specified counter-inductive way; or to argue inductively in the North, but not in the South. Similarly, not every property that can be thought up is a basis for a sound inductive inference—not, for instance, the property of being "grue", that is green until 2400hrs on 31.1.1999 and blue from 0000hrs on 1.1.2000 onwards, or the property of being "bleen", that is blue until 2400hrs on 31.1.1999 and green from 0000hrs on 1.1.2000 onwards.[23]

But even if we exclude all egocentric and arbitrary properties, the sceptic can still put forward rival hypotheses to explain the data. Many natural laws are expressed as functional dependencies, and all can be put into that form. And although often we take it as obvious which function best fits the data, there are infinitely many other functions which fit the data equally well. We have little hesitation in rejecting them, but the sceptic questions our justification for so doing. Clearly, it is not on the basis of any empirical evidence, since all empirical evidence has been taken into consideration already: nor is there any deductive warrant for it in first-order logic. For Hume and the Logical Positivists there was no possibility of there being some further *a priori* justification, and it seemed that our actual inductive practices must be irrational. Once, however, we recognise that reason is not confined to analytic deductive argument, we need no longer despair of justifying our practices. On the face of it, the *a priori* arguments against egocentricity and arbitrariness are cogent. And although there is an enormous infinity of possible functions that fit any finite set of data, it does not have to be the case that they are all equally good.

Consider a sequence of ten tosses of a coin. If we get ten heads, $HHHHHHHHHH$, we may jump to the conclusion that the coin has heads on both sides, or is otherwise biassed. The sceptic, instead of arguing that it is a simple coincidence, may point out that there is a non-denumerable infinity of infinite sequences starting $HHHHHHHHHH\ldots$, and that we have no warrant for supposing that ours is the one that has H every time rather than one like $HHHHHHHHHHTTT\ldots$, or $HHHHHHHHHHTHT\ldots$, or $HHHHHHHHHHHT\ldots$, or .... But we do have some warrant. The sceptic is invoking too many possibilities. By countenancing every sequence that is logically possible, he is in effect reverting to a demand for a deductive justification of inductive inference, that is, asking for the impossible. And the all-H sequence has the opposite merit of being uniquely simple. We can measure the

---

[23] See Nelson Goodman, *Fact, Fiction and Forecast*, Cambridge, Mass., 1979, pp.72-81.

"algorithmic compressibility" of rules generating sequences, and, unsurprisingly, we can specify the all-H sequence more economically than the alternatives that start with ten Hs and then have some tails.

It would be nice to leave it there. Intuitively we reject artificial predicates, such as 'grue' and 'bleen', but the sceptic can still make out that there is no valid distinction between 'blue' and 'green' on the one hand and 'grue' and 'bleen' on the other.[24] Goodman concludes that only inferences based on "projectible" properties are inductively valid, and that blue and green are, and grue and bleen are not, projectible, but gives no adequate specification of what properties are projectible.

In practice we can defeat the sceptic: if he puts forward a gruesome alternative, we can put his hypothesis to the test. But his probing has revealed a potential hole in our theory of inductive inference: we are implicitly assuming something about the nature of reality—that we live in a non-gruesome universe.

§3.7 Degrees of Similarity

Induction carries with it metaphysical assumptions. That the universe is not gruesome may be argued for at two levels: as independently established truths, or as necessary presuppositions of inductive inference, which we must postulate on pragmatic rational grounds. We might be assured that nature is uniform—perhaps theologically by reliable revelation from God—and then we should have adequate warrant for arguing inductively. Or, again, if we were Platonists, and believed in the world of Forms, we should expect the fundamental truths to be universal truths, and think it rational to generalise from the evidence in our possession. We could reasonably use Popperian falsification to winnow likely looking hypotheses, and reckon those that survived severe testing to be substantially true.[25] Once we have concluded that nature is uniform, the suggestion that it might cease to be so tomorrow can no longer be taken seriously. In the next section arguments will be adduced in favour of Natural Kinds, which can be seen as modern successors to Plato's Forms. If those arguments are successful, they show not merely that, synchronically, only a limited number of combinations of features can occur together at the same time,

---

[24] C.Howson, *Hume's Problem*, Oxford, 2000, pp.97-100.

[25] See further below, §4.7.

but that, diachronically, only some successions of earlier and later features are possible; thus constituting an independent argument for the uniformity of nature, in which case we do not so much answer the sceptic as bypass him.

For the present, however, we are taking the sceptic seriously, and are offering a pragmatic justification of inductive reasoning; we therefore have to buttress our argument against niggling doubts. Having to decide, under conditions of imperfect information, what to do, we must try to anticipate. If we are to know anything about what we have not as yet observed, it must be based upon what we have observed: and it must be either like it or unlike it; the assumption that what we have not as yet observed is unlike what we have observed gives no guidance because there are many ways of being unlike, and each particular way proves unsatisfactory; the assumption that what we have not as yet observed is like what we have observed makes sense, and chimes in with our untutored understanding of inductive inference; but it is open to persistent challenge by the sceptic. 'Like', or 'similar to' is a three-term relation: x is similar to y *with respect to* Q. For each value of Q we have an equivalence relation, grouping together all those that are similar to one another with respect to Q. They all share Q-ness. Given any equivalence relation we can pick out those things that share the common quality, and given any quality, represented by a monadic predicate, Q, we can invent an equivalence relation which holds between things that are similar in respect of both being Q. Sometimes, when the common qualities can themselves be strictly ordered, we go further, and ascribe magnitudes. Using a pair of scales we can form equivalence classes of those material objects that all weigh the same. They all have the same weight. And, using the scales again, we can order weights as being heavier and lighter, and, granted some further assumptions, assign numbers to them.

There are a very large number of equivalence relations, and corresponding sets of instances all possessing the relevant quality. At one extreme there is strict identity: $x = y$.
By Leibniz' Law
$$x = y \quad \text{iff} \quad (\forall Q)(Qx \leftrightarrow Qy).^{26}$$
At the other extreme there is the universal relation
$$x \sim y, \text{ where } (\forall x)(\forall y)(x \sim y);$$

---

[26] Actually, it is enough to say $(\forall Q)(Qx \rightarrow Qy)$. See n.27 in next section.

that is the universal relation holds between *any* two items. It is reasonable to claim that two things are more similar to each other if the identity relation holds between them than if only the universal relation does. Indeed, we can say that those things between which the identity relation holds are most similar, and those things between which only the universal relation holds are least similar. So 'more similar to' and 'less similar to' are meaningful terms. But it is difficult to go further and establish an ordering of different degrees of similarity. What we have in effect is a somewhat messy set of partly overlapping, and sometimes incompatible, natural kinds, together with some, not very well formulated, rules for reckoning which natural kinds are more significant or fundamental than others: we assess similarity in terms of natural kinds, rather than *vice versa*.

§3.8 Natural Kinds

For inductive arguments to be cogent, the world needs to be articulated into natural kinds. It is an evident fact that natural kinds exist. The ones we first encounter, and are most familiar with, are not the pure substances and elements of modern chemistry, but the biological species manifested in the fauna and flora around us. We rapidly learn that bulls are dangerous, but it is perfectly safe to say 'Bo' to a cow, and that blackberries are good to eat, and bryony not. Not only do we discover that species exist, but they have to if we are to be able to discover anything. We can distinguish blackberries from elderberries and both from bryony, because there are not very many combinations of features that are actually instantiated. If elderflowers sometimes turned into multi-pipped fruits, or brambles bore large single fruits, we should be in a quandary. Again, if besides silver, there was a silvery metal, soluble in nitric acid but not in hydrochloric, but also magnetic and forming with carbon an alloy as strong as steel, we should begin to be unable to distinguish silver from iron. A doctrine of natural kinds is thus both a necessary presupposition of inductive inference and an evident empirical fact.

Our language contains substantives which refer by means of a number of different features which go together, and such that we can identify individual specimens by reference to some subset of those features. Birds of a feather can be identified either by their plumage, or by their song, or by their shape and size, or by their pattern of flight. A swallow does not sing like a thrush, nor does a swan swoop like a swift. If every pattern of flight was co-instantiated with every pattern of song, every shape and size, and every pattern of colouring, we should have no alternative ways of identifying birds: bird-books would have to be so compendious as to be useless. If there were no natural kinds, not only would communication be impossible, but even thought. Even non-human animals need to be able to classify, and recognise predators and edible prey. Some principle of limited independent variety is necessary, both ontologically, if species are to be distinct, and epistemologically, if species are to be distinguishable.

We are led to a principle of sub-maximality: just as not every similarity is a likely likeness that the future might share with the past, so not every set is a natural kind, nor does every predicate describe a natural kind. Some restriction on set theory, and correspondingly on predicate and propositional calculus, is needed when we are dealing with natural kinds.

Twentieth-century thinkers have been in thrall to symbolic logic, which has served them ill when trying to think clearly about natural kinds. Predicate logic is a logic of predicates, and fails to do justice to substantives. The thesis that all ravens are black is not formulated in terms of ravens, but in terms of the predicate 'being a raven'. Logicians do not formulate ($\forall$ *ravens*)Black(*ravens*), but ($\forall$ *x*)(if *x is a raven* then *x is black*); instead of ravens, we have merely *x*s, dummy substances, with all the work being done by the predicates and the sentential connectives. But predicate logic misleads. Logicians early concluded that negation attached to the predicate: if I deny that the King of France is bald, I ascribe non-baldness to the King of France, not baldness to the Non-king-of-France; from which it follows that we can negate the predicate but not the subject. 'Not-bald' is a quite-all-right predicate, and refers to the property of non-baldness, or hirsuteness: 'not-king-of-France' is not a possible subject, and does not refer to a possible non-person. Predicate calculus does not allow individual variables to be negated—they are only dummies, and are of no account—, but accepts $\neg F$ on a par with F.[27] It thus suggests that non-ravens are on a par with ravens, and that since in predicate calculus

$$(\forall x)(x \text{ is a raven } \to x \text{ is black})$$

---

[27] This is why, as noted in the previous section (n.26), the Identity of Indiscernibles can be expressed by just $(\forall F)(Fa \to Fb)$, and not the more-to-be-expected $(\forall F)(Fa \leftrightarrow Fb)$.

is equivalent to

$$(\forall x)(x \text{ is not black} \rightarrow x \text{ is not a raven}),$$

'all non-blacks are not ravens' is as good a natural law as 'all ravens are black', and some philosophers have tried to persuade themselves that every time they see a non-black thing that is not a raven, they are confirming the law that all ravens are black. It is the wrong conclusion. What we should conclude, rather, is that deductive logic—especially as formulated in predicate calculus—is a dangerous guide in inductive inference. The main sceptical argument depends on taking logical possibilities as being serious and substantial. We are committed to the counter-principle of non-maximality: Not every logical possibility is possible.

It would be easy, but wrong, to conclude that deductive logic has no part to play in inductive inference. In fact, although inductive inferences cannot be represented as deductive ones, they have intimate connexions with deductive logic not only in working out the tests for possible causal factors, but more fundamentally in providing the schema of classification required for marshalling evidence and extrapolating from it. Granted that Nature is articulated in certain natural kinds or sorts, and that these have various causal connexions between them, we may be able to discover them by finding out, through trial and failure, which concomitances we cannot produce, no matter how hard we try. A quasi-Platonist metaphysics underwrites Popper's falsificationist approach, whose rationale can be explicated entirely in terms of deductive logic.[28] We should not throw over deductive logic, but need to find a formulation more sensitive to the substantiality of natural kinds.

The inductive sceptic can be answered. But to do so, we have to make assumptions about the nature of reality, assumptions which it is reasonable to make, but difficult to articulate precisely. We can show that there must be some distinction among properties—between those that Goodman calls "projectible" and those that are not; and we can give reasons why those properties that characterize natural kinds should not obey the standard logic of predicates, but one modified to be appropriate to substantives, which cannot be simply negated. But that does not take us very far, and we have to rely on experiment and observation to tell us what species of things really exist.

---

[28] See, for example, J.R.Lucas, "Causation", in R.J.Butler, ed., *Analytical Philosophy*, Oxford, 1962, ch.2, pp.32-65; or J.R.Lucas, *Space, Time and Causality*, Oxford, 1984, ch.4,, pp.44-67.

§3.9 Limits of Critical Reasoning

A reasonable man has reasons for trusting his reasoning. Although he can make mistakes, the arguments of the previous chapter show that our reasoning powers are not just responses that human beings happen to have, but give us guidance we do well to respect. No natural limits can be set to the power of reason, but human fallibility should make us wary of trusting it unreservedly. We need to question our reasonings, but should not conclude that since any one of them may be mistaken, it must be.

In the face of the sceptic's questions it would be cowardice to cave in, and subside into an easy ignorance about the world we live in, and our role within it. It would be a betrayal of reason also to brush off all questions as impertinent irrelevance. Rather than dismiss all questions out of hand, we should listen to them patiently, but be prepared to question in return, probing to find out precisely what the question is, what its presuppositions are, and what alternative answers are available. Often the sceptic is giving vent to a general discontent, and when made to precisify his question, finds he has had to replace it by more mundane queries which do admit of adequate answers. Often, too, his doubts turn out to be idle rather than substantial, to be allayed by general considerations about the nature of knowledge, rather than particular knowledge of unknown facts. Or the question is revealed as one essentially unanswerable: the sceptic is bemoaning the absence of an answer that could not in the nature of the case be given. In other cases the questions are real questions, but the answers are not really believed; or the sceptic is picking and choosing what to believe and what to reject without having any firm principles to justify the difference in his treatment of them. And finally the shallowness of the sceptical position is revealed when he is asked what answers he would give to his questions, and what his own position is. It begins then to emerge that the difference between the sceptic and the ordinary reasonable man is not so much a difference in assessing particular arguments, as a difference of strategic objectives. The sceptic wants above everything else not to be mistaken: the ordinary reasonable man wants to know. Contrary to Plato's teaching, there is a trade-off between certainty and knowledge. In his insistence on certainty, the sceptic is willing to forgo the possibility of knowledge, comforting himself with the thought that if he does not know anything, at least he does not know anything wrong. The ordinary reasonable man, by contrast, is willing to run the risk of error in his pursuit of knowledge, holding that errors are in any case unavoidable, but are in most cases remediable.

These are good general arguments why reason should not be too critical of reason, and should not seek to abridge its scope. But doubts remain. Philosophers down the ages have questioned whether we can have knowledge of the external world, and, more recently, whether we can really know the internal experience of other men. Many of their arguments fit the schema outlined here, but with individual differences, as well as some arguments peculiar to the specific issue, that deserve individual attention.

Counters against Sceptic's Questions

1. What *precisely* is the sceptic questioning?
2. Is there substantial doubt?
3. Is the sceptic crying for the moon?
4. Sceptic does not really believe—Why not more solipsists?
5. Is the scepticism selective?:
   5.1 Can the boundary be described?
   5.2 Can the boundary be justified?
   5.3 Does it depend on egocentric terms?
6. What alternative position is being offered?

Chapter 4
Explanation and Cause

§4.1   Explanation
§4.2   Why?
§4.3   BeCauses
§4.4   Hume on the Meaning of Cause
§4.5   The Concept of Causal Cause
§4.6   Causal Necessity
§4.7   The Epistemology of Causal Laws
§4.8   Discovering Causal Connexions
§4.9   Causal Reductionism

§4.1 Explanation

Explanation plays a fundamental *rôle* in our understanding of reason and reality. "Inference to the Best Explanation" is a form of reasoning we often adopt, the cogency of which has been defended against the sceptics. It is also a mark of reality.[1]

The search for the ultimate explanation of all things is a driving force in intellectual enquiry. But our ordinary ideas of explanation are confused. We are not clear whether it is only something psychological, or is a deep feature of the nature of things. Although in the preceding chapters we have encountered different sorts of explanation, we sometimes are impelled to hold that there is *au fond* only one basic type of explanation, to which all others should be, in principle at least, reducible. And if there are several varieties of explanation, we are unclear how they are related. Can different sorts of explanation be compatible, if they are genuinely different? Or do some supersede others, or undercut them?

---

[1] item 6 in lists in §8.2, pp.225 and 228.

§4.2 Why?

Explanations are answers to questions, in most cases the question 'Why?' It is, as we have seen, a question easy to ask but difficult to answer, even if, unlike the sceptic, we are willing to wait for one. One fundamental reason, to which I shall return later, is that since explanations are answers to questions, and questions depend on the concepts used in formulating them, and since, as we have seen, the range of concepts available to us is open-ended, the range of possible explanations is open-ended too.[2] Even with unproblematic concepts, it is often difficult to know what sort of answer is being sought. Much depends on the exact form of the question: the question: 'Why are you here?' looks for a different answer from the question: 'Why are you here at the same time as me?'[3] Equally important are the assumptions about what can be taken for granted and about what we think needs explaining: sometimes it is enough to explain that the event being asked about is fairly typical, the sort of thing that often happens; but another questioner may be asking why there should be such a regularity. In the ancient world it was taken for granted that things fell, and only when arrows and javelins went upwards were special explanations called for, and given in terms of some inertial force. If an explanation was demanded for the regular tendency of things to fall, it was couched in terms of the natural *nisus*—things had to go to their proper place, which was somewhere below where they were now. It was Galileo's great achievement to reverse this assumption, and to maintain that being at rest or moving in a straight line was the natural state of affairs for a material object, and that it was deviations from that natural state which required explanation. In so far as the javelin went straight, no explanation was called for: what we needed to explain was why the javelin, and all other heavy bodies, tended to fall. Newton's universal law of gravitation offered an answer, but raised further questions he was unable to answer. Einstein provided an answer, and explained why gravitational mass was the same as inertial mass, by redefining straight lines in terms of geodesics in a curved spacetime. Each 'Why?' we ask is asked

---

[2] See above, §2.10, and below §4.9, and §13.7.

[3] See Peter Lipton, *Inference to the Best Explanation*, London, 1991, chs.3 and 5, esp.pp.35ff., for an illuminating discussion of "contrastive" explanation of a fact set against a "foil".

against a background of unasked 'Why?'s, and each answer that is given to a 'Why?' gives room for further 'Why?'s.

The context and the interests of the questioner are also important. In a law court the issue is the ascription of responsibility; the historian is not trying to determine whom to blame, but to understand how the fears and intentions of many men conduced to a particular outcome. Different emotional attitudes to events give rise to different intellectual thrusts in demands for explanation. Unwelcome events are ones where we are disposed to wonder whether they had to happen; in asking 'Why?', we are seeking reasons why they had, necessarily, to happen: with other surprising cases we may be concerned only to work out how such an event could possibly have happened—particularly in history, we are often concerned to answer "How possibly?" questions rather than "Why necessarily?" ones, as Professor Dray calls them,[4] The difference between "Why, necessarily?" and "How possibly?" questions is of great importance in metaphysics too. Often we feel that there must be an answer to a "How possibly?" question, for else the universe is mysterious and irrational. But it is easy then to slip into thinking that the answer is an answer to a "Why, necessarily?" question, and conclude that everything must be as it is, and that there is no freedom for us to order our affairs as we think best. Many arguments for determinism are based on some equivocation between "How possibly?" and "Why, necessarily?" questions, and we shall need to keep the distinction clearly in mind when unravelling the different arguments for reductionism.[5]

---

[4] W.H.Dray, *Laws and Explanation in History*, Oxford, 1957, ch.6; and W.H.Dray, "Explanatory Narrative in History", *The Philosophical Quarterly*, **4**, 1954, pp.15-27.

[5] See below, §13.7.

§4.3 BeCauses

Aristotle distinguished four beCauses.[6]

> Aristotle's Four BeCauses:
> 1. Material
> 2. Formal
> 3. Efficient
> 4. Final

These sorts of explanation are among those we commonly use. We explain why something is blue by saying that it is made of copper sulphate. Biologists use Formal[7] explanations when they classify specimens, and doctors when they diagnose diseases. Aristotle's Efficient explanation, when we explain an effect by citing an antecedent cause that made it happen, is mis-termed: 'efficient' has a different sense in modern English; Aristotle uses the word τὸ ποιοῦν (*to poioun*) the making or maker. Modern philosophers speak of a "causal" explanation, which is often held to be the pre-eminent type of explanation. Biologists often explain organs by reference to the function they perform, and many human actions can be explained by their purpose, or the end they were intended to achieve. These Final beCauses are now known as teleological explanations.

Formal explanations have been criticized as not being informative: "Why does opium send you to sleep?" "Because it has a *virtus dormativa*." does not give the questioner the answer he was looking for. But often to identify and classify is informative. The doctor's diagnosis can be re-assuring, even though it does not explain why the disease produces the symptoms it does, and by itself offers no cure. Taxonomy is a respectable part of biology, geology and chemistry. It does not explain everything, but is a necessary first step to formulating further questions.

Aristotle sometimes seemed to think that all human action was directed towards achieving some end, but this was a mistake. We sometimes act rationally—in expressing gratitude, for example—without having any ulterior motive: we should, therefore, recognise rational explanations—why someone did something—as a separate

---

[6] Aristotle *Physics* II,3, esp. 194b15-195a26 or *Metaphysics* IV,2; 1013a24-b28; see W.D.Ross, *Aristotle*, London, 1923, pp.71-75.

[7] from Plato's theory of Forms: *Phaedo* 97b-99c.

type of explanation, not always to be subsumed under teleological explanation. Many thinkers, however, are reluctant to accept rational explanations as a separate category. It is easy to be cynical about gratitude, and explain it a means of securing further favours in the future. There are, however, other actions and beliefs which it is difficult for the cynic to explain away in terms of ulterior motives. But these, it is maintained, can be reduced to a purely causal explanation. After all, if a man acts out of gratitude or righteous indignation, we can say that his gratitude or indignation *made* him act as he did. But it is a different sort of 'make' from the 'make' of causal causes. The difference becomes apparent if we consider our reaction to counter-examples. If there is a well-established counter-example to some causal law—if we put a kettle on the fire and it does not boil—we have to revise our laws of nature. But if I fail to show gratitude, no great theories are in jeopardy; it is just that I am not the man people thought I was, but simply a weak, ungrateful specimen of humanity. "The heart is deceitful above all things, and desperately sick" men say of me when they hear of my ingratitude. In making up my mind to do something, I remain free, until I have actually done it, to change my mind. Rational explanations, therefore, are different from causal ones.[8]

We need to expand Aristotle's list further. Explanations vary depending on the focus of the question. A good example is furnished by the bagatelle arrangement in the figure on next page.

Thermodynamics depends essentially on considering not individual molecules, but *ensembles* of them, and calculating the statistical properties of large numbers of un-itemised molecules. Similarly in a running stream, we do not want and are not able to track the movement of individual molecules of water, but note the continuing existence of certain eddies or whirlpools, and may seek and find explanations of these. Often we shift the focus of our questions without realising it. The difference between biological and physical explanation is largely a difference of focus. The biologist focuses his attention on organisms, populations and species, concepts of which the physicist knows nothing, while the physicist concentrates upon atoms and waves, which to the biologist are only of marginal concern.

---

[8] This point is well made by G.H. von Wright, "The Logic and Epistemology of the Causal Relation", in P.Suppes, *et al.*, eds. *Logic, Methodology and Philosophy of Science*, Amsterdam, 1973; reprinted in E.Sosa and M.Tooley, *Causation*, Oxford, 1993, ch.6, pp.105-124, esp.§10, pp.121-124.

§4.3   Explanation and Cause   105

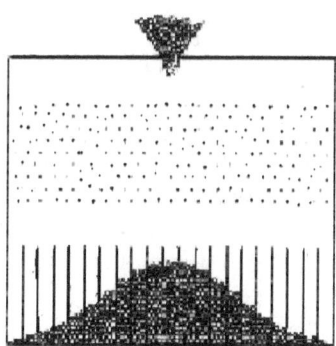

Bagatelle Balls

Bagatelle balls are introduced at the top of a board, and run down through rows of more or less evenly spaced pins, and are collected in boxes at the bottom of the board. If we ask where individual balls will go, or, after the event, why a particular ball ended up in a particular box, we can give no explanation. But if we ask about the collective distribution, we can both predict, with overwhelming probability, and *ex post facto* explain, its over-all Gaussian shape.

Thus biologists explain the oscillations in populations of predators and their prey, say Canadian lynxes and hares, in terms of shortage of food resulting in a reduction of the size of the lynx population, which then allows the unpredated hares to multiply, thereby inducing an explosion in the size of the lynx population.[9] The explanation is convincing, but it is difficult to see how it could be "reduced" to a chemical or physical one.[10]

These different types of explanation have been described as "bottom-up" and "top-down" causation.[11] The jaws of a worker termite are extremely well constructed. If we ask 'why?', we shall be told by the biochemist about the properties of the proteins of

---

[9] J.Dupré, "The Disunity of Science", *Mind*, **92**, 1983, pp.321-346.

[10] See below, §4.9 and §13.7.

[11] I am indebted to Arthur Peacoke for this point, which he made in private conversation. See further, A.Peacocke, *Theology for a Scientific Age*, Oxford, 1990, esp. ch.3, §3.2.b, pp.57-58. See also D.T.Campbell, "Downward Causation in Hierarchical Systems", in F.J.Ayala and T.Dobzhansky, *Studies in the Philosophy of Biology*, London, 1974.

which they are composed. The biologist, however, will tell a different story, about how natural selection has favoured those organisms with the jaws best suited to their life-style. Each of these accounts is explanatory. Both are talking about the same part of the material universe, but are giving different sorts of explanation, because of the difference of concepts employed.

The dependence of explanations on concepts is of crucial importance. Explanations are answers to questions, and questions depend on the concepts used in formulating them, and if, as I shall argue,[12] the range of concepts available to us is open-ended, the range of possible explanations is open-ended too.

If there are irreducibly different types of explanation, there are correspondingly irreducible differences of inexplicability. It is easy not to realise this, because we often use the positive word 'random', not realising that it is an essentially negative concept, opposed to 'explicable'. Arguments against free will often turn on an equivocation in what is to be accounted random. No defence of free will, it is alleged, can be based on the indeterminism of quantum mechanics, since if it were the case that micro-processes in our brains were random, our actions would then be random, and not ones we could be held responsible for. Thus Professor Dennett argues:

> The Libertarian could not have wanted to place indeterminism at the end of the agent's assessment and deliberation. It would be insane to hope that after all rational deliberation had terminated with an assessment of the best available course of action, indeterminism would then intervene to flip the coin before action . . . . [13]

But the explicability that quantum mechanics denies is some sort of physical explicability, whereas the explicability that responsibility requires is a rational explicability, in which the agent explains his actions and the reasons for them. These are very different types of explanation, and it is not to be assumed that the absence of one implies the absence of the other.[14]

---

[12] §4.9.

[13] D.Dennett, *Brainstorms*, Brighton, 1981, and Penguin, 1997, p.295.

[14] See below, §13.4; see also J.R.Lucas, *The Freedom of the Will*, Oxford, 1970, pp.55-59, 109-110.

> **Questions about Explanantion**
> 1. Is Aristotle's list complete?   No
> 2. Are there only a limited number of types of explanation? No
> 3. Can all explanations be reduced to explanations of one type? No
> 4. Does there being an explanation of one type preclude there being an explanation of another type?   No

§4.4 Hume on the Meaning of Cause

Hume complained that he had no idea of cause, since he could have no impression of one. But we do have a concept of cause. We use the word frequently, and though we may be at a loss to give an exact account of its meaning, we think we have a rough understanding of what we mean. Hume confused the concept of cause with the conditions of its application. Both were called "ideas". But my idea *of* causality—of what it is in general to be a cause—is quite different from its application in a particular case— my idea *that* this event is the cause of that. My entitlement to say that this event is the cause of that rests upon various statements in the indicative mood in the past and present tenses: but the concept of cause involves predictions in the future tense, necessity, and certain counterfactual conditionals. I base my assertion that cyanide causes death on reported instances of death following the ingestion of cyanide: but in actually making the assertion, I predict the outcome of people taking cyanide in time to come, impute to it some natural necessity, and commit myself to a number of counterfactual conditionals to the effect that if such and such a person were to take cyanide, he would die.

Hume's account of the meaning of cause yields further insight into the meaning of meaning, and clinches the refutation of the Verification Theory of Meaning in Chapter One.[15] It shows that concepts are different from conditions of application. The evidence for a causal claim must be expressed in the indicative mood and in the present and past tenses, but the content of the claim goes into the future tense and into other moods than the indicative. In going from the evidence to the conclusion that C causes E, we are going

---

[15] §1.2.

> **Hume on Causality**
> Hume makes two valid points about causal connexion:
> 1. There is no analytically necessary connexion between cause and effect;
> 2. The connexion between cause and effect is not perceived by the senses.
> —oOo—
> Hume has run together two different questions:
> 1. What does 'cause' mean? (What is our *idea of* causality?)
> 2. What are the conditions under which the term can be correctly applied? (When are we entitled to have the *idea that* A is the cause of B?)
>
> (1) is an analysis of the *concept* of cause; (2) is an account of the *criteria of applicability*. The word 'idea' can mean either an idea *of* (a concept) or an idea *that* (a proposition).

beyond what we are given, and are sticking our necks out. This is a paradigm instance of the claim made in Chapter One,[16] that we typically make statements that go beyond the evidence for them. The Verification Theory of Meaning is entirely misconceived. It cannot accommodate predictions, statements about other minds, or unobserved objects, it gives a distorted account of causality, and—perhaps the most convincing example of its inadequacy—it cannot account for simple mathematics.

According to the Intuitionists—the Verificationists in the philosophy of mathematics—the meaning of a mathematical proposition is given by its "assertibility conditions". But many people know Pythagoras' theorem, while finding it difficult to prove. Are we to say that they do not know Pythagoras' theorem—not even if they use 3-4-5 triangles to mark out a tennis court—unless they can produce one of the forty seven proofs of the theorem? And can we make sense of there being different proofs of the same theorem unless the meaning of the theorem is separable from that of the proof? I can understand Fermat's Last Theorem though I cannot understand Andrew Wiles' proof of it. Those mathematicians who can understand it no doubt have a deeper understanding than they did before. But they understood well enough what the theorem stated to be excited at the news of its being proved. And

---

[16] §1.2, pp.7,8.

§4.4   *Explanation and Cause*   109

it is difficult to understand what Wiles himself was doing in the years he spent looking for a proof, if he could not know what he was looking for until he had found it.

A similar mistake is made in arguing for the Frequency Theory of Probability. The evidence on which probability judgements are based is, very often, the frequency of some sort of occurrence within an observed collection of instances. But to maintain that this is what probability judgements *mean* leads to absurd complications. Similarly it has been argued that statements about other minds are really statements about the overt behaviour on the basis of which such statements are made.[17]

In each case we need to distinguish the evidence for the assertions I make and the actual meaning of what I say. The evidence is what is available to me, and is characteristically partial and incomplete. The meaning is public, and is constituted by the conventions governing the use of the words in my assertion. It is largely determined by what other statements my assertion implies, and what other statements my assertion contradicts. It is quite possible for a statement to turn out true, although there were no good grounds for asserting it: I may guess that Eclipse will win the Derby, though I know nothing about horses, and have not had contact with those who do. Equally, though more puzzlingly, a statement may turn out false in spite of there having been excellent grounds for asserting it. The doctor had every reason to say that the patient would be able to go to the ball in a week's time, but a drunken motorist mowed him down the next day.[18]

Fundamental Feature of Meaning

When I say something I stick my neck out, and claim *more than* the evidence on which I base my claim.

If I claim that the fire caused the kettle to boil, I may subsequently be shown to be wrong, even though I had good evidence for making the claim.

---

[17] See below, §6.10, §14.2.

[18] See further, S.E.Toulmin, *The Uses of Argument*, Cambridge, 1958, for illuminating discussion.

Hume's mistake about the meaning of cause is a paradigm. Once we understand how he was confused, we can avoid similar confusions in many other branches of philosophy.

§4.5 The Concept of Causal Cause

Once we accept the point that the meaning of a word may be different from the criteria for its correct application, Hume's difficulties no longer worry us. But still, we may ask how we come by the concept, and how it is related to other concepts we ordinarily use.

In our everyday life as agents we often bring things about; we make things happen and sometimes prevent things happening that otherwise would have happened. I make the pot boil, or, more grandly, I cause the pot to boil, by putting it on the fire; and you take care, by placing a fireguard in front of it, that the fire does not set the furniture alight. Often we have to use appropriate means to bring about desired ends. I light the fire by selecting dry wood and tinder, and getting them alight before putting on damp logs from the woodstack. We find it natural to say that we caused both the intermediate means and the ultimately desired state of affairs, and to construe the verb 'to cause' as expressing a transitive relation: I caused the pot to boil by causing a match to ignite, which caused the kindling to catch fire, which caused the fire to burn, which caused the pot to boil. We attribute to the intermediate means the same causal powers as we exercised ourselves in bringing about those means, and through them the ends that we sought to achieve.[19] The notion is crude, and a determined analyst can subject it to the death of a thousand questions. It remains, however, crudely robust. Rather than querying it away, we should accept it as useful, repair its inadequacies, and refine it, when necessary, to occupy a comparable position in our more sophisticated discourse.

The concept of cause I acquire through myself causing things to happen is temporally directed, explanatory, local and singular. I initiate action, typically bringing about my ultimate end by intermediate means, and the reason why it happened is that I decided

---

[19] G.H.von Wright uses the word 'manipulate', which expresses the point well; we manipulate means so as to bring about the desired end. See his "The Logic and Epistemology of the Causal Relation", in P.Suppes, et al., eds. *Logic, Methodology and Philosophy of Science*, Amsterdam, 1973; reprinted in E.Sosa and M.Tooley, *Causation*, Oxford, 1993, ch.6, pp.105-124, esp.§§8,9, pp.118-121.

§4.5   Explanation and Cause   111

that it should. Causes come before their effects, are spatiotemporally connected with them, and to a limited extent explain why they come to pass. Causal explanation implies temporal priority. Explanations need to be informative, and therefore compact. In the language of Cybernetics, they need to have more negative entropy than what they are explaining. I can explain the ripples on a pond by there having been a stone thrown in, but if I reversed the direction of time, and tried to explain them by a fortuitous harmony of movements at the pond's edge conspiring to create concentric ripples all converging on a centre so as to propel a stone upwards and away from the pond altogether, my purported explanation would lack explanatory force because it stood more in need of explanation than what it was supposed to explain.

Causes can be singular. Davidson is right in holding, against the opinion of most philosophers, that a singular causal relation is perfectly intelligible.[20] The concept of a singular one *is* intelligible. Quite apart from the cases where I did it, or you tell me that you did it, some primitive tribes are animists and ascribe agency—which may be completely arbitrary—to everything. It may be superstitious and mistaken, but it is perfectly possible to think that all events are the actions of deities. I forgot to clean my teeth this morning, so the gods made me fall down as I ran across the playground, and graze my knee. Events cause other events, in accordance with the inscrutable ordinances of the gods, who may sometimes overlook my misdemeanours, and on other occasions visit my innocent actions with penal consequences. Singular causation is a coherent concept, and can be defended on metaphysical grounds. Some philosophers seek to explicate time in terms of it. Indeed, granted very few additional axioms, it is possible to derive the Special Theory from a simple transitive asymmetric spatiotemporally continuous causal relation.[21]

Sources of our concept of causal cause

1. First-personal experience of making things happen.

---

[20] D.Davidson, "Causal Relations", *Journal of Philosophy* **64**, 1967, pp.691-703; reprinted in D.Davidson, *Essays on Actions and Events*, Oxford, 1980; and in E.Sosa and M.Tooley, *Causation*, Oxford, 1993, ch.4, pp.75-87.

[21] See further below, §10.2.

Although intelligible, the concept of a singular cause is difficult to use. The inscrutable ordinances of the gods *are* inscrutable, and although someone might have privileged access to their counsels, in practice we need less arcane knowledge if we are to be able to chart our course in the secular world. If I am to achieve my ends by bringing about the appropriate means, I must be able to reckon that means of a recognisable sort will result in a state of affairs of a sort that I do want to obtain. Otherwise I could not cause ends to occur by causing the appropriate means. Admittedly, life might still be possible: there are primitive tribes who sow seeds because that is the right thing to do in spring, and gather harvest because that is what is always done in autumn; but then we say that these tribes have no concept of cause and effect. To have the concept and be able to use it, one must be able to generalise—to universalise—a little, and reckon that things of this sort cause consequences of that sort. At least so far as macroscopic natural phenomena are concerned, we apply and understand causes and effects as instances of *general types* that are connected by some causal law.

Generality is implied not only by the practical requirements of manipulability, but by the desire for explanation. We not only use causal causes to make things happen, but invoke them to explain why things happen. Even in the superstitious example there was some suggestion of failing to clean one's teeth each morning *being bad*: although the gods might have made me fall down in the playground, because I *had* done my morning exercises, or because I *had* done my homework last night, I should be so much at a loss to understand why these virtuous activities should have been visited with untoward consequences, that I should not pick them out as potential causes of my misfortune. If causal causes are to explain, they must identify some antecedent condition as the sort of thing that could be a cause; causes we can discover and use must in some way be universalisable. Thus though singular causes are logically possible—it does make sense to say that this caused that—there are strong conceptual pressures in favour of some sort of generality.

Sources of our concept of causal cause

1. First-personal experience of making things happen.
2. Explaining why things happen.

§4.5 *Explanation and Cause* 113

The concept of cause I gain from my first-personal experience of making things happen carries with it a notion of necessity. But means are third-personal. What sense can I give to the means bringing about the ends? They have no purposes, and form no intentions. But they can necessitate. The fire has no intention of making the pot hot, but it makes it hot all the same. Under normal conditions, if the pot is put upon the fire, it cannot be otherwise than that the pot gets hot. Causal necessity implies universality, but is more than it. Necessity is what distinguishes causal laws from accidental generalisations. It might just happen to be the case that every time I had spilt the salt, I had subsequently suffered bad luck, but I could still maintain that it was only a coincidence, and deny that spilling the salt caused the bad luck. To claim that there *was* a causal connexion, I should have to claim not only that on those occasions when I actually spilt the salt, I subsequently suffered bad luck, but that on any other occasion, *if* I had spilt the salt, *then* I *would have* suffered bad luck. To assert a causal connexion is to go beyond the actual, and to make claims about possible cases as well. The counter-factual 'if I had spilt the salt, then I would have suffered bad luck' follows from 'my spilling the salt necessitated my suffering bad luck', but not from 'whenever I spilt the salt I actually did suffer bad luck'. The necessity of causal laws follows also from their ambition to explain. Although sometimes the question being asked is a 'How possibly?' rather than a 'Why necessarily?' one, the modal force of rationality is usually towards necessity rather than possibility. We understand why something happened by coming to understand why it had to happen.

Sources of our concept of causal cause

1. First-personal experience of making things happen.
2. Explaining why things happen.
3. Third-personal experience of means making ends happen.

---

§4.6 Causal Necessity

Someone might protest, on behalf of Hume, that he had no idea of causal or natural necessity: the concept was not one he had been able to take on board. An explanation is owed of how we come by such a concept. Although Hume was right to point out that causal necessity is not logical (analytic logical) necessity, and that we cannot acquire the concept of causal necessity from simple impressions alone, he was wrong to despair of our ever being able to have the concept of causal necessity at all. It can be extrapolated from our first-personal experience. I make things happen. I have a concept of things being made to happen, and can apply it where it is not I who have made something to happen, but something else, ascribing to it a power I know myself to have. Modern philosophers are queasy at such anthropomorphism, but toy with the possibility that we have an "innate idea", that we had evolved so that our brains were wired up in such a way that we instinctively sought causal connexions, and jumped to conclusions when the evidence provided us with a springboard, in the same way as we seem to be hard-wired to be able to learn languages. Psychologists might be able to devise experiments to determine whether this was the case.[22] If a sense of causal necessity is innate, it could be the case that some people are born without it, in much the same way as some people are born without being able to discriminate red from green. This would explain why Quine and many other mid-twentieth-century philosophers reported that they could not understand what 'causal necessity' or 'natural necessity' meant.

Less problematic is the suggestion that we learn to apply causal concepts by trial and failure: we learn that no matter how hard we

---

[22] Compare J.L.Mackie, *Problems from Locke*, Oxford, 1976, ch.7, p.211, "at the core of <causality> there is the notion expressed by the counterfactual conditional, the notion of what would have happened if this had not, and I have argued that this arises primitively from imaginative projection and analogizing; our tendency to do this and hence to think causally may well be another inborn propensity." See also J.L.Mackie, *The Cement of the Universe*, Oxford, 1974 (pbk. 1989), pp.55-57; see also, Peter Lipton, *Inference to the Best Explanation*, London, 1991, pp.6-8,15-17; N.Chomsky, *Aspects of the Theory of Syntax*, Cambridge, Mass., 1965 ch.1, §8, esp. pp.58-59, N.Chomsky, *Knowledge of Language*, New York, 1986; T.Kuhn, *The Structure of Scientific Revolutions*, Chicago, 1977; and T.Kuhn, *The Essential Tension*, Chicago, 1977, esp. chs. 1 and 2.

§4.6   Explanation and Cause   115

try, some concatenations of events cannot be brought about, and hence, equivalently, that others are inevitable: if no matter how hard I try, I cannot immerse my hand in water without its getting wet, then I know also that the truism "water wets" is an unavoidable law of nature. Although we cannot see necessity, we can learn it from unsuccessful experience. It is a concomitant of our activity as agents. I try, and not succeeding at first, I try and try again. But if, whatever I do, and however much I try, I still do not succeed, I generalise from these particular failures, and conclude that I shall always fail: I cannot succeed, because it is impossible. I may be wrong, but the conclusion is intelligible enough to give content to a concept of natural impossibility, and hence of natural necessity, distinct from the impossibility and necessity that arises from deductive logic. In particular, if certain conjunctions—A without B, taking cyanide and not dying—appear to be impossible, we can reformulate in terms of necessity, and say that A necessitates B, taking cyanide necessarily is followed by death. We thus have a concept of necessity which we can apply not only to occasions when we cause things to happen, but to occasions when things themselves—or events, or whatever—cause other things to happen.

The rational necessity cited in the previous section *is* a respectable concept. It is only in a very limited sense of 'logical' that there is no logical necessity for a cause to be followed by its effect. True, there is no inconsistency in supposing the cause not to have been followed by the effect: it is not a breach of the rules of language to speak of the cause not being followed by the effect. But once we move on from first-order logic, logical necessity is not confined to analytic necessity. We use the word 'logic' in a variety of senses to mark a variety of contrasts. Thus in a passage quoted in the next section (§4.6) Tolman contrasts the inner logicality of the Special Theory with experimental verification, where logicality embraces much more than first-order logic: the Special Theory is to be adopted on grounds of symmetry, continuity and consilience with other theories.[23] These *a priori* considerations not only lead us to adopt the theory, independently of empirical evidence, but confer on it a sense of somehow being necessarily true, and hence also on any conclusions drawn from it. Many people have thought that Newtonian mechanics was necessarily true—Kant offered arguments purporting to prove it. Believing that, they have believed

---

[23] R.C.Tolman, *Relativity, Thermodynamics and Cosmology*, Oxford, 1950, §29, p.53, quoted in §4.7, *ad fin.* on pp.119-120 below.

that if one croquet ball hits another, that other one *must* be moved by the impact. Empiricists may contend that the *a priori* considerations adduced by Kant and others are fallacious. Suppose, for the sake of argument, that they are right: that would only show that many people were wrong in their attributions of necessity, not that they did not have the concept. I may believe Newtonian mechanics on the authority of my school teacher, not on account of any observations I have made or heard about. But I still shall think that momentum *must* be conserved, even though my warrant for so believing will not stand up to sustained criticism. I shall have the concept of causal necessity, even though I am not, according to the empiricists, applying it correctly. Different people may acquire their notions of necessity in different ways: but the obligation to explain how we could come by such a notion has been discharged. Some people may still claim not to be able to understand causal necessity, but must speak for themselves alone.

Sources of necessity
1. First-personal experience: I made it happen.
2. Innate (hard-wired) intellectual reflex (Compare Chomsky).
3. Trial and failure: impossibility is necessity's other face.
4. Rational necessity of consequences of an accepted explanation.

We can give content to the concept of causal necessity, but it is another matter to justify the inference from a bare generalisation to a modal conclusion. Although in practice we seldom have any doubts, in principle it seems a hazardous step to go from a simple generalisation

$$(\forall x)(A(x) \to Z(x))$$

to a causal law, perhaps expressed by a modal proposition

$$\Box(\forall x)(A(x) \to Z(x))$$

where $\Box$ is some sort of natural or causal necessity. One justification is that if a generalisation is due to a causal law, the generalisation is *explained*. It is not just an accidental happenstance, but an underlying feature of the universe that we have come upon. There is a parallel with sense data and material objects.[24] At first sight we may have difficulty in making sense of a scene, but if we can construe a jumble of edges and surfaces as aspects of a building seen from a strange angle, we can comprehend the whole, and see it all as it is. Causal connexions are four-dimensional analogues of material objects. Instead of solidity and impenetrability, they present necessity and ineluctability, and, once posited, make sense of otherwise disparate phenomena. Often the causal law fits in with other laws we have already discovered; our knowledge of nature is cumulative; we can apply causal principles we have already discovered to assess not only the relevance of some factors, but the plausibility of some proposed generalisations.

The inference from a simple generalisation to a causal law, though hazardous, can be defended; but always there is the worrying possibility that our generalisation is only a coincidence, and there is no causal connexion at all. This worry we often resolve by experiment. We contrive to bring about A when it otherwise would not have occurred, and see whether it is accompanied or followed by Z: if it is not, we have falsified the putative generalisation, $(\forall x)(A(x) \to Z(x))$ and can end that line of enquiry; if it is accompanied by Z, we become confident that we are dealing with a causal law, not just a coincidence. Our reasoning is that our intervention was entirely external to the course of events we were examining, and any chance concomitances they may have presented. It might conceivably have been the case that the initial state of the universe happened to be one in which every occurrence of A is accompanied or followed by Z; but we have now intervened *de novo*, thereby disrupting any chance concomitances there happened to be. Anything that survives our interventions is solid, just as resistance to our probing with a stick enables us to feel out the shape of objects at the bottom of a muddy pool.

The argument from experiment assumes free will on the part of the experimenter. On a determinist view of the world, the argument is open to the objection that the same antecedent configuration of the universe that resulted in the experimenter altering things so as to bring about A, had as its consequence also that Z should occur too. In a determinist universe the long arm of coincidence could extend through the experimenter's mind to have him choose to make A happen on just the occasion when Z was going to happen anyway. Determinism, we shall argue later, is false.[25] It is desirable that it be false for many other reasons, but also for this ironical one, that it is only on the assumption of its falsity that we can assure ourselves that seeming causal laws really are causal laws, and not accidental generalisations.

---

[24] See further below, §6.7.

[25] In §13.4.

§4.7 The Epistemology of Causal Cause

The concept of a causal cause has different facets, and so there are different ways of establishing the existence of a causal connexion.

We can have first-personal knowledge of causal causes. I know who made the field flood: I did; I opened the sluice, and let the water in. Other agents may tell me what they have effected, and I can, less reliably, ascribe personal causality to some agents on the strength of their non-verbal behaviour, and attribute to them the reasons they, presumably, acted on. Many causal explanations are personal. Historians, novelists and lawyers offer explanations of the events they recount. These explanations can be complex. Just as I, in the first person, can be aware of many reasons for and against a course of action, so others can third-personally attribute similarly complicated motives to explain what I did. Language affords us an infinite variety of avowal and ascription. Such explanations depend on the possibility of communication, even if in some instances based on behaviour alone.

Other causal explanations are not personal. We should not ascribe agency to natural phenomena, and any knowledge we have of their causal powers must come from some impersonal source. Impersonal sources cannot communicate with us to tell us what they are doing, nor can we empathize with them, and ascribe reasons for their behaviour. We can, however, have recourse to observation, since things, unlike people, are relatively uncomplicated, we can hope to multiply instances, and make up by breadth of observation what we lack in depth of understanding.

Empiricists claim that repeatable observation is the one and only way we can gain knowledge of natural causes. That goes too far. Although our knowledge of causal laws is based on empirical observation, some weight is also given to rational considerations, which go beyond the confines of deductive logic. Even Hume allowed that spatiotemporal contiguity[26] was a mark of causal connexion:

> I find in the first place, that whatever objects are consider'd as causes or effects, are *contiguous*; and that nothing can operate in a time or a place, which is ever so little remov'd from those of its existence. Tho' distant objects may sometimes seem productive of each other, they are commonly found upon

---

[26] 'Contiguity' suggests discrete elements touching each other. In §§12.6 and 12.7 it is argued that time is continuous (and hence space), in which case it is spatiotemporal continuity that is in issue.

§4.7   Explanation and Cause   119

examination to be link'd by a chain of causes, which are contiguous among themselves, and to the distant objects; and when in any particular instance we cannot discover this connexion, we still presume it to exist. We may therefore consider the relation of CONTIGUITY as essential to that of causation; at least may suppose it such, according to the general opinion, till we can find a more proper occasion to clear up this matter, by examining what objects are or are not susceptible of juxtaposition and conjunction.[27]

We are guided also by powerful considerations of symmetry, simplicity, harmony and coherence with other laws. These weigh with us so heavily, that on occasion observations have been discounted. Einstein was confident what the result of the observation on the bending of the sun's rays would be; in the years from 1902 to 1926 the Michelson-Morley experiment was repeated many times, and yielded a positive result,[28] but these were attributed to experimental error; nobody abandoned the Special Theory, because it was so rational, so profound and had such great unifying power. As Tolman puts it:

> . . . the results are to be accepted not only on the basis of the experimental verification which they have received in those cases where it has been possible to test differences between the predictions of relativistic and Newtonian mechanics, but also on the basis of the inner logicality of the theory which has led to them and the harmony of this theory with the rest of physics. The achievement of this logicality and harmony depends on the reconciliation of so many factors that we can feel considerable confidence in accepting results of the theory when necessary prior to their experimental verification.[29]

Hume's concession and Tolman's argument refute extreme empiricism. Constant conjunction is not the sole path to knowledge of causal connexions and natural laws. But Tolman, as well as Hume, relies on empirical observation. Newtonian mechanics and the rest of physics have empirical consequences which have been verified by observation. Only if a theory leads to consequences

---

[27] David Hume, *A Treatise on Human Nature*, Bk. I, Part III, §II, p.75 in Selby-Bigge's edition; see also Bk.I, Part III, §XV, p.173.

[28] For full account see Michael Polanyi, *Personal Knowledge*, London, 1958, pp. 12-13; J.L.Synge, *Relativity, The Special Theory*, Amsterdam, 1958, pp. 161-2; and L.S.Swenson, *The Etherial Ether*, Texas, 1972.

[29] R.C.Tolman, *Relativity, Thermodynamics and Cosmology*, Oxford, 1950, §29, p.53.

which could (logically could) be wrong, is it relevant to our understanding of the natural world—a theory immune to refutation by counter-evidence would tell us nothing of substance about the way things are. It must be possible to envisage falsifying instances without falling into inconsistency. Reason may propose, but ultimately it is empirical observation that decides.

§4.8 Discovering Causal Connexions

Empiricism rules, but only with the aid of reason. Causes have consequences which are testable. If the prime evidence is repeatable observation, the underlying form of a causal law will be some sort of universal implication. A universal implication with simple truth-functional logic is a first stage towards testing a putative causal law, and its logic explains the rationale of Mill's Method of Difference and Method of Agreement.[30] Mill's Method of Difference is a systematic search for falsification of a putative causal law. Suppose it has been suggested that there is a causal law giving rise to the generalisation:

$$(\forall x)(A(x) \to Z(x))$$

In the observed instances there will be many other factors present:

$$A(1) \& B_i(1) \& C_j(1) \& \ldots \& Z(1)$$

$$A(2) \& B_i(2) \& C_j(2) \& \ldots \& Z(2)$$

$$A(3) \& B_i(3) \& C_j(3) \& \ldots \& Z(3)$$

$$A(4) \& B_i(4) \& C_j(4) \& \ldots \& Z(4)$$

$$\ldots$$

where B_i and C_j represent a number of different conditions. In Mill's Method of Difference we vary these, to see if Z still occurs. If on some occasion it does not, say

$$A(5) \& B_6(5) \& C_j(5) \& \ldots \& \neg Z(5)$$

---

[30] See, for example, G.H.von Wright, *A Treatise on Induction and Probability*, London, 1961, ch.4; J.R.Lucas, "Causation" in R.J.Butler, ed. *Analytical Philosophy*, Oxford, 1962, ch.2, pp.32-65; J.L.Mackie, *The Cement of the Universe*, Oxford, 1974, Appendix, pp.297-321; and J.R.Lucas, *Space, Time and Causality*, Oxford, 1984, ch.4, pp.44-67.

§4.8 Explanation and Cause 121

we have refuted the simple generalisation

$$(\forall x)(A(x) \to Z(x)),$$

and must either abandon it altogether, or replace it by one, say

$$(\forall x)((A(x)\&\neg B_6(x)) \to Z(x)),$$

which has not yet been falsified. Mill's Method of Difference thus enables us to refute or refine putative generalisations.

Mill's Method of Agreement enables us to pare down putative laws so as to remove redundant factors. We might have observed

$$A(1)\&B(1)\&C_j(1)\&\ldots\&Z(1),$$

and have supposed that the law was

$$(\forall x)((A(x)\&B(x)) \to Z(x)).$$

But if we vary the condition B, and observe

$$A(2)\&\neg B(2)\&C_j(2)\&\ldots\&Z(2),$$

we shall conclude that B was not an essential part of the sufficient condition of Z. A few moves in symbolic logic will replace B by $B \vee \neg B$, which is tautological, and therefore otiose. Instead of

$$(\forall x)((A(x)\&B(x)) \to Z(x)).$$

we shall have

$$(\forall x)((A(x)\&(B(x) \vee \&\neg B(x))) \to Z(x)),$$

that is to say

$$(\forall x)(A(x) \to Z(x)).$$

If altering some factor makes no difference, then it is reasonable to assume that all the other factors remain unaltered, and that this one factor is itself irrelevant. If altering that factor does make a difference, then again it is reasonable to assume that all the other factors remain unaltered, and that this one factor is at least part of the cause.

Mill's Methods have impeccable logic, but they presuppose certain assumptions, and need further assumptions still, if they are to be carried through to a definite result. They assume that there are many numerically distinct but qualitatively identical As, Bs, Cs and Zs, that is, that observations can be repeated in different places and at different times, and that it does not matter by whom they are made—that their personal hopes and fears will not affect the results. Natural science takes over the Valentian canon of the early church that causal truths should be recognisable *semper, ubique et ab omnibus*, and hence that a mere difference in time, place, or personal attitude, is not *per se* relevant to whether a causal connexion holds or not. This principle rigorously applied would determine the fundamental structure of the universe. Not only would it secure the "absolute conception" of reality,[31] but it would show that space must be Euclidean, since it is only in Euclidean space that objects and events remain invariant under translation and rotation—the transformations of the proper Euclidean group.[32] Many thinkers would be glad to establish that reality was, indeed, thus structured, but it cannot be argued for as a necessary presupposition of all inductive argument. We do not need absolute irrelevance, but only that differences of time, place, or personal attitude do not make *much* difference. It could be that orienting an experiment towards Mecca, or towards the Earth's Magnetic Pole, makes a difference; certainly some observers are better than others. But these factors do not make all that much of a difference. Cases are sufficiently similar to be comparable when working Mill's methods. We do not have to posit a Euclidean space to make causal knowledge possible, but only a space that is locally Euclidean. We could not apply Mill's methods in a space that was extremely contorted, but the somewhat gentle curvatures required by the General Theory in order to explain gravitation are perfectly compatible with our being able to carry out experiments and infer facts from repeated observations.

Granted these modified presuppositions, Mill's Methods offer the prospect of improving our generalisations, paring down redundant conditions, and winnowing out false ones; but by themselves do not reliably reach an end result we can rely on. There are too

---

[31] See Bernard Williams, *Descartes*, Harmondsworth, 1978, pp.65-67, 211-212, 245-249.

[32] See further below, §9.7.

§4.8   Explanation and Cause   123

many factors which could conceivably be relevant. In particular cases we can often discount many such factors by reason of other theories already well established, but we need some general anti-astrological canon of the irrelevance of remote factors, to warrant our ignoring innumerable factors throughout the universe, which could conceivably be causes, so that we can concentrate on those that are serious contenders for consideration.

The Irrelevance of the Remote entitles us to discount the influence of far distant causes, and to confine our attention to the more discoverable causes close at hand. But again we must not hold this to be an absolute principle. The explosion of a distant star might send an electromagnetic pulse that had devastating effects on Earth; and we are still "hearing" the rumbles of the Big Bang. We cannot rule out remote causes absolutely, but if they are mediated, we can take account of the intervening causes nearer at hand. We may take over Hume's requirement of spatiotemporal "contiguity" in the form of a Principle of Locality, which entitles us to disregard the causal influence of remote factors, *unless* mediated through near ones. The Principle of Locality does not rule out absolutely, and unreasonably, the possible relevance of remote factors, but, by insisting that their causal influence be mediated through the intervening interval, secures that our range of enquiry should be reasonably limited. Events at the Pole Star are remote, yet are not without effect on terrestrial navigators: but we do not have to consider what happened 44 light years away; it is enough that in the immediate vicinity of the navigator photons were arriving from a particular direction, and entered his eyes and stimulated the nerves in his retina. The Principal of Locality does not make astronomy impossible, but guards us against unmediated interference from the stars. The Principal of Locality, however, is neither an absolute principle,[33] nor an absolutely necessary presupposition of Mill's Methods: Newton's Law of Universal Gravitation posited a gravitational force that operated across a vacuum without any intermediate processes, and though strongly opposed, it was reluctantly accepted because supported by overwhelming empirical evidence; but its inverse square law implies that the gravitational influence of the stars is negligible, and is the same for all terrestrial events; and its being instantaneous secures us against having to consider the possible influence of temporally remote factors.

[33] See further below, §§9.7, 10.1 and 11.6.

Many thinkers have proposed a Principle of Limited Variety.[34] In contrast to the infinite variety of human affairs, natural phenomena are, we think, relatively simple. We fairly soon cut short suggestions of further possible factors we might test without claiming that they are inherently irrelevant. Originally it was hoped that with its aid, inductive arguments could be made deductively valid; but that, as we have seen, was an illusion.[35] Merely to state that the variety was limited would not entitle a researcher to hold that he had considered all the relevant possibilities, unless the number of relevant variations was given a definite value. But once we abandon the attempt to render inductive arguments deductive, we can construe the Principle of Limited Variety not as an unusable premise, but as a canon of inductive argument which articulates our attitude to natural phenomena, and enables us to discover plausible candidates for being causal laws.

Granted these assumptions we can tighten up Mill's methods, because we can now rationally discount the relevance of many unknown factors, particularly if we can do experiments and concentrate our attention on a single factor which we can alter at will. We can hope to reach a complete and exact account of the causal factors producing a given effect. But that may be more than we really want. Mackie distinguishes among the causal conditions, those on which we should focus our attention by contrast with those which we can largely take for granted. A cause, he says, is an insufficient but necessary part of an unnecessary but sufficient condition of the effect. The scientific exploration of causal explanation is important in its own right, but is not the only reason we seek to discover the causes of things. Often we are guided by practical considerations, and want to pick out from the causal complex revealed by Mill's methods the single factor most easy to manipulate, or the person to be held responsible for the outcome of the whole causal process. Lawyers go further still, distinguishing a *causa causans* from *conditiones sine qua non*. They are concerned to attribute responsibility and blame, as we often are in practical life. But these important matters do not concern us here.[36]

---

[34] J.M.Keynes, *A Treatise on Probability*, London, 1921, ch.xx.

[35] See above, §3.4.

[36] J.L.Mackie, *The Cement of the Universe*, Oxford, 1974, chs. 2 & 3; Peter Lipton, *Inference to the Best Explanation*, London, 1991, chs.4-7.

§4.9 Causal Reductionism

Although philosophers are ready to admit that there are many different types of explanation, they often suppose that one type is pre-eminent. Collingwood argues that some sort of final cause, as in "woman with a cause", is basic, and the modern sense of causal cause a late (and regrettable) development.[37] But most philosophers have held that causal causes are pre-eminent. Leibniz discusses Snell's Law of refraction and points out that Snell and Fermat derived it from the principle of least action:[38] "For when the rays observe in the same media the same proportion of the sines, this is found to be the easiest way, or at least the most determined, for passing from a given point in one medium to a given point in the other."[39] Leibniz claims that this is an instance of a final cause; and while allowing "that the way of efficient causes ... is indeed, deeper and in some fashion more immediate and *a priori*", reckons that "the way of final causes is easier, and is not infrequently of use for discerning important and useful truths which one would be a long time in finding by the other more physical route, . . "[40] Leibniz is wrong to see the principle of least action as a final cause, though right to note the importance of extremal principles as a form of explanation, which can be derived from causal explanation. Final causes can, however, be sometimes explained in terms of causal causes. Darwin's theory of evolution gives a schema for showing how final causes could be explanatory in a world that was entirely governed by causal laws.

The question arises whether the reductions outlined by Leibniz and Darwin can be extended to cover all forms of explanation. Can they all be reduced ultimately to causal explanation? Many think they can. F.H.C. Crick, maintains "the ultimate aim of the modern movement in biology is in fact to explain *all* biology in terms of physics and chemistry".[41] Many biologists oppose such a programme, and often scarcely bother to argue against it, rejecting

---

[37] R.G.Collingwood, *Metaphysics*, Oxford, 1940, Part IIIc, chs.XXIX-XXXII, pp.155-176.

[38] Leibniz, *Discourse on Metaphysics*, chs. XIX-XXII, tr. P.G.Lucas and L.Grint, Manchester, 1953, pp.32-40.

[39] ch.XXII, p.39.

[40] pp.38-39.

[41] F.H.C.Crick, *Of Molecules and Man*, Seattle, 1966, p.10.

it as obviously ridiculous. Their experience of their own disciplines convinces them that the explanations offered are quite all right as they stand, and in no need of being validated by being shown to be really special cases of some other sort of explanation. More than that, they hold that reductionism impugns the autonomy of the explanations they actually offer, and in some way undercuts their validity. Like the reductionists, the anti-reductionists adduce an argument from the success of science: the natural sciences other than physics have been very successful; they have been able to explain and illuminate our understanding. Other biologists, however, feel threatened by the claim that in principle all the things a biologist studies are completely explicable in terms of chemistry and physics. Even if in practice we accept that there are many different types of explanation, and use those explanations that are appropriate to the discipline and the problem under consideration, we are uncomfortable, at least in our metaphysical moments, with their independent co-existence, and feel that in the ultimate analysis the explanations provided by the physicists must be all-embracing, and must furnish us with a complete explanation of everything.

Metaphysical doctrines are at work. The 'must' is a metaphysical must, which overrides all contrary evidence of explanations that seem to resist reduction to physical ones. It is in part an ontological claim, about the nature of reality. the discussion of which must be deferred until Chapter Nine, in part a conceptual claim, about the nature of explanation, holding that in principle all explanations can be derived from a fundamental causal explanation. Certainly, with some explanations it is possible. There have been some successful reductions. Thermodynamics has been reduced Statistical Mechanics: granted Newtonian mechanics, some assumptions about the shapes and elasticity of molecules, and simple statistics, we can offer definitions of the concepts, and derive the principles of thermodynamics in an illuminating and satisfactory way. Genetics has been similarly reduced to the biochemistry of DNA. There have been many more partial reductions. The chemistry of the hydrogen atom has been largely explained by quantum mechanics. We understand some physiological processes because we understand the biochemistry of the reactions involved. The Logicists devised definitions of mathematical concepts in terms of simple logic; and even though the Logicist programme has been beset by problems, and cannot be adjudged a complete success as yet, it may still be amended and carried through to a successful completion. Similarly,

§4.9   Explanation and Cause   127

it is claimed, for all other disciplines. This is the doctrine of Physicalism. It is a doctrine of explanatory reductionism, holding that all other forms of explanation, useful though they may be in particular contexts, can be derived from physics, and are, essentially, only special cases of physical explanation.

But explanations are answers to questions, and so depend on the concepts used to frame the questions, and scientists do not naturally have the concepts of other sciences—it takes time to learn a science and to grasp its concepts. The weakness of conceptual reductionism is well put by Christopher Longuet-Higgins:

> In recent years there has been much interest among chemists in what are now called electrocyclic reactions... Along comes a physicist, expert in quantum mechanics, which, he maintains, explains all chemistry in principle, and we ask him for an explanation of electrocyclic reactions. Does he offer one? No. His first words are 'What *are* electrocyclic reactions?'. In order to answer the question, we shall have to introduce him to chemical concepts that are not part of his intellectual armoury, and even then he may not understand why we asked the question. Actually to answer it he has to become, for the moment at least, a chemist. Only by so doing can he see what principles of physics may be relevant to its answer. Insofar as physics is what physicists do when they are left to get on with their own work, chemistry is not part of physics in any important sense. It has its own concepts and its own problems, the concepts being those that are relevant to the problems. This, of course, is not to deny that physical principles can be brought to bear on chemical phenomena, but the questions must be asked at the higher level before they can be examined at the lower.[42]

Longuet-Higgins argues by example, and there are many others. Even within physics there are many concepts that could not be reduced to more basic ones. In the nineteenth century, it was often felt that we should not be able really to understand electromagnetism, unless we could produce a "mechanical" model, and much work was devoted to models of the ether as an elastic jellylike medium. In the end the concepts of electromagnetism were not "reduced" to those of Newtonian mechanics, but what should count as a physical concept was enlarged so as to include those of

---

[42] H.C.Longuet-Higgins, *The Nature of Mind*, Edinburgh, 1972, ch.2, pp.16-21, esp. p.19; reprinted in H.C.Longuet-Higgins, *Mental Processes*, Cambridge, Mass., 1987, ch.2, pp.13-18, esp.p.16.

electromagnetism. Even the example of thermodynamics is two-edged. Entropy cannot be explained simply by considering just one Newtonian system; rather, we have to consider an "*ensemble*" of them, and *ensemble* is not a Newtonian concept.[43]

For many thinkers the examples are decisive. But in our metaphysical moods, we may feel that they are not conclusive: at some future time, a cleverer thinker may devise adequate definitions of the concepts of each discipline in terms of those of a more basic one, so that in the end the physicalist programme may be carried through.

It is difficult to argue with *may-be*s. But we can show that the metaphysician's *may-be* cannot be universally successful. As with the hoped-for reduction of mathematics, the clinching argument is to be found in logic. Tarski showed that the concept of truth could not be expressed in a formal system of logic that met reasonable requirements of consistency and adequacy.[44] Hence, contrary to the teaching of many Positivists, truth cannot be defined in simple terms. Reductionism fails in this, crucial and seemingly promising, case, and thus fails to hold universally.

Tarski's theorem is recondite, and of no concern to most working scientists, who might maintain that the exception to reductionism was a purely academic one, and that for all practical purposes, reductionism still held good. But truth is not of arcane academic concern alone. The working scientist wants to commend his results as being true. Moreover, it is characteristic of human beings generally that they have a concept of truth, and care about it greatly. Reductionists are committed to the claim that it is in principle possible to explain all human action in terms of fundamental physical laws; but any purported explanation of a particular man's behaviour can be faulted; for some of the things he can see to be true are things he ought not to be able to produce as true, if his output was really determined entirely by mechanical causes.[45] The

---

[43] Of course, physicalism could be made true trivially, if the concepts of physics were enlarged to include the concepts of every science and discipline; but then it would be of no interest.

[44] See above, §2.10.

[45] "Minds, Machines and Gödel", *Philosophy*, XXXVI, 1961, pp.112-127; reprinted in Kenneth M.Sayre and Frederick J.Crosson, eds., *The Modeling of Mind*, Notre Dame Press, 1963, pp.269-270; and *Minds and Machines*, ed. Alan Ross Anderson, Prentice-Hall, 1954, pp.43-59. See also J.R.Lucas, *Freedom of the Will*, Oxford, 1970; Roger Penrose, *The Emperor's New Clothes*, Oxford, 1989; and Roger Penrose, *Shadows of the Mind*, Oxford, 1994.

§4.9 *Explanation and Cause* 129

argument is controversial, but carries conviction. A rational being cannot be represented by a Turing machine. Rational beings exist. So reductionism fails.

The argument against reductionism is a conceptual one. Concepts cannot always be reduced to more basic ones. And if concepts cannot, explanations cannot either, since explanations are answers to questions, and depend on the concepts used to formulate the questions. If the concepts cannot be translated into the terms of a supposedly more basic discipline, the explanations cannot be derived from the explanations of the supposedly more basic discipline.

The result is important, but limited. It rules out one sort of reductionism—explanatory reductionism we might call it—-which claims that all explanations can be reduced to one basic form, and in particular, it rules out physicalism, which claims that all explanations can be reduced to a Hempelian physical explanation in terms of a covering law and initial conditions.[46] But reductionism is often driven by ontological, rather than explanatory, considerations, holding that there is only one form of fundamental substance, and that everything that exists is merely a modification of that fundamental substance, and can be completely explained in terms of it. The arguments of this section do not touch that claim, which will be considered further in Chapter Thirteen. They do, however, have one further positive consequence: if explanations depend on questions, and questions on concepts, and there is no limit to the number of new concepts that we may come to have, there is no limit to the number of new questions that we can ask, and hence to the explanations that we could come to have. Logic rules out there being a Theory of Everything which cannot be further questioned. If there is an ultimate explanation, its ultimacy must depend not on our being unable to raise further questions, but on our not wanting to, because the explanation already given is so satisfying that questions we conceivably could raise no longer worry us.

---

[46] C.G.Hempel and P.Oppenheim, "The Logic of Explanation, *Philosophy of Science*, **15**, 1948, pp.135-175, reprinted in H.Feigl and M.Brodbeck, *Readings in the Philosophy of Science*, New York, 1953, pp.319-352; see also, C.G.Hempel, "The Function of General Laws in History", *The Journal of Philosophy*, **39**, 1942, pp.35-48, reprinted in H.Feigl and W.Sellars, *Readings in Philosophical Analysis*, New York, 1949, pp.458-471.

Chapter 5
Projectivism and Probability

§5.1 Projectivism
§5.2 Degrees of Belief
§5.3 The Marriage of Arithmetic with Boole
§5.4 Assigning Probabilities
§5.5 ... and Statistics
§5.6 The Limits of Ignorance
§5.7 Unprojected Reality

§5.1 Projectivism

Hume could not find any causal relation in the outside world, and concluded that it was something we projected onto the outside world. We had impressions of events, and by a sort of conditioned reflex came to expect the effect, having had an impression of the cause. Instead of causal relations being a feature of reality, they were projected onto reality by our minds. Hume did much the same in regard to secondary qualities and moral qualities. Colour is in the eye of the beholder, and is painted by him onto the world he sees, not something existing in the world in its own right. Similarly moral qualities are not out there in the world, but are ascribed to situations on the basis of our own feelings about them.

Kant can be seen as having done the same for space and time. He accepted Hume's sceptical critique, but whereas Hume thought it was just an empirical fact that human minds worked according to certain psychological laws, such as the association of ideas, Kant held that minds had to work in certain ways, as a matter of rational necessity, if they were to function as minds at all. Not only causality, but time and space were projected on reality by the mind: we do not have sense-experience of them, but project them, the one a condition of outer experience, the other a condition of inner experience, as a means of making sense of our experience generally. Space, time and causality are schemes, scaffolding, into which we use to fit experience. They are not given in experience, but chosen by us, and projected by us onto a world largely of our own creation. Since this is something we have to do if we are to make any sense of sense-experience at all, it is unobjectionable, and can be defended as a necessary and rational prerequisite of all thought. Synthetic *a priori* propositions are *fiats* we adopt for our

§5.1   *Projectivism and Probability*   131

own purposes about how the world is to be construed. They are like spectacles. We have to have them, but we need to recognise that they largely determine what we see.

Modern philosophers mostly follow Hume. Human psychology is what it is—though we should not be here if it had not proved reasonably effective for survival. They are sceptical about the possibility of knowledge and offer projectivist accounts of morality, secondary qualities—and probability. So far as morality is concerned, projectivism is an unsettling doctrine. At first sight it is wildly implausible: we just do not think that there is nothing objectively wrong with cruelty, but merely the fact that we humans are revolted by it. Projectivism is, as Mackie admits,[1] an "error theory". It makes out that the whole of our moral discourse is not what we think it is; and what we think it is, we are told, is entirely invalid. Projectivism does not fit the facts of human discourse. It also fails to account for Corrigibility: the fact that we could be wrong in our moral views is a sign of the objectivity of our claim. Nevertheless, projectivism is urged on us for metaphysical reasons. It makes an austere ontology possible, which requires us to believe that only the world of seventeenth-century science, or some variant on it, exists, and that all else is decoration supplied by our own ingenious minds. Such a world-view is attractive as well as repellent; besides appealing to our masochistic tendencies, it has an aura of scientific authority. We are tempted to explain away our obstinate intimations of objectivity as mere illusion or wishful thinking. Perhaps, after all, there is nothing objectively wrong with cruelty, apart from the fact that we humans are revolted by it; perhaps the real world is colourless and silent, and our perception of the colours and scents of flowers, the song of birds, and the sound of bells pealing over the countryside, are all just the artefacts of our sense organs.

Metaphysics could tell us this. Not only does it need to explain phenomena, but it can on occasion explain them away. And a powerful argument in favour of projectivism is that it looks like being able to offer a convincing account of probability in terms of how our belief structure works, so long as we want to remain consistent.

---

[1] J.L.Mackie, *Ethics: Inventing Right and Wrong*, Penguin, 1977, ch.1, §7, p.35.

§5.2 Degrees of Belief

The Calculus of Probabilities can be argued for, if we interpret probabilities as degrees of belief. The subjective theory of probability, first put forward by Ramsey and then by de Finetti,[2] and subsequently improved and refined,[3] argues that if we are to be consistent in the probabilities we attach to our various beliefs, we must calculate them in accordance with the Calculus of Probabilities.

Beliefs are beliefs of a particular person. I can sometimes say that I am more confident of one thing than I am of another, and so it makes sense to speak of degrees of belief. The claim that I can assign numerical values to these degrees of belief is more questionable: Ramsey suggested that a willingness to take bets at different odds gave an indication of what numerical value a particular person put on his beliefs; but it is difficult to carry this suggestion through—some people are risk averse, and would decline to bet even on very favourable odds, while many others spend money every week on tickets for which the expectation value is markedly less than the cost. That problem, however, does not matter. We are not concerned with what anyone actually does, but with what guidelines, IF numerical values were assigned to my beliefs, I would have to follow in order to be consistent. The key argument is that of the "Dutch Book". If numerical values were assigned to my beliefs otherwise than in accord with the probability calculus, it would be possible to set up a system of bets so that, no matter what actually turned out to be the case, I would lose. I do not have to be willing actually to make the bets. All I have to do is to recognise that if my assignment of a probability to a particular event is correct, then a bet with the corresponding odds would be "fair", that is to say, it would not be advantageous to either side. On those odds it would be a matter of indifference whether to bet on, or against, the event's happening. It is then very easy to argue that p, the probability to be assigned to a belief, must be non-negative and not greater than 1; and that the probability of a tautological belief—a necessarily true one—must be 1, and of an inconsistent—a necessarily false—one must be 0. The additive

---

[2] F.P.Ramsey, *The Foundations of Mathematics*, ed. R.B.Braithwaite, London, 1931, pp.166-18; B.de Finetti, *Theory of Probability*, vol.1, N, 1974.

[3] Most fully by C.Howson and P.Urbach, *Scientific Reasoning*, 2nd.ed., Chicago, 1993, to which I am especially indebted.

§5.2   Projectivism and Probability   133

law for beliefs about mutually exclusive events is also easy to justify. More argument is required to establish the law for conditional probabilities,[4] but it indubitably holds.

In modern times the Calculus of Probability is presented axiomatically. The standard form is due to Kolmogorov. He assigns numerical measures to *sets*. He considers a field, $\mathcal{F}$, of subsets of a set S, closed under complementation, union and intersection, subject to the conditions:

1. $P(A) \geq 0$
2. $P(S) = 1$
3. $P(A \cup B) = P(A) + P(B)$ if $a \cap B = 0$
4. $P(A|B) = \frac{P(A \cap B)}{P(B)}$ provided $P(B) > 0$

On the face of it, Kolmogorov's axioms are assigning numerical measures to certain sets, and they have been described as offering a measure-theoretic interpretation of probability. But although there are some advantages in such an interpretation—Howson and Urbach point out that set theory is language-neutral—there are grave disadvantages: not all sets are measurable, and measure theory is susceptible to Zeno-esque problems once infinitary operations are allowed. (In some recondite areas the distinctions between finite, countable, and uncountable, additivity become important; but until we get to infinity, it is sensible not to worry about how to build bridges over it.)

We do not have to interpret Kolmogorov's axioms as being about measurable sets. The set-theoretic relations of complementation, union and intersection are parallel to the logical relations of negation, disjunction and conjunction, so that Kolmogorov's system of measurable sets is homomorphic with propositional calculus. Indeed, we can regard Kolmogorov's sets as the *extensions* of the propositions, or propositional function, that the logician deals with.[5]

Kolmogorov's axioms are simply postulated. Empiricists might hope that they could be justified by reason of the success of scientific inferences based on them (in some libraries books on probability are shelved in the physics section), but this is like the "justification" of mathematics based on the empirical success of mathematical calculations. We cannot justify laws of thought by their

---

[4] Howson and Urbach, *op.cit.*, ch.6 §c.4, pp.81-84.

[5] Howson and Urbach, *op.cit.* ch.2, §2f, pp.31-32.

empirical success—spin doctors are often succesful—and we cannot just postulate them; moreover, in our every-day thinking measurable sets are not what we assign probabilities to. If we are reluctant to interpret probabilities as degrees of belief, on the grounds that that gives too subjective an account of probability, the main alternative we have to consider is the frequency theory, which interprets probabilities as proportions.

The frequency theory is better mathematically, but worse metaphysically. It is a theory of proportions, or frequency of occurrence in some *Kollektiv* or *ensemble*. If we have a number of coloured balls in an urn, say red balls and blue balls, then the proportion that are red-or-blue is the sum of the proportion of those that are red and the proportion of those that are blue. That is, if the proportion of those that are red is r, and the proportion of those that are blue is b, then the proportion of those that are red-and/or-blue (red $\vee$ blue) is $r + b$; similarly, it is evident that the proportion of those that are not red is $1-r$. The rule for conditionalising probabilities is a simple consequence of the arithmetic of fractions. So it is easy and tempting to try and define probability as a sort of proportion. Von Mises extrapolates from the simple finite class to an indefinitely large, perhaps infinite, one which he calls a *Kollektiv*. He requires a *Kollektiv* to have a "limiting frequency", to which the proportion in question tends, AND which is the same as the limiting frequency of any sub-class picked out by "place selection" alone. We can make sense of this mathematically, so far as denumerably infinite sets are concerned, in terms of "algorithmic incompressibility". Since there are $2^{\aleph_o}$ denumerably infinite sequences, but only $\aleph_o$ algorithms, there is no reason why *Kollektiv*s of any required sort should not exist: but they are somewhat ethereal entities none the less, not the down-to-earth simple proportions that Frequency Theorists claim them to be.

The frequency theory suffers from other defects too: it interprets probability statements as being essentially plural, although we also ascribe probabilities to essentially singular propositions; a doctor saying how long a particular individual is likely to live, for example; or a scientist estimating the probability of a hypothesis turning out to be true. And finally, it is otiose. Thanks to Bernouilli's Theorem, if we have a large number of cases, in which there is a probability of some specific feature being present, the proportion of those that turn out to possess that feature is exceedingly likely to tend towards that probability. Although there are, as

§5.2   Projectivism and Probability   135

we shall see, difficulties in reversing the direction of argument, and arguing from proportions to probabilities, rather than *vice versa*,[6] they should be settled by argument, not by definition. Since there is some connexion anyhow between probabilities and proportions, it is otiose to establish one by definition.

The frequency theory is an objective theory. It is often taken to be the only objective theory. And then in view of its ontological extravagance and other defects, it has seemed that the subjective theory is the only acceptable alternative, and that though our discourse about probabilities is overtly objective, what we are really doing is projecting onto the world the degrees of belief we have in our own minds.

Probability

Several different accounts of probability have been suggested:
1. Subjective Theory; put forward here; probabilities express degrees of belief—the odds on which one would be prepared to bet.
2. Frequency Theory; von Mises; probabilities are simply frequencies within special, indefinitely large "collectives" (*Kollectiv*s).
3. Objective Theories:
    (i) put forward in next section; probabilities are a generalisation of truth-values.
    (ii) Propensity Theory; Popper; probabilities express the tendency of a particular set-up to produce a particular result. (Not discussed here; very similar to 3(i).)

For a tabulation of merits and demerits of each account, see J.R.Lucas, *The Concept of Probability*, Oxford, 1970, Appendix II, pp.213-215.

I.J. Good, "Kinds of Probability", *Science*, **129**, 1959, pp.443-447 gives a useful *résumé*.

---

[6] See below, §5.4.

§5.3 The Marriage of Arithmetic with Boole

If probabilities could be understood only as degrees of belief or as limiting frequencies of *Kollektivs*, the argument for projectivism, at least so far as probabilities are concerned, would be strong. But though these two interpretations do afford a simple justification of the calculus of probabilities, a more general justification is available.

In the account of causal laws in the previous chapter, the logic of the causal factors was a discrete Yes or No of all-or-nothing features which were either definitely present or definitely absent. But in many scientific contexts causal laws are generalised to accommodate variables that can vary continuously; these are expressed as functional dependences. Similarly it seems natural to generalise the discrete Yes or No of truth-values, to accommodate probabilities that can vary continuously between the unqualifiedly true truth-value TRUE, and the unqualifiedly false truth-value FALSE. If we are to have numerical probabilities interpolated between TRUE and FALSE, we shall have to marry the Boolean algebra of propositional calculus with the arithmetical algebra of the proper fractions which we generalise to that of the real numbers in the interval $[0,1]$, with TRUE being represented by 1, and FALSE being represented by 0.[7] Granted a few, very reasonable, assumptions, there is essentially only one way to do this.[8] That is, although we could, if we wished to be perverse, adopt a deviant measure [say between 1 and 2] and deviant rules [for example, if p and q are mutually exclusive, and have probabilities α and β respectively, then

---

[7] Leibniz, Preface to *Théodicée*; reprinted in C.I.Gerhardt, ed., *Philosophische Schriften*, Berlin, 1875-1890, vol.vi, p.29 (see also p.65), saw the reconciliation of *continuity* with points that were essentially discrete, as one of the labyrinths in which our reason goes astray.

[8] I argued this in J.R.Lucas, *The Concept of Probability*, Oxford, 1970; R.T.Cox, "Probability, Frequency and Reasonable Expectation", *American Journal of Physics*, **14**, 1946, pp.1-14, *The Algebra of Probable Inference*, Baltimore, 1961, and I.J.Good, *Probability and the Weighing of Evidence*, London, 1950, had earlier argued to a similar conclusion. For a brief account, see C.Howson and P.Urbach, *Scientific Reasoning*, Chicago and La Salle, 1993, ch.5, §c.4, pp.93-99; or, more fully, E.T.Jaynes, *Probability Theory: The Logic of Science*, Cambridge, 2003, ch.2, pp.24-43.

§5.3   Projectivism and Probability   137

$prob(p \lor q) = ((\alpha - 1) + (\beta - 1) + 1)]$, it would only be a trivial complication of fundamentally the same rule.

We are naturally led to the canonical form of the axioms, by the fact that Boolean Algebra has two operations, conjunction (sometimes known as logical multiplication) and disjunction, both of them commutative and associative, and each with both a universal and an identity element. For disjunction TRUE is the universal element (the disjunction of any proposition with one that is True is itself True), and FALSE is the identity element (the disjunction of any proposition with one that is False has the same truth-value as the original disjoined proposition). For conjunction (logical multiplication) FALSE is the universal element (the conjunction of any proposition with one that is False is itself False), and TRUE is the identity element (the conjunction of any proposition with one that is True has the same truth-value as the original conjoined proposition).[9]

For arithmetical multiplication 0 and 1 fit the bill immediately, as does 0 for the identity under the operation of addition. For arithmetical addition among the non-negative numbers the universal element is ∞[10], but we are familiar enough with logical addition and with $\{1, 0\}$ as an alternative to $\{\text{TRUE}, \text{FALSE}\}$ to recognise 1 both as the maximum possible value for a probability and as the universal element for disjunction.

The argument can be made rigorous, but formal proofs are too lengthy to be given here. Cox and I assumed not only continuity but differentiability, which can be argued for as a reasonable

---

[9] The definition of disjunction in terms of *vel*, or *and/or* and of conjunction in terms of *and* is intuitive and natural. Logical purists, however, can use the features given here to develop Boolean algebra more austerely: they start from the very simple ring, with two "idempotent operations", $\lor$ and $\land$ ($p \lor p = p$ and $p \land p = p$), where the unit element of $\lor$ is the universal element of $\land$, and the unit element of $\land$ is the universal element of $\lor$, The formal feature of duality is emphasized if we replace T by $\top$ and F by $\bot$. Even more austerely, we can write the $\lor$ universal $\bigvee$ and $\land$ universal $\bigwedge$. To carry this through completely, we need to write the quantifiers in "V & A" form: (Vx) for $(\exists x)$ and (Ax) for $(\forall x)$. The latter is not quite correct, but easy to type, as also Λ instead of $\bigwedge$. For this symbolism see J.R.Lucas, *The Conceptual roots of Mathematics*, London, 2000, p.xi. more generally, see P.R.Halmos, *Boolean Algebras*, Princeton, 1963, §1, pp.1-3.

[10] For identity and universal elements, see further §10.3.

requirement on any function representing the probability of the Boolean product of propositions each possessing some probability. But the requirement, though reasonable, is unnecessary. Aczél has proved the essential functional equation from Commutativity and Associativity alone.[11] The axioms of the probability calculus are not mere postulates which we simply choose to adopt; nor do they need to be justified by special assumptions about the nature of probability, as being subjective degrees of belief, or objective frequencies in an ideal *Kollektiv*: rather, they arise naturally as the offspring of any marriage between non-negative real numbers and Boolean entities, which may indeed be beliefs, or sets of some sort, but can be, equally, propositions, or propositional functions.

§5.4 Assigning Probabilities

The probability calculus provides an adequate syntax for discourse about probabilities, but nothing in the way of semantics. Given some probability statements, it tells us how to conjoin, disjoin and negate them, but it does not tell us how we should assign probabilities to particular propositions, or propositional functions, or beliefs, or *Kollektiv*s, or *ensembles*. Whereas once given them, we can manipulate probabilities with a fair degree of confidence, getting them is much more problematic.

The subjective theory has no problem about *estimating* probabilities. It is something we do, and it is a merit of the subjective theory that it does not make out probabilities to be precise, but recognises them as being inherently blurred.[12]. The subjective theory does not presume to criticize any particular estimate we make, but only lays down constraints of consistency if we embark on making many estimates. But this is too lax: not only can multiple estimates be criticized for being inconsistent with one another, but single estimates can be criticized for simply being wrong. If I say on midsummer's day that there is a 90% probability of its snowing before sundown, I may be perfectly sincere, and expressing the actual degree of confidence I have in that prediction, but still I am open to challenge, and unless I can cite some surprising but convincing meteorological evidence, my estimate will be rejected as being wildly wrong. Although I may put a figure on my

---

[11] J.Aczél, *Lectures on Functional Equations and their Applications*, New York, 1966, pp.256-267.

[12] See below, §11.7.

degree of belief about a particular matter, when I articulate it as a probability judgment, I am not voicing a piece of autobiographical information, but making a fallible claim, which may indeed be wrong, but for that very reason can meaningfully aspire to be right.

Objective theories accept that probability judgements may be wrong, and need to be defended, but have difficulty in giving an adequate account of how probability judgements may be justified. Occasionally we can argue on the basis of equiprobable cases. This argument has been unreasonably discountenanced in modern times. Most of the early work on probability was based on equiprobable cases, and although some of the justifications offered for assuming equiprobability were bad, good ones are available. We do not need to postulate positively some principle of indifference, but argue negatively that any difference in probabilities could be explained only in terms of some other difference which we have good reason to reject. If a coin, or a die, or a roulette wheel, has a greater probability of yielding one result rather than any of the others, it would betoken a lack of symmetry, which we should explain by supposing it to be biased. Similarly, we should take it as evidence of para-psychological psychokinesis—or, more likely, of cheating—if each time a pack of cards was dealt, the ace of spades always turned up in one particular person's hand. True dice and unbiased coins and roulette wheels are by definition symmetrical, so as to yield results consonant with each outcome being equiprobable. So, too, a well-shuffled pack fairly dealt out is one where the chance of any particular card being dealt to any particular person is the same as for any other. Often there is confusion between actual, empirical cases, and idealised cases: in the former it is logically possible that there should be unequal probabilities, though if that were the case it would indicate some surprising breakdown of symmetry; in the latter it is stipulated that the dice are true, the coins and roulette wheels unbiased, the dealing fair. These idealised cases are useful when it comes to doing exercises in probability theory, but mask the underlying rationale of equiprobability assumptions, that their being false would call into question the presupposition of deep symmetries in space and time, and the causal irrelevance of mental attitudes *per se*, which are the basis of much of our understanding of the external world.[13] In some cases our preconceptions about how equiprobable cases should be identified

---

[13] See above, §4.8, and below §9.7.

have been shown to be wrong, and we have had to rethink what our criterion of identity should be, and hence a radical revision of ascriptions of particularity.[14]

Although important in physics, where many symmetries are evident, equiprobable cases seldom occur in the biological and social sciences, with their much greater complexity. Sometimes a sensitive use of Bayes' theorem enables us to improve our assignment of probabilities in the light of fresh empirical evidence. But the initial assignment of "prior probabilities" is always open to question, and only in a few cases can we be absolutely confident that the results of our calculations are reliable. Mostly we employ statistics, arguing from a number of essentially similar cases to assign a probability to a general *propositional function* rather than a singular proposition.[15] Given the probability calculus, we can argue convincingly that IF the probability of some sort of an event (say a coin on being tossed coming down heads) is α, THEN it is very probable that in the long run the relative frequency (the proportion of tosses coming down heads) will tend towards α. But can we argue the other way? Can we argue that if the relative frequency is α, the probability is α too?. We face three related difficulties.

One is that the various Laws of Large Numbers never actually give us definite answers with truth-values exactly equal to 0 or 1. By taking larger and larger numbers, we may be able to get nearer and nearer to the extremes, but we never quite reach them. According to probability theory as currently understood, we need to reach them if we are to be able to give a firm interpretation of probabilistic discourse—else we are merely interpreting probabilities in terms of other probabilities: in practice, we are content if we nearly reach them. We are indentifying TRUE and FALSE not with 1 an 0 precisely, but with their *neighbourhoods*. Justification is called for, and will be given, as we deal with the second difficulty, which is that however large our sample, it is only a finite segment, and could be an untypical initial segment of an infinite sequence with

---

[14] See below §11.11.

[15] It is of considerable importance that though we can intelligibly talk of the probability of a singular proposition, it is nearly always to propositional functions that we assign numerical values with confidence. Justified probability statements are inherently general, and import a lack of particularity to the entities of quantum mechanics and other probabilistic disciplines. See further below, §11.11. and §13.6.

§5.4   *Projectivism and Probability*   141

a very different limiting frequency. If I throw a coin ten times, and get ten heads, I may reasonably conclude that the coin is not a fair one, but a two-headed one. Yet if we consider all the 2^{1000} (roughly 10^{300}) possible sequences of one thousand tosses, there will be 2^{990} (roughly 10^{297}) possible sequences which start with ten heads. The problem is insoluble, so long as we confine ourselves to monologous deductive logic. If, however, we consider our actual procedures in the context of two-person logic, we can distil a cogent argument. Whatever the evidence, the sceptic can maintain that it does not entail the probabilistic conclusion we seek to draw from it. We ask him whether that is the response he is always going to make, or whether in principle he can be persuaded by sufficient evidence. If the former, we break off the conversation. He is like the inductive sceptic,[16] crying for the moon, never going to be satisfied by the evidence that could be available. If he is in principle persuadable, we invite him to state his principle precisely. Although most of us are prepared to discount the possibility of a one-in-a-thousand coincidence having occurred, we do not rule out of court the scrupulous researcher who feels queasy at so brusque a dismissal. He will reject the contention that some result is a coincidence only if the odds against it are a million to one. In that case we toss the suspect coin another ten times. If on a number of occasions it comes down tails, he is vindicated, and we were wrong to have jumped to our conclusion that the coin was two-headed: if, on the other hand, the run of heads is continued, we have met his doubts, and justified our conclusion even by his stringent standards.

The two-person dialogue can be articulated in the epsilon-delta notation of mathematical analysis. In formal logic it is expressed by two quantifiers, first a universal quantifier—you, on behalf of the sceptic, pick an epsilon, to say how small a probability has to be before you will discount it—followed by an existential quantifier—whereupon I, on behalf of the main argument, pick a delta, to indicate how many cases would be needed to yield a probability within the epsilon limit. The argument against the sceptic is complicated, but convincing none the less.

In fact the argument is more complicated still. The third difficulty is a generalisation of the first—that TRUE and FALSE are identified not with 1 and 0 precisely but with their neighbourhoods. We do not in general ascribe exact probabilities on the basis of

[16] See above, §3.4.

statistics, but only approximate ones. We have to lay down two limits. We have to lay down limits within which we think the true probability lies, as well as degree of closeness to truth or falsity that is going to be demanded and accepted. Thus if we are wondering what is the probability, α, of a baby's being born a boy, we do not suppose that there is some exact probability, but only that there is an approximate one—round about 0.53, we might think. We have to decide how approximate. We might choose 0.01, so that our claim would be $\alpha = 0.53 \pm 0.01$. The second choice then is to determine how close we must get to 1 or 0 to accept that a proposition with that probability was as good as true, or as good as false—what degree of coincidence we would no longer find credible. We might be prepared to accept that the probability of a baby's being born a boy was 0.53 ± 0.01, if there was only a one in a hundred chance that the results we had observed would have arisen had the true probability been less than 0.52 or greater than 0.54.

We can give a less clumsy picture of these lines of argument, if we think of probabilities not as having precise values, but as having blurred ones.[17] Instead of saying that the true probability of a baby's being born a boy is *in* the neighbourhood of 0.53, we should say that it *is* the neighbourhood of 0.53. Similarly, and more importantly, TRUE is not to be identified with the precise probability 1, nor FALSE with the probability 0: rather, TRUE is the *neighbourhood* of the probability 1, and FALSE is the *neighbourhood* of the probability 0. Blurred neighbourhoods are the result of our projecting two-person dialogues onto monologous discourse.[18]

Probabilities emerge as a, for the most part blurred, generalisation of truth-values. If we can ascribe a truth-value to a proposition, propositional function, hypothesis, belief, utterance, statement, sentence, or well-formed formula, we can intelligibly ascribe a probability to it too. And just as we can be wrong in ascribing truth or falsity, so we can be wrong in ascribing a probability. We can defend our ascriptions, mostly by reference to statistical evidence, but only imprecisely. Most thinkers are of the opinion that the imprecision is only an imprecision of practice, but it will turn out to be an important consideration when we come to try to fathom the "measurement problem" in quantum mechanics.[19]

---

[17] We should note that not all probabilities are thus blurred. When we have arguments for equiprobabilities, they may take exact values, such as 0.5.

[18] A logic for imprecise magnitudes is developed in M.A.E.Dummett, "Is time a Continuum of Instants?", *Philosophy*, **75**, 2000, pp.510-515.

[19] See below, §11.7.

§5.5 ... and Statistics

Statistics has a bad name. Many innocent people have been sent to prison in Britain, or deprived of their children, on the strength of statistical evidence, arrogantly put forward by expert witnesses, and not properly understood by judge or jury. The natural reaction is to disbelieve all statistical evidence. But this would be wrong. Statistical evidence, properly handled, can reveal truth from a welter of confusing figures. What is called for is not wholesale rejection but careful criticism. Only if we understand the argumentation involved, can we be ready to spot errors, or assess counter-arguments.

We need to be wary of the argument from coincidence. If I throw a coin ten times, and get heads every time, I may reasonably suspect that there is something dodgy about it: it could conceivably be a coincidence—there is one chance in 1024 that an unbiased coin would produce ten heads in success just by chance. But when I am reckoning to dismiss that as too much of a coincidence, I may suddenly think that if I got the sequence HHTHHTHTHT, that equally could have occurred only by a one-in-a-thousand chance, so why should I suspect the one more than the other? Coincidences are bound to happen. How can we argue against them?

We can argue against a coincidence having happened provided there is a much better explanation available. But we need to know what that explanation is, and also to consider the possibility of there being available some other explanation which would also explain the figures without resorting to coincidence. In families where there have been several cot deaths parents have been convicted because neither the expert witness, nor the court, took into account the possibility that there might be a genetic link between the deaths. A knowledge of probability and statistics is not enough: a wide-ranging knowledge of the relevant sciences is also required before firm conclusions can be drawn from a set of statistics.

Some general principles can be formulated: the first is that the absence of evidence for a particular hypothesis is not the same as evidence against it. The second is that statistical arguments based on some law of large numbers argue for the truth of *propositional functions*, not particular propositions. We can test whether the assignment of some value to the probability of *a* toss of some particular coin fits the observed results, or of *a* non-smoking male aged sixty living a further five years, but before we apply that result to a particular toss of the coin, or to a particular John Smith, we need to assure ourselves that there are no other relevant factors.

In some cases we can use Bayes' theorem to argue about a particular proposition, but then we need to be explicit about what prior probabilities are being assumed, and ready to recognise any possibility that our assignment may be wrong.

It is likely that in an age of DNA testing there will be many more legal cases involving assessments of probabilities. It is unfortunate that many lawyers in the present age, and therefore many judges, are unversed either in probability and statistics or in the relevant sciences. Much misunderstanding and injustice could be avoided if it were standard practice, whenever statistics were involved, to appoint an *amicus curiae*, someone who understood both statistics and the relevant sciences, to cross-examine expert witnesses, and to explain to both judge and jury what the judgements were that they were being called upon to make.

§5.6 The Limits of Ignorance

One great recommendation of the Subjective Theory of Probability is that it seems to avoid some of the paradoxes of quantum mechanics. Quantum mechanics yields probabilities, probabilities of getting certain numerical results if we make certain measurements. No satisfactory account of what happens when a measurement is made has been forthcoming. An analogy with statistical mechanics is tempting. Quantum mechanics, on this analogy, does not confuse us by giving all the details of an individual system, but characterizes in broad outline the general features of a whole class—or *ensemble*—of systems; and just as temperature, pressure, and other thermodynamic properties are averages of more fundamental properties, such as kinetic energy and momentum, so the probabilities of quantum mechanics are averages over the relevant *ensemble*. When we are about to make a measurement, quantum mechanics is able to describe the system in broad outline, though not in full detail, and can tell us the average value for the magnitude about to be measured in systems thus described. The measurement then reveals the fuller detail that the actual system being measured actually possesses, and did possess prior to the measurement's being made. The measurement does not, on this account, alter the system, but only dispels our ignorance as to which system in the specified *ensemble* we were actually dealing with.

It is a powerful argument, but it assumes that there *are* definite antecedent values of the physical magnitudes which are about to be measured, and that the measuring process simply reveals what

§5.6 Projectivism and Probability

were the values that these "hidden variables" already had. This assumption is false. Quantum mechanics needs probabilities not because we can deal only with large numbers of quantum mechanical states in an *ensemble*, but because it needs to assign weights to possible values of the physical magnitudes (such as energy or momentum) of each particular system.

John von Neumann realised this, and put forward an argument against any determinist hidden variable theory.[20] He pointed out that IF there were hidden variables, these would have to take *definite* values, so that the proposition that some particular magnitude, say energy, had some particular value, say 12 electron volts, would either have the truth-value 1 (or TRUE), or else have the truth-value 0 (or FALSE); but such a theory, with *discrete* truth-values, would not combine with quantum mechanics, which was a theory with a *continuum* of possible probabilities in the interval [0, 1], and not just the two alternatives of discrete value, 0 or 1.

Von Neumann's argument depended on assumptions which could be questioned. But though it could be faulted, it was not refuted, and in due course two further theorems were discovered,[21] resting on assumptions less questionable, but likewise showing that the introduction of hidden variables, which either did, or did not, have some particular value, was incompatible with the continuum of possible probabilities.

It is always dangerous to pontificate about what the latest scientific theory demands of us. And quantum mechanics itself is raising further doubts about scientific assumptions we normally take for granted.[22] But we have to be guided by the best science available; and the best science available requires objective probabilities, which cannot be accounted for simply as the projections of our subjective degrees of belief onto a wholly determinist and determinate world.

Quantum mechanics is philosophically important because:
1. It refutes projectivism.
    (See Chapter 11 for further entries.)

---

[20] J.von Neumann, *Mathematische Grundlagen der Quantenmechanik*, Berlin, 1932; tr. R.T.Beyer, *The Mathematical Foundations of Quantum Mechanics*, Princeton, 1935, ch.III, §2, pp.209-211, and ch.IV, §2, pp.323-328.

[21] One by Gleason, the other by Kochen and Specker, discussed in §11.4. below.

[22] §§11.6, 11.10, 11.11, 11.12, 11.13.

§5.7 Unprojected Reality

If projectivism will not work for probability, it is less likely to work for colours or values. Not that this is a rigid entailment. There would be no inconsistency in supposing that colours and values were painted on the world by us, while probabilities were in the world and discovered by us. But one of the chief arguments for projectivism is economy. It offers an over-all programme for explaining away awkward metaphysical entities in favour of the austere ontology of slightly updated seventeenth-century science. The attraction of such a view is not that it accommodates our experience—it does not, and has to explain it away—but that it offers a single key to all ontology. If the projectivist programme fails for probability, not only may it fail for secondary qualities too, but the argument for pushing it through against the appearances in order to achieve a uniformly economical ontology fails also.

Chapter 6
The Tree in the Lonely Quad

§6.1   Phenomenalism
§6.2   How Do You Know?
§6.3   The Argument from Illusion
§6.4   The Argument from the Senses
§6.5   The Argument from Facts
§6.6   Rebuttals
§6.7   Arguments against Phenomenalism
§6.8   Reality Recovered
§6.9   The Analogy of Feeling
§6.10   Criteria
§6.11   The Argument from Deception
§6.12   Myself and Others
§6.13   Understanding People
§6.14   Conclusion

§6.1 Phenomenalism

> There was a young man who said "God
> Must think it exceedingly odd
>   If He finds that the tree
>   Continues to be,
> When there's no one about in the Quad."

Phenomenalism is the doctrine that the only things that exist are the direct objects of our senses. It was first put forward as a consistent doctrine by Bishop Berkeley, and has in our own age been espoused with great vigour by Professor A.J. Ayer. It used to be known as Idealism, but that name is confusing, as we also understand by Idealism a commitment to high standards of action and aspiration: and there is no connexion between having high standards and having doubts about the existence of trees in unoccupied quads.

Phenomenalism is metaphysical. It offers a minimal ontology, in which all surplus, unobserved, entities have been pared away, leaving only "sense data" as the ultimate constituents of reality, the indubitable starting point from which alone all empirical knowledge must be derived. We mislead ourselves if we suppose that the world contains material objects, tables, chairs, the tree in the quad, and such-like, which exist even when we are not observing them. All we know, all we can know, are the direct objects of observation, and they alone can be properly said to exist. When we talk about the tree in the quad, we are really talking about the sights we should see, and the feelings we should experience, if we went into the quad, and looked in the appropriate direction, or walked in that direction and held out our hands. Material objects are collections of sense-data, actual or possible. Each sentient being can similarly be regarded as a different sort of collection of sense-data; not those that would, or could, be observed by a suitably placed observer, but those that a particular observer has, or might have, and will, or may, have as he experiences his life. It is a form of pluralism: there are many different fundamental entities, all of one type— ideas, impressions, sensations, sense data, or sensabilia—which are neither material objects nor minds, but out of which, by suitable grouping, material objects and minds can be constructed. Since the fundamental entities are neither material nor mental, we can describe phenomenalism as a metaphysics of neutral pluralism.[1]

Because the phenomenalist offers a metaphysical view of the world, he can accommodate—or override—many of its awkward features: it may not accord with our ordinary ways of thinking— but so much the worse for untutored, every-day thinking; it may be cumbersome, but so is much of chemistry and physics. Although, like any other metaphysical system, it needs to save the appearances, it may, because it deals with fundamental truth, massage the truth fairly roughly, in order to fit it to the Procrustean bed that has been constructed. In consequence, it seems to be not so much a philosophical doctrine, as a metaphysical feeling.[2] If a person does not have the metaphysical feeling he will find all the arguments in its favour unconvincing, while if he does have the metaphysical feeling, then he will continue to feel it to be true, however thoroughly the arguments for it are refuted, and as soon as one argument is demolished, he will construct another. Argument appears to have no purchase. We are reminded of Bradley's *dictum* that metaphysics is the finding of bad reasons for what we believe on instinct.

---

[1] Or, since there is *only one type* of fundamental entity, as neutral monism.

[2] See E.M.Forster, *The Longest Journey*, London, 1904, ch.1, for an account of a Cambridge undergraduate's feelings.

§6.2   The Tree in the Lonely Quad   149

Nevertheless, arguments always deserve attention. Many of the arguments deployed are variations on the themes of critical reason discussed in Chapter Three. Some gain support from the superlative assumption that there must be ultimate entities that constitute the foundations of empirical knowledge, some items we can know with absolute certainty. Some obtain purchase through the inadequacy of traditional formulations of the common-sense view. Some are simply fallacious.

§6.2 How Do You Know?

Two lines of approach characteristic of critical reason can be used to argue for phenomenalism: the question "How do you know?", and the doubt "But you must admit that you might be wrong?".

> Arguments **for** Phenomenalism
> 1. How do you know? + inductivism

The "How do you know?" argument for phenomenalism is put very clearly by Stace[3]

> For the sake of clearness, let us take once again the concrete example of the piece of paper. I am at this moment experiencing it, and at this moment it exists, but how can I know that it existed last night in my desk when, so far as I know, no mind was experiencing it? How can I know that it will continue to exist to-night when there is no one in the room? The knowledge of these alleged facts is what the realists assert that they possess. And the question is, Whence could such knowledge have been obtained, and how can it be justified? What I assert is that it is absolutely impossible to have any such knowledge.
>   There are only two ways in which it could be asserted that the existence of any sense-object can be established. One is by sense-perception, the other by inference from sense-perception. I know of the existence of this paper now because I see it. I am supposed to know of the existence of the other side of the moon, which no one has ever seen, by inference from various actual astronomical observations, that is, by inference from things actually experienced. There are no other ways of proving the existence of a sense-object. Is either of them possible in the present case?
>   1. *Sense-perception.* I obviously cannot know by perception the existence of the paper when no one is experiencing it. For that would be self-contradictory. It would amount to asserting that I can experience the unexperienced.

---

[3] W.T. Stace, "The Refutation of Realism", *Mind*, XLIII, 1934, pp.143-155; reprinted in H. Feigl and W. Sellars, eds., *Readings in Philosophical Analysis*, New York, 1949, p.366-7.

2. *Inference.* Nor is it possible to prove by inference the existence of the paper when no mind is experiencing it. For how can I possibly pass by inference from the particular fact of the existence of the paper now, when I am experiencing it, to the quite different particular fact of the existence of the paper yesterday or to-morrow, when neither I nor any other mind is experiencing it? Strictly speaking, the onus of proving that such an inference is impossible is not on me. The onus of proving that it is possible is upon anyone who asserts it, and I am entitled to sit back and wait until someone comes forward with such an alleged proof. Many realists who know their business admit that no valid inference from an experienced to an unexperienced existence is possible. Thus Mr. Russell says, "Belief in the existence of things outside my own biography must, from the standpoint of theoretical logic, be regarded as a prejudice, not as a well-grounded theory."[4]

I might therefore adopt the strategy of masterly inaction. But I prefer to carry the war into the enemy's camp. I propose to *prove* that no proof of the existence of unexperienced objects is possible.

It is clear in the first place that any supposed reasoning could not be inductive. Inductive reasoning proceeds always upon the basis that what has been found in certain observed cases to be true will also be true in unobserved cases. But there is no single case in which it has been observed to be true that an experienced object continues to exist when it is not being experienced; for, by hypothesis, its existence when it is not being experienced cannot be observed. Induction is generalisation from observed facts, but there is not a single case of an unexperienced existence having been observed on which could be based the generalisation that entities continue to exist when no one is experiencing them. And there is likewise not a single known instance of the existence of an unexperienced entity which could lead me to have even the slightest reason for supposing that this paper ever did exist, or will exist, when no one is experiencing it.

Since inductive reasoning is ruled out, the required inference, if there is to be an inference, must be of a formal nature. But deductive inference of all kinds depends upon the principle of consistency. If $P \rightarrow Q$, then we can only prove Q, if P is admitted. From $P \rightarrow Q$, therefore all that can be deduced is that P and not-Q are inconsistent, and that we cannot hold both P and not-Q together, though we may hold either of them separately.

---

[4] B.Russell, *Analysis of Mind*, p.133.

§6.2   *The Tree in the Lonely Quad*   151

> Hence, if it is alleged that a deductive inference can be drawn from the existence of the paper now, when I am experiencing it, to its existence when no one is experiencing it, this can only mean that to assert together the two propositions, (1) that it exists now, and (2) that it does not exist when no one is experiencing it, is an internally inconsistent position. But there is absolutely no inconsistency between these two propositions. If I believe that nothing whatever exists or ever did or will exist, except my own personal sense-data, this may be a view of the universe which no one would ever hold, but there is absolutely nothing internally inconsistent in it. Therefore, no deductive inference can prove the existence of an unexperienced entity. Therefore, by no reasoning at all, inductive or deductive, can the existence of such an entity be proved.

The nerve of the argument is that there are only two ways whereby the existence of a material object may be established, by sense-perception and by inductive inference according to the Humean canon. The claim that reason is restricted to the Humean canon can be countered,[5] and once we allow that inference need not be so narrowly construed, the whole argument falls. Asked how I know that a piece of paper existed last night in my desk, I say first that I saw it there both yesterday evening and this morning, and if pressed argue that there are good reasons for believing it to have been there in the intervening period. A sceptic may go on to question whether they really are good reasons; but he cannot assume, as Stace does, that they are bound to be bad because they do not fit into a predetermined pattern.

But other arguments are available. The sceptic can fault arguments outside the Humean canon, not because they are outsiders, but because they are fallible, and may on any particular occasion turn out to be wrong and lead to a false conclusion. The "How Do You Know" argument is reinforced by the Argument from Illusion.

---

[5] See above, §2.7.

§6.3 The Argument from Illusion

We sometimes make mistakes. We think there is an oasis beckoning to us across a few miles of sweltering desert, when really there is nothing but unending parched sands. The moon seems to be no larger than a sixpence, the distant hills look blue, the stick in the water broken, and when we have jaundice everything is yellow. Similarly with hearing, tasting and feeling. Our judgments, however confidently made, are fallible. We infer that the water is warm, when coming in after skating, we put our hands under the cold tap; but really it is quite cold, though warmer than our chilled fingers. There are no pink elephants in his bedroom, as our delirious friend avers, but we do not think he is telling lies and making the whole thing up. Illusions and delusions do not come marked, so that we know that they are not to be trusted. Dreams sometimes are recognised as such, but not always. Often we are deceived by illusions, and take delusions and dreams for real. In our illusions and delusions we may be misinterpreting our sense-experience, but we are having some sense experience. To avoid error, we should simply report what we actually experience, and leave the interpretation for another time, and perhaps another person.

Arguments **for** Phenomenalism
2. Argument from Illusion:
search for the absolutely indubitable
(but distinguish bare doubt from substantial doubt)

A sense-datum then is that incorrigible minimum of which I can be absolutely sure, and which cannot be thrown in doubt by any further consideration. All our ordinary reports of experience can be thrown in doubt. We cannot believe that we are totally wrong. There must be something we could say which was indubitable. And that indubitable residuum is what we ought to talk about when arguing with a sceptical philosopher or conducting an exercise in critical reason.

But can we make a firm distinction between what we actually experience and the interpretation of what we actually experience? Phenomenalists assume that we can. Once we have drawn the distinction between Reason and Experience, it is natural to look for pure cases of each extreme. And since it is easy to discover a pure

§6.3   The Tree in the Lonely Quad   153

case of Reason unalloyed by Experience in deductive, and especially mathematical, argument, we assume that the contrary case must exist and be equally easy to identify. Even if we do not assume it, the phenomenalist can argue for it, on the ground that there must be minimal sense reports, in which the element of interpretation has been reduced to zero, since if it is not zero, it can be challenged, and we shall have to separate the disputed interpretation from the undisputed evidence on which it is based. But the argument is not cogent. Any particular report of sense-experience can be thrown in doubt—true: but it does not follow that this process can be iterated until we have pared down the report to a bare minimum. For throwing in doubt is not as easy as all that. Arm-chair philosophers find it less difficult than real-life reporters, but always to make a doubt plausible the doubter has to spin an alternative yarn. I see an elephant in a distant field, but on closer approach I recognize it as a haystack covered with a tarpaulin. Such a story throws doubt on such a report. It would be markedly less plausible if the elephant had been observed from close by in a circus. Then perhaps I might be taken in by a couple of clowns in an elephant skin, but surely not by a haystack. A child at a zoo might mis-identify a rhinoceros, but a professional zoologist could not be mistaken in that way, though even he could perhaps be taken in by a very clever dummy constructed by another zoologist. Although we are all liable to errors, we are not liable to all errors, nor all to the same error. The situations in which a haystack can be mistaken for an elephant are different from those in which a dummy can, and both are radically different from those in which sticks seem bent, or daggers appear suspended in front of the guilty observer. In every case we may be wrong, but wrong in a different way, depending on the case and its context. We cannot, therefore, pare down our reports to an irreducible minimum, that can be guaranteed to be mistake-free, for the different mistakes do not form an ordered series tending towards a definite limit, but a heterogeneous collection of mistakes, in different directions and possible only in different and incompatible contexts. In epistemology, as in economics, 'raw' is a relative term. We can contrast our data with our conclusions, as an industrialist can contrast his inputs with his finished products: but no material is absolutely raw, and neither is any information.[6]

---

[6] See further §6.5.

§6.4 The Argument from the Senses

Without the benefit of philosophy we are, nearly all of us, naive realists. We take it for granted that we inhabit a world of real objects, which continue whether we observe them or not, and that when we observe them, we simply perceive them as they are. But as we attempt to formulate our untutored beliefs, we run into difficulties, which the phenomenalist can use to force us into agreeing with him. Science weakens naive confidence. We know that light and sound travel with only a finite velocity. We hear the thunder, the explosion, the pile being hit by the pile-driver, only after the lapse of some temporal duration; and when we observe the stars, what we see is what was happening many years ago. But we cannot hear or see past events. It must be that what we actually hear or see are present events which were caused by past events, and that we infer what happened in the past from what we are experiencing in the present. Similarly, if we try to give a causal account of perception, we have to insert, between the perceiver and the ultimate object he is perceiving, an intermediary which is caused by the object and is what is immediately perceived. We are led to distinguish from the things we ordinarily say we perceive, their effects on us which are the real, immediate objects of perception. So Descartes is led to conclude:

> In fact, we perceive colours only in the sense that we perceive in objects something that produces in us the sensation of colour.[7]

> Arguments **for** Phenomenalism
> 3. Analysis of Perception

But then we are not really perceiving. Rather we are positing that there are in the objects something that causes us to have the sensory experience of colour, much as we posit in stinging nettles something that produces in us the sensation of stinging pain. It is particularly tempting to assimilate sounds to pain. It is not really the bell we hear, we feel forced to concede, since if we put it in a vacuum, we hear nothing. What we really hear is the sound in our ears, caused by the vibrations in the air caused by the vibrations

---

[7] AT VIII; HR I 296; quoted by A.J.P.Kenny, *Descartes*, New York, 1968, p.209

§6.4   The Tree in the Lonely Quad   155

of the bell. We do not really hear bells or the traffic outside, but only the sounds and the noise produced by them. The argument is particularly compelling with sounds. As Berkeley put it[8]

> Sitting in my study I hear a coach drive along the street; I look through the casement and see it; I walk out and enter into it; thus, common speech would incline one to think, I heard, saw, and touched the same thing, to wit, the coach. It is nevertheless certain, the ideas intromitted by each sense are widely different, and distinct from each other; but having been observed constantly to go together, they are spoken of as one and the same thing. By the variation of the noise I perceive the different distances of the coach, and know that it approaches before I look out. Thus by the ear I perceive distance, just after the same manner as I do by the eye.
>
> XLVII. I do not nevertheless say, I hear distance in like manner as I say that I see it, the ideas perceived by hearing not being so apt to be confounded with the ideas of touch, as those of sight are; so likewise a man is easily convinced that bodies and external things are not properly the object of hearing, but only sounds, by the mediation whereof the idea of this or that body or distance is suggested to his thoughts. But then one is with more difficulty brought to discern the difference there is betwixt the ideas of sight and touch: though it be certain, a man no more sees or feels the same thing, than he hears and feels the same thing.

And, indeed, it seems similarly impossible to deny that what we really smell are smells, and what we really taste are tastes, and what we really feel are feels, and what we really see are sights. And, indeed, in a sense this is so. What we have done is to replace the ordinary objects of perception, by ones that we necessarily perceive. In grammatical terms, we have replaced the ordinary external accusatives—bells, fried bacon, honey, velvet, and stars—with internal accusatives—sounds, smells, tastes, feels, sights—thereby transforming fallible, informative statements into necessary, vacuous ones. As a young man I might have been intrigued—or alarmed—if a fortune-teller said she could foretell whom I should be married to in ten years' time: but if, having paid her her fee, she vouchsafed that in ten years' time I should be married to my wife, I should reckon I had not got value for money.

> Arguments **for** Phenomenalism
> 4. Direct Object of Perception
> 5. Assimilation of Sense-experience to Pain

---

[8] George Berkeley, *A New Theory of Vision*, §§XLVI-XLVII.

It is tempting to resist these lines of argument by insisting on an absolute separation between our ordinary mode of discourse and the causal account of perception. But it would be an unreasonable insistence. It is rational to seek for causes, and if we find them, they are to be taken seriously, and my lead us to revise our previous notions. In any case, we sometimes have occasion to talk about our sense-experience rather than what our sense-experience is experience of. I need to tell the oculist how the letter on the screen *looks to me*, not what it really is. Although most of our discourse is about a common external world, sometimes I want to talk about me, and sometimes, even, you may want to hear about me and my sensations. But once we allow that the immediate objects of our senses are sounds, smells, tastes, sights and feels, we are hard put to it to escape from the realm of sense-experience to the external world beyond. Berkeley claimed that it was impossible. The only things that were like ideas were ideas, he said, in opposition to Locke's claim that primary qualities were like the ideas we had of them, (unlike secondary qualities, which were unlike the ideas they produced in us). But Berkeley's argument is broken-backed: 'like' is incompletely specified. In respect of being ideas, only ideas can, indeed, be like ideas. But if I can, as phenomenalists aver, describe a sense-datum as an orange triangle on a green background, then it is perfectly intelligible, and possibly correct, to say that the idea is like, in respect of shape, some other triangle, perhaps in a textbook on geometry, or perhaps marked out by a surveyor on the surface of the earth.

We can talk about sense-experience without being obliged to talk only about it. And argument need not be so restricted that we are unable to argue from sense-experience to what sense-experience is experience of. But it is difficult to keep the discourse and the arguments under control, so as not to say things that give the phenomenalist purchase for his arguments. We are often careless and easily muddled, and then vulnerable to some argument which would persuade us that we could never have knowledge of anything beyond the immediate objects of sense.

Arguments **for** Phenomenalism
6. Difficulties with Representative Theories: Veil of Perception

§6.4   The Tree in the Lonely Quad

Many of the arguments deployed are variations on a limited number of leading themes, which have been separately discussed in preceding sections, and shown to be fallacious. Nevertheless, cumulatively they can be effective. If Locke and the Empiricists were right to hold that our knowledge of the world is based on experience, then the honest and democratic thing to do is to share the reports of one's experience with all who come to listen, but let them make what they like of it. It is unfair to purvey packaged information which has been processed by our fallible reasonings. We should export it raw, and let them process it themselves at home. Not only is this more equal, but it is safer. If some one else makes a mistake, not only shall we be not held to blame, but others, also operating on the raw information we had provided, may correct it: whereas, if all we had offered to the public was the finished article, nobody would be in a position to correct any errors that had crept in while we were processing it. In any case, by confining ourselves to reporting our own sense-experiences we are witnessing to our belief that all observers are on an equal footing, and that there are no mysteries of seeing or knowing that are the peculiar prerogative of an intellectual *élite*. We claim no privileged access to *recherché* forms of reasoning, but humbly confine ourselves to reporting as accurately as we can the sense-experience that has come our way. We provide our share of bricks, and let it be a common endeavour to build them up into the edifice of knowledge.

Arguments **for** Phenomenalism
1. How do you know?
2. Argument from Illusion
3. Analysis of Perception
4. Direct Object of Perception
5. Assimilation of Sense-experience to Pain
6. Difficulties with Representative Theories: Veil of Perception

---

It is difficult not to feel the force of this appeal; particularly in its attempt to get down to the fundamental elements of empirical knowledge. IF Locke and the Empiricists were right, and the mind was a *tabula rasa* on which there were impressed by the senses impressions of the outside world, then the phenomenalists' argument from perception would be strong. And contrariwise, if phenomenalism is false, we shall have to give an account of perception which is not only clearer, but different.

§6.5 The Argument from Facts

The argument from the senses is often strengthened by the assumption—unrecognised—that there are basic facts, a definite class of indubitable entities.[9] Then a reductive argument begins. Any ordinary set of statements cannot state facts, since men, being fallible, sometimes make mistakes. Besides, merely if we think hard enough about any given statement, the original sense of the word 'fact' reappears. If I concentrate hard enough on why I believe there is a tree in the quad, I cease to assume that there is a tree in the quad, and treat that statement instead as a proposition to be proved rather than a premise that is given. In having the question of whether there is a tree in the quad or not brought to my notice I am being begged not to beg the question, and the courtesies of argument demand that I put in doubt what I normally know to be true. There is also what I might call the Yellow-Spot phenomenon in philosophy, namely, that if we focus our attention too hard on any matter for too long, we cease to see it straight. In the dark night of the intellect, which is the philosopher's usual state of mind, it is wise for him occasionally to distract his thoughts and look away, that he may see what he is looking at the better; more especially when he is dealing with facts and certainty. For facts are essentially what is peripheral to the question under examination, what can be taken for granted on this occasion; and therefore by being asked sufficiently earnestly to consider any question sufficiently closely I can be cajoled into giving up fact-status on this occasion for almost any statement: courtesy compels. Only if I am making the minimum possible statement can I be pushed no further: only if I say that there is in my visual field at this moment a red rectangular patch on a cream background, am I safe from possible error: hence, if there are basic facts, only the simplest facts of sense-experience can fit the bill. By attempting to make rigid and absolute the flexible standard, which depends on the circumstances, of what the honest man cannot reasonably refuse to concede, we have ensnared ourselves in a reductionist spiral, demanding an ever lower standard of reasonableness until we reach the phenomenalist's goal, the lowest common denominator of what must be conceded by every reasonable man in any circumstances whatever, that is, what must be conceded by a barely sentient being.

---

[9] See above, §1.6.

§6.5   *The Tree in the Lonely Quad*   159

We start by assuming that a fact is what a true statement states: but this is to misunderstand the part played in argument by the word 'fact'. When we argue, we try to narrow the area of dispute, so as to concentrate our efforts on what is in issue. We use the word 'fact' to flag not what is claimed to be true, but what is agreed to be true by both parties to the dispute. Having agreed on the facts, we can then go on to argue. Sometimes the argument will be about a further proposition of the same logical type as the facts we have agreed on: on the basis of dates not in contention, we argue about another date—say, the date of the battle of Marathon. Often, however, we argue about interpretations or theories or moral judgements, which are of a different logical type from the facts we agree on. It is then dangerously easy to infer that since interpretations, scientific theorising and the conclusions of ethical debate are not facts, they are not true either. By restricting our criterion of truth to that of agreed truth, we eliminate all doubt and dubiety within the province of philosophy; nor can the opponent of this view fault the examples given of what is to be allowed as really true, for only those truths that cannot reasonably be contested are put forward as examples. But since there are few facts, if any, that we cannot in our metaphysical moments be uncertain of, our concept of truth is regressive; our criterion grows progressively and indefinitely more stringent. The more we think, the more nice we become as to what are unquestionable truths; and so not only the propositions of morals, theology and metaphysics, but also natural science, of common sense and everyday life, join the procession to the guillotine.

There are no basic facts: only facts relative to a dispute. Since there is nothing that cannot on some occasion be reasonably doubted, there can be no truths established beyond doubt to all comers, no elemental facts which we just have to accept and on which all else is based. Nothing is never doubtful, though this is not to say that everything is always doubtful. In every dispute we have to start somewhere, but there is nowhere that is the starting point for every dispute. It naturally seems a good idea to build a theory of knowledge upon the facts; and then it is natural to identify the facts with the sense-data we might cite if we were disagreeing about a pattern in the clouds. But once we realise that facts are always with regard to this or that specifiable issue, and not neutral elemental atoms, with regard to any conceivable issue, we need no longer feel impelled to hypostatize them, and conclude that sense-data are hard, brute facts, existing independently of us and the real foundation of all empirical knowledge.

§6.6 Rebuttals

Phenomenalism is very teasing. Often it seems absurd, and we cannot take it seriously. But sometimes we get the bug, and then cannot see how on earth it can be refuted. Phenomenalism seems more like a disease than a position reached through rational argument. But arguments have been put forward, and sometimes seem persuasive. Our first task is to consider them, and see whether they are as compelling as they seem.

Many of the arguments for phenomenalism are sceptical arguments. We need to be aware of the different positions maintained by the sceptic. We can be asked to justify the belief in unobserved objects, but need to be told to whom the justification should be addressed (i.e. what the sceptic's own position is), and what sort of justification he is seeking (i.e. what sort of argument he would in principle be prepared to accept). Otherwise we shall be the target of Hume's guerillas, who themselves have no position to defend, but, whatever we say, profess themselves unsatisfied by it, and demand a further justification. But guerillas win no wars, having no position they can themselves defend. And demands for justification that are intended to be unsatisfiable can be brushed off with contempt.

Some arguments for phenomenalism are based on deductivism. Certainly, if the only valid arguments are deductive arguments, then we cannot argue validly from our having the experience of seeing a tree in the quad to there actually being one, for we *could* (logically could) have been deluded or mistaken: it is not inconsistent to say "I had an experience of seeing a tree in the quad but actually there was not one—it was a *trompe d'oeuil* put up by the Ball committee". But if the sceptic is a deductivist, and demands that 'proof' be taken as deductive proof, he is crying for the moon: he is demanding that the contrary position be unsayable. But it is no merit in a language that it should prevent us from characterizing alternative possibilities; on the contrary, language should be as flexible as possible, not as inflexible. Once we allow that the function of language is to enable us to describe things, we shall expect it to be able to describe what is not the case as well as what is, and so shall not demand that only what is the case shall be describable. It is a logical possibility that we should have an experience of seeing a tree in the quad without there actually being one, but it is not a normal possibility—as witnessed by our needing to explain it in some way: "it was a *trompe d'oeuil* put up by the Ball committee".

§6.6   The Tree in the Lonely Quad   161

The deductivist equates normal and logical possibility, and wants it to be logically impossible—self-contradictory—to describe what it would be like if what was normally impossible actually occurred.[10]

Not all phenomenalists are deductivists. Some allow inductive arguments; some are not sceptics with respect to causality. They may then be led to acknowledge the existence of *unperceived* objects by reason of their causal properties. I may not be able to see the magnet underneath the table, but can still avow its existence on account of the deflection of a compass needle, or the pattern of iron filings, on the top of the table.[11] The tree itself may be unobserved by any human being, but its shadow visible from my window is adequate evidence of its existence none the less. Effects and perceptions merge into each other: the swish of traffic in the wet street may be an effect from which I infer a cause, but equally it may be the cue for my hearing the traffic. An electron microscope is a mechanism which causes patterns to occur in a cathode-ray tube, and perhaps we should not talk of viewing molecular structures with its aid: but should we similarly eschew talk of "seeing" things through an ordinary microscope, a telescope, or in a looking glass?

In modern times scepticism about how we could know of the existence of unobserved objects has been expressed in terms of the Verificationist Theory of Meaning. The meaning of a statement about some material object is simply the method of verifying it, and the way we verify statements about material objects is by seeing, hearing, touching, smelling or tasting them. But Verificationism leads also to solipsism; and if, like Berkeley, we believe in the existence of other people and other minds, we cannot be thoroughgoing verificationists; nor can we be, if we are unwilling to deny knowledge of the future and the past; nor if we are scientists or mathematicians, and reluctant to give up our professional talk of theoretical entities. Some phenomenalists, more consistently, accept a radical reconstruction of their scientific discourse, or become mathematical intuitionists. thereby making their position tenable again, but at the cost of plausibility.[12]

The Argument from Illusion is open to a different type of rebuttal. We are sometimes misled by illusions. But we are not

---

[10] See above, §2.3, §3.1.

[11] See W.F.R. Hardie, "Phenomenalism", *Proceedings of the Aristotelian Society*, **45**, 1945-1946, pp.127-154.

[12] See more generally, §4.4.

permanently and pervasively misled; for, if we were, we should not realise that we had been misled. Although in individual cases we may be deluded, hallucinating, misled, or otherwise mistaken, we can in general distinguish deviant from veridical sense-experience. And hence we have a way, fallible but generally reliable, of knowing when we should be cautious and report only our sense-experience as it seems to us, and when we can use it as a basis for making more ambitious claims about material objects.

The Argument from the Senses is effective against naive formulations of our untutored beliefs, but takes over many assumptions open to question. In metaphysics we seek the ultimate, but should not take for granted that such ultimates exist. There may be no minimum sense data not contaminated by any interpretation. Phenomenalists speak of sense *data*, something *given* by the senses, but this is an entirely wrong view of perception. Sense-experience is not just given, but elicited. We look, we listen, poke, sniff and savour, and sense-experience is the feed-back on these activities.

Rebuttals **against** Arguments **for** Phenomenalism

1. How do we know?
   1a) Indirect knowledge.
   1b) Verificationist Reductionism leads also to solipsism, to mathematical intuitionism, and to denial of knowledge about the future and past, and about theoretical entities.
2. Argument from Illusion shows we can tell difference between veridical perceptions and illusory sensations.
3. An analysis of *how* we perceive does not determine *what* we perceive.
4. Direct and indirect objects: I hear bells, I hear a sound; I married Jane, I married my wife.
5. Most sensations are not painful, but more subtle if less peremptory.
6. Some Representative Theories of Perception are badly expressed, but we do not feel bound by Humean doubts when it comes to science. If we can believe in quarks without ever having seen them, then we might be allowed to believe in the Tree in the Quad which "causes" our tree-like sensations.

§6.7 Arguments against Phenomenalism

The arguments for phenomenalism are not conclusive; some are bad; some are incoherent, presuming the falsity of phenomenalism in arguing for its truth; some prove too much, leading us to deny not only the existence of material objects, but of other persons, and requiring us to abjure all knowledge of the future and the past. But we may be persuaded none the less: we may be convinced by sceptical arguments, accepting the further sceptical conclusions too; or we may simply feel phenomenalist, not driven to it by argument, but just finding ourselves occupying that position. In such cases we have to ask: Can phenomenalism be refuted? If, like Descartes, we adopt the method of doubt, and have been able to affirm our own existence as a solipsistic consciousness, have we good reason to go further, and affirm the existence of an external world? We have. Besides being unable to doubt our own existence, we encounter other inabilities. Although we can avoid seeing, hearing, or feeling things by shutting our eyes, blocking our ears, or not touching with our body, we cannot open our eyes and see things the way we would like to see them, or listen and hear what we would like to hear, or touch and feel as we would wish: we can, through our senses, put questions to nature, but the answers we get are not decided by us, but by nature. Berkeley maintained that the existence of the quires of heaven depended on their being perceived,[13] which in turn depends on our choosing to observe them; but though ostrich-like I may be able to choose not to observe what I do not want to observe, I cannot, conversely, by choosing to observe, observe whatsoever I want, but only what is there for me to observe. The argument is the same as that for causality.[14] Recalcitrance to my will argues for the existence of a reality other than myself with effective power.

But need it be comprised of material objects? Might it not be ideas in the mind of God——

> Young man, your astonishment's odd,
> *I* am always about in the Quad,
> And that's why the tree
> Continues to be,
> Since observed by
> Yours faithfully,
> God.

---

[13] *Principles of Human Knowledge*, §VI.

[14] See above, §4.6.

—or possible sense-data waiting for us to actualise them by choosing to observe?

Descartes was concerned to explain. We, too, may wish not merely to acknowledge the existence of something recalcitrant to our will, but to make sense of our experiences of encountering observations not of our own choosing. Provided reason is not subjected to Humean constraints, and is not confined to deduction and inductive Inference to the Next Case, we can argue from our various sense-experiences to the existence of material objects, as being the best explanation of them. Leibniz gave as a decisive reason for believing in the existence of material objects *la liaison des phénomènes*.[15] We do not merely experience sense-data, but find different sorts of sense-data constantly conjoined. We learn that metals which look like gold are malleable, that if we have a tree-like visual sense-datum and then the kinaesthetic sensations of walking towards it, we shall soon have tactile sense-data of scratchy twigs and impenetrable bark. If we do not believe that these linked sense-data are all due to the tree, we find it very difficult to account for their constant concomitance. Material objects explain why a whole lot of disparate sense-data go together. Phenomenalists cannot explain the invariances of our sense-experience; at best they can only re-state them: those who believe in the independent existence of material objects can explain; they posit the existence of unperceived objects, as scientists posit the existence of unperceived entities. Only a Humean sceptic can deny the cogency of an Inference to the Best Explanation, and such scepticism about the powers of reason is one for which it is impossible to argue by means of reasons that it would recognise as cogent.

Once I am forced to recognise the existence of a reality other than myself with effective power, I am beginning to cut myself down to size. Reality is essentially non-egocentric. So, too, is reason. The more reasonable I am, the less insistent am I on seeing everything exclusively from my own egocentric point of view. Many sceptical arguments lose their charm, once I recognise that they depend on unduly emphasizing some aspect of egocentricity. If I would be a spectator of all time, the past and the future no longer seem entirely

---

[15] G.W. Leibniz, *New Essays on the Human Understanding*, IV, 2, §14, (p.374 in Akademie-Verlag ed.), tr. Mary Morris. *The Philosophical Writings of Leibniz*, Everyman, pp.190-191; tr. P.Remnant and J.Bennett, Cambridge, 1982.

§6.7   *The Tree in the Lonely Quad*   165

unlike the present; other times will not be radically unknowable, as being ontologically different from my time, nor will other minds be ontologically different from my own mind. Similarly, whether or not I happen to be observing something will become irrelevant to its actual existence. Reality having once abated my pride, reason assuages it further, and inclines me to take up a omni-personal, omni-temporal point of view in which I am no longer tempted to reconstruct reality as an emanation of my own will.[16]

Some versions of phenomenalism lead naturally to solipsism, and, *per contra*, if a man believes in the existence of other people, he will believe also in the existence of material objects. For sense-experience is private. I experience what I experience, and you experience what you experience. Then believing, like Berkeley, in the existence of other minds, we can argue against me-phenomenalism because you see the tree when I am not looking, and against you-phenomenalism because I see the tree when you are not looking. It is reasonable then to infer that it should continue to exist when neither of us is looking. We can also use the argument of Locke that a common language presupposes a common external world. Communication would be impossible unless there were things in a common external world for our language to refer to and describe. Although our experiences are necessarily peculiar to us, although for all we know, you may see colours differently from me, there is something common to my experience, your experience, everybody else's, since others use the same words as we do. These common factors can be picked out and talked about. Since they are inter-subjective, it is reasonable to characterize them as objective, as manifestations of, perhaps even as being caused by, some real thing, the same for us all.

Berkeley might acknowledge the force of the argument from intersubjectivity, but deny that it proved the existence of material objects. He might allow that there are common ideas, and yet distinguish them from matter. After all, we see rainbows and hear thunder, but do not believe that rainbows or thunder are material objects. But once we acknowledge intersubjectivity, we are no longer talking about particular sense-experiences, which must be had by some mind, but what is invariant as between many experiences, and therefore not tied to any particular one. We no longer

---

[16] But see further below, §10.5 and §14.8.

can say *Esse est Percipi*. What we are talking about is not something perceived by some person, but something common to what is perceived, or may be perceived, by anyone suitably situated. In some cases it may not be a *material* object, but it is objective, and because accessible to all percipients, not tied essentially to any particular one. Matter, according to Mill, is a permanent possibility of sensation. That cannot be quite right, since the background radiation in the universe—the lingering echoes of the Big Bang—can always be detected, but is not itself matter. But neither is it a sense-datum. Although further conditions are necessary for the adequate characterization of material objects, the argument from inter-subjectivity establishes sufficient objectivity to rule out phenomenalism. Many of Berkeley's arguments are directed against the concept of matter, which he considers too inert to be capable of explaining anything. May-be. But his "notions" run counter to his subjectivist arguments, and we ask: "How different is an idea in the mind of God from an ordinary material thing?" In the end, Berkeley seems not to be establishing phenomenalism or idealism (in the Eighteenth Century sense), but to be replacing a somewhat confused causal theory of perception by one that construes perception as a communication—God telling us what the facts of our lives are. There may be advantages in taking this view—there are certainly disadvantages. But it is not phenomenalism.

Arguments Against Phenomenalism
1. Recalcitrance to Will
2. Invariance over own experience: Leibniz, *la liaison des phénomènes* (*New Essays*, IV:2:14)
3. Non-egocentricity
4. Invariance over experiences of others
5. Maximum Evidence

§6.8 Reality Recovered

The arguments against phenomenalism are diverse, different arguments being appropriate for different thinkers, assailed by different species of doubt. In their different ways they help the doubter recover his ordinary sense of the reality of the external world. They do this very largely by being able to deploy a robust sense of reason, which both neutralises some of the arguments of the sceptic, and gives positive warrant for maintaining the reality of entities the phenomenalist is reluctant to recognise. Reason liberates us from neurotic egocentricity, and Inference to the Best Explanation is a powerful weapon for extending the realm of knowledge beyond any previous bounds.

Reason liberates us from neurotic egocentricity. Modern philosophy is much too preoccupied with ME. Whereas ancient and mediaeval philosophers were primarily concerned with Ontology, the question of what exists, the chief question addressed by philosophers since the time of Descartes has been Epistemology, what can be known, and more specifically, what can be known by me. We can criticize Descartes, as we can criticize Luther, for focusing too much on the personal at the expense of the communal. Reason tells me that I am not the only pebble on the beach. Just as I live in a community of other people, selves like me but different from me, so I think in thought-forms I share with others, and depend on others for much of what I know. Once I listen to reason, phenomenalism loses its grip on me, and doubts about the existence of an external, objective world disappear.

But even if I still feel impelled to visit Descartes in his solipstic prison of isolated self-consciousness, I can reason my way out into a public world of things existing independently of my mind. I infer their existence because they explain both the limitations on my ability to choose what sensations to experience, and the constant correlations between the various sensations I do experience.

These different exercises of reason are illuminating, not least because they are being deployed in favour of one of our most firm beliefs—the existence of material objects—rather than against it, or on behalf of some less commonsensical belief, such as the existence of Platonist ideas, numbers, values, or God. Reality is shown to be under attack from many quarters, and reason shown to have many aspects. Most importantly, reality is intimately connected with reason, though not the same as it, and many of the arguments adduced in defence of the existence of the external world, can be deployed to establish the existence of other entities too. Solipsism, which denies that other people really exist, that is, that other bodies are inhabited by other minds, resembles phenomenalism, and many of the arguments adduced earlier in this chapter can be deployed also with regard to the so-called question of Other Minds. But there are differences too. Consciousness is involved, and is a difficult concept. The science of neuro-physiology and the materialist bias of modern thinking makes us wonder whether in the last analysis consciousness, our own or that of other people, can have any real *rôle* in the scheme of things. Reason itself, in curing us of our neurotic egocentricity, is in danger of denying our existence as *ego*s altogether. We shall need to go on a longer path, and plumb the nature of ultimate reality, before we can reach a reasoned judgement whether we really exist.

§6.9 The Analogy of Feeling

The solipsist, like the phenomenalist, often makes his case by attacking the not-very-well-articulated account of common sense.

The traditional arguments for the existence of minds start with the first person—*cogito, ergo sum*—and argue that there must be something other than oneself, and that one's sense-experience must be a reliable guide to it; and then, having established the existence of the external world, argue that other men's bodies, being visibly similar to one's own, must be inhabited by minds, also similar to one's own. The relations between minds and bodily behaviour has a certain broad similarity to that between material objects and sense-experience, and gives rise to similar objections on the part of the sceptic, and similar counters on the part of the realist.

It is tempting to formalise this as an argument, of a type the sceptic should admit. But unfortunately it then turns out to be an invalid specimen whose invalidity can thereupon be triumphantly exposed. We are tempted, that is, to argue by induction. In one case, my own, I know that my behaviour is linked to states of mind. And so it seems reasonable to argue by analogy that behind other peoples' behaviour lie corresponding states of other minds. But then the sceptic can counter-attack, and point out how unreasonable it is to argue inductively from a single case. Although, as a matter of fact scientists, especially in the mathematical sciences, do not make large numbers of observations, and can often determine either the value of a physical magnitude or the truth or falsity of a physical theory on the basis of only a few readings, yet their sample is only contingently small: their experiments are repeatable, and it is only in cases where theory suggests, what has often been borne out in experience, that repetition will not affect the verdict, that they are content to make do with only a few instances. In the argument to other minds, however, the sample is necessarily limited to a single case. It is not that we could stabilise the correlation between bodily behaviour and states of mind for several other people, but forbear to do so because we know it will only produce the same result: the whole problem arises because we cannot do that, and each one of us knows only himself at first hand, and must, it seems generalise illegitimately from a single instance.

If the only valid arguments are either deductive or inductive, the sceptic can go on to argue that all that we ever see is men's overt behaviour, and that if we ascribe to them mysterious states of mind, we are engaging in invalid inferences which can never be adequately justified. We simply cannot know what other people think or feel, and should acknowledge that such knowledge is impossible, and not pretend to what we cannot have. In fact, although we sometimes talk as though we did at least entertain opinions about other men's minds, since the criterion for the correct use of words lies in their behaviour, their behaviour is all we are really talking about.

§6.10 Criteria

Sceptics often argue for behaviourism by trading on the use of the word 'criterion'. Most of our judgements are uncontested, and depend on a large number of factors, many of which we have barely noticed and may not be able to itemise. If a judgement is contested, we follow the procedure described by Pantin,[17] and look for features about which there can be no doubt and which will enable us to tell in a fairly automatic fashion whether or not the judgement was correct. The criteria are a subclass of all the relevant factors, which have the virtues of being easily itemised themselves fairly indisputably, and together constituting, in practice, though not in logic, a necessary and sufficient condition for the truth of the judgement in question. We cannot count on always being able to formulate complete sets of criteria in particular human affairs; partly because human beings are very complex and very deceitful; partly because we are so familiar with them that we find it difficult

---

[17] C.F.A.Pantin, *The Relations between the Sciences* Cambridge, 1968.

to step back from our immediate judgements, and identify and formulate the factors on which they depend. We have criteria for valid wills in the law, but not for the Good Will in morals, because if we did, our ever-deceitful hearts would soon find it expedient to satisfy them for reason of *amour propre*. Consequently there are often no criteria for the application of personal predicates, or for making correct judgements about states of minds. Philosophers often construe this as meaning that there are no grounds whatever for applying personal predicates, or making correct judgements about states of mind, the word 'criterion' being taken to mean *any* factor whatever on which a judgement may be based. In the proper sense of the word my feeling a pain is not a *criterion* for it being correct for me to say that I am in pain. But this is all too easily taken as meaning that my being in pain is not any ground whatever for my saying that I am. And then we are rapidly led to the conclusion that this, and all similar talk about states of mind, is altogether unwarranted and groundless.

The argument that all we see is bodily behaviour, and the argument that all our words can refer to is bodily behaviour, both rest on the mistake of supposing that what we see or say cannot be more than the cues or evidence which guide us to our conclusions. Our evidence for saying that a man is in pain is the fact that he says so, or is writhing in agony, or is white and drawn, or has an abscess on his tooth: but what we mean, and why we think it important to offer him sympathy, is that he is in pain, suffering something we know what it is like to suffer, which occupies all a man's attention, which he would gladly avoid but cannot ignore. What we mean is *not* our evidence for saying it, any more than it is when on the basis of past experience we predict that there will be a meteor shower tomorrow night.[18] Our evidence is indubitably past: but only an extreme dogmatist would construe a statement about the future as being really about the past. When we say that a man is in pain we are saying more than that he told us, or was white and drawn, or was writhing, although any of these constitutes a good reason for making our assertion. If I say that a man is in pain, and when asked "How do you know?" answer "He told me", I have discharged the onus of justification which my having made an assertion naturally imposes on me. It does not of course follow that I could not be wrong. No matter how good my evidence is, I cannot be sure of not being wrong.

---

[18] See above §1.2, §4.4.

§6.11 The Argument from Deception

Not only, it is said, can inferences from overt behaviour to supposed inner mental states never be justified, but when we do make them, they often turn out to be wrong. We are often taken in by confidence-tricksters. Actors put on the appearance of emotions they do not really feel, and stoics conceal the feeling they really suffer from. The heart is deceitful above all things, and desperately sick. We should avoid all talk of mysterious minds, and concentrate on what we can know, and what does affect us—that is, behaviour. True handsomeness is as handsomeness does. Deceits sufficiently multiplied become livable with. We may be living in a fool's paradise: the apparently benign bods we everywhere encounter may really be malignant demons, who take pleasure in the manifold deceptions they perpetrate on us. But if the deception lasts for ever, if there is no moment of truth, when the real face of demoniacal hate is revealed to us, if the paradise experience was to last us all our life long, should we complain? Only a very foolish fool would carp at a paradise he was to inhabit for ever.

The argument is invalid, and reveals one important difference between behaviourism and phenomenalism. With material objects appearances are, ultimately, conclusive. If the mirage of an oasis beckoning to us across the sweltering desert is followed by an illusion of cool waters and shady palm trees, we do not feel disillusioned the next day, as we set off on our journey again, our waterbags filled, and still savouring the Arab hospitality of the night before. Life could be, for all we know, for all we could know, a singularly coherent dream, provided it is coherent enough, and there is to be no rude awakening into a contrasting reality. So far as things are concerned, we reject Aquinas' doctrine of transubstantiation. The substance of a thing is different from its accidents, but not independent of them, and if all the accidents are unchanged, then so is the substance. But, *pace* the behaviourists, minds are different. This is illustrated by the rather grisly example thrown up by modern medical techniques, where it is desirable to use a drug, such as curare, which relaxes all the voluntary muscles of the body. In effect, it induces complete paralysis, so that all the manifestations of consciousness, even down to the movements of the eye are suppressed. It is also the case that some patients are not anaesthetized by normal doses of anaesthetics. We can envisage therefore the horror story of a patient who is not anaesthetized while an operation is still being performed, and is fully conscious although showing no signs of consciousness to the doctors. He might even survive to tell the story, but in any event it is a conceivable case, conceivable enough to frighten us: and could be so only if consciousness were something different from the clinical criteria, which although usually reliable are not absolutely conclusive.[19]

There is a fact of the matter, about which we could be wrong in any particular instance. So there is a real question, but not one that supports the sceptic's case. Admittedly, we make mistakes about other men's states of mind, as we do also about material objects. But we could not be taken in by the confidence-trickster sometimes if we were not in the habit of generally regarding facial expression, bodily behaviour and the spoken word, as reliable indications of personal integrity. Actors could not simulate, nor stoics dissimulate, except against a background of overt behaviour being a reasonably reliable guide to their feelings. The argument from error proves the exact reverse of what the sceptic concludes from it.

§6.12 Myself and Others

The argument from analogy is not as broken-backed as modern philosophers suppose. As a simple inductive argument it does not work—but why should it have to be construed as a simple inductive argument? We often do agree from a single instance—what Aristotle called ἔκθεσις (*ekthesis*)—so long as we have some reason to believe that the single instance is typical. And we can argue against the contrary thesis—the thesis that I AM DIFFERENT—along the same lines as we argued against the thesis that the future is unlike the past, or that it makes a difference to material objects whether or not I am observing them.[20] The traditional formulation of the problem, as the Problem of Other Minds, makes this obvious. "Other than whose?" is the natural question, and the answer "Other than mine" betrays the inherent egocentricity of the issue.[21] We can go further. Not only does 'other' implicitly involve the first person singular, but the first person singular implies the legitimacy of the other grammatical persons. I could not have learned even

---

[19] See below, §14.2.

[20] See above, §6.6.

[21] See above §3.3 and §6.7.

the use of the first person singular except concomitantly with that of the second and the third. I form my sense of my own identity by comparing and contrasting it with yours and his. The conceptual scheme we actually use is one in which the first, second and third persons are *pari passu*. 'I' in my mouth refers to the same person as is referred to by 'you' in your mouth when you are addressing me. If the sceptic accepts one part of the conceptual structure he must accept it all. He cannot pick and choose. He cannot use our existing conceptual scheme to put its validity in question unless he can state those doubts in a way which does not presuppose the truth of the position he is concerned to question.

The argument can be developed in different ways: it can be deployed *ad hominem* to make an effective debating point; "Who do you think you are talking to?" we ask; and go on "Unless other people have minds, it is pointless to argue with them", thus showing that the solipsist, like other sceptics, does not really believe that other people are automata. His action in speaking belies what his words are meant to say. Alternatively, we can deploy a direct argument, that it is implicit in language and a precondition of our being able to communicate at all that people exist. *Cogito, ergo sum* implies *loquor ergo es*. We can then, not exactly rehabilitate, but reconstruct, the argument from analogy to constitute a cogent cumulative argument for the thesis that people really do have feelings.

§6.13 Understanding People

I am unique. Any inductive argument generalising from my own experience, is precarious, even if not totally vitiated by the narrowness of the base. Nevertheless, any philosopher who instanced himself as his reason for rejecting behaviourism, showed a right instinct. Although I cannot appeal to my own experience as a premise for a simple inductive argument to show that other men have minds, I can turn to myself as a source from which to derive the concepts I need if I am to be able to organize and understand the behaviour of others. We describe other people's behaviour as if they were conscious agents, doing the same sort of thing as each one of us does himself and for the same sorts of reasons. Without these categories of conscious action, it would be impossible, to make sense of, and often even to describe, their behaviour. Even with animal behaviour the ethnologists have needed to borrow heavily from the vocabulary of human affairs in order to make the patterns of observed response intelligible and to suggest to them what further features to look for. With human beings, we are so completely at home in these categories of description that we find it far easier to describe a man in terms of action and temperament than in terms of behaviour or appearance expressed without the aid of specifically personal concepts. I know for certain that a man's behaviour was threatening and that he made as if to attack me, but am utterly at a loss to say which hand was where or how exactly the legs are placed. We all are constantly reading one another's faces, and know whether the boss is in a good mood or not, and whether our remarks are being well received: but only those who are gifted artists can tell what was the exact configuration of lines on the face that betokened impatience and mounting irritation. When we meet a man for the first time, we notice peculiarities of appearance or voice, but with further acquaintance we discount them, and notice only his expression *as* an indication of his state of mind, his words *as* an expression of his thoughts. We not only pay no attention to peculiarities of face and speech, but do not and almost cannot, notice them. If a man has a *tic* which moves his face into a painful grimace, it obtrudes itself onto our notice at first, for it seems to indicate spasms of agony: but soon we hardly notice it at all, because we know that it does not mean anything, while still a flicker of the eyelids will not escape our attention, because it may mean much. We do not see men's behaviour first as behaviour characterized in non-human terms, and then conjecture by hazardous inference that behind it lies some specified state of mind: we ask straight away "Is this man in pain or not?" or "Is he in a good temper or not?", and fit what we see either into the category "Yes, he is in pain", "Yes, he is in a good temper" or into the category "No, he is not in pain", "No, he is not in a good temper". Our answers may, of course, be wrong, and another man may be able to point out features we had overlooked, which could have indicated to us that the other answer should be given. But that is the question we ask, and our whole perception of the situation is structured by that question. We understand people's behaviour in terms of human action and feeling, and would not be able to construe it as we do, if we did not have those categories available from the outset.

The sceptic's claim that we cannot ever see men's minds but only their behaviour is based on a faulty theory of perception, in the

§6.13   *The Tree in the Lonely Quad*   175

same way as the phenomenalists' claim that we cannot see material objects but only the corresponding sense-experiences. In each case there is an acceptable locution in which we see sense-experience or see behaviour, but this does not exclude there being another locution, equally acceptable and more fundamental, in which we see a material object or see a man's mood. In all our perceiving we tend to concentrate on the most important—often the most invariant—features, and to pick these out from amid the welter of irrelevances. The simile of reading is apt. We speak of reading a man's mind, and seeing what he is thinking. When we first learn to read words, we are highly conscious of the different shapes of the letters, and at that stage could be said to see the shapes immediately or directly, and to know what the message was only mediately and indirectly. But when we have been long familiar with reading, we see straight through to the words, and often do not notice and cannot tell what the shape of the letters is. Indeed, we can go further. We get the gist of the message without noticing or remembering the words—sometimes not even remembering what language the message was expressed in. Or we may gain an impression of the style—the personality and the mood of the author, from various *nuances* we often at a loss to itemise. We see *through* one level of phenomena to another; or see that other *level in* the original one. Our knowledge of material objects comes through our sense-experience, our knowledge of other minds through our observation of their bodies: but, normally without any effort, we construe our sense-experience as being perception of material objects, and we see other men's faces, words and actions as expressing their motives. The argument from perception tends towards exactly the opposite conclusion the sceptic wants.

The sceptic may counter that we have to learn to read, and the primitive unreading state is logically prior to the habits of literacy: and that in cases of doubt, we are still forced back to close examination of the letters; and similarly in cases of doubt about how a man's action should be interpreted. All of these may be conceded. We learn to interpret behaviour, just as we learn to read—and just as we learn to see. All perception is learned, but is not any the less perception for that. A person might conceivably—at least for the sake of the present argument let us concede that a person might conceivably—not learn to *use* the *language* of persons: but this would not enable him to talk of behaviour in a less theory-laden and more aseptic way; he just would be unable to talk about, and to a large extent even to notice, behaviour at all. Again, it is true that in cases of doubt, we characterize the letters or the behaviour in neutral terms, and argue which reading or which interpretation is to be preferred. But this does not prove that we either should, or even could, characterize letters or behaviour in terms that were absolutely neutral as between all possible interpretations.[22] Specific doubts about states of mind are common: but far from adding up to a general doubt whether states of mind exist at all, they argue the other way. Only against the background of general non-doubts are particular doubts intelligible at all.

There remains the deep hostility felt by the sceptic at the ontological extravagance of going beyond overt behaviour and positing minds as well as material objects. It can be met in the same way as the similar misgivings felt by the phenomenalist. The additional range of concepts enable us to organize and understand overt behaviour far better than we otherwise could. Ryle gives a brilliant account of the many different ways in which vanity is manifested.[23]

> on hearing that a man is vain we expect him, in the first instance, to behave in certain ways, namely to talk a lot about himself, to cleave to the society of the eminent, to reject criticisms, to seek the footlights and to disengage himself from conversations about the merits of others. We expect him also to indulge in roseate daydreams about his own successes, to avoid recalling past failures and to plan for his own advancement. To be vain is to tend to act in these and innumerable other kindred ways.

The ways are, not only innumerable, but very different. Having at our disposal the concept of vanity, we can see all these different patterns of behaviour as expressions of the same state of mind. Mental concepts enable us to achieve *une liaison des phénomènes* otherwise unattainable; and that is sufficient justification for using them, and believing minds to exist.

---

[22] See, more fully, "On Not Worshipping Facts", *Philosophical Quarterly*, **8**, 1958, pp.144-156.

[23] Gilbert Ryle, *The Concept of the Mind*, London, 1949. pp. 85-87. Compare Jane Austen, *Persuasion*, London, 1818, p.1.

§6.14 Conclusion

The argument of the previous three chapters has been largely negative. Attacks on particular forms of reasoning have been parried. In Plantinga's terminology, we have defeated the defeaters. Some very typical forms of reasoning have been vindicated as generally worthy of credence, though admittedly fallible on occasion. In so far as sceptical metaphysical systems have been based on some critique of reason, they are, in general, mistaken. We can go wrong in our speculations about the nature of reality, but are not bound to. It may be possible to reason aright.

Two further points have emerged which are of importance for metaphysics: we can legitimately reason across categories; from particular instances to general laws; from concomitances to causal connexions; from sounds and sights to events and material objects; from overt behaviour to mental states: and we can legitimately posit entities in order to integrate and explain; the existence of material objects makes sense of the coherence of our visual, auditory and other sense-experience; the existence of minds explains why organisms manifest apparently very diverse patterns of behaviour; Ockham's razor bids us not to multiply entities unnecessarily, but reason can sometimes establish the need for some further kind of being.

Chapter 7
Existence and Reality

§7.1 Universals
§7.2 Existence
§7.3 Platonism
§7.4 Mathematical Platonism
§7.5 Nominalism
§7.6 Conceptualism
§7.7 Natural Kinds
§7.8 Modifying Logic
§7.9 Umbrian Universals
§7.10 Aristotelian Actuality

§7.1 Universals

In arguing against phenomenalism and behaviourism I gave, as a cogent argument for the existence of material objects and persons, the integrating power of the concepts of a material object and of a person. I can make sense of my sense-experience, if I ascribe different sense impressions to the same object: I can make sense of a person's overt behaviour if I construe it as the manifestation of a person's mind. Integrative power is a mark of existence. Earlier, in the account of how we come to know causes, I appealed to there being natural kinds. But do natural kinds really exist? Are we entitled to ascribe existence to sets of sense-data, or to posit a real person behind his observable behaviour? Since Plato first put forward his theory of Forms, the status of universals has been one of the main problems of metaphysics. Do universals exist? or are they only in the mind? or are they just a grammatical feature misunderstood? If they exist, do they exist independently of particulars, or merely concomitantly with them?

The Schoolmen distinguished four possible positions about the existence of universals. Plato had held that the Forms[1] existed

---

[1] Plato uses two words which are standardly translated as Form, but often would better rendered as kind, pattern, shape, species, feature, value. I shall use the stock translation, Form, with the capital letter indicating that it is a term of art; and keep the word 'Species' for Aristotelian universals discussed in the next paragraph; natural kinds may be either Platonic Forms or Aristotelian Species.

independently of their (material) instantiations, and hence before them, *ante res*. A modern physical chemist would be likely to maintain that even before the Big Bang, even if the universe never had existed, oxygen would be a stable nuclear structure, and would be bivalent. Most working mathematicians are platonists, and believe that numbers exist whether or not there are any material objects to which they apply. e and π are more fundamental than the existence of the sun and the moon; the discovery that $e^{i\pi} + 1 = 0$ was a discovery about the nature of reality, on a par with the discovery of America, only more profound.

Biologists are more Aristotelian. They believe in the existence of species, but only as instantiated in specimens *in rebus*. The species of giraffe exists, but only because there are specimens of giraffe. Unlike the Forms, Species are not laid up in heaven, and do not have to be the way they actually are.

The Conceptualists hold that universals exist only in the mind. They think it ridiculous to suppose that there is the idea of a university laid up in heaven. Living human lives in human institutions, we impose classifications reflecting our concerns and needs. Razors are what we shave with, felonies and misdemeanours are forms of behaviour we deem meet for punishment. It is entirely up to us how we classify things, not something to be discovered in the nature of reality.

The Nominalists go further. Their notion of reality has no room for what goes on in the mind: they are concerned with the objective world, and reckon that in the objective world only particulars exist; to exist is to be located in space. Astronauts explore space, but do not find Objective Values there. Universals are not part of the fabric of the world.[2]

Existence of Universals

1. Plato: universals exist *ante res*, independently of their (material) instantiations.
2. Aristotle: universals exist *in rebus*, concomitantly with their (material) instantiations.
3. Conceptualists: universals exist only in the mind.
4. Nominalists: only particulars exist; universals not part of the furniture of the universe.

---

[2] See J.L.Mackie, *Ethics: Inventing Right and Wrong*, Harmondsworth, 1977, p.15.

Each of these positions has been put forward in opposition to some other position, and is to be understood in the context of the alternatives it is intended to supplant and the alternatives put forward to supplant it. Each has something going for it: each is open to serious objections. Often there is an unrecognised shift in what existence is understood to mean. If we can elucidate that, we shall be less confused when we seek to adjudicate between them.

§7.2 Existence

In any case, we feel sure that no further clarity would be achieved by taking the first few steps down that infinite regress that starts with: 'What do you mean by "exists"?' E.T.Jaynes, *Probability Theory: The Logic of Science*, Cambridge, 2003, p.xxviii.

Existence is a counter in argumentative discourse. It licenses discussion by warding off the conversation stopper "But there is no such thing". If I start talking about the greatest prime number, it is the same as if I start talking about the present king of France, or Ryle's youngest son. My discourse, though grammatical and consistent, fails to carry information because it fails to refer to anything. Rather than hear me out as I go rabbiting on, you interrupt, and say "But there is no greatest prime number". That is a conversation stopper. Once it has been alleged that there is no object that my purported referring term refers to, I must either meet the allegation and give it the lie, or else shut up. I cannot go on talking about nothing at all.

In ordinary conversational discourse it is easy to interrupt, and we need take no special pains to guard against failure of reference because should reference fail we shall soon be interrupted and brought to heel. Academic discourse, however, is much more monologous. If you are reading my book, you cannot interrupt. Since I cannot argue from your silence that my referring attempts are being successful, I need to anticipate possible interruptions and deal with them in advance, so that if you were minded to interrupt, you would find the point already dealt with. I forestall your "But it does not exist", or, more colloquially, "But there isn't one", by an existence proof. Existence proofs play a prominent role in mathematics. Once I have proved that the nine-point circle exists, I can go on to talk about it and its centre, and say that the latter is on the Euler line, with complete confidence that I cannot be faulted on the score of talking about nothing at all. Equally if I am disposed to talk about Brouwer's fixed point, I can cite his Fixed

§7.2   Existence and Reality   181

Point theorem to ward off the counter that it does not exist, even though it is a non-constructive existence proof. If someone were to prove that Goldbach's conjecture was true, we should thereafter give short shrift to the computer buff who wanted us to give him a grant while he searched for a counter-example: and *per contra* if it were proved that Goldbach's conjecture leads to an inconsistency, then it would be a reasonable proposal to program a computer to find a counter-example.

An existence claim forestalls the objection that there is nothing for us to talk about. Its force, therefore, often depends on context, and the objection anticipated. The extreme case—*e.g.* the greatest prime number—is where the referring expression is a contradiction in terms. Against such an objection, bare consistency is enough. In first-order logic the Completeness Theorem establishes that any consistent set of well-formed formulae has a model, and consistency proofs for non-Euclidean geometry, non-Desarguian geometry and non-standard models of Peano's axioms, are all we need for us to be able to talk about them with a clear conscience. We are thus led to a minimal Platonism—Hilbertian Platonism, we might call it: we are permitted to talk about anything, if we are so minded, which we can specify without inconsistency. But it is only in few cases that bare consistency suffices.[3] Fictions, too, can be talked about, and shadows, but though discourse about them is allowed to be intelligible, it is not taken seriously—it is not for real.

To exist, then, is usually not just to be talkable about, but to be worth talking about. But it is not easy to be talked about in a meaningful way. I may be very voluble, interlarding my word flow with "You know what I mean", but you may well be unable to know what I mean, because what I actually say gives little guidance as to the real object of my discourse. It is all right if I am talking about large objects in the immediate vicinity—though even there it demands some skill to pick out unambiguously the target at which fire should be directed. But when we want to talk about ideas and feelings and abstract objects generally, it is difficult to identify what it is that another person is talking about. We sometimes use carefully constructed definitions, sometimes examples, sometimes analogies, sometimes metaphors. Only seldom do we succeed in finding a form of words that is absolutely fool-proof: nevertheless

---

[3] See G.M.Hunter, "Is Consistency Enough for Existence in Mathematics", *Analysis*, **48**, January 1988, pp.3-5.

we sometimes succeed in getting our meaning across to another person.

Many thinkers will be dismayed at our inability to tie down completely the topic of our discourse. Although it is a golden precept that we should not be content to use words which will mean what we want them to mean, but should strive to find words that will not mean anything other than what we intend, it is a counsel of perfection to demand that we should actually achieve absolute unambiguity. Even the natural numbers cannot be defined unambiguously in first-order logic—the logic that computers can be programmed to do. Peano's axioms, or any other way of specifying the natural numbers, have weird models, which are not at all what we had in mind when we set out to characterize the natural numbers, but which nevertheless satisfy the specifications we had devised.[4] These unintended models of the axioms for elementary number theory we can obviate if we go to second-order logic, but that involves a certain amount of hand-waving, or accepting ontological commitments which many philosophers would hesitate to make. We can specify the natural numbers unambiguously—"monomorphically"—if we can quantify over predicate variables, that is, talk of all properties. If we concede that properties really exist—as Platonists do—then we have no problem. We can identify the natural numbers absolutely, and be sure that you and I are talking about the same things. But it demands a big initial commitment. And even if we commit ourselves to the existence of properties, we cannot give fool-proof specifications of the objects of our discourse, because second-order logic is not complete, but only Henkin-complete. Whereas in first-order logic every valid well-formed formula, is a theorem, that is to say, every well-formed formula that is true under all interpretations of the axioms, is provable from the axioms by a finite number of applications of some rule of inference, in second-order logic there are well-formed formulae which are true under all intended interpretations of the axioms, but which cannot be proved from the axioms by a finite number of applications of some rule of inference, and so are not theorems. A computer could not be programmed to churn out all the valid well-formed formulae of second-order logic.

The only completeness possessed by second-order logic is Henkin-completeness. Henkin-completeness considers not just the intended interpretations of the axioms, but the weird ones as well.

---

[4] See more fully below, §7.4 of this chapter, pp.193f.

§7.2   *Existence and Reality*   183

Second-order logic *is* Henkin-complete, because every well-formed formula that is true under *all* interpretations, weird as well as intended, is a theorem. Since the range of interpretations is wider, the number of well-formed formulae that come out true in all of them is narrower, and does coincide with the well-formed formulae that can be proved from the axioms. But that is too little. We cannot prove by deduction from the axioms the well-formed formulae which distinguish our intended interpretation from the weird ones. So, although we may be able to convey well enough what our intended interpretation is, we cannot in general do so to a recalcitrant sceptic whose only principle is the avoidance of self-contradiction.

Nevertheless we sometimes succeed in getting our meaning across to another person. Indeed, we seem to do so quite often. It is an important fact about human intercourse that although we sometimes talk at cross-purposes, and may be unduly optimistic about the extent to which our hearers are really with us, we nonetheless do succeed in communicating about abstract matters. We succeed in sharing our thoughts partly because we share values, and so share a common understanding of what meaning is intended. Often examples help, examples both of what I do intend and of what I do not. Given examples of what I have in mind, you can consider other respects in which they are all similar, and pick out the most likely resemblance as being the one I intended. You may check whether you have grasped my point by instancing other examples of what you think I had in mind. Often you will be right, and I shall know that you are with me, because you can go on and make pertinent comments—which could not have seemed pertinent to me if you had misidentified what it was that I was talking about. Since resemblance is a three-term relation, and there are many different respects in which a few examples may resemble one another, I may need to guide you by means of analogies and metaphors, to spot the relevant features that my examples have in common. Sometimes I can.

Fallible though our identifications are, we sometimes succeed in talking about the same thing. It follows that our specification of what we were talking about is not exhaustive. Else, having specified it, we should have nothing left to say about it. It follows further that what we are talking about is not constituted by our specification of it. Our specification was enough to identify it, but there was more to it than simply what we said about it in order to identify it. It follows that to be seriously talkable about implies an existence that goes beyond, and so is independent of, our means of identifying it. We find it difficult to say what that more is, because it differs in different contexts.

§7.3 Platonism

Plato was led into metaphysical claims by his moral concerns. He needed to deny that things are the only things that exist, in order to controvert Protagoras' claim that Man is the Measure of All Things, and morality simply a human convention for human convenience. He was preaching a gospel of moral seriousness, and postulated the Forms to underwrite moral objectivity (*Republic* V, 475e-480). Forms are what enable us to know the difference between right and wrong.

Plato's Programme

1. Plato does not offer a metaphysical system. He changes his mind from dialogue to dialogue, and often is criticizing doctrines he had himself put forward.
2. Much of Plato's argumentation is negative. He wants to controvert Protagoras' claim that Man is the Measure of All Things.
3. Plato was led into metaphysical claims by his moral concerns. He was preaching a gospel of moral seriousness, and postulated the Forms to underwrite moral objectivity.

In Book V he starts with a theory of adjectives. We apply adjectives to various individuals. Communication would break down if I applied adjectives just as I fancied. I have to subject myself to some interpersonal discipline, if language is to be intelligible at all. It is reasonable in some cases at least, to go further, and say that my application of adjectives to particular instances must be in accordance with features they actually possess. I call a cloud white because it has the colour white. It is the colour of the cloud that sets the standard for the correct application of colour words. Similarly the shape of a wheel makes it right to call it circular, wrong to call it square. Nor is this simply a matter of the usage which *we* happen to adopt. In the *Phaedo* (74a9-75b8) he points out that although two sticks are never exactly equal, but only approximately so, we nevertheless have a concept of exact equality. If we had a large number of sticks, each one of which seemed equal to the next, but the first was visibly longer than the last, we should

§7.3 Existence and Reality 185

conclude that some of the pairs of sticks were not exactly equal even though they seemed so. We have an *ideal* of equality, against which we are prepared to check and correct our perceptual judgements. The basis for this judgement lies in the logic of the word 'equal', which expresses a relation that is transitive and symmetric. This is part of what we understand by the word 'equal', and if there is a conflict between this and how we are inclined to apply the word in particular situations, it is the latter that gives way.[5] Similarly with circularity, radial symmetry counts for more than appearances. Protagoras had argued against the claim of the geometers that a tangent touches a circle in just one point: if we observe a wheel on a road, or a hoop on a pavement, or a top lying on a table, we see that they do not touch at just one point, but are evidently touching over some small, but finite, distance.[6] Plato was worried by this argument, but concluded that the fault lay in material objects such as wheels and hoops and tops, and all particular exemplifications of circles.[7]

Plato moved from a theory of adjectives to a theory of nouns. Instead of talking of an abstract whiteness or circularness, we should talk of colours and shapes, among them the colour white and the shape circle. The development of geometry, the study of shapes, made it natural to talk of the square and the diagonal of the square, as we now talk of the Euler line or the line at infinity. In the theory of adjectives tops and pots shared circularness with one another, or possessed it, or participated in it. In the theory of nouns they resembled, or copied, or were modelled on, *the* circle. This is the way we now view chemistry. The Periodic Table characterizes ideal Forms of matter: H_1, C_{12} and O_{16}, each of which has milliions and millions and millions of copies in the universe. Plato is a proto-chemist, and in the *Timaeus* he gives a picture of the Demiurge, a great Lord Nuffield, who has mass-produced models of a few favoured prototypes. Plato did not fully realise that the adjective and the noun accounts were very different from each other, and became entangled in the paradox of the Third Man.[8] Although

---

[5] For a full and careful examination of Plato's argument, see David Bostock, *Plato's Phaedo*, Oxford, 1986, ch.IV, pp.60-115.

[6] Aristotle, *Metaphysics*, II, 2, 997b34-998a4.

[7] Plato, *Seventh Letter*, 343a.

[8] *Parmenides* (132a-133a): Aristotle, *Metaphysics* A, 990b12, Z, 1039a2-3; also *Soph.El.*, 178b36-179a10

> **Platonism**
>
> Platonism holds:
>
> 1. Qualities exist; the furniture of the universe consists not only of things, exclusive space-occupiers, but of qualities, such as fairness, redness and roundness; language depends on our abilities to recognise and classify together the different things that have some quality or qualities in common.
> 2. Abstract entities exist.
> 3. Instead of unlimited variation, certain combinations of qualities often are found, others never.
> 4. Important truths are truths about qualities, species and other abstract entities, not about particular things or specimens.
> 5. Important truths about qualities, species and other abstract entities, are truths that are timeless and impersonal and <in some sense> necessary.
> 6. Irrespective of whether they are known or not, qualities, species and other abstract entities exist, and truths about them are true.
> 7. We come to know qualities, species and other abstract entities and truths about them not <just> by our sense organs but by thinking about them; the concentrated attention of the "eye of the mind", involving not just intellectual acuteness but moral re-orientation.

uncomfortably aware of many problems he had not resolved, and that it was implausible to postulate the existence of Forms of mud or hair, he remained convinced that there was something going for the Forms, and described himself and his disciples as "Friends of the Forms".

Part of Plato's claim should be conceded at once. Abstract entities are talkable about. We can refer to qualities, shapes, patterns, values, and the like, and can talk about them independently of any instantiations they may have. We talk about π and e and the square root of two, the spectrum and the Periodic Table, and a host of other abstract entities, and these form a large part of our interesting discourse. Plato not only licensed talk about abstract entities, but outlined its logic. Abstract entities are not located in space or time, and cannot be possessed by any person. If I am asked where the colour yellow comes in the spectrum, I can answer that it comes between orange and yellow; but if I am then asked where the spectrum is, I am at a loss how to answer. Similarly, I know where silicon is in the Periodic Table, but not where the Periodic Table itself is.

Minimal Platonism allows us to talk about abstract objects. "The quality of mercy is not strained", we may say without fear of being brought up short with the counter "But there is no such thing". Poets as well as mathematicians should be grateful. Still, minimal Platonism is very minimal. Although it is good that abstract entities can be talked about in spite of the philistinism of the vulgar and the metaphysical qualms of the materialists, they are commonly not just talked about, but accorded ontological privileges, needing more justification than that so far given.

Minimal Platonism

Universals are *talkable about*. We can refer to qualities, shapes, patterns, values, and the like, and can talk about them independently of any instantiations they may have.

We do talk about π and e and $\sqrt{2}$, the spectrum and the Periodic Table.

Full-blooded Platonists want to do more than talk. Unicorns and centaurs may be talked about by students of heraldry and mythology, but have no place in serious discourse about the world around us; whereas rhinoceroses and zebras are real, and their species extant. Plato touched upon the questions of whether tunes could exist independently of the notes that composed them,[9] and certainly they can be talked about, and heard silently in the mind's ear. Indeed, unheard melodies may be sweeter than those heard, but they lack massergy; or, more to the point, they have no hearers in the world at large. The species of rhinoceros is not just all the rhinoceroses that actually exist: the species would be the same, even if this or that or the other rhinoceros did not exist. A tune is not just the occasions when it is hummed or sung: it can be

---

[9] *Phaedo*, 85-86.

Beethoven's Tenth Symphony

A manuscript, purporting to be by Beethoven, is found in an attic where Beethoven had stayed towards the end of his life. Initially, everyone is sceptical. But exhaustive tests on the paper and ink discover nothing incompatible with its having been written when Beethoven was alive; the writing seems to be his; and after its first performances musicologists hail it as a genuine work of the master, very much in his style, but developing it in ways that could not have been foreseen, though they can in retrospect be recognised as truly his.

The man who discovered it was himself a music scholar, though by then totally deaf. He refused to publish it until he had himself written a commentary on it, and arranged for its first performance by a specially selected orchestra and choir.

In his commentary he remarks on how the Third Movement begins with a theme tune by a single cello, and is taken up and ornamented by the strings, taken over by the oboes, who develop it until it is almost lost, but is recovered at the end, when it is triumphantly re-asserted by the brass.

This unheard tune surely exists in more than a minimally Platonist sense. It forms an integral part of a great masterpiece. In subsequent years musicologists see its influence on one of Beethoven's extant late quartets.

---

transposed into a different key, and picked up by the wood-wind in an orchestra. Indeed, even though unheard, it could play a part in the course of events, and our understanding of them, as the fictional story of Beethoven's Tenth Symphony in the box above shows.

Equally in a scientific account of the world, explanations are as much in terms of timeless scientific truths as by reference to particular massergy-possessing events. Our world would be a very different world if $carbon_{12}$ were not stable and tetravalent, or sinusoidal functions were not paradigmatically periodic.

Plato never formulated criteria of identity for the Forms, as Frege and the logicists did. He does not offer a metaphysical system. He has a number of insights and arguments, some profound, but he changes his mind from dialogue to dialogue, and often he

§7.4   Existence and Reality   189

is his own severest critic. We cannot distil a definitive doctrine of Platonism from his writings, but his arguments are with us still, and there are many Platonic strands in modern thought.

§7.4 Mathematical Platonism

Although Platonism was never properly formulated by Plato, many thinkers have found themselves best described as Platonists; in the last century, G.H.Hardy, Kurt Gödel, Roger Penrose and most mathematicians.[10] We can best appreciate the content of their Platonism by considering what is denied by them, and asserted by those who controvert Platonism in mathematics.

Intuitionists think of mathematics as a cultural activity, akin to music or dancing. Proving a theorem is like playing a piece of music. It is the activity that is fundamental, not the conclusion. A theorem acquires its meaning from being proved, and has no meaning apart from its proof. It follows that we cannot speak meaningfully of a theorem's being true, or of any mathematical proposition's being true or false, except in the context of a proof or disproof, and hence that we cannot use the principle of bivalence, or the law of the excluded middle, or the law of double negation, to prove something by *Reductio ad Absurdum*. Constructivists maintain that mathematical entities are *created*, rather than merely identified, by definitions, and that, therefore, impredicative definitions are illegitimate. I cannot define something in terms of a class of which it is a member, as its greatest one, for example, because I do not know what the class is, until I know its members, and I do not know this one of its members until I know what the class is. Formalists deny that mathematics is *about* anything. It is, they say, just a game played by making marks on bits of paper. As in chess, certain moves are allowed, and others are disallowed; and as in chess, certain configurations are construed as a defeat, and correspondingly others as victory: in chess checkmate, in mathematics inconsistency.

Platonists, by contrast, believe that mathematical propositions can be true or false independently of our knowing which they are, and consequently that arguments by *Reductio ad Absurdum* are

---

[10] See, for example, G.H.Hardy, *Mind*, 1929, "Mathematical Proof", p.18. Roger Penrose, *The Emperor's New Mind*, Oxford, 1989, and *Shadows of the Mind*, Oxford, 1994.

valid. Likewise they believe that mathematical entities exist independently of our definitions of them, and consequently that impredicative definitions are unexceptionable. And while they concede that it is illuminating to think of mathematics as being merely a game, when we are concerned with syntactic questions, they deny that it is just a game; rather, it is fundamental to our understanding of reality.

Dummett cites Benenson's proof that there are solutions of the equation $x^y = z$ with x and y irrational and z rational.[11] For consider $\sqrt{2}^{\sqrt{2}}$. Either it is rational, in which case the claim is true, or it is irrational. If it is irrational, consider further $(\sqrt{2}^{\sqrt{2}})^{\sqrt{2}}$. Since $(\sqrt{2}^{\sqrt{2}})^{\sqrt{2}} = \sqrt{2}^{(\sqrt{2} \times \sqrt{2})} = \sqrt{2}^2 = 2$, we then have $\sqrt{2}^{\sqrt{2}}$ and $\sqrt{2}$ as the two irrational numbers and 2 as the rational number satisfying the equation $x^y = z$. Intuitionists disallow this proof, because it does not tell us of either $\sqrt{2}^{\sqrt{2}}$ or $(\sqrt{2}^{\sqrt{2}})^{\sqrt{2}}$ whether or not it is rational. The argument is largely one of logic,[12] but can be defended on anti-realist grounds:

> Thinking of a statement as true or false independently of our knowledge involves a supposition of some external mathematical reality, whereas thinking of it as rendered true, if at all, only by a mathematical construction does not. [13]

Can the argument be reversed? Intuitionistic logic goes against the courtesies of conversational interchange, and, more tellingly, against the shared truth-seeking of those engaged in serious argument. I can understand Pythagoras' Theorem without being able to prove it. Our ancestors in pre-historic times constructed 3-4-5 and 5-12-13 triangles in their megaliths, but may well have not actually anticipated Pythagoras; certainly in my own youth I constructed them in my Meccano, and can testify to my own geometrical ignorance at the time. Moreover there are many—forty seven, it is said—different proofs, but all of the same proposition, whose meaning, therefore, must be independent of any of them.

The Intuitionist's emphasis on assertibility conditions for the understanding of the force of the logical constants parallels verificationist theories of meaning. If we reject the latter, and allow that

---

[11] Michael Dummett, *Elements of Intuitionism*, Oxford, 1977, p.10.

[12] See above, §§2.4, 2.5.

[13] p.12.

§7.4   Existence and Reality   191

when we talk of the tree in the quad, we are not talking merely of
the sense-data that an observer suitably situated would experience,
but of a material object independently of whether it be observed or
not, then we should be ready to reject also a logic that rates assertibility conditions above truth conditions. I do not need to know all
about $\sqrt{2}^{\sqrt{2}}$, and in particular whether it is rational or irrational,
in order to talk about it; nor need I know whether $(\sqrt{2}^{\sqrt{2}})^{\sqrt{2}}$ is
rational or irrational, to be able to talk about that. It is enough
that I can identify each of them so that you can know what I am
talking about.

Qualms about impredicative definitions seem equally misplaced.
Once I have indicated the class of entities I am talking about, I can
go on to specify the greatest or the least member of that class, or
some other member specified in terms of its relation to the class
as a whole. The further specification enables my hearer to identify
the entity, but does not bring it into being. If the general characterization of the class was adequate, my hearer already knows the
sort of thing I was going to talk about, and his acceptance of its
existence is prior to the further particulars I subsequently vouchsafe. I can, so to speak, bow in its direction without itemising all
its members, because they are there anyhow to pick up my intent.
If my hearer sets off in that general direction he will find something
that answers to the outline indication offered, and recognise that
that is what was intended.

These objections to mathematical Platonism help to delineate
its positive content, and can be seen to stem from general philosophical positions we have good grounds to reject. Mathematical
Platonism should not be rejected out of hand, and we are entitled
to attach some weight to the fact that most working mathematicians are Platonists. But it is reasonable to seek further, more
compelling arguments in favour.

Positive arguments for mathematical Platonism are very largely
positive arguments for Platonism generally. Much as we can justify positing the existence of material objects on the grounds that
it makes sense of otherwise diverse and confusing sense-experience,
so the existence of universals makes sense of otherwise diverse and
confusing individual instances. If I have the concept of a centroid, I
can understand why each triangle I cut out of a piece of cardboard
has its centre of gravity at its centroid. If I understand group
theory, I can recognise the same pattern in a peal of bells and
in the way a weaver arranges different coloured strands of cotton.

Mathematical Platonism
What does it claim?

1. We can talk about mathematical entities: there is no need to explain them away or give a reductive analysis of them (Contrast Intuitionism or Nominalism).
2. We discover mathematics rather than invent it. Mathematical truth does not depend on our say-so. If Beethoven had been aborted, there would have been no Eroica: but if Pythagoras had never been born, Pythagoras' theorem would still have been true.
3. We can refer to mathematical entities without completely characterizing them, and therefore can quantify over them "Impredicatively" in process of defining them.
4. Mathematical entities have properties independently of our knowledge of them, and so are subject to the Law of the Excluded Middle and the Principle of Bivalence (Contrast Intuitionism).
5. There is open access to mathematical truth. Anybody, even an uneducated slave-boy, can follow a mathematical argument, and acknowledge its force. You do not have to be well situated, either socially or geographically, to do mathematics (Contrast Intuitionism).
6. Mathematics is *a priori*, and hence timeless, placeless, impersonal, and **necessary**.
7. Mathematics is relevant and real. There are certain patterns exemplified in the external world, and mathematics describes the necessary relations between patterns, which constitute the background of natural science and all empirical knowledge.

Patterns integrate otherwise unintelligible instances into an intelligible whole. But, it will be objected "Are not patterns, like beauty, solely in the eye of the beholder?" The answer is "Not always". Admittedly, the patterns Hamlet descried were phantasms of his own imagining, but others can see what we see, and sometimes our view of the pattern is not only shareable but illuminating. In many cases the appearance of subjectivity arises from incomplete specification. This is clearest seen with cardinal numbers, which are the simplest of all relational structures—relational structures with the relation left out. Some have thought that numbers are subjective, since I can view a yard either as three feet, or as thirty six inches, just as I please.[14] But the proper conclusion is not that numbers are subjective: rather, we should recognise that the question "How Many?" needs to be filled out in two different respects: we need to be asked "How many *whats* are there in *what*?", before we can give an answer, but once the question has been fully specified, the answer is fixed and definite, independently of us or our wishes. Different questions specify different types of individual: "How many Colleges in the University of Oxford?" is a perfectly good question, only it specifies a different sort of individual from that specified in the different question "How many undergraduates in the University of Oxford?". Although we can choose what questions to ask, there is nothing psychological or subjective about the answers: it is just that there are different concepts, 'Colleges in the University of Oxford' and 'undergraduates in the University of Oxford', possessing different cardinal numbers. The numerosity of each concept is a given objective fact, depending only on the way the world is, and not at all on how we feel or opine. So too the hexagonal pattern of ice crystals, or the octohedral crystals of alum. It is a matter of human psychology that we can learn to recognise them, but a matter of fact that they are there to recognise.

Sometimes we come to recognise patterns that are deep, and difficult to characterize in simple terms. The style of a painter, a composer, a writer, is extraordinarily difficult to pin down, but recognisable all the same. Sometimes forgers and parodists are successful in producing imitations that pass for the genuine thing, but often they fail, notwithstanding very careful attention to all describable details. It is natural to explain this by positing a *je ne sais pas quoi*, a style, which experts can recognise, although it cannot be fully described in standard terms.

In the case of mathematical Platonism, further, more technical arguments can be adduced; in particular, arguments based on Gödel's theorem. If we consider first-order Elementary Number Theory—call it ENT—purely syntactically, that is, as an *uninterpreted* system of formulae and rules of inference, we then have that

---

[14] G.Berkeley, *New Theory of Vision*, §109; *Principles of Human Knowledge*, §xii. See also Plato, *Republic* VII, 522c-526a; and *Hippias Major*, 300e-302e.

the Gödelian sentence, G, is undecidable in this system, which is to say that neither G nor its negation, $\neg G$, is a theorem of the system:

$$ENT \not\vdash G \quad \text{and} \quad ENT \not\vdash \neg G$$

This, again, is to say on the one hand that the conjunction of first-order Elementary Number Theory with the negation of the Gödelian sentence is consistent, and on the other that the conjunction of first-order Elementary Number Theory with the Gödelian sentence itself is consistent. It follows, in virtue of another theorem proved by Gödel, there are models both of Elementary Number Theory together with the Gödelian sentence, and of Elementary Number Theory together with the negation of the Gödelian sentence. The former is quite straightforward: as we have seen, the Gödelian sentence, though formally unprovable, is actually true. But the latter is weird. It means that there are models of the axioms of Elementary Number Theory in which what are identified as numbers do not behave as what we understand by numbers do. That is to say the axioms of Elementary Number Theory have models that are not isomorphic with one another, and so do not characterize the natural numbers adequately. In fact no first-order characterization of the natural numbers, with addition and multiplication, can characterize them adequately: but we know very well which is the "right" model. We know what the natural numbers are, even though we cannot specify them unambiguously in terms that a computer could take on board. This supports mathematical realism. We are acquainted with the natural numbers, because they exist independently of us, and we apprehend them. A partial characterization is enough for us to be able to recognise them, much as with material objects.

Some philosophers acknowledge the force of this consideration, but resist "neo-realism", suggesting instead that we are led to make more precise what we meant to mean by 'natural number' in much the same way as a novelist may feel that he has not managed to write the story he had intended to.[15] It is a contention that deserves to be taken seriously, but it still has Platonist implications. For it suggests that meanings have a life of their own (contrary to one of Wittgenstein's contentions). We know what we mean by a natural number. If it turns out that the characterization of Peano

---

[15] For instance, R.L.Goodstein, "The Significance of Incompleteness Theorems", *British Journal for the Philosophy of Science*, **14**, 1963-64, p.215.

§7.4   Existence and Reality   195

Arithmetic fails to define it unambiguously, we can go on and pick out the intended model from those not intended, guided by our deeper understanding of the "true" meaning of 'natural number'.
We are guided in a definite direction: we do not have a free choice how the concept of a natural number should be developed. For we *can* give a complete definition in **second**-order logic. In second-order logic the axioms of Elementary Number Theory are "monomorphic", that is to say, they have only one model, and so succeed in identifying the natural numbers uniquely. So if we can avail ourselves of second-order logic, we do not need to posit some platonist acquaintance with the natural numbers in order to distinguish the intended model from the non-standard ones. But second-order logic is itself, on Quine's showing, platonist. If "to be is to be a value of a variable", then qualities and relations must exist if we are to be able to quantify monadic and polyadic predicates. The sceptic faces a dilemma: he can stick with first-order logic, which is ontologically meagre, admitting quantification only over individual variables, referring only to individual particulars, that can be presumed to exist; and which is methodologically pure, being recursively axiomatizable and algorithmic, the sort of logic, as we have said, that even computers can do. But then Gödel's theorem shows the inadequacy of first-order logic, and leads us, *pace* Quine, to look further afield, and in particular to recognise the merits of second-order logic, which is not semantically complete and not recursively axiomatizable. If we avail ourselves of second-order logic, we can characterize the natural numbers categorically and adequately: but at the cost of assuming that qualities and relations are entities over which we can quantify. So, either way, Gödel's theorem pushes us towards some form of platonic realism.
Three final points about mathematical Platonism need to be made. There is open access to mathematical truth. Plato made the point in his dialogue, *Meno*, that anybody, even an uneducated slave-boy, can follow a mathematical argument, and acknowledge its force. Although in the modern world, mathematicians, like musicians, are a cultural subgroup, you do not, *pace* the Intuitionists, have to be well situated, either socially or geographically, to acknowledge mathematical truth. In other disciplines there are authorities: in natural science there are experimental observations, in history primary sources; and in history and the humanities generally, there authorities whose judgements, though contestable, are not much contested. But in mathematics there are no authorities.

> **Merits of Platonism**
> 1. Accounts for the objectivity of values, and of mathematical and scientific truth.
> 2. Accounts for the obligatoriness of values, especially of truth.
> 3. Accounts for the convergence of values and beliefs.
> 4. Articulates sense of discovery rather than invention or creation.
> 5. Licenses Principle of Bivalence, Law of Excluded Middle, Use of Impredicative Sets, and the whole of classical logic.
> 6. Justifies inductive inference.
> 7. Explains animals being able to use cues to recognize significant features of their environment.

Paradoxically, in this, the most difficult of all the disciplines, it is open to anybody to point out a hole in a proof, and to announce to the world the naked lack of truth in the Establishment's proclaimed prodigy.

There is open access to mathematical truth because it is *a priori* and hence necessary. Since it does not depend on who knows it, or where he was when he came to know it, or when he came to know it, it is free from all contingency, and the paradigm of timeless, impersonal truth, not located in space, but valid everywhere, everywhen and for all men. A modal logic that acknowledges necessity and possibility, but has no room for contingency, is markedly different from the logic of everyday life, and makes mathematics a peculiar discipline.[16]

---

[16] See below, §7.10 of this chapter.

§7.5 Nominalism

Metaphysical puritans are made queasy by the lush ontology of Platonism. Entities are not to be multiplied without good reason, because they are not just talked about, but are accorded an ontological status, that sits ill with a down-to-earth view of reality.

Nominalists have a simple view of existence. Things are the things that occupy space, and things are the only things to exist. Only a minimal ability to secure identity of reference is required. If you do not know what I am talking about, I can point it out to you. Anyone persistently unable to locate objects occupying space, would be unable also to carry on conversation with me, and would not be within my field of discourse. The nominalist reckons that only those things can be talked about that can be talked about by anyone that can be talked to.

The underlying metaphysics of materialism, which holds that things *are* the only things to exist, will be addressed later.[17] But the nominalist can also gain some support from logic. For him the correct use of the word 'exist' is that expressed by the existential quantifier in first-order predicate calculus, in which we can quantify over individual variables, but not over predicates. In first-order logic it is correct to say, with Locke, that only particulars exist, in as much as only particulars can be quantified over.[18] And first-order logic has merits. It is complete in a proper and unstrained sense of the word. It is algorithmic, that is to say, the sort of logic a computer could be programmed to do.

Set theory can also be called in aid of nominalism. In set theory it is normal to posit the existence of some *ur*-elements, from which all sets are constructed, thus supporting the metaphysical view that there must be some basic individuals, from which everything else is built up. Set theory also expresses the nominalist's cast of mind in the Axiom of Extensionality which lays down that a set is simply constituted by its members, and has no existence over and above them.

But first-order logic, for all its virtues, fails to give an adequate account of the substances that substantives refer to. And Forms, or Species, are not sets. Indeed, even sets fail to live down to their

---

[17] See below, chs.9 and 13.

[18] John Locke, *Essay Concerning the Human Understanding*, London, 1690, book III, ch. 1 §3.

nominalist pretensions. For though we can make up sets artificially, by specifying each member separately, for example the set $\{a, c, d, g, h, k, l, m\}$, in most cases, where we are not dealing with artificially constructed finite sets, we have to characterize them by means of some general specification. We talk of the *set of natural numbers* without being able to count out each one,

The difference between genuinely extensional sets, characterized by itemising each member individually, and sets characterized by some common specification, is shown by the fact that to deny that any member of an extensional set *is* a member is to contradict oneself; whereas with a set characterized by some common specification it is not self-contradictory, but only false to deny membership to some member.[19] Thus it is self-contradictory to deny that Catherine of Aragon was a member of the set {Catherine of Aragon, Anne Boleyn, Jane Seymour, Anne of Cleves, Catherine Howard, Catherine Parr}, but only false to deny that she was one of Henry VIII's wives. The difference is further brought out by considering counter-factual possibilities. Thus, if I say that all John's girl-friends are blue-eyed blonds, I may be merely observing what happens to be the case, or I may be opining that John is disposed to be enamoured of blue-eyed blonds. What could you infer about a hypothetical Hermione? On the former interpretation, nothing. It had just happened to be the case that Sue, Amanda, Sharon, Caroline and Geraldine were blue-eyed blonds, but that was mere happenstance: on the latter interpretation, however, you could reasonably conclude that Hermione, too, would have to have what it takes to catch John's wandering eye.[20]

Although set theory is nominalist in *ethos*, it does not advance the cause of nominalism, because it fails to represent universals adequately. Quite apart from the modal subtleties of the "open" specification needed in making causal judgments and inductive inferences, there is the general objection that there are too many sets. The world of universals, or Forms, or Species, would be over-populated if every set were one. In order to avoid Malthusian disaster, the selection rules for Forms or Species must be much less generous than those for characterizing sets.

Malthus

The world of Forms would be over-populated if every set were one.

In an infinite world with $\aleph_0$ individuals there are $2^{\aleph_0}$ sets.

---

[19] I owe this point to Dr F.Waismann in a tutorial.

[20] See further below, §7.9.

§7.5   *Existence and Reality*   199

The argument from recognition gives edge to Malthusian worries about over-population. We might maintain that if there were $2^{\aleph_0}$ species, Adam would not be able to name all the species, even if he kept at it for all time. But that argument presupposes that all species must be nameable by means of finite sequences of some denumerable set of symbols, and this might not be so: after all, an algorithmic Adam could not define truth, and many thinkers have claimed to have had thoughts they could not articulate in words. But Adam's human limitations apart, the population of the world of Forms must be not just sub-maximal, but extremely sparse. Scarcity was essential in enabling us to go beyond the identifying features of a natural kind, to there actually being some underlying factor at work.[21] Bird-lovers can identify a greater spotted woodpecker by his long beak and his red rear patch. If these features were not peculiar to greater spotted wood-peckers, they would be useless for identification. It is only because long beaks and red rear patches do not go together with other features—the red breast of robins, for example—that we can use them for identification. And it is only because of the same parsimony of concomitance, that birds themselves can distinguish possible mates from dangerous predators.

The arguments in favour of nominalism can be sympathized with, but not accepted. I cannot have words mean what *I* want them to mean, if I am to be intelligible to others; and I cannot just point to what I want to talk about, unless we have some common background to indicate what sort of thing it is that I am asking you to notice. First-order logic has its merits, but it has its demerits too, and cannot be passed off as the paradigm of logical excellence. Set theory, too, is not a paradigm for our conceptual thought, but shows, rather, the inadequacies of extensionality as an account of natural kinds, which are seen to be necessary, if we are to be able to recognise and identify the things we see and hear. Metaphysicians have tended to go to extremes. They are tempted to deny the existence of universals altogether and allow the existence only of raw sense data, or of overt behaviour, or of simple observations. But those positions are not sustainable. We cannot experience raw data, or accumulate raw observations: to experience is, in part, to interpret: observations have to be classified if they are to be accumulated.

[21] See above, §3.8.

> Set Theory and Natural Kinds
>
> Set theory supports nominalism, BUT
>
> Natural kinds are not sets, because
>
> 1. Malthus: if there were $\aleph_o$ specimens, there would be $2^{\aleph_o}$ natural kinds, and the world of natural kinds would be over-populated.
> 2. Adam: if there were $\aleph_o$ specimens, and $2^{\aleph_o}$ natural kinds, Adam would not be able to name all the natural kinds, even if he kept at it for all time. (But need all natural kinds be nameable?)
> 3. Recognition: in order to be able to identify a specimen as being a specimen of a specific species, the identifying characteristics of the specimen must be peculiar to the natural kinds, and not shared with other natural kinds. Concomitances of characteristics must, therefore be rather rare. (See above §3.8, §4.7.)
> 4. Limited Variety: in order to be able to discover causal connexions, we need to limit our investigations; only if varieties are limited, will we be entitled to infer wide-ranging conclusions from imperfect evidence.
> 5. Negation: to deny that a member of a set is a member of that set is contradictory, whereas to deny that a specimen is a specimen of a natural kinds is only false.
> 6. Modal properties: counter-factual conclusions can be drawn about possible specimens of a natural kinds, but not about possible members of a set.

§7.6 Conceptualism

The argument against nominalism that we need concepts in order to have experience suggests that it is as concepts that universals exist. It is an attractive view for those metaphysicians who yearn for a simple, down-to-earth universe, uncluttered by extra-terrestial entities of dubious standing. The existence of universals is not denied, but they are safely confined to the notoriously fuzzy world of human psychology. And arguments can be adduced in favour of regarding them so: our language and many of our concepts are clearly of human origin and provenance; it is more illuminating to think of justice as a concept developed along with human society than as a Form existing by itself independently of any social context. Food, fuel and razors are functionally defined. Beds are not models of an ideal bed, but are what we use for sleeping on, which

§7.6 *Existence and Reality* 201

may be bunks, hammocks, sofas, or bundles of straw. Even our descriptions depend on our interests. Eskimos, it is said, have many different words for the different shades of white shown by different sorts of snow; Oxford tailors similarly had different names for the different reds in the hoods and gowns worn by the holders of different Oxford degrees; the French use the word *jaune* to describe both yellow daffodils and brown shoes; the ancient Greeks had no word equivalent to our 'yellow', using ξανθός (*xanthos*) for yellowish orange, and χλωρός (*chloros*) for yellowish green. Different cultures group different shade together, applying the same colour word to them all indifferently. 'Yellow' is not the name of a specific colour, with things being called yellow if and only if they participate in yellowness, or resemble the abstract yellow colour.

All this should be conceded. It tells against Plato's theory of adjectives, in which he posited the existence, for each adjective, of a Form, participation in which justified the object's having that adjective applied to it. But Plato himself came to see that his simple theory of adjectives could not be correct, and the fact that the rules for the application of many words depends partly on human institutions and interests does not show that they do not depend on other features too. A Frenchman may call my brown shoes *jaune*, but cannot correctly call them *noir*. What features we notice, and how we interpret them in formulating a description, depend on our *expertise* and the language we use, but what features there are is a matter of non-linguistic fact, something in the nature of things, independent of human artifice.

A sceptic may still argue that abstract entities, though they may be talked about objectively, and are necessary for perception, cannot really exist, because they have no causal powers. Only those entities exist, they say, that can enter into some causal chain of effective events.[22] But causal explanation, like all explanation, operates against a background of assumptions that are assumed to need no explanation.[23] Mathematics generally, like geometry in particular,[24] provides that background, especially for the physical sciences, which are manifestly explanatory. We may on occasion appeal to the background assumptions in order to explain

---

[22] Michael Dummett, *Frege: Philosophy of Mathematics*, London, 1991, p.182: "abstract entities are objective but not actual (*wirklich*); the Equator is causally inefficacious."

[23] See above, §4.2.

[24] See below, §9.9.

something,[25] but for the most part we take them for granted. And the purely mathematical background, because it is pure, and therefore necessary, is most to be taken for granted. But that does not mean that it is not significant. Our world would be a very different world if carbon$_{12}$ were not stable and tetravalent, or sinusoidal functions were not paradigmatically periodic.[26] And these are not psychological facts about human minds, but objective scientific and mathematical truths.

Conceptualism is like projectivism: it makes out that our concepts are simply a matter of human psychology, and not at all dependent on the way the world is, quite apart from human affairs. But human psychology, though important, is not all-important. Just as I can be wrong, and you can be wrong, so we all can be wrong. We may be compelled, sometimes have been compelled, to amend our concepts in the face of awkward facts. Human psychology is amenable to "rational psychology". Locke's nominal essences are important: but his real essences are important too.

§7.7 Natural Kinds

Nominalism and Conceptualism were put forward in order to have an austere metaphysics in which universals were not accorded reality. Since neither is adequate, universals may have to be accepted as part of the fabric of the universe. The Schoolmen distinguished Aristotle's realism from Plato's, and in due course the distinction will need to be made in modern terms; but although he criticized Plato, Aristotle remained very largely a Platonist throughout his life. It is sensible, therefore, to begin by treating Aristotle's and Plato's views on universals together, with Aristotle's claim that they exist *in rebus* rather than *ante res* as a modification, albeit a very important modification, of Plato's version of Platonism.

That there are natural kinds is both an evident fact of ordinary life, of biology and modern chemistry and a necessary presupposition of recognition and of inductive inference. The difficulty lies in determining their logical shape and ontological standing. The Boolean algebra of predicates and set theory is inappropriate. Predicates can be negated, but natural kinds cannot. Since we can describe something as red, we can also describe things—e.g.

---

[25] Graham Nerlich, *What Spacetime Explains*, Cambridge, 1994, ch.7, "What can geometry explain?", pp.169-184, esp. pp.172-173.

[26] See this chapter, §7.3.

§7.7   Existence and Reality   203

traffic lights—as being not red. With natural kinds—in this case colours—it is different. Red is a colour: not-red is not.[27] Predicates can be disjoined: if the traffic light shows just amber or green, you may pass it. But, again, there is no amber-or-green colour. (This is not to say that there are no cases where a negated or disjoined predicate does specify a natural kind. Although we feel queasy at lumping all foreigners together as aliens or wogs; physiologists dealing with the immune system need to classify together all organisms and organic chemicals that stimulate the production of antibodies. And the colour red is constitued of a disjunction of many different shades of red, each of which qualifies as itself a colour.) The Law of the Excluded Middle likewise does not generally apply to natural kinds. We do not have two Species,[28] raven and non-raven, which together make up bird-kind.

That the logic of natural kinds differs from that of predicates and sets also in its modal properties is shown by the case of Flint. Flint was a dog, owned by Mr Pitt, a resident Fellow of Worcester College, Oxford, which had a long-standing rule that dogs were not allowed to live in College. The Governing Body did not want to embarrass Mr Pitt, a much respected tutor of the College, but did not want to rescind the rule either. So it passed a College Order, deeming Flint to be a cat. The union of the set {cats} and the singleton set {Flint} was undoubtedly a set, but would constitute an implausible species. Animal lovers might establish a cat show, but if Flint tried to enter, claiming that the species {cats}∪{Flint} was just as good as the species {cats} he would be shown the door, and told to go to Crufts. Or again, having observed a tendency among feline members of the set {cats} ∪ {Flint} to be aloof and to walk by themselves, we cannot legitimately infer that Flint has these unsociable characteristics.

Although we use predicates to specify natural kinds, their logic is not just the Boolean algebra of predicates, set theory and, its simplest exemplar, propositional calculus. A modified logic is needed.

---

[27] Compare the not-king-of-France in §3.8. above.

[28] Note the capital letter, which warns the reader that the word is not being used exactly as a biologist would use it.

§7.8 Modifying Logic

Predicates and set theory have a Boolean algebra similar to that of propositional calculus, which is complete within its own terms, but does not capture the whole of logic. Sometimes we want to modify statements. There are many modes of discourse besides simple declarative fact-stating sentences. I tell stories. "Once upon a time there was an old man who lived in a cave". I give advice: "you must make a clean breast of it". I reduce the warranty given for my statement: "perhaps there will be a sea battle tomorrow". Or I increase the warranty: "I know there will be a sea battle tomorrow". I can hope, expect, fear, warn, promise or threaten about things to come, and can remember, ponder, relate, or explain, the past. We use auxiliary verbs, or locutions such as 'it is possible that ...' or 'it was going to be the case that ...', or in inflected languages a change of mood or tense. But the modified statement is still something that can be agreed with or disagreed with, accepted or rejected, shared or repudiated. We can construe these various modifiers as unary operators (or functors, or connectives) which operate each on a single (but perhaps complicated) proposition to yield a single (but perhaps complicated) proposition. Although there are some modifiers, such as "I read it in the tabloids, so it must be true", where the modified statement may bear no relation to the original, in most cases the modified statement stands in some relation to the original one. Modal logics consider how our ordinary logic may be modified by some operator, such as 'it is necessary that' applied to propositions. If there are too few links, the modal operator will lose all contact with the connectives of ordinary logic, and modal discourse will be no longer a logic at all. If there are too many, the modal operator will be degenerate, definable in terms of the ordinary sentential connectives, and modal logic will be nothing more than ordinary propositional calculus. We must steer a careful course between the Scylla of having too many rules or axioms, with the result that the modal operator is vacuous or gives rise to inconsistency, and the Charybdis of having too few with the result that our modal discourse is a chaotic one in which none of the ordinary rules of ordinary discourse apply.

Modal logicians symbolize the modal operator by $\Box$, a unary operator with the same formation rules as for $\neg$. What are the axioms and Rules of Inference required to ensure that the propositional content of our hopes, wishes, judgements, or romances, is adequately reflected in the modified propositions themselves? Entailments are essential to meanings; if words are to have their ordinary meanings, analytic propositions must hold as well within the modalised discourse as outside it; and therefore tautologies must remain tautologies when modalised. Since every tautology is a theorem of propositional calculus, and *vice versa*, we stipulate

If Γ is a theorem, so is $\Box\Gamma$,

i.e., If $\vdash \Gamma$ then $\vdash \Box\Gamma$.

This rule of inference is known as the Rule of Necessitation, abbreviated as $R_\Box$, and is characteristic of all modal logics. The Rule of Necessitation ensures that logical theorems remain so when modalised, but does not by itself suffice to legitimise standard inferences in modalised discourse: it enables us to introduce an entailment $\vdash$ into a mode of discourse, but not to use it to make inferences within it. If we are to carry ordinary inferences over into modalised discourse, we need the further rule

If $p \vdash q$, then $\Box p \vdash \Box q$.[29]

Granted the rules of propositional calculus, this rule of inference can equally well be expressed as the axiom

G $\vdash \Box(p \to q) \to (\Box p \to \Box q)$.

The Rule of Necessitation and the axiom G together ensure that modalised discourse is "**inferentially transparent**"—that we can make the same logical inferences within modalised discourse as in unmodalised discourse. They are the **minimum** conditions a system must satisfy in order to be a modal *logic* at all; they govern the interrelation of the modal operator $\Box$ with implication and entailment, $\to$ and $\vdash$.

In order to place the modal operator as fully as possible in the context of propositional calculus, we need also to consider its interrelationship with negation, $\neg$. Does it "commute" with negation, *i.e.* $\vdash \Box\neg p \leftrightarrow \neg\Box p$? If that were a theorem, the modal system would become degenerate, and the modal operator would become vacuous. Although we must eschew the biconditional, the one-way conditional is unobjectionable. Indeed, we can choose which way it should go, deciding whether to regard $\Box$ or $\neg\Box\neg$, which is standardly abbreviated as $\Diamond$, as the stronger. It is natural to choose $\Box$ for three reasons:

first, the modal rule of inference, $R_\Box$, is formulated in terms of it; secondly, since axiom G is equivalent to

---

[29] See Aristotle, *Prior Analytics* I, 15, 34a 22-24.

$\vdash (\Box p \wedge \Box q) \to \Box(p \wedge q),$

we can adopt this as our axiom, and then point out that $\wedge$ is inferentially stronger than $\vee$;

and, thirdly, it seems reasonable to reject $\vdash \neg\Box p \to \Box\neg p$, when we re-write it in terms of $\wedge$ as $\vdash \Box p \wedge \Box \neg p$, which places $\Box p$ under the same constraint of non-contradiction as unvarnished p. (This is not an absolute requirement for every modal operator, as will shortly emerge; but it is a reasonable one.)

If we reject $\vdash \Box p \wedge \Box \neg p$, we are free to adopt the former conjunct of the biconditional as an axiom, or rather its equivalent,

D $\vdash \quad \Box p \to \Diamond p.$

$\Diamond$ is a weaker modality than $\Box$, being implied by it, but not *vice versa*, and not being subject to the ban on contradiction—if we construe $\Box$ as necessary, and $\Diamond$ as possible, we often have occasion to say both that p is possible and that *not-p* is possible.

The modal system which has this axiom in addition to axiom G and the Rule of Inference $R_\Box$ is the system **D**. In it we have four out of the six possible interconnexions between $\Box$ on the one hand and $\wedge$, $\vee$ and $\neg$ on the other, *viz.*

$$\vdash \Box(p \wedge q) \to (\Box p \wedge \Box q)$$

$$\vdash (\Box p \wedge \Box q) \to \Box(p \wedge q)$$
$$\vdash (\Box p \vee \Box q) \to \Box(p \vee q)$$
$$\vdash \Box\neg p \to \neg\Box p$$

but not

Necessity Divided under Disjunction

$\quad \Box(p \vee q) \to \Box p \vee \Box q,$

which would legitimise the inference from He must be either in his rooms or in the library to Either he must be in his rooms or he must be in the library

nor Commutativity with Negation

D* $\neg\Box p \to \Box\neg p,$

which would make negation and the modal operator completely commutative. We cannot add either of these on pain of modal degeneracy. We can therefore argue for the axiom D as giving us as much, in the way of interconnexion between the modal operator $\Box$ and the connectives $\wedge$, $\vee$ and $\neg$ of propositional calculus, as we can hope to have. The system **D** thus constitutes the basic modal logic,

§7.8   Existence and Reality

which preserves meanings and inferences, but does not collapse into simple propositional calculus.

Although the system **D** goes as far as possible in relating the modal operator with the sentential connectives of propositional calculus, it leaves other questions unanswered. It tells us nothing of the bearing of modalised discourse on unmodalised discourse, nor of any relations between iterated modal operators. Various axioms giving rules for such relations can be laid down, giving rise to different modal logics. One option for iterated modal operators is to lay down that the modal operator $\Box$ be idempotent, that is:

4      $\vdash \Box p \leftrightarrow \Box\Box p$

which together with T[30] yields the modal logic called **S4**, Some modal logics go further, and invoke the thesis

5      $\vdash \neg\Box\neg p \to \Box\neg\Box\neg p$,

in which all iterated modal operators are equivalent to the rightmost one. This thesis can be postulated as a separate axiom, but can also be derived from 4 and the "Browerian" axiom

B $\vdash p \to \Box\Diamond p$,

which relates iterated modalities with actuality. The resulting system **S5** is the strongest modal logic. Any axiom to strengthen it further will collapse the modal operators into degeneracy, making the resultant system no different from simple propositional calculus.

S5 captures Leibniz' idea that necessary truths are those that hold in all possible worlds, and the recognition outside logic that universality and necessity are closely allied. The parallel is revealed if in **S5** we have iterated modal operators which do not interact, but are simply distinguished from one another, as it were with subscripts x, y, etc., each modal operator retaining its own modal force separately from the modal force of other operators. That path leads to quantification theory, with $\Box_x$, $\Box_y$, etc. being written as $(\forall x)$, $(\forall y)$, etc., and $\Diamond_x$, $\Diamond_y$, etc. being written as $(\exists x)$, $(\exists y)$, etc.[31] There is thus a close parallel between first-order predicate calculus and modal logic; ultimately the identification of $\Box_x$ with $(\forall x)$ rather than $(\exists x)$ rests upon the fact that $(\forall x)$ is inferentially

---

[30] See below, §7.10.

[31] It should be noted that just as we can develop quantification theory in terms of $(\exists x)$, which can be viewed, instead of $(\forall x)$, so we *can* develop modal logic in terms of $\Diamond$—but at the cost of obscuring the intuitive connexion between $\Box$ and $\vdash$.

stronger than $(\exists x)$, and fits naturally with the suggestion of some logicians that we should view $(\forall x)$ as a possibly infinite conjunction $\wedge \ldots \wedge \ldots$ and $(\exists x)$ as a possibly infinite disjunction $\vee \ldots \vee \ldots$.[32]

Since logic is connected with argument, it was natural to develop it in terms of implication, $\rightarrow$, and negation, $\neg$; but the parallels between $\square$ and $(\forall x)$ and $\wedge$, and also between $\Diamond$ and $\exists$ and $\vee$, are brought out by the two pairs of theorems of **D**:

$$\vdash \square(p \wedge q) \leftrightarrow (\square p \wedge \square q)$$

$$\vdash \Diamond(p \vee q) \leftrightarrow \Diamond(p \vee \Diamond q)$$

and

$$\vdash \Diamond(p \wedge q) \rightarrow (\Diamond p \wedge \Diamond q)$$

$$\vdash (\square p \vee \square q) \rightarrow \square(p \vee q).$$

These bring out the quasi-Boolean character of the modal operators, and enable us to adopt them as giving us a "Boolean-plus" algebra, in which $\square$ is the most highly structured additional operator relative to the Boolean operators.

Boolean algebra applies not only to propositions but to sets and to mereological extensions or parts. We may ask whether "Boolean-plus" algebra has any application to set theory and mereology. It has. Although topology is normally developed in terms of a family of open sets, Kuratowski bases it on a closure operator, $\mathcal{C}$ obeying four axioms analogous to those of the modal logic $S4$.[33]

[K.1] $\mathcal{C}(H \cup L) = \mathcal{C}H \cup \mathcal{C}L$
[K.2] $H \subseteq \mathcal{C}H$
[K.3] $\mathcal{C}\emptyset = \emptyset$
[K.4] $\mathcal{C}(\mathcal{C}H) = \mathcal{C}H$

Kuratowski's topology is based on set theory, but with suitable modifications we can apply his axioms to extensions instead of sets.

---

[32] F.P.Ramsey, *The Foundations of Mathematics*, London, 1931, ch.IX, §B, esp.p.238.

[33] Taken, with changed lettering, from K.Kuratowski *Introduction to Set Theory and Topology*, 2nd ed. Pergamum Press, Oxford, 1972, ch. X, §1, p.123. See also W.J.Purvin, *Foundations of General Topology*, New York, 1964, p.41.

§7.8   Existence and Reality

The first axiom, [K.1], reminds us that his closure operator belongs to the ∨ group, together with ◇ and (∃). The second axiom, [K.2] again seems counter-intuitive, until we remember that it is ⊆ that parallels →, though it appears to point in the opposite direction. The third axiom, [K.3], presents a difficulty, since the analogue in propositional calculus to the emptyset, ∅, is ⊥ or F,[34] which does not feature in presentations of modal logic. What we can do is to reformulate [K.3] in terms not of the empty set, but of the universal set, X, which is analogous to ⊤. Instead of

[K.3] $\mathcal{C}\emptyset = \emptyset$,

we postulate its equivalent,

[K.3'] $\mathcal{J}X = X$

which would parallel the thesis

⊢ □⊤ ↔ ⊤,

where ⊤ is tautology. That thesis holds by reason of $R_\square$. And since ⊢ ⊤ always holds, ⊢ ◇⊤ → ⊤ always holds too, and hence ⊢ ◇⊤ ↔ ⊤. In ordinary topology the empty set, ∅, and the universal set X are both open and closed, and the topological space is said to be connected if and only if they alone are both open and closed.

[K.4], $\mathcal{C}(\mathcal{C}H) = \mathcal{C}H$, stipulates that the $\mathcal{C}$ operator is idempotent, as in the modal logic $S4$.

"Boolean-plus" algebra enriches logic. It yields a variety of modal logics, appropriate for different modalities, quantification theory and topology.

---

[34] See above, §5.3, p.137, n.9.

§7.9 Umbrian Universals

Genuine universals, such as those specifying natural kinds, are characterized by specifications couched in terms of predicates, but the Boolean algebra of predicates admits negation and disjunction too readily. Modal logic restricts unwelcome Boolean operations, and suggests that genuine universals might be characterized by modified specifications subject to the constraints of some modal logic.

Kuratowski's axiomatization of topology was by means of a closure operator, $\mathcal{C}$, equivalent to the $\Diamond$ of modal logic, yielding for each set the closure of that set.[35] We can equally well work with an interior operator $\mathcal{J}$ in place of his closure operator. just as we can formulate modal logic in terms of $\Diamond$ instead of $\Box$. In ordinary topology the interior operator pares down a set, cutting away its penumbra to leave only the core umbra. An operator which operated on a set to cut away artificial and adventitious members, leaving only those that were genuine specimens of the largest species within the set, would lead us from the over-populated world of sets to the more manageable realm of natural-kind universals. Not only would it exclude artificial specifications be formulated, like {cat ∪ Flint}, but also those cases where the meaning of the words we use has been extended by simile and metaphor to cover non-standard cases; we speak of sea dogs, dog-fish and dog-roses. Such terms are perfectly acceptable in ordinary conversation, but are not to be taken as substantial canine substantives in legal or scientific argument. Moreover, it would yield the desirable consequence that the negation of a predicate characterizing a natural kind need not itself characterize a natural kind. Non-ravens do not form a species: non-hydrogen does not have a place in the Periodic Table. We need to seek some "Umbra" operator which will focus on the core meaning of a specification, and exclude the penumbra of meaning and artificial additions or subtractions.[36] Only those specifications which are fully focused, should be accepted as specifying

---

[35] See above, §7.8.

[36] Caution is needed. In modal logic $\Box$ is a stronger operator than $\Diamond$, and in ordinary topology $\mathcal{C}$ is larger than $\mathcal{J}$: but here the umbra is more central, more fully focused, more real, than the penumbra. The difficulty is eased if we think of instances being *within* the umbra, and the relation $\subseteq$, *being included in*. $\mathcal{J}\mathcal{H} \subseteq \mathcal{H}$, so that if this case is covered by $\mathcal{J}\mathcal{H}$, then it is covered by H; Confusion arises because $\subseteq$ and $\rightarrow$ go hand in hand, but seem to point in opposite directions.

§7.9   *Existence and Reality*   211

natural kinds in arguments about nature, or genuine universals in arguments about universalisability.

An interior operator will exclude artificial additions, so that

$\mathcal{J}\{\text{cat} \cup \text{Flint}\}$ is simply $\{\text{cat}\}$.

Thus, we can use the interior operator to pare away artificial additions, and concentrate the artificial specification

$\{\text{cat} \cup \text{Flint}\}$

into just

$\{\text{cat}\}$,

which does specify a natural kind. We need also to exclude artificial subtractions: I should not make an exception for ME, when formulating a maxim of conduct, and by the same token, I should not except J.R. Lucas. The simple interior operator does not rectify such artificial exclusions, which beset applications of the principle of universalisability to moral issues, and may occur in historical argument also. It cannot enlarge $\{\text{dons}\backslash\text{J.R.Lucas}\}$ (that is to say $\{\text{dons except for J.R.Lucas}\}$)

into just $\{\text{dons}\}$,

and so exclude my making an exception in my favour when moralising about the duties of dons generally. To do this, we need to take the complement, apply the interior operator, and take the complement again. For, using overhead bars to indicate complementation,

$$\mathcal{J}\overline{\{\text{dons}\backslash\text{J.R.Lucas}\}} = \mathcal{J}\overline{\{\text{dons}\}},$$

so that

$$\overline{\mathcal{J}\overline{\{\text{dons}\backslash\text{J.R.Lucas}\}}} = \overline{\mathcal{J}\overline{\{\text{dons}\}}}.$$

It is natural, then, to see an analogy between $\overline{\mathcal{J}\,\overline{H}}$ and $\square$, parallel to that between $\lozenge$ and the interior operator. If we call $\mathcal{J}$ the Umbra operator), we might call $\overline{\mathcal{J}\overline{H}}$ the Penumbra operator. Admissible specifications, then, are those that are equal to the umbra of their penumbra. In symbols (keeping $\mathcal{C}$ for the Penumbra operator and $\mathcal{J}$ for the Umbra operator) H has the right logical shape to specify a universal iff $H = \mathcal{J}\mathcal{C}H$.[37]

---

[37] Of course, whether such a specification in some particular case actually does specify a universal is a further question. The condition of being equal to the interior of the closure parallels that of being a regular open set in topology. See P.R.Halmos, *Boolean Algebras*, Princeton, 1963, §4, pp.13-17.

We need to be wary about applying topological principles, which may not actually fit the topic under discussion, to assessments of ontological standing. We have only fragments, rather than a single integrated universe of discourse, and different fragments may have different logics. Natural kinds are articulated into various genera and orders. Although the tree of Porphyry was too schematic, natural kinds do have their various affinities and dissimilarities. In particular, whereas the complement of an open set is invariably a closed set, sometimes the complement of a natural kind *is* a natural kind. The classes of males and females are mutually exclusive and jointly exhaustive, without either being less ontologically robust than the other. Nevertheless, some parallels are illuminating: while we might sometimes have occasion to consider an infinite union of umbras, and accept it as itself being fully focused on an admissible universal, we reject infinite sequences of intersections of umbras, as not being themselves genuine umbras, but only cases of special pleading.[38] Topology may guide us into drawing more subtle distinctions than simple Boolean algebra can provide.

If genuine universals are those for which $H = \mathcal{JCH}$, we are saying that they form a class within which they are, as regards the Umbria operator, modally flat: the condition $H = \mathcal{JCH}$ is used to distinguish the specification from spurious ones, but that once done, iterating the operator, $\mathcal{JC}$, has no further effect. In other respects, however, modal considerations are highly relevant to our understanding of universals.

---

[38] See J.R.Lucas, "The Lesbian Rule", *Philosophy*, 1955, pp.195-213, see http://users.ox.ac.uk/ jrlucas/lesbrule.html

§7.10 Aristotelian Actuality

Aristotle's modal logic[39] includes the thesis

T $\Box p \to p.$

This states that if p is necessarily true, then p is true, and is equivalent to the thesis

T^* $p \to \Diamond p,$

which states that if p is true, then p is possibly true, which the Schoolmen expressed in the adage *ab esse valet consequentia posse* from existence there is a valid inference to possibility. Some modal logics do not have the thesis T: in moral philosophy 'I ought to do it' does not imply 'I do it'. Similarly, tense logics, which distinguish the future from the present, or the present from the past have future and past operators which do not satisfy T.[40] Most, however, do, and are therefore able to make a crucial distinction between actuality on the one hand and necessity and possibility on the other, a distinction which underlies the difference between Aristotle's and Plato's view of universals,

Species differ from Forms. Although species are relatively rare and seem fixed and permanent, so that we are able to draw general distinctions between different species, and do not confuse sheep with cows, or trees with grass, we now know that species evolved gradually over time; from which it follows that one species gradually, over many generations, shaded into another. Indeed, occasionally we find cases where two species shade into each other, not over time but over their present geographical distribution. Contrary to what was once thought, species are not immutable; not

---

[39] I need to emphasize that I am being anachronistic. Aristotle did not know modern modal logic. The doctrines imputed to him and to Plato are not the result of scholarly research, but "rational reconstructions" of positions that can be attributed to them.

[40] In the absence of B we can distinguish an inverse modal operator, $\Box^{-1}$, and thus distinguish the past from the future; since what is possibly possible in the future is possible, the axiom 4 makes $\Box$ have the appropriate modality for the future; but in order to capture our sense of the uniqueness of the past we need a slightly stronger axiom namely 4.3. It should be noted that whereas if we have 4 and B, then we can derive T as a theorem of **S5**, if we had only 5 without T, we should have a weaker system than **S5**, as there would be no way of deriving unmodalised propositions from modalised ones.

only can one transmute into another—as can happen with chemical elements, when radium atoms become radon—but, unlike the elements, there is no fixed form they have to take, and they can evolve in all sorts of different ways, through all sorts of intermediate stages. It follows that biological species are much more dependent on the specimens that instantiate them than chemical elements are on the atoms that instantiate them. They are Aristotelian universals that exist *in rebus*, and do not exist except in so far as specimens of them exist. There is no suggestion of their being prototypes from a select group of possible prototypes, in the way we can imagine the Periodic Table displaying the whole range of possible elements. For many years there were gaps in the Periodic Table, which inspired chemists to look for the missing elements, having quite a good idea of what their properties must be *ante res*, before actually discovering them. Element 85 was a halogen, Element 87 an alkali metal, even when there were no instances known to have these properties. A specimen-less biological species, by contrast, is merely fanciful. We may look for a missing link, thinking that there must be one, but unless and until we find one, we cannot claim that such a species actually exists. Whereas the cosmologically minded chemist can imagine that the elements had to evolve the way they did, because of the atomic structures that quantum mechanics allowed to be stable, the biologist allows himself no such speculations. Maynard Smith puts it well:

> If one was to replay the whole evolution of animals, starting at the bottom of the Cambrian . . . , there is no guarantee—indeed, no likelihood—that the result would be the same. There might be no conquest of the land, no emergence of mammals, certainly no human beings. [41]

The constraints Darwinism lays down are general and elastic. We can see why eyes evolved, and why insects and birds both have colour vision. But mammals, for reasons we can understand but would not have anticipated, lost the ability to discriminate colours and only the primates re-evolved it.

Plato, by contrast, cares little for actuality. He would have been happy with the modal system **D**, which carries over into

---

[41] J.Maynard Smith, "Taking a Chance on Evolution", *New York Review of Books*, **34**, #9, 14 May, 1992, pp.34-36; quoted F.J.Tipler, *The Physics of Immortality*, London, 1995, p.30.

§7.10 *Existence and Reality* 215

modal discourse the meanings and inferential patterns of ordinary unmodalised discourse, and does not collapse into ordinary unmodalised discourse, but deals only with necessities and possibilities.[42] Such a modal logic fits the logic of theoretical chemistry and theoretical physics, and especially that of mathematical discourse. A mathematical proposition cannot just happen to be true: if it is true at all, it must be necessarily true. And similarly with possibilities, a mathematical proposition cannot be possibly true but not actually true. In mathematics the converse of the Schoolmen's adage holds: *Ab posse valet consequential esse*, from possibility there is a valid inference to existence. Two-dimensional non-Desarguian geometry is logically possible; therefore two-dimensional non-Desarguian geometry exists. Whereas normally, as we have seen,[43] bare consistency is not enough to secure that what is referred to actually exists, in mathematics the completeness theorem for first-order logic secures the existence of a model for any consistent set of propositions.

Mathematics, in consequence, seems modally "flat", lacking the crucial realm of actuality between necessity and possibility. The need for necessity in mathematical truth, creates a strain between Platonist ontology and Platonist epistemology. Plato began by thinking that the Forms could be apprehended by the "eye of the mind". Hardy "always thought of a mathematician as in the first instance an observer", and draws the "rather paradoxical conclusion; that there is, strictly, no such thing as mathematical proof; that we can, in the last analysis, do nothing but point"; and on one occasion, according to a story told of him, lived up to this belief. In the course of a lecture he said "It is obvious that ...", and then checked himself, saying "Is it obvious?", whereupon he thought hard for several minutes, and then resumed "Yes, it is obvious". But the necessity of immediate apprehension is not easily communicable. I may point it out to you, as Hardy says, but you may still not twig what I am trying to convey. The Greek word for a pointer $\sigma\eta\mu\epsilon\hat{\iota}ov$ (*semeion*), is also the word used for a mathematical proof, "what Littlewood and I call gas, rhetorical flourishes designed to affect psychology, pictures on the board in

---

[42] Not to be confused with the quasi-topological Umbria and Penumbria of the previous section.

[43] In §7.2.

the lecture, devices to stimulate the imagination of pupils".[44] But rhetoric, though sometimes effective, lacks cogency. Plato saw that he needed to do more than stimulate the imagination of pupils, if he was to secure genuine necessity for mathematical truth, and sought it in the need, if communication is not to break down, to avoid self-contradiction.[45] He finds himself being driven towards a formalist method of proof.[46] The need to avoid self-contradiction, or inconsistency, is not the only source of necessity; indeed, the *Gestalt* of a proof, when it presents itself, can be compelling; but it is difficult to articulate, and the need to establish necessity has been a dominant theme in mathematical thought since the time of Plato.

Demerits of Platonism

1. Dismissal of appearances: does not try hard enough to save the phenomena.
2. Weak epistemology: we do not just see, or intuit, truths but argue about them; we do not see necessity, though perhaps we might feel it.
3. Fails to accommodate contingency (Maynard Smith), and hence (not argued here)
4. Weak on time, and also (not argued here)
5. Fails to accommodate our first-personal experience: I know what it is like to be me, and am quite interested in what you think it is like to be you. Plato only interested in science, not in the humanities.
6. Fails to accommodate our many and continued disagreements.

The Aristotelian modal logic accommodates a different apprehension of reality. Something can just be the case without having

---

[44] G. H. Hardy, *Mind*, 1929, p.18.

[45] See above, §2.1.

[46] *Republic* VI and VII, 509-511, and 533bc. It is noteworthy that Gödel subscribed to a Platonist ontology, while adopting a formalist methodology.

§7.10   Existence and Reality   217

to have to be the case. It is just a matter of happenstance that something is as it is, without there being any rhyme or reason to it. In mathematics it cannot just happen to be the case that, say, there is no even number that cannot be expressed as the sum of two primes, but in everyday life we are often faced with the way things are without there being any explanation why they should be like that. Although reason is a mark of reality, opaqueness is another. "Things ... are what they are, and the consequences of them will be what they will be",[47] and we just have to accept the fact. There is a story of a woman who told Napoleon that she accepted reality: "Begad, you had better" was the Emperor's reply. Reality is there anyway, whether we want it or not, whether we understand it or not.

It is, however, difficult to characterize Aristotelian universals simply in terms of Aristotle's commitment to actuality, because it is heavily qualified. The species *would be* the same, even if some particular member *were* different; possibility tinctures actuality. Much more obviously, in understanding history we need to know not only what actually happened, but the possibilities that were open at the time the crucial decisions were made. Aristotelian species are not simply constituted by things that actually exist, but extend into what might possibly exist. We can characterize them in terms of what they are not, and say that Aristotelian species are independent of any particular instances (in contrast to what the Nominalists claim), but are not independent of all their instances (in contrast to what the Platonists claim).

But it is still a fine distinction between Aristotelian universals which apply to any particular, but only exist provided they apply to some particular or other, and Platonist universals which can apply to any particular, but still exist though there are not any particulars they do, in fact, apply to. Plato and Aristotle both maintain the existence of natural kinds. Plato allows that the Forms may be instantiated—indeed, usually are: the Demiurge has created many instances of $Carbon_{12}$; the Form of $Carbon_{12}$ certainly exists *in rebus*; he differs from Aristotle not in denying that Forms can exist *in rebus*, but in claiming that they can exist without being *in rebus*. But once an Aristotelian species is distinguished from a nominalist set, its connexion with actual instances tends to become more and more attenuated. Even before instances of elements 85 and 87 were

[47] Joseph Butler, *Fifteen Sermons*, No. 7, §16.

discovered, an Aristotelian chemist would be hard put to it not to take them seriously, and agree that the former would have to be a halogen, and the latter a highly reactive alkali metal. Aristotle does not confine his concern to what actually exists at some time, but is concerned also with modal implication of species. The difference between the Platonist and Aristotelian approaches lies not so much in Aristotle's qualified commitment to actuality as in Plato's unconcern with it.

Chapter 8
Appearance and Unreality

§8.1   'Real'
§8.2   Antirealisms
§8.3   Appearances
§8.4   Plato against Appearance
§8.5   Empiricism
§8.6   The Cave
§8.7   Beyond

§8.1 'Real'

The word 'real' has many senses, and has been much misunderstood in consequence. It was, along with other philosophical terms, such as quality, quantity, entity, identity, essence and substance, coined by the Schoolmen in the Middle Ages—*realis, reale* from the Latin *res*, a thing—to mark the distinction between what really existed and what merely existed *in intellectu*, in the mind; and the word still carries connotations of thingness, which can confuse our thinking about reality in the present age.

Austin claimed that 'real' is in modern usage a chameleon word, taking its colour from its surroundings. Just as we often cannot say whether it is good until we know what "it" is—a good knife is quite different from a good meal, or a good opera—so we cannot say whether it is real until we know a real *what*; real butter is contrasted with margarine, real silk with rayon or artificial silk, a real gentleman with a *faux bon homme*, real coffee with *ersatz* coffee, a real grievance with an imaginary one, and so on.[1] Austin has a point. The word 'real' gets its meaning from its opposites—in Austin's phrase, 'unreal' wears the trousers—and is often used to focus the meaning of the word it governs onto the umbra of its meaning, excluding applications on the penumbra. Margarine looks like butter, spreads like butter, can be used instead of butter in cooking, but does not taste like butter, and, unlike butter, is not made from cow's milk. Artificial silk looks like real silk, but does not feel like it, and does not come from silkworms. We contrast

---

[1] J.L.Austin, *Sense and Sensibilia*, Oxford, 1962, ch.VII, pp.62-77.

'real' with 'synthetic', '*ersatz*', 'artificial', 'imaginary', 'illusory', *etc*.

Although the analysis of ordinary language cannot, as was once claimed, give us all the answers in philosophy, it is none the less a useful tool; it can save us from bad mistakes. It is always salutary, when questions of reality are raised, to ask what the contrast is. Anti-realism—some philosophical doctrine denying the reality of some sort of entity commonly believed to be real—is often our best guide to what reality really is; and the traditional opposition between Appearance and Reality can lead to a sharper focus on both these variegated concepts.

§8.2 Antirealisms

Although Austin was right in saying that the meaning of the word 'real' is shown in what it is being contrasted with, his examples are too limited to help us. If we are to rescue reality from the shopkeepers, we need to talk about more philosophical unrealities than margarine, *ersatz* coffee, and artificial silk. What constitutes reality is revealed by what is denied by various versions of anti-realism—philosophical doctrines denying the reality of some sort of entity commonly believed to be real. Dummett gives a good account of realism and anti-realism,[2] listing the following varieties of anti-realism,

1. Phenomenalism
2. Mathematical Intuitionism (Constructivism), and Formalism
3. Behaviourism
4. Instrumentalism
5. Moral Subjectivism
6. Unreality of Time

to which we should add:

7. Unreality of Space
8. Unreality of probabilities (and causes and secondary qualities).

Phenomenalism and Behaviourism, like many other forms of anti-realism, are argued for on verificationist grounds, in which *I* am required to give *my* reasons justifying *my* assertion about

---

[2] Michael Dummett, *Logical Basis of Metaphysics*, Duckworth, 1993; pp.4-8. See also Michael Dummett, *The Seas of Language*, Oxford, 1993, esp. chs.5, 6, 8, 11 and 20. Roger Trigg, *Reality at Risk*, Brighton, 1980, ch.1, criticizing N.Rescher, *Conceptual Idealism*, Oxford, 1973.

objects or people in the *external* world, that is, the world that is external to *me*. Berkeley denied that the quires of heaven were real, because it was up to him whether he perceived them or not. Some arguments against the reality of time turn on the fact that tenses are token-reflexive,[3] and thus covertly egocentric.[4] Similarly, some arguments for behaviourism are covertly egocentric: the 'other' of other minds is defined in terms of some first person, in something of the same way as the *'percipi'* of *esse est percipi* is perception by some first person. Once we look askance at egocentricity, we cease to be bothered about minds that are not mine, times that are, or are not, now, or trees of which nobody can say 'I see it'.

Forms of Unreality
1. Subjective, egocentric.

Since egocentricity is opposed to reality, it is natural to take it that non-egocentricity is a mark of reality. From this it is natural to generalise from me to everyone else; since the sense data of modern phenomenalists are, as a matter of logic, completely dependent on the observer, what is real must, it is assumed, be completely independent of the observer. (It should be noted that this is the contrary, not the contradictory of being completely dependent.) Realists maintain that the tree exists in the quad *whether or not there is anyone there to observe it*. Thus reality is not only independent of the observer, but independent of being actually observed. Some go further, and claim that reality is independent of observation altogether; although there are good reasons for rejecting that,[5] they are responding to a tendency inherent in our concept of reality, captured by Bernard Williams' phrase, "reality is what is there anyway".[6]

Forms of Unreality
1. Subjective, egocentric.
2. Completely dependent on the observer.

---

[3] See above, §3.3 n.8 and §7.3, item 5 in Platonism box, on p.186.

[4] See further below, §10.8.

[5] See later this chapter, §8.4.

[6] B.A.O.Williams, *Descartes*, Harmondsworth, 1976, pp.64-67.

The Absolute conception of what is there anyway captures a large part of the concept of reality, but can be misconstrued as requiring total non-egocentricity. Non-egocentricity is neither a necessary nor a sufficient condition of reality. My pain is real enough, though necessarily mine: ghosts and mirages lack reality, though not peculiarly mine or yours. It is independence of my will, not independence of me that is decisive. Dr Johnson refuted phenomenalism by kicking his foot against a stone. Reality is recalcitrant to my will; although I may choose not to see what is there—the quires of heaven, for example—I cannot choose to see what is not there. Besides the analogy between the solidity of material objects and the robustness of causal connexion,[7] there is a a further analogy with the obduracy of other people. The stone resists my kick, the other chap refuses to go along with my ideas. Although with care we can sometimes move stones, and sometimes cajole other people, material objects cannot be just wished away, and other people have minds of their own, which they can make up for themselves, sometimes differently from what we would have them decide.

Forms of Unreality

1. Subjective, egocentric.
2. Completely dependent on the observer.
3. Dependent on my, or your, will.

Independence fortified by recalcitrance is the mark of reality that leads working mathematicians to some form of Platonism. Intuitionists and Constructivists see mathematics as being merely an activity of mathematicians, without there being any mathematical truth or mathematical objects apart from what mathematicians actually say or do. Mathematical truth and mathematical objects are unreal because they completely depend on mathematicians. Mathematicians are like the observers on whom, according to the phenomenalists, material objects depend; only instead of being passive recipients of sense-impressions, they are active provers and definers.

---

[7] See above, §6.7.

> **Forms of Unreality**
> 1. Subjective, egocentric.
> 2. Completely dependent on the observer.
> 3. Dependent on my, or your, will.
> 4. Dependent on being known or thought about or being constructed.

These accounts of mathematics are reminiscent of versions of idealism, which relied on a coherence theory of truth to have knowledge constitutive of reality rather than trying to correspond to it. Such views are less bizarre in mathematics, which operates at a high level of abstraction, and relies on long chains of deductive argument, but they run counter to the opinion held by most mathematicians, that they are trying to discover truth, and are exploring a world not of their own imagining. For realists knowledge is not constitutive of truth; rather, truth is what knowledge claims to have acquired and is a necessary condition of knowledge; knowledge is "truth tracking", from which it follows that however robust reality may be thought to be, our beliefs about it are always **corrigible**. Statements that aspire to truth suffer a perpetual possibility of being wrong.

If mathematical objects exist independently of our constructions, then they are not just what we say they are. Our definitions are pointers, to enable other people to know what we are talking about, and so long as they are adequate for that in practice, they do not need to have said all there is to be said about them. It is for this reason that mathematical realists do not have to reject all impredicative definitions out of hand. We may legitimately quantify over all the numbers in a certain range, and then define one—say the least—in terms of our quantification, because if the numbers were not brought into existence by our specification of them, the one later defined in terms of the quantification—the least of them all—was already there to be quantified over before we had defined it. The realist demands less of definition and reference than the constructivist, because of his belief that the objects exist in their own right, independently of him. Once again there is an underlying sense of its being there anyway, and independent of our wills, manifesting itself in this case as independence of our knowledge or construction.

> Reality is not constituted by knowledge, but is what knowledge seeks to know.

Mathematics is highly integrated. Some theorems, such as Euler's

$$e^{i\pi} + 1 = 0$$

are recognised as being deep, and tell in favour of mathematical realism. Similarly, common sense urges us to go behind what is apparent and overt, and points out that the existence of material objects and other minds integrates and explains what would otherwise be disparate and inexplicable.[8] Particularly in the case of people, realism explains as well as integrates. We not only recognise the different manifestations of vanity portrayed by Ryle, but understand why the vain person does what he does.

Explanations in terms of human decisions are ultimate. If we want to know why something happened, we can often explain it in terms of what men did, and explain what men did in terms of their reasons for acting. When I know the reasons why someone did as he did, I know all there is to be known. He is, in Aristotle's phrase, ἡ ἀρχὴ τῆς πράξεως (*arche tes praxeos*), the initiator of movement.[9] and the reasons for his decision explain what subsequently happened. Such explanations are not always available, and often are not completely satisfactory, but they offer a level of explanation more satisfactory than that which can be achieved without reference to reasons for action. Their metaphysical importance is shown, in a back-handed way, by the unease generated by determinism and reductive materialism. These purport to go behind rational explanations of our actions, and to reveal them to be totally explicable in terms of the antecedent states of our bodies and their surroundings. Such explanations would, we feel, undercut our status as initiators of actions that came about simply because we decided to do them. If not being an initiator of action derogates from our ontological status, it follows that it is a mark of reality to be an initiator of action, or, more generally, a first cause, the locus of explanation that is not susceptible of further explanation of the same sort.

---

[8] See above, §6.7 and §6.13.

[9] Aristotle, *Nicomachean Ethics*, V, ix, 10, 1136b28.

§8.2   Appearance and Unreality   225

Men are not merely initiators of action, but are relatively independent of their surroundings: if it rains, mountains get wet, but people put umbrellas up and stay dry: if the sun shines, mountains get warm, but people put up parasols, and stay cool. Admittedly, people are not totally independent of their surroundings; but, along with other animals, they are more independent than inanimate objects, and are themselves more independent than other animals. They do not pretend to complete independence, but they do better in the independence stakes than mere things.[10]

Marks of Reality

Aseity implies:

1. being there anyway, and hence Self-subsistent, Impassible.
2. being independent of the observer.
3. being independent of the will, and hence
4. being potentially recalcitrant.
5. being explanatory, and moreover
6. being ultimately explanatory.

Locke held that all things that exist are particulars,[11] and Quine that "To be is to be a value of a variable". Behind these *dicta* lies Aristotle's πᾶσα δὲ οὐσία δοκεῖ τόδε τι σημαίνειν (*pasa de ousia dokei tode ti semainein*), every substance seems to indicate a certain 'this'.[12] Substances are things we can identify and refer to, and it is evident that we do refer to people, and quantify over them, as also quarks and quaternions.

Marks of Reality

1. required to be quantified over by current established practice
   (Quine: "To be is to be the value of a variable").
2. can be publicly identified and referred to.

---

[10] See further below, §§12.8,12.9.

[11] *Essay Concerning Human Understanding*, Book III, ch.3, §1.

[12] Aristotle, *Categories*, 3b10, tr. J.L.Ackrill, Oxford, 1963.

Sceptics may not be ready to accept quarks and quaternions as being *bona fide* substances in the way that material objects are: whereas it is obvious that material objects can be referred to, it may be doubted whether, when we purport to be talking about abstract entities, there is anything that we are really talking about. Such doubts may be met, up to a point, by the fact that we evidently do succeed in talking about some abstract entities. Minimal Platonism is a going concern, but too easy-going to carry real ontological weight: Greek mythologists talk happily together about Zeus and Aphrodite, and devotees of Middle Earth about elves and hobbits; but that does not show that they exist in the real world. And even if by means of quantification over abstract entities, we can characterize the natural numbers uniquely, and be sure that we and other people are talking about the same particular numbers,[13] discourse about abstract algebras or non-Desarguean geometry seems similarly unrelated to reality. Material objects are *there* anyway: abstract entities are not *there*. Bodies not located in space, materialists aver, like God, and the square root of minus one, do not really exist, even though people talk about them. If not being located in space is taken to be a sign of unreality, it would seem that being located in space should be a mark of reality. But that goes too far. Shadows are located in space. It is not location in space, but exclusive space occupancy that is meant. And this, though not a necessary condition of reality, is, by and large, a sufficient one: we can guarantee identity of reference, and exclusiveness secures some degree of recalcitrance—we cannot put anything else in the place where it is, without moving it away.

> **Marks of Reality**
> 1. Exclusive space-occupier.

Yet doubts remain. When fields were first introduced into modern physics, they were felt to be too "iffy" to be real. A field was just a way of registering what would happen to a test particle IF it were placed at a particular point. Space-occupancy was not enough. It was only when it emerged that fields could carry energy that they were admitted to be real, and not a mere notational device. In the Twentieth Century, when energy merged

---

[13] See above, §7.2.

§8.2   *Appearance and Unreality*   227

with mass, the possession of massergy became for many physicists the leading mark of being real. Massergy combined the exclusive space-occupancy and willy-nilliness of matter, the sense of being there anyhow, and not being liable to be wished or imagined away, with the activity of energy, the moving force that gets things done. The moving force that gets things done has causal influence, and it is the possession of causal influence that many scientists regard as the crucial mark of reality. But there are many senses of 'cause', and defenders of the Forms can argue that, although some mathematics is recondite, mainstream mathematics, together with other Forms and species, is an essential part of natural science and our knowledge of causal processes. Platonism need not be minimal, because it draws substantial reality from its involvement in natural science. We add these further marks of reality to our list.

Marks of Reality
1. Has massergy.
2. Has causal influence.
3. Has causal significance.

Some arguments against the reality of time and space depend on the particular *rôle* time and space play in our conceptual scheme, itself largely shaped by metaphysical aspirations not yet articulated. Discussion of them will be deferred until chapters 9 and 13. The arguments for and against Instrumentalism will likewise be deferred to chapter 12. Although some of the arguments have been around for a long time—there was a professor of chemistry in Oxford in the late Nineteenth Century who did not believe in atoms—it was only with the advent of quantum mechanics that the microworld became necessarily invisible even to microscopic eyes, and could not be subsumed into the ordinary public world of material objects, thus raising unavoidable questions about its ontological status. It was also only with the advent of quantum mechanics that probabilities had to be construed realistically, and could no longer be taken as merely pertaining to our beliefs.

Moral antirealism is sometimes driven by a crude rejection of a crude Platonism about values: much of Plato's language is metaphorical, and easily misunderstood by those who want to misunderstand it. Often moral antirealism is fuelled by metaphysical antirealism generally; if matter alone exists, moral principles can only be pie-in-the-sky: but then the fundamental argument is one of metaphysics, not morals. In other cases moral anti-realism is argued for independently of metaphysical beliefs. As such it has no metaphysical implications, but often gives rise to a discontent that is metaphysical. We are not happy with an anodyne Lotus world of pleasurable experiences. We seek challenges; χαλεπὰ τὰ καλά (*chalepa ta kala*), fine things are difficult.[14] We feel a need to be "up against it", finding in the recalcitrance of reality an assurance that life is real and earnest, and has a significance beyond our own mortal life span.

Marks of Reality

1. Not subjective or egocentric.
2. Independent of the observer.
3. Independent of the will.
4. Resistant to will; brute fact; ineluctable, unavoidable; what happens willy-nilly; potentially recalcitrant.

5. Integrative.
6. Explanatory, rational.

7. Independent of whether known or not; contrasted with epistemic.
8. Independent of whether constructed or not (in mathematics).
9. Statements about reality are truth tracking.
10. Statements about reality are corrigible.

11. Required to be quantified over by current established practice. (Quine: "To be is to be the value of a variable")
12. Can be publicly identified and referred to.

13. Exclusive space-occupier.
14. Has massergy (massenergy).
15. Has causal influence.
16. Has causal significance.

17. Independent of surroundings; Impassible.
18. Not explicable in other terms.
19. Self-subsistent; (Aseity).

---

[14] Anthony O'Hear, *Plato's Children*, Oxford, 2005, points out that this is the attraction of sports such as mountaineering.

It is evident that the philosophers' concept of reality, is, like the use of the word 'real' in ordinary language, marked by many different contrasts, which help delineate what reality is. The marks of reality that have emerged, though diverse, are interconnected, and interpenetrate one another. Is it possible to weave these different marks into a coherent characterization? The Schoolmen talked of "aseity", by-itself-ness, being self-subsistent. Aseity combines the independence of being there anyway, and hence potential recalcitrance, should I, or anyone else, seek to push it around, with some ideal of explanatory independence, of being rational, but not being susceptible of, nor needing, any further explanation. Aseity captures the sense of reality being something other than us, a force, if not making for good, at least evincing rationality; but has the demerit of not being determinate in its application, and not being fully realised in the cases considered here. But it would be premature to expect complete clarification as yet; for the most pervasive, and potentially the most misleading, contrast is that between Appearance and Reality.

§8.3 Appearances

Appearance is contrasted with Reality, and not to its advantage. In saying something is real, we exclude our mistakes, our illusions, our limited perspectives, our limited understanding: things are what really they are, not as they appear. Reality is Good, it seems, in contrast to Appearance, which is Misleading and Bad.

But appearances are not all of one piece: the Greek words, φαίνεται (phainetai), δοκεῖ (dokei), give rise to the very different English words 'phenomena', on the one hand, and 'orthodoxy', 'heterodoxy' on the other; the Latin *videtur* has a strong visual connotation, but is used, like the English 'seems', 'semblance' and 'resemble', with a suggestion of fallibility. With some appearances we are impelled to ask to whom did they appear, with others our attention is directed to the subsequently corrected version. The latter, tentative judgements, that seem to be the case, but may well be wrong, should be distinguished from "appearances to", and among these there need to be distinguished those that appear exclusively

> **Appearance**
> 1. Tentative judgement: may well be wrong.
> 2. Autobiographical: not corrigible.
> 3. "From where I sit", "from where you sit": other seats acknowledged.
> 4. What we all (all actual observers) observe: the phenomena which any account of reality must preserve.
> 5. What we all (all actual and possible) observers observe: the phenomena which any account of reality hopes to accommodate.

to me, those that appear to me, but also to you, those that actually appear to us, and those that might possibly appear to us or to other possible observers.

In the first sense I am using the locution 'It appears to me' to give an estimate, in which I try to correct for my own deficiencies and position, and give an account that will be interpersonally valid, but I acknowledge I may fail. I am not talking about *me*, and *my* sense-experience, but about *it*, and you may well be in a better position to know about it, and be able to correct me when I put forward my own tentative judgement.

> Reality corrects appearances

The opposite holds good in the second sense. Then I am reporting how things seem to me, making no attempt to correct for deficiencies of my sense organs, or conditions of observation. It is what I tell the doctor, if I have got jaundice, or the optician, when I am having my eyes tested. I do not turn my head to see the letters close to in order to make out the little letters I am being asked to observe. What is of concern is not what the letters really are, but my impressions, my visual sense-experience, my sense-data. I am being autobiographical, in order that the doctor or optician can help me. And I am the ultimate authority on me. If I say that everything seems yellow, or that the letter appears to be an R, the doctor or optician accepts my say-so as final. There is no room, logically speaking, for saying that I have got it wrong. Apart from deliberate deception or linguistic incompetence (if I did not understand English very well, and thought that 'yellow' meant 'azure'),

§8.3   Appearance and Unreality   231

I cannot be wrong about my own sense-experience. The doctor may find no other symptoms of jaundice, the optician may know that the letter is actually an A, but neither can say that things do not really appear to me yellow, or that it did not seem to me to be an R. In this sense my reports of how things appear to me are infallible: you cannot correct me: what I say goes: I cannot be wrong.

Even if I am not being the infallible me, I still am me, not you, and my ways are not entirely your ways. Without wishing in any way to pressurise you, I may want just to recognise the fact of our being different. My perspective is different from yours, which in turn is different from his and from theirs. But although all different, these perspectives are not all utterly different, or we should not be able to talk to one another about them at all. Besides contrasting how things appear to me with how they appear to you, I may also want to contrast how things appear to me or to you with the invariant core that is the same for all of us. It looks elliptical, but is really round; the ridge of the roof is really level, though from here it looks as if it is going up. This third sense comes between the first two. It is not purely autobiographical and infallible, but it does not invite immediate correction by some superior apprehension of reality. I report that the distant tower looks square, or that the moon seems to be the size of a sixpence. I am not telling you about myself, but about what anyone situated as I am would experience. I could be corrected—someone else, standing where I stood, might say that the tower looked circular, or that the moon was the size of shilling, and I, on reflection or re-examination, might agree. But I could not be corrected by a simple appeal to reality. 'Actually it is triangular', or 'Actually, it is as large as the Pacific Ocean', do not impugn what I said, but only say what I might have gone on to say. Appearances here are contrasted with reality, but are not immediately corrigible by reality, though they are intersubjectively corrigible, and to that extent real with a respected ontological status of their own.

Although as a matter of logic, appearances in this third sense are not immediately corrigible by reality, it has emerged, curiously, and significantly, as a psychological fact, that they are influenced by it. How things appear to an observer *is* affected by knowledge of reality, so that if we can see that an inclined disk is actually a coin, it appears to us as more circular and less elliptical than the geometry of perspective would suggest it should.[15] This "Phenomenal Regression to Real Object" shows how the need for communicators to talk about what is invariant as between the one and the other exerts pressure not only on our language but even on our perceptions.

Whereas appearances in the third sense are what appear to me or to you in the singular, in the fourth sense they are what appear to us in the plural. We have an ideal of competent and impartial observers who will all have the same sense-experience, if under the same conditions, and provide us with a reliable and objective *entrée* into reality. Even so, we can all be wrong. Our ancestors included many reliable and competent observers, who confidently reported that the earth was flat, and that the sun went round the earth. More telling is the fact that we can all be wrong about morals. The biblical "Ye have heard of old time ..., but I say unto you ... " is not a self-contradiction, and may on occasion be true. The moral reformer can make his case; and so too can the knowledge reformer.

> Reality is corrigible, and can be corrected by appearances.

Once we become aware of the limitations of human sensory apparatus, we begin to consider not just what appears to all actual observers, but what would appear to actual and possible observers. If we had microscopic eyes, we should see blood not as red, but as yellow with red corpuscles floating in it; and benzene rings as joined-up hexagons of carbon atoms, with hydrogen ones hanging on. Such speculations are dangerously indeterminate. Once we leave the definite world of actual observers, there are many different modes of possibility that may be invoked. We should be wary of placing too much credence on such speculations. But such speculations have been entertained, and sometimes have proved to be right, and we should note them in listing the different senses given to 'appearances'. With them, reality remains corrigible, but

---

[15] R.H.Thouless, *British Journal of Psychology*, **21** and **22**, 1931. J.J.Gibson, *The Perception of the Visual World*, Cambridge, Mass., 1950, pp.169-172. O.L.Zangwill, *Introduction to Modern Psychology*, London, 1950, pp.30-34. See further below, §§8.5, 9.7.

no longer corrects appearances, but, rather, explains and accommodates them.

These different senses of 'appearance' indicate the different contrasts which go to form our concept of reality. The reality against which the optician assesses his patient's visual acuity is that which corrects appearances while being itself corrigible. The optician has no doubt that the letter seems to the patient to be an R, but no hesitation in concluding that the patient failed to see it correctly. But the optician could, conceivably, be wrong. He might have accidentally turned the translucent screen, so that the bottom left letter is actually a B. In that case we would have the first sense, when I am not talking incorrigibly about me, but corrigibly about some item interpersonally observable. In that sense I use 'it appears to be ' to emphasize my corrigibility. I profess great readiness to evacuate my position if you should wish to controvert me. I am hazarding a conjecture on imperfect information, or I am aware of my own defective sensory apparatus, or limited intelligence. So, paradoxically, both the incorrigible and the corrigible uses of 'it appears' bear witness to the corrigibility of anything we say about reality together with its being the standard against which either sort of appearance is to be assessed.[16]

§8.4 Plato against Appearance

Plato was hostile to Appearances, contrasting them unfavourably with the Forms. Originally it was appearances in the second sense that he was against, because they were subjective, and he was seeking to secure objectivity against the subjectivity of the opinionated. His prime purpose was moral. He was arguing against the moral subjectivism of his time, and sought to show that moral values were objective, because they were realities existing independently of us, and were not constituted by what we happened to think, or what seemed to us to be the case, but were the standard by which our thoughts and actions should be evaluated. Plato's hostility to Appearance was enhanced by his hostility to the self. He thought that self-aggrandisment was the root of all evil, and he associated moral subjectivism with selfishness, and sought to liberate the soul of man from both, holding that it was meant to be a self-less knower, capable of communing with eternal truths,

---

[16] For a fuller account of the different senses of the word 'appear', see P.M.S.Hacker, *Appearance and Reality*, Oxford, 1987, ch.6.

and not subject to the sway of fashion or the attrition of time. He
confused the unreliability of mere opinion with the immorality of
selfishness, and hence conflated appearance in the first and second
senses, and thence, by extrapolation to the other three senses, concluded that appearances in general were egocentric and liable to be
wrong.

Necessities of communication require some measure of intersubjectivity. Plato construed this as a requirement of invariance
over differences of person, and hence also over different points of
view and differences of date, since different people are characteristically at different places at the same time, and often are talking to
one another about what had happened at some different time. It
seemed that necessities of communication required reality to be the
same for all persons at all times in all places, and hence knowledge
must be subject to the Valentian canon, being knowable *semper, ubique et ab omnibus* always, everywhere and by everyone, and reality must really be absolute, impersonal and timeless.[17] But Plato
was going further than the necessities of communication actually
required. He misconstrued the requirement of omnipersonality and
omnitemporality as one of impersonality and timelessness. He was
taking over the characteristic mark of objectivity possessed by material objects, and attributing it to reality generally. We might call
this "Metaphysical Regression to the Thingly Entity" analogous to
the distortion noted in the previous section (§8.3) of our perception
of appearances.

Plato argued further that what is known must be necessary.
If what is known exists necessarily, there can be no contingency
about its existence, nor any changeableness. True science must be
not about appearances, which just happen to be what they are,
and may change, but about unchanging principles, which are always the same because they must be what they are. The sciences
that most closely approximate to this ideal are the mathematical
sciences. Towards the end of his life he discusses which sciences
should be fostered in the Land of the Laws.[18] He has little use
for the domestic sciences, such as weaving and cookery, and comes
down firmly in favour of arithmetic and astronomy. We still feel
that mathematics and mathematical physics are "hard" subjects,

---

[17] See above, §8.2.

[18] *Epinomis* 974d-979d.

and that the biological sciences are somehow "softer", and the humanities are softer still, concerned as they are with the changes and chances of human life, and how things seemed to different people at different times.

If knowledge is necessarily necessary, it must be immune to the assaults of contingent appearances in the fourth, and hence even in the fifth sense. In the seventh book of the *Republic*, Plato dismissed the relevance of observation for ἀστρονομία (*astronomia*), and laughed at those who waste their time lying on their backs looking at the stars instead of getting on with the serious business of calculation.[19] There is a similar story of the Princeton hostess who boasted to Mrs Einstein of the expensive telescope her husband used to discover the nature of the universe, and received the reply: "My husband does it on the back of an old envelope."

We sympathize with Plato and Mrs Einstein,[20] but we nonetheless need to press the question of what view we should take, if the experimentalist, money-spending and banausic though he be, persistently disagrees with the theoretician. The Babylonian astronomers got beyond counting on their fingers, and realised that 10 was a poor base for arithmetical calculation, and that 12, 30 and 60, were much better. It would have been pleasingly rational if the year had been exactly 360 days long, consisting of 12 months of 30 days each. Unfortunately the earth's orbit round the sun the moon's round the earth and the diurnal rotation of the earth on its axis are not synchronized. So although it might have been more beautiful, more rational, if the ratios had worked out neatly, the fact was that they did not. Plato would advise them to be unworried. If appearances did not agree with reason, so much the worse for appearances; it is just what might have been expected with mere appearances, and only goes to show how unreliable they are, and what little use they are as guides to the true reality. It is a tenable position, but at a cost. The Babylonians would have had a beautiful theory, but a useless calendar, which would not have not told them when to expect the rains, when to sow, or when to harvest. Only if a theory leads to consequences which could be wrong, is it relevant to our understanding of the natural world—a theory immune to refutation by counter-evidence would tell us nothing of substance about the way things are. It must be possible

---

[19] *Republic* VII, 529-530.

[20] See above, §4.6.

to envisage falsifying instances without falling into inconsistency. Empirical phenomena may be unsatisfactory in various ways, but they do matter to us. Ἀστρονομία (*astronomia*) as Plato understands it, is not about the stars at all. It should be translated not as 'astronomy', but as 'rational mechanics'. It is a perfectly respectable branch of mathematics, but is no good for telling us where the Pole Star was, or whether there would be a moon to light us back from a party.

Extreme Platonism lacks relevance for us. It is not "News from Nowhere" as the anti-metaphysical gibe would have it, but not news at all, if it has no bearing on us or our concerns. Only if at some remove or other it tells us about us, and me about me, will it have any bearing on our, or my, concerns. An adequate account must preserve the appearances, in order that it may appear to us significant. If I am in a strange town and see a map posted, I need the arrow with the caption "You are here". A dating system is no good, unless we can know what the date is now. It is not enough to have a complete guest list—we sometimes have to ask "who are you?", and need an answer in the first person singular.

Plato has taken non-egocentricity as a mark of reality to an extreme: against that, Aristotle insists that for any science it is necessary σώζειν τὰ φαινόμενα (*sozein ta phainomena*), to save the appearances.[21] Appearances are, in this sense, crucial to reality. A reality which altogether hides itself, and never appears to any of us in any form, under any guise, ceases to be relevant to us, and forfeits its title to being real at all. Potential recalcitrance, rather than bare non-egocentricity, is the essential characteristic of reality: reality not only must not depend on me, but must be able to frustrate my will, if I attempt to push it around heedlessly.

---

[21] Simplicius, *In Cael.* 7.32.18.

§8.5 Empiricism

We endorse Aristotle's criticism. We are empiricists to the extent of demanding that our theories should in the end be vindicated by appearances—appearances in the fourth sense—and in the last resort, when all appeal to experimental error, random fluctuations, unknown intervening factors, or exceptional circumstances, have been exhausted, be rejected if the empirical evidence tells against them.

Many modern thinkers go much further, espousing an empiricism that denies any possibility of a rationalist science, or rationalist morality. Natural science, the Logical Positivists say, is about natural phenomena, period. But they have too narrow a view of reason and an un-thought-out account of natural phenomena. Reason is not confined to deductive logic,[22] and rational considerations play a large part in the natural sciences.[23] Contrary to the teaching of Sir Karl Popper, scientific theories are not exposed to sudden death at the hands of falsifying instances. Experimental error is often, and rightly, invoked to explain away discrepancies between theory and actual observation. When observations cannot be attributed to experimental error, the theory they seem to falsify is not so much refuted as refined. The observations made by Michelson and Morley, it is said, led to the overthrow of Newtonian mechanics. But this, though true, is only partly true. The Special Theory, which replaced Newtonian mechanics, has Newtonian mechanics as a limiting case; and we still use Newtonian mechanics for almost all practical purposes.

> Knowledge is not based on experience alone, but on reason too.

Moreover, sometimes we do not just explain away or accommodate the data of observation, but override them. Hume argued, on empiricist principles, that since there was a minimum spatial interval we could perceive, and likewise a minimum temporal interval we could discern, space and time must be discrete. But we do not accept the verdict of our sensory apparatus as conclusive. We

---

[22] See above, §2.1, n.2, §2.7, §2.10.

[23] See above, §4.7.

mostly think of space and time as continuous.[24] Once we recognise that reason is "thick", and not confined to deductive inferences that cannot be gainsaid on pain of self-contradiction, we can accept that some principles have probative effect in their own right, and may outweigh that of some observations. It is significant that though Einstein could have been refuted by observation, he was not. The principle of covariance, and other symmetries that underlie the General Theory, have great weight, even though it would not be inconsistent to deny them.[25]

> Reason can on occasion override experience.

Although we do need to save appearances, appearances have to be massaged by the criteria of normative reason in order to be saved. They cannot be the "flat" appearances which were taken by the English Empiricists to be purely passive impressions, something that the external world impressed on the mind. In a similar vein, the Logical Positivists spoke of sense-data, items just given from which we were to construct the edifice of empirical knowledge. But though we are subject sometimes to unwelcome interventions from the external world—a flash of lightening, a clap of thunder, a stab of pain—we mostly elicit information about the external world by looking, listening, feeling, sniffing and tasting. Our sense experience is *not* something that just happens to us, but is feed-back on our exploratory activities. We ask questions, and nature gives us answers. And the answers, since they are answers to questions asked, are shaped by the questions. Hence the Phenomenal Regression to the Real Object noted in section §8.3. Only very seldom are we concerned primarily with how an object actually appears to us in the first, autobiographical sense—only if we are at the oculist or trying to paint a picture: almost always we are concerned with the object itself, which we may want to avoid, move, or manipulate, and the answer to that question dominates a merely autobiographical enquiry. The appearances on which empirical knowledge is founded are not the appearances in the first sense, the appearances that might be recorded in an autobiographical account of a stream of consciousness, but are appearances in the fourth sense

---

[24] See further below, §§13.6 and 13.7.

[25] See further above, §12.1.

§8.5   Appearance and Unreality   239

of appearances, that is, which are not necessarily dependent on person, time or place.

> Reason shapes experience, as it makes sense of it.

The pressure of Reason on Appearance goes deeper. Once we move away from the private sense-data of individual persons to what can be observed by people in general, we are led to a public external world in which there are objects, which can be perceived by anyone, at many times and from many points of view, but can equally well exist unperceived. And if it is permissible to explain sense experience by reference to material objects, the possibility cannot be ruled out of our explaining material objects in terms further removed from direct experience. Physicists read what they see in a Wilson cloud chamber as tracks of charged particles. The complicated apparatus devised by experimental scientists can be see as instruments of torture to force nature to reveal her secrets, and the observations are construed as answers to the question asked by the experimenter rather than what might be seen by an uninformed bystander. What we see with our eyes is so much a question of what we are looking for, that text books in biology show diagrams of cells, not photographs taken through microscopes. To the uninformed observer photographs taken through microscopes, like X-ray photographs, are just a blur. The eye has to be trained if it is to see what there is to be seen. Similarly the ear. When I twiddle the tuning knob, I pick up foreign stations with a lot of interference. Even if I can make out what language is being spoken, I cannot distinguish the message from the noise—unless it is English, when I can pick out what is being said in spite of much interference. Psychologists and physiologists sometimes tell us in consequence that the retina and inner ear are really part of the brain; and without presuming to opinionate about physiology, we should accept the moral, that the appearances the empiricists cherish are not opposed to reason, but largely shaped by it.

The concept of appearance is fuzzy at its remoter end. The appearances we all observe are not clear-cut, because it is not clearcut who *we* are. Are we the we who can read X-ray photographs and understand Wilson cloud chambers? Or the we that includes me, who cannot see anything through a microscope, nor pick out the theme tune from the rest of the orchestration? It seems Philistine to construe the range of actual observers narrowly. I hesitate to intrude my imperceptiveness as a barrier to the advancement of science; I am inclined to believe that when scientists say that they can see something of consequence in their apparatus, they are telling the truth. I extend the range of actual observers to focus on the competent, gifted and highly trained, to include what can be observed with the aid of apparatus, and even further to include what may be observed with even better apparatus, and, indeed, what might be observed if we had better sense-organs. We slide from the fourth to the fifth sense, and consider how the world would appear to those enjoying the beatific vision, or possessing microscopic eyes.

§8.6 The Cave

In Book VII of the *Republic* Plato likens our ordinary experience to that of prisoners in a cave, in which they can see only dim shadows of real objects they are unable to look at directly. A few favoured souls, however, may undergo a conversion, which enables them to escape from the cave and see things properly in normal daylight. They would see things as they really are, and come to understand the why and the wherefore of the succession of shadows seen in the cave. Although what we see with our ordinary eyes are only transient appearances, true philosophers can see with the eye of the mind a permanent reality which is not subject to human whim or fashion, and which can give us guidance and illumination.

The Twentieth Century has given better analogies than the cave. The early films were all black-and-white, and viewers in the cinema saw only a monochrome representation of the real world, which they saw in all its coloured magnificence when they came out of the cinema into broad sunshine. Early television was similarly monochrome, and in any case there is a contrast between the images shown on the screen and what we can see in the outside world.

> **Plato's Cave**
>
> Black & White TV *v.* Coloured World

The analogy is compelling: the images are only appearances, which only partially represent a reality not mediated through cinema or television. The contrast between the images of uninformed experience and the realities that give rise to them is intuitive and plausible. Nevertheless, Plato has been severely criticized by modern philosophers. They are sceptical of the eye of the mind. True, we do use visual metaphors for intellectual feats of understanding: but they hesitate to posit an eye of the mind on a par with the genuine eyes we can identify in our heads. Can Plato give any other account, they ask, of how we could know what the outside of the cave was like, were we able to get there? And, without waiting for an answer, contemptuously dismiss the whole account as an idle simile offering us again only News from Nowhere.

But Plato was not just offering us information about the world of Forms. The true philosopher, having seen the Forms with the eye of the mind, could return to the cave, and see the same images as other men saw, but with understanding of why they were as they were. And Plato was not the only thinker to seek knowledge of a reality beyond the appearances we all can share. The ancient atomists and their modern successors portray a world markedly different from the one we experience, claiming that it lies behind it and can explain it. All the phenomena of ordinary life are, it is hoped, to be explained in terms of the position and its time-derivatives of the atoms. If we had microscopic eyes, says Locke,[26] we should be able to see into the real nature of things, and understand why natural phenomena appeared to us as they did. Plato's cave cannot be dismissed as an idle metaphor, unless much of modern chemistry and physics is to be ruled out of court also.

> **Scientists' Cave**
> Coloured TV *v.* Black & White World

Some philosophers are willing to do just that.[27] We do not have microscopic eyes, and so are in principle unable to verify what the scientists say. But such criticisms make little impact. We do not need microscopic eyes: optical microscopes and electron microscopes serve instead. And in any case we believe what the scientists tell us not because we can somehow see it for ourselves, but because what the scientists tell us *explains* what we can see for ourselves. Our warrant for believing in a reality beyond appearance

---

[26] John Locke, *Essay Concerning Human Understanding*, II:23:11-12

[27] Susan Stebbing, *Philosophy and the Physicists*, London, 1937.

is inferential, not sensory. Reality is rational, and inference to the best explanation can give us knowledge of it.

A similar two-part defence of Plato's own account can be mounted. Although most of us cannot read an X-ray photograph, some can; and similarly some sensitive souls can read the book of nature and the hearts of men and can see how things cohere, and that All is Well. Some who go on long Wordsworthian walks in the Lake District may sufficiently sharpen their sensibilities to be aware of deeper realities; some never lose the gleam perceived by childhood innocence, and even in adulthood see the fields bathed in orient light; many have a sense of the numinous in certain hallowed places. We could, even, give credence to a sixth sense possessed by seventh sons of seventh sons. We cannot confidently set limits to what might appear to people in the fifth sense of 'appear'. Sceptics can insist that the fourth sense be tightly delimited, but then they have to allow that Reason enables us to go beyond the limits of appearances in that restricted sense. Although the reasons that might be adduced for holding natural scenery indicative of a Deity upholding it, are not the same as those arguing for the atomic theory of matter, they cannot be dismissed out of hand. The explanatory schema outlined aims to explain everything, thereby revealing its significance: it makes up in width what it lacks in detail. It may fail, but it is not foredoomed to failure.

Plato's Cave (*Republic* VII, 514ff.)

How can Reality be more real than Appearance? How can we, inside the Cave, know what it is like outside? God might tell us; it might be revealed in mystical experience, or by communing with nature during long walks in the Lake District; we might have an extra sense; (in the kingdom of the blind the one-eyed is king). Then it is

 Black & White TV *v.* Coloured World

Alternatively, we might know because it was more **explanatory**

drive for economy—only primary qualities

then

 Coloured TV *v.* Black & White World

Locke-Mackie thesis.

Microscopic eyes see the real essences of things, in which there are no secondary qualities: secondary qualities merely painted onto reality by us.

Most thinkers in the present age are readier to accept the world of the atomists than the world of the Forms. Their world is much more austere than Plato's. Whereas for Plato the appearances within the cave were much dimmer and more monochromatic than those in the world outside, for the atomists the reverse is true, and it is reality that is devoid of colour and scent and sound, being constituted of corpuscles possessing only the primary qualities of configuration and motion. Its austerity is seen as a virtue. For our warrant for accepting that atomism gives us a true account of reality is its explanatory power; and explanations need to practise economy. To explain colours monochromatically is to explain: Plato's glorious polychromatic world may be much lovelier than the greys of the cave, but cannot be offered as an economical explanation of them. The world the microscopic eyes would see, did they exist, is knowable without them, because of its explanatory power: whereas Plato needs, and in the opinion of his critics fails, to provide a convincing account of the eye of the mind, or in its absence some other warrant for holding that the world of the Forms actually exists.

§8.7 Beyond

Explanations give rise to further questions, which in turn demand further explanations. The classical atomists, or corpuscularians, as we may call them to distinguish them from the exponents of modern atomic theory, whose atoms are anything but unsplittable, explained secondary qualities, such as colours, sounds and scents, in terms of primary qualities, such as position and motion. But questions arise about these too, and in the Twentieth Century physicists have sought deeper explanations, which sometimes they can give, in terms of quantum mechanics and Einstein's General Theory. It is tempting to extrapolate from the explanation of secondary qualities in terms of primary qualities, and to envisage these in turn being explained in terms of "nullary" qualities. Certainly, the search for explanations gives rise to a progression of deeper and deeper explanation, and in so far as explanatory power is a mark of reality, we have an ordering of greater and greater—or deeper and deeper—reality. But there is a trade-off between explanatory power and experiential adequacy. Berkeley and many others have complained that the world of the atomists has no room for the colours, sounds and scents that make up a large part of life as we experience it. It has not been established that explanatory power is the sole mark of reality, nor that scientific explanation is the only one capable of leading us from one ontological type to another. Reason is many-faceted, and it may be that the further reaches of reality do not have to be more featureless than the appearances we already know.

Although reality is intimately connected with reason, it is not the same as it. Sometimes reality is contrasted with reason, as when we have to recognise as a simple brute fact the opaque necessity of a natural law that reveals itself in the impossibility of conjoining the cause with the absence of the effect. The independence and potential recalcitrance of reality has been a recurring theme. The reality of various different sorts of entity has been impugned on the grounds that, being in some way dependent, they lack the independence that genuinely real entities would possess. Absolute aseity was the mark of the God of Parmenides and the philosophers, and other entities aspire to some measure of aseity in order to be accorded some degree of reality. But, as we shall see later,[28] independence is not unconditional, and is available only at considerable cost.

Marks of Reality
1. self-subsistent.
2. truth tracking.
3. corrigible.

The criteria of reality are diverse. Some are based on some contrast with some form of unreality, others on some positive feature—explanatory power, causal power, or the possession of massergy. It is difficult to integrate these criteria into one coherent whole. Indeed, some—rational transparency on the one hand and brute actuality on the other—seem directly opposed to each other. Yet the attempt to integrate these different intimations into one coherent whole has been the driving force in metaphysics, and is the reason why some of the marks of reality have been recognised as such. Since the different marks of reality are diverse, it is not obvious that they can be ordered in any sort of way. But the word *realius*, 'more real', makes its appearance in the late twelfth century,

---

[28] §12.7.

§8.7　　　　　　　*Appearance and Unreality*　　　　　　　245

soon after *reale* itself. The sense of there being degrees of reality is strong. Although it should not be accepted uncritically, it should not be dismissed cavalierly. It underlies the Ontological Argument, and will become easier to appreciate as we explore that.

Marks of Reality

1. not dependent merely on me
1.1 corrigible
1.2 not subjective
1.3 independent of whether constructed or not
2. resistant to will; brute facts; what happens willy-nilly
2.1 causally efficacious
2.2 has massergy
3. rational, explanatory
3.1 required (to be quantified over) by well-established theory (Quine: "To Be is to Be the Value of a Variable")
4. independent of the observer
4.1 not transient; permanent
4.2 independent of whether known or not; contrasted with epistemic
5. independent of other things (cf. Faraday's arguments for the real existence of fields).
6. completely determinate (EPR)
7. has *haecceitas*

A final list, tentatively grouped, and in items (6) and (7) looking ahead to chapter 12 (quantum mechanics). No list can be fully complete, because there always may be further ways in which entities fail to be all they ought to be.

Chapter 9
The Search for the Ultimate

§9.1   The Ontological Argument
§9.2   "Existence Is Not a Predicate"
§9.3   The Search for the Superlative
§9.4   The Logic of the Mostest
§9.5   Togetherness and *Res Extensa*
§9.6   Corpuscularianism
§9.7   The Plenum and the Void: Arena and Explanation
§9.8   Penultimate Imperfections

§9.1   The Ontological Argument

The ontological argument has run for a long time, regularly refuted, regularly re-appearing in a new form. Something can be learnt from its longevity. Its proponents must be on to something, or it would not have survived its many refutations. But equally, it must have been much misformulated, or it would not have seemed evidently fallacious to its many critics. Perhaps it does express a deep philosophical intimation. But certainly it has been taken to prove more than it really can establish. Like many other philosophical arguments it has suffered by being made out to be more rigorous than in the nature of the case it can be. For some philosophers addressing some questions it may have been decisive in leading them to adopt one of the few options open to them: but it is quite inconclusive for others, with different presuppositions of different problems, and cannot be reduced into a valid proof cogent for all comers and compelling them to accept the conclusion it claims to demonstrate.

The two traditional proponents of the ontological argument put it forward in different contexts. Anselm's *Proslogion* was primarily a prayer addressed to God, and the argument occurs as a digression, a put-down for the Fool, who said in his heart that there is no God. Descartes, having shut himself up and got himself into a solipsistic hole, needed God to undo the damage of the malicious demon, and to give some warranty that appearances were not altogether deceptive, but were, by and large, a reliable indication of reality.

The context is important for assessing what the argument was really establishing. Thus, although Descartes uses the language of

§9.1   *The Search for the Ultimate*   247

traditional Christianity, the God whose existence he proves does not do very much for Descartes in the way of forgiving his sins, assuring him of salvation, or offering a hope of a future life. The only perfections God has that signify are those of existing and not being a deceiver. Reliable reality is what Descartes needs and that is all that the ontological argument in his hands can properly prove.

Anselm's argument addresses a different problem. He is dealing with the Fool, *Insipiens*, who is not serious about metaphysics, not engaged in the problem of God, not greatly bothered. Anselm needs to convince the Fool that he should not take a short-term egocentric view, but should be in earnest, because life is real. We easily overlook the tenor of his argument because the crucial word, *reale*, had not yet been coined. Anselm had to make do with the unspecific *maius*, 'more' or 'greater'. God is, by definition, the mostest; and the mostest must exist, or it would not be the mostest, but less most than it would have been if it had existed. It is an intuitively attractive argument. Kant would rather have a hundred thalers that actually exist than a million imaginary ones. But it depends on glossing *maius* in a particular way. Otherwise we can easily parody the ontological argument with one arguing that the devil must exist, since a devil that did exist would be more diabolical than a merely imaginary one. That *maius* means 'more real' is implicit in Anselm's argument, in that he takes what is also *in re* as more than what is *in intellectu* alone; it is explicit among those who later spoke of God as the *Ens Realissimum*.

That the *Ens Realissimum* should exist seems incontrovertible, the more so if we put it into Greek, where to affirm that τὸ ὄν ἔστι (*to on esti*), 'Being exists', looks fairly tautological, and equally if we are more emphatic and say τῷ ὄντι, τὸ ὄν ὄντως ἔστι, (*toi onti to on ontos esti*), 'In reality, reality really exists'. But this indisputability is purchased at a price. We may be able to maintain without fear of contradiction, that reality exists, but do so at the price of not being able to say what it is like. We cannot in the same logical breath establish whether it exists (*an sit*) and what sort it is (*quale sit*): the two questions are incompatible and, as sometimes in physics, cannot both be answered at once. Anselm may ask whether ultimate reality exists, and may be able to argue that it does; but may not, at that juncture, take a position on its nature or essence, bar the single fact that it exists.

But Anselm's Fool was not a modern atheist, who is deeply concerned about reality, but concludes that it is not personal. For him other arguments, if other arguments there be, are needed to show that only if the ultimate reality is a person can we make sense of things and give a satisfactory account of ourselves and the world we live in. Against the insipid man, or the Cartesian solipsist, however, it makes a point. It directs our attention to something other than ourselves, something that is not the mere creation of our whim or imagination, something which sets a standard against which our own thoughts and judgements are evaluated. It has protreptic force: it bids us be *serieux*; reality, ultimate reality, exists, and once we recognise that fact, it is reasonable to be ultimately concerned with ultimate reality. It is a pointer: it points us in the direction of ultimate reality, and urges us to begin the search. But it does not, and cannot, lay down what it is we shall find it to be.

Anselm was half aware of this. The language of the *Proslogion* shows a significant shift from the personal language in which he addresses God—*Ergo, domine, qui das..., da mihi,.... quia res... et hoc es....* And then there is a sharp change to the neuter. *Et quidem credimus te esse aliquid...* and thereafter it is always *aliquid*, or *id*, or *id ipsum, quo maius cogitari non possit*, and the neuter is taken over in the standard scholastic definition *Ens Realissimum*, not *Ens Realissimus*. But later Anselm lapses—if 'lapse' be the right term—back into the personal mode of address, and takes it for granted that the Ultimate Reality he has proved to exist is the Christian God who created the world and raised Jesus from the dead. And thereby Anselm, and Descartes too, laid themselves open to the standard refutation, canonically expressed by Kant, though going back to Gaunilo, Aquinas, Caterus and Gassendi.

§9.2 "Existence Is Not a Predicate"

Existence, said Kant, is not a predicate. In modern symbolic logic we can say that we should turn the E round and instead of writing $E(x)$ write $(\exists x)$, and say existence is not a predicate but a quantifier. If that be the case, we cannot argue that a Perfect Being would have all predicates, and hence, among them, that of existence. Kant distinguishes *in intellectu* from *in re*, not as a simple distinction easily overreached, but a fundamental one. *In intellectu* goes with well-formed, not self-contradictory, syntactic: *in re* with a definite proposition, actually true. Semantic questions of existence always are to be decided *a posteriori* by evidence, and cannot ever be settled *a priori*. And hence, once we have specified the nature, or essence, of anything, whether Ultimate Reality, the Supreme Being, or the traditional God of the Judaeo-Christian tradition, we cannot go on to define Him into existence.

The contention is a fair one against one version of the ontological argument, but is not in general true, nor a cogent criticism of all versions. Although Kant asks rhetorically ". . . if . . we admit, as every reasonable person must, that all existential propositions are synthetic, how can we profess to maintain that the predicate of existence cannot be rejected without contradiction?", in fact we can. Mathematicians regularly affirm that there exist prime numbers between 12 and 21, that the nine point circle exists, and the like; contrary to Kant's own view, at least some of these judgements are analytic.[1] Moreover, as was shown in the previous chapter [Existence and Reality], there are many uses of 'exist' which cannot be represented simply as a quantifier. If we restrict ourselves to first-order logic, then indeed, the ontological argument cannot be formulated within it: but that may reveal an inadequacy in first-order logic rather than in the ontological argument itself.

Even within first-order logic questions of existence arise that cannot be dealt with in purely quantificational terms. We often need to assume a non-empty universe of discourse—one in which some things exist—before we can use quantifiers at all. Questions of existential import arise when we use universal terms, as they do also with definite descriptions. Such questions of existential import can to some extent be dealt with in terms of existential quantifiers, but other senses of the word 'exist' are altogether distinct, and are

---

[1] *Critique of Pure Reason*, A 598, B626; tr. Norman Kemp Smith, p.504.

used, indisputably, to express assessments of ontological privilege. We can see this if we consider, once again, the statement:

> There exist prime numbers between 12 and 21

and the purported inference from it to the conclusion:

> Numbers exist.

Anyone who sought to use that inference as a knock-down proof of mathematical realism would show that he did not understand what was at issue. We may be able to cite the way we talk about numbers as evidence against nominalism, but the fact that we use the existential quantifier in mathematics does not mean that we accept the existence of the natural numbers in the sense that the nominalist denies.

There are many disputed questions of ontological status. Besides the fundamental questions of whether the natural numbers exist, mathematicians have sometimes had doubts about negative numbers, real numbers and imaginary numbers. Outside mathematics, philosophers have, as we have seen,[2] doubted whether material objects exist, and whether other minds exist; they have also doubted whether space exists, whether laws of nature exist, whether atoms, electrons, or quarks exist. In each case we can understand what is at stake. It is not a linguistic question—we may speak with the vulgar, but assign or deny a fundamental significance to the locutions they use and what those locutions refer to. In some cases the doubts of the philosophers may have been silly, but it is difficult to dismiss them all without abandoning philosophy altogether.

---

[2] Chapter 6.

§9.3 The Search for the Superlative

The *Ens Realissimum*, whatever else it may be, is superlatively real. And that brings difficulties about the logic of the superlative, especially when applied to 'real'.

Grammatically, superlatives are formed, along with comparatives, from the positive adjectives, which are the simplest. Logically, however, the comparative is the basic form, and both the positive and the superlative is formed from the comparative. The Ultimate Reality is something nothing else can be real-er than,

Plato, when he first put forward the theory of Forms, thought that every adjective denoted some abstract universal. 'White' denoted the colour white, 'square' denoted the square shape, and similarly 'great' denoted the property of greatness, 'big' of bigness, 'little' of littleness. But then there was a paradox. Simmias was big in comparison with Socrates, little in comparison with Phaedo: my fourth finger is big in comparison with my little finger, little in comparison with my middle finger: a very beautiful ape would be hideous as a human. Plato at first thought these puzzles showed the unreliability of the senses, which could easily be bamboozled into seeing inconsistent properties present in the same thing at the same time. Later he realised that the puzzles were puerile, and evaporated once we recognised that the positives were back-formations from the logically more primitive comparatives. Words like 'great', 'big' and 'little' do not denote qualities or ascribe properties in the way that words like 'white' or 'square' do. To say that the middle finger is big is to say that it is *bigger than* most of the others: to say that Socrates is short is to say that he is *shorter than* most men. Only if the range of comparison is explicitly stated or evident from the context do we know what is meant by saying Socrates is short. He is short *for a man*, but not short for a boy: indeed he is taller than most boys. How much shorter than the average man or taller than the average boy someone needs to be in order to be short or tall is not clear. A man who was only very slightly shorter, or taller, than the mean, or median, man in his group of comparison, would not be accounted short or tall.

The superlative is more obviously definable in terms of the comparative. In ordinary usage the greatest is the one which is greater than all the others, the biggest the one which is bigger than all the others, the least the one which is less than all the others. On reflection we recognise that sometimes there may not be a single one that outstrips all the others, as when two boys come first-equal in a form order. It is useful to distinguish a strict **maximum** which alone is greater than everything else from those elements in an ordering that are merely **maximal**, that is to say that each of them is not exceeded by any other element, even though it does not itself exceed the other maximal elements. Whether there is one maximum element, or some maximal elements, or none at all, depends on the ordering generated by the comparative.

Comparatives are often, though not exclusively, expressed in English by means of the form '...er than', and with one exception,[3] every phrase of that form gives rise to an ordering. Ordering relations are transitive: if I am taller than you, and you are taller than Tony, then I am taller than Tony. In this they resemble equivalence relations, which express different ideas of similarity, but whereas equivalence relations are symmetrical, and therefore reflexive, ordering relations are irreflexive and therefore asymmetric: although I am the same age as myself, I am not taller than myself, and although if I am the same age as you, you are the same age as me, if I am taller than you, you are not taller than me.

Orderings can be classified by reference to their macrostructure or "global" structure, and also by reference to their microstructure. Globally, orderings may be serial or non-serial, and linear or partial. A transitive irreflexive relation gives rise to a serial ordering if for every element there is a further one bearing that relation to it: thus 'greater than' gives rise to a serial ordering among the natural numbers, since for every natural number there is a greater one; whereas, by contrast, 'less than' gives rise to a non-serial ordering among the natural numbers, since there is no natural number less than nought. Obviously, in a serial ordering there is no maximum element, nor any maximal elements.

Linear orderings (also known as strict orderings, or connected orderings) are ones for which the "law of trichotomy" holds:

Given any two elements, either the one is greater than the other, or the other than the one, or they are both, in that respect, the same.

Thus

---

[3] *other than*

Either I am taller than you, or you are taller than me, or we are both the same height.

We can picture a linear ordering by means of a Hasse diagram. Each node represents an element, and those higher up and greater than those lower down. It is clear that not all orderings are linear—for instance the relation '— is divisible by —', or in the Special Theory of the relation of causal influenceability; such orderings are called partial. In a partial, non-serial ordering there may be maximal elements, or, for instance if the ordering is a lattice, a maximum element. If the ordering is non-serial and linear, there must be a unique maximum element.

For there to be an *Ens Realissimum*, that than which nothing is more real, it must be permissible to speak of one thing being more real than another. It is not obvious that we can, since our assessments of reality are, as we have seen, highly heterogeneous; but on the other hand, since there are some underlying principles, it may be possible. And, indeed, we do sometimes recognise degrees of reality: the greatest prime number and the square circle are logically impossible, whereas the golden mountain only happens not to exist. Hallucinations, dreams, delusions, illusions, shadows, and rainbows are successively less unreal. Perhaps we can give sense to 'real-er than', Anselm's *maius*, and begin to obtain purchase on his argument.

Even if we can give sense to 'real-er than', it may not lead us to an *Ens Realissimum*. It is possible to read Hegel as positing an unending series of apprehensions of the truth, each an improvement on its predecessors, but each in turn giving rise to an antithesis which needs a new synthesis to reconcile the opposites. The account of reason given in chapter two suggests that it always outruns our attempts to pin it down, and comprehend it completely. In so far as Reality is equated with Reason, we are committed to a doctrine of "more-than-ism", whereby we are always travelling successfully and effectively, but never arrive at an end of journeying.

The case is different, however, if we understand Reality substantially, as the ground of our being. Some Axiom of Foundation seems to be called for. An infinite succession of supports, with none firmly grounded on firm ground, fails to support. The world is, according to one myth, supported by a giant elephant; and the elephant stands with his four feet on giant tortoises. But what do the tortoises stand on? Reason reaches upwards, ascending through an infinite progression of further flights of understanding: but Substance, if it is to do its job of supporting existence, rests upon a descending, and finite, precession of different degrees of Reality, ending with at least one that is an unsupported supporter.

Even so, we have not proved the existence of an *Ens Realissimum*. Anselm is careful in his terminology. *Aliquid quo maius nihil cogitari possit* indicates not a maxim**um** real being, but one that is only maxim**ally** real. It is unsurpassed by anything else, but not necessarily itself surpassing all others. Nevertheless later in *Proslogion* 2, Anselm assumes that there is only one unsurpassable being—*id quo maius cogitari non possit*—in which case it is a supreme being, as Descartes throughout assumes. Plato said so too, according to reports, in his lecture. Certainly, we speak of the Ultimate Reality, much more readily than of the Ultimate Realities; and though we may have occasion to invoke the "Gods of the Copy Book Headings", we think of them as subordinate deities. The polytheism of the Olympians was felt by the philosophers to be unsatisfactory, and even the dualism of good and evil, though evidently representing our own fractured moral experience, was too fractured to constitute an over-arching framework for explaining everything. If it is not all-embracing, then there are realities outside it, and we shall seek a deeper account which encompasses them as well as it.

Plato had a sense of *beyond* when he said that the Form of the Good was ἐπέκεινα τῆς οὐσίας πρεσβείᾳ καὶ δυνάμει (*epekeina tes ousias presbeia$_i$ kai dunamei*) beyond all reality in dignity and power. Although beyond all reality, the Form of the Good nevertheless *exists*, not only substantially, as the ground of our being, but rationally, as the ultimate goal of all enquiry, οἶ ἀφικομένῳ, ὥσπερ ὁδοῦ ἀνάπαυλα ἂν εἴη καὶ τέλος τῆς πορείας (*hoi aphikomeno$_i$, hosper hodou anapaula an eie kai telos tes poreias*).[4] Plato has, as it were, created a "logical superlative", by considering *All* the members of the ordering together, instead of each of them singly. The practice of mathematicians is illustrative. In transfinite set theory the finite ordinals can be neatly characterized as the set of all their predecessors: we start with the empty set Λ, which we can write as 0, and then say that the first (1st) ordinal is the set

---

[4] *Republic* VII, 532e.

of its predecessor(s), *i.e.* $\{0\}$, that is, the set of the empty set $\{\Lambda\}$, which we can write as 1, the second (2nd) is the set of its predecessors, that is $\{0, 1_{st}\}$, and similarly the third (3rd) is the set of its predecessors, that is $\{0, 1_{st}, 2_{nd}\}$, and so on. We can then introduce "limit ordinals", and define $\omega = \{0, 1, 2, 3, \ldots\}$, the ordinal that comes after all the finite ordinals. And so, applying this to metaphysics, we might, perhaps, talk of an omega *realissimum*, comprehending an endless succession of ever more real realities.

But we need to be wary. The dual approach of ordinary and limit ordinals gives access to Cantor's paradise, but harbours the risk of inconsistency. Can we not talk of all ordinals? And then of the ordinal of all ordinals? But then we could construct its successor, an ordinal not hitherto considered. It is the same as with the cardinal number of all cardinal numbers. The trouble lies in the word 'all', which is ambiguous as between each separately and all together.[5] At a children's party we may say 'Now we are six', as supporting the claim that we are too old to cry; alternatively, it may be followed by 'we can play ring o'ring o'roses': in the former sense, 'all' could be replaced by 'each'; each of us is six, so each of us is too old to cry; but each of us cannot play ring o'ring o'roses on his own—nobody can play unless there are five others also playing. We can tease out the difference in terms of different dialogues:[6] in the one, if you name an instance, I can say whether it is one of them—if you ask whether Samantha was one of those at the party, I can tell you whether she was or was not. In the other case I must be more pro-active. It is not enough to wait until you mention names, and then say whether or not they fall within the group my 'all' comprises: rather, I must have already comprehended the whole group together as some sort of unity, in order to say something about it as a whole.

When I use the word 'all' in this sense, I do not merely hold myself in readiness, to answer about whatever example you care to cite: I claim to have some comprehensive principle, covering them all. It is that which is lacking in the case of the ordinals. Presented by you with any ordering, I can say whether it is an ordinal or not: but I do not have a comprehensive view of ordinals. Church and Kleene proved that there is no recursively related notation-system

---

[5] See above, §2.6, and below, §9.5.

[6] See above, §§2.5, 2.6.

which gives a name to every constructive ordinal.[7] Although if you produce a putative ordinal, I can say whether it really is one or not, I cannot communicate to you, since I do not possess myself, an ability to instance, in due course, every one of them. I can wave my hand over all the ordinals, but I cannot hand you them one by one. So far as metaphysics is concerned, we have a much weaker grasp of reality than we do of finite numbers: if talk of an ω point of ultimate reality were to be allowed at all, it suggests, that contrary to Plato's aspiration, it is one to which we were journeying purposefully but could never arrive at or comprehend completely.

The Ontological Argument does not prove that Ultimate Reality exists. Rather, it is a pointer to a quest. Some of the arguments are hand-waving, and may lead us into the inconsistencies of the Cantorian Absolute; but they delineate what the Ultimate Reality would have to be like, if it was to be genuinely ultimate and indisputably real. We may fail to find it, but it is not stupid to seek it. Physicists seek a Grand Unified Theory of Everything, and discuss what it would be like if we had one. At this point the ontological argument begins to merge with the cosmological argument.[8] But since explanatory power is one mark of reality, that is not surprising. At the very least, it is not far-fetched to seek some unified schema of explanation, and were we to think we had one, it would be natural to hold that we had a correspondingly unified order of reality, in which the Ultimate Reality would be that in terms of which everything was to be explained. And within that context it would be inconsistent to deny that Ultimate Reality existed.

---

[7] A.Church and S.C.Kleene, "Formal Definitions in the Theory of Ordinal Numbers", *Fundamenta Mathematicae*, **28**, 1936, pp.11-21.

[8] See Kant, *Critique of Pure Reason*, Transcendental Dialectic, Bk II, ch.iii, §5, A 608-609, B 636-637; and J.L.Mackie, *The Miracle of Theism*, Oxford, 1982, pp.81-84.

§9.4 The Logic of the Mostest

Although the ontological argument cannot determine the nature of Ultimate Reality, the search for the superlative generates certain guidelines. If it is ultimate, it cannot depend on anything else: it has to be self-subsistent, self-explanatory. It has to have what the theologians called *aseity*, by-itself-ness. At relatively low levels relative independence and relative self-sufficiency are, we shall see, marks of reality; but, as we shall also see, purchased at the price of increased sensitivity and responsiveness.[9] Such a trade-off runs counter to a natural supposition that the *Ens Realissimum* is superlative in every way. Descartes said that it possessed all perfections. But it is not possible to be superlatively everything at once. Philosophical theism found it impossible to reconcile God's omnipotence with His omniscience. Either He was free to change His mind, and not do what He had been going to do, in which case He was not omniscient; or He always knew what He was going to do, in which case He was not able to do anything other than what He knew He was going to do, and so was not omnipotent. There are many other incompatibilities among superlatives. The most simple is the least complicated; perhaps it is not a virtue to be complicated, but if we use the term 'multi-faceted' instead, it does seem requisite that Ultimate Reality should be multi-faceted, so as to be all-embracing. Not only as regards aspects, but simply as regards number, maximality seems also to imply minimality. The universe should encompass all the many things that are prominent in our experience and thought, but also, as the word implies, be one.

Some of the tensions between different excellencies can be assuaged by careful re-articulation of the concepts involved. Omniscience cannot mean 'knowing everything whatsoever'. It is no derogation from God's omniscience that He does not know that $2 + 2 = 5$. An omniscient being can only be required to know all truths; and propositions about the future choices of free agents, as also about the outcome of purely probabilistic processes, are not as yet true, and do not constitute possible objects of knowledge. Provided we do let ourselves be beguiled by Plato and other philosophers, into supposing that knowledge could not be genuine

---

[9] See below §10.7.

knowledge unless it was infallible,[10] we can reflect that in ordinary life we often know what we are going to do without feeling constrained thereby in our freedom of choice. Philosophers are prone to misconstrue concepts, attributing to them rigidity against the usages of ordinary common sense. Particularly when attempting to describe the ultimate, they tend to exaggerate the importance of some features beyond their normal range of significance. Nevertheless, careful attention to ordinary usage and robust common sense will not resolve all incompatibilities. Not all superlatives can be massaged so as to be compatible. The metaphysician cannot have it all at once, but must compromise one excellence in order to make room for another, balancing their respective excellences as best he can, hoping in some way not yet articulated, to get the best trade-offs available.

> The Ultimate should have the superlative virtues of being unique, single, singular, simple—BUT ...

We may go for simplicity, and hold that the Ultimate Reality is one, a Parmenidean Deity, a single all-embracing but profoundly simple totality. But then we have the problem of accounting for the variety of the universe as we know it, and the perpetual flux of change. Philosophical monotheism distances God, who is singular and unlike anything else, from His created universe, which is able to manifest itself in a multitude of ways; but philosophical monotheism still has difficulty in accounting for, or at least justifying, the manifold and often unwelcome changes and chances of this fleeting world.

Instead of simplicity, a metaphysician may choose to major on plenitude. Leibniz did. His mostest led him to postulate many—as many as possible—monads, each monad possessing as many properties as possible. Spinoza, by contrast with Leibniz, was a monist, holding that there was only one ultimate reality, *Deus sive natura*, but, like Leibniz and unlike Parmenides, ascribing to it maximal complexity. Spinoza's modern representative is Einstein. His *Deus sive Natura* is spacetime. It is the one ultimate reality; all variety is

---

[10] See above, §3.2.

accounted for in the General Theory by local contortions of spacetime, which are modifications of the one fundamental substance.

The fourth possibility is minimalist pluralism. Like Leibniz, the classical corpuscularians postulated many ultimate substances, but ones that were as simple as possible. Their corpuscles were counter-Anselmian absolutes, that than which it is impossible to imagine anything lesser. Whereas Leibniz' monads can be thought of as idealised persons, necessarily not qualitatively identical, the corpuscles were idealized things, each featureless, and hence qualitatively identical, though numerically distinct.

Metaphysical Options

	Minimal (Simple)	Maximal (Complex)
Monism (One)	Philosophical Theism (God has no parts)	Spinoza-Einstein (Spacetime Universe)
Pluralism (Many)	Corpuscles (Minimal Properties)	Monads (Maximal Properties)

Each of these paradigms is open to objection, but each has something going for it. It would seem that simplicity and complexity, unity and plurality, cannot all be realised at once, yet all seem to be called for. The apparent contradiction between different *desiderata* can be eased by noting that it is in different respects that Ultimate Reality is required to be simple or complex, one or many. The Universe is by definition one, but comprising all things is also many. Ultimate Reality, if it is to be relevant to us and real for us, must accommodate the manifold changes and chances of our fleeting existence, but integrate them into a comprehensible unity. It may be that our different intimations as to what the Ultimate Reality must be like, are directed not so much towards the ultimate, but some penultimate, or ante-penultimate, reality. Even if the truly ultimate reality is a single, simple unitary Being, the penultimate reality, may be able to manifest itself in a multitude of ways.

Newton was a Unitarian Corpuscularian, believing in God the Father, who in the beginning created atoms and the void. Superlative excellencies, not all realisable in the Ultimate, may be manifest in some penultimate reality. The four ideals of mostestness should not be seen as mutually exclusive and final, but as complementary and tentative, not as definite characterizations of the Ultimate, but only as glimpses of Penultimate or Ante-penultimate Realities.

§9.5 Togetherness and *Res Extensa*

Togetherness is a key notion in metaphysics. The Great Chain of Being binds the disparate levels of Reality into One Coherent Whole; communication enables persons to be members of the Kingdom of Ends, the Republic of Letters, or the Communion of Saints. Maximal monism holds that Reality is one integrated manifold. Descartes' *res extensa* met the need of being a single whole while yet having parts.

The modern study of the part-whole relation is called mereology, and understands the part-whole relation as a partial dense ordering relation.[11] In order to constitute a coherent whole, parts need in some way to be *together*—otherwise they would be in no better case than Leibniz' disparate monads. They need, on occasion, to be neighbours; they need to share a common boundary, or be next to each other. But nextness seems to argue for discreteness, and hence for a pluralism of separate entities, always in danger of falling apart.

Plato had many dark sayings in his later dialogues, the *Parmenides* and especially the *Philebus*, about τὸ πέρας (*to peras*), the bounded, and τὸ ἄπειρον (*to apeiron*), the unbounded, and about the more and the less and the Great and the Small, and Aristotle seems sometimes to be engaged in what we might describe as prototopology.[12] Plato and his successors puzzled long over the continuum, being already aware that the square root of

---

[11] Some writers construe the part-whole relation as an antisymmetric relation, so that each whole is part of itself. Here, however, 'part of' will be taken to be an irreflexive transitive relation, and may be read as '*proper* part of'.

[12] See especially, Kenneth M. Sayre, *Plato's Late Ontology*, Princeton University Press, 1983; M.J.White, *The Continuous and the Discrete*, Oxford, 1992, and David Bostock, "Aristotle on Continuity in *Physics* VI," in L.Judson, ed., *Aristotle's Physics: A Collection of Essays*, Oxford.

2 was not a rational number, so that the set of all rational numbers whose square was less than 2 was not next to the set of all rational numbers whose square was more than 2, but was separated from them by a gap, occupied by the irrational real number $\sqrt{2}$. Eudoxus almost succeeded in giving a satisfactory account of the continuum, but it was not until Dedekind and Cantor that a really rigorous treatment was finally achieved. In each case they were working with the *linear* ordering the numbers naturally have, and made essential use of linearity. Almost all subsequent work has taken for granted the numerical background of their work, but that is not essential. Topology, or *Analysis Situs*, as Kant called it, is essentially non-numerical, and can be developed axiomatically without any reference at all to numbers.

Whitehead hoped to go further, and with the aid of suitable definitions ground topology in mereology. His method of Extensive Abstraction was a generalisation of Cantor's definition of a real number as a sequence of nested intervals. A sequence of convergent parts would define a point, and also the neighbourhood of that point. Other limit elements could also be defined—lines, surfaces, *etc.* and hence point-wise connectedness, and sharing a common boundary generally. Unfortunately, there were irremediable flaws in his programme, and topology cannot be based on the *part of* relation alone.[13]

For most metaphysicians it is enough that we *can* characterize continuity for a *linear* ordering without any appeal to the arithmetical properties of rational numbers. If temporal instants are linearly ordered, as will be argued later,[14] then, as the Greeks half realised, it must be continuous; and if time is continuous, and movement in space is possible, space must be continuous too.

There would be some metaphysical advantage in having the continuity of space dependent on the continuity of time: it would strengthen the claim that time was more fundamental than space. But that thesis can be supported by other arguments, and it would be better if the concept of *res extensa* as a connected continuous whole could be developed from the concept of a maximal monistic reality. And although Whitehead's Cantorian approach failed,

---

[13] For fuller discussion, see J.R.Lucas, *The Conceptual Roots of Mathematics*, London, 2000, §§10.6-10.8, pp.282-290.

[14] See below, §13.7.

a Dedekindian approach will work, provided we strengthen the Boolean algebra of parts in the same way as the logic of natural kinds was distinguished from the Boolean logic of sets.[15] Kuratowski's topology is based on set theory, but with suitable modifications we can apply his axioms to extensions instead of sets. The first two axioms apply straight-forwardly, but the third axiom, [K.3], presents a difficulty, since there is no empty set, ∅, in mereology (though we can define what it is for the intersection of two extensions to be empty). As in §7.8 we reformulate [K.3] in terms not of the empty set, but of the universal set, X, which does carry over to mereology. The parallel condition for mereology is that the universal extension is, and it alone, both open and closed.

It thus appears that we can strengthen the Boolean algebra of mereology by the addition of a single unary operator in much the same way as we can strengthen propositional calculus by the addition of a modal operator, and set theory by the addition of a closure operator. The crucial question is whether we can interpret Kuratowski's closure operator as telling us anything relevant to our present concerns. Arguably, it can. The closure operator has a "least upper bound" property. Kuratowski proves his theorem 3:

$\mathcal{C}(A)$ is the smallest closed extension containing A;

in other words $\mathcal{C}(A)$ is the intersection of all closed extensions F such that $A \prec F$.

or, as it might be expressed, the closure of A is the minimum envelope that envelopes it. Much as Dedekind defines $\sqrt{2}$ as the least upper bound of all those rational numbers whose square is less than 2, so here we can identify $\mathcal{C}(A)$ as (A)'s least larger extension.

The closure operator, so to speak, adds to an extension its boundary. With that understanding we can characterize what it is for two extensions to be separate, and hence also what it is for two extensions to be connected. Even if they do not overlap, two extensions are not separate unless the boundary of either also fails to overlap the other. And contrariwise, two extensions are connected if the intersection of one with the closure of the other is non-null. A single extension is an unseparated whole if there are no two parts of it which are mutually separate and conjointly exhaustive of it.

---

[15] See above, §§7.8, 7.9.

§9.5   The Search for the Ultimate   263

We can also re-instate Whitehead's Cantorian approach. The pathological Abstractive Classes that vitiated Whitehead's programme, were ones which were not properly nested, but all converging on a boundary point of each extension, and can therefore be obviated if the successive members of an Abstractive Class are not merely part of their predecessors, but each has its *closure* part of its predecessor, itself an open extension. Cantor was able to secure this condition by stipulating that the two end-points of each successive interval were respectively greater than or less than the endpoints of the preceding interval. Without linearity this cannot be secured by specific stipulation. Granted a closure operator, however, we can ensure that even in the general case there is genuine nesting, so that it is impossible for an Abstractive Class to converge to a boundary point, which could be the point of convergence of another pathological Abstractive Class.

Among genuine, non-pathological Abstractive Classes Whitehead defined another, antisymmetric ordering relation, *cover*. An Abstractive Class covers another Abstractive Class iff each member of the former has some member of the latter as a part. If two Abstractive Classes each cover the other, they define the same limit entity. An Abstractive Class that is covered by every Abstractive Class it covers is minimal, and its limit entity is a *point*.

Points and other limit entities, such as lines and surfaces, defined by means of Abstractive Classes, which do cover other Abstractive Classes without being covered by them, are counter-Anselmian absolutes, where each part has another nested within it, but there is no part nested within them all. There is a downward serial succession of smaller and smaller parts though with no minimal part, which can none the less be comprehended as constituting a different sort of entity. Points, unlike atoms or corpuscles, are not parts; but they can feature in an account of *res extensa* that does have parts, as what is pointed to by an infinite succession of nested parts, the totality of a serial ordering—its end-point, so to speak.

Once we have introduced into *res extensa* points by means of genuinely punctiform Abstractive Classes, we can develop standard point set topology, with the Abstractive Classes constituting the neighbourhood of each point; and then interior and exterior points, point-wise connexion, local connectedness and dimensions.

Although *res extensa* admits not only of many parts but of points as well, its maximality is limited. It is minimal in the range of qualities admitted, allowing only primary qualities; in consequence it has difficulty in accounting for the variety of the world. Indeed, it might seem at first as though only one magnitude could be ascribed to each point, thereby constituting a simple scalar field: but this is too *simpliste*; besides scalars we can ascribe vectors and even tensors, and in each case we can consider not only the magnitude at one instant, but the rate of change—the first derivative with respect to time—and indeed second and higher derivatives. Descartes talked of vortices, using these to account for the discreteness of material objects in terms of a fundamentally continuous—almost fluid—*res extensa*, and has been criticized for this.[16] Such criticisms can be parried. By an exercise of charity we can see Descartes as feeling towards the $\nabla \times \vec{E}$ and $\nabla \times \vec{B}$, **curl** E and **curl** B, of differential geometry, and the explanatory power of electromagnetic fields.

Such charity demands greater resources than have so far been provided. Differential geometry requires not just continuity but *smoothness*.[17] For Descartes there was no problem. He assumed that *res extensa* was what could be characterized by Cartesian geometry, which would secure for it not only the standard topology of the real numbers, so that the magnitude of any part can be assigned a real number as its measure, but smoothness as well, so that it constituted a *differentiable* manifold. We can, however, make do with fewer assumptions than Descartes. Granted that the points of *res extensa* form a continuous locally connected space of

---

[16] See for example A.J.P.Kenny, *Descartes*, New York, 1968, ch.9, pp.214-215.

[17] The standard example to show the difference is the function $x\sin(\frac{1}{x})$ as x tends towards 0. Since $\sin(\frac{1}{x})$ is always less than 1 and more than -1, $x\sin(\frac{1}{x})$ tends towards 0 as x tends towards 0, and the function is continuous in the neighbourhood of 0. But the differential $\frac{d}{dx}x\sin(\frac{1}{x}) = \sin(\frac{1}{x}) + x\cos(\frac{1}{x})$ fluctuates wildly as x approaches 0. Although the value of the function gets smaller and smaller as x approaches 0, it wiggles uncontrollably. If we take the function as giving the position in a particular direction of an object, then its velocity alternates more and more rapidly the closer it approaches 0. That would be physically impossible: so we stipulate that there should be no uncontrollable wiggles—that the manifold should be smooth.

some definite dimensionality, each can be assigned coordinates and some scalar magnitude. Provided we can assign a real number to each point in space, $f(x,y,z)$, we can calculate the *gradient* of the field,

$$\nabla f(x,y,z) = \frac{\partial f(x,y,z)}{\partial x} + \frac{\partial f(x,y,z)}{\partial y} + \frac{\partial f(x,y,z)}{\partial z}.$$

Although a scalar field is an assignment of *numbers*, the operator ∇ operates on it *whatever* the numbers are in a particular case. We can abstract from any particular assignment of numbers, and consider *just* the operator, independently of any actual assignment. We borrow numbers briefly, but give them back almost at once. Differential topology can thus be developed by considering only those properties of a differentiable manifold that are preserved under any diffeomorphism; and yields, by means of a subtle use of a differential operator,[18] a primitive notion of direction, and the conceptual framework for the General Theory.

§9.6 Corpuscularianism

The fourth metaphysical option outlined in §9.4 is minimal pluralism, which postulates many fundamental entities with minimal properties. There is an inherent difficulty in the Many-Minimal combination. Whereas Leibniz could have many fundamental substances, because each, being maximally complex, could differ from every other in some respect or other, metaphysical atomism, or corpuscularianism, as it is called here, to avoid confusion with modern atomism, had difficulty in securing that its minimal entities, were numerically distinct. Since they were all alike, or in technical terms since they were all qualitatively identical, there was a problem of how they were to be distinguished from one another, if they were, indeed, individual entities.[19] In order not to fall foul of the Identity of Indiscernibles, some quasi-quality was needed, some parameter too evanescent to qualify as a quality proper, but sufficient to distinguish one corpuscle from another. This was provided by space.

---

[18] See C.W.Misner, K.S.Thorne and J.A.Wheeler, *Gravitation*, New York, 1973, §9.2, pp.227-229 and G.Nerlich, *The Shape of Space*, 2nd ed., Cambridge, 1994, ch.4, §4.2, p.101.

[19] See below, §12.11.

Each corpuscle occupied a different position in space, but position occupied was not an essential property of a corpuscle, since it could change. Whereas in Aristotle's scheme of things each thing had its proper place towards which it tended to move, corpuscles were free to occupy any position that was vacant. The only restriction was on multiple occupancy. Two corpuscles could not occupy the same place at the same time. Hence impenetrability. We can see why Locke was uneasy about solidity. It was not really a primary quality but a logical requirement of corpuscles being minimal substances, each with its own identity, but, possessing no qualities of its own, necessarily having *a* position, though there was no particular position it necessarily possessed.[20]

Corpuscularianism thus managed to have many entities, all possessing the same—that is, no—qualities, yet none the less numerically distinct. But, in securing a satisfactory criterion for corpuscles' being different, it created for itself a problem in telling when they are the same. If two positions were occupied by a corpuscle at different times, how could we tell whether it was the same corpuscle on each occasion or two different ones? Since there were no qualities, we could not identify an individual corpuscle by its characteristic qualities. Nor could we identify it by its position at any given time, since its position was not a peculiar property, but something that could change from time to time. The only available characteristics of a corpuscle was the position it occupied, or some time-derivative of position. Thus spatiotemporal continuity was the only feature each corpuscle possessed on its own; and granted

---

[20] The possibility of distinguishing between corpuscles by reason of their having different velocities or accelerations was not explored: we can imagine a cloud chamber showing two fundamental particles passing through each other rather than bouncing off each other, being identified by their velocity as much as by their position. But if two corpuscles were distinguished by having some time-derivative different, then almost always they would differ also in respect of the basic parameter itself. Hence if we are going to secure pluralism by having the qualitatively identical ultimate entities distinguished by some quasi-quality, nothing is gained by having this quasi-quality a differential of a parameter rather than the parameter itself.

impenetrability, we could use it as a criterion of sameness.[21] If there was a spatiotemporally continuous path from the position of a corpuscle at one time to its position at another, then it must be one and the same corpuscle, since, thanks to impenetrability, there could never be a case of two spatiotemporal paths coming together at, or diverging from, a single point. We could, therefore, regard each corpuscle as an individual entity, a substance, with an identity of its own, having *haecceitas*, this-ness. There was no logical impropriety in Newton's wanting to rewrite the book of *Genesis*: "In the beginning God created corpuscles and the void" and it is entirely appropriate to apply to corpuscles Maxwell-Boltzmann, rather than Bose-Einstein, or Fermi-Dirac, statistics.[22]

Same and Different Times, Places and Things

Different things cannot be in the same place at the same time. The same thing cannot be in the different places at the same time.

But

The same thing can be in the same place at different times.

Space and time provided the foil to the corpuscles. The corpuscularians secured numerical distinctness by having different cor-

---

[21] Sir Michael Dummett finds this problematic. He argues that if we adopt the general schema of a physical magnitude being a real function of time, "there is no reason provided by the *concept* of a physical magnitude why its magnitude should change continuously: if it is constrained to change continuously, it can only be so constrained by the laws of physics, and not by conceptual necessity". (M.A.E.Dummett, "Is Time a Continuum of Instants?", *Philosophy*, **75**, 2000, p.501.) But it is not being denied that corpuscles might change, *e.g.* their mass, discontinuously; it is only that if they changed their position discontinuously, then, in the absence of their having some other identifying feature, we should be unable to identify a particle at one time as being the same particle as one at some other time.

[22] See below, §12.11.

puscles occupying different positions, and identity by having individual corpuscles follow spatiotemporally continuous paths. Space consisted mostly of the vacuum, or void, places where a corpuscle might be but was not, together with the places actually occupied by corpuscles. Whereas Descartes' space was plenum, a field everywhere, properly referred to by a noun, *res extensa*, Newton's was a void, at best an attenuated adjective, describing where corpuscles might be, but usually were not. Consisting mostly of unactualised possibilities, the Corpuscularians' space could be faceably accused by its critics of being not a substance, but a nonentity, a mere nothing, which could not be intelligibly said to exist. But it had to have some features, which meant that it was some sort of entity that could be talked about, and not a complete nonentity. It had to be continuous. The chief reason was that time is continuous,[23] and spatiotemporal continuity was the criterion of identity for corpuscles. The arguments for the continuity of *res extensa* were also pertinent: only if the many corpuscles were all located in one integrated space, could they together comprise a single universe. A third argument from featurelessness told against the alternative which is occasionally suggested, namely that space is discrete. But if space were discrete, there would be a smallest interval, and hence a preferred length; and a space made up of discrete tiles is not homogeneous, and is likely not to be isotropic, having some preferred directions. The space of the corpuscularians had no preferred magnitude, no preferred position and no preferred direction. These three considerations justified the assumption that spatiotemporal continuity was available to provide a criterion of identity.

These negative features stemmed in part from the void's being mostly only an unactualised possibility of occupation, but also from the *descriptive* role of corpuscularian space. Space needed to have as few features as possible, so as not to foreclose any possible configuration of the fundamental substances, the corpuscles, and hence, in a seeming paradox, had to be maximally symmetric. For the same reason space needed to be at least two-dimensional, since otherwise the corpuscles, being impenetrable, could never get past one another, and would be stuck always in the same spatial order.

The very featurelessness of the Corpuscularian void was itself a feature, giving rise to further features, which could be properly

---

[23] See below, §13.6.

§9.6 *The Search for the Ultimate* 269

predicated of space. Even if space was not a substance, it needed to be referred to by a substantive, 'space', which might well be diginified by a capital letter, 'Space'. In spite of being τὸ οὐκ ὄν, (*to ouk on*) to the Greek atomists, and for the Corpuscularians a manifold of attenuated adjectives indicating where corpuscles might, but for the most part did not, exist, Space none the less had some degree of reality. Unactualised possibilities, it seems, are not totally unreal.[24]

The Features of Featurelessness

Newtonian Space is:
1. Continuous, because
    (a) Time is continuous,
    (b) Only a continuous space can embrace all the corpuscles together in a single universe,
    (c) Needed to provide criterion of identity,
    (d) Discrete space would contravene 6. and 5.
2. Connected; else it would not be a single space, housing all that there is.
3. Has at least two dimensions; else order of corpuscles would be forever fixed.
4. No preferred position.
5. No preferred direction.
6. No preferred distance.

---

[24] See further below, §14.8.

§9.7 The Plenum and the Void

Voltaire reported that he had left space a plenum in Paris, and found it a vacuum in London. Our modern concept of space, having disparate parentage, is under tension, a tension going back to the late Middle Ages, when there was a controversy among the Schoolmen over the rationality and omnipotence of God. Duns Scotus and the Realists argued that God was reasonable, and could only act reasonably. William of Ockham and the Nominalists wanted to stress the omnipotence of God, and claimed that He could do whatever He willed, at any place whatsoever. All places were alike accessible to Him. Hence the homogeneity of space. Corpuscularianism took over these considerations and made them its own. Space needed to have as few features as possible, so as not to foreclose any possible configuration of the fundamental substances, the corpuscles. Descartes, Spinoza and Einstein, by contrast, were Scotists, seeking a causal understanding of *Deus sive Natura*. The void, therefore, seeks to be as descriptively flexible as possible, but is weak on explanation: *res extensa*, by contrast, tries to explain, if only in outline, why events happen, but is weak on describing and identifying them.

The dual parentage of space endows it different ambitions. It aspires to the modest unobtrusiveness of the void, a recognition that its role is to provide an inconspicuous background, against which the protagonists of reality can show their mettle. But it also inherits from *res extensa* substantial self-assertiveness, a claim to be the ultimate reality, and able to explain everything. The aims are incompatible. They manifest themselves in the distinction we now make between geometry and geometrodynamics. Geometry describes: geometrodynamics explains. Geometry is available to all the empirical sciences offering a flat canvas for portraying the phenomena they deal with, which may then be explained according to the principles appropriate for the particular science in issue. Geometrodynamics, by contrast, seeks to explain within the terms set by fundamental theory, and is prepared to stipulate a different geometry in order to secure a better explanation. Instead of the level playing field of Euclidean space, Einstein posited a space-time so contorted that a freely falling cricket ball could be said to be following a geodesic. We should not be affronted at his apostasy from Euclid, but simply recognise the difference between the

§9.7   *The Search for the Ultimate*   271

aims of geometrodynamics and geometry. Causality, which concerns events that happen and have to happen, posits the plenum—a field, developing according to laws which should one day explain why everything is as it is—and needs to be distinguished from the spatiotemporal framework, which provides the means of locating events and referring to them irrespective of their role in any causal process—a vacuum, devoid of features that might constrain possible dispositions of corpuscles.

Geometry v. Geometrodynamics
1. Geometry is an Arena.
2. Geometrodynamics offers an Explanation.

—oOo—

These different aims exert different conceptual pressures:

1. Characterization comes before explanation, so geometry needs to be as flexible as possible, and causally inefficacious;
2. Explanation needs to be in accordance with observation, and should not be prescriptive.

—oOo—

(Time can likewise be understood in two ways:

1. the concept of Time being Ripe does make sense;
2. but is to be avoided as much as possible, so as to seek more illuminating explanations.

See §13.1.)

But it is the same space. Similar logical pressures apply. Maximal monism holds that Reality is one integrated manifold: minimal pluralism locates its many minimal entities in one all-encompassing void, which although itself a non-entity, manages to embrace all that does exist in a single universe. The former requires the different parts of the plenum to be integrated into one whole, and hence to be a topological manifold: the latter requires the different occupancies in the void to be integrated into one occupier, which again has to be a spatial manifold. *Res extensa*, if it is to be a connected whole of extended parts, has to admit limit elements, and hence extensionless points and questions of dimensionality, and thus is spatial: and the void, however much of an nonentity it is supposed to be, has global features none the less, which confer on it not only continuity, but a standard topology with at least two dimensions.

If space has at least two dimensions, questions of geometry arise. Featurelessness requires that there be no preferred distance; geometrical structures should be invariant under magnification; and if geometrical structures are to be invariant under magnification, then their geometry must be Euclidean: for, as John Wallis discovered in the Seventeenth Century, only in Euclidean geometry can we have similar triangles that are not congruent;[25] that is, only in Euclidean geometry can there be figures of the same shape, but different sizes. In the Elliptic geometry of Riemann and the Hyperbolic geometry of Bolyai and Lobachevsky the shape of a figure determines its size: thus on the surface of a sphere a triangle each of whose vertices is a right-angle must be an octant of the sphere, and must have sides of length one quarter of the circumference. (This example shows also that Elliptical geometry has a preferred distance—the circumference of the sphere. In Hyperbolic geometry there is a preferred area—the area of a triangle whose angles add up to $0°$.) Euclidean geometry is thus more *flexible* than its rivals; it keeps open a wider set of possibilities, and thus is more flexible and more friendly to empirical science. Indeed, only if we have a "flat" geometry of zero (or almost zero) curvature, in which shapes are independent of size, shall we learn to identify shapes and discuss them with other people. Paradoxically, the very featurelessness of the void requires it to be maximally symmetric.

> Shapeliness implies Euclid

Necessities of communication exert further Euclidean pressures. Having material bodies, we necessarily occupy different positions when we talk to one another, and are in the habit of moving around in a space that is at least two-dimensional, and seeing things from

---

[25] See J.R.Lucas, *The Conceptual Roots of Mathematics*, London, 2000, ch.2, §2.2, pp.34-39; or "Euclides ab Omni Naevo Vindicatus", *British Journal for the Philosophy of Science*, **20**, 1969, pp.1-11.

different points of view on different occasions. Shapes are seen from points of view which may be nearer or farther from the shape being observed, and may be oriented at different angles with respect to the shape. We can express these changes on the points of view by groups of transformations: in the one case by the group of translations, or displacements; in the other by the group of rotations. These two groups of transformations can be combined into a single group, which in the Theory of Groups is known as the Proper Euclidean group. Euclidean geometry is the geometry of shapes that remain invariant under transformations of the Euclidean group. If you and I are talking about some object, the way it will appear to you will be different from the way it will appear to me. But if I describe the dish as circular, as it "really" is, rather than elliptical, as it appears to me, and the window pane as rectangular rather than an oblique quadrilateral, then you will recognise those descriptions easily, because from your point of view too, that is how they "really" are. Hence it is that even when I am trying to report how some shape appears to me, what I see seems to me to be more like what it "really" is than what would be warranted by the retinal images in my eyes.[26] Necessities of communication pressure us to talk about what is the same for the talker and the person being talked to. And the shapes that are the same for different people talking from different places and at different angles to the shapes they are talking about, are the shapes that are invariant under the Proper Euclidean group of transformations, that is, the shapes of Euclidean geometry.

These are *desiderata*, not hard facts. We may be forced to adopt a non-Euclidean geometry, as navigators were, when they sought to describe the surface of the globe.[27] Description and explanation are not utterly separate activities, and we may need to conform our canons of descriptive flexibility to the facts elicited in our search for adequate explanations. Luckily, it seems, as far as our best

---

[26] See above, §8.3, referring to R.H.Thouless, *British Journal of Psychology*, **21** and **22**, 1931. J.J.Gibson, *The Perception of the Visual World*, Cambridge, Mass., 1950, pp.169-172. O.L.Zangwill, *Introduction to Modern Psychology*, London, 1950, pp.30-34.

[27] And sometimes the global properties of geometry do explain. See Graham Nerlich, *The Shape of Space*, Cambridge, 1976 and 1994, ch.2; and Graham Nerlich, *What Spacetime Explains*, Cambridge, 1994, ch.7, esp.§7.3, p.172.

> **The Proper Euclidean Group**
> consists of:
>
> 1. Translations (or Displacements);
> 2. Rotations.
>
> Euclidean geometry is invariant under these transformations.

explanations go at present, that space *is* Euclidean, or nearly so. But this is, so far as the plenum and the void are concerned, a contingent matter. Only if we delve deep into quantum mechanics can we find an *a priori* argument for some fundamental Euclideanness in the nature of things.[28]

> **Wish List for Geometry**
>
> 1. Shapes independent of sizes.
> 2. Invariant under change of position and direction. (Also
> 3. Parallel lines very useful for Cartesian geometry.)
>
> These all in the optative mood.
> Hope for an imperative requirement of
> 4. Pythagoras' theorem from Parseval's in quantum mechanics (see §12.10).

Res extensa is similarly under pressure, though from epistemological accessibility rather than from descriptive flexibility. It is constrained by various symmetries needed to make empirical knowledge possible.[29] Although the range of explanations that might, conceivably, account for the development of *res extensa* is very wide, only those within a limited range could be discovered empirically by finite mortals. In order to argue inductively from

---

[28] See below, §12.10.

[29] See above, §4.8.

§9.7   *The Search for the Ultimate*   275

observations to general laws, we need some canons of irrelevance if we are to be able to identify those factors that are genuinely causal. We need the principle "Same cause, same effect", which could never be applied if *any* difference of spatial or temporal position precluded a situation's being counted as the same. The mere fact that one set of observations were made in Oxford, and another in Cambridge, does not of itself mean that they are qualitatively different; nor should it matter which way the apparatus was pointing, unless there was some causally relevant feature, such as a magnetic field, involved. Events are deemed to be the same irrespective of position or orientation. The same argument applies as for the recognition and description of shapes. Only if our description of causal processes is invariant under translation and rotation, that is, under the operations of the Proper Euclidean group, will their position and orientation be causally irrelevant. (Again, this requirement is not absolute. Position-indifference and direction-indifference could be secured in a space of constant curvature, but then translation would not be distinct from rotation. If the curvature were sufficiently small, the distinction would not signify. Indeed, the curvature need not be constant, provided it is sufficiently small. The General Theory, which works with a spacetime that is Riemannian rather than Euclidean, typically requires spacetime to be "locally Euclidean".)[30]

Subject to similar pressures, the mathematics in the two theories are sufficiently similar for either to be able to accommodate the account given by the other. Although the plenum theory abhors a vacuum, it can contemplate a scalar field that is almost everywhere zero, but having a Dirac delta function at the points where there are corpuscles: and although the corpuscularians are not happy with fields in empty space, they can hypostatize the forces that would act on a test particle were it to be at a particular point, and might even postulate an ether to explain them.

The tension between fullness of description and economy of explanation underlies different treatments of the "Incongruity of Counterparts". Leibniz criticized Newton's account of space, claiming that it could be replaced by a purely relational account. Space was simply a system of actual or possible relations. In particular,

---

[30] See above, §4.8.

he claimed, all spatial relations would be unaltered if East were interchanged with West, so that there was no real difference between them. Euler and later Kant picked on this as revealing a fundamental flaw in Leibniz' relationism.[31] There is a global difference between spaces which are not orientable, like a Möbius strip, and the orientable spaces we normally work with: on a Möbius strip a triangle can be moved continuously round so as to be superimposed on its mirror image; in a three-dimensional non-orientable space, a left-handed glove could be moved around so as to fit a right hand. Orientability is, like continuity and dimensionality, a global property of a space as a whole. It is thus a further feature of space required by the ideal of being as featureless and flexible as possible. Much as we want to be able to talk about shape independently of size, so we want to be able to distinguish between mirror images and describe them as being different from each other.[32] But if space is orientable, vortices can spin in two distinct ways, left-handed and right-handed, clockwise and anti-clockwise. North and South Poles, spin up and spin down, positive and negative electricity, matter and anti-matter, all fall out of a theory of vortices in an orientable space. On his return journey a later Voltaire might find parity conserved in Paris, and the TCP theorem already in its *salon*s a topic of polite conversation.

---

[31] *Leibniz' Third Letter to Clarke*, §5, p.26 in *The Leibniz-Clarke Correspondence*, ed.H.G.Alexander, Mancheser, 1956, and Kant, "Concerning the ultimate foundation of differentiation of regions in space", reprinted in G.B.Kerfers and D.E.Walford, eds. *Kant: Selected Pre-Critical Writings*, Manchester, 1968, and in J. van Kleve and R.Frederick, eds. *The Philosophy of Left and Right*, Dordrecht, 1991. (Kant later changed his mind: see his *Prolegomena to Any Future Metaphysic*, §13, tr. P.G.Lucas, Manchester, 1953, pp.41-43.)

[32] By far the most illuminating account of this issue is given by Graham Nerlich, *The Shape of Space*, Cambridge, 1976 and (2nd ed.) 1994, ch.2, "Hands, knees and absolute space".

§9.8 Penultimate Imperfections

Each of the paradigms outlined in the previous sections had its defects. The Parmenidean God of minimal monism was unique, simple, independent of all else, the sole self-sufficient substance, the ground of its own being and that of everything else. But His imperturbable invariance is belied by the Heraclitean flux of experience; and, more seriously, philosophical theism has never come up with a satisfactory account of how God acts in the world, and why He does not intervene to prevent the many evils we have to endure. Although the Christian churches have taken over some Parmenidean doctrines, and claim that God is utterly simple, being "without body, parts, or passions",[33] the account they actually give of the Godhead is, as the Moslems complain, very complicated. Any account of a personal God must be complicated, and one which each year remembers the suffering of God at Passiontide, must forgo any claim to Parmenidean simplicity, or self-sufficiency.

The Ultimate Reality needs to be one integrated whole, but also many-fold in order to account for the diversity of things and the occurrence of various events. The *Deus sive Natura* of maximal monism meets many of these requirements, and can claim to be in many respects the mostest; in the General Theory the writhings of spacetime not only constitute all material objects, but claim to be able to explain all events. These claims, however, have not been substantiated in detail, and modern science owes as much to minimal pluralism as to maximal monism: the world we know is a world of material objects, located and sometimes moving about in a Euclidean or nearly Euclidean space, by virtue of forces very different from those of gravity.

The corpuscles were superlatively small, and the void, though all-encompassing, possessed as few features as possible, but for that very reason possessed quite a few, enabling it to provide us with a framework in which to describe events, but lacking the substantial causal muscle required for explanation.

Each of Leibniz' monads was in its way maximal, encompassing within itself a representation of the whole universe; but the Preestablished Harmony is so implausible that it is difficult to take

---

[33] Article 1 of the 39 Articles.

monads seriously. In the next chapter, however, a modified monadology will be outlined, more realistic, but still preserving some of his insights.

Leibniz' monads are the successors of Descartes' *res cogitantes*, just as Spinoza and Einstein take over his *res extensa*. Although historically Descartes came before Leibniz and Spinoza, thematically we should see the positions reversed: Spinoza and Einstein as articulating maximal monism, and Leibniz as articulating maximal pluralism, and Descartes as trying to accommodate them both. Notoriously he failed. Although he was much closer to the facts in acknowledging that both minds and bodies exist, he failed to give a satisfactory account of how mind and matter interact. But he was closer to the facts, and any world-view that deserves to be taken seriously must accommodate some sort of dualism, and succeed in harnessing together the two horses that Descartes failed to ride.

Each ideal of mostness has its defects and each is under pressure to take on board the excellences of the others. But not every superlative excellence can be possessed at once. The absence of some excellences, as we become aware of them, drives us to seek a deeper understanding of what excellencies Ultimate Reality ought to possess. Thus far the most we can claim to have achieved is to have sketched inadequate pictures of what Penultimate, or Antepenultimate, Reality might be like. But the inadequacies and loose ends of this chapter give some indication of how we should proceed.

Chapter 10
Points of View

§10.1 Locality
§10.2 Causal Cones
§10.3 Minkowski Spacetime
§10.4 Windowed Monads
§10.5 Covariance
§10.6 Perspectives
§10.7 McTaggart and Mellor
§10.8 Tense and Temporality

§10.1 Locality

Newton's Law of Universal Gravitation was always open to the complaint that it involved "Action at a Distance", contrary to the Principle of Locality. But it was very well established empirically, and had to be accepted. Similarly in contemporary quantum mechanics we seem to have correlations between measurements that defy the Principle of Locality, but have to be accepted nonetheless.[1] Although locality is a characteristic mark of causal connexion, it is not, as Hume supposed,[2] an essential one. Nor is it merely a uniformity we have found to hold for the most part—else we should feel little compunction in accepting that in some cases it happened not to hold. It is clearly an *a priori* principle, though not an absolutely necessary one.

In Chapter Four the Principal of Locality was argued for as a desirable presupposition for making Mill's Methods of Agreement and Difference work, an anti-astrological canon that precluded the possibility of there being unrecognised remote causal factors influencing the events under consideration.[3] But though the Principle of Locality does the job, it is not the only way of securing the Irrelevance of the Remote; in fact, the inverse square law is itself adequate.

---

[1] See below, §11.6.

[2] See above, §4.7.

[3] §4.8.

More fundamentally, the Principal of Locality is presupposed as a criterion of identity. Spatiotemporal continuity provides a criterion of identity for corpuscles, and similarly it enables us to pick out those that may be at work in a causal process. Once again, the requirement is not absolute: if there were a finite number of corpuscles, and occasionally one would apparently go out of existence, while at the same time another would apparently pop up somewhere else, we might reasonably reckon that it was the same corpuscle, which had on that occasion moved with an infinite velocity from the one place to the other. And it might also be feasible without its aid to identify which causal factors were actually at work: a hero in science fiction might have a gravity shield, whereby he could shield himself from the gravitational influence of the sun, the moon, or the earth, and thus determine what force each, in the absence of the shield, was exerting on him; more plausibly, we might discover in retrospect that changes in the earth's position were instantaneously mirrored in changes of the gravitational field around Neptune.

Leibniz' complaint against Newton's Law of Universal Gravitation was that it was "occult",[4] that is, inexplicable. It is only if causal factors are spatiotemporally connected, that we can understand how they can be causes of effects. Locke thought so too. When he first asked himself how bodies produce ideas in us, he replied "manifestly by impulse and nothing else. It being impossible to conceive that body should operate on what it does not touch (which is all one as to imagine it can operate where it is not), or, when it does touch, operate any other way than by motion", from which he went on to argue "If, then, bodies cannot operate at a distance ... it is evident that some motion must be thence continued by our nerves or animal spirits, by some part of our bodies, to the brains or the seat of sensation, there to produce in our minds the particular ideas we have of them". But after the publication of Newton's *Principia*, Locke acknowledged that gravitation did operate on matter at a distance, and changed the fourth edition of the *Essay*, to say that impulse was merely the only way we could

---

[4] For example, by Leibniz, *Fifth Letter to Clarke*, §35, p.66 in *The Leibniz-Clarke Correspondence*, ed.H.G.Alexander, Manchester, 1956.

§10.1   Points of View   281

conceive bodies to operate in.[5] Action at a distance may be established by inductive arguments as a natural uniformity, and we may be led to conclude that it is an ineluctable law of nature, but we cannot see how we could go further by some abductive inference to the best explanation,[6] and come to understand why it had to be so. But given the minimalist features of corpuscularianism, even action by impulse was also conceptually opaque. How could corpuscles interact at close quarters? In the ancient world the atoms had sometimes been thought to have hooks, which enabled them to interact causally and to join up to form larger entities, but if they were *point*-particles, they could not have hooks, nor any shape whatever. They could only collide. But this would be a rare occurrence—much too rare in fact, if space was continuous, since even an infinite number of point-particles would occupy a space of measure zero, and would almost always miss each other, in a space that was a continuum.

> Himpacts Hardly Hever Happen

Moreover it was assumed, perhaps too readily, that when they did collide, they would bounce off each other, as in a collision between perfectly elastic bodies. But if they did happen to collide, then since they were point-like and impenetrable, they would need an infinite force to reverse their motions instantaneously. When a miss is as good as a mile, and a hit engenders infinite forces, action by impulse is as problematic as action at a distance. Only if substance is extended, can it reliably interact with its neighbourhood. Laplace's equation

$$\frac{\partial^2 V}{x_1^2} + \frac{\partial^2 V}{x_2^2} + \ldots + \frac{\partial^2 V}{x_n^2} = 0$$

---

[5] See *Essay Concerning Human Understanding*, II, Ch. IV, p. 58, Ch. VIII, p. 136, and Ch. XI, pp. 176-7; and *Essay Concerning Human Understanding*, 11, 8, §§11-12. I am indebted to J.L.Mackie for drawing my attention to this. See also Reply to Second Letter, p. 468; quoted in A.S.Pringle-Pattison's edition, p. 68n.

[6] See above, §2.7.

expresses a condition on the value of a potential at a point with respect to its neighbourhood for a space of n dimensions, which will yield the wave equation

$$\frac{\partial^2 V}{x^2} + \frac{\partial^2 V}{y^2} + \frac{\partial^2 V}{z^2} = \frac{1}{c^2}\frac{\partial^2 V}{t^2}.$$

which expresses the condition that the potential at any point is equal to the average value for the neighbourhood.[7]

Locality can explain, granted a field theory. And granted the ontology of *res extensa*, Locality should obtain. For although, as we saw in §9.7, the plenum, like the void, has to be Euclidean or almost Euclidean, the arguments were not all the same. Both were subject to the Proper Euclidean group on account of their being position- and direction-indifferent, but the void was further pressured towards Euclidean-ness by the requirement that its shapes, and geometrical figures generally, should be independent of size. Maps and scale models are good descriptive tools, but experiments in general do not work if scaled down to suit the convenience of the experimenter. Although causality has to be date- and position-independent, it needs to take account of duration and distance, as Galileo pointed out. If elephants were twice as large, their weight would be increased eightfold, but the cross-section, and hence the strength, of their bones, only fourfold, so that their legs would not be able to carry them. No causal law could have duration completely irrelevant—else the cause would not have to precede the effect. If we are to have an explanation of change, there must be differences at different dates, and explanations must explain not only effects' being different, but their being different at a *different* date from their causes.

Maximal monism cannot afford to have spatial distance altogether irrelevant because of the austerity of its basic vocabulary: if only primary qualities are to be admitted, and causal laws, properly formulated, are to be date- and position-indifferent—that is, they should not contain absolute temporal or spatial arguments—it follows that they must be able to have differences of date and position as relevant parameters. Causal laws should, therefore, be expressed at least as differ**ence** equations, and granted the togetherness of

---

[7] See more fully, J.R.Lucas, *A Treatise on Time and Space*, London, 1973, §48, pp.243-245.

§10.1   *Points of View*   283

res extensa, we reach the infinitesimal in the limit, and are led to the conclusion that causal laws should properly be expressed as differ**ential** equations, and hence that any causal influence across a finite spatiotemporal interval is by means of intermediate processes.

Once again the argument is persuasive, but not conclusive. Date-indifference is not an absolute requirement. Cosmologists now believe in the Big Bang, which constitutes an absolute zero for our dating system; and it has been suggested that the constants of nature change—exceedingly slowly—with time. Time could ripen on its own,[8] Jerusalem could be the one still point in the whole universe, light could go faster when directed towards Mecca. Strange things are conceivable. And the fact that they are conceivable shows that our concepts of space and time are not tied to those of cause and effect by some deductive necessity, as is often made out, but only by the limitations of mortal men and rational considerations on the excellence of nature. Theories in conformity with the Principle of Locality and those of date-, position-, and direction-indifference though not the only possible ones, are to our minds more Lovely, and in any case more Likely to be discovered.[9]

Locality requires finitude. If the propagation of causal influence were instantaneous, it could scarcely be subject to any requirement of continuity, for it would not be mediated through intermediate positions, but would jump immediately from cause to effect. The requirement of continuous propagation is therefore a requirement that causal influence can be propagated only along spatio-temporally continuous paths at finite speeds.[10] It could still be that the speed of propagation was different along different paths. Indeed, the speed of light is lower in a material medium than *in vacuo*. It conceivably could be different in different directions *in vacuo*, or in different parts of space, but that would contravene the featurelessness of the void. It is reasonable to suppose that the maximum speed of propagation is the same everywhere and in all directions.

Thus if we accept the stipulation that casual influence can be propagated only along spatio-temporally continuous paths, we are committed to a finite maximum speed of causal propagation. And if we are serious about the isotropy and homogeneity of space, and the homogeneity of time, we are committed to this finite maximum speed of causal propagation being the same in all directions and on all occasions.

---

[8] See further below, §12.1.

[9] The epithets 'lovely' and 'likely' are Peter Lipton's; see his *Inference to the Best Explanation*, London, 1991, ch.4, pp.61-64.

[10] Here and throughout this book I use the word 'speed' when only magnitude is in issue, and the word 'velocity' when it is a vector with a direction.

§10.2 Causal Cones

IF there is an upper limit to the speed of propagation of causal influence, then for any one place at any one time the universe will be divided into two regions: a region of causal influenceability; and a region which can neither influence nor be influenced by anything going on at the time and place in question. The boundary is a cone, or, if there are more than two spatial dimensions, a hypercone. The ordering will be only partial: events which are each in the other's light cone can be ordered, but with events which are each outside the other's cone each will neither influence nor be influenced by the other. The manifold of such events will constitute a space markedly different from the Euclidean spaces we are familiar with. It will be a Minkowski space, the spacetime of the Special Theory.

Early in the twentieth century, A.A. Robb, quite independently of Einstein and Minkowski, showed that, provided there was more than one spatial dimension, a partial ordering relation of causal influenceability would yield a definition of orthogonality between a timelike and a spacelike direction, and hence orthogonality between two spacelike lines, from which congruence between line segments, and hence a metric, can in turn be defined. Granted a metric, we can pick out the paths of light rays along the surface of each cone, characterized by their being maximal and hence unique and linear.[11]

---

[11] A.A. Robb, *A Theory of Time and Space*, Cambridge, 1914; 2nd ed. (*Geometry of Time and Space*) Cambridge, 1936; and *The Absolute Relations of Time and Space*, Cambridge, 1921. Robb's work attracted little attention at the time, but has been properly recognised in recent years, and has been developed further by J.A.Winnie, "The Causal Theory of Spacetime", in J.S. Earman *et al.*, eds., *Foundations of Space-Time Theories*, Minnesota Studies in the Philosophy of Science, Minneapolis, 1977, pp.134-205. Roberto Torretti, *Relativity and Geometry*, Oxford, 1983, ch. IV, §4.6, pp. 121-129. David Malament, "Causal Theories of Time and the Conventionality of Simultaneity", *Noüs*, XI, 1977, pp.293-300. An earlier treatment is to be found in H.Mehlberg, "Essai sur la théorie causale du temps", I and II, *Studia philosophica*, Lemberg, **1** and **2**, 1935 and 1937, pp.119-260 and 111-231; tr. in H.Mehlberg, *Time, Causality and the Quantum Theory*, Reidel, Dordrecht, 1980. E.C.Zeeman, "Causality Implies the Lorentz Group", *Journal of Mathematical Physics*, **1**, 1964, pp.490-493, has a somewhat similar approach; see also E.H.Kronheimer and R.Penrose, "On the Structure of Causal Spaces", *Cambridge Philosophical Society Proceedings*, **63**, 1967, pp.481-501.

§10.2   Points of View   285

The causal approach has been seized upon by some philosophers to argue for a reductionist account of space and time, and criticized by others for that very reason. Admittedly, if a reductionist account were acceptable on other grounds, the causal approach would increase its appeal. But the rejection of reductionism does not vitiate the causal account, which amplifies our understanding of *Res Extensa* by bringing in causality, as well as showing the effect this must have on the topology of spacetime.[12]

Cones force us to take perspectives seriously. We have to associate with each point its own cone, dividing spacetime into what is, and what is not, accessible from that particular point. Each cone delimits a range of possible "frames of reference", themselves equivalence classes of (1+3)-dimensional coordinate systems that are invariant under transformations of the three spatial axes by the Proper Euclidean group.[13] The cones are not optional extras, as coordinates are in ordinary geometry: geometry can be done without coordinates, though often they are convenient to use. But even if we take an absolute view of Minkowski spacetime and do not adopt any one set of axes, but view all points equally, its topology still attributes to each point its own view of spacetime. The View from Nowhere as it has been called[14] is inadequate: our view of reality, if it is to encompass all aspects of reality, must be a view from everywhere, embracing all perspectives.

---

[12] Graham Nerlich, "Special Relativity is not Based on Causality", *British Journal for the Philosophy of Science*, **33**, 1982, pp.361-388, (reprinted in Graham Nerlich, *What Spacetime Explains*, Cambridge, 1994, ch.3, pp.58-90) criticizes the causal approach not only because it has often been espoused by reductionists, but also because it forecloses the possibility of there being "tachyons", which go faster than light. But tachyons have never been observed, so that a version of the Special Theory that does not allow for them is, thus far, empirically adequate. But see also Brent Mundy, "The Physical Content of Minkowski Geometry", §7, *British Journal for the Philosophy of Science*, **37**, 1986, pp.45-49.

[13] Physicists characterize frames of reference as being "rigid", but this is not entirely happy, since rigid rods alter their length when moving at high speeds. In practice, however, the reader can blur these distinctions, and think of each cone as repesented by a coordinate system with its origin at the vertex, its line of rest vertical, and its (hyper-)plane of simultaneity horizontal, which would be a stationary frame of reference.

[14] Thomas Nagel, *The View from Nowhere*, Oxford, 1986.

§10.3 Minkowski Spacetime

Robb's work attracted little attention when it was published, and the ways in which the Special Theory was originally developed laid little emphasis on the conical structure of spacetime. They imply it nonetheless. Even Minkowski's programme of integrating time with space into a single spacetime leads to its having a structure markedly different from a simple 4-dimensional Euclidean space. Time is not just a fourth dimension of a par with the three dimensions of space, and even when integrated into spacetime, remains different, giving rise to a Lorentz signature $(-,+,+,+)$,[15] instead of the standard $(+,+,+,+)$ for a 4-dimensional Euclidean space.

This consequence follows from the need, inherent in any programme of integrating time and space as much as possible, for some standard trade-off between time and space—one second, say, for 186,000 miles. Of course, it does not in principle have to be that. But if it were infinite, as with Newton's instantaneous gravitational force, then instead of a single Minkowski spacetime we should have merely the Cartesian product of two manifolds, $S^1 \times S^3$, one-dimensional time and three-dimensional space. Ultimately this may be the true state of affairs. But the programme of integrating time and space as much as possible argues in favour of there being some finite trade-off between time and space, which then should constitute a "universal speed",[16] that is to say, one which, when compounded with any speed, yields just itself as a resultant.

There are different rules we might have for compounding velocities (in the same direction). Under the Galilean transformation characteristic of Newtonian mechanics, if one frame of reference is moving away from another at a velocity v, then a body which according to that frame is moving with velocity u in the same direction will be assigned a velocity $u + v$ in the other frame. The composition rule for velocities (in the same direction) is simple addition. $u \oplus v = u + v$. With this rule there are two velocities which yield the same result whatever velocity they are compounded with, namely $\pm\infty$. In general it can be shown that for any reasonable composition rule, there is just one speed (two velocities in opposite

---

[15] Or $(+,+,+,-)$: the former way is better in as much as it puts time first; but since we talk of speed as distance divided by duration, the latter expression comes to us more easily.

[16] See above, §5.3.

§10.3   Points of View   287

directions) which will yield the same result whatever other velocity they are compounded with; and, correspondingly, for any such universal speed, there will be a rule for compounding velocities. If the universal speed is c, the composition rule for compounding two velocities u and v in the same direction will be:[17]

$$u \oplus v = \frac{u+v}{1+\frac{uv}{c^2}}.$$

The programme of integrating time and space as much as possible thus leads to a finite universal speed. Geometrically, this would be represented by an "isotropic" line, a line that makes the same angle with every line that intersects it. In Euclidean space no such real line exists—we have to invoke imaginary numbers to satisfy the required equations. In Minkowski space, however, such lines can exist, because the Lorentz signature $(-,+,+,+)$ expresses the fact that the time dimension is seen as including a factor i, or $\sqrt{-1}$. Whereas in a Euclidean four-dimensional space the distance between two points (x_1, y_1, z_1, w_1) and (x_2, y_2, z_2, w_2) is $(x_1 - x_2)^2 + (y_1 - y_2)^2 + (z_1 - z_2)^2 + (w_1 - w_2)^2$, in Minkowski space time the "distance" (or, better, "separation") between two events (x_1, y_1, z_1, t_1) and (x_2, y_2, z_2, t_2) is $(x_1 - x_2)^2 + (y_1 - y_2)^2 + (z_1 - z_2)^2 - (t_1 - t_2)^2$. This difference is forced on us if we want to carry through the programme of integrating time and space as much as possible, and gives to Minkowski space a topology quite different from that of ordinary Euclidean space: points on a line representing the universal speed all count as being close to one another, and the sheath of such lines through any one point divides the spacetime into two distinct regions.

Two different approaches yield the same result. The causal approach naturally gives rise to sheaves of causal influenceability: spacetime falls apart into a separate space and a separate time, if the universal speed is infinite, and if it is finite, involves $\sqrt{-1}$ and a Lorentz signature $(-,+,+,+)$ which in turn require sheaths of null lines through every point. Either way we are led to cones.

---

[17] Alternatively, we can keep the simple addition rule and change what is being added. Instead of velocities, we can consider "rapidities", which are related to velocities by the hyperbolic tangent $tanh$. A measurable magnitude can be "regraduated" so as to fit a different composition rule (see the reference given in §5.3, n.11); in particular, it can be regraduated to fit a simple addition rule (and hence also a simple multiplication rule). One possibility we have to consider in metaphysics is that some magnitudes we ascribe to some sorts of reality—energy, perhaps—are massaged to be simply additive; the measuring requirement creates the magnitude measured.

§10.4 Windowed Monads

The Special Theory leads us to take perspectives seriously. Somewhat surprisingly the argument can be reversed. From an austere account of perspectives we can, granted a few defensible assumptions, be led to the Special Theory. And we can, moreover, see this as the culmination of one trend in seventeenth-century metaphysics, an attempt to embed a plurality of discrete *res cogitantes* in a universe constituted of a single continuous *res extensa*.

Each frame of reference is a map of the world, an equivalence class of coordinate systems with a common perspective on the world, and is often—and significantly—by physicists called "an observer". We can ask how these maps must be correlated if they are to be all maps of the same world. Normally we impose fairly stringent conditions on maps—much more stringent than Leibniz imposed on his "expressions". Frames of reference may move with respect to one another in all sorts of ways, but in the Special Theory we confine our attention to "inertial" frames of reference, that is, frames of reference moving at uniform velocities with respect to one another. We ask how these coordinate systems must be correlated if they are to be all maps of the same world. More mathematically we ask what transformation is needed to transform the map offered by one into the map of the same world as given by another.

Although Leibniz lived long before the advent of the Special Theory and it is anachronistic to offer an exegesis of frames of reference in terms of monads, it is none the less illuminating.[18] It is difficult at first to make sense of monads, but the modern world of computers and cyber-space offers some help. A modern monad is a nerd with a computer, to which he is dedicated, and with which he spends all his time. Although he is still located in the physical world, in which we live and move and have our being, it is a matter of indifference to him. His whole life is in cyberspace, googling, searching, down-loading, sending and receiving E-mails, posting messages on his web-site, contributing to chat shows. He need not, though some nerds do, understand how his computer works, and the subtleties of service-providers and the internet generally: it is enough simply to be able to surf, to send and to receive. Leibniz' monads, however, differ from our nerds: they do not interact or communicate. The integration of the monads into an apparently communicating community was spurious. His

---

[18] For another such exercise, see §12.1.

monads were windowless, and did not communicate with one another. Theirs was a *pre*-established harmony, It is as though all our computers had been pre-programmed by Mr Gates to have all the E-mails we were to receive, all the results of searches we might undertake, and all the programs and documents we might download, already cached in our personal PC, so that there was no need to connect to a landline or broadband; it was all there already. The pre-established harmony, is a *machina ex deo*, entirely lacking plausibility. It lets Leibniz off the hook of having to give an account of how the monads communicate with one another, but is a fatal defect of his metaphysics. But provided we address the question of how *res cogitantes* could communicate with one another, and do not rely on antecedent pre-programming by an omniscient manufacturer of software, we can come to see how personal perspectives are possible in a single well-integrated universe.

Actually, nerds can sometimes turn their attention away from their computers, and be aware of the world around them. We have many windows on the world, and our different senses interact with it in different ways, giving us a wide variety of information. We need to accommodate the fact that observers can both communicate directly with one another and also view them as physical objects occupying a definite position in spacetime. If we are to integrate *res cogitantes* into a universe constituted of a single continuous *res extensa*, the means of communication between different *res cogitantes* should be a causally explicable process in *res extensa*, and therefore with a finite speed of propagation.

Radar presupposes a finite speed of transmission of the electromagnetic impulses—if there were no gap between transmission and reception of the reflected pulse, we could not know how far away the object was: and although the communication of information between monads is not necessarily non-instantaneous, and even if by means of some finitely propagated causal process, not necessarily by means of the same finitely propagated causal process as the acquisition by monads of knowledge of the external world, economy suggests that the same causal process is involved in each case. Windowed monads communicate with one another by means of radio, propagated at the same universal speed as the radar pulses by means of which they probe and find out about the external world.

One further assumption needs to be made explicit, the association between each frame of reference at a particular point—the preferred origin of its coordinate system. It is given in the Special Theory by the topology of Minkowski spacetime,[19] and taken for granted in ordinary life—the minds we are familiar with are embodied, and therefore have a spatiotemporal position that can be located in any frame or reference. Observers can be observed: that is, not only can they observe objects in their common world, and communicate with one another as observers, but can also locate one another as objects, along with all the other objects each locates in his view of the world.

Granted this much, it follows, most surprisingly, that two observers, seeking to harmonize the accounts they give of the world common to them both, must use the **Lorentz transformation** to translate the coordinates assigned by the one into the coordinates assigned by the other.[20]

If frames of reference are not windowless, but can

1. communicate with one another, and
2. can locate one another within their own frame of reference,

the transformation correlating their respective assignments of dates and positions must be
the **Lorentz transformation**.

---

[19] See above, §10.2

[20] The argument is given in J.R. Lucas, *A Treatise on Time and Space*, London, 1973, §44, pp.211-224, and J.R. Lucas and P.E. Hodgson, *Spacetime and Electromagnetism*, Oxford, 1990, ch.4, §§4.1-4.4, pp.123-143; it is available on the web at http://users.ox.ac.uk/ jrlucas/polychro.html. The original argument is due to Milne and Whitrow; see G.J.Whitrow, *The Natural Philosophy of Time*, Edinburgh, 1961, ch.II §8, pp.171–173 and ch.IV §§3–4, 2nd ed. Oxford, 1980, ch.5, esp. §§5.2-5.4, pp.230–253; and E.A.Milne, *Modern Cosmology and the Christian Idea of God*, Oxford, 1952, ch.III and IV; and *Kinematic Relativity*, Oxford, 1948, ch.II, esp.§24; see also C.W.Kilmister, *Special Theory of Relativity*, Oxford, 1970, ch.2, pp.14–19, and G.Stephenson and C.W.Kilmister, *Special Relativity for Physicists*, London, 1958, ch.1§7, pp.16–19 and C.W.Kilmister, *The Environment in Modern Physics*, London, 1965, ch.4, pp.46–53.

§10.4   *Points of View*   291

It is a surprising result, the more so since the Lorentz transformation with very few other assumptions will yield, again most surprisingly, the Maxwell equations, which are the foundation of all electromagnetism.[21] We may be sceptical and ask how it could be possible to produce such a juicy rabbit out of an empirically empty hat; what would be said were there to be observations which falsified the Lorentz transformation? There are, admittedly, several empirical assumptions being made, which though plausible and generally accepted, could be false.[22] The derivation given here does not show that windowed monads must use the Lorentz transformation for translating the coordinate systems they use on pain of self-contradiction, but only that if certain *desiderata* such as economy, isotropy, causal explicability, are to be secured, then the Lorentz transformation gives the means whereby their different sets of coordinates can be harmonized. Where Leibniz had to invoke a pre-established harmony to bring his windowless monads into communal togetherness, the Lorentz transformation can re-establish harmony between the disparate perspectives of different observers viewing the same external world.

---

[21] See J.R.Lucas and P.E.Hodgson, *Spacetime and Electromagnetism*, Oxford, 1990, chs.5 and 6.

[22] See J.R.Lucas and P.E.Hodgson, *Spacetime and Electromagnetism*, Oxford, 1990, §4.5, pp.143-147. R.B.Angel (*Relativity: The Theory and its Philosophy*, Oxford, 1980, pp.110–115.), in particular, questions whether it can be taken for granted that there is a finite maximum velocity for the propagation of causal influence, pointing out that Action at a Distance is not a contradiction in terms, and that Newtonian mechanics, which admits infinite velocities, is not inconsistent. Hence, he argues, the argument must fail, or it would have ruled out Newtonian mechanics *a priori*. But this is to limit the *a priori* to the analytic. It is not that the rules of language make it meaningless to talk of action at a distance, but that such a notion does not fit in with our rational view of reality, for the reasons given in §10.1, so far as we have been able to form one.

§10.5 Covariance

Einstein's approach was different. He was concerned to bring out deep similarities hitherto obscured by differences of perspective. He asked "Under what conditions will an electromagnetic wave appear the same to different observers?", "Under what conditions will different observers reckon that an event occurred at the same time?", and "What must be the case if Maxwell's equations are to have the same form in different frames of reference?". He had a strong sense of sameness, and sought similarities underlying a wide variety of superficially different conditions. We can see his Special Theory as widening the range of conditions under which electromagnetic phenomena were essentially the same, to include, besides date, position and orientation, uniform velocity as well. That is to say, electromagnetic experiments yield the same observations not only in laboratories at different times, in different places and in different directions, but also in laboratories moving at a uniform velocity with respect to one another. Maxwell's equations, which express the laws of electromagnetism, are *covariant* with the Lorentz transformation: or, to put it the other way round, if Maxwell's equations are to have the same form in frames of reference moving with uniform velocity with respect to one another, then the rule for translating the coordinates in one frame of reference into the coordinates in another frame of reference must be given by the Lorentz transformation.

Covariance is a difficult concept. We need to distinguish some features that are *invariant* under the Lorentz transformation from others that are *covariant* with it. Different transformations preserve different features—transformations of the Euclidean group preserve shapes, and distances.[23] These features are said to be invariant under transformations of the Euclidean group. Similarly in the Special Theory the spacetime separation between two events is invariant; it is a magnitude that is the same whatever inertial frame we adopt. In contrast to this the wave equation

$$\frac{\partial^2 \phi}{\partial x^2} + \frac{\partial^2 \phi}{\partial y^2} + \frac{\partial^2 \phi}{\partial z^2} - \frac{1}{c^2}\frac{\partial^2 \phi}{\partial t^2} = 0$$

involves x, y, z, and t explicitly, but is similar none the less. It has the same *form*. Whereas invariance expresses complete independence of coordinate systems, covariance is correlative with the

---

[23] See above, §9.7.

coordinate system employed. It undoes the arbitrariness inherent in choosing a particular origin and set of axes. (There is a certain irony in the fact that Descartes, who was the proponent of the absolute conception of reality, also introduced coordinates, which give the position of points from an arbitrarily adopted point of view.) It shows up what is similar, not independently of, but in spite of, our arbitrary choice of coordinates.

Einstein sought similarities, and held that they were characteristic of the fundamental laws of nature. He used it most notably to formulate his General Theory, where he needed to get away from the rigid rectangular Cartesian coordinates that had until then been taken for granted. His principle of general covariance laid down that laws of nature should be expressed covariantly, that is, in the same form in all coordinate systems. But that was an inadequate specification: any putative law *can* be expressed covariantly, granted sufficient elaboration. Einstein was applying a further, unarticulated condition, that the covariant formulation should be reasonably *simple*. Implicit restrictions on possible choices of coordinates determine what can be conveniently expressed in covariant form—in the Special Theory only *inertial* frames of reference are admissible, that is, only frames of reference moving with *uniform* velocity with respect to one another; it is only in the General Theory that accelerated frames are taken into account, and similarities sought between even them.[24]

We can see Einstein as starting from the assumption that any point can be the origin of a coordinate system, and trying to get away from the arbitrariness of choosing to adopt some particular coordinate system. Although he uses coordinates to express the Laws of Electromagnetism, he seeks to minimise the significance of the particular coordinate system adopted, and bring out in stark relief the underlying truths which do not depend on the coordinate system adopted. An objector might complain that the mere use of coordinates conceded at the outset the possibility of each point having its own perspective; but the real moral to be drawn is that in spite of his downplaying the significance of any choice of coordinates, Einstein's theory confers on every point its own importance as the origin of a highly significant coordinate system.

---

[24] For a fuller discussion, see R.B.Angel, *Relativity: The Theory and its Philosophy*, London, 1980, ch.10.

§10.6 Perspectives

There are many different approaches to the Special Theory, but each leads to the same conclusion, that spacetime is articulated in such a way as to assign to each point its own way of dividing the spacetime of which it is a member into three regions: the past, which may have influenced the Here and Now; the Future which may be influenced by the Here and Now; and the Elsewhere and Anywhen, which could neither have influenced the Here and Now, nor be influenced by the Here and Now, and may be assigned a present, past or future date according to the frame of reference actually adopted. Although we can view spacetime from nowhere in the impersonal, unlocated way of modern science, we do not form an adequate view of it unless we realise that each point has its own view differing systematically from that of every other point. If we simply exclude what is local and personal, our account of reality will leave out much that is undeniably real, and we shall be driven to the double-talk of the

> .... faith-healer of Deal,
> who said "Although pain is not real,
> when I sit on a pin,
> and it punctures my skin,
> I dislike what I fancy I feel".

Hitherto we have assumed that objectivity is opposed to subjectivity, and that in order to obtain a proper conception of reality, we must factor out anything that is local or personal. We are moved by two considerations: what is subjective is up to us, and therefore arbitrary, whereas reality is what it is whether we like it or not; and although when I know something, it is a fact about me that I know it, it is not a fact about me whether I really know what I think I know. Thus Bernard Williams speaks of knowledge presupposing "an absolute conception of reality", a reality that is there *anyway*, independently of any thought or experience.[25]

Two arguments for the impersonal, absolute conception of reality:
1. What is subjective is up to us, and therefore arbitrary.
2. Knowledge depends on reality, not *vice versa*.

---

[25] B.A.O.Williams, *Descartes: the Project of Pure Enquiry*, Penguin, 1978, pp.64-65, 239, 245-249, 301-303. See also T.Nagel, *The View From Nowhere*, Oxford, 1986, pp.14-15, and A.W.Moore, *Points of View*, Oxford, 1997, *passim*.

Each consideration carries weight, but neither requires us to eschew everything that is personal or local. Reality is recalcitrant: it is there *willy nilly*. But so is much of our experience: the faith-healer of Deal cannot wish away his pain. Much that is in the eye of the beholder is not *just* in the eye of the beholder, and is not simply a matter of the beholder's say-so, but is open to discussion and criticism. The art critic can be wrong. He claims the new exhibit is beautiful, but if I say it is ugly, I could conceivably be right, much as the army doctor may be right when he says the malingerer is not really in pain, but only pretending.

Similarly, while it is an important truth that knowledge depends on reality, not reality on knowledge, the reality we know may nonetheless include, and to that extent depend on, some non-arbitrary thoughts and experiences of the knower. Reality is there *anyway*; positive thinking will not make it go away; nor can coherence with our other thoughts, or with the thoughts of others, preclude the possibility of its nonetheless proving them wrong. Although in coming to know things the questions we ask largely depend on us, the answers are not of our own choosing. Even if the questions are about us, so that the answers do, to some extent depend on us, they do not do so entirely. Knowledge is not just what we think it to be: but it can be about us, even about what we think.

If I am an artist, and am drawing a picture of a house, the shapes I shall inscribe on the paper will depend on the position from which I am drawing; The shape of, say, the front door will be different from what it would be if had positioned myself differently. But though in either case what I draw on the paper will be different, and will depend in part on the position taken up by the person doing the drawing, there will be an important similarity between the different drawings. Although it is up to the artist where he chooses to draw from, it is not entirely up to the artist what shapes and colours he inscribes on the paper. He can get the perspective, or the colour, wrong. (Sometimes he may do so deliberately, in order to achieve some other effect: but again, he may fail.) It makes sense to complain, "It is not a true likeness".

We are not obliged to accept the absolute conception of reality, though we can see why it has been adopted by most philosophers. As we move from the familiar scene of ordinary life to the remote landscape of ultimate reality, the availability and scope of first-personal information diminishes, as does also the possibility of effective intervention on our part in the course of events. It is natural for the metaphysician to be a spectator of all time,[26] taking an entirely impersonal view of the underlying structure of things behind the changes and chances of our fleeting experience, and hence construing it as that which is invariant, the same whatever personal, temporal, or spatial perspective we adopt, the actual shape of the door which the artist seeks to portray, the truth to which knowledge seeks to attain. But, though there is much to be said for this understanding of reality for many purposes, it is a limited view, factoring out all features which are of significance to a full, stereoscopic view of the world we live in and ourselves as its inhabitants.

We have two possible conceptions of reality. In the one case—the "absolute conception of reality"—we abstract from all points of view, and give an entirely impersonal account of the invariant features of reality that do not depend on any particular point of view—the view from nowhere: in the other—which we may call "the perspectival conception of reality—we do not leave out the point of view, but take it into account in such a way that other points of view can be accommodated. In the former, reality is contrasted with the appearances "from where I sit":[27] in the latter, it seeks to accommodate those appearances, being the reality which saves appearances by contrast with empty speculations which do not.

The account of atoms and the void is entirely impersonal, describing corpuscles whose number and identity are the same for everyone, and a space with a Euclidean geometry whose magnitudes and features are the same for all observers. Frames of reference, on the other hand, are observer-centred and offer accounts which, though observer-dependent, are sufficiently similar in content to be accessible to other observers. 'We make a comparable distinction in our every-day use of ordinary language. We can use third-personal language to refer to people independently of who we are, whom we are talking to, where we are situated, and at what time we are talking; but we mostly use an egocentric language, in which I refer to myself as 'I', to the person I am talking to as 'you', the place where I am situated as 'here', and indicate the temporal relation of the events I am talking about to the time at which I am talking by the

---

[26] Plato, *Republic* VI, 486a8.

[27] See above, §8.3.

appropriate tense. Scientists use the impersonal mode, describing an invariant reality that is the same for everyone, everywhere, and at all times; and some philosophers have held that it is in general better to do so.[28] We can, indeed, adopt an impersonal, untensed discourse, using only the third person with names and a tenseless verb with dates, but we find it difficult not to use tenses, and difficult, not to say misleading, not to use the first person of ourselves. I can refer to myself by my name, and say "J.R. Lucas *be* born on June 18th, 1929", but save in exceptional circumstances, I should be being economical with the truth if I referred to myself simply as "J.R. Lucas". Hearers are entitled to know that it is the person speaking to them that is being referred to. On many matters he is the authority on himself, and if people were to doubt his word, they would be impugning his honesty, whereas if they doubted what he said of a genuine third person, they would be merely questioning the reliability of his sources. The pressure to use tenses is stronger still. Although I could use an unconjugated verb, and say "J.R. Lucas *be* born on June 18th, 1929", I feel impelled to use the past tense, and say "J.R. Lucas was born on June 18th, 1929", even though the date gives adequate indication of when the event took place, which was before the present time of utterance. The reason is that in some cases it makes a great difference whether I am speaking in anticipation or am merely reporting in retrospect. Not only am I authoritative if I announce my intention to act, but I can be reasoned with, and perhaps dissuaded from acting, whereas past events, no matter how doleful, cannot be undone. The future is open, and to some limited extent, it is up to us how it eventuates: whereas the past is fixed and unalterable; there is less room for doubt about it, and no room for debate whether to make it happen one way or another. So, rather than use the eternal sentences of Quine, we *conjugate*. We make systematic changes, depending on the person who is speaking, the person he is talking to, the place where is situated, and the time he is talking at, changes which, although altered by the context, preserve an essential similarity of content, which remains, so to speak, covariant under the transformation from one speaker to another.

---

[28] W.V.O.Quine, *Word and Object*, New York, 1960, pp.193-194, 208, 226-227; or *Elementary Logic*, New York, 1965, p.6; or N. Rescher, "Truth and Necessity in Temporal Perspective", in R.M.Gale, ed., *The Philosophy of Time*, London, 1968, pp. 183-220.

We can extend the idea of covariant conjugation. As I view Minkowski spacetime, I see cones showing which parts of spacetime are causally accessible from the vertex of the cone, and which are causally inaccessible. And for many purposes I need to pick on some point, and adopt *pro tem* a coordinate system consonant with its cone as my frame of reference, and do all my calculations from that particular point of view. To the outsider it might seem that to adopt a particular point of view would be a fatal derogation from the ideal of objectivity. But it is not. Although it is *my* view *pro tem*, I do not insist on its absolute authority against all comers, but allow that you have your view, and others have their views, each recognising the validity of the other views, and each equally authoritative. I, so to speak, conjugate my view, and can phrase what I want to say in terms that you could use, equally truthfully, to say what you wanted to say. We do not have to confine our conversation to items that are the same for all of us, but, provided we conjugate appropriately, can share our different perspectives with one another. In mathematical terminology, we can discuss objectively not only things that are invariant, but those that vary covariantly with respect to our different standpoints. Reality need not exclude the personal and local, but can embrace such perspectives and accommodate them, in particular, the tenses we naturally use when not under pressure from philosophical orthodoxy. But these are deeply suspect, and need to be vindicated against the received opinion of traditional philosophers.

Conceptions of Reality

Absolute	**Perspectival**
Invariant	Covariant
Impersonal	Personal
Tenseless	Conjugate
Valentian Canon	Secondary Qualities (See §14.7)

§10.7 McTaggart and Mellor

McTaggart argued that time was unreal, because tense was essential to time, and tense was self-contradictory. On the first point he was right, on the second confused.

Tense was self-contradictory, he said, because any attempt to explain the passage of time in terms of tensed language alone led to our having to ascribe all three tenses, past, present and future, to one and the same event, and each of the three tenses is incompatible with the other two.[29] He concluded that only tenseless discourse was free from contradiction, but since this left out the specifically temporal features of time, no consistent account of time could be given. In discussing this contention, we need, first, to distinguish two claims: a strong one that tensed discourse—the A series in McTaggart's terminology—is by itself sufficient for all temporal discourse; and a weaker one that the A series is a perfectly consistent part of temporal discourse which also includes tenseless discourse—the B series in McTaggart's terminology. We need, secondly, to distinguish the claim that the A series is free from self-contradiction from the exercise of giving an adequate philosophical exegesis of it. Once we make these distinctions, we no longer have even the appearance of inconsistency in our philosophical exegesis of tensed language. It is indeed true, as McTaggart claims, that for any event it at some time *be* future, it at some time *be* present and it at some time *be* past, and this may well be a key part of our account of temporality. But there is no objection to a philosopher who seeks to *be* a spectator of all time using untensed language to talk about time. If the B series is forbidden us, we may be unable to talk philosophically about time; and indeed, life would be awkward if we had no dates, no calendars and no diaries; but discourse exclusively in terms of the A series would not be self-contradictory. It would still be true to say that for any event it was once future, either was or is or will be present, and will be past, but it does not follow from this that we can generate an inconsistency by following McTaggart down an infinite regress of ever more complex tenses. If we stick to tensed language there is not even an appearance

---

[29] J.E.M.McTaggart, "The Unreality of Time', *Mind*, pp.457-474; reprinted in J.E.M.McTaggart, *Philosophical Studies*, London, 1934; and in R.Le Poidevin and M.MacBeath, *The Philosophy of Time*, Oxford, 1993, pp.23-34, esp. pp.31-34. See also J.E.M.McTaggart, *The Nature of Existence*, i, Cambridge, 1927, ch.xxxiii.

of inconsistency. McTaggart tries to generate one by construing these tensed locutions tenselessly, and each time the ensuing inconsistency is resolved by distinguishing the tenses, construing the resulting, more complexly tensed, locution tenselessly again. That does, indeed, produce an infinite regress. But it is one generated by McTaggart's seeking an all-time philosophical exegesis, not by the incoherence of tensed discourse. At most it could show that we cannot give a tenseless account of tensed discourse. Maybe not. But that is a far cry from showing that tensed discourse is itself incoherent, or that the combination of tensed and tenseless discourse we ordinarily use is in any way defective.

Although McTaggart's argument is fallacious, it has been defended by a number of distinguished thinkers.[30] Le Poidevin reformulates McTaggart's argument in terms of three tense operators, P for past, N for present and F for Future. These are exclusive:
$Pp \rightarrow \neg(Np \vee Fp)$
$Np \rightarrow \neg(Pp \vee Fp)$
$Fp \rightarrow \neg(Pp \vee Pp)$
He secondly seeks to express the fact that every event and every time *be* at some time past and at some time present and at some time future. He says:

> Every event exhibits all A-series positions. Or to put it in different terms, each tense operator is applicable to every true proposition:

$(Pp \wedge Np \wedge Fp)$

He then points out that this last thesis is inconsistent with the three earlier ones. He allows that the last thesis is false "if we read the conjunctive proposition as *present tensed* (as the embedded proposition p is present-tensed)". "At no time is it the case that some event is past, present and future. Rather, it has these different A-series positions at different times." He goes on to suggest that instead of the simple conjunction first proposed, we should have:

$(Pp \text{ at } t \wedge Np \text{ at } t^* \wedge Fp \text{ at } t^{**} \wedge \neg(t = t^* \vee t = t^{**} \vee t^* = t^{**}))$

---

[30] M.A.E. Dummett, "A Defence of McTaggart's Proof of the Unreality of Time", *Philosophical Review*, **69**, 1960, pp.497-505, esp. pp.502-503; reprinted in M.A.E. Dummett, *Truth and Other Enigmas*, London, 1978, ch.20. D.H.Mellor, *Real Time*, Cambridge, 1981, pp.98-102; reprinted with corrections in R. Le Poidevin, and M.MacBeath, *The Philosophy of Time*, Oxford. 1993, pp.47-59. R.Le Poidevin, *Change, Cause and Contradiction*, London and Basingstoke, 1991.

But this is not a satisfactory response to McTaggart's challenge, since it makes use of B-series times, t, t^* and t^{**}. If tensed theory is correct, the truth conditions must be given in *tensed*, not tenseless terms, and so we must rephrase in tensed terms. This Le Poidevin attempts to do, but like McTaggart, finds fault with each attempt he makes.

Leaving aside the natural response that it is quite possible to believe that tensed language is essential without thereby debarring oneself from using tenseless language too, we can still meet McTaggart's challenge by constructing in tensed language a way of expressing omnitemporal truths. For every event we hold it to be the case that at some time it will be past, and at another time it is present, and at another it was future. We *can* express in tensed terms the tenseless existential quantifier 'at some time' by the disjunction of all three tense operators. If every event is such that at some time it will be past, then either it was the case that it will be past, or it is the case that it will be past, or it will be the case that it will be past; in symbols:

$$(PPp \vee NPp \vee FPp)$$

Similarly if every event is such that at some time it is present, then either it was the case that it is present, or it is the case that it is present, or it will be the case that it is present:

$$(PNp \vee NPp \vee FNp)$$

Similarly again, if every event is such that at some time it was future, then either it was the case that it was future, or it is the case that it was future, or it will be the case that it was future:

$$(PFp \vee FNp \vee FFp)$$

If we conjoin these three disjunctions, and state

$$((PPp \vee NPp \vee FPp) \wedge (PNp \vee NPp \vee FNp) \wedge (PFp \vee FNp \vee FFp)),$$

we have no inconsistency.

Mellor accepts McTaggart's critique of tensed discourse, but rejects the claim that tensed discourse is essential to time. Time, he holds, is real: but tenses are *merely* our perspective on time. Tenses are essentially token-reflexive, or indexical.[31] Token-reflexive terms depend on the context of utterance, and so are seemingly subjective.[32] The present tense is used of events contemporary with the time of speaking, the past of events that happened before the time of speaking, and the future of events expected to take place after the time of speaking. No exclusively non-token-reflexive translations of tensed utterances can be given, nor can their truth conditions be expressed in exclusively non-token-reflexive terms. Rather, the truth conditions of tensed utterances are functions of the time of their utterance as well as the tenseless facts of the case. And so, Mellor concludes, tense is unreal.

But it does not follow. Mellor does not succeed, any more than McTaggart, in showing that tensed language is inherently self-contradictory, only that it is token-reflexive. But that is no surprise. Quite naturally, a philosopher, if asked to provide an exegesis of tense, will try to give it in terms of untensed language. We normally use both tensed language—McTaggart's A series—and tenseless language—McTaggart's B series, freely translating from one to the other, as convenience dictates. If either is the occasion of difficulty, we use the other. But courtesy to the questioner does not imply any deficiency in the language being explained.

Mellor is much concerned about sentences and truth conditions, and concludes, quite rightly, that tensed facts do not exist. But that is not because they are tensed, but because facts generally do not exist. The word 'fact' is a treacherous term: it takes its sense from what it is being contrasted with, and systematically varies according to the topic under discussion.[33] It would be a fact in a Court of Law that the deed complained of was done eight years ago, so that a legal action is out of time, although a historian, adducing it as evidence for the agent's motives, would date it in the standard way.

'Truth-making condition' is likewise a term of art. Different utterances are made true by different sorts of conditions. What

---

[31] See above, §3.3, n.8.

[32] See for example W.V. Quine, *Word and Object*, New York, 1960, pp.170f., 191-194, 208, 226-227; W.V.Quine, *Elementary Logic*, New York, 1965, p.6. J.J.C.Smart, *Philosophy and Scientific Realism*, London, 1963.

[33] See J.R.Lucas, "On Not Worshipping Facts", *The Philosophical Quarterly*, **8**, 1958, pp.144-156.

makes it true that $e^{i\pi} + 1 = 0$ is very different from what makes it true that Queen Anne died in 1714. Often, if we are in dispute as to when we went on that holiday in Majorca, we shall look up diaries and calendars: but on finding the corpse with *rigor mortis* not having set in, I shall conclude that the murder was committed only a short time ago. Truth conditions, like facts, are too variable and too insubstantial to bear any argumentative weight.

It remains that tenses are token-reflexive. But this does not show them to be unreal. We can see this most clearly if we consider that we conjugate not only over tenses but over persons. I use the first person of myself, the second person of the person I am talking to, and the third person of other people. The first- and second-persons are obviously token-reflexive, the third person not necessarily so. But we do not conclude that the first- and second-persons are unreal. We recognise that for certain purposes—writing scientific articles, for example—an impersonal mode of speech, often couched in the passive voice, is appropriate; and on occasion we need to be told to whom 'I', 'you', 'he', 'she', 'we' or 'they' refers. But we do not make out that because 'I' when uttered by me refers to me, but when uttered by you refers to you, first- and second-personal language is contradictory. Rather, as already argued,[34] we reckon that first- and second-personal language is needed if we are to be able to identify third persons by asking 'Who are you?' and being told 'I am John Smith', or whatever.

Mellor contrasts the reality of time with tenses being *merely* our perspective on time. But the force of that contrast fades, as we ponder the cones implicit in Minkowski spacetime, and recognise that covariance may be as much a mark of reality as invariance.

---

[34] In §10.6.

§10.8 Tense and Temporality

McTaggart argued that tense was essential to a realistic account of time. If so, tenseless accounts of time are radically defective, giving only a partial characterization of time, and leaving out its essential temporality. We need to distinguish two criticisms: a general one against extreme non-egocentricity, and a more telling one, specific to our understanding of temporal terms.

It is a valid criticism of the absolute account of time given by philosophers, and taken over by the classical physicists, that if we confine ourselves to timeless, impersonal and unlocated discourse, we leave out the links with experience that make our discourse relevant. It is like doing celestial mechanics, but with no connexion with the stars in the sky.[35] If I am in a strange town and see a map posted, I need the arrow with the caption "You are here". It is not enough to have a complete guest list—we sometimes have to ask "who are you?", and need an answer in the first person. So, too, with time. A dating system is no good, unless we can know what the date is now; a story that begins 'Once upon a time' is as clearly fictional as one beginning 'A certain man went down from Jerusalem to Jericho'. It matters very much whether an unpleasant experience is going to happen to me, or is already over,[36] just as I am much more alarmed if it is going to happen to me rather than to someone else who has been brain-washed to have all my memories and to think that he is J.R. Lucas.

But it is not only relevance that is in question. If we confine ourselves to timeless, impersonal and unlocated discourse, we may leave out not only the links with experience that make our discourse relevant, but also those that make it meaningful. We give content to terms such as 'earlier' and 'later' from our antecedent understanding of words such as 'yesterday' and 'tomorrow', 'ago' and 'soon'. If we did not have tensed language, we should not be able to give temporal content to 'earlier' and 'later', which might mean, for all we knew, 'hotter' and 'colder', or 'above' and 'below'.

Against this, it might be objected that we can understand stories beginning 'Once upon a time', which are not anchored by token-reflexives in our actual experienced world.

---

[35] See above, §8.4.

[36] A.N.Prior, "Thank Goodness, That's Over", *Philosophy*, **34**, 1959, pp.12-17; reprinted in A.N.Prior, *Papers in Logic and Ethics*, ed. P.T.Geach and A.J.P.Kenny, London, 1976, pp.78-84.

Admittedly, novels are read and understood, even though containing no genuine token-reflexives, but we understand what the third-personal descriptions mean only because we already know from our ordinary discourse what first- and second-personal terms mean. Similarly we understand what the tensed narratives in a novel mean only because we already know from our ordinary discourse what tensed terms mean.

Tensed discourse is necessary not only to give content to an earlier past and a later future, but to provide some anchorage in reality. The present tense, is an essential mark of temporality, as is shown by the arguments of those who deny the reality of all, or some parts of, time on account of the absence of an adequate present. St Augustine's argument of the Ever-Shrinking Present takes for granted that the unshrunk stretches of past and future time do not qualify, and concludes that the shrunken present instant, not being an interval, a *distentio*, will not do either.[37] Modern Philosophers who espouse "Presentism" likewise witness to the necessity of the present tense.

Tenseless accounts of time lack

1. Connexion with us, and relevance.
2. Direction (difference between earlier and later).

3. Presentness.

St Augustine concluded that time was a *distentio animi*, an extension of the mind. Kirwan points out that this will not do as a definition of time,[38] but we can make sense of it as a characteristic feature of time, if we regard ourselves as *agents*, looking forward to the future, as we make up our minds about what we are going to do. It is the experience of reaching out to the future, and deciding which possibilities to grasp and make real, that gives us our basic intimation of temporality. Our ordinary experience is not just a passive solipsistic experience, but of ourselves being agents deliberating about what to do in the future and owning up to what we

---

[37] See below, §12.6.

[38] Christopher Kirwan, *Augustine*, London, 1989, pp.184f.

have done in the past. To be a person is to be an agent—*ego ergo ago*—and to use the first person singular is to allow the use of the second person by others, with the possibility of communication, in which we ask questions in order to elicit answers. Equally the use of the first-person plural presupposes communication between us, whereby we reach agreement about the reasons we shall act on: and communication presupposes time.[39] Thus, a sense of temporality stems from first-personal experience, and conjugating over person and over tense are concomitant with each other.

If a tenseless account of time is no more temporal than an impersonal account of personality is personal, the account of time given by the classical physicists is seriously defective.[40] Time for them is a one-dimensional continuum, homogeneous and isotropic, lacking both the directedness, which is a prominent feature not only of human experience, but of biological and even of physical phenomena as well[41] and the uniqueness of the present, which is of supreme importance when human action is under consideration.

Physicists have laboured to remedy these defects. The Second Law of Thermodynamics, that entropy increases with time, is not temporally isotropic, and there are deep conceptual links between entropy, information, explanation and causality, which help explain why the Second Law should be the way it is, but have not so far yielded a convincing characterization of time. It would be wrong to condemn all such efforts as necessarily futile. Deep understanding may come of them. But it is a curious exercise to factor out the directedness of time, which is a feature of everyone's experience of it, and then to labour to put some direction back again to it.

Tenses secure not only the directedness of time, but the special status of the present. This too should concern the physicist, since it is implicit in every light cone he draws, but it is only in another branch of physics, to which we now turn, that the present is decisively vindicated.

---

[39] This is contested by M.MacBeath, "Communication and Time-Reversal", *Synthese*, **56**, 1983, pp.27-46.

[40] See for example, K.G.Denbigh, *Three Concepts of Time*, Berlin, 1981.

[41] See further below, §11.12.

Chapter 11
Quantum Mechanics

"The quantum theory of fields is the contemporary locus of metaphysical research." H.Stein[1]

§11.1   Unhistory
§11.2   The Inner Cave
§11.3   Discreteness and Continuity
§11.4   From von Neumann to Kochen-Specker
§11.5   From EPR via JSB to GHZ
§11.6   Non-locality
§11.7   The "Measurement Problem"
§11.8   Knowing and Being
§11.9   The Uncertainty Principle
§11.10 Nullary Qualities
§11.11 Indiscernability and *Haecceitas*
§11.12 Quantum Realism
§11.13 Quantum Philosophy

§11.1 Unhistory

Historically, quantum mechanics was forced on physicists by empirical evidence. Black-body radiation and the photo-electric effect could not be explained in terms of classical physics, and quantum mechanics was developed in order to make some sort of sense of bizarre experimental observations. But with the benefit of hindsight, we can begin to see the rational pressures that shaped our twentieth-century attempts to understand the physical world.

---

[1] "On the Notion of Field in Newton, Maxwell and Beyond", in R.H.Stuewer, ed., *Historical and Philosophical Perspectives in Science*, Minnesota Studies in the Philosophy of Science, **5**, Minneapolis, Minn., USA, 1970, p.285; quoted by M.L.G.Redhead, "A Philosopher Looks at Quantum Field Theory", in Harvey Brown and Rom Harré, eds., *Philosophical Foundations of Quantum Mechanics*, Oxford, 1988 (pbk 1990), p.9.

It is a dangerous exercise.[2] All too easily we read into the past principles that exist only in our imagination, and endow our reason with a sensitivity it would never have developed, without the brute given-ness of experimental evidence. Nevertheless, it is a useful exercise, enabling us to see well-worn truths in a new light. We are now able to see the Special Theory as the culmination of Newtonian theories of space and time, though it took the Michelson-Morley experiment to force us to re-think in that direction.[3] With quantum mechanics, if we set it against the foil of classical corpuscularianism, we see the different alternatives that we might have in a theory of matter; and the weaknesses of classical corpuscularianism enhance the cogency of its development into quantum mechanics.

The Corpuscularian philosophy leaves the following loose ends:
1. It yokes together discrete point-particles and continuous space;
2. It assumes a certain set of primary qualities, which presuppose
3. 3-dimensional, Euclidean space;
4. It entirely ignores epistemology.

For quantum mechanics is not simply an *alternative* to classical mechanics. Rather, it accepts the physics of classical corpuscularianism, but seeks to go beyond it. It seeks to remedy some of the blemishes on the corpuscularian schema of explanation, by going a step further than corpuscularianism, and offering more fundamental explanations, both physical and metaphysical. Explanation is a rational activity. Although constrained by the need to save the appearances, explanations are not explanatory unless they conform to certain rational ideals. And in the development of quantum mechanics, we can detect the pressure of certain canons of rationality, and dimly discern some rational ideals.

---

[2] Also undertaken in §10.4.

[3] See J.R.Lucas and P.E.Hodgson, *Spacetime and Electromagnetism*, Oxford, 1990, ch.8.

§11.2 The Inner Cave

Quantum mechanics is a metaphysics of the Cave. Behind the world of appearances lies a more fundamental and more real world, which explains how things appear to us, and the underlying course of events, and which is accessible to thinkers who think hard, and really want to know the nature of things. As with classical corpuscularianism, the explanatory power of quantum mechanics is its warrant of truth. It stands or falls by its ability to account for phenomena, and explain what hitherto had been un-understood. But though there is no independent access to it by means of some insight into the Form of the Good, explanatory power is itself a fief of Reason. The Greek atomists and many of the early corpuscularians were persuaded, in advance of empirical vindication, by the rational merits of its tenets. Even more so with quantum mechanics, where in spite of the extraordinary difficulty in making sense of it, there seems to be some intellectual necessity about the theory, quite apart from its confirmation by experimental observation.

Unlike classical corpuscularianism, however, quantum mechanics posits not just a Cave, but an Inner Cave. When the corpuscularians thought that they had escaped from the cave of mere appearances into the light of day, they misled themselves—they had only come from an inner cave to an outer one, in which we still saw only shadowy representations of the real cosmos. The corpuscularian philosophy assumed a certain set of primary qualities. If we had microscopic eyes, we would be able to see the primary qualities of the ultimate constituents of matter, and it was these that determined their secondary qualities, and all their other powers and properties. The great economy of explanation was a weighty argument in favour of corpuscularianism, but raised the question of why the primary qualities were so important, and whether they did not need to be explained in their turn. Quantum mechanics, being not so much a rival to classical corpuscularianism as a development of it, takes us further—if not right into the outside world of full enlightenment, at least remedying some of the defects of current theories. A better Fundamental Theory of the Universe would go behind Locke's primary qualities to ones more basic still—"nullary qualities", so to speak; and posit a cosmos with properties that were inherent, not contingent.

Optative Physics

A Desirable Fundamental Theory of the Universe would

1. Go behind Locke's primary qualities to ones more basic still—"nullary qualities"??
2. Posit a space with properties that were inherent, not contingent.

Quantum mechanics does this. The ψ-functions it ascribes are highly abstract, and remote from experience, but have intellectual coherence and rational appeal. The Fourier analysis of periodic functions requires an abstract infinite-dimensionsal Hilbert space in which Parseval's theorem serves as an analogue of Pythagoras' theorem in establishing a quasi-Euclidean metric.[4] We thus have a picture. A periodic function can be expressed as a superposition of pure sinusoidal functions of different frequencies, and these latter can be represented by different axes in Hilbert space, and their superposition as the corresponding ray in Hilbert space. Although Hilbert space in general has a denumerable infinity of dimensions, we can make do with three. We can picture a ψ-function, representing the state of a quantum-mechanical system, as a searchlight beam moving across the sky, searching for enemy bombers. The direction of the beam will be measured by the angle it makes with the North, the East and the vertical axes (or any other three orthogonal axes we choose to adopt), say θ, ϕ and χ, with Pythagoras' theorem yielding:

$$cos^2\theta + cos^2\phi + cos^2\chi = 1$$

Each squared cosine gives the probability that if the relevant operator is applied, the beam will align itself along the corresponding axis.[5]

Fourier analysis is bad news for the learner. Although Schrödinger's wave approach and Heisenberg's Hilbert-space approach are *au font* equivalent, there being two approaches have given rise to a bewildering variety of symbols and ideas. Nearly all involve the letter ψ. In Schrödinger's approach ψ is a function, a periodic function representing a wave, on which we perform various operations with operators—energy operators, momentum operators, position operators, and the like—and then find solutions for the resulting equations, which tell us what energy levels, what values for momentum or position, are possible. Heisenberg represented quantum-mechanical operators as matrices, for which we could work out what vectors were "*eigen*-vectors", vectors, that

---

[4] See above, §9.7.

[5] According to standard expositions of quantum mechanics it should be seen as a single ray, but, as will be argued in §11.7, a beam is a better representation.

§11.2 *Quantum Mechanics* 311

is, which were transformed by the matrix into a vector aligned in the same direction, but with a magnitude multiplied by some real number (possibly, just the number 1), its *eigen*-number. Dirac developed this into an extremely elegant formulation in terms of vector spaces, in which the state of a quantum-mechanical system was represented by a "ket vector", $|\psi\rangle$, which can be expressed as a sum of orthogonal vectors in Hilbert space. The fact that these approaches are equivalent adds greatly to the power, the beauty and the profundity of quantum mechanics: but the way most writers about quantum mechanics slide around the different symbolism and different methods of argument make for very difficult reading.

Classical corpuscularianism has a problem in relating the world outside the cave—the world of science—to what we see in the cave—the world of experience. Quantum mechanics has a similar problem in relating the world of corpuscularianism to a more profound one behind it. The relation is represented by operators— self-adjoint Hermitian operators which operate on the ψ-functions or $|\psi\rangle$ vectors that represent the state of a quantum system. These operators have certain *eigen*-values, the set of *eigen*-values depending on which operator we are considering, and for each *eigen*-value there is a probability, depending on which ψ-function we are considering, of getting that *eigen*-value. These *eigen*-values are often called values of 'observables'. It is a deeply misleading name. Most of the magnitudes of which the *eigen*-values are measures are several steps remote from actual observation. I do not observe energy or momentum, and the natural philosophers of the Seventeenth Century had difficulty in distinguishing them, and in framing adequate concepts. The alternative term, 'dynamical variable', is preferable, but I shall talk of 'classical physical magnitude'. It makes the distinction, overlooked by Bohr, between the inner cave, in which there are material objects, inter-personal communication and shared experiences, and the outer cave of classical corpuscularianism, in which there are particles possessing mass and moving in space. It also fits with Einstein's phrase 'element of physical reality', but uses the word 'classical' to limit the force of the word 'physical': there should be no suggestion that only elements of classical physical reality are real; ψ-functions and $|\psi\rangle$ are not elements of classical physical reality, but are, we shall argue, physically real none the less.[6]

---

[6] See below, §11.12.

§11.3 Discreteness and Continuity

Classical corpuscularianism found it difficult to reconcile discreteness with continuity. Its ultimate entities, the atoms, were discrete, but they existed in a continuous space. Any pluralist metaphysic is bound to deal with a plurality of discrete ultimate entities, but faces a problem of how they can interact. If we reject Leibniz' heroic expedient of denying interaction altogether, we are bound to posit an all-encompassing medium for them to interact in, a medium which is unified topologically, as space is. Classical corpuscularianism has a pluralist metaphysic of discrete individual entities, but integrates them into a monistic all-encompassing continuous space.

But there were problems in accommodating absolutely discrete corpuscles in an entirely continuous space. In order to be absolutely discrete, the corpuscles had to be *point*-particles, ἄτομοι (*atomoi*), logically unsplittable, as well as being impenetrable, so as to enable each to maintain its separate existence. Though point-particles were impenetrably solid, they could be packed into an infinitesimal volume—and would, granted the inverse-square law of attraction all collapse into an infinitesimal volume, which would be always getting smaller, but could never actually be a single point. Moreover, point-particles in a more-than-one-dimensional space would almost never collide; and if they did, would have to be subject to infinite forces in order to effect an instantaneous change of velocity.

Quantum mechanics marries discreteness and continuity in an entirely different way. Beginners in quantum mechanics are encouraged to think of an orbit like the petals of a flower: a stable orbit is a standing wave which has one, two, three, four, five, six petals, but not two and a half petals. There are other manifestations of discreteness within a matrix of continuity: a polygon can have three, four, five, six sides, but not two and a half sides. And although some mathematicians have been able to work with fractional dimensions, in our ordinary understanding the number of dimensions of a space is necessarily a whole number.

In quantum mechanics discreteness and continuity are integrated by means of periodic functions. A periodic function is one that regularly returns to the same value after a certain interval, for example

$$\sin(x) = \sin(2n\pi + x).$$

Although such a function is continuous, the number of periods is counted in whole numbers.[7] This discreteness is not the logical

---

[7] See more fully below, §11.10.

§11.3   *Quantum Mechanics*   313

discreteness of entities unsplittable because they have no size, but an as-it-happens discreteness of intervals whose magnitude is determined by physical laws. It is not linked with individuality, and is the discreteness of an accountant's accounts, rather than of an ontological pluralist. Quantum mechanics can, in consequence, accommodate solidity. It tells a long story, about energy levels, and permitted jumps from one to another, instead of the excessively short story, told by the corpuscularians, of logically impenetrable and unsplittable point-particles. The quantum-mechanical account has more "give" in it, which enables it to explain the phenomena of colliding molecules of gas, and the elastic rigidity of metals, but has to take for granted the value of Planck's constant as a given fact.

Classical physics admits only discrete truth-values, and is entirely Either-Or. Quantum mechanics admits a continuum of probabilities, and can often allow a Both-And. Where classical physics insists on impenetrability, which is a concomitant of exclusive space-occupancy, quantum mechanics allows the superposition of alternative states of affairs. This parallels a large part of our thought, which is Both-And. We often consider cumulative cases, with arguments on either side. These arguments continue to coexist: it is only when we have to decide, that we come down on one side or the other. The thinkers who in the early days of quantum mechanics suggested that electrons had free will, were misunderstanding what the physicists were trying to tell them. But the parallel between the process of making up one's mind, and a superposition of different states collapsing into one definite *eigen*state, is a genuine parallel, which has important implications for the nature of time.

§11.4 From von Neumann to Kochen-Specker

The marriage of discreteness and continuity gave issue in probability theory. Quantum mechanics uses probability theory, and needs the probabilities it uses to be objective probabilities, not cloaks for our partial ignorance of the exact composition of *ensembles*. John von Neumann had seen this, but his argument was not generally accepted, and in due course David Bohm faulted it by producing a hidden-variable theory none the less, and in 1966 John Bell showed which of von Neumann's assumptions could be challenged. Yet though von Neumann's actual argument could be faulted, it was not refuted: it was revealing the fundamental difficulty in adding hidden variables to quantum mechanics: the whole point of hidden variables was that they had values, and for any specified value either definitely did have, or definitely did not have, that particular value; quantum mechanics, on the other hand, was combining ideals of continuity with those of discreteness in its own idiosyncratic fashion, which could not accommodate the requirements of discreteness inherent in a hidden variable theory.

This is brought out by Gleason's Theorem,[8] which can be seen as a development and refinement of von Neumann's putative proof, and exploits the difficulty of introducing hidden variables, yielding discrete truth-values, into an essentially probabilistic theory. In ordinary quantum mechanics a system, $|\psi\rangle$, does not, unless it is an *eigen*-vector of some operator, *have* a definite value of that physical magnitude, but only a probability that IF the operator operates on the system, THEN the value of the physical magnitude would turn out to be one of the *eigen*-values of that operator. A hidden-variable theory claims that there is a hidden variable, λ, which together with $|\psi\rangle$ determines what the value of the dynamic variable is. It acts like a projection operator, picking out one *eigen*-value, and rejecting the others. But, provided that there are three or more possible *eigen*-values, it is impossible to do that consistently.

The proof is a topological one, turning on the impossibility of *continuously* mapping a *discrete* set onto a *connected* surface. Then there cannot be a smooth transition for occasions when a physical magnitude, say energy, has one definite value, say 12 electron volts to occasions when it has another, say 16 electron volts; there will have to be jumps.

---

[8] C.Piron, *Foundations of Quantum Physics*, New York, 1976, p.86.

§11.4   *Quantum Mechanics*   315

An intuitive way of seeing that this cannot be,[9] is to picture the inside of a three-dimensional sphere: a projection operator is like a set of orthogonal axes, that is, three diameters at right angles to one another, one of them picking out two preferred antipodal points (which could be coloured red) and the other two marking the two antipodal pairs of rejected points (which could be coloured blue). Then if the North and South Poles were red, the whole equator would have to be blue; similarly for any other pair of antipodal points, there would have to be a great circle of blue points, and we should be unable to place enough red points, to get each set of diameters at right angles to one another having one of the diameters on red.

Gleason's theorem can be proved rigorously, though the assumptions on which their proof is based, can be questioned. The argument given by Kochen and Specker is likewise rigorous,[10] but formidably difficult to follow, involving 117 different unit vectors, which cannot all be coloured so that any triad of orthogonal axes will have one red and two blues. This is an argument where the path of wisdom is not to try and make the argument one's own, but to accept it on the authority of the many clever and dedicated men who have examined it closely, and found no fault in it.[11]

Even the Kochen-Specker proof can be evaded if we impose sufficiently radical surgery on our normal understanding of science. Many physicists have tried to formulate a version of quantum mechanics which is determinist while remaining faithful to the facts, This can be done—in a manner of speaking. We can formulate the following "Hidden Variable Theory".

---

[9] Due to F.J.Belinfante, *A Survey of Hidden-Variable Theories*, Oxford, 1973, pp.38-39, a fuller discussion is given on pp.63-67; see also M.L.G.Redhead, *Incompleteness, Non-Locality and Realism*, 1st ed., Oxford, 1987, pp.124-125.

[10] S.Kochen and E.Specker "The Problem of Hidden Variables in Quantum Mechanics", *Journal of Mathematics and Mechanics*, **17**, 1967, pp.293-328.; reprinted in C.A.Hooker, ed., *The Logico-Algebraic Approach to Quantum Mechanics*, vol.1, Dordrecht, 1975.

[11] For a careful, but intelligible, exposition of these arguments, see M.L.G.Redhead, *Incompleteness, Non-locality and Realism*, Oxford, 1987 and 1989, ch.1, §1.5, pp.27-30, and ch.5, §5.1, pp.119-131; I am greatly indebted to this work.

> **Spoof Hidden Variable Theory**
>
> The state of a quantum system is given by
>
> 1. a ket vector $|\psi\rangle$, and
> 2. a hidden variable λ.
>
> λ takes positive integral values
> For any dynamical variable ("observable") A, with associated operator $\hat{A}$, and *eigen*–values $a_1, a_2, a_3, \ldots$ [ordered by magnitude]
> the A-value of $(|\psi\rangle, \lambda)$ is a_λ
>
> This is fully determinate: for any system we can tell what the value of λ was by making a measurement, and seeing which *eigen*–value emerged. Admittedly, we do not have a law of development; the Schrödinger equation tells us how $|\psi\rangle$ evolves, but not how λ does—but one cannot have everything.

This spoof hidden variable theory fails because there is no law of development for the hidden variable, λ. The theory allows us to say what λ *was*, after the event, but not what λ is going to be, before we measure it; λ is a dangler; it has no grip on the theory, it plays no part, except to register what we already know *ex post facto*. A hidden variable theory can be constructed, provided we sufficiently relax the conditions on what constitutes a respectable theory, but at the cost of their credibility. In order to be a genuine hidden-variable theory, a theory must satisfy various criteria, which for the most part have not been fully formulated, and often are only recognised when a theory emerges which seems unsatisfactory in some respect. It is only because we have implicit standards of what can properly count as a theory, that we can say that serious theories with hidden variables are inconsistent with quantum mechanics.

If we accept that quantum mechanics is not going to be supplanted or supplemented, the implications for philosophy are momentous. In the first place we are led, as we have seen,[12] to objective probabilities for singular propositions, and hence to reject projectivism in one of its most favourable cases. Probabilities cannot always be explained as projections of our partial confidences, nor swept aside as a merely statistical property of frequencies found

---

[12] See above, §5.6.

in *ensembles*, but are to be ascribed objectively either as generalised truth-values to singular propositions, or as propensities to particular quantum-mechanical systems. It tells against projectivism generally. Although we still *can* explain secondary qualities and values as the projections of our sense-experience or attitudes onto a colourless, valueless real world, the argument for our doing so for reasons of metaphysical economy no longer applies.[13]

Secondly, if quantum mechanics requires objective probabilities, it cannot be completely determinist. For many physical properties—the mass of non-radioactive elements, the position of material objects, the movement of the planets—predictions can be made with an overwhelming probability of their coming true, but for some physical properties there will be a non-negligible probability of their becoming this, and a non-negligible probability of their becoming that. And sometimes it will make a significant difference which way they turn out. If our fundamental physical theory is not deterministic, many Laplacian arguments, which seem to undermine the autonomy of different types of explanation, can no longer be sustained.[14]

Quantum mechanics is philosophically important because:
1. It refutes projectivism.
2. It refutes determinism.

---

[13] See above, §5.7.

[14] See below, §13.2.

§11.5 From EPR via JSB to GHZ

Einstein was a determinist. He did not believe that God played dice. In the positivist atmosphere of the 1930s, and against the background of the widespread (mis-)understanding of Heisenberg's Uncertainty Principle[15] a realist construal of objective probabilities seemed implausible, and in view of the extreme difficulty in making sense of "the collapse of the wave function" the force of von Neumann's argument was parried.

Einstein tried to prove the existence of hidden variables—and paved the way for a further argument showing them to be impossible. In his original example he considered two particles, initially together which then separated to be at some considerable distance from each other.[16] By measuring the momentum of one, we could, thanks to the conservation of momentum, know the momentum of the other. But we could also measure the position of the other, and hence know both its position and its momentum, contrary to the Heisenberg Uncertainty Principle. This seemed to show that although quantum mechanics was not able in general to *measure* both the position and the momentum of a particle at any one time, it made sense to *ascribe* both. Each particle *had* a definite position and a definite momentum, even though we could not measure them both at once. And from this it would follow that quantum mechanics was in some sense incomplete: there was a fact of the matter—"an element of physical reality"—which went beyond the purview of quantum mechanics. This argument supported the then prevailing view that quantum mechanics was like statistical mechanics: it gave useful, statistical information about what happened in a large number of cases, but fuller information about each individual particle was in principle available, and from it a completely deterministic account of its future trajectory could be calculated. The fuller information was comprised by the hidden variables, which, together with those already in use in quantum mechanics, would belong to a complete theory, containing quantum mechanics as a part.

---

[15] See below, §11.9.

[16] A.Einstein, B.Podolsky and N.Rosen, "Can Quantum-Mechanical Description of Reality be Considered Complete?", *Physical Review*, **47**, 1935, pp.777-780; reprinted in J.A.Wheeler and W.H.Zurek, eds., *Quantum Theory and Measurement*, Princeton, 1983, pp.138-141.

§11.5   *Quantum Mechanics*   319

Modern versions of the EPR (Einstein-Podolsky-Rosen) argument use examples based not on position and momentum, but on "spin"—a quantum-mechanical concept akin to polarization in classical optics. Two photons, which originally were together and polarized in some direction, are separated. When they are at a considerable distance from each other, and so, presumably, no longer interacting, each comes to a polaroid screen, which will either let it through or absorb it, always letting it through if the angle of polarization of the screen is the same as the angle of polarization of the photon, always absorbing it, if the angle of polarization of the screen is at right angles to the angle of polarization of the photon, and if the angle of polarization of the screen is at θ^o to the angle of polarization of the photon, having a probability of $cos^2\theta$ of getting through, and a probability of $sin^2\theta$ of being absorbed.[17] According to quantum mechanics the polarization of the two photons is correlated: that is to say, if the two polaroid screens are both set with their direction of polarization the same, then either both photons get through, or both photons are absorbed. This correlation is analogous to the assumption in the original EPR paper that the two particles had the same momentum, though in opposite directions. The correlation decreases if the polaroid screens are inclined to each other, and if they are at right angles, then a photon gets through one if and only if its partner does not get through the other. In general, if the polaroid screens are inclined to each other at an angle of θ^o, the probability of the photons either both getting through or both being absorbed is, $cos^2\theta^o$.

Einstein argued that this correlation could not be due to the polaroid screen on one side influencing the behaviour of the photon on the other side, and that it must be due to each photon having acquired some common property while they were interacting, which would account for their linked behaviour subsequently. But this cannot be so. If, for instance, each photon had the same direction of polarization, then IF the polaroid screens were both oriented to be aligned in that direction, we should, indeed, find that they both would let through photons from the same pair; and similarly IF they were both aligned at right angles to the direction of the photons' polarization, they both would absorb photons from

---

[17] I am greatly indebted to T.Maudlin, *Quantum Non-Locality and Relativity*, Oxford, 1994 and 2002, for this exposition.

the same pair: But if the polaroid screens were set at different angles to each other, discrepancies would inevitably occur, since their correlation, according to quantum mechanics, would depend *only* on the alignment of the screens with each other, while according to the hidden variable hypothesis, it should depend on the alignment of each screen with the supposed direction of polarization of the photon pair. The mathematics works out easily if we take each polaroid screen being aligned at an angle of $30°$, one clockwise and one anti-clockwise to the supposed direction of polarization of the photon pair, so that the screens are inclined at $60°$ to each other. Then, since $cos^2 60° = \frac{1}{4}$, and $cos^2 30° = \frac{3}{4}$, the probability of a pair of photons of both getting through or both being absorbed is only $\frac{1}{4}$ according to quantum mechanics, but would be $\frac{3}{4} \times \frac{3}{4}, = \frac{9}{16}$, were the hidden variable hypothesis true.

Against Einstein-Podolsky-Rosen

Quantum mechanics says that the results of making measurements on correlated entities depends *only* on the settings of the measuring apparatus.

The hidden-variable theory says that the results of making measurements on correlated photons depend on the direction of polarization of the photons as well as the settings of the measuring apparatus.

In some circumstances the supposed effect of the direction of polarization on the two results does not cancel out.

So the hidden-variable theory is incompatible with quantum mechanics.

It is for experiments to determine which is right.

This is only one example of a hidden variable account, and makes many assumptions which can be faulted. J.S. Bell produced an entirely general argument to show that no hidden variable account could be consistent with quantum mechanics.[18] Instead of considering correlated photons, whose passing through or absorption by a polaroid screen could be measured, Bell considered anti-correlated particles whose spin in a particular direction could be

---

[18] J.S.Bell, "On the Einstein Podolsky Rosen Paradox", *Physics*, 1, 1964, pp.195-200; reprinted in J.A.Wheeler and W.H.Zurek, eds., *Quantum Theory and Measurement*, Princeton, 1983, pp.403-408.

§11.5   Quantum Mechanics   321

measured; and instead of supposing that the hidden variable was the direction of polarization of the pair of photons, he merely supposed that there was *some* hidden variable λ, which might be a set of variables or even a set of functions, but which, for convenience sake, was represented as a single continuous variable. It was still the case that each measurement could yield just two possible results, which were symbolized as $+1$ and -1 (instead of "got through" and "absorbed"). Thus there were two measurements to be made, one on each particle, the results of which would depend on

1 the settings of the measuring device,

and, if the hidden variable hypothesis were true,

2 λ;

and the result of each measurement would be $+1$ or -1.

Bell considers the case where each measuring device can be set to measure spin in two directions, which we can represent by $\vec{a}$ and $\vec{a}'$ for the settings of measuring device A, and $\vec{b}$ and $\vec{b}'$ for the settings of measuring device B; Thus each particle could be measured in two ways, depending on the settings of the measuring devices. If the hidden variable hypothesis were true, the result of measuring will be a function of the hidden variable, λ, and of the setting, which we can represent as: $A(\lambda, \vec{a})$ or $A(\lambda, \vec{a}')$, and $B(\lambda, \vec{b})$ or $B(\lambda, \vec{b}')$. For the sake of conciseness, let us represent these results as a, a', b and b', and the joint results as $ab, a'b, ab'$ and $a'b'$, remembering that these are, according to the hidden variable theory, functions of λ. Now consider the value of

$$ab + a'b + ab' - a'b'.$$

It can be factorised as

$$a(b + b') + a'(b - b').$$

Each term is ± 1, so that either $(b+b') = 0$, or $(b-b') = 0$; hence the whole expression must have the value ± 2. If we take the modulus of this, we can say that the hidden variable theory assigns definite values to what would be the result of measuring the spin of the two particles, such that the function of those values:

$$|ab + a'b + ab' - a'b'| = 2.$$

But this result is inconsistent with quantum mechanics. According to quantum mechanics the correlation between the results of measuring the spin of two anti-correlated particles depends *only* on the settings of the measuring device, and if they are inclined at an angle of θ, the correlation is $cos^2\theta$. If, once again, we align two of the settings of the measuring devices, so that $\vec{a} = \vec{b}$, have $\vec{a}'$ inclined to $\vec{a}$ at an angle of $30°$ clockwise, and $\vec{b}'$ inclined to $\vec{b}$ at an angle of $30°$ anti-clockwise, so that $\vec{b}'$ is inclined to $\vec{a}'$ at an angle of $60°$, then $ab = -1$, $a'b = -\frac{3}{4}$, $ab' = -\frac{3}{4}$ and $a'b' = -\frac{1}{4}$ so that

$$|ab + a'b + ab' - a'b'| = 2\frac{1}{4}.$$

Bell's Argument

Quantum mechanics says that the results of making measurements on correlated entities depends *only* on the settings of the measuring apparatus.

Hidden-variable theories say that the results of making measurements on correlated entities depend on the value of the hidden variable as well as the settings of the measuring apparatus.

Bell constructed a function of the results of alternative measurements on an anti-correlated pair of entities. If these results depended on the value of a hidden variable, they would be confined between certain limits. But for certain pairs of alternative measurements, quantum mechanics yields values outside those limits.

Contrary to the EPR argument, quantum mechanics with regard to some functions *is* complete. There is no room to insert a hidden variable.

Since Bell's original paper, there have been many variants put forward, with different assumptions and simpler working.[19] In particular, Greenberger, Horne and Zetlinger have devised a proof involving three particles that avoid some of the doubts and difficulties

---

[19] See for example, J.F.Clauser, M.A.Horne, A.Shimony, and R.A.Holt, *Phys.Rev.Lett.* **23**, 1983, pp.880 ff.; P.Heywood and M.L.G.Redhead, *Fund. Phys.*, **13**, 1983, pp.481 ff.; A.Stairs, *Philosophy of Science*, **50**, 1983, pp.587 ff.; H.R.Brown and G.Svetlichny, *Found. Phys.*, **20**, 1990, pp.1379 ff.; R.Penrose, *Shadows of the Mind*, Oxford, 1994, pp.246-249.

raised by earlier versions.[20] But the arguments are difficult. Although we can be clear about what quantum mechanics predicts, it is harder to get a grip on hypothetical hidden variable theories. In particular we may well suspect that the Bell Inequality involves multiplying numbers which could only be elicited under incompatible conditions. If the measuring device A is set at $\vec{a}$, it cannot be set at $\vec{a}'$, and so the expression $|ab + a'b + ab' - a'b'|$ is a nonsense. But that is to misconstrue the nature of the argument. The argument is a *Reductio ad Absurdum*. The hypothesis is that some hidden variable theory is true, rather than quantum mechanics. And in a hidden variable theory each particle had definite properties, whether or not they are measured. On that basis it would be perfectly acceptable to consider what would be the result of measuring a property, even if the measurement is not, and cannot be, carried out. Hidden variables confer counter-factual legitimacy. So, granted the assumption of there being some hidden variable, there are, under any conditions, definite values $\vec{a}$ and $\vec{a}'$ at any given time, even if we cannot discover what they both are. Hence also, IF some hidden variable theory is true, THEN $|ab + a'b + ab' - a'b'|$ is not a nonsense, and has a definite value, which is inconsistent with some particular predictions of quantum mechanics.

Any standard hidden variable theory makes predictions which are different from those made by quantum mechanics for some of the possible settings of the measuring device. It could, of course, be that quantum mechanics was wrong—not merely incomplete, as Einstein supposed, but definitely wrong. Experiments to decide between quantum mechanics and a hidden variable theory were difficult to conduct, but finally Aspect and his collaborators in Paris were able to devise one that excluded the possibility of some communication between the measuring devices at the speed of light, and was sensitive enough to allow for inefficiencies in the measuring devices. The results were inconsistent with hidden variable theories, and vindicated quantum mechanics.[21] The results, though

---

[20] D.M.Greenberger, M.A.Horne, and A.Zetlinger, "Going Beyond Bell's Theorem", in *Bell's Theorem, Quantum Theory, and Conceptions of the Universe*, ed.M.Kafatos, Dordrecht, 1989, pp.69-72; L.Hardy, *Phys.Rev. Lett.*, **68**, 1992, pp.2981 ff.

[21] A.Aspect, J.Dalibard, G.Roger, "Experimental Tests of Bell's Inequalities, using time-varying analyzers", *Physical Review Letters*, **49**, 1982, pp.1804-1807.

not absolutely conclusive—further experiments might yield other results—seem decisive.[22] In any case quantum mechanics has been confirmed by other experimental observations to a very high degree of accuracy. Any theory to supplant or supplement quantum mechanics needs to have very strong credentials. These are conspicuously lacking in those that call in question the assumptions on which either the Aspect experiment or the Kochen-Specker proof is based.

The EPR argument, intended to show that quantum mechanics was incomplete, and needed to be supplemented by a hidden variable theory, achieved the opposite, proving that quantum mechanics was as complete as possible, that no reasonable hidden variable theory could be true, that quantum mechanics was through and through probabilistic, and hence that physical determinism must be false.

In Brief

Quantum mechanics cannot be supplemented by a hidden varible because:
1. They won't fit in; we cannot paint discrete truth-values onto a continuum of possible probabilities
   (von Neuman, Gleason and Kochen-Specker).
2. There is no room for them; (Bell and Aspect).

But there is an even more surprising import of Bell's argument and Aspect's experiment: quantum mechanics is not only indeterminist, but is also non-local.

[22] See R.Penrose, *Shadows of the Mind*, Oxford, 1994, pp.247-248.

§11.6 Non-locality

The Einstein-Podolsky-Rosen argument assumed the Principle of Locality: the behaviour of one particle could not be influenced by the setting of a distant measuring device. Aspect's experiment took great pains to exclude influences propagated with the speed of light. The result of his experiment showed that, even when apparently separated, the two particles still formed one entangled quantum state. It might be possible to explain this by positing some curious topology for quantum-mechanical systems, whereby apparently distant entities were really quite close to each other,[23] but failing that, we should have to allow some instantaneous or almost instantaneous transmission of information, quite contrary to the thrust of Einstein's Special Theory.

It is easy to misunderstand this result. Some people have thought that we could construct a "Bell telephone", by means of which we could send "unstoppable and unjammable" messages faster than light.[24] But we cannot choose what message to send. We can only choose what question to ask about the quantum-entangled system: we can choose which direction to set our spin detector; that is, we can choose whether to ask "Is it spin up or spin down? in the direction that points towards the Pole Star?", or "Is it spin up or spin down? in the direction that points towards Sirius?", or "Is it spin up or spin down? in the direction that points towards Betelgeuse?", or in any other direction we like, but we cannot choose what answer we shall get. And it is only the answer, together with the question that it is the answer to, that determines the answer given a long way off to a similar question. Aspect's experiments do not show that there is "action at a distance", but only "passion at a distance".[25]

Even though the non-locality revealed by Aspect's experiments does not reinstate action at a distance, it has significant implications, some of them disturbing. If locality is not required in quantum mechanics, neither need it be required of hidden variable theories intended to supplement quantum mechanics. The deterministic theories devised by Bohm *are* consistent with quantum

---

[23] As in Minkowski spacetime; see above, §10.3.

[24] See N.D.Mermin, *Physics Today*, April 1985, p.38.

[25] I owe this phrase and much else to M.L.G.Redhead, *Incompleteness, Non-locality and Realism*, Oxford, 1987; and 1989.

mechanics, operating with "pilot waves" to guide the particles into the right paths. And even the Kochen-Specker contradiction could be escaped at the cost of further non-locality assumptions.[26] These theories are generally rejected out of hand, for failing to meet our normal requirements of what a theory should be, much as the spoof hidden variable theory of §11.4 would be rejected as unworthy of serious attention. But if quantum mechanics itself is non-local, why should we not accept alternatives to quantum mechanics that are no more bizarre?

But non-locality is not bizarre—not unless Newton's theory of gravitation was bizarre. Admittedly, Action at a Distance was felt to be a blemish, but one that could be accepted, given the theory's intellectual elegance and empirical support. It was only in the Twentieth Century, with the advent of Einstein's Special and General Theories, that the principle of locality was elevated into an absolute principle. Aspect's experiments force us to re-think again. Locality assumptions have two functions in scientific thought. They tell us of the relative unimportance of distant factors, and require that all causal influences be mediated through intervening distances by some process. The former is important when we are trying to isolate a cause and effect:[27] the latter is a regulative principle we have for an explanation's being satisfactory. More generally, we can see them as the spatial surrogates of the analytical method. Analysis yields understanding by concentrating on the parts separately. If they are spatial parts, concentrating on any one means not attending, or not attending very much, to any other. And this will not lead to our ignoring relevant factors so long as any influence distant factors have is mediated through the part under our immediate observation. Locality assumptions hold out a promise of explicability, and provide a means of accommodating extraneous influences, but are not essential to science. Newton's law of gravitation flouted it, and if Aspect's results can be explained only as some form of passion at a distance, so be it.

Nevertheless, the violation of locality goes deep. It makes quantum mechanics appear to be much more holistic than other scientific theories, not just with regard to Aspect's experiment, but in

---

[26] M.L.G.Redhead, *Incompleteness, Non-Locality and Realism*, Oxford, 1987, pp.137-152.

[27] J.R.Lucas, *Space, Time and Causality*, Oxford, 1984, p.57.

§11.6   *Quantum Mechanics*   327

all cases of quantum entanglement. Quantum systems are typically not separable into their constituent parts, but have to be considered as a single whole. And that is an important message for the metaphysician. We cannot always follow Descartes' analytical method.[28] Valuable though it often is to analyse problems and things, considering each part separately, it cannot always yield the whole truth, and therefore should not be applied without regard to circumstance. We should follow Plato rather than Descartes, and recognise that the philosopher needs to be συνοπτικός (*sunoptikos*), taking the broad view as well as the narrow one on account of the inter-connectedness of things.

> **Bell and Aspect**
> Bell's argument and Aspect's experiments show not only that quantum mechanics is indeterminist,
> but that it is **non-local**.

Non-locality is important also for our understanding of time. Throughout the twentieth century it was widely believed that the Special Theory had demoted time. Not only was time merely one of four dimensions of spacetime, but the distinction between past, present and future depended on the choice of frame of reference. There were no hyper-planes of absolute simultaneity, and one observer might regard a distant event as present, another as past, and a third as something still to take place. The Special Theory, it seemed, constituted a conclusive argument against the importance of tense. But the "conclusive argument" depended on the premise that the speed of light was an absolute maximum. If superluminal speeds are possible, particularly if there are instantaneous transmissions of information, the argument against the reality of tense is broken; but further consideration is needed before we have a positive argument in favour.

---

[28] Descartes, *Discourse on Method*, Part II, tr. J.Veitch in Everyman ed., London, 1912, pp.15-16; E.Anscombe and P.T.Geach, *Descartes Philosophical Writings*, London, 1954, pp.20-21; J.Cottingham, R.Stoothoff, D.Murdoch, *Descartes: Selected Philosophical Writings*, Cambridge, 1988, p.120; AT VI p.18.

> Summary
>
> According to quantum mechanics the correlation between the results of measuring the spin of two anti-correlated particles depends *only* on the settings of the measuring device, and not on any value of a supposed hidden variable.
>
> If the measuring devices have a space-like separation, and are not influenced by any hidden variable, the propagation of causal influence between the measuring devices must be instaneous, or at least much faster than the speed of light.
>
> —oOo—
>
> Perhaps we should not mind it too much: perhaps the Special Theory concerns only electromagnetic phenomena, and the instantaneous transmission of influence is unobjectionable elsewhere in physics.

§11.7 The "Measurement Problem"*

Thought about quantum mechanics has been much confused by the so-called "Measurement Problem". It is a problem, but it is not primarily a problem about measurement, though we can see how in the intellectual atmosphere of the time, it came to be construed in terms of our assigning values to physical magnitudes.

One of the strongest arguments for the subjective view of probability was that it obviated the problem. A quantum state, or wave function, $|\psi\rangle$, is typically a superposition of different possible states, or wave functions, which, on a measurement being made, instantaneously or almost instantaneously collapses into a single one. It is difficult to make physical sense of this, but easy if the original $|\psi\rangle$ was a probabilistic characterization of an *ensemble*, with the measuring process giving fuller information about one particular member of the *ensemble*. Probability characterizations do not move at all, but can change instantaneously on receipt of

---

* In this section especially, as throughout this chapter generally, I am conscious of my ununderstanding of quantum mechanics. I stick my neck out at my peril. But if I am proved wrong, knowledge will have been advanced a little, whereas if I remain safely silent, my reputation may be intact, but ignorance will remain unabated.

§11.7   Quantum Mechanics   329

new information. I may know that a colleague is either in his rooms in college or else in the Bodleian library, and so the corresponding probability distribution is concentrated on his being in these two areas. If I then telephone him in college, and he answers the phone, the probability distribution for his being in the library immediately vanishes, and that for his being in his room increases to unity. But it would be absurd to say that one part of the probability distribution had instantaneously travelled from the library into the college, up the stairs and into his room. The instantaneous collapse of the wave function is not due, on this interpretation of quantum mechanics, to something's moving with a speed greater than that of light, because a wave function is only a probability, and a probability is not a thing at all.

The subjective view of probability looked like working for those quantum interactions which take place when we were measuring some physical magnitude of a quantum system, since in that case our concern is only with information, and if $|\psi\rangle$ gave only the probability distribution of an *ensemble* of similar particles, there would be no need to speak of an instantaneous motion of anything. But most quantum interactions are not measurements. We measure quantum systems only occasionally, but they are interacting all the time. When we think about quantum mechanics, we too readily abstract from the messiness of real life, and consider ideal cases, artificially isolated from outside interference. These are illuminating, but untypical. Except in carefully designed experiments, quantum systems are constantly subject to interference, and being made to interact with other systems. When they do, they become entangled, and often "collapse" into an *eigen*-state of the interfering system. In physics laboratories, it may well be a measuring device, with *eigen*-states corresponding to the *eigen*-values of the physical magnitude being measured. Outside physics laboratories, where the interfering system has not been carefully designed, its *eigen*-states may be entirely different from those of any measuring device ever designed, and may have *eigen*-values of no interest to any physicist.

Whether or not the interfering process is designed to elicit a measurement, there is a problem: the system evolves discontinuously—the "collapse of the wave function"; instead of being a superposition of many different *eigen*-functions, it jumps into being a single *eigen*-function, contrary to the Schrödinger equation, which prescribes continuous development. It is difficult to make sense of this. Roger Penrose suggests that the effect of gravitation is responsible: if gravitation is expressed as in the General Theory as a curvature of spacetime, it is intuitively plausible that a superposition of two differently curved spacetimes is unsustainable, and must result in one or the other being actualised. Adding second-order terms to the Schrödinger equation, might represent the effect of gravitation;[29] Others have suggested that the universe is filled with mini-projectiles, which knock the system off course and into an *eigen*-state;[30] an intuitively more acceptable account invokes the "Gambler's Ruin" of probability theory.[31] But probability theory can be invoked in a different respect.[32] We talk of probabilities as though they were precise, but recognise in our use of them that they are imprecise. We give odds of three to one, but do not think to distinguish them from a marginally different figure; if there is a fifty-fifty chance of something happening, we often will put in an 'about'. Nor is this only a matter of uninformed usage. The inference from frequencies to probabilities will not go through unless we are ready to identify truth with the *neighbourhood* of 1, and falsity with the *neighbourhood* of 0.[33] If we accept that probabilities are blurred concepts, we can see that in an interaction with a large system, there will be many, many *eigen*-vectors, so that the state-vector of the system is likely to come into the neighbourhood of some *eigen*-vector. We can picture the state-vector as a search-light beam. The beam moves. It is not a single ray, but a narrow pencil, with the light-intensity falling off rapidly at the edge. If the penumbra, so to speak, of the beam lights up an enemy aeroplane, the beam locks onto it with full intensity. Similarly, if the state-vector of a system comes into the neighbourhood of an

---

[29] Roger Penrose, *The Emperor's New Mind*, Oxford, 1989, and *Shadows of the Mind*, Oxford, 1994.

[30] G.C.Ghirardi, A.Rimini, and T.Weber, *Physical Review* D, **34**, 1986, pp.470ff.

[31] Philip Pearle, "Combining stochastic dynamical state-vector reduction with spontaneous localization", *Physical Review* A, **39**, 1989, pp.2277-2289.

[32] See, more fully, J.R.Lucas, "Prospects for Realism in Quantum Mechanics", *International Studies in the Philosophy of Science*, vol.9, no.3, 1995, pp.225-234.

[33] See above, §5.4.

§11.7   *Quantum Mechanics*   331

eigen-vector, it locks on to the *eigen*-vector. In most cases the difference, both then and subsequently, in the development of the state-vector is minuscule, but in those cases where a measurement is really being made, the accompanying difference can be great. Although the projection of the state vector of the whole interacting system plus measuring apparatus onto the small Hilbert sub-space of the system alone may initially lie well away from the projection of the *eigen*-vector, yet the small displacement in the large Hilbert space of the combined system (the whole interacting system plus measuring apparatus) may rapidly lead to the state-vector of the small system aligning itself along an *eigen*-vector.

The "locking on" metaphor is suggestive, but still only a metaphor. Since the Schrödinger equation is deterministic and preserves solid angles, something more is needed to give substance to *locking on*. Sir Michael Dummett outlines an Intuitionist logic for a fuzzy realism which may be appropiate to quantum states.[34] Alternatively, Philip Pearle's "Gambler's Ruin" provides a bridge from continuity to discontinuity. If stochastic processes are continually taking place between different *eigen*-vectors, then generally and in the large, the results will mirror the initial probabilities, but occasionally an unlucky one will be ruined, and forced out of the game. This would happen appreciably often only when probabilities in the neighbourhood of 0 or 1 were involved.

Thus far, we have only considered a conceptual argument about probabilities. We may ask if there is anything physical to say. We need to consider not Hilbert space, but Schrödinger's wave mechanics. Instead of a searchlight beam being nearly aligned with an *eigen*-vector, we should have a wave function and a Fourier expansion of it with one of the terms having a frequency very close to that of the wave function itself. We are familiar with closely adjoining frequencies. In the old amplitude-modulated (AM) sets one could hear, besides the intended station, the output of others with neighbouring frequencies. The wireless set could resonate to them, and if the amplitude was being altered, could select them out of the incoming radio wave. In the quantum case the interacting

---

[34] See M.A.E.Dummett, *Thought and Reality*, Oxford, 2006; "Is time a Continuum of Instants?", *Philosophy*, **75**, 2000, pp.510-515. Dummett's general argument against physical magnitudes' having precise real-number values is unconvincing: but that is no reason why some should not be imprecise.

system has very many *eigen*-frequencies, and it is likely that there is one sufficiently close to that of the ψ-function for it to resonate so strongly as to become the sole resonating frequency.[35]

To return from these highly speculative speculations: quantum-mechanical systems are interacting all the time, and so their wave functions are collapsing all the time. Schrödinger's cat is not left as a superposition of dead cat and alive cat until the experimenter looks in to see how she is: the whole experimental set-up is not—cannot be—properly isolated from outside interference, and is being continually bombarded by cosmic rays, gamma rays, visible light and physical vibrations. Throughout the experimental period the superposition of the two cat states is being made to collapse: a cat-alive one if no radium atom has disintegrated and set off the apparatus; and a cat-dead one if the apparatus has been triggered, and the hydrogen cyanide released. No superposition could exist in the real world for more than a few nanoseconds without being interfered with by some adventitious factor and shaken down into some *eigen*-state or other.

If quantum-mechanical systems are continually being confronted by a moment of truth, when various possibilities are winnowed out, leaving one definite state of affairs, there is an ontological difference between the future and the present and past. Although I may not know it—may be unable to know it—there is a definite fact of the matter, whether some atom in Betelgeuse has or has not emitted a photon. The date I should ascribe to it, in order to have my theory of electromagnetism working smoothly, may depend on the frame of reference adopted. But as of now, the atom either has or has not emitted a photon: If it has not, the emission is still in the future; if it has, the emission is either present or past.

On a realist construal of quantum mechanics, then, there is a real, world-wide distinction of tenses. Although according to the Special Theory there is no hyper-plane of absolute simultaneity, the Special Theory takes account only of electromagnetic phenomena. If we are to take account of quantum mechanics also, we see a

---

[35] Other resolutions of the measurement problem have been suggested, most notably the Many-Worlds interpretation: but it is deeply implausible—it flouts Ockham's razor to an extravagant degree.

> **Quantum mechanics is philosophically important because:**
> 1. It refutes projectivism.
> 2. It refutes determinism.
> 3. It vindicates tense.

world-wide hyper-surface[36] of simultaneity, as interacting quantum mechanical systems come to have definite *eigen*-values for their physical magnitudes instead of a probabilistic spread of possible values. Tense is real.

§11.8 Knowing and Being

The corpuscularian philosophy took no account of the problem of knowledge: Newton thought of space as the *sensorium* of God, with God knowing where everything was by immediate apprehension. The universe was bathed in divine omniscience, and we were encouraged to take a God's-eye view of the world, in which we were concerned about how things were, but not about how we could come to know them. Quantum mechanics, by contrast, is all the time raising the question "How do we know?". It arose originally to accommodate difficulties in explaining radiation, the interaction between matter (very ontological) and radiation (light-like: rather epistemological); and works with "operators", representing interactions with potential observers, rather than the observer-independent evolution of states. Of course, there are observer-independent states, the ψ states on which the operators operate. But the ψ states are remote from observation. We can posit their existence, but we cannot say what they are, unless they are operated on, when they seem to jump into an *eigen*-state of that operator.

There is a great range of questions we can ask: "Where is it?", "What is its momentum along the X-axis?" "What is its angular momentum around the X-axis?" "What is its energy?", and

---

[36] In Newtonian mechanics it is a hyper-plane: hyper because it is three-, not two-dimensional; plane because Newtonian dates are entirely independent of position. If Einstein's General Theory is accepted, Spacetime is not everywhere flat, so that the hyper-surface separating the future from the past is not a hyper-plane.

> ### Classical *v.* Quantum approach
> Classical physics offered a reasonably clear ontology, but no epistemology. Newton took a God's-eye view of the universe, knowing by immediate omniscience where each point-particle was, and what its velocity was. The question "How do we know?" was unaddressed, and unanswerable. Quantum mechanics by contrast includes the interaction between knower and known as part of what it has to account for.

very many more. To any such question there will be a definite answer; but the answer will not tell us what value the system had in respect of that magnitude immediately before the question was asked. Immediately before the question was asked, the system had only various probabilities of giving some one of the definite values (*eigen*-values) allowed by that question. Operating on the system—asking the question—forces the system to get into an *eigen*-state of the operator—to give a definite answer by ticking one of the boxes provided on the questionnaire. Whereas in classical corpuscularianism coming to know the state of a system did not seriously affect what the state of the system actually was,[37] in quantum mechanics the process of coming to know does alter the state of what was known. After the alteration the system will have some definite *eigen*-value of the operator that brought about the alteration: that is, from the system there will have been elicited a definite answer to the question asked. The answer will tell us what the state of the system is then, as a result of the question being asked, but not what it was before the question was asked.

---

[37] Thus Niels Bohr, *Essays 1958-1962 on Atomic Physics and Human Knowledge*, London, 1963, p.59: Ultimately, this viewpoint rests on the fineness of our senses, which for perception demands an interaction with the objects under investigation so small that in ordinary circumstances it is without appreciable influence on the course of events. In the edifice of classical physics, this situation finds its idealized expression in the assumption that the interaction between the object and the tools of observation can be neglected or, at any rate, compensated for.

§11.9 The Uncertainty Principle

The Uncertainty Principle is the best known corollary of quantum mechanics, but also widely misunderstood. Its name, and the first expositions of it, have made it appear to be an epistemological thesis, a limit on what can be known. We cannot know the precise position and momentum of a quantum mechanical entity, because our bumbling attempts at determining the position alter its momentum, and *vice versa*. But true though that may be, it does not go to the heart of the matter, for however skilful and unbumbling we were, we still could not determine the precise position and momentum of a quantum mechanical entity, because they are not there to be known. Not even God can know the precise position and momentum of a quantum mechanical entity. The trouble lies not in the apparatus—which might be improved—but in the questions, which exclude each other. It is like the problem we have tuning an old-fashioned, amplitude-modulated (AM), wireless. The more closely we tune in on a radio station, the more blurred the acoustic response, and *vice versa*. It is not just that our condensers and aerials are imperfect—though they are—but that all there is in reality is a very complicated radio wave which we can analyse in different ways. If we consider it as a very precise station frequency, we cannot register relatively rapid variations in amplitude, because they would constitute an alteration of the station's frequency. If, on the other hand, we want to take note of such acoustic variations of amplitude, we have to take account of frequencies in a band around that of the station, and thus may pick up unwanted messages from neighbouring stations. The difficulty lies not in the apparatus, but in the choices we make. So too with a quantum mechanical entity. The more we regard it as localised in one spot, the less we can ascribe a single definite momentum to it; and the more we see it as moving with a uniform speed, the more widely dispersed it seems, and less concentrated in any one position.

Since the Uncertainty Principle is not an epistemological one about the limits of our knowledge, but an ontological one, about the nature of the known, we ask how deeply it is embedded in quantum mechanics. At one level we can show how it emerges so far as position and momentum are concerned, from the position and momentum operators.[38]

---

[38] Readers who dislike formulae can safely skip the next paragraph.

The position operator, $\hat{X}$, is given by $\hat{X}|\psi\rangle = x|\psi\rangle$:
the momentum operator, $\hat{P}$, is given by $\hat{P}|\psi\rangle = -i\hbar\frac{\partial}{\partial x}|\psi\rangle$.
So
$$\hat{X}\hat{P}|\psi\rangle = x(-i\hbar\frac{\partial}{\partial x}|\psi\rangle),$$
and
$$\hat{P}\hat{X}|\psi\rangle = -i\hbar\frac{\partial x}{\partial x}|\psi\rangle - x(i\hbar\frac{\partial}{\partial x}|\psi\rangle).$$
Hence
$$\hat{X}\hat{P}|\psi\rangle - \hat{P}\hat{X}|\psi\rangle$$
$$= x(-i\hbar\frac{\partial}{\partial x}|\psi\rangle) - (-i\hbar\frac{\partial x}{\partial x}(|\psi\rangle) - x(i\hbar\frac{\partial}{\partial x}|\psi\rangle))$$
$$= +i\hbar|\psi\rangle,$$
or, leaving out the $|\psi\rangle$,
$$\hat{X}\hat{P} - \hat{P}\hat{X} = i\hbar.$$

From this we can see that the uncertainty principle is a concomitant of quantum mechanics having the *operators* it has. So far as the $|\psi\rangle$-functions are concerned, all is determinate, just as are the wireless waves outside the house. It is the way the macro world, for example our apparatus, interacts with them that produces the ambiguity. If we adopt the Hilbert-space model, we can locate the trouble in different operators having different sets of orthogonal axes associated with their *eigen*-vectors. Operators with the same set of orthogonal axes commute: roughly we can say that as a result of the first operator, the system is in an *eigen*-state of that operator, and on applying the second operator, since the system is already in an *eigen*-state of that operator too, it remains so.

More carefully,[39] if the two operators, $\hat{F}$ and $\hat{G}$, have the same *eigen*-functions, we can expand the $|\psi\rangle$-function as a sum of those *eigen*-functions:
$$|\psi\rangle = \sum a_n|\psi\rangle_n,$$
and work out the result of operating first with $\hat{G}$ and then with $\hat{F}$:
$$\hat{F}\hat{G}|\psi\rangle = \hat{F}\hat{G}\sum a_n|\psi_n\rangle = \hat{F}\sum a_n\hat{G}|\psi_n\rangle = \hat{F}\sum a_n g_n|\psi_n\rangle$$

---

[39] Readers who dislike formulae can again safely skip this paragraph.

§11.9 Quantum Mechanics 337

$$= \sum \hat{F} a_n g_n = \sum a_n g_n f_n.$$

If we then work out the result of operating first with $\hat{F}$ and then with $\hat{G}$:

$$\hat{G}\hat{F}|\psi\rangle = \hat{G}\hat{F}\sum a_n|\psi_n\rangle = \hat{G}\sum a_n \hat{F}|\psi_n\rangle = \hat{G}\sum a_n f_n|\psi_n\rangle$$

$$= \sum \hat{G} a_n f_n = \sum a_n f_n g_n,$$

we see that the result is the same, since f_n and g_n are real numbers, and their product is the same irrespective of their order.

Thus we see that all operators would commute if they all had the same *eigen*-vectors, but only then; that is, only if there were a preferred set of axes in Hilbert space, corresponding to a preferred set of frequencies for the wave functions. We are led then to wonder whether there could be a theory analogous to quantum mechanics, but having all the operators commuting. There is no compelling reason for thinking that Hilbert space should be axes-indifferent. And thinkers have speculated that there might be some "unique basic rhythm of the universe".[40] If this speculation is rejected—and the fact is that position and momentum operators do not commute— and we suppose the underlying waves to be as amorphous and featureless as possible, it follows not only that there are non-commutating operators in quantum mechanics, but, what is often not sufficiently recognised, that there are more than just two families. It is not just that position and momentum are "complementary", but that in general eliciting the value of one classical physical magnitude precludes eliciting the value of many other classical physical magnitudes, which often are similarly "incompatible" among themselves.

We are led also to speculate on the connexion between the operators and the classical physical magnitudes (or dynamical variables) the values of which the operators elicit. Why does $-i\hbar\frac{\partial}{\partial x}|\psi\rangle$ tell us what the momentum, $\hat{P}$, of a system is? The short answer is that it is a carry-over from classical mechanics when articulated in its Hamiltonian form. Only if we have the operators we do have, will the physical magnitudes they elicit from the underlying quantum states have the relations with one another they need to have, if they are to be plausibly identified with the classical physical magnitudes we already know. There is force in this contention: but still it leaves us hankering after a deeper explanation yet to be discovered.

---

[40] G.J.Whitrow, *The Natural Philosophy of Time*, Edinburgh, 1961, ch.1, p.46. See below, §12.8.

§11.10 Nullary Qualities

There are very many self-adjoint Hermitian operators that could operate on a ψ-function, or $|\psi\rangle$, and elicit one out of the set of *eigen*-values for that operator. Only a few of them are of interest to contemporary physicists. The classical physical magnitudes are not quite the same as the primary qualities, and spin is altogether a newcomer, though it might claim a distant parentage in Descartes' vortices.

The nullary qualities are not operators, but the characteristics of the ψ-functions, or $|\psi\rangle$ vectors, themselves. These are periodic functions (represented by rays in Hilbert space), which can be characterized in terms of a set of basic sinusoidal functions (or orthogonal axes in Hilbert space). There is no one preferred set of basic sinusoidal functions (or orthogonal axes in Hilbert space) but a wide variety of different ones, with different operators having their own set of basic sinusoidal functions (or orthogonal axes in Hilbert space). It follows that any characterization of basic sinusoidal functions (or orthogonal axes in Hilbert space) is not canonical, being no more fundamental than any other. The basic entities are the ψ-functions, (or $|\psi\rangle$ vectors) themselves, together with the fact that they *are* periodic (or that they are vectors in a *Hilbert* space).

It is easy to see that these entities are more abstract and remote from ordinary experience than the primary qualities of classical corpuscularianism, but more difficult to make out that they are more rational. Yet this can be argued. For whereas with the ordinary space of classical corpuscularianism, it appears to be a contingent question whether it is Euclidean or not,[41] with wave functions (or their Hilbert-space representation) it is built into the very concept of such a space that such a theorem should hold. Quantum mechanics is thus purer than classical corpuscularianism. Instead of primary qualities, it has periodic functions, which under Fourier analysis turn out to be subject to Parseval's theorem (or vectors in Hilbert space, likewise subject to a profound Pythagorean rule). And although we use the traditional trigonometric names, sine and cosine, in discussing periodic functions, they can be characterized purely mathematically, without any appeal to everyday geometry with its Euclidean presuppositions.

[41] See above, §9.7.

§11.10 Quantum Mechanics

The differential calculus gives us the general rule for the differential coefficient of x^n, namely

$$\frac{dx^n}{dx} = nx^{n-1}$$

which, conversely, gives us an easy rule for integrating all polynomials—except those of the form x^{-1}, that is to say, except those of the form $\frac{1}{x}$. Yet clearly there is such a function, $log(x)$, which can be defined in terms of its differential properties (by considering $\int_0^x \frac{dy}{y}$), and it has an inverse, $exp(x)$, which can be written e^x, where e is the base of natural logarithms, $2.71828\ldots$ Thanks to Taylor's theorem, we can expand the exponential function as Maclaurin's series:

$$e^x = x^0 + \frac{x}{1} + \frac{x^2}{1 \times 2} + \frac{x^3}{1 \times 2 \times 3} + \ldots + \frac{x^n}{n!},$$

(where $n! = n \times n-1 \times n-2 \times \ldots 3 \times 2 \times 1$)

We then consider the function e^{ix}, where $i = \sqrt{-1}$, which has the most remarkable property, discovered by Euler,

$$e^{i\pi} = -1,$$

from which it follows that $e^{2i\pi} = (e^{i\pi})^2 = 1$ and hence that $e^{(x+2ni\pi)} = e^x$. Thus we see that e^{ix} is a periodic function, with period 2π.

If we expand e^{ix} as Maclaurin's series, remembering that $i^2 = -1$, and separate the real and the imaginary parts, we have

$$e^{ix} = \left(1 - \frac{x^2}{2!} + \frac{x^4}{4!} \ldots \right) + i\left(x - \frac{x^3}{3!} + \frac{x^5}{5!} \ldots \right),$$

which mathematical readers will recognise as $\cos(x) + i\sin(x)$, or, as it is sometimes written, $cis(x)$; only, whereas the expansions of cos and sin are ordinarily derived from their trigonometrical properties, here the expansions are used to *define* the functions.

It is easy then to see that if we consider the expansion of e^{-ix}, since the real part consists entirely of even powers of x, it will be the same, that is $\cos(x)$, while the imaginary part will have all its signs reversed, but will otherwise be the same; that is it will be $-\sin(x)$. So $e^{-ix} = \cos(-x) + i\sin(-x) = \cos(x) - i\sin(x)$
Also since $e^{ix} \times e^{-ix} = e^{ix-ix} = 1$ it follows that

$$(\cos(x) + i\sin(x)) \times (\cos(x) - i\sin(x)) = \cos^2(x) + \sin^2(x) = 1,$$

which is normally taken to be an expression of Pythagoras' theorem in trigonometric terms. To this extent, then, quantum mechanics can claim that its entities are more rational than those of classical corpuscularianism or modern materialism.

> **Thanks to Euler**
>
> Euler's theorem (writing $\sqrt{-1}$ rather than i)
>
> $$e^{\sqrt{-1}\pi} = -1$$
>
> shows us:
> 1. that $e^{\sqrt{-1}\pi} \times e^{\sqrt{-1}\pi} = -1 \times -1 = +1$
>   so that $e^{2\sqrt{-1}\pi} = 1$
>   and hence that $e^{2n\sqrt{-1}\pi x} = e^{\sqrt{-1}x}$
>   that is to say $e^{\sqrt{-1}x}$ is a periodic function of x with period n;
>
> 2. that if we expand $e^{\sqrt{-1}x}$, separating its real and imaginary parts, as $cos(x) + \sqrt{-1}sin(x)$,
>   then since $e^{\sqrt{-1}x} \times e^{-\sqrt{-1}x} = e^{(1+-1)\sqrt{-1}x} = e^0 = 1$,
> $(cos(x) + \sqrt{-1}sin(x)) \times (cos(-x) + \sqrt{-1}sin(-x)) =$
> $(cos(x) + \sqrt{-1}sin(x)) \times (cos(x) - \sqrt{-1}sin(x)) =$
> $cos^2(x) + sin^2(x) = 1$,
>   which is the trigonometric version of Pythagoras' theorem, and can be generalised to any number (even an infinite number) of dimensions.
>
> The first gives a deep way of combining continuity with discreteness, the second a deep way of securing that probabilities add up to unity.
>
> > Thank you, Leonhard Euler

§11.11 Indiscernability and *Haecceitas*

Locke held impenetrability to be a primary quality. It caused difficulties, but played an essential role in individuating corpuscles. It was a key feature of corpuscles in classical corpuscularianism that each corpuscle could be individuated, having its own identity, and being in principle capable of being re-identified as the same corpuscle as it was before. Newton re-wrote Genesis to start with the sentence: In the beginning God created atoms and the void. Although all the corpuscles were, in classical corpuscularianism, qualitatively identical, they were numerically distinct, and could be distinguished from each other by the requirement that two corpuscles could not occupy the same position at the same time.

The atoms and molecules of classical mechanics give rise to Maxwell-Boltzmann statistics. In calculating the thermodynamic properties of gases, we count as two different cases the case in which this molecule is here and that molecule is there, and the case in which that molecule is here and this molecule is there. In quantum mechanics, however, such calculations give results which are not borne out by experiment. To get the right results we need to use Bose-Einstein (or Fermi-Dirac) statistics, in which we count as only one case that in which this photon is here and that photon is there, and that in which that photon is here and this photon is there. The natural interpretation is that photons, and other "Bosons", (and electrons and protons and other "Fermions"), are not entities to which the words 'this' and 'that' can be meaningfully applied. Indeed, as Bohr points out, "whenever customary ideas of the individuality of the particles can be upheld by ascertaining their location in separate spatial domains, all application of Fermi-Dirac and Bose-Einstein statistics is irrelevant . .".[42]

We are led to a similar conclusion by reflection on the Heisenberg Uncertainty Principle, for it precludes our being able to use the classical criterion for re-identification: if the position of a subatomic particle is sharply defined, its momentum, and hence its trajectory, is undefined, so that there is no spatio-temporal continuous path by means of which we can tell whether an entity at one time is the same as, or different from, an entity at another time.[43]

Bosons and fermions, then, lack "this-ness", or *haecceitas*, "haecceity", as Duns Scotus and the later Schoolmen called it. Although grammatically nouns, they have the logic of adjectives. If we are considering a photograph, we may well think that we would have a different photograph if that black patch were exchanged with this white one. But if that black patch were exchanged with this black one, we should not have a different photograph, but the same one. Instead of regarding them as particular particles, we should

---

[42] Niels Bohr, *Essays 1958-1962 on Atomic Physics and Human Knowledge*, London, 1963, p.91.

[43] For a much fuller account, in which alternative conclusions are explored, see Steven French, "Identity and Individuality in Classical and Quantum Physics", *Australasian Journal of Philosophy*, **67**, 1989, pp.432-446. See also Steven French, "Identity and Individuality in Quantum Theory" *Stanford Encyclopedia of Philosophy*, February 2000, http://plato.stanford.edu

think of them as excitations of a field: a field which is electronically excited here and electronically excited there does not become a different field if it is electronically excited there and electronically excited here.

A useful parallel is modern money. Although in the old days when all transactions were made by means of coins, it would have been possible to trace the history of an individual coin, it is impossible to do so now in the age of cheques and credit transfers. If I earn £100 from writing an article, and £100 from examining a thesis, and spend £100 on my electricity bill and £100 on my water bill, there is no saying which incoming £100 went to pay which utility bill. Lawyers use the word 'fungible' of goods whose whole point is the function they perform, and no distinction is made between numerically distinct items which perform the function equally well. If I borrow a pound of caster sugar from you, I have adequately discharged my debt by giving you a pound of caster sugar, even though it is not the self-same pound—which my family has eaten—but a pound of the same sort and quality. Money is a peculiarly apt comparison, since on account of its historical origin, it is invariably discrete. We can pay someone one hundredth of an American dollar, but not one seventh or one thousandth. Quantum mechanics is discrete too. Moreover, suitably favoured systems can sometimes run short-time overdrafts, and "borrow" enough energy from their neighbours to get them out of a hole.

Aristotle held that it was characteristic of substance that it could be referred to as 'this': Πᾶσα δὲ οὐσια δοκεῖ τόδε τι σημαίνειν (Pasa ousia dokei tode ti semainein).[44] And conversely what lacks individual identity lacks substantiality. The subatomic entities of quantum mechanics are not substances; they lack the hard reality of the corpuscles of classical corpuscularianism and the atoms of modern materialism. The ontological argument for materialism fails.[45] Although it remains true that we are made of matter, that truth is no longer the end of the story. Ultimately we are constituted not of separate impenetrable atoms, each pursuing its own path, as it collides or interacts with other atoms, but of a shimmering flux of superposed excitations, κυμάτων ἀνήριθμον γέλασμα (kumaton anerithmos gelasma), the innumerable laughter of waves.[46]

---

[44] *Categories*, 3b10.

[45] See below, §13.6.

[46] Aeschylus, *Prometheus* 90. Compare Keble's "many-tinkling smile of

> **Quantum mechanics is philosophically important because:**
> 1. It refutes projectivism.
> 2. It refutes determinism.
> 3. It vindicates tense.
> 4. It refutes classical materialism.

§11.12 Quantum Realism

The insubstantiality of quantum entities raises doubts about their reality, and has been taken by some to support some form of anti-realism. The fact that nullary qualities are more recondite than primary qualities, seems to tell against the reality of whatever it is that constitutes the stuff of quantum mechanics. Throughout the twentieth century philosophers have been drawn to instrumentalism when they try to think about quantum mechanics. Thus Sir Michael Dummett writes ". . . instrumentalists . . . . . regard theoretical entities as useful fictions enabling us to predict observable events; for them, the content of a theoretical statement is exhausted by its predictive power. This is one case in which the view opposed to realism is made more plausible by empirical results; for a realist interpretation of quantum mechanics seems to lead to intolerable antinomies."[47] But the antimonies are intolerable only if we take the primary qualities—the categories of classical corpuscularianism—as paradigms of reality. IF it is an essential mark of reality to be an individual located in space, to have a definite velocity, and to trace out a spatiotemporally continuous path in spacetime, then subatomic entities fail to be real. But so do the sounds and scents and colours of our everyday world. Scientists have to work hard to meet Berkeley's criticisms of their silent and colourless universe: and if by argument they can vindicate the claims of classical corpuscularianism and modern materialism to reality, they must allow the possibility of quantum mechanics'

> Ocean", and Einstein's more prosaic "There is no place in the new kind of physics for both the field and matter, for the field is the only reality." quoted by R.Sorabji, *Matter, Space and Motion,* London, 1988, p.40: and Millič Čapek, *The Philosophical Impact of Contemporary Physics,* Princeton, 1961, p.319.

[47] *The Logical Basis of Metaphysics,* London, 1991, p.6.

making good a similar claim to a comparable reality. Quantum systems do not have sharp values for both position and momentum at the same time, and this runs against our belief that real entities should have primary qualities. But once we go beyond primary qualities, there is no call on real entities to have them, any more than Newtonian atoms need to have determinate colours. Moreover, although quantum-mechanical states do not in general possess definite classical physical magnitudes, the ψ-function, $|\psi\rangle$, is perfectly determinate, and can be seen as an entirely determinate ray in Hilbert space, with a definite direction, or as a superposition of wave functions with different frequencies and different weights. It is just that the relevant description is not in terms of standard primary qualities, such as position and momentum. And even if the single ray is replaced by a slightly fuzzy beam, it is still moderately determinate. To this extent, then, quantum-mechanical entities have a faceable claim to reality.

Still, quantum mechanics does lack the inexorable grittiness of classical corpuscularianism and modern materialism, being indeterminist and lacking haecceity. But these, though they argue against determinist materialism, do not support a general anti-realism: rather, they shift the focus of realist concern upwards, from the sub-atomic entities themselves to the framework in which they operate. Instead of the time-dependent Schrödinger equation,

$$i\hbar\frac{\partial \Psi}{\partial t} = \hat{H}\Psi = -(\frac{\hbar^2}{2m})\Delta\Psi + U(x,y,z)\Psi,$$

we should consider the time-**in**dependent Schrödinger equation,

$$(\frac{\hbar^2}{2m})\Delta\Psi + [E - U(x,y,z)]\Psi = 0,$$

which tells not how the probabilities of a quantum-mechanical system develop, but what configurations of energy-levels are possible. It is these that give us an understanding of physics and chemistry. Spectroscopy and valency are not explained by the history of particular protons or electrons, but an understanding of the structures within which any photon or electron, that is, any photonic or electronic excitation of the field, must operate. Quantum mechanics not only leaves room for a different form of explanation, but positively requires it.

> **Quantum mechanics is philosophically important because:**
> 1. It refutes projectivism.
> 2. It refutes determinism.
> 3. It vindicates tense.
> 4. It refutes classical materialism.
> 5. It requires different levels of explanation.

§11.13 Quantum Philosophy

Quantum mechanics has been a two-edged sword in philosophy. At first it supported a subjective or frequency theory of probability, with no great break with the received view of modern materialism, but in the end it has entirely subverted these views, requiring an objectivist view of singular probability, and instantaneous, or almost instantaneous passion at a distance.

The syntax of the calculus of probabilities was determined by the need to marry Boolean and arithmetical algebra.[48] If the conjunction of any proposition p with the truth-value TRUE is to be p, the probability assigned to TRUE needs to be 1; and if the conjunction of any proposition p with the truth-value FALSE is to be FALSE, the probability assigned to FALSE needs to be 0. Further argument shows that we can, without loss of generality, subtract the probability from 1 to obtain the probability of the negation, have the multiplication rule generally for the conjunction of independent propositions or propositional functions, and the addition rule of the disjunction of mutually exclusive propositions or propositional functions. It follows that the probability of all the alternatives must add up to 1. Bernouilli's theorem and various Laws of Large Numbers also follow, leading to the conclusion that in a large *ensemble* the frequency of the various alternatives is likely to be approximately proportional to their probabilities. Proportions, expressed as fractions, add up to 1, and this made Einstein's interpretation of quantum mechanics appear eminently reasonable. Its failure forces us to rethink: instead of a number of different sorts of impenetrable, entirely separate, entities, we have a single entity, itself differently sorted; instead of proportions adding up to unity, we have the generalised Pythagoras' theorem:

$$cos^2\theta_1 + cos^2\theta_2 + \ldots cos^2\theta_n + \ldots = 1,$$

---

[48] See above, §5.3.

The general feel is inclusive rather than exclusive, elastic rather than rigid, holistic rather than exclusively analytical. Furthermore, although it may seem rather hard to accuse classical corpuscularianism and modern materialism of being static, there is a sense in which quantum mechanics is dynamic in comparison with them. Time is much less assimilated to space in quantum mechanics than in its predecessors: it characteristically turns up as an independent variable, most notably in the Schrödinger time-dependent equation, and it is tensed by the tide of collapse sweeping through the universe.

Quantum mechanics thus supports a metaphysics very different from that of classical corpuscularianism and modern materialism. Instead of the principle of impenetrability, it has that of superposition: instead of the hard **Either Or**, it accommodates **Both And**, allowing many different possibilities to co-exist until the moment of truth, when interaction forces a quantum mechanical system into an *eigen*-state, with a definite numerical value for the appropriate magnitude. It suggests a world of potentialities, the future being open to many different possibilities, some of which become actual in the present, remaining fixed and unalterable thereafter.

Quantum mechanics is metaphysically important because:

1. It represents a further stage in pushing back the explanation of things: no longer in terms of primary qualities, but of "nullary qualities".
2.
   (i) Instead of impenetrability, it has superposition,
   (ii) Instead of **Either Or**, it has **Both And**,
   (iii) Instead of proportions, it has Pythagoras' theorem.
3. Not just analytic, but holistic too.
4. Dynamic; takes time seriously.

Chapter 12
Time

§12.1 Time and Change
§12.2 Leibniz and Relationism
§12.3 Spacetime
§12.4 Time and Electromagnetism
§12.5 Tense and Modality
§12.6 Augustine, Instants and Intervals
§12.7 The Topology of Time
§12.8 The Metric of Time
§12.9 Time and Experience
§12.9 Tense and Reality

§12.1 Time and Change

The preceding two chapters vindicate our intuitive understanding of time. We are not obliged to filter out all sense of tense and transience in order to reach a proper conception of reality, as something invariant over time and person; because the need for non-subjectivity is met by covariance, and, provided we conjugate appropriately, we can do adequate justice to the existence of standpoints other than our own. Furthermore, conjugation is not only permissible but mandatory if we are to do justice to the modal implications of quantum mechanics. Any form of realism compatible with quantum mechanics must distinguish the merely possible future from the actual present and unalterable past. Even the austere physicist must have a tensed understanding of time. Nevertheless, time is under attack from many sides. The arguments are diverse, and need to be dealt with separately—and in some cases repetitiously—in order not only to buttress the reality of time, but to sharpen the distinction between time on the one hand, and change and cause and space and spacetime on the other, and to articulate the reasons why it has the topology and metric that it has.

Since time has links with many parts of our conceptual structure, some philosophers have thought that we could construct an adequate characterization of time not in purely scientific terms, but in terms of other basic concepts. Aristotle famously said that ὁ χρόνος ἀριθμός ἐστιν κινήσεως κατὰ τὸ πρότερον καὶ ὕστερον (*kineseos kata to proteron kai husteron ho chronos arithmos estin*) time is the number (he should have said μέτρον (*metron*), measure, for he was normally sensitive to the distinction) of change with respect to *before* and *after*.[1] But that is only a characterization of time, not an eliminative definition: 'with respect to *before* and *after*' shows that time is not said to be an aspect of change as such, but only that time is the *temporal* aspect of change.

Arguments Against Time

1. Time can be explained away in terms of change, or cause.
2. Time is just an order of events.
3. Time is just an aspect of Spacetime.
4. Time depends on Tense, and Tense is Egocentric.
5. The Special Theory shows that the distinction between past, present and future depends entirely on our choice of frame of reference.
6. The more we think about time, the more we realise that what we are thinking about takes no time at all.

We cannot define time simply in terms of change, for then we should not be able to distinguish one and the same poker being red at one spatial extremity and black at another from its being red at one time and black at another. Similarly, we may say of the sky that it is red, and we may say of the sky that it is not red but blue; and this may be because we are speaking of it on different occasions, but it may also be because it is red in the West, but blue in the East. We apply incompatible predicates to one and the same thing, and resolve the contradiction by distinguishing the two cases by some parameter, t. Although it is tempting to identify that parameter, t, with time, it does not have to be so: it could be space or direction.

Although we cannot distil from change a complete characterization of time, it is often held that change is a necessary concomitant of time. After all, how can we tell that time has passed, except by reference to some concomitant change—the movement of clock hands, the burning of a candle, the increasing pangs of hunger, the changing of the seasons, the fading of beauty? Even if I am

---

[1] *Physics* IV, 11, 220a25.

a solitary thinker, isolated from all external stimuli, I am still a process: if I am embodied, my bodily functions are going on, and in any case my thinking is an activity, and I turn my attention now to this, now to that, object of concern. It is difficult to portray change-less time, and tempting, therefore, to maintain that it cannot exist. Shoemaker, however, gives an entirely convincing argument for the possibility of time without change.[2] He imagines a tripartite world, in one part of which everyone and everything freezes into immobility every other year. In one of the remaining parts, everyone and everything freezes into immobility every third year, and in the other every fifth year. What happens after twenty nine years? A verificationist[3] would have to make out that the 31st of December of the 29th year was followed immediately by the 1st of January in what most people would take to be the 31st year.

The reason most people would give for rejecting the verificationist view was that it ran counter to the simplicity and regularity of natural laws. Three regular cycles of two years, three years and five years respectively are much simpler than the convoluted ones that except the years when the other two happen to coincide with the first. We have a choice. We can refuse to give any weight to rational considerations which point to anything beyond immediate empirical experience; but then will have no justification for any predictions or inferences to some recondite explanation: or we can ascribe some weight to canons of simplicity and regularity, and must then be ready to allow some inferences to some things that

---

[2] S.Shoemaker, "Time without Change", *Journal of Philosophy*, **66**, pp.363-381; reprinted in S.Shoemaker, *Identity, Cause and Mind*, Cambridge, 1984, and in R.Le Poidevin and M.MacBeath, *The Philosophy of Time*, Oxford, 1993, pp.63-79. See further, W.H. Newton-Smith, *The Structure of Time*, London, 1980, ch.2. I put forward a less convincing, though still, I think, cogent, argument in my *Treatise on Time and Space*, London, 1973, §2, pp.10-11.

[3] Aristotle's definition is generally taken to be based on verificationist assumptions: thus Shoemaker, *op.cit.*, pp.363ff.; W.H.Newton Smith, *The Structure of Time*, London, 1980, p.14; R.Sorabji, *Time, Creation and the Continuum*, London, 1983, p.74f.; E.Hussey, *Aristotle's Physics: Books III and IV*, Oxford, 1993, p.142; but this is contested by Ursula Coope, "Why does Aristotle say that There is No Time Without Change?", *Proceedings of the Aristotelian Society*, CI, 2001, pp.358-367.

cannot be empirically verified.[4] Once we abandon extreme empiricism, and allow some weight to rationality, we see that although we may need change in order to measure time, time does not need change in order to exist.

Changeless time implies Action after a Duration analogous to Action at a Distance. The same arguments apply. On the one hand we want to have time causally inefficacious, like space, in order that we can repeat experiments and observations, so as to establish causal connexions and natural laws: on the other we may be forced by empirical evidence to posit a theory in which the Principle of Locality does not hold, and causes can operate across a temporal duration or a spatial distance without any intervening process.[5]

As with space, we need to distinguish two different *desiderata*. It is a presupposition of repeatable experiments and observations, that a mere difference date should not signify. Results should be the same on Wednesdays as well as on Tuesdays, in September as well as in August, in Cambridge as well as in Dover. This requires date-indifference, as it does position-indifference. Time, like space, should be invariant under translation. Granted these essential symmetries of space and time, we can hope to discern causal connexions between natural phenomena, and discover natural laws, simply on the basis of many instances, and without any recourse to humane insight, so as to empathize with agents. If we go on to seek explanations, we are likely to look for local intermediate chains of causality. Action at a distance is an affront to our aspiration towards adequate explanation, but does not preclude our being able to discover the regular course of natural events. Newton's law of gravitation and Shoemaker's cycle of thirty-year freezes are discoverable, although not explicable in an acceptable way.

Although the two *desiderata* are distinct, they are connected. If space and time define the arena on which causal processes are played out, we deem them to be altogether inefficacious, playing no part in the evolution of events, but only setting the scene within which causes operate. If there are spatial or temporal vacua, however, mere distance or duration must play some part. At midnight on December 31st of the thirtieth year, everything springs into life, simply because 365 days have elapsed since midnight on December

---

[4] See above, §8.5, and quotation from Tolman in §4.7.

[5] See above, §10.1.

31st of the twenty ninth year. After the year's rest, the time is ripe for renewed activity. And if time can ripen since midnight on December 31st of the twenty-ninth year, it might also be able to ripen since the beginning of time, if there was one. Not all dates need be on a par: it could be that something was due to happen tomorrow not because of anything today, but because it was the date appointed at the beginning of time. The normal presupposition of date-indifference would not be enough to rule this out. All that is required is that for the most part experiments and observations should be repeatable, much as the requirement on spacetime, if science was to be feasible, was only that it should be locally Euclidean, not that it should be absolutely so.[6] It could be that most processes were date-indifferent, but that some were not, and would in their own good time result in events that happened when they happened for no other reason than that it was the right time for them to take place.

Space and Time as Arena and Explanation

1. Corpuscularian space is where things can be, but mostly are not. It is a many-dimensional manifold of mostly unactualised possibilities.
2. Time is when things can happen, and mostly do. It is a one-dimensional manifold of mostly actualised possibilities.

—oOo—

3. Action at a Distance is conceptually possible, but difficult to explain.
4. Action after a Duration is conceptually possible, but difficult to explain.

—oOo—

5. Position-indifference and direction-indifference are necessary presuppositions of scientific discovery of causal connexions.
6. Date-indifference is a necessary presupposition of scientific discovery of causal connexions.
   BUT these requirments are not absolute. It is enough that spacetime be locally Euclidean; and cosmologists postualte a Big Bang, a special date when our universe came into existence.

---

[6] See above, §§4.8, 9.7, 10.1.

Once we allow that the mere effluxion of time *can* (conceptually can) be a cause of something's happening, and that time, and similarly space, are not, of conceptual necessity, causally inefficacious, we may legitimately wonder whether, although change will not serve for characterizing time, perhaps cause might do. Not only is time intimately connected with cause, but, as we have seen,[7] Robb was able, granted an asymmetric transitive relation of causal influenceability, to develop a theory of "conical order", giving rise to the light-cone structure of Minkowski spacetime.

Caveats are still in order. We need to note the modal point, that we are dealing not with actual causal connexions, but with possible ones. If the relation of causal influenceability is asymmetric, the anisotropy of time will be explained; but can we justify the asymmetry of causal influenceability? can we rule out backward causation? and, more germanely, why should teleological explanations—explanations that look towards the future—be ruled out?[8] More generally, we can ask how we come by a concept of causation—in many accounts we cite temporal antecedence as a feature that distinguishes causes from effects. We can also ask how we can apply it to the world around us, without being able to rely on the causal inefficacy of time.

These questions can be answered, some satisfactorily. We can acquire the concept first-personally.[9] And then, if we ground our concept of causality in that of agency—my bringing it about that a desired effect should occur, we can accommodate teleological explanations, and distinguish them from ordinary causal ones. I do something in order to make something else happen: why did I do it? in order to make the something else happen; why did the something else happen? because I did the something. We can further elucidate the 'make' in terms of causal necessity. The concept of causal necessity is itself grounded in agency.[10]

---

[7] §10.2.

[8] Huw Price, *Time's Arrow*, Oxford, 1996, argues that this may well be a mistake. Other thinkers explain causal cause in terms of necessary and sufficient conditions, and identify the direction of causation by the cause's being explanatory of the effect, and not *vice versa*. The argument given here does not absolutely rule out that possibility, though it is difficult to see how it could be carried through.

[9] See above, §4.5.

[10] See above, ch.4, §4.6.

§12.2 Time

It is also conceivable that we should come to know causes second-personally. The Creator might have told us—or, more likely Newton—how He had arranged things;[11] or, indeed, time, though not completely inefficacious, might be sufficiently so for us to be able to discover natural laws which implied some action after a duration; after all, in Shoemaker's fable, the two-, three- and five-year cycles were discoverable in the ordinary way.

We may be able to explicate time in terms of causal influenceability—but only if causal influenceability is construed as an asymmetrical, and hence inherently temporal concept: the word Robb uses to say that one event is causal influenceable by another is 'after'. We may also be able to explicate causal influenceability in terms of causality and causal explanation, but since the concepts of cause and causal explanation are themselves grounded in that of agency, the temporality of time would, still, stem from our being agents, who look towards the future as the time when we can do what we choose to do.

§12.2 Leibniz and Relationism

Leibniz held that time and space were not substances, but only systems of relations.[12] He had low view of relations, regarding them definitely inferior, ontologically speaking, to qualities. We do not. We regard qualities and relations as on a par: qualities are simply monadic relations. They may both of them differ from substances, but relations are no more insubstantial than qualities. Moreover, time and space are not just relations which happen to obtain between actual things and actual events, but systems of relations that could obtain between possible events and possible things. Just as space is not just where things are, but is where things can be, so time is not constituted by the events that actually happen, but must also accommodate events that might possibly happen. Time, like space, has a very definite, highly integrated structure. It is, we shall argue, continuous and one-dimensional. Like Leibniz, we take it for granted that it is directed and not cyclic. If time has to be talked about as a whole, and has topological properties ascribed to it as a single whole entity, it needs to be referred to by a substantive noun, and cannot just be analysed

---

[11] Compare §§4.5, §9.7, and §10.1 above.

[12] *Fifth Letter to Clarke*, §§33, 47ff.; reprinted in H.G.Alexander, ed. *The Leibniz-Clarke Correspondence*, Manchester, 1956.

away, and so may, like space, qualify for being *pace* Leibniz, a substance after all, though very different from the impenetrable point-particles of classical corpuscularianism.

Although Leibniz' account fails to do justice to the way we think about time, it has a crude down-to-earth attractiveness that resonates with many modern sentiments. Its verificationist question "What difference would it make if the whole universe had started half an hour sooner?" seems unanswerable, and an ontology that admits only things and events is clearly more economical than one that tangles with invisible space and tenos time. But the attractions are superficial. It only gets off the ground because of the high degree of symmetry we ascribe to time and space, which makes Leibniz' verificationist questions difficult to answer. It does indeed make no difference whether an experiment is done today or tomorrow, or in Oxford or in Cambridge. If the world had begun half an hour sooner, there would, we assume, be no discernible difference, because only on that assumption can we argue from repeated observations to laws of nature. But that was only to be expected, if time and space are to satisfy the conditions necessary for their being an arena, in which events can be located and described without prejudice to the causes we may posit to explain them. Once it is recognised that time and space, as we understand them, are, and need to be, highly symmetrical, in order not to obtrude on our causal investigations, we cease to be vulnerable to Leibniz' challenges. Again, although at first it seems very down-to-earth to think of space and time as simply the relations that things bear to one another, we come to realise, when we think about it, that measuring distances and durations is not a simple matter, but highly "theory-laden": in laying off lengths by means of a foot rule, we are making assumptions about the Euclidean nature of space; and obviously measuring durations by means of a pendulum, hair-spring, or atomic, clock, or by the earth's rotation, or by its orbit round the sun, depends on periodic processes having isochronous intervals. Without these assumptions we should be unable to assign numerical values to distances or durations, and the whole relationist programme would collapse.

Relationism fails.[13] Many other attacks, however, can be mounted, which like that of Leibniz, concede that our concepts of time and space are well-founded, but construe them as being aspects of something more fundamental, such as spacetime.

---

[13] For a fuller discussion, see J.R.Lucas, *Space, Time and Causality*, Oxford, 1984, ch.9. See also C.Hooker, "The Relational Doctrines of Space and Time", *British Journal for the Philosophy of Science*, **22**, 1971, pp.97-130; and Graham Nerlich, *The Shape of Space*, Cambridge, 1976 and *What Spacetime Explains*, Cambridge, 1994, chs.1 and 2.

§12.3 Spacetime

Minkowski famously announced

> Henceforth space by itself, and time by itself, are doomed to fade away into mere shadows, and only a kind of union of the two will preserve an independent reality. [14]

Many understood this to mean that time was altogether relative and unreal, though Minkowski was careful not to say that. Spacetime was, on his view, an independent reality: it was only that time *by itself* was not. Spacetime had *aseitas*:[15] time, although not illusory or fictitious, did not. Whereas temporal duration was an invariant quantity under the Galilean transformations, it is not under the Lorentz transformation, which preserves only spacetime separations, but neither spatial ones nor temporal ones separately. This is important, and shows that time by itself is not an independent variable in electromagnetism, but does not show that it is unreal. Although Minkowski spacetime can be described as a four-dimensional manifold, its metric (and hence also the topology based on it) is radically unlike that of a Euclidean four-space. The Lorentz signature $(+ + +-)$ marks a fundamental difference between timelike directions and timelike separations on the one hand and spacelike directions and spacelike separations on the other.

Mathematicians are tempted to discount this difference between timelike and spacelike separations, arguing that they can transform Minkowski spacetime into a simple four-space by setting $ict = x_4$. It is a tempting move. A transformation that converts simple exponential functions into periodic ones suggests that there might be some fundamental periodicity which underlies the fundamental rhythm of the universe, and would explain why there are many rhythms all in harmony with one another; and why many different ways of measuring time all keep time with one another.[16] But so far as we know, there is no preferred period, and the details of any such explanation are altogether obscure. More tellingly, the topological difference between Minkowski spacetime, with Lorentz

---

[14] H.Minkowski, "Space and Time", An Address delivered at the 80th Assembly of German Natural Scientists and Physicians, at Cologne, 21 September, 1908; reprinted in A.Sommerfeld, ed., *The Principle of Relativity*, New York, 1923, p.75

[15] See above, §8.2.

[16] See above, §11.9.

signature $(+++-)$, and a simple Euclidean 4-space, with Lorentz signature $(++++)$, is profound. Although Minkowski spacetime does bring out some significant similarities between time and space, these fall far short of showing that $ict = x_4$, or that the dimension of time was simply a fourth dimension of space divided by ic.[17]

Minkowski's spacetime also lends strong support to the picture of a "block universe", and suggests that we should reject our ordinary experience of time in favour of a much more abstract and mathematical concept, with the future already in existence, just waiting to occur. We are to picture world-lines in Minkowski spacetime as already timelessly existing and ourselves as going along a world-line encountering our pre-determined future as it takes place—in Weyl's words

> The objective world simply *is*, it does not *happen*. Only to the gaze of my consciousness, crawling upward along the lifeline of my body, does a section of this world come to life as a fleeting image in space which continually changes in time.[18]

But this is only a picture. Although Minkowski spacetime, a four-dimensional manifold with Lorentz signature, seems more integrated and solid than a Cartesian product of a three-dimensional space with a one-dimensional time, exactly the same picture is available in the latter case: we can equally well think of a world-line timelessly existing in Newtonian space-and-time—the Galilean transformation can be seen as just a special case of the Lorentz transformation in which the speed of light is infinite. Both pictures are available, both misleading, both non-obligatory.

The reason why the block universe undercuts the reality of time is that it makes out that our sense of the passage of time is merely psychological, and that in reality time simply *is*, with no distinction between past, present and future.

---

[17] For further arguments against simply construing t as an imaginary fourth dimension of space, see C.W.Misner, K.S.Thorne and J.A.Wheeler, *Gravitation*, New York, 1973, §2.3, Box 2.1, p.51.

[18] H.Weyl, *Philosophy of Mathematics and Natural Science*, Princeton, 1949, p.116.

§12.4 Time and Electromagnetism

The anti-realist arguments of McTaggart and Mellor failed.[19] Tensed discourse is not self-contradictory, though it does depend on the point of view of the speaker, and needs to conjugate accordingly; once, however, the distinction is drawn between covariance and invariance, the conjugation of tenses ceases to be a reproach. But then the Special Theory seems to come to the aid of the sceptics. The very fact that it gives rise to different points of view has been taken to show that none of them are of more than limited validity. Whereas it was a complaint in the previous section that spacetime altogether lacks tense, the complaint against the Special Theory, when not formulated in terms of Minkowski spacetime, is that it makes out the choice of a frame of reference to be entirely arbitrary, with a corresponding arbitrariness in the ascription of the terms 'past', 'present' and 'future'. An event could be both future and past, depending on which frame of reference we had decided to adopt: future with respect to the frame of observers on Earth, past with respect to that of a distant Astronaut moving at a high velocity relative to the Earth. The ascription of futurity, presentness, or pastness is, therefore, purely relative, a matter of our arbitrary, subjective, egocentric choice, and so indicative of no real property of the event.

But that argument attributes too much significance to electromagnetism. A frame of reference does not determine what is currently going on at distant places, but only what dates should be ascribed to them in order to make electromagnetic phenomena coherent. As far as electromagnetic phenomena are concerned, we have no means of telling exactly when a distant event—an event in the "Absolutely Elsewhere and Anywhen"—takes place; but for any given frame of reference, IF we ascribe the same date to all events on a particular hyper-plane of simultaneity, then the laws of electromagnetism apply neatly and yield harmonious results. So far as the Special Theory goes, simultaneity is a rather superficial and frame-dependent property, which we find useful for assigning dates to different events in different places, but which is not of fundamental importance in accounting for the propagation of causal influence. The ascription of presentness, pastness, or futurity, to events outside the light cone is nominal rather than real, and has no bearing on their ontological status.

---

[19] §§10.8 and 10.9.

But that is not the end of the argument. Physicists are reluctant to confine the Special Theory to being merely a theory of electromagnetism; they take it to apply to space, time and reality generally, and it is natural to construe it as ranging over the whole of physics, and not just electromagnetic theory. Any God's-eye view of what is really past or present as opposed to what is really future must impose a privileged frame of reference that is contrary to Einstein's principle that there are no privileged observers, that is to say, no special inertial frames of reference. The claim that there are no privileged inertial frames of reference expresses a deep symmetry, not to be lightly given up merely in order to accommodate old-fashioned views about time.[20]

There is force in this rejoinder, but it is not decisive. History tells against our precluding on *a priori* grounds the possibility of there being a preferred frame of reference. Newton had similar difficulties with Absolute Space. Newtonian mechanics is relativistic, in the same way as electromagnetism. Newton's laws of motion come out the same in any uniformly moving frame, so that it is impossible to tell, within Newtonian mechanics, whether we are moving with respect to Absolute Space or not. Newton recognised this, but maintained, correctly, that Absolute Space was nevertheless a coherent notion, and opined that the centre of the solar system might be at rest in it. Later, when electromagnetic theory was being developed, Michelson and Morley sought to determine the rest frame of the ether, and if they had succeeded, we should have

---

[20] For further discussion of these arguments, see Howard Stein, "On Einstein-Minkowski space-time", *Journal of Philosophy*, **65**, 1968, pp.5-23; and 'A note on time and relativity theory", *Journal of Philosophy*, **67**, 1970, pp.289-294; and "On Relativity Theory and the Openness of the Future", *Philosophy of Science*, **58**, (1991), pp. 147-167. See also M.Capek, *The Philosophical Impact of Contemporary Physics*, Princeton UP, 1961; and "Time in Relativity Theory: Arguments for a Philosophy of Becoming" in J.T.Fraser, *The Voices of Time*, London, 1968; O.Costa de Beauregard, "Time in Relativity Theory: Arguments for a Philosophy of Being" in J.T.Fraser, *The Voices of Time*, London, 1968; R. Weingard, "Relativity and the Reality of Past and Future Events", *British Journal for the Philosophy of Science*, **23**, (1972) pp.119-121. R.Sorabji, *Necessity, Cause and Blame*, London, 1980, pp.114-119; R.Torretti, *Relativity and Geometry*, Oxford, 1983, pp.249-251. N. Maxwell, "Are Probabilism and Special Relativity Incompatible?", *Philosophy of Science*, **52**, (1985), pp. 23-43.

§12.4　　　　　　　　　　Time　　　　　　　　　　　359

undoubtedly taken that as being at rest in Absolute Space. Similarly now, if some superluminal velocity of transmission of causal influence were discovered, we should be able to distinguish frames of reference, and say which were at rest absolutely and which were moving. If, for instance, we were able to communicate telepathically with extra-terrestial beings in some distant galaxy, or if God were to tell us what was going on in Betelgeuse now, then we should have no hesitation in restricting the Principle of Relativity to the phenomena of electromagnetism only. Hence it cannot be an absolute principle foreclosing absolutely any possibility of absolute time.

These are not mere possibilities. In many of the models that cosmologists use—solutions of the field equations of the General Theory—there is a world-wide cosmic time that flows, if not evenly and uniformly, at least generally and universally. There are thus also preferred hyper-surfaces (not necessarily flat) of simultaneity constituting a world-wide present and separating a real unalterable past from a possible future not yet actualised.

Not every symmetry is suitable for thinking about time and space. In electromagnetic theory time is symmetrical under reflection, although in reality, as will be shown in the next section, it is not.[21] Similarly, Einstein's principle that there are no privileged observers was propounded in the context of electrodynamics. So long as we confine our attention to electrodynamics, we have good reason for adopting the Lorentz transformation as our way of correlating positions and dates in different inertial frames of reference; but it does not follow that that is the way we must ascribe positions and dates to distant events, and that no other ascription could be correct.

---

[21] Perhaps, though, the comparison should be with parity, which comes to the same thing in one dimension, but is different if there are more than one. It is, we firmly believe, a feature of our three-dimensional space that it is orientable, that is to say that incongruous counterparts cannot be brought to coincide by any continuous translation or rotation; clockwise and anti-clockwise corkscrews are essentially different. In electromagnetism the interchange of positive and negative charge, or of North and South magnetic poles, is accompanied by a corresponding change of clockwise and anti-clockwise. It appears that the product of Time × Charge × Parity is a fundamental invariant, in which case the anisotropy of time is secured by the deep difference between positive and negative charge. Martin Gardner, in his *The Ambidextrous Universe*, 1964, 2nd ed., Penguin, 1982, pp.193-197, and *The New Ambidextrous Universe*, New York, 1990, pp.203-208, gives an accessible account of these matters, and warns against greeting an extra-terrestrial visitor who extends his left hand to us!

§12.5 Tense and Modality

Putnam, Rietdijk and Lango have a fallacious argument for a tenseless view of time, because of alleged inconsistencies in our ordinary concept of simultaneity, arising from there being different frames of reference.[22] If we change the frame of reference, we change the hyper-plane of simultaneity, that is, we change the events to be reckoned simultaneous, and correspondingly, those reckoned to be future or past. If we consider two observers in two frames of reference moving with a uniform velocity with respect to each other, they will have different hyper-planes of simultaneity, and an event that is future to one will be past with respect to the other. Hence, they argue, there is no absolute distinction between present, past and future.

There is clearly something wrong with the argument. It depends on a confusion between two-termed and three-termed relations. It assumes that simultaneity is a two-termed relation, whereas in point of fact simultaneity is a three-termed relation, and in the Special Theory we always have to ask "simultaneous with respect to what frame of reference?". Simultaneity with respect to a given frame of reference *is* an equivalence relation, so that if one event is simultaneous with another and that other is simultaneous with a third, then the first is simultaneous with the third. But simultaneity with respect to *different* frames of reference is not an equivalence relation at all. The argument depends on a simple equivocation in the use of the term 'simultaneous'; no event in the past of an observer in a given frame of reference can also be, in that frame of reference, simultaneous with his Now.

The argument fails: but behind the fallacious argument is another, more substantial one. There could not be any *modal* difference between past, present and future, because the correct ascription of these terms depended on the frame of reference chosen, and that choice was arbitrary.

---

[22] H.Putnam, "Time and Physical Geometry", *Journal of Philosophy*, **64**, 1967, pp.240-247; reprinted in H.Putnam, *Mathematics, Matter and Method, Philosophical Papers*, I, Cambridge, 1979, pp.198-205; C.W.Rietdijk, "A Rigorous Proof of Determinism Derived from the Special Theory of Relativity", *Philosophy of Science*, **33**, 1966, pp.341-344, and "Special Relativity and Determinism", *Philosophy of Science*, **43**, 1976, pp.598-609; John W. Lango, "The logic of simultaneity", *Journal of Philosophy*, **66**, 1969, pp.340-350.

But, we have seen, there *is* a modal difference between past, present and future states of a quantum-mechanical system. The future is a superposition of state vectors, representing different possible future states. The present is the moment of actuality, when the state vector "collapses" into a definite *eigen*-vector, with the past being likewise definite and unalterable. Any realist construal of quantum mechanics insists upon this difference between past, present and future. These, of course, are states of affairs, not dates. Different possible states of affairs project onto the same future date. But the difference between the future, where the states of affairs are as yet indeterminate, and the present and past, where the states of affairs are unalterably determinate, is stark. We may not be able to know what the state of a distant star at present is, but there is an ontological matter of fact as to whether it is a superposition, or has collapsed into a single *eigen*-state. Contrary to the received understanding of the Special Theory, there is a hyperplane (or, in the General Theory, a hyper-surface) of present-ness sweeping through the universe, representing the moment of truth when possibilities become one definite actuality.

Possibilities and actualities are best expressed in terms of modal logic. As of now, it is possible that you will marry Jane. If you marry Jane, it will be possible that you will have children carrying some of Jane's genes. So it is, as of now, possible that you will have children carrying some of Jane's genes. In formal logic we can express this inference as

$$\Diamond\Diamond p \vdash \Diamond p,$$

which is equivalent to the more familiar thesis **4**

$$\vdash \Box p \to \Box\Box p,$$

the characteristic axiom of **S4**. The accessibility relation, Q, in the Kripke model is transitive, and admits of there being many different branches, representing different possible courses of events, but without the branches being required to unite subsequently. This corresponds to there often being exclusive alternatives open to us. As of now, you can marry either Jane or Jean, but next year, if you have by then married Jane, you will no longer be free to marry Jean. Life with Jean will then be a might-have-been. We often wonder how things might have panned out if our decisions, or circumstances, had been different at an earlier stage in our lives.

It is different with the past. From where we are now, there is only one possible past. A few philosophers have denied this, and have thought that if memories fade sufficiently, there could be alternative pasts leading to the present as we know it.[23] But though our knowledge of the past may be abridged, the reality remains the same. If we accept this,[24] the appropriate thesis for expressing the fixity of the present and past in standard modal logic is **S4.3**

$$\vdash \Box(\Box p \to q) \lor \Box(\Box q \to p),$$

where $\Box$ is a backward-looking strong modal operator expressing a present-or-past modality.[25] It is more intuitive to stick with the previously used future possibility operator, $\Diamond$ and its converse, $\Diamond^{-1}$, and express the unlterability of the past by the thesis[26]

$$\vdash \Diamond \Diamond^{-1} p \to (p \lor \Diamond^{-1} p \lor \Diamond p),$$

where the accessibility relation, Q^{-1}, for $\Diamond^{-1}$ is not only transitive, like Q, the accessibility relation for $\Diamond$, but linear.

A temporal view of the universe will therefore have a tree-like structure, generated by a many-one ordering relation, with many possible future courses of events, but only a single actual course of present and past events. The future therefore is represented by many different limbs branching to the future, the branches showing the different possibilities still open, and the past by the trunk, which is single and definite, the present being the topmost point of the trunk, just before the branches begin to branch out. The passage of time is marked by the dropping off of branches, which

---

[23] Jan Lukasiewicz, "On Determinism", in L.Borkowski, ed. *Selected Works*, North Holland, 1970, pp.127-8; reprinted in Storrs MacCall, ed., *Polish Logic*, Oxford, 1967, pp.38-39; quoted by A.N.Prior, *Past, Present and Future*, Oxford, 1967 p. 28.

[24] In my *The Future*, Oxford, 1989, ch.10, pp.184-189, I give three arguments for doing so.

[25] For alternative formulations see A.N.Prior, *Past, Present and Future*, Oxford, 1967, pp.26-31. The standard formulation given in G.E.Hughes and M.J.Cresswell, *An Introduction to Modal Logic*, London, 1968, ch.14, p.261 is $\vdash \Box(\Box p \to \Box q) \lor \Box(\Box q \to \Box p)$; the shorter version given above is due to P.T.Geach.

[26] I owe this formulation and much else to Storrs McCall.

Jean and Jane

On the left we see that the fact that it was possible that I should be married to Jean does not imply that I ever was, or am, or ever shall be, married to her. The light lines indicate *might have beens*, eventualities that were at one time possible, but no longer are. Possible courses of events that are still open are indicated by slightly thicker lines, stemming from Now, and from nodes that are as of now still possible. The heavy line below Now indicates the unalterable past. On the right we see that if it ever will be the case (Then) that I was married to Jane, then either I am now (Supposed Now 2) or I was (Supposed Now 3) or I shall be (Supposed Now 3). There are many possibilities open to us in the future (many of which will come to nothing), but for those that actually occur, only one past course of events, which is by then unalterable.

are no longer live options, and a corresponding lengthening of the trunk, the remaining branches being future possibilities that are still really possible. The dead branches are might-have-beens, no longer really open possibilities, but still connected by virtue of there being some time in the actual past when they were really open possibilities.[27] But though we lose the might-have-been possibilities no longer open to us, we gain the actuality of the present, and the definiteness of our deeds. Time is the passage from possibility through actuality to unalterability. Transience should no longer be a matter for regret, but welcomed as the condition of our aspirations being crowned by achievement.

The tree-like structure reflects the fact that there is only a partial ordering of possible actions and events. Some philosophers, however, have spoken of a partial ordering with alternative times,

---

[27] For a full development of the branch model of time, see Storrs McColl, *A Model of the Universe*, Oxford, 1994. See also J.R.Lucas, *A Treatise on Time and Space*, London, 1973; and *The Future*, Oxford, 1989.

> **Moods and Trees**
> 1. The future is open and possible.
> 2. The present is actual and real.
> 3. The past is unalterable and necessary.
>
> —oOo—
>
> This shows that the tenses are anchored in reality,
> and in particular that
> a) Time has a direction,
> b) The present is uniquely distinguished.

future or past.[28] It is largely a question of terminology. We—most of us—do believe that there are alternative possible future courses of events, and may be able to imagine alternative courses of events in our actual past: but these are possible courses of events, not dates. It may be that next year you will marry Jane, and it may be that next year you will marry Jean, and these are two distinct possibilities: but there is only one next year, and in it only one of those possibilities can be actualised. We project many different future possibilities onto one time axis of strictly ordered dates. More formally, we argue that if p is an event which is possible, but merely possible, then $\Diamond \neg p$ as well as $\Diamond p$, but we cannot have $\Diamond (p \wedge \neg p)$. Although I can go to Cambridge tomorrow, and not go on the day after tomorrow, I cannot both go and not go at the same time. Although we can remove apparent contradictions in colloquial usage by specifying different dates, once the propositions are fully specified, the order of their dates is fixed by whether or not, for different choices of proposition, we have $\Diamond \neg p$ and $\Diamond p$; p and q are the same date if and only if $(\Diamond \neg p \wedge \Diamond p) \leftrightarrow (\Diamond \neg q \wedge \Diamond q)$.

There is no difficulty in doing this in our ordinary way of speaking, since we have to hand both McTaggart's A series and his B series. But to quell doubts about the ability of tensed discourse to meet all the requirements for talking about time, it is worth pointing out that we can elucidate the relations *before* and *after* in terms of tense. We imagine ourselves at the time of one of the events, and ask whether the other would be, at that time, past,

---

[28] A.N.Prior, *Past, Present and Future*, Oxford, 1967, pp.27-29, pp.127ff.

present, or future; if past, it was before, if present, it was at the same time as, and if future, it was after, the event we had imagined ourselves being contemporaneous with. We are, of course, so familiar with using both dates and tenses, that this clumsy definition seems otiose; and in our ordinary usage take *before* and *after* to give a simple linear and strictly connected ordering of dates.

A simple linear and strictly connected ordering is in ordinary parlance one-dimensional. The modal approach thus establishes the one-dimensionality of time.[29]

§12.6 Augustine, Instants and Intervals

St Augustine put forward the argument of the ever-shrinking present.[30] He found that whenever he tried to identify the present, he always found that some of what he had taken to be the present was not present, but already past, and some was not present, but was still future. He concluded that no time could properly be said to be present.

Augustine's puzzle is resolved if we keep in mind the grammatical point that the words 'present', 'past' and 'future' are adjectives, and insist on knowing what noun they are being used to qualify, and whether these nouns refer to *instants*, punctiform moments of time with zero magnitude, or *intervals*, stretches of time, to which some positive magnitude can meaningfully be ascribed. We can apply the words 'present', 'past' and 'future' to dates, and phrases that mark the beginning or end of some process, such as 'the moment of death'. But we can also apply them to intervals—my years at Oxford, or the time you spent on the Rural District Council. Often some word referring to an interval is meant in all three cases,

---

[29] Some care is needed, because topology assigns dimensionality to *continuous* manifolds, and we have not yet estblished the continuity of time. The word 'connected' also has a different sense in topology from that used here; similar care is needed in distinguishing the modal and topological uses of the word 'open'.

[30] *Confessions*, bk XI, chs.XII-XXII, xiv-xxix. The argument was well known in antiquity: Aristotle gives it in *Physics*, IV, 10, 217b34-218a8, (discussed by Michael Inwood, "Aristotle on the Reality of Time", in Lindsay Judson, ed., *Aristotle's Physics*, Oxford, 1991, pp.151-163). For a sympathetic account of Augustine's whole philosophy of time, see Christopher Kirwan, *Augustine*, London, 1989, chs. VII, VIII and IX.

Augustine's Ever-Shrinking Present

Past   Present Year   Future
─ ─ ─ ─ ─ ─ ✱✱✱✱✱✱✱✱✱✱✱✱✱✱✱✱✱✱✱✱✱ + + + + + + +

Past   Present Term   Future
─ ─ ─ ─ ─ ─ ─ ─ ─ ✱✱✱✱✱✱✱✱✱✱✱✱✱✱✱✱ + + + + + + + +

Past   Present Week   Future
─ ─ ─ ─ ─ ─ ─ ─ ─ ─ ✱✱✱✱✱✱✱✱✱✱✱✱✱✱ + + + + + + + + +

Past   Present Day   Future
─ ─ ─ ─ ─ ─ ─ ─ ─ ─ ─ ─ ✱✱✱✱✱✱✱✱✱✱ + + + + + + + + +

Past   Present Hour   Future
─ ─ ─ ─ ─ ─ ─ ─ ─ ─ ─ ─ ─ ✱✱✱✱✱✱✱✱ + + + + + + + + + + +

Past   Present Minute   Future
─ ─ ─ ─ ─ ─ ─ ─ ─ ─ ─ ─ ─ ─ ✱✱✱✱✱✱ + + + + + + + + + + + +

Past   Present Second   Future
─ ─ ─ ─ ─ ─ ─ ─ ─ ─ ─ ─ ─ ─ ✱✱✱✱✱✱✱ + + + + + + + + + + +

Past   Present ?Limit?   Future
─ ─ ─ ─ ─ ─ ─ ─ ─ ─ ─ ─ ─ ─ ─ | + + + + + + + + + + + + + +

No Present Interval at all

so

No Time at all

as when we talk of last year, this year, and next year: and then it is unproblematic to say, for example, that the past, present and future years together constitute the whole of time.

Augustine invites us to focus on the present. But whatever interval we propose as being *the* present interval, he counters by considering smaller intervals, only one of which is present, and the others either past or future. Provided we remember always to specify what sort of interval we are talking about, Augustine's puzzle disappears. I can talk about the present age, the present century, the present year, the present month, the present week, the present day, the present hour, and so on, just as I can talk about the local town, the local district, the local parish, the local street, and so on: and the fact that the present week contains not only today, but yesterday and tomorrow too, is no more puzzling than the fact that the local parish contains not only the local street, but several other streets as well. Change the noun, and you change the application rules for the qualifying adjectives. It is, however, easy not to specify what sort of interval we are talking about; ordinary usage allows us to apply the phrase 'the present' to any convenient interval, and often to supply a suitable term to fit the context. And then if we stress the uniqueness implicit in the *the*, we cannot light upon any interval better qualified than the others. Only if we shift to instants, is there a unique present instant, alone deserving the accolade of presentness. Thus under pressure, we distinguish *the* present instant from all past and future time. Consistency might lead us to talk of instants throughout, but we run into difficulties with Lebesgue measure theory and higher-order infinities, as we wonder whether time is constituted of all past, present and future instants. Instead we mix modes, and think of the past and future intervals, and the present instant, dividing the one from the other, but also uniting them in so far as it is the common boundary of each.

Augustine's Argument against the Reality of Time
1. Only the Present is Real.
2. No temporal interval is altogether Present.
3. Only an instant can be properly called Present.
4. An instant does not have extension.
5. Time does have extension.
6. Time is not Real.

In the next section it will be argued that the argument of the ever-shrinking present should be seen as anticipating Cantor's definition of a real number by means of a Cauchy sequence of nested intervals, and establishing that time is a continuum, with 'the present' uniquely referring to an instant dividing the past interval from the future interval. But that leaves Augustine's argument apparently intact. The present instant, being an instant, has no duration, so that Augustine could conclude that it did not exist for any time at all, and so was not time. Augustine presents us with a dilemma: on the one hand the present instant is quintessentially temporal; on the other hand, time is essentially an interval, a duration. And an interval, it seems, cannot be made up of instants. For instants are of zero magnitude, and no matter how many instants we have, they still will only have zero magnitude. Obviously for any finite number:

$$0 + 0 + 0 + 0 + \ldots + 0 + 0 = 0,$$

and that still holds if we go to the limit:

$$\Sigma_{n=1}^{\infty} 0 = 0.$$

The argument seems incontrovertible, and would show that no stretch of time can be made up of instantaneous *nows*. We can only escape its paradoxical conclusion if we recognise, with Cantor, that there is more than one sort of infinity, and that the argument shows only that

$$0 \times \aleph_o = 0,$$

but has nothing to say about $\aleph$s (alephs) greater than $\aleph_o$. Cantor showed that the number of real numbers in an interval, say that between 0 and 1, was greater than $\aleph_o$, for each real number between 0 and 1 can be expressed as an infinite decimal, $0.a_1 a_2 a_3 \ldots\ldots$. If there were only $\aleph_o$ such numbers, we could arrange them in a list:

$0.a_1 a_2 a_3 \ldots\ldots$
$0.b_1 b_2 b_3 \ldots\ldots$
$0.c_1 c_2 c_3 \ldots\ldots$
$0.d_1 d_2 d_3 \ldots\ldots$
$\ldots\ldots\ldots\ldots$

But then we see that the list has left out a number between 0 and 1, namely $0.(a_1 + 1)(b_2 + 1)(c_3 + 1)(d_4 + 1)\ldots\ldots$, which differs

§12.7   Time   369

from the n_{th} member of the list in the n_{th} decimal place.[31] So
the number of real numbers between 0 and 1 is greater than $\aleph_o$.
Hence, provided that a temporal interval is a continuum, like the
real numbers, it need not follow from each instant's having zero
magnitude that the interval must have zero magnitude too.[32]

Modern measure theory enables us to resolve the puzzles that
confused the Greeks and St Augustine. The ever-shrinking present
does not show that time has no duration. Rather, it provides a key
argument in unveiling the topology of time.

§12.7 The Topology of Time

Many questions have been raised about the topology of time:
whether it is continuous or discrete; whether it is necessarily one-
dimensional; whether it is connected; whether it is cyclic; whether
it had a beginning, or will have an end.

Many thinkers have thought that time must be discrete. Hume,
no mathematician, gave an argument which now, with the benefit
of modern analysis, it is a useful exercise to unpick.[33] More seriously, some scientists wonder whether there may be a minimum
duration, a chronon (about 10^{-24}) seconds below which we cannot go, and which represents a temporal atom, so to speak, an
indivisible, though extended, moment.[34] There may emerge some
argument for a natural unit of measurement, as we shall see; but
even so, if we could think of it having any magnitude at all, we
could think of its duration having only half gone. If a photo-finish
enables us to distinguish between two events, we can think of an
event that a more sensitive photo-finish would show to be later
than the earlier and earlier than the later event. Time, as we think
of it, is dense, not a set of discrete units. If time were discrete,

---

[31] If the digit, f_n say, $= 9$, then for $f_n + 1$ we write 0.

[32] It would be tempting to suppose the opposite, that any set of more than $\aleph_o$ entities must have a non-zero magnitude; but Cantor showed that that was not the case. Some ordinal properties are required, as well as a cardinality greater than $\aleph_o$.

[33] See J.R.Lucas, *The Conceptual Roots of Mathematics*, London, 2000, ch.9, §9.6, pp.243f.

[34] See, for example, G.J.Whitrow, *The Natural Philosophy of Time*, Edinburgh, 1961, pp.156, 257.

we should expect space to be discrete too. But space is many-dimensional, and would have to form some sort of lattice, if it were composed of discrete units; and lattices, if homogeneous, are not isotropic. We can have a lattice that is homogeneous, in that it makes no difference if it is translated along any straight line; and we can have a lattice that is isotropic, in that it has spherical symmetry, and can be rotated about its origin—though then the origin is different from other points, and translation makes a difference; but we cannot have both.

Time is not only dense, but continuous. Augustine's argument of the ever-shrinking present does not show time to be unreal, but, as was suggested in the previous section (§12.6), constitutes a version of Cantor's definition of a real number by means of a Cauchy sequence of nested intervals. Alternatively, we can use Dedekind's approach. The thought that the present instant both divides and in a sense unites the past and the future was known to Aristotle, and emphasized by the Neoplatonists of late antiquity. If we reconstruct that thought in terms of a Dedekind cut, we have an argument for holding time to be a continuum from the Ever-Present Present. It is an argument about the way we have to think about time. We do not think that there are any gaps in the existence of the present—certainly, if it is the present that secures the reality of time, the existence of gaps would imply that time was continually dropping out of reality and popping in again. It would be unreasonable to suppose that there could be occasions when there was a past and a future, but no present in between; that there could be a crack between today and tomorrow. But if there is in all cases an instant corresponding to the division between the future and the past, then those instants constitute a linear continuum, with the order-type of the real numbers.[35] Conceptually, then, we think of time, as a continuum.

Arguments for the Continuity of Time
1. Ever-shrinking Present → Cantor's real numbers
2. Ever-present Present → Dedekind's real numbers
3. Assumptions of Science

—oOo—

These are purely conceptual arguments, about how we think—have to think—about time.

---

[35] See E.V.Huntington, *The Continuum*, Harvard, Mass., 1917, ch.5, or G.H.Hardy, *A Course of Pure Mathematics*, Cambridge, ch.1, §15, pp.24-27.

§12.7   Time   371

A further argument for the continuity of time comes from the natural sciences. Many natural laws connect temporal durations with spatial distances, or some other magnitude, often in the form of differential equations, some of them second-order with respect to time. The distance traversed by a body under constant acceleration—for example, a body falling freely under gravity—varies with the square of the time. If after two seconds a body has fallen 64.4 feet, we ask "At what time would it have fallen exactly half that, namely 32.2 feet?", and are told "$\frac{\sqrt{2}}{2}$ seconds after it was let go". Only if time is continuous does this answer make sense. And although we could reconstruct physics replacing differential equations by difference equations, the result would be clumsy and counter-intuitive. We thus have an argument from science based on rational considerations leading to a conclusion beyond the bounds of empirical verification.[36]

Arguments for the Continuity of Time
1. Ever-shrinking Present
2. Ever-present Present
3. Assumptions of Science

Physical Science is formulated in terms of real numbers, and on occasion uses irrational numbers to date particular instants.

—oOo—

Science could conceivably be better expressed in ways that did not presuppose real numbers—quantum mechanics might lead us to adopt a fuzzy realism with an Intuitionist theory of numbers. But present theories, so long as they are not superseded, support time's being continuous.

If time is continuous, the question of the dimensionality of time in the full topological sense arises. Time is one-dimensional. That follows from the openness of the future and the unalterability of

---

[36] See above, §12.2. For a verificationist counter-argument, see M.A.E.Dummett, "Is Time a Continuum of Instants?", *Philosophy*, **75**, 2000, pp. 497-515; and further, Ulrich Meyer, "Dummett on the Time-Continuum", *Philosophy*, **80**, 2005, pp.135-139; and M.A.E.Dummett, "Hume's Atomism about Events: A Response to Ulrich Meyer, *Philosophy*, **80**, 2005, pp.141-144.

the past.[37] Also, if time were more than one-dimensional, it would be possible to twist time in one dimension around an axis in some other dimension, so as to reverse its direction, which would be contrary to the anisotropy—the directedness—of time.

Time is necessarily connected (in the topological sense) in a way that space and persons are not. There is only one time, whereas there could be two disconnected spaces (as in Quinton's night-time dream world[38]), and there are many societies with whose members we do not interact at all. This follows not from the need for a token-reflexive anchoring of temporal discourse—the same would apply to space—but from the truth behind "Presentism".[39] Although it is not true that only the present is real, it is true that the reality of the present secures the reality of other tenses. 'Once upon a time' not only indicates fiction by the studious vagueness of token-reflexive reference, but acknowledges the connectedness of time by purporting to provide some sort of reference in the one and only time we have. Although a story might be told of two entirely separate times, which we could understand, because we could imaginatively project ourselves into each of the time sequences, there must be some relation between the events in the one fictional time sequence and those in the other, if the story is not to fall apart into two separate stories which just happen to be bound up in one book between one set of book-covers. If any events in the one influence any events in the other, those events stand to each other in some over-arching temporal relation. Equally, if anyone in either time sequence communicates with anyone in the other, or knows anything about anyone or anything in the other. Rather than think of there being two separate times, we should read the story as being about two separate worlds. Separate spaces are—just—possible, but time is necessarily connected and unique.

---

[37] See above, §§11.7, 12.5.

[38] Anthony Quinton, "Spaces and Times", *Philosophy*, **37**, 1962, pp.130-147; reprinted in Robin Le Poideven and Murrary MacBeath, eds., *The Philosophy of Time*, Oxford, 1993, pp.183-202.

[39] See above, §10.6. For Presentism see J.Bigelow, "Presentism and Properties", *Noûs*, **30**, 1996, pp.35-52; T.Sider, "Presentism and Ontological Commitment", *Journal of Philosophy*, **96**, 1996, pp.325-347; N.Markosian, "A Defense of Presentism", in D.Zimmerman, ed., *Oxford Studies in Metaphysics*, I, Oxford, 2003.

§12.7 Time

Because of the periodicity of many natural processes, many thinkers and poets have thought of time being cyclic, and looked forward to the time,
> When with the ever-circling years
> Comes round the age of gold.

We might argue against cyclic time that it would no longer be anisotropic: for any event that was after the present and seemingly in the future, would have already happened, and therefore be in the past. But that objection could be countered by refining anisotropy, and requiring only that time be *locally* directed, as we do when we say that Australia is East of Britain, and America East of Australia, though America is West, not East, of Britain. The branch model of the universe, however, rules out time's being cyclic. Future states of affairs are possible, past ones unalterable. If the future state of the universe is modally different from the past, there is no possibility of the past recurring. It remains possible, of course, that at some future date it will so happen that the state of the universe is the same as it was at some date in the past. That could happen; but there could not be any law requiring it to happen. Time could not be cyclic, nor could the course of events in the universe be reliably recurrent.

Had time been cyclic, it would have had no beginning and no end. Not being cyclic, it might be beginningless and endless, or it might have a beginning, or it might have an end, or it might have both. Many arguments have been adduced for and against a beginning, or an end, of time or of the world. Kant argued in his First Antimony that it was equally impossible to deny or to affirm that the world (or as we should say "the universe") had a beginning.[40] It is, according to Kant, impossible to deny that the world had a beginning, because then we should have to hold that an eternity had elapsed before the present time, and this would mean that an infinite—*unendlich*—series had come to an end. As always where infinities are involved, it is difficult to get a firm grasp of the problem. If our only concept of the infinite is the potential infinite, Kant's argument makes sense—Wittgenstein said he would be surprised to meet someone who had just counted down from minus infinity to zero: but mathematicians have no difficulty in dealing with a regression of order-type ω^*, the order-type of the

---

[40] *Critique of Pure Reason*, A426/B454ff. tr.Norman Kemp Smith, London, 1929, pp.396ff.

negative integers $\ldots -5, -4, -3, -2, -1$, and before the echoes of the Big Bang were first detected, physicists had no difficulty in understanding Hoyle's theory of continuous creation, and believing that the universe had existed from everlasting.

When we speak of infinite time having elapsed, we tend to assume that some metric has been given, and think of an infinitely large interval. But metrics, as we shall see, are not always given, and cannot be automatically taken for granted. We can measure in various ways, and what is a finite interval according to one metric may be an infinite one according to another: the transformation $y = log(x)$ transforms the unit interval from 0 to 1 into the infinite interval from $-\infty$ to 0. Kant himself speaks not of infinite intervals, but of "an infinite series of successive states of things".[41] But, since time is dense, there will always be an infinite series of successive states of intervals before any instant other than the first instant (if there is one). This is shown by the argument of Achilles and the tortoise, and by Aristotle's argument of the dichotomy. If we take a robust view, and insist that there is nothing wrong with an instant's being the limit point of an infinite series of antecedent successive states of things, then there is nothing wrong with an infinite series of antecedent successive states of things *simpliciter*, and Kant's argument against beginningless time, or a beginningless universe, collapses.

Kant's argument against a beginning of the universe is based on the causal inefficacy of time. If time is simply the arena in which events are caused and themselves cause other events, then there could not be a beginning to the universe, because there would be, *ex hypothesi*, nothing earlier to have caused it to come into existence. But we do not have to regard time as causally inefficacious.[42] The universe could have come into existence simply because the time was ripe for it to do so. Or we may be led to deny that *every* event has an antecedent causal cause. It might be that the universe just wobbled into existence, as some cosmologists seem to suggest. Theists distinguish God from the created universe, and explain its coming into existence as a *fiat* of His creative will, which could be antecedent to the creation without being part of it.

It is more difficult to think of time itself, as opposed to the universe, having a beginning, or an end. We imaginatively project

---

[41] A426/B454.

[42] See above, §12.1.

ourselves to the date in question, and cannot coherently envisage a present that had no past, or a present without a future. We can, mathematically, posit a closed one-dimensional continuum containing its limit points at either or both ends. Prior has formulated tense-logics with first or last instants. But there is a difficulty in interpretation. According to the modal account, time might, or might not, have had a beginning; the converse Kripke accessibility relation, Q^{-1}, of the converse modal operator $\Diamond^{-1}$ could be serial, but does not have to be, so far as the modal properties of $\Diamond^{-1}$ are concerned. It is different with regard to the end of time. Q needs to be serial; else no possibilities would be open at the end of time, and we should lose the distinction between past and future. It may seem strange that there should be a modal argument against there being a last instant of time, but not against there being a first one. The reason is that the present, the moment of actuality, is more like the past than the future. The actual present, like the unalterable past, is unique, in contrast to the many possibilities afforded by the future.

Other aspects of the concept of time tell against there being either a last or a first instant. The present instant is not only what divides the past from the future, but, as some of the later Neoplatonists averred, is also what unites them; that is to say, the present instant is both a later (upper) bound of the past, and an earlier (lower) bound of the future.[43] At the beginning, or end, of time it would still serve as a boundary of the future, or the past; but it could not constitute a *common* boundary of the both. And so would not be a possible present, as we understand it. It would seem, then, that if we give full weight to conditions of temporality, time must be thought of as a topologically open, not a closed, interval.

The Topology of Time
1. Time is linear (§12.5);
2. Time is topologically continuous (§12.7);
3. so Time is one-dimensional.
4. Time is topologically connected.
5. Time is not cyclic.
6. Time is topologically open, without a first or a last instant.

---

[43] Some of the Schoolmen found this difficult, and tried to distinguish the last instant at which something was still from the first instant at which it was moving, and worried about the state of affairs between those two instants.

§12.8 The Metric of Time

We think time is more difficult to measure than space, because we cannot take up a minute or an hour, and lay it off alongside an earlier or later minute or hour, as we can, we think, with an inch or a foot (though even these latter measurements are not as simple as we assume).[44] We measure time by processes, occasionally linear, like King Alfred's candles, or the water clocks of antiquity, but mostly periodic ones. Periodic processes have the virtue that granted the causal inefficacy of time, we have good reason for believing that each period will, indeed, have the same duration, that is to say, that they will all be isochronous.

The basic assumption of isochronicity is open to attack from two sides. It can be made to seem trivial. We often *can* regraduate magnitudes to make them amenable to simple arithmetical operations.[45] We can do this with duration to make it simply additive. If some physical process is described by a transformation, $T(t)$, of the relevant physical features after a duration t, We can regraduate the measure of the duration so that there is a modified transformation, $T'(t')$, such that if after a (modified) duration a' the original state of the system has been transformed by $T'(a')$, then after a further (modified) duration b' the original state of the system has been transformed by $T'(a' + b')$; that is $T'(a' + b') = T'(a').T'(b')$. This means that if ever any process returns to its original state, we can regraduate the measure of duration, and correspondingly modify the physical law of development of the system, so that $T'(1') = I$, the identity operator, and for any a, $T'(a' + 1) = T'(a').T'(1') = T'(a').I = T'(a')$. We thus seem to have made periodicity trivial. But not necessarily. The transformation T had to be modified to T', and the cost in complication could have been horrendous. We are in the same position as we were with Shoemaker's argument for changeless time: we could then have denied the existence of changeless time, but at the cost of great complication in the laws of nature. We could do the same now. Extreme empiricists see this as a simple choice open to us, which we are free to make either way; and say that the theory is "underdetermined by the data". But this is to ignore the pressure of rationality. We are not free to choose either way: one

---

[44] See above, §12.2.

[45] J.R.Lucas, *A Treatise on Time and Space*, London, 1973 and 1976, §14, pp.78-84.

§12.8 Time 377

choice is much less reasonable that the other. (This is not to say that there are never cases where the considerations are more evenly balanced, and we do—at least until further evidence turns up or deeper understanding gives us definite guidance—have simply to make a choice.)

The basic assumption of isochronicity is open to attack also on the ground that the causal inefficacy of time is an unwarranted assumption. It is assumed in Newtonian mechanics and the Special Theory, but in the General Theory the curvature of spacetime varies from point to point, and explains gravitational attraction. If we probe, we find once again a delicate mixture of *fiat* and fact, which can easily confuse us, and is difficult to disentangle. Even when space was a homogeneous, isotropic vacuum, magnets were known to have preference as regards direction. These were ascribed to magnetic fields, which were assumed to exist just in order to explain the behaviour of magnets and iron filings. Although now the ether, posited to exist in the late Nineteenth Century, is ridiculed, it can, more charitably, be seen as an analogous attempt to provide a separate noun for the verb 'to undulate', so as to keep space itself empty and free of causal entanglements. In some cases it has seemed rational to opt for space and time being causally inefficacious, and to posit fields to explain why things happen as they do: in other cases we have opted for geometrodynamcics, in which space and time do not just constitute the arena, but are themselves participants in causing the course of events to be what it is.[46] Either way, there are disadvantages as well as advantages. Often it is unclear which way it is most reasonable for us to go.

We are, however, fortunate when we come to measure time: we are not compelled to make difficult choices, because, as it happens, all our different ways of measuring time cohere. Pendulum clocks, based on gravitation, keep the same time as sundials, based on the conservation of angular momentum, and atomic clocks, based on quantum mechanics. We can imagine its not being so: some cosmologists have played with the thought that the constants of nature vary with time, and that the time of Newtonian mechanics and gravitation is a logarithmic function of the time of radioactive decay and the expansion of the universe.[47] But there is no convincing evidence that this is so. The music of the spheres has the

---

[46] See above, §9.7.

[47] P.A.M.Dirac, *Proceedings of the Royal Society*, A, **162**, 1938, pp.199ff.; E.A.Milne, *Kinematic Relativity*, Oxford, 1948; E.Teller, *Phys.Rev.*, **73**, 1948, pp.801ff.

same harmonics as the resonances within the atoms. We might, then, be led to suppose that in Whitrow's felicitous phrase, "there is a unique basic rhythm of the universe".[48] But this would imply too much. It would indicate, as we have seen, a preferred set of orthogonal axes in Hilbert space, and corresponding pressure on all (?respectable?) operators to commute, contrary to their actual behaviour.[49] Furthermore, the basic rhythm would have a period, which would then define a chronon, a fundamental unit of time, so that time—and hence also space—would not be metrically amorphous. There are yet further difficulties to negotiate. Even if there were periodic processes with different periods, there would, we might argue, be a "great year" when they all coincided. And that great year's duration, or the dates at which it began and ended, might have cosmic significance, analogous to that of the thirtieth year in Shoemaker's cycle.[50] But it is only if the ratios of periods of the various processes are rational numbers, that this result follows. If there are some whose ratios are irrational numbers, there is no recurrence, and there could be a basic rhythm without a basic unit.

If there are periodic processes, they can be expressed as a Fourier series of sinusoidal functions, the paradigm example of which is the general solution of the wave equation.[51] There are strong arguments in favour of this equation as the canonical expression of the principle of causality. If causes are to be able to operate at locations away from where they originate, it will be natural that causal influence should travel at a uniform, finite, "universal" speed, which will be represented in Minkowski spacetime by an isotropic line, involving the imaginary number, i, $\sqrt{-1}$; which in turn will make it natural for processes developing over time to be expressed by sinusoidal functions, which are inherently periodic. Periodicity is not restricted to temporal processes—crystals have a periodic structure in space: but it is peculiarly characteristic of temporal processes, and highly desirable if our measurement of time is to depend more on fact than on *fiat*. It may be that it is rationally required that our desires should be met.

---

[48] G.J.Whitrow, *The Natural Philosophy of Time*, 1st ed., London and Edinburgh, 1961, p.46.

[49] See above, §11.9.

[50] See above, §12.1.

[51] §10.1.

§12.9 Tense and Reality

Time and tense have survived the attacks of the antirealists scathed but not subverted. The arguments against their reality have been met. The concepts of time and tense are not self-contradictory, and programmes for explicating them in terms of change, cause, relations, or spacetime, have failed to deliver any reason for regarding time or tense as merely an aspect of something else. We still may obtain deeper understanding through their links with personality, consciousness, experience and agency, but these are unlikely to support any sort of anti-realism. We have, in Alvin Plantinga's phrase, defeated the defeaters, but in the process have had to refine further the concepts of time and tense, and the interplay between them.

Time is under the same tension as space, on the one hand to provide the arena, on the other to constitute an explanation, for the course of events. In the former role it needs to be tenuous and insubstantial, in the latter juicy and obtrusive. It is not a conceptual necessity that it should be causally inefficacious, but it is a *desideratum*. The thinker, who is a spectator of all time, can project himself in his thoughts to any time, and imaginatively see things from an arbitrarily chosen point of view; in doing so, he wants to be unhampered by temporal constraints; and so deems time to be tenuous and causally inefficacious. But tenuous time cannot be that tenuous, much as the featureless space of the corpuscularians by reason of its featurelessness possessed certain features. Although we can range over all time in our thoughts, the present presses in on us, and obtrudes upon the tranquillity of our speculations the need for action now. And because time is essentially tensed, it has to be continuous, one-dimensional, directed, non-cyclic and without a last instant.

Speculative freedom requires date-indifference, and date-indifference is secured if time is invariant under translation, but other symmetries are not to be sought or imposed. Although for the purposes of electromagnetic theory all inertial frames of reference are on a par, this equivalence cannot be generalised to the General Theory or quantum mechanics.[52] The constancy of the speed of light implies that time is no more invariant under magnification than space,[53] though it is metrically amorphous, with no fundamental unit of duration. Nor is time symmetrical under reflection.

---

[52] See above, §§12.4 and 11.7.

[53] See above, §9.7.

This anisotropy of time is in contrast to spatial directions, which are symmetrical under reflection.

Although the traditional canons of scientific enquiry lead naturally to a tenseless view of time—thus assimilating it to the dimensions of space—scientific developments in the twentieth century point in a different direction, and quantum mechanics, in particular, vindicates an understanding of time which is essentially tensed. If time is real and essentially tensed, reality is not the impersonal invariant absolute that it is often taken to be, but a covariant complex to understand which we have to be ready to conjugate over tense. And if we conjugate over tense, we might legitimately conjugate over persons too. A possible metaphysics is beginning to take shape. It would have the virtue of completeness that the Platonist ideal of timeless, impersonal and unlocated truths lacks. IF completeness is a *desideratum*, then rather than ignore every feature that is not the same from every point of view, we need to register the importance of points of view, and in considering each, consider also how its perspective would alter if any other point of view were adopted. We can distinguish between the necessary egocentricity of any observer reporting what he observes, and the purely arbitrary choice I, and every other person, is entitled to make. We can see why philosophers and scientists have sought an "absolute" conception of reality that is invariant over all observers, but can meet their reasonable demands by accepting covariance as well as invariance as marks of objectivity. We can thus preserve the desirable purity of the Platonist ideal without having to overlook much else of importance. Great though the attractions of the View from Nowhere at Nowhen by Nobody are, the need for completeness in our view of reality overrides them all.

But the received wisdom of our age is against the lush ontology of such a metaphysics. We are in thrall to a reductionist metaphysics of materialism in respect of what ultimately exists, and physicalism in respect of what ultimate explanations must be. The arguments for reductionism, therefore, must be articulated and answered.

Chapter 13
Reductionism

§13.1 Pervasive Pressure
§13.2 Laplace
§13.3 Isolation and Chaos
§13.4 Indeterminism
§13.5 Supervenience
§13.6 Haecceity
§13.7 Levels of Explanation
§13.8 The Virtues of Irrelevance
§13.9 Pluralist Monism

§13.1 Pervasive Pressures

There are many intellectual pressures towards reductionism. We are heirs of classical corpuscularianism, and are often unwilling materialists under our skin. There are arguments from the success of science and for the unity of science, and for the unity of the world in which we and scientists operate. These give rise to different reductionist theses, which are usually confused, and reinforce one another, but need to be distinguished, and dealt with separately.

The strongest version of reductionism is physicalism, which was discussed in Chapter Four. Physicalists are ready to extrapolate from the success of science, and imagine that one day we shall have reduced all other sciences to physics, which will be a grand unified theory of everything. And this is implausible, since explanations depend on concepts, and not all concepts are susceptible of reductive analysis. Against this the physicalist may protest that the argument of Chapter Four, does not show that the concepts of chemistry and biology are among those that are irreducible to physical ones; he takes it as am established fact that all those he is interested in are so reducible, citing instances of successful reduction. But the claim that the concepts of physics were adequate is not supported by history. In order to effect the reductions it was necessary sometimes to invoke concepts—*ensemble*, for example—which lay outside the purview of physics as it then was. The physicalist might take this as evidence that the boundaries of physics are not as fixed as is often supposed, and that just as they had to be enlarged to take account of electromagnetism and quantum mechanics, so they might need to be expanded further. They might.

But it is a dangerous argument. Physicalism could be made true trivially, if physics was enlarged to include the concepts of every science and discipline; but then it would be of no interest. In order to have clout, physicalism must explain everything within some limited scheme of explanation. There is no *a priori* argument that there must be such a scheme, nor any *a posteriori* evidence that there actually is one.[1]

Materialists espouse an ontological rather than explanatory version of reductionism. Even the Archbishop of Canterbury, a chemistry master once told his class, is 59% water. But that is hardly the whole truth about Archbishop of Canterbury. To leave out the *way* matter is arranged, is to leave out almost all the important facts. Mathematicians allow that sets are important, but do not suppose that relational structures are merely sets. Furthermore, quantum mechanics has deprived matter of its substantiality. The fundamental particles of matter lack *haecceitas*, thisness. Atoms are composed of protons, neutrons and electrons, which in turn are made up of quarks and even more recondite entities, but are not *just* composed of them: the constituents do not just constitute them; it is their constitution that determines which constituents are needed; each atom is not particularly instantiated by any particular constituents, but can be equally well instantiated by any of the requisite generic type. Instead of the materialist ontology of classical corpuscularianism, an edifice resting on a ground level of fundamental particulate entities, we have a less grounded one, an ontology more like a ship floating in a sea of unindividualised ὕλη (*hule*), stuff, which supports the ontology without exerting any directed metaphysical pressure on it.

Mere materialism, then, is of little consequence. It becomes threatening when the claim is not only that everything is made of matter, but that the matter of which everything is made up is subject to rigid causal laws, which completely determine its future development. Although quantum mechanics has destroyed the scientific support for such a hypothesis, it retains its hold over our philosophical imagination. More importantly, it provides a matrix on which we can tease out the really difficult question, which has

---

[1] R.Healy, "Physicalist Imperialism", *Proceedings of the Aristotelian Society*, **79**, 1978-1979, §XII, pp.191-211, gives a useful account of different varieties of physicalism.

§13.1   Reductionism   383

often seemed to require some reductionist answer, namely how different levels of explanation can be reconciled with there being only one world; and how they can be autonomous while all operating in the same arena, and interacting with one another. For there seems to be a natural hierarchy of the natural sciences, with physics at the bottom, and chemistry above physics, and then the biological sciences above chemistry. If each level can in principle be reduced to the next level below, then we have a unified science, which naturally commends itself: if levels cannot be explained in terms of lower ones, we seem to be introducing mysterious principles, perhaps some vital force. Although in our ordinary way of thinking, minds are very different from matter, dualism, which posits minds as fundamental substances in addition to matter offers no coherent account of how they interact. Just as dualism of substance is unsatisfactory, so dualism of explanation is unsatisfactory, because it fails to give an account of how different schemes of explanation cohere. Biologists who posit a vital force, an *élan vital* or various entelechies, do not advance their subject, and do not produce any explanation of the relation between their subject and more basic ones. Reductionists do. Only if we accept that all explanations reduce ultimately to physical explanations, can we banish obscurantist appeals to mystery.[2]

Or so it seems.

---

[2] For a robust exposition, see Steven Weinberg, *Dreams of a Final Theory*, London, 1993.

§13.2 Laplace

At the beginning of the Nineteenth Century Laplace put forward a thesis of universal determinism: given the exact position and velocity of every particle in the universe an infinite intelligence could calculate the exact position and velocity of every particle in the universe at any later—or any earlier—date. In Newtonian mechanics each particle has three coordinates to express its spatial position, and three to express its velocity. In Lagrange's generalisation we have three "position coordinates", q_1, q_2, q_3, and three "momentum coordinates", p_1, p_2, p_3.

Laplace was a materialist, working with simple Newtonian mechanics, but he need not have been dealing with material particles at all, and could have worked with very different variables. Classical electromagnetism is as determinist as classical mechanics. Any fundamental science will do; a materialist metaphysic is not essential. All that is required is that we have a certain set of basic variables, $x_1, x_2, x_3, \ldots x_n$, and a set of functions, $f_1, f_2, f_3, \ldots f_n$, one for each variable, so that given a set of values $a_1, a_2, a_3, \ldots a_n$, for the basic variables at any one time, t_0, their value at any other time, t_i, will be

$$x_1 = f_1(x_1, x_2, x_3, \ldots x_n; t_i),$$

$$x_2 = f_2(x_1, x_2, x_3, \ldots x_n; t_i),$$

$$x_3 = f_3(x_1, x_2, x_3, \ldots x_n; t_i),$$

$$\ldots\ldots\ldots\ldots\ldots$$

$$x_n = f_n(x_1, x_2, x_3, \ldots x_n; t_i).$$

In many cases it is reasonable to impose conditions of continuity and differentiability with respect to t and to the various x_is. Granted certain further conditions on these functions to ensure that they are, and remain, independent of one another, we have a completely determinist system, giving a perfect Hempelian explanation extended to cover the whole universe.

Many objections to Laplace's thesis have been put forward, some of them fatal. Nevertheless, it is illuminating to suppose it true, in order to see whether his version of determinism implies physicalism. If there is a complete account of reality evolving according to some deterministic law, then the configuration of the

§13.2 Reductionism 385

universe at any given time will be completely dependent on preceding configurations and the law of development, and that is how things will have to be. A Laplacean Deity, surveying the whole universe, would be able to see the trajectory of each point-particle, and *in a sense* know the precise state of affairs at any given time. Such knowledge, however, would be in many ways uninformative. If I knew the positions and movements of each molecule of water in a stream over a given period, I would be inundated with a wealth of irrelevant information. I should need to stand back, and discarding much of the information available, concentrate on a few features, such as bubbles and eddies, which had some continuing identity as they were swept along by the current. Similarly a Laplacian Deity would need to "disattend" to much, if he was to see the wood, and not just the trees. Instead of following the fortunes of each helium molecule in a given volume of gas, he would do better to consider the mean kinetic energy of all the molecules in a given *ensemble*. The concepts of thermodynamics highlight certain invariances and tendencies which are obscured by all the detail vouchsafed by the complete Laplacian picture.

Similarly the chemist and the biologist have each a different focus, which enables them to concentrate on different features, talk about different things, and offer different sorts of explanation. The chemist does not view the whole universe, but only very limited parts of it. The biologist will focus on those sub-systems in which the organism being studied is present. To the physicist these sub-systems, if viewed as they develop over time, will seem to be simply collections of one-dimensional curves in phase-space, but the chemist and the biologist will point out to him similarities between certain curves with the irrelevant detail left out. The chemist will say that each of these is an aqueous solution of silver nitrate reacting with a chloride ion, and the precipitate subsequently being decomposed by light; the biologist will say that the organism is breathing, and taking up oxygen from the atmosphere and expelling carbon dioxide. The chemist does not want to know the temporal history of fundamental particles, but why certain general features are manifest. He is interested in the Schrödinger time-**in**dependent equation, which will, he hopes, tell him about stable electron orbits in atoms and molecules, rather than the Schrödinger time-**dependent** equation, which traces out the history of one particular system. His interests are different from the primary interest of the physicist, and he seeks answers to different questions couched in terms of different concepts. IF the physicist can learn the relevant concepts, he will be able to group together a range of different sub-systems in which the projection of the curve representing the development of the whole universe has a particular shape, and recognise each of them as an instance of the chemical or biological topic in question. But as we have already seen,[3] these may be concepts the physicist, as such, is not familiar with. He will be able to assure himself that the curves are indeed in accordance with the fundamental laws of physics, but will not himself, *qua* physicist, possess the concepts needed to classify the different curves together as instances of one chemical reaction or one biological organism respiring.

> **Laplace though wrong is illuminating**
>
> In a Laplacian world the "noise" would smother the "signal". To filter the signal out, a Laplacian Deity would have to know a lot of non-physics

Of course, many physicists in the actual world *can* acquire the relevant concepts of chemistry and biology, so as to be able to understand what the chemists or biologists are talking about. But that is because they are not just physicists, strictly construed, but intelligent human beings. We have to distinguish between two Laplaces, Laplace the physicalist and Laplace the Laplacian Deity. Laplace the physicalist is strongly reductionist, but the Laplacian Deity need not be *explanatorily* reductionist, because, being infinitely intelligent, he knows all there is to know. Anything mortal scientists can know, he can know too.

But that does not make the case for physicalism. Physicalism claims that all true explanations can be *derived* from his all-encompassing explanation, and that there is no room for any other explanation that could not be so derived. But explanations are answers to questions, and questions are posed in terms of concepts, and as was proved in Chapter Four, not all concepts are reducible to simpler ones.[4] Laplace the physicalist may protest it was not proved that the concepts of chemistry and biology are among those

---

[3] See above, §4.9.

[4] §4.9.

that are irreducible to physical ones; and may claim that all those he is interested in are so reducible, citing instances of successful reduction. But in order to effect the reduction, Laplace the physicalist may have to appeal to Laplace the Laplacian Deity and ask him to provide some concept—*ensemble* say, or heterocyclic reaction— which lies outside the purview of his original physics. Certainly, the claim that the present concepts of physics are adequate for a successful reduction of all those of other sciences is not supported by history. But, the physicalist might argue, the boundaries of physics are not as fixed as is often supposed: physics has had to expand its concepts to take account of electromagnetism and quantum mechanics; and might need to expand them further. It might. But it is a dangerous move. Physicalism only has clout because it is saying something shocking: that the explanations given by other sciences are merely special cases of physical explanation. Although some revision of what counts as a physical explanation is acceptable, indefinite expansion trivialises the claim. Thermodynamics can be swallowed, but biology is indigestible.

Laplace the Laplacian Deity is less procrustean. He is a physicist without being a physicalist. He allows that there may be different types of explanation, and that higher-level ones, "top-down" explanations, are not necessarily derivable from lower-level "bottom-up" ones.[5] Higher-level sciences have a certain sort of autonomy, "explanatory autonomy" as we may call it. Their characteristic explanations cannot be derived from those of the Laplacian physicist, not because they invoke some mysterious principles, some *élan vital*, but because of the poverty of the physicist's vocabulary.[6]

Non-implications
1. Determinism does not necessarily imply materialism
2. Determinism does not necessarily imply physicalism

---

[5] See above, §4.3, or more fully D.T.Campbell, "Downward Causation in Hierarchical Systems", in F.J.Ayala and T.Dobzhansky, *Studies in the Philosophy of Biology*, London, 1974.

[6] See above, §2.2 and §4.9.

But it is an inadequate concession the Laplacian Deity is making: even if chemical and biological processes could not be *explained* in purely physical terms, they were *determined* by purely physical conditions; in any particular instance the situation the chemist or biologist was interested in would develop according to Laplacian laws into another one that the chemist or biologist would describe in their own terminology, and would offer their own explanations of the development, which might, indeed, be illuminating, but could not account for the course of events being what it was, since that was already done, and completely done, by the Laplacian account. The explanations of the higher-level disciplines would not be fully autonomous; however interesting and insightful, they would have to be compatible with the underlying Laplacian law. Chemical and biological, and similarly psychological and rational, explanations could never lead to predictions which went beyond, or were at variance with, those the Laplacian Deity could, in principle, make. As John Searle puts it: " ... since everything can be accounted for in terms of those particles and their relations, there is simply no room for freedom of the will".[7] Many scientists, biologists in particular, are unhappy. They crave a greater autonomy. They hold that their disciplines yield genuinely new knowledge, which not only explains things more illuminatingly, but charts things happening that could not have been deduced from Laplacian principles even by an infinite intelligence with perfect information. We might say that they seek "ontological autonomy", since the necessity implicit in determinism implies ontological status. Much as causal connexions can be seen as 4-dimensional analogues of solids,[8] so conversely ineluctability suggests metaphysical solidity.

Laplacianism is not quite the threat it is taken to be, but it is a threat none the less. It need not rule out our having other disciplines, such as chemistry and biology; and it can allow that the explanations afforded by these disciplines are not mere sub-theories of physics. But it will imply that the explanations afforded by those disciplines will have only subordinate status, because in principle it is possible to predict everything that will happen to the stuff out of which everything is made.

> In a Laplacian universe, there could be illuminating explanations that were not reducible, but they would not be fully autonomous.

---

[7] John Searle, *Minds, Brains and Science,* Harmondsworth, 1984, p.86.

[8] See §4.6.

§13.3 Isolation and Chaos

There are many objections to Laplacianism, not all of them fatal. Laplace claimed that a Laplacian Deity could predict the state of the universe at any given date. But actual systems are in practice unpredictable: in order to be determinist, systems need to be isolated from outside influence—else a wandering asteroid might destroy the whole system, however fully its own initial conditions had been specified. Often we can discount the influence of remote causes, and discover reasonably accurate and reliable laws: often, but not always. Hence, it is argued, the Laplacian Deity cannot always predict. But the argument does not work. For the universe as a whole *is* isolated. There is nothing outside it that could disturb it; everything has, *ex hypothesi* been taken into consideration. IF—and it is a big IF—the state of the whole universe at a time has been completely and precisely specified, then the Laplacian Deity has all the information he could possibly need for him to calculate unerringly how things will be at any other date.

Practical Arguments against Laplace
1. We cannot isolate systems absolutely
2. We cannot specify initial conditions with absolute precision

---

But it is a big IF. At the beginning of the twentieth century, Poincaré pointed out that gambling machines worked because differences too small for the gambler to control resulted in differences that were large enough to be significant. A roulette wheel will end up either red or black, but it is impossible to give it an initial twist that will ensure its ending up black: the smallest difference may lead it to ending up red instead. This seems surprising. If we consider not just a single point in phase space, but a small finite neighbourhood, representing not just the original system but those very like it, we can argue that for systems, such as roulette wheels, with only a finite number of possible values for their variables, the n-dimensional "volume" in phase space will remain constant under the Laplacian transformation, so that states of the system that started being closely alike will end up being closely alike still, and also that in the fulness of time, systems that go on changing will come back to close to their original state. But the argument is flawed. Although volumes in phase space do remain the same under

Laplacian transformations, their shape does not: What may have started as a small spherical ball may be distorted into a spread-eagled shape, some parts of which are at a great distance from others. Thus two systems that are closely alike at first may diverge and end up in very different states. It follows that, whatever might be done in principle by an infinite intelligence, many actual systems are in practice unpredictable, because finite intelligences can achieve only limited accuracy, and the remaining, ineliminable imprecision may make a significant difference in outcome.

Much study has been given in recent years to "chaotic" systems, which are subject to unpredictabilities, much as roulette wheels are. Surprising results have emerged. Although detailed predictions are impossible, some persistent patterns develop, which sometimes remain stable under a considerable range of boundary conditions. Some thinkers have seen in imprecision and chaos a rescue from determinism. We can never specify the state of a system with absolute precision, and if very small differences—the beating of a butterfly's wings in India—can lead to very considerable consequences—say, a hurricane in Florida—then we shall not be able in practice to predict the future course of the world's history, although we may be able, none the less, to predict the formation of some stable patterns, which we may regard as "emergent features", beyond the ken of simple physics, but interesting and significant all the same.

But, again, the rescue does not work. It may show that epistemologically we shall never be able to make physical predictions in practice, but it does not show that ontologically we are free. We may not be able to determine the state of the universe with absolute precision, but on the assumptions of classical materialism there is an absolutely precise state of the universe. God, or Laplace's infinite intelligence, could know it; or, in any case, even if unknown, it was there to be known. And that, absolutely determinate state of the universe, whether known or unknown, would determine the state of every succeeding (and preceding) state of the universe with absolute precision. Chaos theory remains important, and has much to tell us about how we should understand the actual universe we live in, but is powerless to exorcise the demon of Laplacian determinism.

Chaos theory, then, is powerless to exorcise the demon of Laplacian determinism. But quantum mechanics can. Quantum mechanics is the fundamental physical theory, and if quantum mechanics is indeterminist, as was argued in the previous chapter, Laplacian determinism loses all plausibility.

§13.4 Indeterminism

As with materialism, so with physicalism, the conclusive refutation comes from quantum mechanics. Quantum mechanics is the fundamental physical theory, and, as it seems, no more fundamental theory can be forthcoming; and quantum mechanics is indeterminist.[9] Even an infinite intelligence, given the exact position and velocity of every particle in the universe, would be unable to calculate the exact position and velocity of every particle in the universe at later dates. Nor would he be able to do so, were he given full information about fields and charges instead of positions and velocities.

There has been much misunderstanding of this argument. It is objected that it does not prove free will, or re-establish traditional modes of thought; and that the introduction of some degree of randomness does not make the universe more rational. The argument of Professor Dennett quoted in Chapter Four[10] is put forward also by Professor Nowell-Smith:

> "A genuinely uncaused action could hardly be said to be an action of the agent at all; for in referring the action to an agent we are referring it to a cause"[11]

and Professor Smart:

> "... if one of our actions happened by 'pure chance' in the sense in which, according to modern physics, the change of state of a particular radium atom occurs by pure chance, then this action would not be one for which we could be held *responsible*."[12]

In short, if our decisions are random, they are not much to be proud of, and are not ones we can seriously be held responsible for.

But the argument is fallacious, turning on an equivocation in the meaning of the word 'random'. Randomness is a negative concept; a random event is one that is inexplicable. And once we recognise that there are many different types of explanation,[13] we see that there are many different types of randomness, and that

---

[9] See above, §11.4 and §11.5.

[10] §4.3.

[11] P.H.Nowell-Smith, "Freewill and Moral Responsibility", *Mind*, LVI, 1947, p.47.

[12] J.J.C.Smart, "Free-Will, Praise and Blame", *Mind*, LXX, 1961, p.296.

[13] See above, §4.3; and J.R.Lucas, *The Freedom of the Will*, Oxford, 1970, pp.55-59, 109-110.

an event or an action may be random in one sense, inasmuch as it cannot be explained in one way, but not random in another sense, since it can be explained according to some different canon of explanation. Thus an action may be random in that there is no complete physical explanation of it, while being perfectly explicable as a rational response to the circumstances. "He wrote the cheque because he had promised his nephew £100 if he got his colours for cricket" explains his action perfectly well, irrespective of whether there is an explanation in physical terms of the movement of the molecules that make up his hand. It may be that there is no such explanation. The physicist would then regard them as random from his point of view. But it would not follow that the action could not be explained in terms of reasons, or that it was random from a moral point of view, and not something we can hold the uncle responsible for.

The randomness objection fails, but that is not to say that we should construe quantum mechanical indeterminism as a positive argument for free will or for the autonomy of disciplines and sciences other than physics. The significance of the indeterminism of fundamental physics is not that it proves anything, but that it disproves a purported disproof. Laplacian physicalism claimed that all other modes of explanation could be reduced to that of a determinist physics, because, being determinist, it left no room for any other independent type of explanation. If, however, our fundamental physical theory is not determinist, that claim fails. It does not follow that the counter-claim is true: only that it has not been shown to be false. In a phrase of Alvin Plantinga's, the indeterminism of quantum mechanics "defeats the defeaters".

For many thinkers it is enough to defeat the defeaters. Our conceptual structure is a house of many mansions, and we operate with many different modes of thought, and different types of explanation. This is where we start from, and though some seek an absolute starting point from which we can establish the whole of our thought, many are prepared to accept accepted ways of thought as *prima facie* acceptable, and will abandon them only for good reason. Metaphysicians, armed with the ultimate, seem to be possessed of good reasons, and it could be the case that our whole edifice of thought was undermined by scientific physicalism. In that case, accepted modes of thought would have to be abandoned; but if the challenge of physicalism can be met, then there is no need to do more. Accepted modes of thought remain acceptable.

But this response does not satisfy everyone. Having once been shaken out of unthinking acceptance of accepted ways of thought, the metaphysician wants not only to defeat the defeaters, but to scrutinise accepted ways of thought to see if there are positive reasons for accepting them. He finds it difficult to picture what is happening. There are atoms and molecules which we can identify and re-identify, but as he tries to track their paths in time to come, he gets, instead of a definite causal chord as in the Laplacian picture, only a vapour trail. It just does not seem to make sense. And the answer is that indeed it does not: he is looking at the wrong level. At the level of molecules and atoms, all is confusion. Only at some much higher level does an intelligible pattern occur. IF atoms or molecules were ontologically fundamental, he would have a good reason for thinking that he ought to examine everything at the level of atoms or molecules, but since they are not, there is no reason why he should insist on being confused at their level rather than seek understanding at some other.

These two considerations fall short of providing a positive account. But they do not merely defeat the defeaters: they pave the way for a more positive approach, involving different types of explanation and different levels of discourse.

§13.5 Supervenience

The failure of Laplacian determinism has been thought to secure the ontological autonomy that biologists crave. But that is too quick. It removes one argument against ontological autonomy, but there are many other intellectual pressures towards a reductionist metaphysics. Even though there are irreducible conceptual differences between the sciences, they all study one world, and are interlinked by a web of inter-scientific explanations. The physicist may have to ask the chemist "What are electrocylic reactions?",[14] but having been told, will set about discovering the physical explanation for them. The biochemist gets his problems from biology, but his answers from chemistry. The scientists may be talking different languages, but they are all talking about the same *things*, which are *au font* physical things subject to the laws of physics.

This, ontological rather than explanatory, dependence is expressed by the doctrine of supervenience. Supervenience is a concept used by moral philosophers, and recently taken over into the

---

[14] See above, §4.9.

philosophy of mind to express a form of metaphysical dependence analogous to that supposed by the materialists.

In reaching value-judgements we need to consider the "facts of the case". If I am asked whether a particular car is a good car, I need to consider things like safety, petrol consumption, manoeuvrability, commodiousness, ease of parking, *etc.* My evaluation depends on factors such as these. We can see that this is so, if we consider the case of someone's reaching different judgments about two cars that seem similar in all respects. If I praise one car, and say that it is good, and condemn the other as being bad, you may reasonably ask "What is the difference?" And if I say that there is no difference, save that the one is good and the other is bad, you will suspect that I am being irrational. It is perfectly reasonable to say of two cars that they are similar, except that one is red and the other is yellow: but to say of two cars that they are similar, except that one is good and the other is bad, goes against the logic of the word 'good'. Likewise in the law-courts, and when we pass moral judgement on men's actions, we hold that like cases should be judged alike. If the goose has been convicted of serious wrong-doing, then so should the gander, unless there is a significant difference between what each of them did. Judgements are not free-floating, doling out praise and blame as the wind catches them, but are tied, in some way to be elucidated, to the facts of the case. This is not to say that they are defined in terms of the facts. To describe something as good, or to call an action right, means more than merely to relate the facts about it: but the judgement, if it is to be a proper, that is to say rational, judgement, must be based somehow on the facts.

Psychologists and neuro-physiologists hold that the mental phenomena of our experience must be supervenient on the physiological events in our brains. They do not claim to be able to *define* mental events in terms of physiological ones: but they do hold that they depend on them in some other, but substantial, way. Thus Papineau argues "We surely don't want to allow that two worlds can be psychologically different though physically identical. This would be tantamount to accepting dualism."[15] We can express

---

[15] D.Papineau, "Irreducibility and Teleology", ch.2 of David Charles and Kathleen Lennon, *Reduction, Explanation and Realism*, Oxford, 1992, p.49.

§13.5 *Reductionism* 395

this formally in terms of there being a *function* from the physiological (or factual) to the mental (or evaluative). The function need not be one-one; typically, it is many-one. Cars can be good in many different ways: many different neuro-physiological states will be experienced as painful. But the *same* neuro-physiological state cannot be sometimes painful, and sometimes not; nor can a car that is the *same* in all respects as another be evaluated differently.

The doctrine of supervenience is attractive, and contains an important truth. But it is not as simple as it seems. As always, the concept of similarity is treacherous: we think that *the same as* is a simple two-termed relation, whereas in fact it is three-termed. We may say "a is the same as b", but we need to be clear about the respect in which a is the same as b; I may be same as you in respect of nationality, or interest in philosophy, but different from you in respect of age or height. Two numerically distinct neuro-physiological states may occur at the same time but in different locations, or at different times in the same location, or at different times and at different locations. If they occur in different people, one may well be more sensitive to pain than the other. The princess in the fairy story could feel a pea through twenty four mattresses, and a modern teenager, brought up to be in touch with her feelings, might be equally pained by discomfort, whereas a young Spartan, intent on proving his manhood, might experience no pain when in a similar neuro-physiological state. Different people are different, not only by the canons of ordinary life, but in their physiology. One man's meat is another's poison. The neuro-physiologist may want to abstract from the physiology of the whole body, and concentrate on the brain alone, but he might well be wrong to do so. He could try to obviate this difficulty by confining his attention to one person, and maintaining that two similar neuro-physiological states in the same person should then give rise to the same experiences. But not necessarily so. Familiarity can breed competence, and it can also breed boredom. Whether or not the same neuro-physiological state had already occurred may be a relevant factor.

These qualifications do not destroy supervenience. The neuro-physiologist could still cite two identical twins in the same neuro-physiological state at the same time, and we might be willing to concede that at least they should be having the same mental experience then. But all that has been shown is that it is not always a straightforward matter to say what neuro-physiological states should count as being the same. Circumambient factors—personal chemistry, previous experience—may bear upon whether the neurophysiological state, narrowly defined, should count as being the same or not. With moral and legal evaluations it is even more so—so much so that we have the adage *Circumstances alter cases*. Exact similarity may be a plus or a minus in evaluating. Symmetry may enhance the architectural merit of a building, but a perfect copy of a work of art is a forgery. A private individual buying a second car is unlikely to think one exactly like the one he already has will be a good buy, whereas a business man building up a fleet, will think the opposite. The last thing a woman wants when buying a dress to go to a dance is one the same as one someone else's, whereas a few years earlier it was vital that she should have the same sort of shoes as were all the rage with her class-mates. Repeated actions are, from a moral or legal point of view, often quite different from those done only once.

Whether or not two actions of some person are to count as the same, depends on whether being repeated is morally or legally significant. That is to say, the criteria for sameness of an action are not exclusively "factual". We have to evaluate them in order to determine whether some difference between them is significant. The criteria of "factual" similarity depend on moral, or legal, evaluation.[16] This very much alters the import of the principle of supervenience. It would be easy to construe it as implying some strong principle of "universalisability", to the effect that factually similar situations should be evaluated similarly. Likewise the neuro-physiologist might construe supervenience as requiring neuro-physiologically similar brain states to be accompanied by similar mental experiences. But all that is actually required by

---

[16] See J.M.Brennan, *The Open Texture of Moral Concepts*, London, 1977, ch.1, §§11,12, pp.50-58, for an excellent account, to which I owe much. J.Griffin, "Values, Reduction, Supervenience, and Explanation by Ascent", in D.Charles and K.Lennon, eds. *Reduction, Explanation and Realism* Oxford, 1992, ch.11, pp.297-321, makes the important point that in value-judgements the concepts of the natural or the factual is fuzzy-edged. This is due in large part to ambiguity in the meaning of the word 'fact', which varies with the question is issue. See J.R.Lucas, "On Not Worshipping Facts", *Philosophical Quarterly*, **8**, April, 1958, pp.144-156. With the natural sciences, however, it is reasonable to hold that the concepts involved are not incurably fuzzy-edged, and that firm distinctions can be drawn between physics, chemistry, biology, *etc.*

supervenience is that if the evaluation, or mental experience, is different, there should be *some* difference in the factual situation, or neuro-physiological state. What this difference is may depend on the evaluation or mental experience. That is to say, although the difference in any particular case can be described in purely factual, or purely neuro-physiological, terms, we cannot explain in purely factual, or purely neuro-physiological, terms, *why* the difference cited should be a *relevant* difference.[17] Normally we think we know what differences are significant. In the natural sciences we take it for granted that differences of time, location and person are not, *per se* relevant;[18] hence the humour of the limerick:

> There was a young man in Dover,
> Who bowled twenty-five wides in an over,
>   Which had never been done
>   By a clergyman's son
> On a Tuesday in August in Dover.

But clearly we cannot automatically assume that personal factors are irrelevant to moral or legal evaluations nor to mental experience generally; and sometimes, as the examples given show, differences of time or location may be relevant too. And, although in the natural sciences we call on the principle of locality to discount the influence of remote causes, we cannot plausibly do that where human minds and memories are involved. The Laplacian circumvents the problem of relevance by having the whole universe as that on which everything else depends; that is to say, *every* state of the universe is to count as being different from every other one. But that, as we have seen, gives rise to other difficulties. Apart from inflating the noise/signal ratio to astronomical proportions, it is manifestly false that we take the whole universe into consideration when we make moral or legal judgements, and runs counter to the neuro-physiologist's contention that it is the state of the *brain* that is relevant to mental experience. Although the Laplacian could still insist on his, somewhat diffuse, sense of supervenience, nevertheless, once the spell of Laplacianism is broken, any further principle

---

[17] A.Rosenberg, makes a similar point with regard to the biological sciences: " there is no precise physical property ... correlated with the evolutionary property of fitness", in his "The Supervenience of Biological Concepts", *The Philosophy of Science*, **45**, 1978.

[18] See above, §4.8, pp.122,123.

of supervenience needs to count only some situations as being relevantly different, but, as we have seen, though the difference is one that *can* be specified in the terms, factual or neuro-physiological in our examples, of the base discipline, *which* differences are to be counted as relevant depend on the higher-level discipline.

The principle of supervenience is like that of universalisability. Kant's injunction that we should act only on those maxims which we can will to be universal laws of nature commends itself to us as being a natural concomitant of rationality. Many modern philosophers, most notably Professor R.M. Hare,[19] have adopted it as the key feature of moral discourse, but have run into difficulties in formulating maxims that are both universal and account for the subtle variations of the individual case. The difficulties can be diminished if we distinguish two principles of universalisability, a weaker as well as a stronger one. The stronger one follows Kant's formulation, and requires us to have maxims or laws or moral principles, under which particular judgments may be subsumed. In Hare's presentation they are major premises, which, in conjunction with factual minor premises specifying the conditions of the particular case, entail the judgment to be made in that particular case. The weaker principle of universalisability does not require maxims to be formulated in advance of a judgment, but only that if we reach different judgments in apparently similar cases, we can justify the difference in our judgment by citing some relevant difference between the cases. Advocates of the strong principle of universalisability claim that they can accommodate the differences brought to their notice by practitioners of the weak principle of universalisability, by successive emendations of the maxims they have adopted. Brennan's principle of supervenience counters this claim by showing that the *rationale* of including just the differences that emerge from the weak principle of universalisability depends on the moral point of view. If one killing counts as murder and another does not, then there must indeed be a difference between the two cases, and this difference is one that can be described in non-evaluative terms. But we cannot say why the different cases we count as murder are so counted without explaining that they are all *wrongful* killings of a peculiarly wicked sort.

---

[19] R.M.Hare, *The Language of Morals*, Oxford, 1952, (pbk.1964), esp. §§5.2-5.4, pp.80-86.

§13.6   *Reductionism*   399

Supervenience straddles the ground between dualism and reductionism. Unlike dualism, it does not maintain that there are two totally separate realms, with utterly different substances obeying altogether different laws. There is only one world, and different items in it are interconnected. But the interconnections are not all one way. Although a difference in the higher level requires there to be a difference in the lower level, what that difference is depends on the higher level, and cannot be explained in terms of the lower level alone.

§13.6 Haecceity

In classical atomism each atom can be individuated, having its own identity, and being in principle capable of being re-identified as the same atom as it was before. Newton re-wrote Genesis to start with the sentence: "In the beginning God created atoms and the void". Although all the atoms were, in classical atomism, qualitatively identical, they were numerically distinct, and therefore, together with the atoms and molecules of modern physics, give rise to Maxwell-Boltzman statistics. In calculating the thermodynamic properties of gases, we count as two different cases the case in which *this* molecule is *here* and *that* molecule is *there*, and the case in which *that* molecule is *here* and *this* molecule is *there*. In quantum mechanics, however, such calculations give results which are not borne out by experiment.[20] To get the right results we need to use Bose-Einstein statistics, in which we count as only one case that in which *this* photon is *here* and *that* photon is *there*, and that in which *that* photon is *here* and *this* photon is *there*. The natural interpretation is that photons, and other "Bosons",[21] are not entities to which the words 'this' and 'that' can be meaningfully applied. They lack "this-ness", or *haecceitas*, "haecceity", as Duns Scotus, and the later Schoolmen called it. Although grammatically nouns, they have the logic of adjectives. If we are considering a photograph, we may well think that we would have a different photograph if that black patch were exchanged with this white one. But if that black patch were exchanged with this black one,

---

[20] For an early recognition of this, see Niels Bohr, *Essays 1958-1962 on Atomic Physics and Human Knowledge*, London, 1963, pp.90-91.

[21] Many subatomic particles, such as electrons and protons, are "Fermions", not "Bosons", and obey Fermi-Dirac statistics: but that does not concern us here.

we should not have a different photograph, but the same one. A useful parallel is modern money. Although in the old days when all transactions were made by means of coins, it would have been possible to trace the history of an individual coin, it is impossible to do so now in the age of cheques and credit transfers. If I earn £100 from writing an article, and £100 from examining a thesis, and spend £100 on my electricity bill and £100 on my water bill, there is no saying which incoming £100 went to pay which utility bill. Lawyers use the word 'fungible' of goods whose whole point is the function they perform, and no distinction is made between numerically distinct items which perform the function equally well.[22] If I borrow a pound of caster sugar from you, I have adequately discharged my debt by giving you a pound of caster sugar, even though it is not the self-same pound—which my family has eaten—but pound of the same sort and quality. Money is a peculiarly apt comparison, since on account of its historical origin, it is invariably discrete. We can pay someone one hundredth of an American dollar, but not one seventh or one thousandth. Quantum mechanics is discrete too, somewhat contrary to what we might have expected. (And suitably favoured systems can sometimes run short-time overdrafts, and "borrow" enough energy from their neighbours to get them out of a hole.)

If sub-atomic entities lack *haecceitas*, they fail to qualify for being ultimate substances. Πᾶσα δὲ οὐσία δοκεῖ τόδε τι σημαίνειν (*Pasa de ousia dokei tode ti semainein*), said Aristotle, introducing the concept, "Every substance seems to indicate a this".[23] The absence of thisness, *haecceitas*, indicates insubstantiality. Bosons (and fermions also) are too insubstantial to carry the weight of being the ultimate things, about which a Laplacian intelligence could make predictions and retrodictions with absolute certainty. Atoms, perhaps, may be the ultimate material substances, but though physicists may come to understand atoms in terms of alpha rays, beta rays, gamma rays, electrons, kaons, muons, neutrons, photons, pions, protons, quarks, and the like, these latter will not be ultimate substances.

Quantum mechanics argues against Laplace's materialism as well as his determinism. This will make it easier for the Laplacian Deity to spot significant higher-level patterns. Much irrelevant

---

[22] I owe this insight to Dr M.J.Lockwood, Fellow of Green College, Oxford.

[23] *Categories*, 3b10.

§13.6   Reductionism   401

detail he had to disattend to will turn out to be insubstantial. Supervenience will have to be construed as a many-one, not a one-one, function; for although a high-level difference implies a low-level difference, the converse is not true. And the message is general. Chemists and biologists ignore much detail the Laplacian regarded as relevant. When they point out to him the configurations that are relevant to their disciplines, he can hardly see the wood for the trees. In order to attend to the relevant aspects, he has to disattend to the others. But to do this with a good conscience, he has to assure himself that the "disattended to" features would make no difference—no difference, that is, so far as the aspects relevant to the other disciplines are concerned. The absence of haecceity should soothe his conscience, assuring him that what he is not noticing does not matter.

It should help him in another way. The Laplacian view of the universe is modally flat, in that it gives us just the history of what actually happened. But the chemist and biologist are interested in counterfactual features: the chemist is concerned with what would have happened if the silver nitrate solution was more dilute, or was reacting with fluoride or bromide ions; the biologist if the organism was hot, or exposed to greater concentrations of carbon dioxide. Silver nitrate to the chemist is not one momentary configuration of part of the universe, but a stable chemical which will manifest its properties under a variety of conditions. The biologist studying an organism is deeply unconcerned with many of the details the physicist finds important, but does find its homoeostatic behaviour highly significant—when circumstances are different, organisms respond appropriately, so as to maintain some parameters the same, the different circumstances notwithstanding. Biological concepts are not only constitutionally "iffy", but counterfactually so. The biologist does not identify a single linear curve in Laplace's phase space, but a whole collection of them, a cord, so to speak, representing not just the actual course of the universe but a range of courses that would have happened had the initial conditions been slightly different. It is all one to the bird whether this or that oxygen molecule gets absorbed by his lungs: either would be equally serviceable in re-oxygenating his blood, either would be equally melodious in his song to defend his territory or to attract a mate. The search for ultimate understanding leads us away from individual this-ness, and towards a welter of interchangeable, unidentifiable, discrete amounts.

> **Fundamental Arguments against Laplace**
> 1. Quantum mechanics is indeterminist.
> 2. We cannot specify in purely physical terms *which* physical differences are significant in higher-level explanations.
> 3. Subatomic entities lack this-ness.

§13.7 Levels of Explanation

Explanations are answers to the question 'Why?'. Before that question can even be asked, we need to know of *what* the question is being asked. For each particular sort of question there is some sort of entity of which it is appropriate to ask that sort of question. We can ask why atoms form compounds, why people do things, why animals behave in certain sorts of ways. These concepts—atom, organism—are often reducible to lower-level concepts, but can, on account of irrelevance or the lack of *haecceitas*, thisness, be realised by many lower-level states. Thus it is that there can be explanations at a higher level without there being equally illuminating ones at the lower-level. As we saw in Chapter Four,[24] if a succession of bagatelle balls are allowed to run down a board with pins evenly spaced, the course of each ball and the place where it ultimately lands up on the bottom of the board is effectively unpredictable. But if there are slots at the bottom, so that the place where each ball lands up is not altered by subsequent balls, and we feed in a large number of balls from the same starting point, a pattern emerges, which approximates to a Gaussian distribution. Though individually each bagatelle ball moves randomly, collectively they form a Gaussian distribution. Individually we can make no predictions and offer only skimpy, probabilistic explanations: but collectively we can explain the intelligible overall pattern of the whole.

Downward causation, then, can make sense. Many have doubted this. Jaegwon Kim, who has spent many years thinking about mental causation, argues that "upward determination"—an ontological thesis akin to that put forward in this chapter—cannot be combined with downward causation. He supposes that a mental property M is causally efficacious with respect to a physical property P^*, and that a given instance of M causes a given instance of P^*. This instance of M is there because it is realised by a physical

---

[24] §4.3, p.105.

property, say P. Since P is a realisation base for M, it is sufficient for M, and it follows that P is sufficient for P^*. In which case we should reckon that P is the cause of P^*, and M only an epiphenomenon.[25] But though the lower-level state P is sufficient for M, what M causes is not a unique lower-level state P^*, but a disjunction of such lower-level states, describable in higher-level terms as M^*. I have a mental state M of intending to open the door. I get up and open the door. A very large number of physical states could count as opening the door. The explanation, M causes M^* at the higher level does not constitute a sufficient condition for P^*, but at best a sufficient condition for P^*, or $P^{*'}$, or $P^{*''}$, or .... The key point is that although the open door is not obviously a "mental" event, what counts as the door being open is seen from the point of view of an agent, and so is a concept belonging to higher-level discourse, not lower-level discourse. Because the mapping of lower-level states onto higher-level states is many-one, the causal relation between the two lower-level states is many-jointed, and the fact that there is a causal relation between them mediated through the higher-level states does not imply that there is a simple and direct causal relation between the two lower-level states which are the realisations of the two higher-level states through which they are connected.

The issues become clearer if we repeat the exercise of §13.2, and once again suppose that Laplace was right. IF Laplace was right, there would be a lowest-level description of the state of the universe, P, which would cause a subsequent lowest-level description of the state of the universe, P^*, and thus pre-empt any other causal account through some higher-level state. We might still have the higher-level causal account, but it would be otiose so far as causality was concerned (though perhaps not as regards illuminating explanation). Even if we could calculate the exact course of each bagatelle ball from its antecedent circumstances, the result would be uninformative, and we should still contrast the uninformative web of individual paths with the intelligible overall pattern of the collective whole. Similarly, even if we could calculate a causal connexion between some state of a neurophysiological system and a subsequent state of a muscular response, we might be able to understand it better if we could focus on the wood of mental events

---

[25] Jaegwon Kim, "Non-Reductivism and Mental Causation", in J.Heil and A.Mele, eds. *Mental Causation*, Oxford, 1999, p.207.

instead of the particular neurophysiological tree. But Laplace is wrong, and so there is no warrant for pre-empting the intelligible causal account which goes through higher-level concepts. Predictions based on physical theory about the course that will be taken by any particular bagatelle ball fuzz out into a cloud of probabilities. The only prediction we can make is about the distribution of balls in a long succession of experiments, and the only cause we can assign to its over-all Gaussian shape is in terms of the general set-up of the experiment.

The same general account holds good at each level of explanation: if we were to track each atom of oxygen, hydrogen and carbon, involved in some biological process, we should suffer from a surfeit of irrelevant information. Only if we changed our focus, and concentrated on long-lasting tangles of inter-acting elements, would we discern physiological processes of respiration, excretion, reproduction and the like. In neither case would we be postulating mysterious entities with mysterious powers: only bagatelle balls ran down the board, and they were guided by no agency apart from their impacts with the evenly spaced pins; only atoms constitute cells and organisms. What is new at the higher level of organization is the type of explanation invoked. In chemistry and biology we give chemical and biological explanations of processes which indubitably involve the entities of physics, but are not explained in the way a physicist explains things. When the chemist hears the physicalist claim "It is all in the Schrödinger equation, he may nod in agreement, but what he understands by the Schrödinger equation is the Schrödinger time-**in**dependent equation,

$$(\frac{\hbar^2}{2m})\Delta\Psi + [E - U(x,y,z)]\Psi = 0,$$

not the Schrödinger time-**dependent** equation. The question to which a Hempelian explanation would be an appropriate answer is not the question he is asking. He is asking about the structural properties of the cuprammonium ion which confer its chemical properties and deep blue hue, and the answer will be in terms of stable energy levels of *any* cuprammonium ion, not the development over time of some particular microphysical system.

Because their explanations are different, the Laplacian physicalist on the one hand and the chemist and biologist on the other differ in two other respects: first, that what they are talking about

§13.7 Reductionism 405

is not the same as he wants to talk about; and secondly, that although the higher-level whole is composed of lower-level parts, the parts are not *particular* parts. The would-be Laplacian would like to talk about the evolution of the whole universe: but even if that were possible, it is not what the chemist and biologist want to talk about; what they want to talk about is only a very small part of the universe—a chemical compound or a particular organism—irrespective of what happens elsewhere and elsewhen. They are not tracing the evolution of one particular history of the whole universe, but a fragment of a large number of possible histories that all resemble one another as regards that fragment. The difference of topic as between the chemist or biologist and the physicalist is like the difference between the whole set of bagatelle balls, whose Gaussian distribution can be explained by probability theory, and the particular single bagatelle ball, whose movements the Laplacian physicalist would ideally hope to predict.

The different disciplines discuss different topics. But the topics are related. Our explanatory pluralism must not only allow their being different sorts of explanation, but provide some account of how they can be interconnected. Besides the many explanations that lie altogether within one discipline, there are interdisciplinary explanations, in which a higher-level discipline frames questions for some lower-level discipline to answer. These questions are, typically, of the form 'How Possibly?' rather than 'Why necessarily?',[26] and carry no determinist overtones. The physiologist asks the biochemist how blood can be oxygenated in respiration, and the biochemist tells him about the chemical properties of the haemoglobin molecule, and the strength of its linkages to oxygen, carbon dioxide. His answers enlighten the physiologist, but give no grounds for thinking the future is foreclosed by the present, or that respiration is merely a matter of the chemistry of haemoglobin; if there is discovered a species of crab whose blood is based on vanadium instead of iron, it does not impugn the veracity or value of the biochemist's account of haemoglobin. Lower-level explanations for the most part supplement, but do not supplant, explanations sought or offered at a higher level. Sometimes, however, they do. If there is carbon monoxide around, the animal will die on account of haemoglobin's greater affinity for it. Similarly, the plant moved, because it was washed down stream; the city prospered because it

---

[26] See above, §4.2.

was on a trade route; the civilisation flourished because it enjoyed an equable climate. But such explanations only sometimes apply, and explain only some general features. Some maritime expeditions end in disaster because of storms or tidal waves; and all naval expeditions operate at sea level; but if we want to understand why ships have gone around the world, we have to consider the reasons why men travelled where they did, reasons which discounted the risks of storm and tide, and which did not rule out any destination, so long as it was at sea level.

If we want to give a causal account of events, it is no use going for the lowest level, and hoping that we can give a complete and adequate account at that level. As yet we do not know that we have reached the lowest level; and at the lowest level we have reached we have no predictability, and no substances. At higher levels we can make limited predictions about certain classes of entities: to predict that gold will not tarnish, or that iron will rust does not tell us everything, but within wide limits these are reliable predictions. So, too, in biology, and ecology and ethology; and even, sometimes in sociology: we can make predictions at the higher level, about what will happen generally speaking, in an organism, in a population, in a species, in a society, though unable to predict at the lower level what will happen to a single molecule, to a particular animal, a specimen, an individual member of a society.

Causal accounts are important. Like explanatory power, they confer reality, If we can give a causal explanation at a higher level, and cannot do so at a lower level, then we should not suppose that the lower is more real than the higher. Equally for explanation generally. If from the standpoint of the higher level we can reach an understanding not available at the lower level, then, again, that is a mark of reality that the higher level possesses and the lower does not. These considerations are not conclusive, but are decisive here. They are not conclusive: they could be over-ridden by other considerations which indicated that the lowest level was ultimate, and without question wore the metaphysical trousers. Classical materialism claimed such ultimacy, and the progress of the natural sciences seemed to support it. But closer examination has shown these claims to be unwarranted; and the many different types of explanation scientists and others have developed lead us to acknowledge corresponding types of reality, but linked together in a hierarchy of levels.

What explanations are explanatory, and what concepts are needed to formulate them, are questions to be decided by the different disciplines involved, and not laid down by a Procrustean programme of what explanation ought to be. What levels are appropriate depends on what explanations are most explanatory. Explanation, not ontology, wears the trousers. If there had been an ontological bedrock of fundamental substance, it would have provided purchase for a rebuttal on behalf of ontology, and if there had been a fundamental scheme of explanation, it would have established a dominant order of explanatory schemata, which would have kept all others in their—subordinate—place. In the absence of these, we are led to attribute a due measure of reality to the entities referred to by concepts at different levels of explanation. Not that all explanations are equally good—some may be rejected altogether. But many are good enough to confer some warrant of ontological respectability, and are sufficiently autonomous not to be undercut, even if placed within some over-arching hierarchy of different types of explanation.

§13.8 The Virtues of Irrelevance

Ontological reductionism failed because the fundamental particles of matter lacked *haecceitas*, thisness. In place of the materialist ontology of classical corpuscularinism, an edifice resting on a ground level of fundamental particulate entities, we have a less grounded one, an ontology more like a ship floating in a sea of unindividualised ὕλη (*hule*), stuff, which supports the ontology without exerting any directed metaphysical pressure on it. Instead, reality is accorded to entities playing a key role in explanations. Since some explanations straddle different levels, entities at different levels are related too. The cuprammonium ion is constituted of atoms and sub-atomic entities; the organism is constituted of chemicals, themselves mainly composed of carbon, hydrogen, oxygen and nitrogen; the society is composed of individual men, women and children. The relation, however, is not one of specific, but only generic, composition: the cuprammonium ion would not be a cuprammonium ion unless it was composed of some copper atoms or others, but it does not matter which; its deep blue hue is due to the emission of photons of a wavelength rather less than 400 nanometres, but it does not matter which photons are emitted, and it would not matter if none were emitted over an interval of a nanosecond, because, the energy levels being what they are, another photon would be emitted pretty soon.

At higher levels, however, we do not have absolute indeterminacy, but regard the differences that do exist as being nevertheless irrelevant. We can plausibly imagine ourselves distinguishing this atom from that atom, and maintaining that in the lungs of everyone now alive, there are 50 oxygen atoms that were once in Julius Caesar. But that does not make us the same as Julius Caesar. Nor does the fact that, apart from my teeth, I have in my body hardly any atoms that are the same as those I was born with, impugn my being the same person none the less. Criteria of identity vary greatly in the different disciplines, but are seldom sameness of component; I am not an indispensable member of society. If I had not been born, or died in my youth, England would still be England, even though it could not exist were there no Englishmen alive.

Irrelevance makes it possible to separate ascriptions of reality from the existence of any particular constituents, but it shapes our concept of reality in a further way. Thanks to the extraordinary stability of the nucleus, most atoms can continue to exist over long periods of time, but are otherwise very much at the mercy of surrounding reagents. Iron rusts, limestone weathers, wood rots. We learn about the oxygen cycle and the rain cycle, and come to see oxygen atoms being endlessly recycled by chemical processes. Although tenacious of existence, they are largely passive, reacting to reagents, and subject to many changes and chances in their long drawn-out lives. Though distinguishable in principle, oxygen atoms, are not differentiated in practice. We have no grounds for picking on one oxygen atom rather than another as a key factor in explaining a chemical or biochemical reaction. If they are there, they can be used, combined with, or pushed around, but any one of them is as good as any other, and things happen to them rather than any particular ones being the initiating causes of events. Although they have *haecceitas*, their thisness is to all intents and purposes irrelevant, and no significant information is enshrined in the particular history of any single particular oxygen atom.

Organisms are less at the mercy of circumstances, but often in practice they play the part of interchangeable units rather than unique individuals. Although worms have *haecceitas*, so that this worm is a different worm from that worm, either will do as a meal for the bird: they are, as bird-food, fungible. In the world there are differences, but to the bird they are irrelevant. Irrelevance thus is crucial, but comes at a price. It is crucial ontologically, because it allows the mapping from lower-level to higher-level states to be many-one, and not just one-one, thus precluding any claim that the higher-level entity depends on any particular lower-level ones (as well as also securing the autonomy of different types of explanation). A higher-level state can be realised by many different lower-level states, because the differences, though real at the lower level, are irrelevant from the higher-level point of view. What is important from the higher-level point of view is not the particular lower-level constituents that realise it, but the bare fact that there are suitable lower-level constituents available to constitute it according to its principles of constitution. It is the pattern, the process, that is important, not the particular elements that, as it happens, form the pattern or take part in the process. It is important that the pattern be instantiated, or that the process actually happens, but it is irrelevant whether it is these particular constituents or those, that instantiate the pattern or take part in the process.

Irrelevance comes at a price. Although it is a given in subatomic physics, and secured in chemistry by the qualitative identity of atoms of the same element (or isotope, to be more precise), at higher levels qualitatively different cases have to be deemed the same, the real differences between them being deemed irrelevant. But irrelevance in one respect is secured at the cost of greater sensitivity to external circumstance in another. Either worm will do as a meal because the bird can see either, and recognise it as a worm. The dinosaurs were susceptible to cold, and when the sun went down they ceased to be active. Our ancestors, the first mammals, could avoid being eaten by being warm-blooded, and hence capable of operating by night. They were more independent of their environment than the reptiles, but also more sensitive to it, sweating when it was hot, and shivering when it was cold. Homeostasis confers independence from adventitious circumstance, but needs feed-back, which makes for sensitivity to obstacles to be obviated. Animals beat plants, mammals beat reptiles, man beats other mammals, in the independence—or, perhaps better, aseity[27]—stakes, but at the cost of being more responsive to—one might almost say 'more aware' of—the world they live in.

---

[27] See above, §8.7.

§13.9 Pluralist Monism

The World-view that emerges from our critique of Reductionism is a Pluralist Monism. It is pluralist in positing different kinds of explanation, and denying that they can all be reduced to one fundamental type. It is monistic in not positing different sorts of fundamental substance. Its pluralism derives ultimately from the irreducibility in principle of all concepts to some basic ones, and the actual fact that many of the concepts we use are not in practice definable in terms of physics. Since the questions that explanations are answers to make use of such concepts, explanations are similarly irreducible. Explanations differ not only in the terms they use, but in the entities they are about. Since these entities are essential to explanation, they have some ontological status. They exist, not merely through some whim of ours, wanting to mythologize about them, but because they are integral to our understanding and knowledge of the world: τὸ παντελῶς γνωστόν παντελῶς ὄν (to pantelos gnoston pantelos on)[28] It is tempting, then, to go for ontological pluralism as well as explanatory pluralism, and posit the entirely separate existence of every sort of entity involved in explanation: but that lands us in insuperable difficulties when we try to explain how entities of different sorts interact. Once we distinguish 'How Possibly?' from 'Why necessarily?' explanations, we can see how higher-level sciences can frame questions that the lower-level sciences can answer, without its following that the lower-level sciences can frame and answer all the questions asked by the higher-level sciences. Different sorts of explanation are indeed irreducibly different, but not totally disconnected. Supervenience connects, but does not imply reductionism, because it is often a many-one, not a one-one, function from the lower to the higher level. It can be a many-one, not a one-one, function from the lower to the higher level, because at the subatomic level there is not *haecceitas*, thisness, and at higher levels, differences, even if distinguishable, are deemed irrelevant, or made to be irrelevant by some homeostatic process that compensates for any adventitious alterations of circumstance.

Since explanations at different levels cannot all be reduced to simpler, or more basic, ones, they are autonomous. And since reason is a mark of reality, explanatory autonomy confers ontological autonomy. Atoms, molecules, cells, organisms, demes, populations,

---

[28] Compare Plato, *Republic* V, 477a2.

§13.9   *Reductionism*   411

species, tribes and societies, all can be said to exist, to be the proper objects of concern, referred to by nouns in good ontological standing. They exist, but not separately. Though each exists in its own right, it does not exist as a separate kind of substance, but is made up of other substances, and goes to make up yet others. But—crucially—it is not *just* made up. The constituents do not *just* constitute the higher-level entity: rather, the constitution of the higher-level entity determines which constituents are needed; and it is not particularly instantiated by any particular constituents, but can be equally well instantiated by any of the requisite generic type. The requirement of supervenience captures the togetherness of different substances at different levels, without implying a one-way dependency of the higher on the lower. Things cannot exist or happen at the higher level without things existing or happening at the lower level, but what sort of lower-level things are needed is determined by higher-level considerations, which often cannot be adequately expressed in lower-level terms.

Reductionist arguments have a metaphysical drive. Ontological reductionism—materialism—identifies ultimate reality with the smallest possible entities, the elementary particles of fundamental physics. Explanatory reductionism—physicalism—identifies ultimate explanation with the explanations that will be vouchsafed by some future physical theory of everything. Materialism fails because the elementary entities revealed by physics are not particulars, but only an indeterminate substrate. Physicalism faces an initial difficulty that the concepts needed for its reductions are not always forthcoming in practice, and sometimes not available in principle; and a final refutation in the indeterminism of quantum mechanics. But though reductionism fails to find ultimacy, it can claim to offer unity, another desirable feature of a metaphysical system, and one that eludes most other systems. If reductionism is false, we still need to account for the unity of the universe and the hierarchy of sciences. Pluralist monism holds that there is only one stuff, but that it is organized in complex ways, and different explanations are appropriate at different levels of organization. The different types of explanation are inherently many: they cannot all be reduced to one type, but we can sometimes show how higher-level phenomena are realised through lower-level processes. We can reasonably extrapolate to the claim that it is always possible in principle to explain how higher-level activities can come about through the operation of lower-level laws, so long as we keep reiterating the point that such explanations are "How possibly" explanations, not "Why necessarily" ones, and therefore have no Procrustean or reductionist implications.

We find it difficult to accept. We are imbued with Laplacian assumptions, and think that the lower level must be basic, and that a change at the lower level must *cause* a change at the higher level, and not *vice versa*. It is difficult to rid ourselves of this preconception. We need to remind ourselves that supervenience does not imply temporal precedence or succession: there is no suggestion that the events at the lower level precede those at the higher. They are concomitant, and to that extent the causal relation could go either way. More importantly, what goes on at the lower level is too indeterminate to be plausibly identified as *the* cause. If we focus on the higher level we can detect entities and processes about which we can ask sensible questions, and hope to find adequate answers. These entities and processes represent a large number of different actual and possible accounts at the lower level: the early bird I am observing is the same bird as ate a number of early worms, and as would have eaten a number of other early worms had those he actually ate not been available. No single lower-level account corresponds to the higher-level account, and no lower-level account has the definiteness that would qualify it for causal primacy.

It is difficult for modern man to accept fully the shift of concern in the questions asked and the entities about which they are asked. Modern man is inclined to be a metaphysical masochist, drawn to any world-view that denies his humanity by cutting him down to merely animal or thingly size. Even when forced to acknowledge that Laplace's picture no longer holds, he still is conditioned by Laplacian and materialist assumptions when he comes to consider the nature of man. The quantum-mechanical revolution in physics has not penetrated the deeper levels of his mind. Nor ours. We still feel that if we are made up of matter, as we are, the material particles of which we are made up must be what makes us do all the things we do. We need to exorcize such thoughts, and recognise that in reality we are dealing with countless wave-functions, merging into one another indeterminately, and developing indeterministically. And at higher levels, where there are particular atoms, particular cells, particular specimens, they are typically, from an even higher standpoint, interchangeable with and replaceable by, others of the same generic type. Instead of thinking of the particular determining the general, we have to think of the general

§13.9   *Reductionism*

as the only definite entity we are dealing with, and its structure determining the shape of the whole. Against such a background we need feel no temptation to reconstrue human decisions as being really produced by "those particles and their relations";[29] instead, we should accept them at face value as being themselves the cause of the movement of various bits of matter. We should re-instate our common-sense view of human action in an external world against a pervasive materialism which seems to leave no place for humanity. That view can be faulted on many grounds, but is robust enough to remain plausible—many would say inescapable—none the less. In order to oust it, we needed not only to distinguish and counter the different arguments urged in its favour, but to offer an alternative which accommodated the strong points of the materialist metaphysic, in particular its insistence on the unity of the universe.

Reductionism fails. The arguments of this chapter not only defeat the defeaters, but suggest a pluralist monism, which accommodates the traditional diversity of explanations that common sense demands, while securing the oneness of the world, which it was reductionism's ambition to provide.

---

[29] See above, §13.2.

Chapter 14
Persons

§14.1 Minds and Bodies
§14.2 Consciousness
§14.3 A Mind of One's Own
§14.4 Fusion and Fission
§14.5 In Praise of Bodies
§14.6 The Subjective View
§14.7 Secondary Qualities
§14.8 Conjugating Viewpoints

§14.1 Minds and Bodies

If reductionism is false, we can hope to give an un-mysterious account of the interaction between minds and bodies that preserves the autonomy of the mental. At present we have very little idea of how a pattern of retinal stimulation evokes a mental image of, say, a snake in the jungle, or how a decision to attack it, or to run away, results in the corresponding action. But we may progress. I see the snake, and am inclined to have a go at killing it, thereby impressing my mates; but then I think of my responsibilities as the sole breadwinner, and deem discretion the better part of valour. We can imagine how an innate response produces the adrenalin that makes the first response possible, and how established neural patterns bring to mind affection and concern for the family in the future. In each case our understanding will be of the "How Possibly?" kind, not the "Why, necessarily"; if the physiology were to dictate the sequence of mental processes, they would be wooden and inflexible, quite unlike the variegated responses of our actual life. But once we no longer have a metaphysical argument for overall reducibility which would justify a procrustean strait-jacketing of mental activity into rigid patterns, the claim that it can be done because it must be, loses all plausibility.

At the physiological level no intelligible pattern emerges; a number of physiological states succeed one another. The way they develop is perfectly compatible with the principles of physiology, but other courses would have been equally compatible. Granted the first-personal concepts of consciousness, we can see the physiological states as instantiating the conflicting considerations present to my mind as I wrestle with them, and finally decide what to do.

I can make sense of the broad, first-personal picture, but lose my bearings as I descend to more limited processes at a lower level.

Descartes' dualism required a causal interaction between fundamental substances of a radically different kind: we have not found any fundamental substances in our search for the Ultimate Reality; the one reality we have found is amorphous and lacks the thisness that is the characteristic mark of substance. The interactionism outlined here is an explanatory interactionism, suggesting how different explanations can co-exist and interpenetrate with each other, by virtue of their asking different questions at different levels of complexity of the same sort of stuff. The me whose sensations I am conscious of, and which carries out the decisions I make, is a material me, composed of the same matter as in the cells of my body and the oxygen molecules I breathe in: but it is not just that matter that happens to constitute my body now; my body has a history, which involves many material particles now dispersed far from where my body is, and would be the same body if largely composed of different matter from that of which my body is currently composed. To focus too much on my current components would be to stop focusing on me. We cannot replace asking about me by asking about my components, though we can see how answers to questions about my current components can be fitted into answers to wider-ranging questions about me generally. Although sometimes answers to questions about my physiology, biochemistry, chemistry, or physics, will have an important bearing on the decisons I take, and what I manage to achieve, for the most part they are irrelevant, since if one process was not available, another would do just as well. Minds and the persons they embody are exceptionally independent of circumstances, being able to achieve their purposes by some means or other in spite of adventitous obstacles and difficulties.

> ### Aseity
> Just as men are more independent of their surroundings than other animals, so minds are more independent still, have greater aseity, and are correspondingly more real.

It is the principle of Aseity. Independence of circumstance confers ontological status. Minds, embodied in persons, can be called substances, not because they are ultimate non-composite entities, but because they are referred to by key terms we use in explanations of a sort extremely in our discourse. Although there is an indefinite plurality of possible explanations, explanations of why someone did something predominate and differ from those put forward to account for natural phenomena. Mental deliberation, as we have seen,[1] has a "dialogue" logic of *prima facie* cases, objections, rebuttals, and conclusions subject to *ceteris paribus* clauses: the natural science generally, and physiology in particular, aims to have a "monologous" logic of necessary and sufficient conditions which ill accords with the process of ratiocination, and precludes there being any simple match between the physiological stimulus of seeing the snake and ensuing response, and the thoughts that actually went through the man's mind. It is reasonable, therefore, to draw this major distinction among the many different sorts of explanation, and re-introduce dualism, a dualism of topics, based on a dualism of questions, rather than a dualism of substance; that is to say, among the many different types of question we ask, the biggest distinction is between impersonal questions from an external point of view, and those about persons from a personal point of view. Answers to the latter typically involve a vicarious first-personal stance, in which possible reasons for actions are canvassed and assessed, in a situation seen, as it were, first-personally by the person concerned. To do this, it is not enough to stand in another's shoes; we have to try to get inside his skin, and feel as he does, and see with his eyes. We deem him to be a conscious being with a viewpoint peculiarly his own.

Dualism

We reject Cartesian dualism which holds that bodies and minds are just two different kinds of fundamental substance, but Descartes was not wrong in picking out minds as what a large part of our discourse was about.

Dualism is not, fundamentally, ontological, but a dualism of stand-point, the (first-)personal and the impersonal, based on a fundamental difference in types of explanation.

---

[1] See above, §1.5.

§14.2 Consciousness

Consciousness has long been a problem for philosophers. It is a difficult concept, or, rather, bundle of concepts,[2] but has been made more difficult by philosophers approaching it from the wrong direction. If we start with the impersonal, tenseless view from Nowhere, we find it difficult to construct a plausible concept of consciousness, just as nineteenth-century scientists found it difficult to reinsert the arrow of time into a physics from which it had been filtered out. Often the correct response to a philosopher who demands a convincing account of consciousness, is like that of the yokel who, asked for directions by a lost motorist, replies "If I wanted to get to Dunchideock, I wouldn't start from here". Philosophers already have some concept of consciousness. Rather than trying to explicate consciousness in purely impersonal or third-personal terms, we should remind them of their first-personal knowledge of themselves, and encourage them to make use of resources already available to them if they want to gain understanding of other men and some other animals.

Theories of meaning are largely to blame for the philosophers' self-imposed blindness, who tell themselves that the behavioural criteria for consciousness are all that can be at issue, because, when we say something, we can only mean what the grounds are for our saying it.[3] That this is false in the case of consciousness can be seen if we consider the gruesome case of patients who were administered an ineffective anaesthetic together with an all-too-effective dose of curare, which completely paralysed them, so that they were able to feel the surgeon's knife without being able to make it known to him that they were still conscious. They were conscious, though there were no signs of consciousness. Hence, consciousness is not constituted by the overt evidence of being conscious.

The conclusion has been resisted by some philosophers in the grip of a theory of meaning which leads them to argue that it is only by reason of the patients' subsequent testimony that we know of their terrible experiences. If the patients had died, or if they had been given an amnesic drug that made them forget the horrible things they had undergone, then, so the argument runs, there would have been no fact of the matter, beyond the evident absence of overt indications of consciousness, and we should have no warrant

---

[2] See below, this section p.420.

[3] See above, ch.1, §1.2.

for saying that they ever were conscious of the operative procedures being performed on them. But this is absurd, as well as callously inhumane. I should view entirely differently the prospect of an operation in which I was going to be genuinely unconscious from one in which I was going to suffer all the agonies of unanaesthetized surgery, even if later I was going to die or be made to forget it. As with verificationist arguments generally,[4] so with consciousness; the criteria for ascribing consciousness are one thing, but what we mean when we ascribe consciousness is something more.

Our concept of consciousness is not clear-cut, but is, rather, a cluster of concepts, with a corresponding multiplicity of criteria—those used by an anaesthetist dealing with a human patient, those used by a biologist deciding to anaesthetize an organism before vivisection, those used by an ecofreak, asking a tree's permission before cutting it down for fuel. With human beings we distinguish the questions whether someone is aware of something, and whether he is self-conscious. It is easy to confuse these different senses. Often the best safeguard is to ask what the opposite is, what consciousness is being contrasted with. Often we start by ascribing on the basis of limited criteria the full consciousness that is characteristic of personhood, and subsequently have to modify it, when it becomes evident that other criteria are not satisfied. Our ancestors were animists, ascribing personality to trees and hills and springs, but we back-track, allowing only that trees are alive. Homeostatic behaviour is a necessary, but not a sufficient, condition of something's being conscious. We find it extremely implausible to ascribe consciousness to totally inert minerals—even the ecofreak does not ask the coal's permission before burning it. But the homeostatic behaviour of plants is not enough to make us think they are conscious; and the doubts extend to the behaviour of animals moving away from noxious environments and towards food supplies, or engaging in reproductive activity, which may seem at first sight to be instances of conscious behaviour. But we withdraw the ascription of consciousness, if subsequent investigation shows a machine-like insensitivity to the real needs of the actual situation. The apparently well-thought-out behaviour of a sphex wasp making nests wherein to lay her eggs might seem at first to be evidence of the wasp's consciously carrying out a plan of action. But it turns out to be an automatism, triggered by certain stimuli, even when

---

[4] See above, §1.2, §4.4.

§14.2   *Persons*   419

wildly inappropriate.[5] Dennett makes much of sphexishness, as showing how wrong we are to ascribe consciousness on the basis of apparently purposive behaviour; but his argument is two-edged. In seeking to rebut the ascription of consciousness to the sphex wasp, he allows that the apparently purposive behaviour constitutes some *prima facie* evidence in favour of the ascription, and in arguing that the ascription ought none the less be withheld in this case, he indicates another criterion for consciousness, which, if present, would strengthen the case for regarding an organism as, indeed, being conscious. The absence of what we might call holisitc assessment in cases of sphexishness not only counts against the sphex wasp's being conscious, but suggests that where this criterion is satisfied, an ascription of consciousness may be justified.

"Holistic assessment" has proved a problem for workers in artificial intelligence, who know it as the "Frame Problem". They are now able to program machines to behave in fairly complicated ways, but not to adjust themselves to the wide range of circumstances which they are likely to encounter. Organisms have evolved to be able—within reason—to adjust. Although they occupy some particular ecological niche, there is a much greater range of variation within that niche than any machine thus far constructed can accommodate itself to. It is a mark of consciousness not to be so severely limited in its responses. Although often we need to concentrate on the matter in hand, disregarding everything we take to be irrelevant to our present purpose, tunnel vision is a defect: we need to be alert to the emergence of unforeseen factors, which may disrupt our carefully contrived plans. Wide-ranging responsiveness to the environment is taken as evidence of awareness, itself a central facet of consciousness.

With human beings (and perhaps some other "higher animals"), a further facet of consciousness is the ability to stand back, and reconsider the whole situation, oneself included. It emerges from the ability to adjust to unexpected variation of circumstance; for this involves an ability to stand back and consider not only the circumstances but also the programs, what they can accomplish, and hence in what circumstances they are appropriate. If I am alert to my environment, I may become aware of factors adverse to my

---

[5] D.C.Dennett, 1984, *Elbow Room*, Oxford, ch.1, §3, pp.10ff. Further examples, telling both ways, are given by Roger Penrose, *Shadows of the Mind*, Oxford, 1994, pp.407-408.

> **Consciousness**
>
> Different Contrasts:
>
> (1) Medical: as opposed to being asleep, anaesthetized, concussed, in a coma.
> (2) Responsive: as opposed to being inert, like a mineral.
> (3) Sensitive: as opposed to being merely homeostatic, like a vegetable.
> (4) Alert: as opposed to having tunnel-vision, ?like a sphex wasp?.
> (5) Self-conscious: as opposed to not being able to stand back, and reconsider.

present plans, and I may then need to weigh up the *pros* and *cons*, and decide whether to continue with the plan I had adopted, or to modify or abandon it. I am led to detach myself from myself and my situation, and re-assess the situation from a new standpoint, which can be seen as a higher standpoint in as much as it is more detached, and less in thrall to immediate circumstance. Standing-backness and self-criticism are peculiarly characteristic of consciousness. Its first appearance among animals—the discovery on the part of tits how to peck through the tops of milk bottles, of rabbits how to gnaw through the plastic guards around growing trees, of household pets how to find their way home over long distances—attract notice and are commonly cited as evidence of animals being conscious like us. The full transition from being conscious to being self-conscious appears fairly late—only in human beings, and often not even then. But the first origins of this transition seem to be deep in the concept of consciousness. The conscious organism is something separate from its environment, acting homeostatically so as to preserve itself, and reproduce its kind, capable, to some extent, of adjusting its strategies to fit the situation in which it finds itself, and hence with some power of reflection.[6]

Thus far we have distinguished three inter-related marks of consciousness: 1. homeostatic behaviour that suggests the agent has a goal which is pursued in spite of adventitious alteration of circumstance; 2. some plasticity of behaviour, revealing a sensitivity

---

[6] See Bernd-Olaf Kppers, *Information and the Origin of Life,* (tr. Manu Scripta), Cambridge, Mass., 1990.

§14.2   *Persons*   421

to a wide range of circumstance and an ability to size up the situation as a whole, and adjust behaviour to the whole of it, and not just a few salient features; and 3. some degree of independence from physical environment. What leads us to ascribe, on the basis of these criteria, actual consciousness is its explanatory power. As we saw in chapter six, if we can integrate a wide variety of different pieces of behaviour as manifestations of a single state of mind, as we can with Ryle's depiction of the different manifestations of vanity,[7] it is rational to posit that there is, in fact, a mind at work. We can understand diverse pieces of behaviour, provided we posit the existence of a person, conscious of himself and how he appears to others; therefore it is reasonable to make this posit, just as it is reasonable to believe that electrons exist, because by so doing we can explain many diverse phenomena. The same line of argument that justifies our rejecting phenomenalism and believing in material objects as the reality that gave rise to phenomenal appearances, justifies also the ontological assumption that certain patterns of behaviour are to be understood as the actions of conscious beings.

The arguments for ascribing consciousness are presumptive, not conclusive. They can be defeated, as Dennett seeks to defeat the ascription of consciousness to the sphex wasp. There is room for rational disagreement over whether, and to what extent, animals are conscious. Ants show considerable flexibility of response to their environment: do they feel pain? Is is cruel to pull of the wings of house flies? In contemporary Britain there are many who believe that foxes feel fear when pursued by foxhounds, but that fish do not feel pain when pulled by a fish hook in their mouth, and that therefore hunting should be banned, but angling allowed.

Often it is the consequences of imputing consciousness that seem to tell most against making any such ascription, and it is useful to consider what follows from regarding an organism or machine as conscious. We are most keenly aware of the moral consequences: we think it wrong to cause animals pain, unless for a sufficiently good reason, whereas we have no qualms in cutting down a tree or boiling unanaesthetized carrots. If computers were conscious and sufficiently self-aware, we might feel it incumbent to consult them about their own future, perhaps even give them the vote. But these moral consequences are not fundamental: rather, they flow from

---

[7] See above, ch.6, §6.13.

a metaphysical view of conscious beings as centres, each having a view of its own upon the world. We should not cause people pain, because they are sentient beings, for whom pain is, from their point of view, bad. In attributing to them a point of view, we attribute to them a privileged authority on what that view is. I am the authority on me. What I say about me goes; not absolutely—I may be lying, dissimulating or malingering, or I may misunderstand the English language, or even misreport my own feelings; but these are only subsidiary derogations from my being generally the person peculiarly entitled to speak about me, and to have my words believed. I may have a terrible disease or a horrible wound, and the doctors may expect me to be in great pain: but if I assure them that I feel no pain, and my actions confirm that I am being truthful, then the doctors have to accept my word for it, and perhaps look for other explanations—perhaps I have had the operation under hypnosis, perhaps I have had acupuncture, perhaps I am one of those unfortunates who can feel no pain. Conversely, if I feel pain, I am to be believed, even though there is no discernible cause for it. It may be "only psychological", it may be some malfunctioning of the nervous system, but it cannot be denied without imputing to me dishonesty. Similarly in the case of animals, except that there we have no distinction between behaviour generally and the special sub-class of linguistic behaviour: if we read their behaviour as that of a sentient being, we believe it in the absence, or even against the evidence, of physiological explanation—if a rabbit squeals, I think it is hurt or frightened even if I can see no cause of pain or ground for fear, whereas if a tyre squeals, I give it no probative force and disregard it as soon as I can account for it as the result of friction on the road's surface. If we came to regard computers as conscious, we should give more credence to their output than to their hardware, and be prepared to agree that something was wrong even though the most exhaustive examination failed to reveal it, provided the output, either by means of direct symbolism or through suitably modulated aversive behaviour, indicated that this was so. Once this point is reached, moral consequences follow: the artefact has a right to consideration, because it has a view of its own which cannot be subsumed under views available to us apart from its explicit avowals or significant actions.

Consciousness has different facets and different aspects. Our ascriptions of it are always fallible, but can be justified. They explain. IF the reductionist programme could be carried through, their explanatoriness would be merely an illumination for us, and ontological parsimony would still counsel not regarding sentient beings, and in particular, persons, as anything very special. But since no reduction can be carried through, ontological parsimony counsels in favour of regarding persons as fundamentally real, since only by doing so, can we make sense of diverse phenomena. If we can attribute feelings and motives, and more generally empathize with other men, and to a more limited extent with other animals, we can achieve an understanding of their reactions and behaviour in the characteristically complicated, and often unique circumstances in which they are situated. We try to see things from their point of view, because there is no other way in which we can see things coherently. But once we accept they have a point of view, which is in the same ontological class as ours, we are impelled to take into consideration not only our own hopes and fear but theirs also. And then we are in deep waters.

§14.3 A Mind of One's Own

Locke explicated personal identity in terms of memory, and common sense has since accepted a Lockean position which makes memory-claims, along with character traits and first-personal avowals, the definitive criteria of personal identity. Such an account seems to fit our actual practices, acknowledges the prime importance of the first-personal standpoint, allows for the intelligibility of Dr Jekyll and Mr Hyde, and the various Miss Beauchamps, and for the widespread human hopes and fears of a life after death, and all this without being very strongly committed to any particular metaphysical scheme. But it has been criticized, because it fails to guarantee uniqueness. The memory claims of any one person could be put forward by another person, sincerely believing that he was the same person that the first claimant genuinely believed himself to be. Just as physical appearance and behaviour can be duplicated, so memory claims, character traits, and avowals of identity can, in principle, be duplicated too. Whatever evidence we might have for identifying one claimant as the person he claimed to be, it is logically possible that there could be another candidate with exactly the same features, and therefore equally worthy to be identified as the same person. Having unreservedly accepted the first as the genuine claimant, we should be nonplussed on encountering the other; we might, like Buridan's ass, conclude that since they cannot both be, they neither of them can be, the person they both claim to be; or, perhaps more reasonably, we might seek some further surety for uniqueness.[8]

One feature that cannot in our world be duplicated is bodily continuity, and many modern philosophers have concluded that bodily continuity is the constitutive condition of personal identity, as it was of corpuscles, and still is of atoms. But there are difficulties, both in practice, and in principle.

With few exceptions, bodily continuity is not a criterion we actually use. Only with patients intensively watched over in hospital and prisoners securely locked in their cells, can we be sure that they are bodily continuous with their previous selves. Nearly always we rely on faces and self-avowals. That point, by itself, is not decisive. Criteria are features which serve as handy indicators; they are subject to constraints of practicality: they need to be accessible, easy to apply, and reasonably reliable under commonly prevailing conditions, but do not need to exhaust the whole content of the concept, nor to be infallible, nor even reliable under conditions which seldom, if ever, obtain. In order to delineate the concept, we are concerned not just with criteria, but with constitutive conditions. But once we relax the certainties of ordinary life, and take seriously the possibility of two claimants with qualitatively identical characteristics and memories, we cannot rule out in principle the counter-factual possibility of someone's splitting bodily, amoeba-like, into two.[9] In the corpuscularian philosophy spatiotemporal continuity was a constitutive criterion of identity, because corpuscles possessed no essential qualities, beyond occupying some place or other at any one time, without there being any place that any one corpuscle necessarily occupied at any given time.[10] But it is only a contingent, not a necessary truth that material objects and human beings do not divide or join up like rain drops. If they did, our concepts would be very different from

---

[8] B.O.A.Williams, "Personal Identity and Individuation", *Proceedings of the Aristotelian Society*, LVII, 1956-1957; reprinted in B.A.O.Williams, *Problems of the Self*, Cambridge, 1973, I, pp.1-25.

[9] A.M.Quinton, *The Nature of Things*, London: Routledge and Kegan Paul, 1973, p.95.

[10] See above, §9.6.

what they are.[11] Even if we adopt the metaphysics of modern materialism, bodily continuity would not have for human bodies the pre-eminent position it has for atoms, because human bodies are processes rather than things, processes involving a continual flow of energy and matter, with no particular material particles reliably continuing as permanent constituents of any human body.

Although bodily continuity cannot make good the inadequacies of the traditional account, the criticisms made of the traditional account are cogent. Personal identity is necessarily unique, but every characterization of a person in terms of memory claims about the past or other present mental features, habits, or abilities, can be duplicated. We can secure uniqueness only if we look not just to the past, but to the future, not just to the passive, but to the active, and not just to the actual, but to the possible. Once again, we must conjugate. We need to conjugate over tense and mood, considering not only the actual present and unalterable past, but the possible future; we need to conjugate over voice, considering ourselves not only as the subjects of experience but as the initiators of action; and over person, considering not only third-personal ascriptions of identity, but first-personal avowals, and second-personal discourse.

Locke held 'person' to be a forensic term, whereby people were held responsible for what they had done, and blamed for what they had done amiss. But though at this present time I can only remember having done some particular deed in the past, at one time I was deliberating, and was making up my mind whether I should do it or not. At that time it was not a matter of my merely having certain experiences, putative memories of having done it in the past, but of my forming an intention for the future and actually carrying it out. I was an agent, not passively experiencing but actively doing. And until I had carried out my intention, it was an open question whether or not I actually would. Although now that I have done it, the deed is done beyond recall, it was at one time only a possibility, with its being still up to me whether or not it would actually be realised.

The importance of future possibility is shown by an example from *Alice Through the Looking Glass*. Tweedledum and Tweedledee were more than ordinary identical twins: they shared consciousness and experiences. Each knew what the other was doing, felt the other's pains, and remembered what the other had

---

[11] See K.M.Wilkes, *Real People*, Oxford: Oxford University Press, 1988, ch.1 for reasoned scepticism about the extent to which counter-factual hypothetical experiments should weigh with us.

done. We might be tempted to say that there was only one person, Tweedle, but with two bodies. Bilocation seems perfectly intelligible, and would have advantages for busy modern man, with 2.8 engagements for every available hour. While one of me was dutifully present at a meeting, my happier half could be reading a good book, buying a surprise present for my wife, or having lunch with a useful contact, only occasionally interrupted by the need to know which proposal my dutiful half should vote against. With four arms and four eyes I could make much better use of my time than I currently do. So long as there were unity of control, and my dutiful half could not vote against the better judgement of my liberated half, it would be right to regard me as two bodies with but a single mind, and therefore just one person. It would be quite different if there were, or at least potentially could be, some conflict. Then there would be two of us, perhaps in very close telepathic communication, and often of one mind on matters of importance, but not necessarily agreeing on all things. If, as Alice was assured, Tweedledum can quarrel with Tweedledee, then they are indeed two separate centres of decision-making, and not two arms of the one unified Tweedle. Tweedledum has a mind of his own, different from Tweedledee's, since he can make it up differently. Even if they always in fact agree, they could differ, and so are different. Having a mind of one's own is being able to make it up differently.

> Tweedledum and Tweedledee Agreed to have a battle; For Tweedledum said Tweedledee Had spoiled his nice new rattle.
>
> Just then flew down a monstrous crow, As black as a tar-barrel; Which frightened both our heroes so, They quite forgot their quarrel.

The future encompasses many possibilities, whereas the present consists of only one actuality, and the past of only one unalterable course of events. In talking about the future, therefore, we have to consider all possibilities: if Tweedledum and Tweedledee can decide to attempt different things, then, whatever the harmony hitherto, there is some future possibility in which one is trying to counter what the other is trying to do; if Tweedledum and Tweedledee cannot decide to attempt different things, then among all the possible future courses of events there is none that represents the one trying to thwart what the other is endeavouring to achieve. And since we are already in the realm of possibility, there is no room for a further appeal to possible duplication to confuse identity. If we are faced with two people both plausibly claiming to be the same person, let them meet each other. If each denounces the other as an impostor, then we can be at least sure that they are not both the same person in the way that Tweedle, were it not for the possibility of battle, might have been: one of them at least is an impostor. We may not be able to tell which, and we may have another Tichborne case on our hands; but that will be good news for the lawyers rather than bad news for the philosophers. If on the other hand, each treats the other with fraternal affection, taking him for granted as a fully accredited and completely apprised fellow-worker in a common field of endeavour, we have a bilocated person enjoying two bodies but with only one will. When we survey the future, either there is a possible course of events in which the two putative Tweedles fight, or there is not: if the former, they are different persons, Tweedledum and Tweedledee, not both Tweedle; if the latter, there is only one person we are dealing with, Tweedle. There is no third alternative: having considered all possibilities already, there are no further ones to generate further putative persons. Moreover, the all-or-none character of all possibilities secures the all-or-none character also of individual identity. When dealing with individuals, there is no room for a nicely calculated less or more: each someone is definitely a one, as well as necessarily not anyone else. By considering all the possible actions of an agent, we secure that each is one and all alone, and ever more shall be so.

Locke can be fairly charged with having neglected the future in his account of personal identity, but Williams cannot, and in "The Self and the Future" argues from the self's future concern for itself: but concern presupposes the possibility of action and thus of intention.[12] I am afraid of being tortured: and therefore I take action to avoid it. If I did not, other things being equal, try to avoid being tortured, I could not be said to be afraid of being tortured. So we can ask at different stages in Williams' account who would try to take avoiding action. Suppose the torturer were to drop his

---

[12] B.O.A.Williams, "The Self and the Future", *Philosophical Review*, LXXIX, 1970; reprinted in B.A.O.Williams, *Problems of the Self*, Cambridge, 1973, 4, pp.36-63.

guard, and leave the prison door open: it would be the person who was going to be the inhabitant of A's body at the time of torture who would self-interestedly want to escape. The decision-maker is the person who can try to avoid the threatened evil, and is concerned to do so. Often puzzle cases in the philosophy of mind are constructed in which we are invited to imagine ourselves in some dreadful situation paralysed or completely under the control of a mad scientist. But such situations are, not only fortunately but necessarily, untypical. We are, first and foremost, agents: were we not agents, it is doubtful whether we could be patients either—consciousness is very largely a feedback on endeavour—and we certainly could not have the concept of a person that we do have. *Ego, ergo ago.* As I contemplate the dreadful things that might happen to someone, I identify with him whose actions then, should circumstances turn out to be less unpropitious than currently portrayed, I can decide upon now.

Since each rational agent can make up his mind what he should do, and to a large extent carry his decisions into practice, it matters very much to us with whom we are dealing. We need to be able to distinguish different agents because they have different patterns of behaviour, and these differences may matter to us very much. Individuals signify, not simply as idiosyncratic obstacles we need to learn to manipulate if we are to achieve our ends, but as sources of value, differing from us in some important respects, but none the less valid and worthy of our own affirmation and respect.

We can look at this in a Leibnizian way. There is a tension between the necessary uniqueness of the self and the possibility of multiple instantiation of any set of qualities. So long as we are dealing with only a finite set of qualities, they specify some *infima species*, which only contingently and not necessarily has only a sole specimen. If, however, we move into the infinite realm of possible courses of events, we can specify an individual uniquely by an infinite specification characterizing every response he might make under every set of conditions. If two putative persons would respond to every situation in the same way, then they are one and the same person, numerically identical: if there could be some discordant response, they are to that extent qualitatively as well as numerically distinct. Instead of needing the bodily continuity of the corpuscularians to guarantee the separate individuality of each entity necessarily located in space, each monad differs from every other one by virtue of the way it actualises the infinite potentiality

§14.3   *Persons*   429

open to it as an agent. The Leibnizian picture of individuals as infinitely complicated monads, each qualitatively different from all others, is important as a prophylactic against a scepticism that has prevented many philosophers from conjugating over persons. They have been confined to the third person by qualms about the first-personal approach. But while we should sympathize with those who are in the grip of a theory of meaning, we need not share their affliction. We have experience, most notably of other people but also of concepts, which, because they go beyond anything that could be programmed or specified from outside, seem to us to be indubitably real. People have style. Not only men of letters in their literary output, but all of us in our ordinary activities, do things in our own characteristic and inimitable way. Although a well-trained classicist can produce a passable parody of ancient authors, extended imitation is soon distinguished from the real thing, because the real is original, with unanticipated features which *ex post facto* are recognised as being absolutely right, but which did not conform to any antecedently specified rule. At a much lower level it is often the mark of someone's having understood a concept that he is able to apply it in new cases that lie altogether outside the existing rules, and, at a slightly higher level, of his having got inside a poem or play that he can make critical comments that go beyond the most that the most assiduous student could have mugged up. In the non-denumerably infinite welter of possible performances of possible monads we can distinguish the rational from the irrational even though we do not have any explicitly formulated rule to tell us how to do it. In mathematical terms people are capable of non-algorithmic reasoning which is right without being rule-bound, and individual without being random. Hence it is that we are, most of us, robustly immune to doubts whether we can meaningfully ascribe to another person a first-personal standpoint and private experiences all of his own: we have on occasion felt the force of a individual personality, different from anything we could have thought up for ourselves, yet rational none the less; and that gives us confidence to believe that we are dealing with something real, an entity that is the same on different occasions of encountering it, an entity such as we hold ourselves to be. If I recognise something as a person, I recognise that he has his own first-personal standpoint, and can use the word 'I' to express it in the same way as I do to express mine: and if I re-identify him as a particular person, I ascribe to him the same coherent identity as I assume for myself in my view of my own affairs. Were it not for this, I should not be interested in the identity of individuals, but should be content to identify species, as I am with flowers. Although in each case I may turn out to be wrong in my identification of a person, the point of the claim is to establish him as an *alter ego*, a particular *alter ego* with whom I have had dealings in time gone by, or may have dealings in time to come.

If I regard someone as an *alter ego*, as someone who can use the word 'I' to express it in the same way as I do to express mine: I shall want to address him in the second person: I ask *you* to give your own account, in the first person, of what you did and why you did it, the view you now take of your actions, your opinions about current affairs, and your plans for the future. Personal identification is important because it opens up the possibility of dialogue in which the person concerned can give a first-hand account, and when he uses the first-person singular, we shall know to which person the word 'I' in his mouth refers. The fact that we often have to ask people their names has not been sufficiently attended to. It proves the prime importance of the first person even where mere criteria are concerned, and is becoming increasingly important as other ways cease to be available in consequence of the meagre information provided by electronic means of communication.

Potential disagreement is constitutive of personal identity. If two people can disagree, they are different persons: if they cannot, they are the same person. But it does not provide a convenient criterion. Faces and avowals are what we commonly use, and are nearly always reliable, sometimes supplemented by other bodily features, character traits, and memory claims. These work well enough in practice, though if the world were very different, we should be unable to rely on them as much as we do. Underlying all personal discourse is our seeing persons as agents, each an $\dot{\alpha}\rho\chi\dot{\eta}$ $\tau o\hat{u}$ $\kappa\iota\nu\epsilon\hat{\iota}\nu$ (*arche tou kinein*), an initiator of action, with a mind of his own, which he makes up for himself, and can make up differently if he so decides.

§14.4 Fusion and Fission

The prime importance of the first-personal approach should guide us when we come to consider Derek Parfit's difficult cases. It is the point of ascribing an identity, not the criteria which have served us well in more mundane circumstances, that should carry the most weight with us. In so far as we can make sense of fusion and fission thought experiments, we need to ask how the story is to be told from the inside before attempting to say how we, on the outside, would respond.

Let us deal with fusion first. There is an obvious difficulty, analogous to that in spare-part surgery. Transplants are commonly rejected, just because, as we have seen, human bodies are not material objects but processes, more like flames or eddies than pieces of furniture or wooden ships, and what counts is not the material particles composing a body at any one time, but the metabolic flow of matter and energy, and the information implicit in the organization of the organism. In the same way, any hypothetical experiment involving the fusion of two personalities would have comparable difficulties in integrating disparate memories into one coherent and plausible history of the putative person. Of course, a story can be told of a mad scientist getting hold of me, and implanting some of the memories of Fiona, and of my waking up with apparent memories of my first pony, Queen Charlotte's Ball, a London season, triumph at Badminton, and my marriage at St George's, Hanover Square, to a sprig of aristocracy. But apparent memories are not, contrary to the opinion of many philosophers, accepted always without question. In the quiet watches of the night I vividly remember many exploits, sometimes as Napoleon, sometimes as Pericles, sometimes, less properly, as the Sublime Porte, surrounded by eunuchs and concubines, all eager to gratify my merest whim; but these impressions, however vivid, are rejected because they do not fit in with the rest of my remembered experience; and, though less spectacularly, some waking memory-impressions are likewise subject to critical scrutiny, and in spite of the fact that I could have sworn that I posted the cheque, I ruefully concede that I must have misremembered it as I find the cheque in its envelope still nestling among the other papers on my desk. Memory, though generally reliable, is not of its nature infallible, and we only accept those memories which do not run counter to the rest of what we know and understand. One look in the mirror will convince me that I was never the deb of the year, half a minute on a horse that I could never have gained even a rosette at a pony-club rally. Just as the the body rejects intruded cells, so each man's autobiography rejects intrusive matter which cannot be accommodated within what is already known and understood; and although the immune system of the body can, at great cost and risk, be sufficiently suppressed to allow transplants to be made, the suppression of the critical faculties required before I could be content to accept Fiona's memories as my own would be so great as to leave me a completely irrational, and barely self-conscious, being. No first-personal account of fusion is coherent: although I may by my own free decision share the rest of my life with another, merging my individual will in our joint choices, and coming to know all her memories as she recounts them, neither of us can know the other's early memories first-hand, and our sharing could never conceivably become a complete coalescence.

Much the same is true of fission, though not so absolutely. Each one of us needs to be able to make sense of his future as well as of his past. A person, as Lockwood maintains, arguing from a very different starting point, is essentially a diachronic concept:[13] we should take it as definitive of mind that it encompasses its own past actions and reaches out towards what is to happen. As Glover emphasizes, our identities are very largely what we ourselves create.[14] If I could not form a coherent view of my own future, I should not have a coherent concept of myself. I find no difficulty in envisaging a future in which I am bilocated, but formidable difficulties in making sense of the prospect of my being two mes, not of one mind with each other. I should not want my Abel-self to be slain by my Cain-self, undeterred by Swinburne[15] and anxious to secure his sole claim to be me. So I decide now not in either of my successor selves to slay my other self. But will this decision stick? After all, it is always possible to change one's mind. I might, I suppose, make sure by deciding now to separate, like Abraham and Lot, but our experience with actual identical twins makes this seem unnatural, and in the face of such a prospect I am much

---

[13] Michael Lockwood, *Mind, Brain and the Quantum*, Oxford: Blackwell, 1989, pp.279ff.

[14] Jonathan Glover, *I: The Philosophy of Psychology and Personal Identity*, Harmondsworth: Penguin, 1988.

[15] R.G.Swinburne, "Personal Identity", *Proceedings of the Aristotelian Society*, **74**, 1973-74, p.237.

§14.4 *Persons* 433

more likely to resolve very firmly not to change my mind. If that possibility is excluded, or if intentions do not survive the process of fission, then I am already no longer a person, and nobody can be identified with me. In order for there to be any question of my continuing to exist, I must be able to form intentions and stick to them. In that case, I shall resolve not only that we shall, neither of us, hurt or thwart the other, but that we shall stick together through thick and thin. Tweedle will rule out the possibility of a battle, and will remain, so much as in them lies, still just Tweedle, though bilocated Dumly and Deely. So, too, the tribe of Lucas clones will stick together, like a pack of wolves, each abiding by the decision made in the original position, each identifying himself as part of the pack, quite possibly using only the first person plural; and should any have the misfortune to be separated from the pack, likely to fade away and die through inanition and loss of identity.

Difficulties remain. The two most notable are the division of consciousness and the unforeseen fission. It could be the case that Dum and Dee did not know, until told, what the other was doing. But this often happens in ordinary life, where I do not know what I am doing until I tell myself and consciously recognise it. More pertinently, in the real-life split brain cases there is some division of consciousness between, as it were, two centres of consciousness. But we should note our response: a few philosophers excepted, we continue to regard the patient as a single person, because for the most part he is able to make over-all decisions and integrate his behaviour into a coherent pattern. This no accident. Consciousness is not entirely separable from decision-making, but is, as we have seen, largely a feed-back on action.[16] If we are of one mind what to do, we shall be mutually aware of how we fare in consequence.

Fission is not altogether symmetrical with fusion. With fusion, whatever memories may have been implanted in me, I shall have to decide whether to own them as memories of my own actions, or disown them as fantasies that can have played no part in my real life. In the case of fission that I have considered, I was able to decide antecedently what I should subsequently do, and impose on

---

[16] Admittedly, Foster, among others, offers an account of the unity of the stream of consciousness without any explicit reference to decision-making, but I am unpersuaded of its success. See his "In Self-Defence", in G.F.Macdonald, ed., *Perception and Identity*, London: Macmillan, 1979, pp.175-182.

my future an orderly theme. But what if an individual is divided unawares? If I did not know I was fissile, and it just happened to me? I meet someone who looks like me, behaves like me, has all my memories, aspirations and ambitions, and who says he is me? Do I regard him as an impostor to be killed, or an *alter ego*, to be cherished and cooperated with? Answers give out: but perhaps the questions have run out too. I share Dr Wilkes' scepticism both as regards the feasibility of surgical Parfitry. and its relevance to our understanding of the concept of a person. The very fact that our actual concepts have been developed against a particular background of fact means that our criteria are likely to pick on contingent rather than necessary features as reliably characteristic of what it is to be a person, or to be the same person as one previously identified. *Habeas corpus* makes sense in humdrum England, but would have been of no avail to Ariel seeking his liberty from Prospero's spell-enforced servitude. If the transmigration of souls were an established fact, if we lived in one of Shorter's imaginary societies, if most of our pupils behaved, and avowed having experiences, like Miss Sally Beauchamp, if our colleague Dr Jekyll alternated in behaviour with the altogether unelectable Mr Hyde, our concepts and forensic practices would be very different. So too with other, non-personal concepts. If the world were very different, our concepts would be different too. We should not have the concept of a material object if we lived in an aqueous medium, in which beneficial and noxious chemicals were diffused, but with no definite sources or boundaries: we might then have a purely olfactory experience, in which we could distinguish various sorts of "good—here—now" and "bad—here—now", but no numerically distinct objects we could re-identify and manipulate. Hence it is reasonable to meet difficult fission possibilities by pointing out that we should not have the concept of a person, if agents did not continue over extended periods of time, pursuing long-term plans, remembering what they had done, and what they had decided to do. I should not be conscious of myself as a self if I could not decide what I was going to do, and always forgot what I had done and what I had been going to do. Not that I have to have complete plans for all my future life or complete memory of all my past doings: I can tolerate a large measure of present indecision and forgetfulness. But once I am not totally undecided and amnesiac, I can take steps to transcend my limited abilities. I can write memos to myself, to remind myself of what decisions I either have made or need to make, and I can keep a diary. Thus, granted only the minimal capacities required of our being agents at all, we can extend our effective forward planning and backward memories to connect our present selves with our future concerns and previous deeds. It is only if we are hopelessly restricted to the present that we cannot get a grip on the future and past, and then we should no longer be agents at all, and should not know ourselves as such.

So, if we cannot rule out puzzle cases absolutely, we can at least marginalise them, either by reckoning them so bizarre that they altogether undercut the notion of one's having a first-personal view of oneself as a person, or, if any reasonable power of decision-taking is left, by extending it to cover the difficult cases, and taking them into account as we envisage possibilities and form life projects, and by discounting awkward possibilities by definite decisions. If we are to have a concept of an agent, he must be able, at least a little, to extend himself towards the future and to own his deeds done in time past, and any such extension is itself extensible. I can make up my own mind what I shall do, and it is the mark of its being my mind that I can make it up for myself, differently from you.

§14.5 In Praise of Bodies

If in our minds we can range freely over space and time, we might suppose that we could do without our bodies altogether. Plato thought so. Many religions teach that our mortal flesh is an encumbrance to purity of spirit, and popular ideas of life after death envisage some sort of disembodied existence.

But there are difficulties. Minds have been shown to be largely independent of bodily circumstance, but not absolutely so. Over a wide range it does not matter which particular atoms, molecules, physiological processes are involved, but it does not follow that it does not matter whether any atoms, molecules, physiological processes are involved. As far as explanations are concerned, minds are often the ultimate entities: but as far as ontology is concerned, they are not ultimate simples, but rather patterned composites. And although it is the pattern we should be primarily interested in, it is relevant question whether the pattern is actully instantiated or not.

But how relevant? A strong Platonist holds that universals exist *ante res*, and could in principle work out theoretic chemistry from quantum mechanics, not much caring whether any particular element or compound was actually to be found somewhere in the universe or not. Disembodied minds, it might seem, are in the same case. Might we not work out what their personal qualities must be, and assess their moral worth? I can imagine myself without a body—perhaps looking down at my own funeral, and seeing my body committed to the flames or the earth, but how could people recognise me thereafter, if I did not have a face? Indeed, could I have visual experience if I was not located anywhere? The argument that led to the perspectival view posited windowed monads who could not only communicate with one another—the radio rule—but interact causally with one another to the extent that each could observe where others were located—the radar rule—for which they needed sense organs to observe, and bodies to be observed.

Some philosophers find these difficulties insuperable; Sir Peter Strawson wittily observes, alluding to the Apostles' Creed, that it is just as well that the orthodox believe in the resurrection of the body.[17] Some of the difficulties, however, though real, are not insuperable. After all, in the E-mail community we may never have met or heard those we have converse with, but know them only by the different addresses at the head of messages that flash up on our VDUs. Cyberspace affords a model of a universe of windowed monads, who do not essentially have visual experience, and are known by their E-mail addresses rather than their faces. Although we, who are sighted, use screens, blind people can use E-mail, with auditory and tactile substitutes for visual display units. Some of the adolescent young live primarily in a world of text-messaging, only occasionally emerging to eat, and make sure their parents are still around. Although we need some sensory input and some motor output to do E-mail or surf the web, we are not dependent on any particular sense or any particular mode of operation. We can imagine a world of nerds, each being able to register a unique E-mail address at some designated site.

McTaggart would have found such a world intelligible, and answering, though perhaps a trifle austerely, to his ideal. In spite of difficulties over initiation into such a community of souls, learning their language and, more particularly, establishing intersubjective referents for common nouns (we could posit that they all have a natural—"innate", one might almost say—ability to surf the web), they could have meaningful dialogues about mathematics, not only

---

[17] P.F.Strawson, *Individuals*, London, 1959, p.116.

elementary number theory, but analysis, the theory of groups, and perhaps even analytic geometry. Such a picture presupposes that each communicating entity is an individual, and reliably the same individual, who has exclusive and secure control over the use of his own identification number in authenticating messages, so that there is no danger of messages to or from john.lucas@merton.ox.ac.uk going to, or being attributed to, the wrong person. Such a cyber-society, in which we had no eyes or faces, seems conceivable. Admittedly, if its members never had had any embodied existence, they might have rather little to talk about, and could become boring, unless they developed advanced mathematical interests. (Minds that had been embodied in some previous existence would fare better; they could remember and recount scenes and sounds from their yesteryears, and reminisce about the hardships they had endured, and the successes they had achieved.) But possible boredom apart, would disembodied minds be at disadvantage compared with their embodied colleagues?

They might be. It depends on how their existence is structured with regard to what they can do and what may be done to them. Minds differ in being able to decide differently. In the world we live in, we are not always able to carry out our decisions. There is a gap between aspiration and achievement. Our aspirations are often thwarted by the untowardness of circumstance or the interventions of others. In a disembodied existence, we should not be able to do things by means of our bodies, but we can conceive of our being able to do things by some form of telekinesis. I will that the mountain be removed to another place, and lo! it is removed. But what if you would not have it so, and will that it stay put? We cannot both be telekinetically omnipotent.

If I am to operate in a non-solipsistic universe, there must be a gap between aspiration and achievement. I am free to aspire only on condition that wanting is not the same as getting. In the public world I am necessarily not the only pebble on the beach, but if I am to be not merely a pebble, but to have a mind of my own, there must be some realm where my mind can roam unfettered by the vetos of others or the recalcitrance of reality. I need some privacy of intention, if I am to have a mind of my own: and I must operate in a public realm, if I am to be en effective agent. The distinction between public and private is a deep conceptual one, deeper than the traditional distinction between the bodies and minds we are acquainted with, linked only contingently by discoveries in neurophysiology and our everyday experience.

In cyber-space I can send E-mails to all and sundry, but am often the victim of spam—unwanted E-mails inviting me to download porn, or make $10,000. I can protect myself by setting up filters that siphon off E-mails containing certain words or the $ sign. Adolescent nerds might gang up on an unpopular one, and agree that they each would block his E-mails to them. It could happen on a world-wide scale. The fashion-setters might decide that my views were insufficiently PC to deserve a hearing, and declare that it was uncool for anyone not to block E-mails emanating from john.lucas@merton.ox.ac.uk. I could go on composing E-mails to my heart's content, expressing ever more politically incorrect views, but it would be the freedom of impotence. Only if I am the only effective person in the world, can I be both omnipotent and invulnerable. If there are others like me, then I shall be able to do some things, but unable to prevent them doing others, and unable sometimes to prevent them preventing me from achieving what I want.

Although I am quite fond of my body—a poor thing, but my own—I can imagine myself dispensing with it; but I cannot imagine there being absolutely no distinction between the public and the private, between an omnipersonally accessible world and my own first-personal perspective, with the concomitant possibility of my aspirations being frustrated, and my being vulnerable to unwelcome concatenations of public events.

I and **Me**

I can in my thoughts imagine that **I** am free of all material constraints, and can occupy any location in space and time

But

in point of fact it is not possible for **Me** to be without a material body, or to be located at any other place or time.

§14.6 The Subjective View

In the austere world of windowed monads there is a tight correlation between the perspective of any frame of reference—the coordinates assigned to a particular point—and its position in the external world. With human observers there is a correlation, but not a tight one: the letter on the optician's screen may be an A, but the patient truthfully reports his seeing an R. If our prime concern is the nature of the external world, it does not matter much. One observer's errors can be corrected by the observations made by others. But once we seek to include the subjective as part of reality, we have to consider the status of genuine but mistaken reports, together with other purely subjective experiences.

Many thinkers shy away from acknowledging purely subjective experiences on account of Wittgenstein's argument against private language. But that argument does not prove as much as is commonly supposed. Wittgenstein argues that my use of language must be corrigible to count as a use of language at all, and that if there are no public criteria, I cannot be corrected by anyone else. And from this he concludes that I cannot be corrected at all. But I can be corrected by myself. I often make mistakes, and correct them as soon as I make them; and, less often, come to realise later that I was mistaken, and then silently withdraw my previous usage. Wittgenstein sneers at the man who, dubious about the truth of what he reads in a newspaper, buys another copy of the same newspaper; but if it were a later edition, it would not be futile—occasionally errors in earlier editions have been corrected in later ones. Often, of course, they are not; and similarly, often I don't realise I was wrong, or won't admit it. But equally often in my use of public language my mistakes go uncorrected. With my private thoughts there is a crucial difference between those that are in principle incorrigible and those that may on occasion be uncorrectable in practice. In practice my later self may fail to notice and correct mistakes made by my earlier self, but this does not make my usage incorrigible in principle. I can be wrong in my use of my own private language, and that is enough to make it a rule-governed activity, and hence a language, and not mere babbling.

Wittgenstein's argument works only against a private language in which what I say is absolutely ungainsayable. When what I say is gainsayable, if only by me, my saying it (or even only thinking it) is not an inherently idle exercise. Its relevance, however, is tenuous, if it is open to correction only by my subsequent correction. Often, however, it is open to correction in other ways too. Often I use a public language to tell you about my subjective experiences: you then can understand me, and can also contradict me: the problem is not one of intelligibility, but of warrant. How can you have grounds for correcting what I say about my own private experience? But the case is not hopeless. A sceptic insinuates that he and I do not see blue and yellow the same way; my experience of blue is like his of yellow, and *vice versa*. It is clear that we cannot settle the matter by reference to the external world. We both call the sky blue and primroses yellow, but that does not touch the question of how we see them. But I can show him a spectrum, and ask him to point out the *lightest* colour. If he deems the lightest colour to be the one at the further end of the spectrum away from red, then I shall believe that he is seeing as yellow what I see as blue: but if he deems the lightest colour to be the one in the middle, next to red, then I shall have some warrant for believing that he sees as yellow what I see as yellow. Again, the sceptic insinuates that he and I do not see red and green the same way. I show him a spectrum, and draw his attention to the extreme blue end, asking if it shows tinges of red or of green. If beyond indigo he sees violet, his experience of red is the same as mine: if the colour beyond indigo is reported as having a greenish hue, I think he may be onto something.

Musical notes have a much more definite intrinsic structure, and we could go a long way in establishing that a man who was not tone-deaf had auditory experiences much like ours. Most of our experience is not purely sensory, and fits in with other experiences to form a more or less coherent whole, which not only registers the world around us, but reacts to it in various ways, some of which may issue in action. I sympathize less with someone who tells me he is in great pain, when I see him engaged in lively banter with members of the opposite sex. It may be that he is putting on a brave show, but I begin to look out for other signs: does he avoid certain positions, situations, topics? does he show the same gay abandon when not in company? can he concentrate with equal vigour on dull and boring work without being distracted by his excruciating pain? Pain is not just a sensation: it is something which obtrudes itself on our attention, and which we are averse from. Pleasure is what we have when we enjoy what we are doing, and is usually a concomitant of our doing it well, and wanting to do it again. Other feelings are more specific, often responses to events, and often connected with aspirations or intentions, which could be realised in subsequent action. Although we may misunderstand them or misreport them—psychotherapists spend their time freeing patients from such errors—we usually have sufficient self-knowledge to chart our feelings and describe them reasonably well to others. I share my perspective with you. It would not be possible if we did not both inhabit the same public external world, which provides a common anchorage for many of the things you and I both experience, but it does not require that most of what I tell you obtains its meaning from its being about something in our common external world. You know what I am talking about because I tell you, using a common language which is much used for communicating perspectives as seen from the point of view of the speaker and intended to be understood by the hearer.

I can talk about much more than my sense-experience and basic feelings. I can express my point of view about all manner of subjects, including value-judgements and wide-ranging attitudes to public events and private aspirations. Since all our sense-organs select what they sense, and all our narratives select what they report, it is a mistake to condemn the subjective view as failing to make the grade of objective respectability. Rather, we should recognise that we have different objectives. Sometimes we are down-playing the subjective, and trying to report on a reality as absolutely conceived. But it is equally legitimate to be concerned to convey some thing more personal, seeking to enable others to see things the way I see it. Poets and novelists sometimes succeed in enabling us to alter our own perspectives. So, too, painters and sculptors. A picture is not a photograph. A photograph does not pick out what is significant from what is not, whereas a picture, in showing what the artist thought was significant, may teach us to recognise the significance of what had hitherto eluded us. We conjugate. And in expressing a first-personal subjective view, may communicate to others a second- or third-personal understanding, which in turn may illuminate, enlarge, or deepen, their own first-personal understanding.

§14.7 Secondary Qualities

If first-personal subjective views can convey truth, secondary qualities need no longer be discountenanced. The colours, sounds, smells and tastes that appear to me are not for that reason unreal. Although appearances can be contrasted with reality, they can also convey perspectival information. In the table in §8.3,[18] it is not the first sense of appearance that is in issue, but the fourth. Secondary qualities are not just what I, in the first-person singular, say they are, but what we, in the first-person plural, agree about. They may be subjective, but they are inter-subjectively monitored. There is nothing of arbitrariness or subjective whim about them. They are candidates in good standing for telling the truth about the world as it really is.

Nevertheless, they are discountenanced. The standard opinion, first formulated by Democritus, and of great importance to Descartes, and popularised in the English-speaking world by Locke,[19] excludes them from any fundamental account of the world, in favour of primary qualities, which alone are accounted real. In the real world things really do have shapes and sizes, and can be counted and measured, but though we speak of them possessing colours, and emitting sounds and scents, we are, it is alleged, only painting our sensations on to them, attributing to them qualities they do not really possess, on the strength of how they appear to us.

Primary and Secondary Qualities

Primary: bulk, figure, number, situation, motion or rest, ?solidity/impenetrability?, mass, energy, momentum, parity, charge, ?spin?.

Secondary: colours, sounds, smells, tastes.

---

[18] p.230.

[19] See G.S.Kirk, J.E.Raven and M.Schofield, *The Presocratic Philosophers*, 2nd ed., Cambridge, 1983, p.410. John Locke, *Essay Concerning Human Understanding*, Book II, ch.8, §§9-25, ch.23, §§9-12. See also Reginald Jackson, *Mind*, **38**, 1929, pp.56-76; reprinted in C.B.Martin & D.B.Armstrong, *Locke and Berkeley*, New York & London, 1968, pp.53-71. Jonathan Bennett, *Locke, Berkeley, Hume: Central Themes*, Oxford, 1971, ch.IV, pp.89-123. J.L.Mackie, *Problems from Locke*, Oxford, 1976, ch.1, pp.7-36.

§14.7 *Persons* 443

The metaphysics of projectivism, discussed in Chapter Five, supports this view. Projectivism has the great virtue of ontological economy, as well as fitting in with the scientific world-view. Since, however, we cannot economize on objective probabilities, if we are to make sense of quantum mechanics,[20] the argument from economy is broken-backed. But still, the argument from the scientific world-view carries weight. Whereas primary qualities were ones that entered into scientific explanations, secondary qualities did not, and did not play any part in explaining our perception of them. It was a telling criticism in the Seventeenth Century which had had hopes of explaining all secondary qualities in terms of primary qualities; but now we are seeking deeper explanations still, by means of theories that do not take primary qualities to be fundamental qualities, but rather answers to questions elicited by a certain sort of operator. Secondary qualities may, indeed, be explicable: but so, it is hoped, are primary qualities, which in any case no longer have the primacy in our scientific thinking that they once had.[21] In any case, to explain is not to explain away. The Special Theory explains in terms of its position and relative velocity why each light-cone has the shape it has, but that does not make it any the less real. Even if secondary qualities can be explained, it does not follow that they are unreal.

We may be concerned merely to describe the world, but even then, it is claimed, secondary qualities are unsatisfactory because they are inherently first-personal, depending on the observer's autobiography, rather than omni-personal, independent of the particular idiosyncrasies of the observer. Primary qualities, by contrast, are said to be observer-independent. If I see three cows in the field, each with four legs, there really are three cows in the field, each with four legs. I can go to a shop, and order twelve yards of curtain material, confident that when it arrives, it will appear to be twelve yards long, whereas the paint I chose at the same time may seem quite different when I put it on the woodwork. Similarly with sound, the whistle sounds different to me as the train speeds by. When I come in from a snowball fight, even the water from the cold tap feels warm. If I have a fever, sweet delicacies seem

---

[20] See above, §§11.4 and 11.5.

[21] See above, §11.10.

nauseous. Locke asked if porphyry was black at night.[22] and we wonder whether chlorophyll was green in the Jurassic age.

These attacks on the descriptive integrity of secondary qualities can be met. Shape and size are in equally bad case. They, too, vary with the position of the observer.[23] And although we may be able to assign numbers which do not vary from one observer to another, measuring is a highly theory-laden procedure, not the simple reading off of some intrinsic quality.

In observing shape and size we can, as Descartes' examples of the distant tower and statues show, draw the distinction between how something appears to us, and how it really is.[24] But so we can with colours and sounds. I realise now that I was looking at the paint chart under artificial illumination in the shop, whereas it is being seen by daylight in the house. Similarly with sound, I attribute to the Doppler effect the change in how the whistle sounds to me as the train speeds by, and believe that the note was really the same all the time. In the same way we differentiate between describing sensations of warmth and coolness and ascribing a temperature, which is intended to be a real quality of an object. I can say that the cold water feels warm to my chilly hand, though really it is 40°F. I can also say that the wine was really quite sweet, though it tasted sharp after the baked Alaska.

Doubts about the reliability of our sense organs are most persistent in the case of colour, for good reason. It has been hitherto the case that we are not so much aware of the variability of apparent shape as we are of the variability of apparent colour; the reason is that when we are conversing, we are necessarily conversing at the same time, and therefore occupying different positions; so we learn to talk not about the apparent shape and size of things, which would be different for each of us, but about a "real" size, which is the same for us all, wherever we happen to be. With colour, however, the pressure to talk about real colours rather than apparent colours has, for most of man's history, been much less insistent: when we converse we converse at the same time, and since illumination has varied with time, but not significantly with space, and

---

[22] *Essay Concerning Human Understanding*, II:8:19.

[23] See phenomenal regression to real object in §8.3.

[24] Descartes, *Meditation VI*, tr. in Everyman ed., London, 1912, p.131; E.Anscombe and P.T.Geach, *Descartes Philosophical Writings*, London, 1954, p.113.

§14.7   *Persons*   445

has varied only from daylight to dark, there has been no need to distinguish a "real" colour of an object from its apparent colour as seen under daylight. With the advent of artificial illumination, the situation is changing. We are learning to differentiate between how an object appears under various different sorts of artificial light from its "true" colour, which is an invariant relation between incident and reflected light.[25] In so far as we can make this distinction, the secondary quality of colour is in the same case as the primary quality of shape. If we are *describing* the world as it was long ago, then it really *was* green, even if there was nobody around to see it. The contrast is between the autobiographical statement of experience, as I, you, he, she, or anyone, might have stated it, and the publicly accredited account of what there is in reality, according to the rules of the English language. Green then is what things really are, and if I report something's being green, when I am in good health, good sight, and am observing under normal conditions, it does not just appear green, but really is green. If I want to alter the colour of a material object, I dye it; I do not put on coloured spectacles, or alter the illumination under which I view it. Green is a real objective property of material objects, not as it may appear to me, you, him, her, or anyone, but as we all characterize it.

From the descriptive point of view secondary qualities are in the same case as primary qualities. We factor out each individual standpoint, and adopt a person-invariant mode of discourse, just as we do for primary qualities. In each case we attribute them to the external world, being able to make the distinction between what they really are, and how they appear to us, and being ready to allow correction to our reports of what is really the case, either on the strength of the testimony of others, or on coming to realise that our observations might have been skewed by some adventitious circumstance.

Jonathan Bennett argues that secondary qualities are peripheral, whereas primary ones are central:[26] if I am colour-blind or tone-deaf, I can manage quite well, whereas if I am shape-blind, or

---

[25] Similarly with coloured filters: in my motorcycling youth, I used to wear greenish-yellow goggles; when I first put them on, everything seemed greenish yellow, but soon I began to see things as they really were. When I took the goggles off, the effect was reversed, but again, it soon wore off.

[26] Jonathan Bennett, *Locke, Berkeley, Hume: Central Themes*, Oxford, 1971, ch.IV, pp.89-123.

unable to estimate distances or durations, I shall for ever be trying to put square pegs into round holes, bumping into obstacles, and failing to arrive in time. This is true. Colours, in particular, are peculiar, in being remarkably separate from most other features. (It is a pity that philosophers have tended to take statements about colour as paradigms. The fact that the word 'good' is unlike the word 'yellow' shows not that the former is non-natural, but that the latter is non-typical.) But there are degrees of non-centrality, and they cut across the primary/secondary distinction. Primitive tribes have weak powers of shape-discrimination, but need to be well able to discriminate sounds.

> **Primary and Secondary Qualities**
> Four different grounds of distinction:
> 1. Direction of Scientific Explanation.
> 2. Observer-independent v. Observer-dependent
> 3. Central v. Peripheral
> 4. Dispositional v. Non-dispositional

Locke assimilates the observer-independent v. observer-dependent ground of distinction to a dispositional v. non-dispositional one.[27] He compares colour with sensations of warmth, and taste; and these with pain. For something to be painful, it has the *power* of causing pain in a sentient being. The definition is entirely in terms of the pain which it would cause if a person were to be affected. It seems reasonable, he argues, to construe the term as a dispositional one, ascribing to the object said to be painful simply a power which in turn is characterized by the sensations of a sentient being, so that if there were no sentient beings, there would be no pain, and hence no painful objects or processes. In the same way, the word 'poisonous' refers to a propensity of a substance, no doubt due to its chemical structure, to damage organisms which come in contact with it: but there is no further special quality of being poisonous. And again, if there were no organisms, there would be no poisonous substances. He then suggests that just as a substance's being poisonous is simply its having a disposition to cause damage on someone who takes it, so its being green is simply

---

[27] John Locke, *Essay on the Human Understanding*, II,8, §§8-22.

its having a disposition to cause green visual sensations in someone who views it.

But the argument does not survive scrutiny: sharp objects can cause pain, and bullets wound or kill, but even if there were no sentient beings, flakes of flint would still be sharp, and moving objects would still possess kinetic energy and momentum. Almost every quality has some relational aspect, and can therefore be construed as being at least covertly dispositional. Although secondary qualities can, indeed, be construed as being "constitutionally iffy", so that to say that chlorophyll is green is to ascribe a disposition which manifests itself in suitable perceivers calling it 'green'; its being dispositional no more downgrades it ontologically, than the fact that a magnetic field manifests itself in suitable magnetic needles aligning themselves along it, shows that magnetic fields do not "really exist". Locke's argument seems to be an attempt to shift the boundary between *pukka* qualities and suspect dispositions, so as to reclassify all sorts of erstwhile respectable qualities as being dispositional in the last resort. But then shapes and sizes can be construed as dispositions to remain unaltered under transformations of the Euclidean group.

Still, there is some distinction to be drawn. Being poisonous is not merely a power, but a power to produce effects *in us*. Bernard Williams cites the example of 'amusing'.[28] To call something amusing is on the face of it to ascribe a property, in much the same way as to call it green: but it is a property relative to human interests and tastes. It would be awkward to describe incidents in the Jurassic age as being amusing at the time they took place; and similarly, it is argued, we should not describe anything as being green then, in the absence of any observers who could see it as green. All we should do is to say that the leaves would have looked green to us, had we been there to see them, since they contained chlorophyll, whose chemical structure makes it reflect light with wavelength around 600 nanometres. But there is an important difference between something's being amusing and its being green. Tastes and interests vary: Queen Victoria was not amused by many of the things her contemporaries found amusing, but her water colours

---

[28] Bernard Williams, *Descartes*, Penguin, 1978. p.243. See also, David Wiggins, Truth, Invention and the Meaning of Life, *Proceedings of the British Academy*, LXII, 1976.

showed the same trees as green as were so observed by her subjects. Against this it can be argued that ascriptions of colour are also variable, and do, in fact, vary with language and culture. The Greeks had no word for yellow, using the word χλωρός (*chloros*) for greenish yellow, and ξανθός (*xanthos*) for orangeish yellow.[29] But it is a different variability. There are differences over where to draw boundaries—whether turquoise should be counted as green or blue—but, apart from colour-blindness, no radical differences over central cases. Were that not so, we should not identify some people as colour-blind.

The colour-blindness argument tells both ways. It is effective in showing that our perception of colour is not like our sense of humour, nor radically dependent on culture and language. But it reveals also how much our judgements about colour depend on the majority of mankind agreeing. Where there is a serious division of discriminatory ability—whether phenol-thio-urea tastes bitter or not—we hesitate to attribute either bitterness or tastelessness to it, and speak only of how it appears to different people.[30] It can then be argued by extrapolation that the ascription of colour, being similarly observer-dependent should be construed similarly safely. Although "locally" there is agreement, the agreement is only local, being found among a certain range of human observers, but not extending to members of other species, nor even to all members of *homo sapiens*.[31]

It is quite reasonable to consider the senses of non-human animals. Mammals other than primates are colour-blind. Many a dog-owner must have wondered what a dog's world would be like, somewhat shadowy, no doubt, but full of exciting smells. Dogs and birds, we believe, can hear sounds of a higher pitch than we can, and it is a profitable topic of contemplation to wonder what it would be like to be a bat, using sonar to locate its surroundings. The world of an electric eel might be even more interesting

---

[29] This seems less strange when we look at a spectrum, and note how small is the band that looks yellow to us.

[30] Jonathan Bennett, "Substance, Reality and Primary Qualities", *American Philosophical Quarterly*, **2**, 1965, part II, §1, p.9.; reprinted in C.B.Martin and D.H.Armstrong, *Locke and Berkeley*, New York & London, 1968, p.105. A convincing counter is put forward by P.M.S.Hacker, *Appearance and Reality*, Oxford, 1986, ch.4, §3, pp.150-159.

[31] Bernard Williams, *Descartes*, Penguin, 1978, pp.241-245.

§14.8 *Persons* 449

philosophically, though perhaps rather dull if actually experienced. But we must be wary of a covert anti-anthropomorphism in these speculations. If in our avoidance of mere "local" perspectives, we rule out all human observers, we have to be ready to say what sort of observer would be allowed. Newton's universe was observed by God. He knew where everything was in His *sensorium*, because He had created everything, and sustained its continuing existence by an act of will. But God need not be colour-blind. If God is allowed as a non-local observer, we cannot exclude secondary qualities from our absolute conception of reality. If God's non-local observing is disallowed, if we seek a conception of the world as it is independently of all observers, we are in danger of evacuating it of all empirical content.[32] The final test is observation. An account that does not save the appearances is not relevant to us, and is not about the world we live in. We cannot purge our account of the world of secondary qualities on the ground that they are observer-dependent and therefore local, because the resulting absolute conception of reality without observation is idle.

§14.8 Conjugating Viewpoints

Although our bodies are located in physical space, and can move only relatively little and relatively slowly, our minds can range over all space and all time, as well as being able in some cases to project themselves into other men's minds. I can imagine that I am at some other place at some other time than the here and now of my actual bodily location: when I went to catch my plane at Heathrow, I had already bought my ticket; by the time you get this letter, I shall already have left the country. In each case the 'already' indicates a different date from that of speaking. Reichenbach gives an illuminating account of tense structure, distinguishing a "reference point" (R) from both the time of speaking (S) and that of the event being spoken (E)about.[33] S and E are not under our control, but we can choose R as seems most illuminating. Reichenbach is able to bring out the difference between the simple past, or aorist, tense as in 'I went to Cambridge yesterday' which simply says something about yesterday, namely that it was a Cambridge day, and the perfect tense, as in 'I have been in Cambridge', which says something

---

[32] See §8.4 above.

[33] H.Reichenbach, *Elements of Symbolic Logic*, New York, 1947, §51, pp.287-298.

about me now—for example, I could go on to say "so I know where Magdalene is". Similarly, we can at the cost of some circumlocution distinguish the simple future, 'I shall be dead by then' from the analogue of the perfect 'I am about to die'; and likewise we can say 'I shall be about to lecture then' and 'I was going to write to you' as analogues to the pluperfect and future perfect. The distinction between the future simple and the analogue to the perfect is difficult to draw, but important philosophically: the Schoolmen distinguished situations described by the latter, as ones where the future was present in its causes; and failure to keep the distinction in mind has led to many thinkers accepting some form of fatalism.

I can conjugate complex tenses, because in my mind I am unfettered in my ability to adopt different points of view; similarly, I can conjugate over person and number, because I can project onto others the emotions, intentions, ambitions and aspirations of which I have first-personal experience myself. I may be wrong, and any ascription I make may be proved wrong by irrefutable third-personal evidence. But I can be right, and just as in my own understanding of myself, I can always stand back, and review the views I had hitherto held, so I may always have fresh insights as I seek to understand other people.

Most important is the second-person singular.[34] I come to know thee better and correct my previous misapprehensions about thee, by entering into dialogue and conversing with thee. In doing so, I not only discover thy mind, but develop my own attitudes and sympathies and insights. I become more myself in relation to thee.

It follows that there is not a simple unitary *ego*, as assumed by many thinkers, which remains unaltered as the person I really am. Rather, I am an overlapping set of variegated personalities, the different *me*s realised in different contexts with regard to different people. A portrait painter once exclaimed on seeing his subject "I see seven archbishops: which one am I to paint?". So it is with all of us. The father, the Captain, the colleague, the pupil, the swain and

---

[34] Modern English is unfortunate in having almost lost the words 'thou', 'thee' and 'thine'. French and German have still kept it, and can distinguish intimate togethernesses, where it is appropriate *tutoyer* from the more public occasions where I address you more distantly as *vous* or *Sie*. At the risk of seeming absurdly old-fashioned, I shall here use 'thou', 'thee' and 'thine' to express the personal second-person singular as distinct from the impersonal 'you'.

the lover are different, with different, and sometimes incompatible, characteristics, which cannot be massaged into one complete and coherent whole. Personality is not only infinitely complex, but to some extent indeterminate.

And yet there is only one person. A parallel with quantum mechanics suggests itself. There we reckon that there is only quantum-mechanical reality, but different operators elicit different physical properties of it; so with personality, the same self is understood and described in different ways by different persons who have inter-acted with him. We are resonators. When I am on the same frequency as thee, thou pickest up one signal coming over on that frequency, whereas when I am in the ward room, the common room, or the pub, my mates detect a different message coming over amidst the general noise.

Paolo and Francesca were consigned by Dante to purgatory. Though for a season lovers can revel in each other's existence, sweet nothings pall, and honeymoons go sour, if the happy couple do not move on, and begin to consider what, as an item, they are going to do. There is a necessary progression from the second person singular to the first person plural (or better, in Greek, the first person dual). We are also impelled to do things together by external pressures. Although man is much less dependent on his environment than other animals or other things, he is not self-sufficient. I am mortal, and need the cooperation of another, if my name and genes are to last beyond my own death. In a multitude of other ways we need help if we are to survive and achieve our aims. Man is a social animal who needs must cooperate with his fellows.

If thou and I cooperate with each other we cooperate in a common enterprise. Together we lift the stone. The reason why each of us heaved and strained was that we wanted the stone lifted. Purposes, motives, and reasons for action generally, can be shared. They have a different logic from that of bodies, things and material objects generally. Thou and I can have the same purposes, motives and values, though not the same body: ideals are not privative, as ordinary possessions are—my having an ideal does not preclude thy having it; often the contrary. Values and aspirations can inter-penetrate one another, whereas things are impenetrable, exclusive space-occupiers. (Sometimes, of course, values are opposed, and one cannot be realised without abandoning the other; but usually they are not inherently exclusive, and often we can find ways of realising them both.)

Cooperation is best explicated by means of the Theory of Games. In many simple cases it is obvious what each must do for both to benefit; but three crucial ones, the Rule of the Road, the Prisoners' Dilemma, and the Battle of the Sexes, reveal external pressures on us to conjugate. The Rule of the Road arises where there are two or more outcomes with equally good pay-offs for all concerned. If we all drive on the left, we all avoid collisions: but equally if we all drive on the right. There is no way whereby each of us, guided solely by the light of nature, will arrive at the same strategy as everybody else. We need an antecedent agreement, a convention, a rule, which we all recognise and all abide by. I cannot make a go of it in the first person singular alone. I have to regard myself as one of us, and accept as my own the arbitrary convention rule agreed upon by everybody else. Language is the most important example. With few exceptions, it is only by convention that certain sounds have their meanings. There is no way we can reason out why in English 'Nay' indicates a negative, while in Greek ναί (*nai*) means 'Yes'; and in English 'OK' means Yes, while in Greek οὐχί (*oukhi*) indicates a negative. Words mean what they mean by convention, not nature. But once established, conventions constrain us as well as enabling us. I may be an anarchist, and deny the right of the Queen-in-parliament to make laws about how I should drive my car, but if I am wise, I will drive on the left, simply because that is what other, unliberated, drivers do, and I would rather pass them safely than have a head-on collision. I may be an existentialist, and seek to avoid the bad faith of doing the done thing, but unless I take care to keep to the grammatical rules of the French language, I shall not be able to share my thoughts with my fellow intellectuals, or obtain a following in the national press. These and many other ties bind me, and incorporate me into society. *We* have to have rules.

Rules are important, but inconveniently rigid. If I am a motorist, I need to be sure what the other driver is going to do, and I need to be able to tell on the basis of limited information. I cannot enter into an intimate and wide-ranging I-thou relationship with him, but only a limited, and therefore somewhat impersonal I-you or I-he relationship; and he likewise with me. The first-personal *we* implies a third-personal *they*. We avoid the accident, because each of us can know what other drivers in that situation are going to do. Similarly with language, similarly with dancing, similarly with etiquette.

The Prisoners' Dilemma proves how self-defeating the me-first strategy can be. For not all activities are mutually beneficial. If the Fierce Bad Rabbit takes the Good Rabbit's carrot, it may be good from the Fierce Bad Rabbit's point of view, but it is very much not so from that of the Good Rabbit. Taking whatever you want may seem like a good policy at first, but is less so if other people adopt it too, and help themselves to your possessions whenever they can. We are all losers in a free-for-all, because the benefits of taking whatever one wants, are outweighed by the disadvantage of having one's own things nicked. We all do better if each forgoes the opportunity to steal, and enjoys the benefit of not having his possessions stolen. Since we are all worse off if we consider only our individual selves, it makes obvious sense for each of us to identify with us all; then we shall all benefit by our each forbearing to maximise his own pay-off at the expense of everyone else. Once again, I cannot make a go of it in the first person singular alone. *I* have to regard myself as one of *us*, and be ready to forgo my own individual interest for the sake of our collective good.

The Battle of the Sexes shows that it is self-defeating to consider only future outcomes. If I resolutely let bygones be bygone, and take no account of what has already been done, I lay myself open to manipulation by unscrupulous others. We need to conjugate over the past as well as the future. Just as we make the transition from the immediate present to the future, as we urge agents not to go just for immediate pleasure, but to consider the long-term future as well, so we are impelled to widen the range of our consideration, and to take in the past as well as the future, since it turns out to be imprudent to be guided by prudential considerations alone.

It is tempting to generalise, and identify with all humanity over all time, adopting utilitarianism as the policy that allows personhood to flourish in caring for the whole of mankind. But there are many fellow human beings. If one is to love them all equally, one cannot love any one of them specially. The Utilitarian can have an I-them relationship with humanity in general, perhaps even rising to an I-you one, but not an I-thou relationship with anyone in particular. I can appreciate his rational benevolence, and may benefit from it, but in its impartial administration to all and sundry it will again seem impersonal, and un-self-enhancing. Utilitarianism treats men as units, not as individuals, recognising that different outcomes have different pay-offs for different people, but not accommodating each person as an agent, with his own interests and ideals he aspires to achieve by his own actions.

We need to conjugate. A full concept of personality needs to consider the possible as well as the actual, in order to delimit separate selves, and to take into account the past and the future as well as the present, and to recognise that the first person singular must be accompanied by the second person singular and the first person plural, if it is to develop into a coherent concept. These developments engender further tensions: Each is a definite individual, ultimately responsible for what he decides to do, while being also an indeterminate shimmering of different personalities, revealed and developed in different personal relationships. Each is unique, of infinite complexity, transcending all stereotypes and neat classification, while needing also to be a safe pair of hands, who can be relied on to do his bit when required.

Chapter 15
Inconclusions

§15.1 The Restoration of Reason
§15.2 The Pressure of Reason on Reality
§15.3 Personal Reason and Reality
§15.4 Recalcitrance and Actuality
§15.5 Metaphysical Argument
§15.6 Questioning Quest

§15.1 The Reasonableness of Reason

We can reason wrong, and all our reasoning needs to be subjected to scrutiny. Nearly always it is possible for the scrutineer to find fault with the reasoning, and to reject it as unconvincing, but very often sceptical conclusions can be countered. Although in the individual case the sceptic may be right, the general strategy must be wrong, since it precludes all possibility of success. If not every exercise of reason is inherently flawed, there must be some means of distinguishing good reasoning from bad, and it is up to the sceptic to indicate, at least in outline, what his criterion for reasoning being good reasoning is. Once articulated, the criterion itself is open to scrutiny, and often can be shown to be inappropriate because it is too stringent. Many sceptics have shown themselves to be deductivists, who will not accept any argument unless it is a deductive one, and will not accept any premise unless it is analytically true, pointing out, when presented with any non-deductive argument or any non-analytic premise, that it is logically possible that it should be wrong. But to demand that it should not be logically possible for arguments and premises to be wrong is to demand that anyone controverting them should be contradicting himself, and breaking the rules that make language intelligible. The sceptic will be persuaded only if effective opposition is unsayable. But if no alternative can be even formulated, what is being proposed excludes nothing, and so is vacuous. The sceptic whose demands come down to the requirement that we only mouth sweet nothings is one we need not take much notice of.

In other case the sceptic is not one who is making unreasonably stringent demands, but one who is being selective in his scepticism.

455

He does not practise what he preaches; or rather, he practises himself what he preaches against in others. It is easy to be an occasional solipsist, but difficult not to formulate it in a language learnt from others.

Scepticism can be countered, because reason is two-sided. The sceptic's objections can be objected to, his position scrutinised as well as our own. The two-sidedness of reason gives a perspective which oversteps the limitations many philosophers have sought to impose on the range of reason. Monologous argument, based simply on the avoidance of self-contradiction, is not the paradigm, but merely a limiting case of a dialogue in which one party is a nonentity, with the only shared concern between the two parties being that they should be mutually intelligible. Most dialogues have further aims. Often there is a shared concern to know the truth, and then arguments by *Reductio ad Absurdum* are available, since either party is prepared to suppose the opposite "for the sake of argument", and then allow that it leads to inconsistency, or other absurdity, so that the supposition must be rejected, and its negation admitted to be true. Many disciplines are constituted by more particular shared concerns, which furnish the background for, and give direction to, the arguments that take place between practitioners. Historians want to understand why people acted as they did, and therefore admit exercises in empathy and *verstehen*, which physicists would regard as wholly inappropriate to their subject. Not that these shared concerns are immune to questioning. On occasion we may articulate the background assumptions of the biologist, the historian, the lawyer, or the literary critic, and consider whether they are justifiable and appropriate for those seeking the understandings which, it is hoped, these disciplines can provide. But those are separate enquiries, and need not be undertaken whenever biologists, historians, lawyers, or literary critics are engaged in their subjects. Their arguments may properly be scrutinised on occasion, but are not to be rejected, or discountenanced as not being genuine arguments at all. The sceptic is entitled to ask questions, but ought to wait for answers; and then will often find his doubts resolved, his objections met, and the received view rehabilitated. The principle of credulity, though not sacrosanct, often wins through.

Determined sceptics can still resist. Even logic can be cut down to size by strenuous feats of incomprehension, and refusal to concede any inference unless compelled to do so on pain of otherwise

§15.1   *Inconclusions*   457

being trapped in inconsistency. Modal logic means little to those who lack the concepts of necessity and possibility. A logician can take an algorithmic view of logic, conceding only what can be established by means of a step-by-step proof; and in that case the so-called "valid" well-formed formulae—those that are true under every reasonable interpretation of the axioms—of second-order logic which are not theorems will not be reckoned themselves to be true, seeing that there is an element of hand-waving in quantifying over *all* predicate variables, and a suspicion that to do so presupposes the existence of Platonist universals. A sufficiently thick-skinned sceptic can maintain that first-order logic, Peano's axioms with the fifth expressed as an axiom schema, give him all that he needs.

Even so, his position is not impregnable. Gödel's First Incompleteness Theorem shows that in any first-order formulation of elementary number theory there are well-formed formulae which cannot be proved in that theory, but are evidently true. The only recourse for the sceptic is to not understand 'true', as some of his brethren have been able to not understand 'necessary'. But to not understand 'true' is suicidal for anyone propounding a philosophical thesis. If he cannot commend what he says as true and worthy to be believed, he is no longer engaged in dialogue with us, and is merely exercising his vocal chords. A philosopher is necessarily a truth-seeker. Else he is not engaged in philosophy at all, and cannot command our attention. Truth is an indispensable concept. And, as Tarski's Theorem shows, it cannot be defined in terms of algorithmic provability. Although I can always be called on to justify any statement I put forward as true, there is no system of step-by-step proof which will lead to all truth: but there *is* a step-by-step proof that shows this to be so for each step-by-step system considered.

This final refutation of the sceptic turns on a tension within reason itself. Reason needs to have its reasons, but aspires to a truth which goes beyond any limited set of reasoning. Reason outruns its own original reasonings, though from its new vantage point it can see the rationality of its new position, being able to survey the whole scene, rather than checking it step by step. The change of stance occurs again and again in mathematical reasoning. We learn to count, one number after another, and soon we generalise to a general concept of (natural) number. Such a generalisation *is* hand-waving, of a kind Dedekind deemed inadmissible. But Dedekind's own characterization of the natural numbers requires second-order logic: he needs to quantify over *all* systems (sets) that include the first number and its successors. We cannot itemise them individually, and Keferstein could retort that to generalise over all systems was just as dodgy as to generalise over all numbers.[1] If we do not allow second-order logic, but seek to make do with just first-order logic, together with an axiom schema in place of Peano's Fifth axiom, we are no longer able to characterize the natural numbers uniquely, and will find that, however much we tighten our specification, it will cover other entities besides the natural numbers. Even to move from Peano's first four axioms, which can reasonably be regarded as simply defining what it is to be a natural number, to some version of the fifth axiom, embodying some principle of recursive reasoning, requires a recognition that *all* attempts to deny the conclusion of a recursive argument *must* end in inconsistency. Mathematicians are constantly being impelled to generalise, to get the hang of an argument, and to apply it in new and unprecedented circumstances. Although properly concerned to take care not to be wrong, they are not so keen to be certain that they are not wrong that they will forgo all possibility of being right. And the same holds for thinkers generally, though it is less easy to prove to the determined sceptic that he must mend his ways, or else cease to be a thinker of thoughts worthy to be believed.

Reason is not merely analytic. In §2.4 it emerged that although first-order logic is complete in the sense that every well-formed formula true under all interpretations *is* derivable from the axioms by successive application of a rule of inference, second-order logic is not complete in this sense. In second-order logic, the logic in which we can quantify over predicate variables as well as over individual variables, there are well-formed formulae true under all reasonable interpretations; and it is only in second-order logic that we can characterize the natural numbers uniquely, postulate various axioms of infinity, and define the concept of being finite. It would be unreasonable to deny that second-order logic was logic; and hence it would be unreasonable to deny that there are logical truths that are not analytic. Synthetic *a priori* propositions are possible, and hence we may seek some *rationale* of the laws governing natural

---

[1] See Dedekind's letter to Keferstein, translated and printed in J.van Heijenoort, *From Frege to Gödel*, Harvard University Press, 1967, Boston, Mass., esp. pp.100-101.

phenomena being what they are. A theory may be justified *a posteriori*, but we still ask *why* it is true. We are impelled to follow Plato's programme, and τὰς ὑποθέσεις ἀναιροῦσα (*tas hypotheseis anairousa*), seek to establish them, not as mere postulates, but as, in some sense, rationally required.[2] This was done for the axioms of the probability calculus in §5.3, where no *a posteriori* justification would have been in order. General "qualitative" constraints arising from what we were trying to do in introducing probabilities gave rise to specific numerical results. In something of the same way general conceptual requirements on time and space gave rise to their having specific topological and geometrical features; and parity of esteem between different points of view interacting and communicating with one another led to the Lorentz transformation and the Special Theory.[3] Kant had attempted to provide a comparable justification for Newton's laws of motion.[4] Einstein similarly appealed to the homogeneity of space and time in his 1905 paper on the Electrodynamics of moving bodies.[5] Although quantum mechanics was forced on us by empirical observation, not theoretical considerations, the unhistorical account of Chapter Twelve picks out some conceptual pressures shaping it.

Reason has been rehabilitated. Although at first it seemed that we should cut reason down to size in order to secure its cogency, it turned out that the opposite was the case. The Logical Positivists had identified reason with logic, and construed logic as being nothing but a form of rule-following that must be followed on pain of unintelligiblity. But not even logic was just a form of rule-following. However fully we formulated logic in terms of axioms and rules of inference, there would be further inferences evidently valid, though not covered by the formal system that had been formulated. There was room for the inferences which guide us in seeking laws of nature, and which lead us to assume the existence of material objects and other minds. We are entitled to be sceptical about scepticism,

---

[2] Plato, *Republic* VII, 533c7.

[3] See above, §10.4.

[4] *Metaphysical Foundations of Natural Science*, ch.3, pp.536-553, tr.J.Ellington, Indianapolis, 1970, pp.95-117.

[5] "*Zur Elektrodynamik bewgter Köper*", *Annalen der Physik, 17, 1905*; tr. W.Perrett and G.B.Jeffrey in A.Sommerfeld, ed., *The Principle of Relativity*, Methuen, 1923; reprinted by Dover.

and to rehabilitate common-sense beliefs as being generally worthy of credence, in spite of their being fallible, and sometimes actually wrong. We should, indeed, be modest in our assertion, but not in our aspirations. We may reason wrong, but can be led by reason to truths that hitherto had passed all human understanding.

> **Defeaters Defeated**
> Deductivism Defeated.
> Constructivism Defeated.
> Intuitionism Defeated.
> Projectivism Defeated.
> Phenomenalism Defeated.
> Solipsism Defeated.
> Behaviourism Defeated.
> Nominalism Defeated.
> Conceptualism Defeated.

§15.2 The Pressure of Reason on Reality

Reason inclines towards more-than-ism, but as we attempt to think about reality, we find ourselves driven towards nothing-buttery. Its strength stems in part from a residual atomism, a sense that the world is made up of tiny point-particles, themselves paradigmatically thing-like, infinitely small, infinitely hard, infinitely simple, each one capable of existing entirely on its own. In part also reductionism is driven by the need to have a unified account of the universe. Descartes' dualism failed on this crucial point. Although his account fitted the phenomena, it failed to offer any sort of account of how the mental and the material interacted. Metaphysicians try to avoid the problem of interaction by having only one world, accepting the supposed consequence that all mental activity is basically material.

> Reductionist Tendencies in Reality
> 1. Ultimate Things.
> 2. Unity of Science.

Modern physics has undermined materialism. Atoms do, indeed, exist, but they are no longer point-particles, infinitely small,

§15.2   Inconclusions   461

infinitely hard, infinitely simple, but themselves consist of sub-atomic entities, which are not paradigmatically thing-like, lacking haecceity, or any continuing individuality. The ontological pressure towards nothing-buttery has gone, because there is now nothing plausible to come after the 'but'. The argument from unity has been met by a more careful analysis of explanation. Explanations involve concepts, and not all concepts can be reduced to some basic set of simple ones. Once it is established that truth cannot be defined in simple terms,[6] the reductionist programme of defining all concepts in simple terms has to be abandoned, and we can allow in principle, what has long been evident in practice, that the concepts used in biology, psychology, history, or aesthetics, are not to be reduced to those of chemistry, physiology, ethology, or social science. If the concepts cannot be defined, neither can the explanations. We cannot derive all the explanations of biology from those of a more fundamental science, such as chemistry or physics. Even if there were a complete physicalist account of the universe, the chemist and the biologist would still focus their attention on only part of what the physicist wanted to tell them. From the fluctuating flux of radiation and sub-atomic interchange, the chemist would focus on long-lasting concatenations of protons and neutrons and their accompanying electrons: these are the atoms which enter into chemical processes with other atoms to form moderately long-lasting molecules; amid the changes and chances of the physicist's world these are centres of permanence, which exist on their own, and persist in spite of physical interactions. Explanatory power confers ontological status. We regard atoms, cells, organisms, demes, species, and above all persons, as real, because it is in terms of them that explanatory explanations are framed.

Moreover, owing to the indeterminism of fundamental physics, no Laplacian predictions are possible, which would determine what could be correctly predicted by other disciplines. The autonomous predictions and explanations of the different sciences are unrivalled. There is no over-arching Theory of Everything which could in principle provide perfectly precise predictions and explanations, that would constitute a Procrustean bed into which all other predictions and explanations must be accommodated. Different predictions can be made in different disciplines, but only with as much precision as the subject matter allows, and without foreclosing the

[6] See above, §2.10.

possibility of other predictions being made in other disciplines. The concepts of the different sciences can be applied to a wide range of "Laplacianly different" situations, so that their predictions and explanations can hold good, not having to take account of many differences relevant at some lower level. As I look on a turbulent stream, I can be sure that I shall see eddies, though I cannot say exactly when they will form, or where they will be.

The two main arguments for reductionism have been defeated. The ideal of ultimate thinginess has evaporated, and we are being led to take explicability as a leading mark of reality. It is on account of the latter that the nothing-buttery of reality not only is defeated, but gives way to more-than-ism. Explicability implies rationality, and reason is more-than-ist. Reshaped reality is much more rationalist than has been fashionable in the Twentieth Century. It owes more to Plato and Leibniz than to modern materialism. Matter matters less. It is patterns that are important, not the indeterminate Aristotelian $\hat{v}\lambda\eta$ (*hule*), that they are composed of. Biology is becoming more based on information theory than biochemistry, dealing with largely independent, self-subsistent quasi-monads, whose ontological status is based on their explanatory power. Chemistry still has far to go. The quantum mechanics of atoms larger than hydrogen is too complicated for a purely theoretical understanding, but there is in principle an explanation to be discovered of the chemical properties of substances and their reactions, of why atoms of carbon$_{12}$ are plentiful and atoms of carbon$_{13}$ are rare, whereas atoms of chlorine of different atomic weights are abundant.

Under the pressure of reason our concept of reality has changed. We can no longer embark on a search for the ultimate thing-like things of which everything else is constituted, and whose movements determine the whole course of events, for thinginess disappears as we press onwards and downward to the ultimate constituents of matter. Reality resides not there, but in the processes and other entities that possess a measure of independence, and play an important part in the course of events. It has always been taken for granted by practitioners of the various disciplines, but pooh-poohed by ontological and explanatory reductionists. With their arguments defeated, the traditional view can be reinstated, but buttressed by a more careful justification, explicitly appealing to the relevance of reason to assessments of reality, and offering an account of how entities at different levels interact.

§15.2 Inconclusions

A key element of that account is *robustness* of those entities. They are the same entities in spite of many minor, and sometimes some major, variations of lower-level circumstance. The early bird who fails to find the early worm, is still the same early bird, and will make do with a later meal of a lunch-time worm. The molecule of gas is still the same molecule, though bumped into by other molecules, and made to change its velocity; or irradiated by an electromagnetic field, and having its electrons absorb and emit light as they change their energy levels. Molecules, however, are not all that long-lasting. They react with chemical reagents to form different molecules, and although some—those composing rocks and mountains—have lasted a very long time, they are all subject to attrition in the fulness of time. Some molecules may, indeed, survive a very long time, but if they happen to be involved in a chemical reaction, there is nothing they can do about it. Biological processes, by contrast, can counteract the impacts of change. They can adapt to adventitious alterations by themselves altering in other ways. In the case of cells the range of adaptability is small, in the case of whole organisms larger, and in the case of species larger still. We focus on what is relatively independent of surrounding circumstances, regarding as relevant only those factors that make a substantial difference. What is taken to be relevant or taken to be irrelevant differs in the different disciplines, but there is a growing degree of independence—or aseity as the theologians would term it—as we ascend the hierarchy. Independence, however, comes at a price. In order to offset the influence of altered factors, a process, or more generally an entity, has to alter itself in some other respect. I maintain the same body temperature by sweating if it is hot, and shivering if it is cold. Aseity requires sensitivity.

Reality has been reshaped by reason and aseity. But in an integrated universe, the more self-subsistent an entity is, the more it has to take account of what is going on in the rest of the world, and respond appropriately to it. Aseity implies not a detachment from temporal existence, but an involvement, possibly a painful involvement, in it.

> Reason inclines towards More-than-ism, Reality towards Nothing-buttery.
>
> How are they to be reconciled?
>
> Pluralist Monism:
> 1. Many types of explanation;
> 2. One Universe.
>
> One universe organized hierarchically, with different levels corresponding to different types of explanation, and showing different degrees of self-subsistence.

§15.3 Personal Reason and Reality

The pressure of reason on reality restores the status of persons as entities ranking highly on the score of aseity, a status further enhanced by the argument of Chapter Ten, in which Leibnizian monads were windowed, so as to be integrated in a single monistic universe in the spirit of Spinoza and Einstein.

Plato thought the Forms must be impersonal and timeless, and this requirement was taken over not only by the theologians, but by Descartes in what Bernard Williams describes as the "Absolute Conception of Reality", and modern philosophers generally.[7] Reality is what is there anyway, and, according to the understanding of most thinkers, excludes the personal. The impersonally of the Absolute chimes in with our sense of the real being other than us, recalcitrant, unyielding, unfriendly, uncaring of our concerns. But we exaggerate. We eviscerate reality of all personality needlessly. Reason demands an objectivity that is not the mere plaything of my wishes and whims, but does not have to exclude everything about me: being contrasted with the subjective does not imply being opposed to the personal. My pains, my wishes and whims, and more importantly my intentions and sense-experience, do not by themselves constitute reality, but are real none the less. Just as the mark of reality is covariance as much as invariance, so reason requires us to conjugate rather than confine ourselves to the impersonal passive.

---

[7] Bernard Williams, *Descartes*, Harmondsworth, 1978, pp.64-67. See above, §8.2, p.221.

Conjugation provides the rationale of empathy, *verstehen*. My understanding of others is based on my understanding of myself. I project onto others the emotions, intentions, ambitions and aspirations of which I have first-personal experience myself. I may be wrong, and any ascription I make may be proved wrong by irrefutable third-personal evidence. But I can be right, and just as in my own understanding of myself, I can always stand back, and review the views I had hitherto held, so I may always have fresh insights as I seek to understand other people. They and I are potentially infinite in our complexity.

Important consequences follow. Our knowledge of human affairs is differently based from our knowledge of natural phenomena, and the epistemological difference both supports and is supported by an ontological one: in Chapter Six it was shown that knowledge of other minds was possible, and in Chapter Fourteen that human beings are beings with a much greater claim to reality than entities such as molecules or cells or organisms. Although importantly influenced by the considerations noted in the previous section, our knowledge of natural phenomena is none the less primarily based on repeated observation. Instances can be multiplied if they are sufficiently similar, but people are awkwardly un-alike. Not only is each person unique in some high-flown sense, but each is capable of making up his mind on quite mundane matters differently from what we should expect, and sometimes does. Instances can only be unreliably multiplied, and many situations are single, susceptible of only a one-off explanation. It would be impossible to give explanations of historical events, if they had to be like the explanations we give of natural phenomena, as is shown by the failure of attempts to explicate historical explanation in accordance with the Hempelian paradigm.[8] Fortunately, we have other resources. The somewhat meagre resources of reason noted in Chapter Four,[9] are enriched by the indefinitely extendible supply of self-knowledge. Much as I can imaginatively project myself to another date, and pluperfectly recount how events would have seemed from that standpoint, so I

---

[8] C.G.Hempel, "The Function of General Laws in History", *The Journal of Philosophy*, **39**, 1942; reprinted in H.Feigl and W.Sellars, eds., *Readings in Philosophical Analysis*, New York, 1947, pp.459-469; P.L.Gardiner, *The Nature of Historical Explanation*, Oxford, 1952; and W.H.Dray, *Laws and Explanation in History*, Oxford, 1957.

[9] §4.7.

can put myself in another's shoes, and assess the situation as if I had been Napoleon before the battle of Austerlitz, or Caesar wondering whether to cross the Rubicon. Sometimes, perhaps, I can go further, and get inside somebody's skin and feel how Cleopatra or Medea might have felt—though such error-prone imaginative exercises may be best left to poets and novelists. Even the cautious judgements of academics are highly fallible, and where judgements differ, there is no decision-procedure to vindicate one view or convict another of error. As with our ordinary deliberations about what to do, there is only a continuing conversation, in which different arguments are put forward, objections raised and countered. In the course of such conversations, some men seem to be wiser judges than others, and we are inclined to accept their judgement, even when we cannot articulate arguments that the view they favour is better than opposing ones. We defer to the authority of the wise in history and literary criticism, as we do in every-day decision-making, because we cannot reach an answer without exercising judgement, and their judgement seems better than ours.[10]

The rehabilitation of reason is complete. Not only are we entitled to be sceptical about scepticism, but our understanding of reality, which had often been taken to be opposed to reason, has been re-shaped, giving us ontological warrant to affirm the legitimacy of empathy and humane insight, and to validate the judgement of the individual thinker. But although we may indeed be led by reason to truths that hitherto had passed all human understanding, we should not assume that we can, by reason alone, be led into all truth.

§15.4 Actuality

With reality thus enriched, reason restored could overreach itself, and suggest an all-encompassing rationalism that could hope to explain everything. The argument against Plato's concept of ἀστρονομία (astronomia) needs re-evaluating, if reason is no longer confined to analytic deductions that must be conceded on pain of self-contradiction. It is still the case that a study that is immune

---

[10] See above, §1.7.

§15.4 Inconclusions 467

from refutation by empirical evidence is not a natural science at all, but the history of science puts a different gloss on falsification. The negative result of the Michelson-Morley experiment started by falsifying the luminiferous ether theory of electromagnetism, but has become the entirely predictable corner-stone of the Special Theory, which we can now see, is the natural and rational development of Newtonian mechanics,[11] so much so that when later experiments yielded positive results, scientists attributed them to experimental error, their confidence that the Special Theory really was true being based not only on experimental observation but on "the inner logicality of the theory".[12] There have, in fact, been many cases where the predicted result did not occur, and our understanding of the laws of nature had to be revised in consequence. Nor is this surprising: the considerations of continuity, symmetry, simplicity, harmony, and coherence with other laws, which constitute Tolman's inner logicality, though powerful, are diverse and do not always bear in the same direction. Moreover, our intimations of simplicity and harmony are themselves subject to criticism and reassessment—often induced by the effort to find a new explanation which will accommodate discordant observations. Although scientific theories must be falsifiable, and so can be refuted, often it turns out that they have not be so much refuted as refined.

The same is true of the humanities. Our predictions and interpretations all too often fail to fit the facts, but this can lead to a deeper understanding of human nature as we wonder how someone could act in the way he did. It is a recurrent theme in great literature, how characters are driven to act out of character by some inner necessity we can only appreciate as we try to make sense of what is portrayed.

Extreme rationalists might thus hope that in the fullness of time, chastened on occasion by the empirical refutation of bad theories, or inadequate understanding, we should ultimately arrive at a fundamental schema of explanation, which, while remaining falsifiable, remained also always unfalsified.

Although opaque impenetrability was the characteristic mark of thinginess, we sometimes think that its opacity is more a function of our limited understanding than of the inherent unintelligibility of

---

[11] As argued in J.R.Lucas and P.E.Hodgson, *Spacetime and Electromagnetism*, Oxford, 1990, ch.1.

[12] Quoted from Tolman in §4.7, above, p.119.

things. Many things that were obscure are now understood, many brute facts of yester-year have lost their brutishness, as scientific understanding has enlightened us about the *whys* and *wherefores* of their nature. We are thus tempted to move towards a Platonism which was not as dismissive of mere appearances as Plato was, and could in principle work out a complete world system from a purely Platonist stand-point, while managing in doing so to save the appearances too. There would be no contingency in the world: only in our understanding of it. Duns Scotus and Leibniz would approve. From a God's-eye point of view, if we could arrive at it, all would be plain; for He acts always for good reason, and having ordered all things, can understand completely why they are as they are.

But it cannot be. Indeed, we cannot want it to be. A full-blooded Theory of Everything leaves no room for human freedom. If men are free, their free choices will have consequences which can be explained only in terms of the choices they actually made. It is possible to kick against the pricks. Sometimes we do what is reasonable and right, and sometimes our unreasonable choices can be explained by reference to psychological or physiological facts. But if we are free, and it is up to us what we do, Things will happen for no other reason than that our decisions were what they were. Even if we were never unreasonable or bloody-minded, the most a rationalist could hope for would be an *ex post facto* understanding of why we acted as we did; as we deliberate, we assess weighty considerations of either side, and our judgement is ours alone, and may differ from that of other decision-makers, without any being unreasonable or wrong. The *ex post facto* understanding available to students of human affairs offers the rationalist only an eviscerated rationality, that has no predictive power, and does not guide the course of events in any forceful way.

Not only would a forcefully rational universe be incompatible with human freedom, but it would eviscerate also our sense of reality, which is equivocal in its relation to reason. Although reality demands to be understood, it often also presents itself as being opaque to reason, as something that must be simply accepted just as it is, something other than us, oppressive, making us feel small. The smallness is, in fact, correlative with our desire for mastery. The sense of reality being "what is there anyway", although not opposed to everything personal, is opposed to its being subject to our whims, wishes and wills. It is something we may find ourselves

§15.4　　　　　　　*Inconclusions*　　　　　　　469

up against, something other than us, to which we have to conform rather than having it conform to us. Reality may be reshaped by reason, but it must be by a chastened reason. Rationalism readily overreaches itself, massaging reality so that it loses an essential feature of reality—its recalcitrance. Where we can understand it, we feel less oppressed by its ineluctability. It is partly, of course, that understanding restores some, although only a limited, measure of freedom. Freedom is not the recognition of necessity, but where necessity is recognised, it is easier to come to terms with it, and know its limits, and hence to know in what respects we are free, and can make up our own minds about what should be done. More importantly, however, it is because we identify with reason, and once we see the reason why something has to be, we see its so being as something we endorse, and as no longer contrary to our will. If we understood why everything was as it was, we should no longer repine at its being so, but accept it as a concomitant of our rational affirmation of the world. Hence, if reality is to remain possibly recalcitrant to our will, it must be the case that not everything is as it has to be. There must be some contingency in the universe.

There is. The possibility of a perfectly non-contingent universe is ruled out not only by human waywardness, but by quantum mechanics. Things happen because in the event it is one quantum-mechanical possibility that is realised rather than another. We can make probability judgements about whether a radium atom will disintegrate within the next half-hour, and our judgements will be vindicated by the behaviour of large numbers of radium atoms over time: but we can neither predict nor explain when a particular radium atom will in fact disintegrate. The fact that quantum mechanics is governed by objective probabilities means that no further explanation is in principle possible, just as the freedom of the will means that on occasion people will be obdurate, and say No to the most reasonable requests. Each in a different way manifests the impenetrable opacity that we think of as the characteristic feature of things. Not everything is as it has to be. Both with human affairs and with natural phenomena there is an irreducible element of happenstance in the way that things turn out. The cookie crumbles. It might have crumbled differently. But that is the way it actually did crumble, and actuality rules.

Actuality replaces recalcitrance as a key mark of reality. It ties together personality and time. The reality forced on us by a realist construal of quantum mechanics is one where possible futures are actualised at a present moment of truth, and thereafter are unalterable necessities. It is the actual present which separates the future from the past that requires a tensed view of time, rather than the tenseless view of time given by a purely Platonist, modally flat, metaphysics. A philosopher may be a spectator of all time, but must himself be in time, and experiencing its transient flux. Being a person in time, he makes up his mind for himself what he shall do, and his choices are his own, and not necessarily transparent to others. I may choose to open my mind to you, but I may choose not to. My freedom of choice may be opaque to your understanding. A world in which I am free to make up my mind as I think best is a world in which you are faced with the consequences of my decisions, which may or may not be intelligible, but must simply be accepted as facts. All the time wave-functions are collapsing and other people are making decisions, and that is the world in which I, and you, and all of us live, and make our own way as best we can.

§15.5 Metaphysical Argument

Metaphysics seldom provides conclusive arguments. Because a World-view must account for everything, it must take everything into account, and therefore is always vulnerable to some new fact or consideration which may entirely alter the way we look at things. It must, therefore, be always provisional, and metaphysical arguments generally are tentative rather than conclusive.

Unfavourable comparisons are made with other disciplines, which sometimes have clear decision-procedures,[13] and invariably have strict canons of relevance, and widespread recognition of what arguments are worthy of serious consideration. But practitioners of other disciplines secure cogency at a price. They can argue cogently about matters within their field, because they have limited objectives, and share background assumptions. It is easy for them to secure cogency if matters about which they cannot argue cogently are outside their consideration. Not only is their argumentation limited in scope, but it is also fragile. When in the Nineteenth Century non-Euclidean geometries were discovered, they were thought to have shaken the foundations of all rational thought. The *esprit de géométrie* could provide incontrovertible deductions from

---

[13] See above, §1.6 and §1.7.

§15.5   *Inconclusions*   471

axioms, but if the axioms were put in question, it was powerless. Metaphysical arguments, by contrast, although error-prone, are less fragile. They have no limitations on what may be relevant, and may draw support from wide-ranging considerations, and present a cumulative case for a synoptic, holistic view. Often they are trying to articulate vague intimations,[14] which become clearer and more precise when criticized and attacked.

If a view seeks to take everything into account, it is inherently self-referential. Self-reference provides a characteristic style of argument in metaphysics. Logical Positivism failed because according to its own principles its tenets were deemed nonsensical, and similarly Marxists and Freudians were debarred by their own philosophies from being able to commend their doctrines as being true. Scientific materialism has a much stronger claim to be accepted, but is open to the same difficulty, that if it were true, then its proponents' commendations and our responses would be merely the inevitable outcome of an antecedent state of the material universe, with no normative force in the commendations, and no rational deliberation actually bringing about our acceptances. Many thinkers have sensed this as an insuperable objection to scientific materialism,[15] but it has proved very difficult to articulate the argument clearly. Self-reference is a slippery concept, and it is only with the aid of mathematical logic that we can tie it down securely. Gödel devised a self-referential argument to prove that

---

[14] As for example in Chapter Nine where a vague idea of a universe comprising a multitude of different entities, which need to be integrated into a coherent whole, while still retaining their diverse identities, is gradually articulated and refined. Ideas of togetherness, nearness, nextness, crystallize out, giving rise to sharper concepts of continuity and connectedness. And then smoothness emerges as something more or less assumed, but not explicitly, and is added to our characterization of a manifold.

[15] H.W.B.Joseph, *Some Problems in Ethics*, Oxford, 1931, ch.1, pp.14-15; J.E.M.McTaggart, *Philosophical Studies*, London, 1934, p.193; C.S.Lewis, *Miracles*, London, 1947, ch.3, esp. p.27. H.H.Price, "The Self-Refutation of Naturalism", *Socratic Digest*, IV, 1948, p.98; J.D.Mabbott, *Introduction to Ethics*, London, 1966, pp.115-116; E.L.Mascall, *Christian Theology and Natural Science*, London, 1956, ch.6, §2, pp.212-219; Norman Malcolm, "Conceivability of Mechanism", *Philosophical Review*, LXXVIII, 1968, §§22-27, pp.67-71; Warner Wick, "Truth's Debt to Freedom, *Mind*, LXXXII, 1964, pp.527ff.

truth outruns provability, and in a similar fashion, though independently, Tarski showed that the predicate '... is true' cannot be defined in first-order logic. Not only in our views about reality, but in the account we give of reason itself, we face a choice: if we try to cut reason down to size, and give an austere economical account of it, we deny ourselves the concept of truth, and the means of commending our account as one worthy to be believed; if we acknowledge that we do have a concept of truth, we are committed to reason's being more than can be accommodated by any algorithmic ("mechanical") account of proof. "More-than-ism" makes many thinkers queasy. But the alternative of "nothing-buttery" is even harder to stomach. Without a concept of truth, reason ceases to be itself. Indeed, what is the point of having proofs, if they do not lead to truths? Not only is reason under threat, but equally the reasoner himself. We can re-examine Descartes' *cogito, ergo sum*, remembering that to cogitate is not just to have mental experiences, but is to engage in truth-seeking meditation, and see that if I have no concept of truth, I cannot be a cogitator, and have no claim to exist as an autonomous thinking being. If reason is cut down to size, there is no room for little me as a reasoner. And, *per contra* any metaphysical system large enough to authorise me to say *sum*, I am, is likely to lead to the great I AM.

§15.6 Questioning Quest

But we must not jump to conclusions. We have intimations rather than inferences, and where we do have inferences, they are mainly negative. Many of them were ones that defeated the defeaters. Traditional common-sense beliefs are not undermined by contentions currently canvassed to discredit them. Reason is not confined to vacuity; anti-realism is unwarranted. It is sensible then to regard reason as substantial and realism as sensible.

These negative conclusions are comforting, even though somewhat lacking in exciting positive content. They support a humanist outlook, in reinstating a common-sense view of the world, and in resisting threats from scientific advances that seem to undermine our freedom to act as we think best, and our status as originators of action and centres of value. Reason emerges as not only substantial but original and personal. We have free will, and are capable of using it not only responsibly but constructively and creatively. If reason admits personal creativity, it follows that there is not a single, monolithic scale of value, by means of which everything can be graded and compared with everything else, but a multiplicity of different excellences, each good in its own way, though necessarily failing to achieve the excellence acknowledged by some different first-personal reasoning. Many contemporary problems are dissolved once we recognise that in the house of reason there are many mansions, and that reasons range from those shared by all to those spoused by only a few rational agents, or even by only one. Reality is in large part reasonable, but necessarily not always so. It is essentially independent of us, and sometimes opaque to our understanding and recalcitrant to our will, not because of a brute thinginess, but because of an unforeseeable and inexplicable actuality in an indeterminist universe, and the fact that other people are free to make up their minds not as we would have them do, but as they think fit. Instead of thinginess, the independent existence of reality is due to its role in explanation and its robustness in the face of altering circumstance—with a greater degree of rationality and aseity being a mark of greater reality.

It is tempting to extrapolate to a maximum, and posit an Ultimate Reality that is maximally rational and maximally self-sustaining. But, as we have seen, the logic of the superlative is treacherous: not all perfections are compatible with one another; philosophical theism found it impossible to reconcile the omniscience of a Parmenidean Deity with His omnipotence. But similarly the minimal pluralism of the corpuscularians, the maximal pluralism of Leibniz, and the maximal monism of Spinoza and Eistein, were found to be untenable, at least in their traditional form. But now that we have seen that not all excellences can cohere with one another, we have to select a coherent set of excellences, guided by further intimations about what is reasonable and good, together with our revised understanding of what it is to be real, if we are to seek an Ultimate Reality. Traditionally maximal aseity has led theologians once again to posit a Parmenidean God, entirely self-sufficient and complete in itself, untroubled by the changes and chances of this fleeting world. Such a being is conceivable, but sits ill with the view of reality developed here. Not only should we have little reason to care for a God who cared nothing for us, but we should have little reason to believe in his existence; for a Parmenidean God secures independence by being entirely separate, thereby precluding all interaction with sublunary men, whereby they might come to know him. The self-sustaining independence that is a mark of reality as it needs to be understood in an integrated universe is not achieved by static separation, but by dynamic interplay. Aseity is achieved not by a thing-like impassiveness, but by sensitive adjustment. Maximal aseity would require maximal sensitivity, which in a personal being that had values and cared about the course of events, would imply extreme vulnerability. The ideal of self-sustainingness is not ἀπάθεια (*apatheia*) the calmness of the ancient Stoics or the impassivity of the Buddha, but an engaged compassion that registers all that is wrong, and responds to it as best it can.

Maximal aseity may be only an ideal. If it existed, it would qualify as being more real than anything less self-sustaining, but further argument would be needed to show that Ultimate Reality was actually instantiated. Some argument may be adduced from the requirement of rationality,[16] and the revised view of reason. If the Ultimate Reality is to be rational, its rationality would need to be a personal rationality rather than the impersonal one of the Absolute conception. If the Ultimate Reality is to be maximally rational, it must be one which, unlike standard causal explanations, does not give rise to demands for further explanations. Poets have suggested that personal explanations, explanations giving reason why an agent acted as he did, can be completely adequate—so that no further explanations seem to be called for—that the Love that moves the sun and the other stars is an ultimately satisfying explanation.

It may be. But I cannot prove it. I can share my thoughts, but not compel yours. A World-View is personal, though reasoned too. It is first-personal expressing the way I see the world, as a picture shows how I see a scene, or a poem how I feel as I encounter some aspect of life: but it is also reasoned; I don't just feel this way about the world; not only have I had to think about it, but I have had to take account of many objections that can be raised against various theses I am inclined to maintain. It is a dialectical exercise, with critics, actual or potential, always butting in with their objections and counter-arguments. But it also has to be, in some small way, a work of art, putting forward not just a series of arguments, but a coherent whole. The arguments are intended to be good arguments, but often I have to rely on some finer judgement about various

---

[16] Compare Kant's claim in §9.3 above, that the Ontological argument merges with the Cosmological argument, and that the Ultimate Reality should be identified as the locus of the Ultimate Explanation.

§15.6 Inconclusions 475

contentions pointing in different directions, as I seek a reflective equilibrium in which no consideration is overlooked, and all are woven together into one coherent whole.

There is a necessary tentativeness about the conclusions I have reached. I can offer them to the reader for his consideration, but I cannot press them upon him by coercive argument, which it would be irrational for him not to accept. Still, these are conclusions I have reached, and though the arguments for them are not coercive, they nevertheless weighed with me, and may weigh with others.

In any case, my conclusions do not conclude the matter. The creativity of reason suggests that there may be no end to wondering and explaining. Plato yearned for an ultimate state of understanding, οἷ ἀφικομένῳ ὥσπερ ὁδοῦ ἀνάπαυλα ἂν εἴη καὶ τέλος τῆς πορείας (hoi aphikomeno$_i$ hosper hodou anapaula an eie, kai telos tes poreias), where we could be at rest, having arrived at the end of our search,[17] but in the Ontological Argument the inference from the comparative—that some things are more real than others—to the superlative—that there is an *ens realissimum*, a most real something—was always suspect, and perhaps we should construe the intellectual quest after the manner of Hegel and Gregory of Nissa, as a journeying rather than a final destination, an ἐπέκτασις (*epektasis*) always reaching out to what lies in front rather than resting content with what has been already attained.

---

[17] *Republic* VII, 532e2-3.

Aczel, J - 138
Anselm - 246-8, 253, 258, 262
Anti-Realism - 220-29, 304-6, 357, 379, 472
Aquinas, T - 171, 248
Aristotle - 2, 18, 25, 27, 31, 37, 103-4, 107, 172, 178(f), 179, 185, 203, 205(f), 213-8, 224-6, 237, 260, 265, 342, 347, 349(f), 365(f), 369, 374, 400, 462
Aseity - 225, 228-9, 244-5, 256, 355, 409, 415-16, 463-4, 473-4
Aspect, A - 323-7
Augustine, St - 305, 365-9
Austin, J L - 219-20
Ayer, A J - 3-5, 84(f), 147
Baye's Theorem - 89-90, 140, 144
Behaviourism - 13, 75-6, 118, 129, 168-77, 178-9, 220-1, 417-23, 428, 433-4, 460
Bell, J S- 314, 320-7
Berkeley, George - 75, 147, 155-6, 161, 163, 165-6, 193(f), 221, 243, 343
Bernoulli's Theorem - 134, 345
Boole, G - 136-8, 203-4, 208-10, 212, 261, 345
Bose-Einstein - 266, 341, 399
Cantor, G - 255-6, 260-2, 367-70
Carroll, L - 34, 65, 425-7, 433
Causation - 97, 103-6, 107-9, 110-130, 154-6, 161-2, 196, 198-202, 222-3, 227-8, 224-5, 253, 269-70, 274, 278, 279-91, 298, 306, 326, 328, 350-4, 357-9, 374, 376-7, 379, 382, 388, 393, 402-4, 406, 412, 415, 436, 474
Chaos - 389-90
Chomsky, N - 114(f), 116
Christianity - 246, 248-9, 277
Cones - 284-5, 298, 303, 352, 357, 443
Corpuscularianism - 88, 258-9, 262, 265-70, 274, 278, 280-1, 296, 308-13, 333-4, 338-40, 342-4, 351, 354, 379, 381-2, 407, 424, 428, 434, 473
Corrigibility - 131, 223, 228, 230-3, 244-5, 439
Crick, F H C - 126
Darwin, C - 126, 214

Davidson, D - 111
Dedekind, R - 39, 260-2, 369-70, 457, 458(f)
Democritus - 9, 442
Dennet, D - 106, 391, 418, 421
Descartes - 11, 78-9, 81-2, 122(f), 154, 163-4, 167, 221(f), 246-8, 254, 256, 259, 263-4, 267, 269, 274-5, 278, 286, 293-4, 327-8, 356, 415-6, 442, 444, 460, 464, 472
Dirac, P - 266, 274, 311, 341, 377(f), 399(f)
Dray, W.H - 64(f), 102, 465(f)
Dummett, M.A.E - 142(f), 190, 201(f), 220, 266(f), 300(f), 331, 343, 371(f)
Egocentricity - 82-3, 91-2, 99, 164-8, 172-4, 221-3, 228, 234, 236, 247, 296, 304, 340, 357, 380
Einstein, A (see Einstein-Podolsky-Rosen) - 6, 55, 88, 101, 119, 235, 238, 243 258, 266, 269, 278, 284, 292-3, 311, 318-20, 323, 325-6, 343, 358-9, 459, 464 Einstein-Podolsky-Rosen - 318-20, 325
Elementary Number Theory - 35-7, 44, 67, 182, 193-5, 437, 457
Epicurus - 9
Epimenedes Paradox - 35, 67
Epistemology - 3, 5, 83, 96, 104(f), 118-20, 153, 167, 215, 216, 228, 245, 273, 308, 333-5, 390, 465
Euclid - 122-3, 181, 269, 271-4, 278, 282, 284-7, 292, 296, 308, 310, 338, 351, 354-6, 447, 470
Euler, L - 180, 185, 224, 276, 339-40
Fermat, P de - 108, 125
Finetti E de - 132 (f)
Fourier Analysis - 310, 331, 338, 378
Freud, S - 4, 64, 471
Galileo - 101, 282, 286, 355-6
General Theory - 53, 55, 88, 123, 238, 243, 258, 260, 264, 274, 293, 326, 330, 333(f), 359, 361, 377, 379
Gleason's Theorem - 145(f) 314-15, 324
Gödel, K - 2-3, 34-40, 44-6, 66-7, 69-71, 129(f), 189, 193-5, 216(f), 457, 472

Hegel, G W F - 253, 475
Heisenberg Uncertainty Principle - 318, 335-6, 341
Heraclitus - 277
Hilbert Space - 181,310-11, 331, 336-38, 344, 378
Hobbes, T - 64
Howson, C - 89-90, 93(f), 132(f), 133, 136(f)
Hume, D - 5-6, 49, 50, 53-4, 76-7, 80, 84, 89, 92, 107-10, 114, 119-20, 123, 130-1, 151, 160, 162, 164, 237, 279, 369, 371(f)
Instrumentalism - 220, 227, 343
Intuition - 21-22, 63-4, 76, 90, 93, 108, 137(f), 161, 162, 189-90, 195, 208(f), 209, 220, 222, 240, 247, 315, 330-1, 347, 371, 460
Kant, I - 4-6, 8, 39, 56-7, 116, 130, 146, 247-9, 256(f), 260, 276, 373-4, 398, 459, 474(f)
Kochen, S - 145(f) 314-5, 324, 326
Kolmogorov, A - 133
Kuratowski, K - 209-10, 261
Laplace, P-S - 281, 317, 384-412, 461-2
Leibniz, G - 55, 94, 125-6, 136 (footnote) 164, 166, 208, 258-9, 265, 276, 278, 280, 288-9, 291, 312, 353-4, 428, 462, 464, 468, 473
Locke, J - 75, 114(f), 156,-7, 165, 197, 202, 225, 241-2, 265, 280, 309, 340, 423, 425, 427, 442, 444, 446-7
Lorentz Transformation - 284(f), 286-7, 290-2, 355-6, 359, 459
Lucretius - 9
Mackie, J L - 114(f), 120(f), 124, 125(f), 131, 179(f), 242, 256(f), 281(f), 442(f)
Marx, K - 4, 471
Materialism - 75-6, 106, 147-53, 161-8, 171-2, 175-7, 187, 190-1, 197, 222, 226-7, 234, 239, 250, 277, 339, 342-6, 382, 387, 390-1, 400, 406, 411, 413, 415, 421, 424-5, 431, 434, 443, 445, 451, 460-2, 471
McTaggart, J E M - 209-302, 304, 357, 364, 436, 471(f)
Mellor, D H - 299-303, 357

Mill, J S - 24, 120-5, 166, 279
Minkowski, H - 284-7, 290, 298, 303, 325(f), 352, 355-7, 378
Mises, L von - 87(f), 134, 135
Monads - 94, 195, 258-59, 278, 288-91, 353, 410-13, 428-9, 436, 439, 462, 464
Moore, G E - 3, 5
Natural Kinds - 93, 95-7, 178, 199-200, 203-4, 211-12, 261
Neumann, J von - 145
Newman, J.H - 64(f), 145, 314, 318, 324
Newton, I - 83, 88, 101, 116, 119-20, 124, 127-8, 237, 259, 266-8, 276, 279-80, 286, 291(f), 307(f), 308, 326, 333-4, 340, 344, 350, 353, 356, 358, 377, 384, 399, 449, 459, 467
Occam, W of - 177, 269, 332(f)
Ontology - 3, 5, 96, 126, 131, 135, 147, 165, 167, 182, 187, 195, 197, 203, 211-12, 216(f), 224, 226-7, 231, 244-5, 246-50, 256, 282, 313, 332-5, 342, 353-4, 357, 361, 380, 382, 388, 390, 393, 402, 407, 409-11, 416, 421-3, 435, 443, 447, 461-2, 465-6, 474(f), 475
Pantin, C F A - 169
Parmenides (see also Plato) - 258, 260, 277, 473
Peacocke, A - 105(f)
Peano, G - 40-2, 65, 181-2, 194, 457-8
Pearle, P - 330(f), 331
Penrose, R - 129(f), 189, 284(f), 324(f), 330, 418(f)
Planck's Constant - 79, 313
Plato - 1-2, 8, 10, 14, 19, 21, 27, 28, 68, 77-80, 103(f), 178-9, 184-91, 193(f), 195, 201, 203, 213-17, 227, 233-6, 240-3, 251, 254, 256-7, 260, 296(f), 327, 410(f), 435, 459, 462, 464, 466, 468, 475
Platonism - 3, 10, 93, 97, 167, 178n., 179, 181-2, 194, 186-97, 203, 215-18, 221(f), 222, 226-7, 236, 369, 375, 380, 435, 457, 468, 470
Poincar, A - 40, 71, 389
Popper, K - 51-2, 93, 97, 135, 237

Positivism - 2, 92, 128, 237-8, 318, 459, 471
Principle of Locality - 123-4, 279-83, 325-7, 350, 397
Probability - 77-9, 87-93, 105, 109, 120(f), 130-46, 180, 227, 257, 310-11, 313-4, 317-20, 324, 328-31, 333-4, 340, 344-5, 402-5, 443, 459, 469
Projectivism - 93, 97, 114(f), 130-1, 135-6, 142, 145-6, 202, 331, 333, 361, 364, 372, 374, 379, 443, 449-50, 465
Protagoras (also, see Plato) - 4, 14, 184-5
Pythagoras - 108, 190, 192, 273, 310, 338-40, 345-6
Quantum Mechanics - 53, 88, 106, 127, 144-5, 214, 227, 243, 273, 279, 307-46, 347, 361, 371, 377, 379-80, 381-2, 387, 390-2, 399-400, 402, 411-12, 435, 443, 451, 459, 462, 469-70
Quine - 2, 114, 195, 225, 228, 245, 297, 302(f)
Ramsay, F P - 132 (f)
Reichenbach, H - 82(f), 87(f), 449
Russell, B - 33(f), 39, 49, 50, 82(f), 84(f), 150
Ryle, G - 21, 34(f), 176, 224, 421
Scepticism - 6, 7-8, 20, 47, 54-5, 66-8, 73-99, 100-1, 130-1, 141, 151-2, 160-1, 63-4, 167-70, 172-7, 183, 188, 195, 201, 226, 241-2, 291, 357, 424(f), 428, 440, 455-9, 466
Shoemaker, S - 349-50, 353, 376, 378
Schoolmen - 78(f), 219, 229, 269, 341, 374(f), 399, 450

Schrodinger - 310, 316, 329-32, 344, 346, 385, 404
Smart, JCC - 52, 302(f), 391
Socrates - 8, 25, 28, 73
Solipsism - 66, 75, 99, 161, 162, 163, 165, 167, 168, 173, 246, 248, 305, 437, 456, 460
Spacetime (see also Special Theory) - 101, 258, 269, 274, 277, 284-92, 294, 298, 303, 308, 327, 330, 333(f), 343, 347-8, 351-2, 354-7, 359
Special Theory - 53, 88, 111, 115, 119, 237, 252, 284, 285(f), 288, 290, 292-4, 308, 325-8, 332, 348, 357-8, 360-1, 377, 443, 459, 467
Specker, E - 145(f) 314-5, 324, 326
Stace, W.T - 149, 151
Supervenience - 393-99, 401, 410, 411-12
Swinburne, R G - 20, 26(f), 83, 84(f), 87(f), 432
Tarski, A - 67, 128, 457, 472
Tense - 52-3, 56, 107, 213, 221, 297-306, 327, 332-3, 343, 345-6, 357, 360, 364, 372, 374, 379-80, 417, 425, 449-50, 470
Tolman, R C - 115, 119-20, 349(f), 467
Urbach, P - 132(f), 133, 136(f)
Verificationist Theory of Meaning - 107, 161
Walsh, W H - 3 (f), 5, 64(f)
Whitehead, A N - 260-2
Williams, B - 4(f), 122(f), 221, 294, 427, 447, 464
Wittgenstein, L - 3, 5, 194, 373, 439
Wright, G.H von - 85(f), 104(f), 110(f), 120(f

www.ingramcontent.com/pod-product-compliance
Lightning Source LLC
Chambersburg PA
CBHW031540300426
44111CB00006BA/119